THE CRUSADE IN THE
LATER MIDDLE AGES

THE EXPEDITION OF THE FRENCH AND GENOESE TO BARBARY
(M. CLXV. P. 399.) MS. HARL. 4379, FOL. 60 VO.

THE CRUSADE IN THE LATER MIDDLE AGES

by

AZIZ SURYAL ATIYA

M.A., PH.D., F.R.HIST.S., Etc.

HON. PROFESSOR OF MEDIEVAL (INCLUDING ORIENTAL) HISTORY
IN THE UNIVERSITY OF BONN
SOMETIME CHARLES BEARD AND UNIVERSITY FELLOW OF THE
UNIVERSITY OF LIVERPOOL, AND HISTORY TUTOR IN THE
SCHOOL OF ORIENTAL STUDIES, UNIVERSITY OF LONDON

With 2 coloured and 8 monotone plates and 4 maps.

METHUEN & CO. LTD. LONDON
36 Essex Street, Strand, W.C.2

First published in 1938

PRINTED IN GREAT BRITAIN BY
BUTLER AND TANNER LTD., FROME AND LONDON

PREFACE

THE conception embodied in the title *The Crusade in the Later Middle Ages* is a comparatively new one. The older view as expressed by a series of writers from Wilken (1807) to Grousset (1934–6) was that the crusade as a movement came to an end with the fall of 'Akka and the termination of Latin dominion in the Holy Land in 1291. During the last fifty or sixty years, however, various scholars, with increasing show of reason, have questioned the validity of the standard doctrine. As a result of their activities, extensive masses of unpublished material on the crusade in the fourteenth century were brought to light in the publications of the 'Société de l'Orient Latin' and in the *Archives de l'Orient Latin* under the editorship of the comte Riant, one of the greatest pioneers of the new school of thought. Delaville Le Roulx then wrote his work on *La France en Orient* and Iorga his biography of Philippe de Mézières, and both dealt with many aspects of our subject. The latter has also published a large number of documents on the crusade in the fifteenth century in his six series entitled *Notes et Extraits pour servir à l'histoire des croisades au XVe siècle*. In the meantime, a few monographs on persons and events related to the crusade in our period appeared in Germany and France (see Bibliography). The result of these activities is that the conception of the crusade according to the old school of thought has been seriously modified although that conception still finds notable support, as for example in the case of M. René Grousset in his recent work.

Our debt to all these scholars has been acknowledged in the proper place in the footnotes. On the other hand, it is essential here to note as justification for the present essay, that the longer works of Delaville Le Roulx and Iorga which cover the fourteenth and part of the fifteenth centuries are mainly biographical in character—the one concerned mainly with the life of Boucicaut, marshal of France, and the other with that of Philippe de Mézières, Chancellor of the Kingdom of Cyprus, and, later, tutor of Charles VI of France. The crusade is treated in both works on account of the fact that both Boucicaut and Mézières espoused its cause for the greater part of their lives. Without minimizing the achievement of either scholar, we may be justified in saying that the wider outlook on the crusade as a general movement remained secondary to their original thesis. It is this gap which we propose to fill in our present study—the first to deal with the subject in its entirety from the Western as well as the Oriental sides. The plan of our work was formulated in a course of lectures on the 'Relations between the East and the West in the Later Middle Ages' delivered at the University of London School of Oriental Studies some years ago. Close research in a subject of this kind, and a period of this length, necessitated visits to most of the famous depositaries of manuscripts in Europe and the East; the material and other difficulties involved need not be stressed. A fair estimate of the crusading impulse and its expression, as we have been fully and consistently aware, cannot be made without a thorough and comprehensive examination of the western as well as the eastern sources; and this examination we have attempted in the following pages. On two occasions, in connexion with the crusades of Pierre de Lusignan and Jean de Bourgogne respectively, we found it essential to visit Alexandria and Nicopolis for accurate topographical knowledge and for the reconstruction of the two famous battles of 1365 and 1396. For the topography of the Mahdiya region, the scene of the expedition of Louis de Bourbon in 1390, invaluable information has been received from Professor H. A. R. Gibb, to whom we are also indebted for reading our manuscript and for his many and valuable suggestions on the Oriental side of this study.

As will be noted, we have divided the work into four parts. The first of these consists of a general view of the later medieval world in regard to the crusade; and the second includes treatment of the enormous mass of propagandist literature in the West, of which accounts of pilgrimages are an outstanding feature. In the third, we have surveyed the state of Eastern Christendom, the relations between Europe and the Mongols, and Latin missionary activities in the Near, Middle and Far East, along with the bearing of these neglected subjects upon the crusade in our period. In the fourth we have traced the history of the crusading movement itself, expedition by expedition. At the close of the last section, we have briefly outlined what we call 'counter-propaganda' and 'counter-crusades', in other words the reaction of the East to Western attacks. This reaction, in its manifestations from the age of Saladin to that of Suleiman the Magnificent, demands special treatment and we were tempted to offer a detailed account of it, but its doubtful relevance to our thesis and the exigences of space compelled brevity. The story of the crusade of Nicopolis, already dealt with in a separate published study, has been much curtailed in this work; for the generous appreciation that study has received in England and abroad, we express our gratitude.

To the University of Liverpool and to numerous friends and colleagues in many countries, we are indebted for assistance, sympathy and encouragement. We wish to mention in particular that easier access to a vast amount of material in the German manuscript collections was made possible in the Oriental Seminary of the University of Bonn, thanks to the good offices of its learned Director, Professor Paul Kahle. We again owe much to Miss Gertrude Winter for unsparing effort in her intensive revision of our text and footnotes. Mr. Hunt of the

Palaeography Department in the University of Liverpool has also helped in the transcription of the Munich MS. of Ramon Lull which appears in Appendix I.   Professor R. A. Furness has kindly read Chapter XV, and Mr. D. M. Dunlop has assisted in the task of proof-correction.   Our greatest debt remains that to Professor G. W. Coopland, not only for reading manuscript and proofs, but for his invaluable suggestions and encouragement at all phases of the work.   To him in the last resort the completion of that work is due.   It is also our privilege and our duty here to record our permanent debt to the enlightened policy in matters of research of the Egyptian Education Authorities in Cairo and London; notably, His Excellency Muhammad El-Ashmawy Bey, Under-Secretary of State for Education, and Messrs. J. M. Furness and V. Watson, former and present directors of the Egyptian Education Office in England, without the material assistance which they have freely given, the accomplishment of our task would have been long delayed or impossible.

A. S. ATIYA

March 1938

CONTENTS

ix

PART III

THE EAST AND THE CRUSADE

PART IV

THE CRUSADES

APPENDICES

ILLUSTRATIONS

MAPS AND PLANS

THE CRUSADE IN THE
LATER MIDDLE AGES

PART I
INTRODUCTION

CHAPTER I

THE BACKGROUND

The changing world in the Later Middle Ages: old ideals and new facts. Europe and the Crusade: historical developments against war in the East; events and factors in favour of the movement. The Levant and the Crusade: strength of Egypt and Syria; rise of the Ottoman Empire. The West and the Tatars: missionary work and rapprochements for union against Islam; failure. Dawn of Modern History

THE crusade, both as a holy war and as an act of devotion, was the perfect expression of one aspect of the medieval mind. The concrete form of ideals of chivalry and faith, the movement was more generally accepted and approved than had been the case with any previous manifestation of Western ideas since the fall of the Roman Empire. The extraordinary focusing of attention and action, which is its most striking characteristic, may indeed be regarded as an immense demonstration of the ideal of the Christian Commonwealth. Like all great political theories of the past, present, and future, the idea of a Christian Europe under Pope and Emperor was never completely accepted. The exceptions which prove the rule were large; quarrel between theory and practice can at every phase be demonstrated. Hence we may expect to find with the development and progress of the contest between Empire and Papacy that the fervour and unity of the crusading movement become seriously diminished. The Crusades may have been the foreign policy of the Papacy, but they were at times the foreign policy of Europe, and as the struggle between lay and religious powers becomes a narrower and, perhaps, meaner thing, and as commercial and national interests override older considerations, we shall find corresponding changes in the nature of the Crusade. Those changes will, it is hoped, be sufficiently evidenced in the course of this examination of the movement against Islam

3

in the fourteenth century.[1] Here we may note some of
the main phases and consequences of the process.

At the fall of the Hohenstaufen, and the beginning of
the Great Interregnum, the Papacy, while apparently
triumphant in the narrower issues, reflected in its own state
the profound changes upon which medieval society was
entering; and the loss of unity as between the two great
institutions of the Early and Central Middle Ages, partly
cause and partly result, affected all Christendom, and along
with it, the Crusades. The Empire was in process of super-
session by kingdoms, trade leagues, great feudatories, and
republics: the Papacy lost the essence of its past when
Boniface VIII failed to vindicate his claims to Hildebrandine
power. The Babylonish Captivity, the Great Schism and
the Conciliar Movement are links in a chain of causation,
but may be more profitably considered for our purpose as
results and symptoms of change. That the Crusade of the
fourteenth century should not be the Crusade of the eleventh
is but another expression of the same evolution.

Turning now to look more closely at the immediate background and environment of the fourteenth-century Crusade,
we need only review briefly at this stage the position and
powers and stage of development of those authorities and
organizations to whom advocates of the Crusade in the fourteenth century might reasonably look for initiative and
activity. In the complex of fourteenth-century history we
have to note the forces and motives which encouraged some
to condemn, and others to foster, projects for a Crusade.
These may be classified as political, religious and economic,
and they include sharp changes in the Levant and Eastern
Europe, the conscience of the Papacy, the activities of
religious and secular Orders, and, perhaps most important,
the efforts of the pilgrims and propagandists of the Age.[2]

[1] Although the present study covers the Later Middle Ages, the fourteenth century actually includes the main stages in the movement under
consideration and is therefore taken throughout as representative of the
whole period.

[2] The political, religious and economic history of the Later Middle Ages
as a whole, is the necessary introduction to the present study and any summary, even of essentials, is made the more difficult by the fact that the crusade
in the period under review covers a much wider field than the early crusades.

At the opening of the fourteenth century, the Holy Roman Emperor had neither the men nor the money to enable him to carry any plan of crusade to a successful issue, no hereditary rights round which the special interests of a dynasty could be centred and expanded from generation to generation, and even no fixed capital from which centralized government might be developed. Germany itself had, indeed, supplied two great military religious orders—the Order of the Sword and the Teutonic Order—whose sole vocation was to fight the battle of Christ against unbelievers. The activities of both organizations were, however, deflected from the Holy Land to the heathen marches of Prussia and beyond. There was little hope of finding in the Empire a man who would conduct a holy war, and the contemporary had to seek a leader elsewhere.

England and France, the two countries which had given so many valiant fighters for the crusade in the past, were now themselves on the verge of a ruinous conflict which was to last almost as long as the Middle Ages, longer than a century. The Hundred Years' War drained the resources of both kingdoms and kept the flower of their chivalry constantly occupied with the warfare on French soil. Although there was still much sympathy for crusading as an ideal on both sides of the Channel, the much-needed practical support for the cause did not materialize until the *rapprochement* between Richard II and Charles VI produced a temporary cessation of hostilities. It was during this breathing-space that the Crusade of Nicopolis (1396) was made possible against the Ottoman Turks in Eastern Europe. But peace was short-lived, and the early years of the fifteenth century saw a resumption of the Hundred Years' War. In addition to a foreign policy which discouraged any serious thought of the crusade, England had her constitutional struggles, the interminable unrest in the marches of Wales, the wars on the Scotch border, and, at a later stage, the Wars of the Roses.

We have therefore confined this survey to the main factors in Western and Oriental history which have a direct bearing upon the crusade. The reader is asked to supplement this introductory chapter by the standard general histories and on special points by the works listed in the Bibliographies to vols. VII and VIII of the *Cambridge Medieval History*.

On the soil of France, apart from the battles of the Hundred Years' War in which the French chivalry suffered such heavy loss, the death of Charles V and the accession of the infant Charles VI in 1380 retarded the movement towards French unity for a generation.   From the quarrels of the regency developed the rivalry of Burgundy and Orleans, and with the murder of Orleans in 1407 the feud widened into the long struggle between Burgundians and Armagnacs which in turn developed into that grouping of forces, 'Nationalist' party against Burgundians and English, which was interrupted by the arrival of Joan of Arc in 1429.   The gradual liberation of France, and the final expulsion of the English, left French rulers with tasks of consolidation and hopes of expansion.   France, which to the East had been *par excellence* the crusading country, limited her share to pious hopes and expressions of encouragement to others.

Behind all these movements, wars and struggles, there was an increasing, but still vague, feeling among the separate peoples of Europe, which has often been described as the 'awakening of nationalities', a useful term if the appropriate reservations are constantly kept in mind.   The older conception of the Pope and the Emperor enjoying full hegemony over the rest of Christian mankind, though not yet eradicated from the legist's mind, had largely disappeared; and the theory of universality in the governance of the world had, in the Later Middle Ages, been increasingly divorced from practice.   Within separate kingdoms, however, men's loyalties, ingrained in feudal and domainal habit, stood more for their county than for their country.   Broadly, this was the case at the outset of the fourteenth century.   The power of the feudal nobility was, in increasing measure, ceasing to be justified by the evident necessity for such power which had existed in earlier days when the control of local government and the conduct of provincial defence were beyond the ways and means of the central authorities, if indeed we can legitimately speak of central authorities.   The march of events in the fourteenth and fifteenth centuries demonstrated to the 'menu peuple' that, in the changing circumstances of the age, it was in their interest to support a royal master for their protection both from the injustice and

THE CROWN OF THORNS WITH THE CROWNS OF ENGLAND AND
FRANCE, SYMBOLICAL OF UNION FOR THE CRUSADE.
MS. ROYAL 20 B. VI, Fol. 1 vo.

exactions of their immediate feudal lords and from foreign invaders. Thus we notice the grouping of widespread interests round the person of the King and a continuous weakening in the old local ties. It is easy to overrate these new tendencies and misinterpret them by the use of the modern term 'nationalism'. What happened was that the members of each 'nation' began to discover that their individual interests were identical with those of their king, hence the nascent feeling of 'royalism' which is often mistaken for 'nationalism'. The sum-total of the whole argument in its bearing upon the present study is that the new orientation fixed men's eyes on their kings, and with the new concentration on home troubles and home aggrandisement, 'international' co-operative movements based on wider motives, such as the crusades, grew more and more remote from realities with the waning of the Middle Ages in England and France.

At the end of the thirteenth century Spain and Italy, regarded as geographical units, show a considerable degree of similarity. Each contained a number of independent powers. The division of Spain into the kingdoms of Aragon, Castile, Leon, Navarre and Portugal retarded the re-conquest of the Andalusian realm of the Naṣrides, but the Spaniards were ardent exponents of the Crusade against Islam—if fought within the Peninsula. In Italy, on the other hand, the existence of independent Republics intensified the spirit of competition for trade markets in the East and for all that wealth and leisure implied in matters of progress and culture. Hence the Italians were indifferent, if not hostile, to a war which would adversely affect their trade interests.

The Spanish conception of the holy enterprise was more or less confined to the struggle against the Muslims in south-western Europe which consequently minimized their contribution to the fight for the salvation of the Holy Land. The West, on the other hand, throughout the whole history of the crusade, remained comparatively apathetic towards the idea of fighting the Muslims in Spain, except possibly in the case of attacks by the mixed host of Englishmen, Rhinelanders and Flemings on Lisbon and its liberation from Arab

dominion in 1147.[1]   When Ramon Lull recommended to
the Council of Vienne (1311–12) a crusade by way of Spain
and North Africa to Egypt and Syria, no one seems to have
devoted much attention to his cry.[2]   Not until the consolidation of Spain after the fall of Granada (1492), was
that country in a position strong enough to encourage any
thought of fighting Muhammadanism outside the Peninsula;
and even then when Columbus was sent for the first time by
the Western trans-Atlantic route to explore the possibilities
of union between Europe and the Tatars against Islam, the
whole course of human history was on the verge of a complete change as a result of the impending discovery of the
New World.[3]

In Italy, we find a world of republics and principalities
bent on advancing their material interests in the East.
When it suited their expanding trade to participate in the
crusade, they did so without hesitation.   Examples are not
wanting.   The classical one is that of the part played by
Venice in the Fourth Crusade which ended in the destruction
of the Empire of Constantinople in 1204.   The Genoese
were the initiators of the Barbary Crusade of 1390, though
not so much in defence of their faith as of their trade, an
attitude which they demonstrated by supporting Duke Louis
de Bourbon in the siege of al-Mahdiya only until the Berber
Sultan restored to them their commercial privileges.[4]
While the Venetians, throughout the Later Middle Ages,
sought papal dispensation to carry on their trade with
Egypt, the Genoese, acting under menace of excommunication,[5] continued to be the foremost agents for selling young
slaves to reinforce the Mamlūk army.   With the growth of
Ottoman ascendancy in Asia Minor and in Eastern Europe,
the Italians were the first to court their alliance and beg for

---

[1] Osbernus, 'De Expugnatione Lyxbonnensi', ed. Stubbs in *Chronicles and
Memorials of the Reign of Richard I* (Rolls Series 1864), I, cxlii–clxxxii; also
under title 'Crucesignati Anglici Epistola' in *Portugaliae Mon. Hist.*, I,
392–407; H. A. R. Gibb, 'English Crusaders in Portugal,' in *Chapters in
Anglo-Portuguese Relations* (ed. E. Prestage, London, 1935), 1–23.

[2] *vide infra*, Cap. IV.

[3] *vide infra*, Cap. X; cf. Bertrand and Petrie, *Hist. of Spain*, 195 et seq.,
237 et seq.

[4] *vide infra*, Cap. XVII.   [5] *vide infra*, Pt. I *passim*.

trade privileges. Contemporary authority is not lacking for the view that the Duke of Milan was treacherous enough to inform Bayezid of the forthcoming Crusade of Nicopolis and thus put him on his guard against the last serious attempt in the Middle Ages to save the East.[1] Little help towards the holy cause could be expected from states which, openly and unscrupulously, placed their material interest before all pious considerations. Such help as was furnished by Venice on various occasions, was more or less wrested from the Republic after long negotiations and procrastinations.

On the purely religious side, the Papacy naturally had been the main pillar of the crusading movement. Yet here, again, as in the political sphere of European history, the march of events was equally discouraging. The three periods and the three series of problems of the Babylonish Captivity, the Great Schism and the Conciliar Movement absorbed much of the public attention that might have been devoted to the Crusade. Moreover, thinkers of the time began in varying degree to question older views as to the authority of the Pope. Of the milder type we have, among others, Marsiglio di Padua (1270–1334), the famous author of the *Defensor Pacis* and his French helper Jean de Jandun (ob. 1328), William of Occam [2] (1280–1347), John of Goch (1400?–75), and John of Wesel [3] (ob. 1489). Of the violent and extremist type it is sufficient to mention John Wyclif (1327–84) and his Lollard disciples in England and John Huss (1369–1415) and his noble follower Jerome of Prague in Bohemia. In a world of such passion and such controversy, and such forced expenditure of intelligence on problems touching the very foundations of medieval society, the need for holy war was thrust into the background.

On the economic side, too, there was much that was symptomatic of the passing of the old order. The Black Death (1347–50) with its 'cataclysmic' effects on manual

[1] Froissart (ed. Kervyn), XV, 252–4; Serviteur de Gui de Blois (in Kervyn's *Froissart*), XV, 465; Chronicon Flandriae, in *Corp. Chron. Fland.*, I, 346; cf. Atiya, *Crusade of Nicopolis*, 62–3, 182. (Reference will be made in future to the last work as *Nicopolis*.)

[2] Flick, *Decline of the Med. Church*, I, 194–204.

[3] C. Ullmann, *Reformers before the Reformation* (2 vols., Edinburgh, 1855–60), I, 17 et seq., 217 et seq.

labour in the West contributed no mean share to the tangle
of causes which ultimately led to the outbreak of the
Jacquerie (1358) in France and the Peasants' Revolt (1381)
in England. It is not within the scope of the present
study to attempt an estimate of the effects of the great
pestilence on the economic unrest on both sides of the
Channel. One thing, however, is clear. The generations
that lived in these eventful years and suffered these calamities must perforce have ceased to look far beyond their
own borders.

It might appear from the multiplicity of the signs of
change here reviewed that in the Later Middle Ages the
crusade became a moribund ideal beyond human power to
resuscitate. This opinion, indeed, has been held by a series
of distinguished historians, and the view is still expressed
that the expulsion of the Latins from the Holy Land in the
last decade of the thirteenth century marked the end of
the holy war.[1] It must now, however, be recognized that
the crusade and the crusading impulse outlived the Kingdom of Jerusalem as it had existed on the Asiatic mainland for at least two centuries, during which projects for
Eastern expeditions remained one of the vital forces in
European politics notwithstanding all the adverse circumstances already enumerated. This is the sum-total of the
thesis underlying the whole of the present study, and at this
juncture we may indicate certain of the forces which kept
the crusade alive in the minds of the statesmen, churchmen,
and 'common' people of the age.

Events in the Levant during the fourteenth and fifteenth
centuries were moving with much rapidity and in such a

---

[1] The latest work published on the history of the crusades by René
Grousset (*Histoire des croisades et du royaume franc de Jérusalem*, 3 vols.,
Paris, 1934–6) ends with the fall of 'Akka in 1291. Grousset has conceived the illuminating idea of dealing with the crusades in three distinct
periods marked by three preponderant movements—first, Muslim anarchy
and the establishment of the Frankish Kingdom of Jerusalem; second, a
state of equilibrium between the Muslim and Frankish monarchies; and
third, the rise of the Muslim monarchy and the predominance of anarchy
among the Franks. A clear and valuable study of the early crusades, this
work is to be included among those which take the 'standard' view that
the crusading movement ended with the thirteenth century.

direction as to keep the West aware of the growing Saracen menace to the few remaining Christian outposts in those regions. Moreover, the calamities threatening the Catholic nations in east central Europe at the hand of the Ottoman Turk, had a most disquieting influence on the rest of Christendom. The fall of 'Akka in 1291, although long foreseen, caused great alarm and indignation in Europe. The complete consolidation of Syria under Muslim rule for the first time since the beginning of the crusades at the end of the eleventh century appears to have fostered the spirit of aggression among the Mamlūk Sultans of Egypt and their Amīrs, who pursued their career of conquest further north into the Christian Kingdom of Lesser Armenia. Owing to her proximity to the empire of the Egyptians in northern Syria, Armenia became their next objective and its forts were destroyed one by one, its prosperous towns pillaged and its fields laid waste. The Armenian people represented the latest triumph of Catholicism in the East. In the early years of the fourteenth century, their kingdom was on the edge of ruin; and, to save it from utter extinction, they renounced their old creed, submitted to the authority of Rome, and appealed to the West for succour. Leaving on one side the controversial subject of the genuineness of the Armenian conversion, we may say that a moral duty fell upon Western Europe to protect and preserve from destruction this much-oppressed kingdom. In spite of this, Armenia was finally annexed by the Amīr of Ḥalab (Aleppo) in 1375 and King Leo VI was captured and carried to the Citadel of Cairo where he remained in chains until 1382. This disaster aroused great indignation in Europe and stirred up the enthusiasm of western people for the crusade. The fate of the little Latin Kingdom of Cyprus under the House of Lusignan was not very much better than the lot of her Armenian sister on the mainland. Although protected by the waters of the Mediterranean, she survived her by only a few decades. As soon as the Egyptians were able to equip a fleet and launch it against Cyprus, the fate of the island was sealed. Three naval expeditions in 1424, 1425 and 1426 brought pillage and destruction on the kingdom and ended in the capture of

King Janus, who, like Leo the Armenian, was carried in chains to Cairo. He was released only after the payment of a heavy ransom, and after swearing allegiance to Sultan Bursbai and promising to pay him an annual tribute. The Egyptian chroniclers concur in telling us that Janus recovered his freedom after becoming one of the Sultan's Mamlūks and his viceroy (Ṣāḥib, Mutamallik) in the kingdom that had been his own. What effect these successive disasters had in the West, remains to be seen in the following pages. The turn of Rhodes, too, was soon to follow in the expeditions of 1440, 1443, and 1445.[1] Although Egypt fared ill in its attempts to overthrow the Knights of St. John, the Egyptian wars formed a precedent for Muslim attacks on the island fortress and prepared the way for the final expulsion of the Order from Cyprus at a later stage by the Ottomans in the reign of Sultan Suleiman the Magnificent. While these conflicts were bringing to a speedy and tragic end the inefficient rule of Latin Christianity in the East, the Ottomans had been marching with bewildering rapidity towards the heart of Catholic Christendom in Europe. The defeat of the united forces of the West outside the city of Nicopolis in 1396 and the final destruction of the shadow of the ancient empire of Constantinople in 1453 had ensured the hold of the Turks over the Balkans and enabled their armies to follow the road of invasion to Buda and to Vienna. As early as the reign of Murad I (1359–89), the Sultan, according to French pilgrims, had sworn to 'come to France when he had finished with Austria' and had also pledged himself to ride to Rome and turn the altar of St. Peter's into a manger for his horse.[2] Even if Europe was not in the mood to make any further attempts to subdue the East and save the Holy Land from the unbeliever, it seemed as though a crusade would be needed to save Eastern and Central Europe from the Turkish menace.

The Papacy, despite its trials and tribulation during the periods of the Babylonish Captivity, the Great Schism and the distracting influence of the Conciliar Movement, never lost sight of the Crusade. The earnest attempt of the papal

---

[1] *vide infra*, Cap. XIX.   [2] *Nicopolis*, 2.

curia to convert the Tatars to Catholicism and so secure their help and support for an effective crusade [1] is only one demonstration of the activity of the Church. To say that the Avignonese papacy had become subject to the will of the kings of France and that it had completely neglected its duties, in which the crusade remained a vital element, would be both misleading and unjust. Contemporary documents prove beyond all doubt the weakness of such contentions. Clement V (1305–14), the first of the Avignonese popes in the period of the Babylonish Captivity, seems to have accumulated the large sum of 300,000 gold florins to be used for the cause of the crusade. When Clement died before the realization of his project, the money was left in the Château de Monteux in the diocese of Carpentras in the custody of his nephew, Bertrand de Got, vicomte de Lomagne, who retained the treasure, probably aiming to appropriate all or part of it to himself. John XXII, who succeeded to the papal chair, wished to recover this money and put it to its proper use according to the express will of his predecessor. Hence a protracted process was opened in the course of which several appeals were issued to the Kings of England and France to settle this and the more important matter of the crusade.[2] Of the support given by Clement VI to King Hugh de Lusignan at the battle of Smyrna (1344) and to Humbert de Viennois in the crusade of 1345, by Innocent VI to Pierre I de Lusignan in his attack on Adalia (1361), by Urban V to the crusaders of Alexandria (1365) and to the enterprise of Amedeo VI of Savoy (1363–6), and by other popes and anti-popes to the Barbary

---

[1] *vide infra*, Cap. X.

[2] This long case has been brought to light by the publication of the majority of documents connected with it. *vide infra*, Cap. III, analysis of propagandist documents of the reigns of Philippe le Bel and Clement V; see also P. Ehrle, *Archiv für Litteratur und Kirchengeschichte*, V, 5, 16, 125–36, 143–6; *Rev. de Gascogne*, XXXII, 1–20; L. Guérard, *Documents Pontificaux sur la Gascogne—Pontificat de Jean XXII*, I, no. 42 (p. 52 et seq.) and no. 149 (p. 236 et seq.). For other documents on the crusade in the pontificate of John XXII, see also Guérard, op. cit., I, nos. 77, 85, 128, 134, and II, nos. 186–7, 191–4, 210, 214, 235, 289–301; Baluze (ed. Mollat), I, 174; *vide infra*, Cap. III on projects of crusade by Philippe VI and John XXII.

expedition (1390) and the crusade of Nicopolis (1396), much will be said in the following pages.

The creation of a great number of new orders in the Later Middle Ages helped to keep the idea of holy war in the mind of the chivalry of the West. The Brotherhood of the Templars was suppressed by the General Council of Vienne (1311–12), but the old established Order of St. John, the Order of the Sword and the Teutonic Order continued to flourish. All owed their origin in the main to the crusading movement. Now, during the period under review, a multitude of organizations seem to have sprung up under the auspices of princes and nobles, high and low, on all hands [1]; and it is indeed difficult to dissociate these creations from the spirit of the crusade which had given rise to the older ones. Four of these are worthy of special note: first, Philippe de Mézières' noble but abortive conception of the 'Militia Passionis Jhesu Christi',[2] a form of armed 'League of Nations' to end the Schism in the Church and faction in the States of Western Europe, to re-conquer and retain the Holy Land for Catholic Christendom, and to watch over the morals of man; second, the 'Order of the King of Cyprus' which was instituted for the defence of the Island, and to which many of the noble pilgrims on their way to the Holy Land were admitted and entrusted by the Kings with its symbolic dagger [3]; third, the 'Toison d'Or', which was probably the most prosperous of all, as it was patronized by the Dukes of Burgundy, whose wealth and influence made it strong; and fourth, the 'Escu d'Or', founded by the Good Duke, Louis II de Bourbon, who commanded the Barbary Crusade.[4]

In an age of faith, the idea of saving the Holy Places could not possibly sink into complete oblivion. No doubt, there were periods of indifference and forgetfulness towards a cause for which so much Christian blood had been shed in

---

[1] Huizinga, *Waning of the Middle Ages*, 74–81.

[2] For details, *vide infra*, Cap. VII.

[3] The ceremony of consecration is described by Felix Faber in his first Evagatorium in 1480; trans. A. Stewart, in *Palestine Pilgrims' Text Society*, I, 25.

[4] *Chron. du Bon Duc*, ed. Chazaud, 12–15.

bygone centuries. Yet, reminders of the state of the Christians of the East and the duty incumbent upon their fellow-men in the West were numerous. Travellers came back from the Levant with tales of suffering, sacrilege and misery; but perhaps the most potent of reminders were the wandering princes of Christian Kingdoms, now extinct or on the verge of extinction at the hand of the Saracen. The first and perhaps the most moving of these cases was that of King Leo VI of Armenia, who, after having lost his country and his crown, and after having been incarcerated in Cairo for seven long years (1375–82), was at last released on the payment of his ransom by the Church [1] and on condition that he should not return to his native land. The King went to and fro in the West, and after visiting the courts of both Urban VI and Clement VII,[2] retired to Paris where he lived on charity until he died in November 1393 without leaving an heir to his lost kingdom.[3] The Western journeys of Pierre I de Lusignan, 1362–5, too, served as another reminder of a totally different kind. Owing to the high place occupied by this 'athleta Christi' in the fourteenth-century movement, his travels in Europe will be considered in detail at a later stage in this study.[4] In the fifteenth century the main emissaries of the East came from the crumbling Empire of Constantinople. After the crushing defeat of the Latins at Nicopolis in 1396, Manuel II Palaeologos was forced to swear allegiance to the Ottoman victor, Bayezid I. Seeing, however, that the downfall of

---

[1] Leo sent Schaban, Count of Gorigos, his son-in-law, to Avignon to explain to Clement VII the miserable state of the King and Queen of Armenia in Egypt. Moved to pity, the High Pontiff published a series of bulls dated 4 July 1381 to the Archbishops of Tarragona, Saragossa, Toledo, Saint James of Compostella and Seville as well as to the Chapter of Braga enjoining upon them to raise the necessary funds for the deliverance of the Armenian captives. *Vat. Arch.*, Reg. 293, fo. 135 vo; Reynaldus, VII, 446; Dulaurier, *Rec. des Hist. des Crois.*, *Documents arméniens*, I, 722; cf. Valois, *France et Grand Schisme*, II, 221–2, n. 5.

[2] Valois, l.c.

[3] Makhairas's *Chron. of Cyprus* (ed. Dawkins), I, 98–9 (§ 113) and II, 98 n.; Stubbs, *Lectures*, 227; J. A. Gatteyrias, *L'Arménie et les Arméniens* (Paris, 1882), 118–19; Fortescue, *Armenian Church*, 29; *Nicopolis*, 15–16, 165 n. 56.

[4] *vide infra*, Cap. XIV.

his last stronghold in the forsaken city of Constantine was merely a matter of time, he departed on a 'mendicant Pilgrimage' to the West, hoping against hope that he might rouse his fellow-Christians to come to his aid and save the miserable remnant of his Empire. He wandered from one court to another in Italy, France and England during the years 1399–1401. Benedict IX, the Roman Pope, responded by sending Paul, Bishop of Chalcedon, and Ilario Doria, Knight of Genoa, 'to England and other parts' to preach the crusade against the Turks. The Duke of Milan gave Manuel some valuable presents, and Charles VI of France granted him a pension of 30,000 crowns. In England, he was met by Henry IV himself at Blackheath and taken to the royal palace at Eltham for Christmas. On his return, however, Manuel found that his beleaguered capital was saved for a time, thanks to Timur's victory over Bayezid I in the battle of Angora (28 July 1402) and not to the imperial intercession at the courts of Europe.[1] After the fall of Constantinople and the flight of the last of the Palaeologos dynasty to the Morea, one of their number, Thomas Palaeologos, took refuge in Rome in 1461, bringing with him the head of St. Andrew the Apostle. His presence added to the anger of Pius II against the Turk and made him determined to fulfil his project of crusade at any cost.[2] The sad fate of dwindling monarchies and the wanderings of august kings and emperors among the peoples of Western Europe could not but inflame the ardour of men and women among whom the crusade was still a living memory.

Last but not least was the great energy displayed in the writings of pilgrims and propagandists of the Later Middle Ages for the old cause. The enormous body of literature

[1] *Nicopolis*, 119–20, 199 notes 11–13 (*Papal Letters*, IV, 308; PRO MS. E. 101, Bundle 330, no. 17; *Letters of Henry IV*, 56–7); Finlay, *Greece* (ed. Tozer), III, 481; Vasiliev, *Emp. byzantin*, II, 320–3; Schlumberger 'Un empereur byzantin à Paris et à Londres', in *Rev. des Deux Mondes* (11 Dec. 1915) and in *Byzance et croisades* (reprint, Paris 1927), 87–147; Jugie, 'Voyage de l'empereur Manuel Paléologue en Occident,' in *Échos d'Orient*, XV (1912), 322–32.

[2] *vide infra*, Cap. IX on the crusade of Pope Pius II; see also Vasiliev, op. cit., II, 266.

emanating from the pen of these enthusiasts is indeed one of the permanent monuments of the time and justifies the special attention which will be accorded to it in the following pages. If the crusade had aroused so much sympathy in Europe, how can we account for the meagreness of its outcome and the ultimate failure of the movement as a whole? The futility of all efforts to save the Holy Land might be ascribed in part to the circumstances of European politics already outlined in this chapter. On the other hand, the state of the Islamic world was yet another principal element in the frustration and collapse of the crusading movement. It would be idle to dwell on all the events and institutions which formed the basic strength of Egypt in Asia and of Turkey in Europe, although a brief survey of some of these seems both necessary and helpful.

Egypt in the fourteenth and fifteenth centuries was one of the most prosperous countries in the world. The description of Cairo and Alexandria by late medieval travellers, frequently quoted in the first part of this study,[1] and the accounts of the contemporary Egyptian chroniclers, read like a fairy tale. In dealing with the social and home life of the Mamlūks, Stanley Lane-Poole suggested that

'we must turn to the Thousand and One Nights, where, whatever the origin and scene of the stories, the manners and customs are drawn from the society which the narrators saw about them in Cairo in the days of the Mamlūks; and the various articles of luxury that have come down to us, the goblets, incenseburners, bowls, and dishes of fine inlaid silver and gold, confirm the fidelity of the picture'.[2]

The chief source of this fabulous wealth was not Egypt itself, whose arable land was limited to a comparatively small and narrow strip of soil on the banks of the Nile in times when the modern irrigation system was unknown. It was not only in articles of luxury that the natural resources of Egypt were defective, but also in some of the primary raw materials, necessary for the maintenance of a large army. Egypt had no forests to supply timber for the

---

[1] *vide infra*, Chapters (VIII and IX) on Pilgrims, Travellers and Propagandists.

[2] *Hist. of Egypt in the Middle Ages*, 251.

construction of fleets and no mines to furnish the Sultans
with the raw metals for the manufacture of implements of
war.   The secret of the prosperity of the country was trade.
Egypt, and for that matter Syria also, happened to be in
possession of the nearest and most practical termini of the
Eastern trade routes by the Red Sea and by the Euphrates
and Persia to India.   Other routes to Caffa, Trebizond and
Armenia existed, but they did not rival the former in
facility and cheapness; and, moreover, it must be remembered that the market-towns of Christian Armenia were
closed by the Egyptians after that country had been seized
by them in the course of the fourteenth century.   The
merchants of the West had no choice but to resort to the
markets of Alexandria, Damascus and other important
towns in the Mamlūk Empire for their trade requirements.
The solidity and efficiency of an elaborate and centralized
administrative system,[1] without equal except perhaps in
some of the Italian republics, ensured a regular and un-
diminished revenue for the Sultan's coffers.   This money
was not, at least wholly, spent on luxuries and amusements
for the ruler in power.   The major part of it was used for
the maintenance of a standing army, sufficiently well-
equipped and well-trained to stem the tide of invasion by
the crusaders from Western Europe on the one side and
by the Mongols from the heart of Asia on the other.   This
army was annually reinforced by a few thousand young
Mamlūks purchased for the Sultan and his generals partly
by Muslim agents who imported their goods by land, but
chiefly by Christian merchants and especially the Genoese
who transported their acquisitions from the markets of
Caffa and the Balkans by sea.   It was a lucrative trade,

[1] Gleanings on this interesting subject may be made here and there in the
Egyptian chronicles, but perhaps the best direct sources are:

(a) Zoubdat Kachf el-Mamālik—*Tableau politique et administratif de
l'Égypte, de la Syrie et du Hidjaz sous la domination des sultans mamlouks du
XIIIᵉ au XVᵉ siècle*, par Khalîl eḍ-Ḍâhiry; ed. P. Ravaisse (Paris, 1894).

(b) al-Qalqashandī, Ṣubḥ al-Aʿasha, in which Fatimid and Mamlūk institutions are treated together.

Secondary authorities include Godefroy-Demombynes, *La Syrie à
l'époque mamlouke*; van Berchem, *Matériaux pour un Corpus Inscriptionum
Arabicorum*; and Bjorkmann, *Staatskanzlei im islamischen Agypten*.

and the Italian merchants unscrupulously defied all the papal bulls prohibiting it on pain of excommunication.[1]

It is unnecessary here to moralize on the baseness of such transactions on the part of the Italians, offending as they did against the law of God and the interests of their fellow-Christians, or to dwell too long on the ruthless and unscrupulous character of that enormous medieval 'foreign legion' of Mamlūks. Whatever the rights and wrongs of the case, the fact remains that, with the passing of centuries since their introduction into Egypt and their ultimate ascension to power in the state, the Mamlūks had succeeded in fashioning one of the most redoubtable systems of medieval warfare, whose efficiency was proven in the long succession of encounters with the crusaders of the East. The abundant contemporary Arabic literature dealing with the Mamlūk art of war,[2] may indeed form a worthy basis for a much-needed and independent work on the subject. At present, however, it will be illuminating to indicate briefly some of the outstanding characteristics of that system. The victory of the Mamlūks in battle was not necessarily the outcome of sheer valour. In this, the Western combatants were equal, if not superior to them. It was a question of tactics which aimed at the dislocation of the enemy phalanxes and the confusion of his lines. The skill of the Mamlūk fighters in archery and the type of horse they used, helped considerably towards this end. Mamlūks were trained from early youth, not only to become great swordsmen and lancers, but also and in particular to achieve excellence in the use of the bow and arrow; and constant drilling during the rest of their lives increased their attainments in this sphere. Then the Mamlūk horse, lean but swift in action, presented a marked contrast to the heavy Western horse; and, again, the Mamlūk soldier was lightly clad while his Western opponent was mailed in steel. Even if we overlook the conditions of battle under a fierce Eastern sun, a point which Philippe de Mézières, chancellor of the Kingdom

---

[1] More specific details of this matter are furnished in the followng chapters, especially Cap. II and VI.

[2] See section on counter-propaganda in Cap. XIX and bibliography under Art of War in Oriental MSS.

of Cyprus, made clear in his *Songe du vieil pelerin*,[1] this contrast alone is sufficient to explain the defeat of the Christians and give us reason to marvel at whatever triumphs they may have achieved. The mobility of the Mamlūk line of battle enabled them both to harass their enemy on all sides and to adapt their own formation and tactics to any unforeseen development without much difficulty. When hard-pressed in sieges, too, they knew what the West did not know till very recent times—the use of 'poisonous gases'. Missiles and Greek fire served their purpose well as long as the walls of a beleaguered city remained intact. On the other hand, a gap in the wall or the boring of a mine—a favourite practice in European warfare—would lead to a precarious battle at close quarters and the uncertainty of hand-to-hand fighting with a steel-clad enemy. To stop the onrush of besiegers into their stronghold, the Mamlūks hit on the ingenious idea of baking inflammable discs capable of emitting thick fumes of sulphur and ammonia.[2] These were placed in the defective parts of walls and in mines and set alight. Even if such gases were not strictly poisonous according to the standards of modern civilization, they were sufficiently pungent and obnoxious to deter and demoralize the mailed knight in his slow movement.

On the religious side, it is extremely doubtful whether the Mamlūks viewed the principle of holy war (al-Jihād) in the same light and with the same earnestness as the apostles of primitive Islam. Composed of Christian renegades who had betrayed their God and renounced their faith, or recruited from distant regions and tribes of obscure origin, they often gave themselves up to excesses, debauchery and orgies of the worst type. Yet in public they affected such a holy appearance and manner as to silence their critics. On the other hand, the spirit of al-Jihād was consonant with their warlike instincts, and this word was therefore continually used to intensify the enthusiasm of all Muslims in their contests with the crusaders. One very important feature of the Arabic literature on the art of war was the

[1] *vide infra*, Cap. VII.
[2] Baktūt al-Rammāḥ (B.M. MS. Or. 3631, i), ff. 216 ro—217 ro.

form in which it was presented as advice for holy warriors (mujāhidīn). The Mamlūk soldier, however ungodly he might have been in the past, became a holy warrior (mujāhid) in his contest with the Christians; and when he fell in battle, he became a holy martyr (shahīd).

The Ottoman Turks had much in common with the Mamlūks, at least in regard to the matter of warfare. Their tactics were similar, their horse was identical, and their attention to the art of using the bow and arrow was equal. They also had their 'foreign legion', but on a much smaller scale, in the Janissaries,[1] although some writers are apt to antedate the importance of this future *corps d'élite*. Their war too, was a holy war (Jihād) with a somewhat more genuine feeling about it than in the case of the Mamlūks. It is also noteworthy that, whereas the Mamlūk Sultanate, like the Holy Roman Empire in the West, was purely elective in principle—and hence suffered from the unending quarrels and many crimes caused by disputes over succession—the Ottomans had an established dynasty with fixed hereditary rights; and one of the happy features of its early history was the unbroken chain of strong monarchs who laid the foundation of a vast empire. On the other hand, it would be an error to magnify the power of the Ottomans beyond its definite limitations in the four-teenth century. Their European conquests were in great part made easy by the impotence of the countries which succumbed to their yoke. Further, the Ottomans were only one of many independent Turkish dynasties in Asia Minor, and far from being the strongest or wealthiest of them. It was not until the fifteenth century that the process of Turkish unification in Anatolia by means of a series of marriages, intrigues and conquests was complete. The Timurid invasion of the peninsula in 1402 either suppressed or at least reduced to impotence all the indepen-dent Turkish principalities and with them the remaining Christian fortresses on the Asiatic mainland. Bayezid I sustained the most humiliating defeat of his career and

---

[1] *Nicopolis*, 73–5 and 186 n. 56–61; Hasluck, *Christianity and Islam under the Sultans*, II, 483–93; Lybyer, *Government of the Ottoman Empire in the time of Suleiman the Magnificent*, 91–3.

became Timur's prisoner for the rest of his life at Angora, but the Ottoman realm was intact beyond the Hellespont —a fact which may account in part for Ottoman recovery and supremacy over sister states in Asia. If the Crusade of Nicopolis (1396), either by accident or by design, had been postponed for six years until the time of the battle of Angora (1402), the power of the Ottomans might have been wrecked for ever, their rule in Europe nipped in the bud, and—who knows?—the dream of uniting the forces of the West and of the Far East in conjunction with Timur the Tatar against the Mamlūks realized and the Holy Land regained for Latin Christianity.

In the Balkans, the conditions that heralded the greatness of the Ottomans were of a different nature from those affecting Asia Minor. Their origin may be traced to the year 1345 when the usurper Kantakuzenos invited a detachment of Orkhan's army to cross the strait and assist him in his civil war with the child-emperor John V Palaeologos and the Dowager-Empress his mother. In return for this service against his own fellow-countrymen, Kantakuzenos undertook to marry his daughter Theodora to the Sultan and to allow his men to carry into slavery whomsoever they captured among the reluctant Greek followers of the legitimate emperor. This was the beginning of the end of the ancient empire. The Ottomans never retired from Thrace and they unremittingly pursued their triumphant career after the deposition of Kantakuzenos. The field was too rich and the booty too tempting to be given up without a struggle. This struggle proved to be beyond the power of the imperial host to sustain. Byzantium had fared ill at the hands of the Latins in the Fourth Crusade in 1204. When the Latin Empire of Constantinople was recovered by the Palaeologi in 1261, it was a weak and divided land, composed of several petty fiefs under Latin and Slavonic lords organized on an alien feudal model. The old imperial theocracy was but a shadow of the past and the country had become the prey of conflicting institutions, interests, races and creeds. The hatred of the native Greeks for their arrogant foreign masters was aggravated by the planting of Latin Catholicism in their country.

This absence of political independence and, what meant even more to the Greek, the great menace to Eastern Orthodoxy, changed the whole outlook of the inhabitants of the Empire towards the Ottoman invasion. The advent of the Turk in their midst was not considered as calamitous as it has often been painted; for the new invader, though replacing the Latins in their lordship of the land, promised to be more tolerant in religious matters. The Greeks would willingly forfeit that slender hope of political independence, if only they could save their church from ruin. The Ottomans appeared in the Balkans at this juncture and made use of these circumstances to establish their sway on European soil. This baffling situation has its analogy in earlier Byzantine history, when the 'Jacobites' of Egypt treated with 'Amr ibn al-'Āṣ and accepted the Covenant of Caliph 'Umar to save their Church and country from the ruthless government of the Melkite Christians in the days of Heraclius. Although the analogy is not altogether a perfect one, in each case the surrender of liberties to an invading race with a totally different religion was regarded as the lesser of two evils.

The idea of the crusade in later medieval times was not confined to Europe and the Levant. It was hoped that a third party—the Tatar—would enter the field against the Muslims. In order to estimate the extent and limitation of Mongol collaboration in holy war, it may be helpful to outline the main features of the Mongol state in the period under review. During the fourteenth century their empire consisted of four distinct divisions—first, the Kipchak realm in the steppes of south Russia; second, Persia whose government was disputed by a multitude of dynasties until Timur put an end to all of them; third, the Chaghatai Empire, named after its founder, a son of Chingiz Khan who held the greater part of Central Asia; and fourth, the Far East under the dynasty of Qublay Khan. At the close of the thirteenth century, the Mongols were still largely pagan, and this gave rise to the great contest between the Christian missionary and the Muslim traveller and merchant, each trying desperately to win them for his faith, and the struggle ended in the complete triumph of the latter. For the purposes of missionary activity, the Roman Church created three large Oriental Sees—first, the 'Vicaria Tartariae Aquilonaris', comprising the Custodia Gazariae (Khazars) on the north-western shores of the Black Sea as well as the Sea of Azof and the 'Custodia Sarai' between the Black Sea and the Caspian; second, the 'Vicaria Tartariae Orientalis', comprising the 'Custodia Trapezundis' (Trebizond) and the 'Custodia Thauris' (Tabrīz) which extended over Greater Armenia, Mesopotamia and Persia with the town of Soldaia as the seat of the Archbishop of Sultanieh; third, the 'Vicaria Tartariae seu Kathay', with Cambalec (the Arabic Khān Bāliq and the modern Peking) as the seat of its archbishop until the expulsion of the Mongols from China about the middle of the century.[1] The contiguity of Mongol dominion to the Holy Land together with the great hatred of Tatar emperors for the Mamlūk sultans encouraged the Latins in their effort to bring this new race within the fold of Catholicism and ultimately save the Holy Land with their aid. The failure of this movement was not entirely due to the Mongol adoption of Islam as their state religion, but, as we hope to show, rather to the inability of the crusading countries to take united action at the right moment. The death of Timur on 19 January 1405 precipitated the dismemberment of his vast empire and the final downfall of Mongol

[1] Golubovich, *Biblioteca Bio-Bibliografica della Terra Santa*, II, includes three useful maps outlining the Roman Catholic provinces in the East during the Later Middle Ages:

(*a*) The Mediterranean, comprising the Holy Land, 'Romania', Morocco and Tunis.

(*b*) 'Vicaria Aquilonare' and 'Vicaria Orientale'.

(*c*) Asia showing the formation of the 'Vicaria Tartariae seu Kathay' and the rest of the 'Vicaria Orientale', which includes 'India Prima Inferior' to the Ganges, 'India Secunda' beyond the Ganges to roughly the borders of China. 'India Tertia Magna Superior' is shown as lying well within Tibet and China as far as Cathay.

See also Bretschneider, *Notices on medieval geography of Central and Western Asia*, 96–7. In the same volume, the author has published a map of the Mongol Empire made in 1331 and found in the Imperial Library of Peking. This map confirms the outline adopted in the present study. Further material of general interest is also available in J. K. Wright's *Geographical Lore of the Time of the Crusades* (New York 1925), 265–98.

power and influence in the Near East.   Thus all hopes of
a Romano-Tatar crusade to crush Egypt and save the Holy
Places were extinguished in the course of the fifteenth
century.

In the meantime, other great movements had shaken the
very foundation of the medieval world.   The revival of
classical scholarship had changed the old conception of
life and learning, and the age of discoveries opened up
new fields for expansion and furnished Europe with new
bones of contention.   The interests of the West became
more oceanic than Levantine, and the zeal for the crusade
was on the wane.   Egypt, hitherto head of the Islamic
world, succumbed to the conquering arm of the Turk
(1517) and sank into the obscurity of one of the darkest
ages in all her history, while the dawn of Modern History
broke over Europe with the Renaissance.

PART II
PROPAGANDA AND PROJECTS

CHAPTER II

BIRTH OF AN EPOCH

Fall of 'Akka (Acre).   Thaddeo of Naples, first propagandist of period.
Nicholas IV.   Charles II. of Anjou.   Fidenzio of Padua

THE capture of 'Akka by the Egyptians in May 1291 may
be appropriately regarded as the end of one chapter and
the beginning of another in the history of the crusades.
The three or four decades immediately following the
collapse of the Latin Kingdom in the Holy Land formed
a period of propagandist activities in the West for the
recovery of the lost heritage of Christ.   To this end, many
notable men of letters and religious dignitaries of the
fourteenth century devoted their efforts with some success.
The new expeditions, though rightly bearing the name of
crusades, differed considerably from the old enterprises in
constitution and results.   With them, however, they had
one common object, at least in theory, the conquest of
Syria and Palestine.

Towards the close of the thirteenth century the Latin
possessions in the Holy Land consisted of Anṭarṭūs, Jubail,
Ṭarābulus (Tripoli), Beirūt, Ṣaida (Sidon), Ṣūr (Tyre),
'Akka, and Ḥaifa, strung out along the coast of Syria and
Palestine.   Both as a trade emporium and as a fortified
town, 'Akka appears to have been greatly superior to the
others—an assumption which is confirmed by the descriptions of it given by medieval Arab geographers.[1]   The
Egyptians realized the importance of 'Akka; but pressed
by war with the Tatars, they signed a treaty with the Latins
on 3 June 1283 [2] renewing a ten-years' truce, meanwhile

---

[1] Qazwīnī (ed. Wüstenfeld), II, 148–9; Yāqūt (ed. Wüstenfeld), III,
707–9; Abulfeda (ed. Reinaud and de Slane), 242, 43; Dimashqī (ed.
Fraehn and Mehren), 213.

[2] Maqrīzī (ed. Quatremère), II, i, 221; 5 Muḥarram A.H. 681.

continuing their preparations for war. The chance soon
came in 1289 when the Christians unwisely broke the terms
of peace by ill-treating Muslim merchants in Ṭarābulus
and 'Akka.[1] The Mamlūk Sultan Qalawūn (1279–90)
at once took the offensive and after seizing Ṭarābulus, set
siege to 'Akka in the summer of 1290. Even his sudden
death in November of the same year [2] did not move the
rulers of Egypt from their resolution to bring their operations against the Christians to a successful issue. After
hard fighting and heavy losses on either side, 'Akka succumbed to Sultan Khalīl (1290–93), Qalawūn's son, on
Friday 18 May 1291.[3] After 'Akka had been taken by
storm, its fortifications levelled to the ground, its garrison
massacred, and its women and children carried into slavery,
the fate of all the remaining towns still in the hands of the
Christians was sealed. They surrendered with little or no
opposition within the next two or three months.

The human aspect of the fray inside 'Akka is perhaps
nowhere described more vividly than in the account of

[1] Bohtor (B.N. MS. Ar. 1670), fo. 10 vo; Rukn-al-Dīn Baibars, (al-Tuḥfa
al-Mulūkiya fī al-Dowla al-Turkiya, Vienna MS. Mixt. 665) fo. 50 vo-51
ro; Ibn al-Furāt (Vienna MS. A.F. 124), fo. 63 ro and 88 vo et seq.;
Dhahabī (Duwal al-Islām, B.M. MS. Or. 1558), fo. 113 vo.

[2] Muir (Mamelukes), 41; article 'Kalā'ūn' in EI.

[3] A list of the Western sources for the history of the fall of 'Akka has been
compiled by Comte Riant in his introduction to Thaddeus, v–ix, and it is
therefore unnecessary to repeat them here.

On the Arabic side, in addition to works mentioned in a previous note,
see Rukn-al-Dīn Baibars (Zubdat-al-Fikr, Oxford MS. Pocock 324), fo.
200 ro–216 ro; Maqrīzī (Sulūk, Cambridge MS. Qq. 276), fo. 152 ro et
vo; 'Imad al-Dīn of Ḥamah (Abul-Fida, cf. BGAL for editions; Cairo MS.
Hist. 68M), non-foliated, last six folios; al-'Omarī (Aya-Sofia MS., Sect. 16,
vol 3), fo. 649 et seq.; al-Dhahabī (al-'Ibar, B.M. MS. Or. 6428), fo. 169
ro–170 ro; al-Tilmisānī (John Ryland MS. 93), fo. 29 ro et vo; Ibn
Kathīr (Oxford MS. Marsh. 676), fo. 36 ro–37 ro; al-Ḥusainī al-Fāsī
(John Ryland MS. 80), fo. 27 ro.

Fairly full accounts of the fall of 'Akka and the remaining Christian
possessions in the Holy Land may be found in several secondary authorities:
Michaud, IV, 454 et seq.; Wilken, VII, 719 et seq.; Kugler, 406–7; Stevenson, 349–55; Condor (Latin Kingdom), 386–413; Ruville, 342–4; Weil
(Abbasidenchalifat), 161 et seq.; Muir (Mamelukes), 39 et seq.; Röhricht,
Gesch. d. Königreichs Jerusalem, 1004–32; Mitteil. d. öster. Inst. XV, 1–58,
and Forschungen zur deutsch. Gesch. (1879), 96–126.

Thaddeo of Naples [1] who was an eye-witness of the fall of the city. Little is known about him. In the *Hystoria*, he is described as 'Magister civis Neapolitanus', who had resided in Syria for several years.[2] He is afterwards found at Messina where, in December 1291, he wrote his story of the disaster. He was evidently a man of mature age at this time, and one may therefore deduce that he must have been born during the first half of the thirteenth century. The non-apologetic attitude which he takes in regard to Jean Gresti, captain of the French contingent and towards the flight of King Henri II de Lusignan,[3] the rival of Charles of Anjou as claimant to the Crown of the Kingdom of Jerusalem, reveals that he is neither French nor a partisan of the Angevin dynastic claims. He is no merchant, for though he states that the Pisan and Venetian settlements in 'Akka discharged their duties while the fighting actually continued, he deprecates the behaviour of the Italian merchants in taking to flight as soon as they saw the enemy pouring into the town.[4] Comte Riant suggests that he was either a Templar, on the ground that he consistently praises the profession of arms,[5] or more probably a clerk—a preaching friar, as evidenced by his knowledge of the Scriptures which he quotes freely; there is no categorical evidence to confirm the conjecture. Such is the meagre material available for Thaddeo's own life.

As a source the *Hystoria* contributes hardly any fresh evidence on the details of the siege. The only incident related not met with elsewhere is one of little import. Two hundred priests and members of religious orders,[6] says the author, gathered together in the form of a battalion and, without other arms than the Cross which led them, hurled themselves on the lines of the enemy only to be cut to pieces by the sword. It is difficult to explain this suicidal

[1] Despite the fact that the *Hystoria de Desolacione et Conculcacione Civitatis Acconensis et Tocius Terre Sancte* was edited as early as 1873, it seems to have escaped the attention of most subsequent historians of the crusade. The date of its redaction is placed by Comte Riant, pp. xj–xij, in December 1291, within three months of the fall of 'Béryte'.

[2] ib., ix, 39; 'in partibus Syriae olim degenti'.

[3] ib., x, 25, 26.   [4] ib., 25–6, 28, 31, 38.

[5] ib., x.   [6] ib., 14–16. 'De presbiteris religiosis crucesignatis.'

attempt which merely exposes the ill-advised tactics of the Christian host. Yet we may search in vain for a contemporary annalist who equals Thaddeo in the liveliness of his description of the events of the day. The horrible tumult[1] of war furnishes him with material. The unspeakable massacre, the desecration of churches, the riderless horses trampling down children abandoned by their parents, the suicide of women who preferred to plunge into the sea in search of death rather than fall into Saracen hands—all these aspects and more are depicted with mastery and with the intimate knowledge of a close observer.

The main value of Thaddeo's chronicle, hitherto unknown or overlooked, is that it is written chiefly as a document of propaganda for the crusade, the first of its kind within the period here considered after the fall of 'Akka. It is presented in the form of an 'Epistola' addressed to the whole of Christendom.[2] His treatment of the subject shows that it was not his intention to convey a complete historical picture with all the details and facts of the siege. Thaddeo chooses, eulogizes, deprecates and above all describes many of the scenes which seem most suitable to rouse the feelings of all good Catholics against the victors of the day. He speaks without restraint about their violence against women, not even excluding those who had taken the veil.[3] The houses of God, too, were subjected to a desecration of the worst type. Sacred images were snatched from the altars and tied to the tails of camels

---

[1] ib., 59. 'De tumultu populi, civitate jam capta.' He says, 7–8, '. . . ex omni parte se intuencium absque fuge remedio in hostium potestate, tanquam in medio sagene, conclusos, & a feritate barbarica tam infeliciter captivatos, per miserande civitatis plateas, vicos, domos et angulos, universaliter est auditus, quem sua sonoritate in Dei aures, . . . Tunc clamaverunt omnes de profundis miseriarum tribulantis ad Dominum, &c.'

[2] ib., xii.

[3] ib., 9–10. 'Tunc virgines ejus lamentantes, in pallorem converse, subite facte sunt squalide; pro eo quod intacta pudoris claustra virginei, sacrilegus heu! proh pudor! predo violenter infregit & temerariis contactibus violavit: nunc prostitute fuerunt omnes a lascivientibus canibus & oppresse, que, vel, amisso conjuge infra juventutis floride adhuc teneros annos, caste viduitatis domi Deo tributa solvebant, vel, virginalis amore mundicie, Christo Domino in monasteriis sub sacre religionis observancia se perpetuo dedicarant, vel ad sobolem procreandam vacabant amplexibus pudicicie conjugalis.'

to humiliate the powerless defence.[1]   The narrative, taken
as a whole, is in reality a homily and an exhortation with
the events of 1291 as a mere frame and text.   Thaddeo
sees the hand of Providence in it all.   These disasters
are God's punishment of the Christians for their sins, and
the infidels are the instruments with which He displays
His wrath.[2]   The ways of the Almighty, however, are
not without aim; for, seeing the indifference of His flock
to the fate of the Holy Land, He gives them this cruel
reminder of their duty to save it.   Thaddeo ends his
epistola with a number of invocations or 'exclamacii' addressed to God, to the Holy Pontiff, to all the kings and
princes of Christendom, and finally to all good Catholics
to take up once more the cause of the crusade.   To the
Omnipotent he prays [3] for fortitude and mercy that Christians may overthrow His cruel enemies who do not honour
His name.   He exhorts the Pope as vicar of Christ among
nations to eradicate paganism and redress the injury to
the Saviour that his name may be honoured throughout
the world.[4]   Then he solicits all kings and princes to cease
their dissensions and act, not singly, but as one body in
the bosom of the Church Militant. [5]   Lastly he exhorts
all the faithful to avenge the bloodshed of Christians on
Eastern soil and by force of arms to save the Holy Land
which is 'our heritage'.[6]

---

[1] ib., 31, 33, 37–9.   [2] ib., 48–55.
[3] ib., 63–4. 'Exsurgat igitur in fortitudine sua Deus noster . . .   Pre-
sumpcionis quoque tante temeritatem arguat, adversus ejus omnipotenciam
in jactancie contumacia se jugiter erigentem; festinus jam ipse de celo
virtutum Dominus in adjutorium veniat sui populi christiani, ut inimici
ejus in ire sue iracundia dissipenter: . . . ut contra gentes que bella volunt
& ejus potenciam non verentur, jam non Deus misericordiarum appareat,
sed ut Dominus pocius timeatur ulcionum.'
[4] ib., 64–5. 'Exsurgat & Christi vicarius in nacionum exterminium
paganarum, & Redemptoris injuriam vindicet a quo imperium ipse accepit &
regnum super omnes, qui ubique terrarum nomen reverentur & invocant
Salvatoris'.'
[5] ib., 65; '. . . necnon in membra tam honorabilia corporis mistici
Ecclesie militantis'.
[6] ib., 65–6; '. . . unanimiter proficiscantur . . . ut vindicetur Christianus
sanguis . . . gladius, in manu valida . . . ut expurgatis exinde sordibus
bestiarum, quibus tanto fuit abhactenus tempore prophanata, Terra Sancta,
hereditas nostra, &c.'

Thaddeo does not suggest any definite plans as to the manner in which the crusade should be conducted, but confines himself to exhortations.   The other task, he leaves to his propagandist successors, whose work he anticipates, and to the Church and state authorities to whom he addresses two of his 'exclamacii'.   Of all the crowned heads in Europe at this time, the wearer of the papal tiara, Nicholas IV [1] (1288–92), was the most ardent to promote the crusade. As Brother Jerome d'Ascoli of the Franciscan Order, this Pope is to be remembered as apostolic legate in the East under Gregory X.   This may help to explain his keen interest in the affairs of the land beyond the sea.   It was he who furnished Giovanni de Monte Corvino with letters to Arghūn, Qublai Khan and the Nestorian Patriarch Mar Jabalaha with a view to further missionary work in the Far and Middle East.[2]   A Christian East would ensure the destruction of Muslim supremacy in the Holy Land.   Further, he strove hard to establish peace on a firm foundation in Europe in order to unite all the forces of Latin Christianity for the crusade.   By asserting papal suzerainty with success over the Kingdom of Sicily as against the claims of Aragon, he gained a permanent follower in the person of Charles II whom he crowned as undisputed King of Sicily and Apulia.   Outside Italy, he intervened between Edward I and Philippe le Bel to bring about the cessation of hostilities between England and France and unite the forces of the two kingdoms to overthrow the Saracen.   In the Empire he obtained a pledge first from Rudolf of Hapsburg (1273–91) and on his death from Adolf of Nassau (1291–8), King of the Romans, to espouse the cause of a crusade.   He even invited John II, Emperor [3] of Trebizond, to assist in the forthcoming holy war.   It appeared from the active propaganda [4] of the

---

[1] *Liber Pontificalis* (ed. Duchesne), II, 467; *Platina of Cremona*, II, 118–22; Gibbon (ed. Bury), VIII, 251–3; Milman (*Latin Christianity*), VI, 447–53; Neander (*Christian Religion and Church*), VIII, 384; Robertson, VI, 290–91, 315, 394, 436–7, 476; Gregorovius (*Rom*), V, 485 et seq.; Mosheim (*Ecclesiastical Hist.*), II, 517; Finlay (ed. Tozer), IV, 349–50; Giesler, III, 126–33.

[2] *vide infra*, Cap. X.   [3] Finlay (ed. Tozer), IV, 349–50.

[4] Heidelberger, 1–9; Delaville Le Roulx, *France en Orient*, I, 13 et seq.

Pope that the whole world was about to crush the empire of the Mamlūks for ever; but time passed—there was neither union in Europe nor action in the East except that undertaken by Nicholas himself. Even before the overthrow of the Latins in the Holy Land with the fall of 'Akka, he had taken the necessary measures for a declaration of war against the Egyptians. In 1291, when the fall of 'Akka was imminent, he declared an embargo on all commercial intercourse with territories subject to the Sultan in arms, horses, iron, timber, foodstuffs and 'alia quaecumque mercimonia' without discrimination, on pain of excommunication and perpetual loss of civic rights.[1] This declaration was confirmed by the Pope in a letter addressed to the Genoese;[2] but ultimately he had to limit it to a period of ten years in regard to foodstuffs. The object of this policy was to reduce the Sultan's revenue to a mere pittance and even starve him to submission. Though not the first of its kind, the precedent thus set was to be of great historical importance as will be shown in detail at a later stage.[3]

Nicholas IV had surrounded himself with many who shared his aspirations and intentions for the Holy Land, and he listened to their advice on the matter of the crusade. Pre-eminent among these was Charles II of Anjou (ob. 1309). His father had left him a legacy of personal interest in the affairs of the East. Charles I (ob. 1285) had made a claim to the crown of the Kingdom of Jerusalem and his son and successor had not renounced it.[4] Moreover, Charles I seems to have had active communication with the Christians of the East.[5] In addition to this heritage, was the fact that Charles II had become vassal to Pope Nicholas, the supreme and ardent exponent of the crusade, which must have intensified the King's interest in the Holy Land. At any rate he had formulated his views on

[1] Reynaldus, *ad ann.* 1291, no. 27; cf. Heyd, II, 25.
[2] Reynaldus, *ad ann.* 1290, no. 28; *Annal. Jan.*, 341; cf. Heyd, II, 26.
[3] *vide infra*, Cap. VI and XII.
[4] B.N. MS. fr. 6049, f. 183 vo–190; cf. Le Roulx, op. cit., I, 16 and note.
[5] 'Lettre des Chrétiens de Terre Sainte à Charles d'Anjou' (A.D. 1260), ed. Delaborde in ROL (1894), no. 2, 206–15. A detailed analysis of this letter appears in Cap. X.

the project of crusade. A 'passagium generale' against so overwhelmingly strong a monarch as the Sultan of Egypt in the present circumstances, he asserted, would be folly.[1] The landing of the forces in Egypt would be prevented without difficulty and the climatic conditions of the East would reduce the capacity of the host of the Cross to fight with the same vigour as the Muhammadans. On the other hand, a trade war against Egypt—the central market of East and West—would achieve what other means of warfare might fail to accomplish. It would also be cheaper to maintain, for only fifty galleys, fifty transports and 1,500 men were needed to enforce the permanent boycott of Egyptian goods and to punish all 'the bad Christians' [2] who might tend to sacrifice the common cause of Christendom for their own individual gains by carrying arms to Egypt. The King of Cyprus, the Templars and the Hospitallers could provide ten galleys and the rest might be levied by the Holy See. Charles suggested, or perhaps, more accurately, supported the idea of the unification of all military orders into one body,[3] an idea already current in the West since the meeting of the Council of Lyons (1274) where Ramon Lull [4] had fought in vain to persuade the Church to act in that direction.

Another adviser to Nicholas on his project for crusade was Fidenzio of Padua, a Franciscan friar of whose life little is known beyond what may be gathered from his own report [5] and the scanty material in the annals of the

[1] Delaville Le Roulx, op. cit., I, 16–19.

[2] ib., 17; 'li mauvais crestiens'.

[3] *Vit. Pap. Aven.* (ed. Mollat), III, 150. 'Item tempore Nicolai Papae IV, propter perditionem terre sancte que tunc fuit, quia Romani clamabant fortiter et alii populi eo quod succursus sufficiens ad defensionem ipsius terre non fuerat missus per eum, ad excusationem quodam modo sui, et ut appareret se velle remedium apponere circa negocia terrae sanctae, refricavit seu reassumpsit verba unionis predicte et tandem nichil fecit.' Delaville Le Roulx, op. cit., 18, note 1, also quotes this passage from the original edition of Baluze, II, 182.

[4] *vide infra*, Cap. IV.

[5] *Liber Recuperationis Terrae Sanctae*, B.N. MS. Lat. 7247, ff. 85–126, first analysed in brief by Delaville Le Roulx, op. cit., 19–25. Heidelberger, 6–7, summarizes Le Roulx's analysis, although the views of the latter scholar call for further scrutiny and consideration. The *Liber* has since been edited

Minorite Order. Grouped together, these references only present a series of disconnected landmarks in Fidenzio's biography. Nevertheless they bear sufficient evidence of his multiple activities and the importance and originality of his plan for a crusade. Of his childhood and his early education, nothing is known except that he had a military training before deciding to take the vows of a Franciscan.[1] In 1266, he became Provincial Vicar of the Minorite Friars in the Holy Land,[2] and we may therefore assume that he had already been there long enough to justify his preferment to that dignity. Fidenzio's life in the Holy Land was certainly one of great trial, for the fortunes of the Christians had sunk to a very low level during that period and their derelict fortresses beyond the sea succumbed to the Saracens one by one. Fidenzio himself was an eye-witness at the fall of Ṣafad to Baibars Bunduqdārī in 1266. Two years later, when Antioch was seized by the Egyptians and many of its Christian inhabitants were carried into slavery, Fidenzio risked his life by crossing to the Mamlūk camp to inspire and fortify the captives. Ultimately, he managed to reach the Sultan's court where he presented a twofold plea,—first for the termination of hostilities by the conclusion of a truce, and second, for the grant of a safe-conduct to the members of his Brotherhood.[3] His mission, however, does not seem to have borne fruit, as subsequent events prove. In 1274, he was at the Council of Lyons, where Pope Gregory X (1271–6) asked him to prepare a report on the project.[4] Instead of responding immediately to the papal request, Fidenzio returned to the East and travelled far and wide for some years in Egypt, Syria, Cyprus, Armenia, the Empire of

by Golubovich, in the *Biblioteca Bio-Bibliografica della Terra Santa*, II, 9–60, to which reference is made here.

[1] Golubovich, op. cit., II, 2.

[2] ib.

[3] ib., 2–3, 24–5, 29.

[4] ib., 4, 9. 'Felicis recordationis dominus papa *Gregorius* Sancto Spiritu inflamatus totis visceribus liberationem Terre Sancte desiderans, . . . michi mandavit in concilio Lugdunensi ut in scriptis ponerem qualiter Terra Sancta acquiri posset de manibus infidelium, et qualiter acquisita possit a Christi fidelibus conservari.'

Constantinople, Turkey and Persia,[1] probably with the object of making further inquiries into the subject of the report which he ultimately dedicated in 1291 to one of Gregory's successors, Nicholas IV.[2] During that period, however, Fidenzio is known to have been in Europe in the course of 1286 when he acted as mediator between Venice and Pope Honorius IV (1285–7) for the lifting of an interdict which Martin IV (1281–5) had imposed on the Republic of St. Mark.[3]

Judging from the above-mentioned facts about his life and work, Fidenzio was well-qualified to give sound advice on the matter of the crusade. His extensive travels in the Near and Middle East, his long residence in Syria, his acquaintance with the Sultan and his court, his experience with the Mamlūk army and Mamlūk warfare, and moreover, his knowledge of the Arabic tongue [4]—all these must necessarily have added considerable weight to the force of his argument. On the other hand, it is essential to bear in mind that Fidenzio's plan was completed while 'Akka was still in the hands of the Latins,[5] and as a result his views were partly based on a situation which no longer existed after the fall of the city on 18 May 1291.

The *Liber Recuperationis Terre Sancte* is divided into two large parts. The first part consists of a general

[1] Golubovich, op. cit., II, 5–6, 25.   [2] ib., 9.

[3] ib., 1–2; Eubel, *Epitome Bullar.*, no. 1575; Sbaralea, *Bullar. franc.*, III, 563.

[4] Golubovich, op. cit., 3.

[5] ib., 19; 'nam modo, id est tempore quo libellus iste scriptus est, currunt ab Incarnatione Domino Jhesu anni mille cclxxxxj; a Machometo autem citra currunt anni sexcenti lxxxviiij'.

The mention of the Hijra year, unusual in medieval documents of the West, is of great importance here as it narrows down the completion of Fidenzio's *Liber* to the first three days of January 1291: (A.H. 689 = A.D. 14 Jan. 1290 to 3 Jan. 1291), that is, more than five months before the fall of 'Akka. This is confirmed at a later stage;—first when Fidenzio suggests that the crusading fleet should be stationed in presumably Christian waters, 'in Cipro, vel in Accon, vel in insula A(n)terodi, vel in Rodo' (ib., 49); second, by the explicit statement that 'Accon est civitas Christianorum, et ibi est dominium Latinorum' (ib., 54).

In his preface to the *Liber* (ib., 6), Golubovich inadvertently refers to the above statements as occurring in chapters 15, 72 and 77 instead of 14, 71 and 79 respectively.

history of the Holy Land from time immemorial up to the time of its loss by the Christians to the Saracens, indicating the causes thereof and the necessity for its recovery.[1] The second and more relevant part deals with the practical aspects of a successful crusade for the recovery of the Holy Places as well as the ways by which it may be retained under Christian dominion.[2] In the first place, the author prescribes a return to the strict practice of Christian virtues [3] as a necessary preliminary to the success of efforts to save the right and lawful heritage of Christ. On the other hand, in the case of war with so formidable an enemy as Egypt, virtue is insufficient. The strength of the hostile forces, the geographical points at which the landing of the crusaders might be possible, the routes leading to Syria and Palestine, the nature of the fleet, the constitution of the army—all these and many other factors must be examined in detail to enable the leader of the crusade to calculate with the utmost exactness all the possibilities of victory and of defeat. Fidenzio spares no effort to fulfil this task in the latter section of his memoir.

The host of God, he lays down, should consist of twenty to thirty thousand horse and a considerable body of infantry whose number, unfortunately, he leaves undefined.[4] Numbers, however, do not ensure victory. Men must be strongly armed, well disciplined and united.[5]

---

[1] ib., 9 et seq. The peoples that held the Holy Land at various times were, according to Fidenzio, the 'gentiles' (*gentilium diversorum*), Jews, Assyrians, Romans, Christians and Saracens. By the first Christian domination, he refers chiefly to the Syrian Christians whose "infectio, variatio, effeminatio, indiscretio, divisio, defectio, derelictio' (ib., 12) led to the loss of the Holy Places. The author devotes a long chapter to 'Machometo et vita ejus' (ib., 16–19) and enumerates the qualities of the Saracens as 'infidelitas, feditas, crudelitas, cupiditas, sagacitas, stolliditas, instabilitas' (ib., 19). The concluding chapter of Part I urges the return of the Holy Land to Christendom—'Quod Terra Sancta debet esse Christianorum' (ib., 26–7).

[2] ib., 27 et seq. 'Quomodo Terra Sancta posset acquiri et qualiter deinceps valeat conservari.'

[3] ib., 35.

[4] ib., 28. 'Et puto quod sufficere possunt xxxᵃ milia equites Christiani, vel saltem xxᵃ milia cum alio adjutorio. . . . Oportet etiam quod in exercitu Christianorum sint pedites multi.'

[5] ib., 'Decenter armati—Bene ordinati—Ad unionem dispositi.'

His account of Saracen tactics, and their use of the arrow and the light horse in battle is intended to put the crusaders on their guard against the errors of their predecessors.[1] His advice for effective reconnaissance (*De exploratoribus*) is of interest, since it is here that he draws attention to the skilful system whereby the Sultan kept himself informed by his agents of the actions of the Christians, not only in the parts adjacent to his own country, but also in remote regions.[2] After dealing with the qualities and virtues befitting the leader of the host,[3] Fidenzio suggests that war with the Saracens should be waged by two forces, simultaneously by sea and by land.[4] He strongly upholds the sea blockade of Egypt which could be successfully carried out by means of a fleet consisting of forty or fifty galleys, but not less than thirty—all well equipped with men and war material.[5] Their first duty would be to intercept all those ungodly and insubordinate Christians who, in search of worldly gains and in defiance of the penalty of excommunication imposed by the Church, continue to trade freely with the enemy. Moreover, a sea blockade of the coasts of Egypt and other countries subject to Muslim rule would be an effective weapon against Saracen prosperity owing to the Saracens' ignorance of the art of navigation.[6] Describing the Mamlūk gains from commerce, Fidenzio reports that from Alexandria alone comes a daily income of one thousand 'old besants' or more than

---

[1] Golubovich, op. cit., 28–30.

[2] ib., 33. 'Soldani Sarracenorum multos habent exploratores, et omnia facta Christianorum volunt scire non solum in partibus propinquis, sed etiam in partibus remotis.'

[3] ib., 41.

[4] ib., 46. 'Unus exercitus eorum debet pugnare contra Sarracenos per mare, alius autem exercitus debet pugnare contra eos per terram. Isti autem duo exercitus debent pugnare contra Sarracenos eodem tempore, ut majorem jacturam faciant et inferrant Sarracenis.'

[5] ib.; 'et bonum esset quod essent l vel xl vel xxx ad minus galee, bene armate et bene parate, tam in personis, quam in omnibus hiis que sunt necessaria ad bellum'.

[6] ib.; 'quia Sarraceni Egipti et alii Sarraceni qui impugnant Christianos Terre Sancte, non poterunt navigare nec aliquas merces, aut aliqua alia per mare deffere, &c.' This, of course, is not absolutely true, as will be shown later in this study.

a thousand florins, which the Sultan may spend on the equipment of Saracen horsemen.[1] If the Christians cease to frequent Egypt, the Saracens would lose all this income and thus sustain a heavy blow.[2] Fidenzio then speaks of the means of deflecting the Indian trade from the Red Sea and Egypt to Persia and Christian Armenia.[3] Another point in favour of the blockade is the possibility of preventing the importation of young men from the shores of the Black Sea (Mare Majus) to reinforce the enemy's army of Mamlūks.[4]

There are three ways by which the crusaders can approach the Holy Land.[5] The first is the land route across Europe to Constantinople, and then through Anatolia (Nacolim) and Armenia; this has the advantage of avoiding the difficulties involved in transport of horses and a large store of provisions by sea. The 'peregrini Christiani' who proceed by this way march through friendly Christian countries, with the exception of Muslim Turkey, and even Turkey is subject to the dominion of the Tatars who are not hostile to Christians.[6] The army must be accompanied by guides (*ductores, pedotos*) to lead them by cities which will cater for their needs, and by interpreters conversant with the languages of nations through whose territories they will journey.[7] The second way of reaching the Holy Land is by the sea route from Venice and Genoa, which is also a good one; but it is difficult to find the ships necessary for conveying such a great number of men and animals.[8] The third route is by land as far as Brindisi (Brundusium) and then by sea across the Adriatic to Durazzo (Duratium),

[1] ib., 47. 'Audivi etiam dici quod Soldanus omni die . . . habet de Alexandria circa mille bisantios veteres, qui valent ultra mille florenos, de quibus Soldanus potest stipendiare multos equites Sarracenos.'

[2] ib. 'Si vero Christiani non vadant in Egiptum Sarraceni amittent emolumentum pecunie et erit dampnum maximum Sarracenis.'

[3] ib., 48–9.   [4] ib., 49.

[5] It is interesting to note in passing that Fidenzio systematically uses the word 'pellegrini' or 'peregrini' for crusaders, a fact which shows the close connexion between pilgrim and crusader in the author's mind and throws more light on the theory of the common origin of both movements.

[6] ib., 51. 'Turchi subduntur dominio Tartarorum, qui etiam non essent ausi nocere Christianis, habito mandato regis Tartarorum.'

[7] ib., 52.   [8] ib.

then on to Constantinople whence the rest is identical with the latter stages of the first route. It would not be necessary on this third route to prepare a large fleet for the conveyance of all the 'peregrini' at the same time, as this could easily be carried out by a few ships going backwards and forwards from the one side of the sea to the other.[1] Fidenzio does not specify which of these three routes should be adopted by the crusaders. In all probability, he deliberately left the final decision to the discretion of the leader of the host and his circumstances. The terminal points which the author recommends for the host before advancing into Syria are equally accessible by all three routes. He does, however, take into consideration the nature of the harbours in which the crusaders' galleys may be anchored, thus implying at least the partial use of the sea route. These coastal towns appear in the *Liber Recuperationis* as 'Soldinum'[2] and 'Portus Pallorum'.[3] Each of these two ports has its merits. The waters of Soldinum (St. Simeon) are suitable for harbouring the smaller craft which may sail up the Orontes as far as the walls of Antioch, and the town itself is situated on the borderland of Armenia and Syria. Portus Palorum, on the other hand, lies on

---

[1] Golubovich, loc. cit. 'Et quia transitus ille brevis est, cito possent naves ire Duratium et inde reverti Brundusium et transportare omnia animalia et omnia necessaria exercitui '

[2] St. Simeon, Suweidieh, Sudinum, Soldin or Sollino, near the mouth of the Orontes or Nahr (River) al-Asi, sometimes confused with Seleucia which is situated slightly to the north of Suweidieh (see Droysens' Handatlas, Map 74). Rey (Périples des côtes de Syrie et de la Petite Arménie, in AOL., II C, 333), falls into an error which has again been adopted by Delaville Le Roulx, I, 23 note 3 and Golubovich, op. cit., II, 52, note 2.

[3] P. Pallorum, Pallora, Pallori, Palli, Antipalli, Pals or Plas appears in the XIVth Century Mediterranean maps of Marino Sanudo (1307), Pietro Visconte (1318), Pizigani (1367), the famous Catalan map of 1375 and in Fidenzio's own map reproduced by Golubovich. Probably the only recent historical maps in which P. Pallorum can be traced are Spruner-Menke's (Handatlas, Orient no. XI, see Pallora) and Rey's (op. cit., in AOL, II C, facing 328–9, see P. de Palli). Otherwise, this town seems to have disappeared completely from modern maps. It is known to have been situated a few miles south-west of Lajazzo or Ayas on the gulf of Alexandretta at the mouth of R. Mamistra (also known as Sehiun, Jahan or Pyramus in different periods). Cf. Desimoni, Actes passés à l'Aias &c., in AOL, II C, 436; Röhricht, *Bibl. Geogr. Palaest.*, 600–1.

the shore of the deeper waters of the Gulf of Alexandretta where the larger galleys may be anchored off the Armenian coast,[1] and the fact that this port is well within Christian Armenia might help to safeguard the army landing there against any surprise attacks by the enemy—a point which, though not mentioned explicitly by Fidenzio, could not have escaped his observant eye. The suggested route of the campaign justifies the choice of these towns rather than Ṭarābulus and 'Akka which were still in the hands of the Latins at the time Fidenzio wrote his *Liber Recuperationis*. The crusaders might march from Armenia to the South into Syria without fear of being intercepted by the enemy. He advises the leader of the host to proceed immediately to Antioch, which he regards as inadequately guarded by a small garrison. In order to ensure the success of fighting on the Asiatic mainland, however, it is essential to cut communications between Egypt and Syria. This can easily be done with the collaboration of the fleet. Syria itself is not heavily garrisoned. The danger always comes from Egypt, and the maritime inefficiency and limitation of the Egyptian navy as compared with that of the Christians are not to be ignored by the crusaders. Much damage can be done to the coastal towns of that country which is highly vulnerable from the Mediterranean. The Nile is the main artery connecting the interior with the sea and its mouths must therefore be blockaded by Christian galleys. These, too, will put an end to Saracen piracy and thus make the sea safe for Christian traffic. Meanwhile, the economic war against Egypt should be carried to a successful issue.[2] Fidenzio's work concludes with a number of chapters on the conditions which will ensure the maintenance of the Holy Land in the hands of the Christians, once they have conquered it. A sufficient garrison, the custody of the sea, a stable government under the presidency of one leader, and, last but not least, a life of Christian humility[3] are factors which should not be overlooked in the constitution of the newly acquired land of promise.

---

[1] Golubovich, op. cit., 52, 55–6. 'Naves enim magne possunt stare in Portu Palorum, parva vero vasa possunt locari in fluvio Soldini' (56).

[2] ib., 56–8.   See above for further references.   [3] ib., 58–60.

While these considerations were being examined in Rome, the disastrous news of the fall of 'Akka and all the remaining Christian outposts on the Syrian coast reached the West. Nevertheless, the efforts of Nicholas IV to enlist all good Catholics for the crusade failed. Delaville Le Roulx [1] thinks that the moment was an auspicious one for a crusade. The King of France, he says, had asserted his superiority over his feudal lords and England had suppressed all turbulence in both Wales and Scotland, while the House of Hapsburg had become supreme in the Empire and Aragon had re-conquered the Balearic Islands; all were therefore free to take up the Cross, but none showed any serious intention of sailing to the East. Le Roulx's verdict is not strictly accurate; for the contest between the French crown and the feudal nobility persisted to the end of the Middle Ages; and England had no peaceful neighbour in either Scot or Welsh, even if we overlook her constitutional difficulties and the imminent outbreak of war with France. It is true that the Hapsburgs then had no Investiture troubles and that Aragon ruled the Balearic Islands; but Germany was still very far from being united, and Aragon had its own troubles with its Christian neighbours while the Moors remained a hostile power within the Iberian Peninsula. In Italy the leading maritime republics of Venice and Genoa had their rivalries, and neither of them was sufficiently enthusiastic about papal interdictions and wars which would only ruin their trade and the basis of their prosperity. Though individually each monarch was religious-minded enough not to lack interest in the cause of a crusade, there existed neither the harmony which would unite all against the Saracen nor the stability at home which would give each of them a free hand to act outside his own country in remote regions. It is a striking feature of our subject that all the crusading expeditions of the Later Middle Ages were conducted not by Western Kings, but either by nobles or by the Kings of Cyprus.

Realizing the dangers of delay and eager to bring the forces of England, France and the Empire into unison for immediate action, Nicholas IV decided to take the initiative

[1] op. cit., I, 25.

himself. Out of the papal coffers, he equipped a fleet of twenty galleys which were to be reinforced in the Cypriote seas with fifteen more supplied by Henri II de Lusignan.[1] This was intended for the defence of Armenia against Saracen incursions and for an attack on the coasts of Asia Minor as well as the coast of Egypt in the neighbourhood of Alexandria. Evidently the execution of such a plan was beyond the capacity of this small force, and Nicholas died on 4 April 1292 before realizing that his fleet had failed to achieve anything.

On reviewing the events of the last decade of the thirteenth century, it becomes perfectly clear that Christendom lost all and gained nothing in the Holy Land. The pontificate of Nicholas IV witnessed the end of the last vestige of the Kingdom of Jerusalem in Syria with the fall of 'Akka. Yet the importance of Nicholas's reign cannot be exaggerated, for most of his actions anticipated the very lines of policy which were to be followed closely for more than a century by his own successors as well as by the crusading princes of Europe and of Cyprus and the Knights Hospitallers, soon to become the Knights of Rhodes. The modest tract written by Thaddeo of Naples introduced a new branch of literature which, in volume and importance, occupied a notable place in the literature of the age. The efforts of Nicholas to create an atmosphere of peace between England and France became the main concern at the papal Curia throughout the disastrous period of the Hundred Years' War. Alliance with the Tatars, though considered before his time, was destined to become an ideal of subsequent popes and propagandists for many years. The unification of all the military Orders of Religion became a watchword in almost every work of propaganda written in the fourteenth century. The sailing of the Pope's fleet to Cyprus fixed that island as the normal rendezvous of many future crusades. The attempt to defend Armenia seemed to point to the impending fate of that unhappy country whose proximity to Egypt rendered her an easy prey for Mamlūk revenge and Mam-

---

[1] Golubovich, op. cit., I, 16; Heidelberger, 8; Heyd, *Histoire du commerce*, II, 28; Wilken, VII, 779–80.

lūk raids and ravages until her final extinction as an independent kingdom. The project of a campaign on the
coast of Asia Minor was a forerunner of the crusades which
resulted in the capture of Adalia and Smyrna about the
middle of the century. The idea of attacking Alexandria
came to fruition in 1365, when Pierre I de Lusignan and the
knights of many European states surprised and sacked that
city. Last but not least, the failure of the expedition of
1292 was an omen of the ultimate futility of all efforts to
recover the Holy Places from Muslim hands. In a word,
the pontificate of Nicholas IV saw the birth of a new epoch
in the history of the crusades.

CHAPTER III

PIERRE DUBOIS AND THE REIGN OF PHILIPPE LE BEL

General tendencies of the reign. Diplomatic propaganda: Pierre Dubois and Guillaume de Nogaret. Advice of men of action: Jacques de Molay, Foulques de Villaret, Henri II de Lusignan and Benito Zaccharia. The Church: Prince Hayton, Guillaume Adam and Guillaume Durant 'le Jeune'. Other propagandists: Galvano de Levanti and Ramon Lull

IT is needless to say that the reign of Philippe le Bel was one of the most momentous periods in the annals of medieval France.[1]   The laying of the foundation of absolutism, the modest beginning of the French 'Parlement', the extension of royal authority in matters of taxation and jurisdiction outside the King's 'demesnes', the humiliation of the Roman Curia and the establishment of the Papacy at Avignon, the abolition of the Order of the Templars and the confiscation of their property, and, last but not least, the encouragement of members of the legal profession and the 'tiers-état', of men of action and of servants of the Church to put forward their views on the promotion of the crusade —these are some of the events which mark the importance of the age of Philippe IV in French as well as European history.   Of attractive appearance yet seemingly modest in character and exacting in religious observances, Philippe was a man of strong will, unscrupulous and unchivalrous, and, unlike St. Louis his grandfather, was always ready to further the interests of the monarchy at the expense of feudatories and popes without discrimination.[2]   The capital

[1] A. Coville, in Lavisse et Rambaud (*Hist. Générale*), III, 11, describes it as 'une énigme'.

[2] Guillaume l'Écossais, a monk of St. Denis, quoted by Coville, loc. cit. See also Giovanni Villani (*Croniche Fiorentine* Eng. trans. by Rose E. Selfe and P. H. Wicksteed, London, 1906), 278, who says that 'King Philip was a lord of a great heart, and in his life did high emprises'.

47

event of the reign was the King's contest with Boniface VIII. The Papacy had indeed emerged victorious from its struggle with the Hohenstaufen; but the realization of the old Hildebrandine theocracy became impossible in fact. The theoretical supremacy of the 'sacerdotium' over the 'regnum' in both spiritual and temporal affairs was tolerated by the growing monarchies in many countries of Europe, notably in France, as long as the Popes did not attempt to enforce the hegemony of the Church over the strong lay powers. It was a state of unstable equilibrium. During the reign of Philippe le Bel, the three Popes—Honorius IV (1285–7), Nicholas IV (1288–92) and Celestine V (1294)—remained comparatively inactive in face of the French monarch; but with the accession of the strong Boniface VIII (1294–1303), came the rupture which ended in the triumph of the French King and the transfer of St. Peter's chair to Avignon. This event had its repercussion on the projects for crusade. The Popes, Philippe thought, were then in his grip near French territory and could be heavily taxed to fill his own treasury. The crusade appeared to be the most plausible pretext to justify in the eyes of the world the extraction of money from the Church; [1] and so Philippe declared himself for the cause of holy war against the Saracens. This gesture was taken seriously by men of all classes of medieval society, who came with definite plans for the accomplishment of the King's wishes. Works of the highest interest were submitted to the Pope, the King and the Council of Vienne (1311–12) by men who had spent many years in the Levant and by others who had never gone beyond the sea; and although no crusade was undertaken by Philippe le Bel, their ideas enriched the propagandist literature of the age.

Foremost among the King's advisers on this matter was

[1] Philippe seems to have been hard-pressed for money throughout his reign, and continued to devise means for new exactions from both Church and laity. For this aspect of his reign, see G. Picot, *Doc. relat. aux États Généraux sous Philippe le Bel*; Isambert, Jourdan et Decrusy, *Rec. gén. des anciennes lois françaises*, III, 316 and 333, and IV, 521; G. Dupont-Ferrier, *Institutions financières de la France à la fin du moyen âge* (Paris 1930–2), I, 191 note 2, and II, 9, 30–1, 135, 138, 141, 146, 193, and 337. The last work includes full references to the subject.

Pierre Dubois [1]—a medieval 'radical',[2] 'publicist',[3] and 'pamphleteer'.[4] He was born in the district of Coutances in Normandy between 1250 and 1260, studied at the University of Paris where he heard Thomas Aquinas [5] (ob. 1274) deliver a sermon, and attended the lectures of Siger de Brabant on the Politics of Aristotle.[6] In 1300, as an accepted legal authority, he handled several cases for Philippe IV and Edward I. He is believed to have died after 1321.[7]

In his leisure time he wrote numerous memoirs, most of which he submitted to the King, on matters of social, ecclesiastical, military and financial reform. Though holding no high office in Philippe's administration, he was in favour with the King who listened to his advice. His ideas, like Philippe's character, might recall the age of the Renaissance rather than the early decades of the fourteenth century, for they were both bold and unconventional. A staunch supporter of the French monarchy, he hoped that the King of France might be elected Emperor and establish his universal authority, not only over the West, but also over the East. This turned his attention to the project

[1] In Latin documents, Petrus de Bosco.

[2] Powicke, in *Historical Essays*, 169 et seq.

[3] Langlois (*De Recuperatione*), xv, calls him 'le premier publiciste de son temps'; Zeck, *Der Publizist Pierre Dubois*, and R. Scholz, *Publizistik zur Zeit Philipps des Schönen* (Stuttgart, 1903), *passim*.

[4] The most important of his numerous pamphlets are:

    (a) *De Recuperatione*. First edited by Bongars as anonymous, II, 316–61; then by Ch. Langlois separately (see Bibliography).

    (b) *De Abbreviatione*. Cf. Wailly, in *Acad. des inscript.*, XVIII, ii, 435–494, and *B.E.C.*, 2e ser., III, (1846), 273–315.

    (c) Three memoirs against the Templars, ed. Boutaric in *Notices et Extraits* XX pt. ii, 85 et seq.

    (d) *Pro Facto Sancte Terre*. Memoir to Philippe le Bel advising him to persuade Clement V to crown him Emperor. In same vol. of *Notices et Extraits*.

    (e) *Opinio cujusdam suadentis regi Francie ut regnum Jerosolimitanum et Cipri pro altero filiorum suorum, ac de invasione regni Egipti. . .* Langlois, Appendix, 131–40.

    (f) Pamphlets against Boniface VIII, ed. P. Dupuy, *Hist. du différend de Boniface VIII et Philippe le Bel* (Paris, 1655).

[5] Langlois, 53.   [6] ib., vii–viii.

[7] Molinier (Sources), III, 196, no. 2871.

of crusade to recover the Holy Land, reconquer the Empire
of Constantinople and even invade Egypt. To this end,
he wrote two important tracts.[1]

Perhaps the most important of Dubois' works is the *De
Recuperatione Terre Sancte*. Although apparently concerned with the recovery of the Holy Land, this is a document advocating general reform in all branches of the
society of the age. In it, Dubois regards the holy war
simply as a means to a bigger end. He urges the suppression of papal power in temporal matters,[2] the confiscation
of all the property of non-conventual monasteries,[3] and the
establishment of a general council similar to the modern
League of Nations under the patronage of the King of
France for arbitration and preservation of peace in the
West.[4] He supports marriage of the clergy,[5] the substitu-
tion of girls' public schools for convents and the teaching of
the vernacular [6] besides Latin. Finally he proposes the
constitution of a regular army with definite regulations for
recruitment,[7] the simplification and codification of all laws,
the establishment of new and more efficient modes of procedure,[8] and emigration to and colonization of the lands
beyond the sea.[9] Singularly modern in his main ideas,
Dubois retains many characteristics of the medieval [10] mind
in his belief in astrology,[11] in his conception of history [12] and
above all in his methods of reasoning. As a schoolman and
a medieval logician, Dubois often resorts to hair-splitting in
his arguments, and the setting forth of his doctrines involves quotations from the Bible, the Canon Law, the Digest
and Aristotle. He shares with his contemporaries their

---

[1] *vide supra*, 49 n. 4.   [2] *De Recuperatione* (ed. Langlois), 33.
[3] ib., 35 et seq.   [4] ib., 7, 11 and 82.
[5] ib., 85. See also p. 51; cf. Mézières below, Cap. VII.
[6] ib., 47, 51, 60–3, and 70.
[7] ib., 15, 92, 114 et seq.   [8] ib., 74–8.
[9] ib., 7 and 92.   [10] ib., Introduction, xix.
[11] ib., 6. 'Tamen hujusmodi angeli, ac etiam celum per suum notum, cum
influencia corporum que sunt in ipso, licet fortiter inclinant et movent
homines ad opera etc.' Cf., *De Abbreviatione*, fo. 11 vo, where he also
says 'influencia solis et lune aliarumque stellarum humana corpora disponunt
ad agendum'.
[12] ib., 130.

hopes and aspirations for the fulfilment of the crusade, though his motives may differ considerably from theirs. The *De Recuperatione*, written between 1306 and 1308 and presented to the Kings of France and England and to the Pope, formulates many of these ideas and motives. It is divided into two distinct sections—the first[1] originally intended as a circular to all the princes of Europe, and the second[2] specially composed for his own royal master and for no one else.

Dubois chooses the land route for the German, Hungarian and Eastern European crusaders to avoid the difficulties of transporting large numbers of horses. Meanwhile the French, the English, the Spanish and the Italian contingents who do not fear the sea may journey by the maritime route to the Holy Land.[3] There should be no discord among the nations represented in the crusade; and the leadership of the host in each district must be entrusted to a single 'dux belli' with a number of centurions (*centuriones*) under his command. Every centurion in turn leads eight cohorts, each consisting of twelve men.[4] For the finance of the expedition, Dubois suggests several sources from which the King can draw sufficient funds to ensure the permanent conquest of the East. These include the abolition of the Order of the Knights Templar and the confiscation of their property,[5] and the imposition of death duties on the estates of all deceased clergy amounting to half the revenue of cardinals and a quarter of that of other members of the Church hierarchy. In the case where a clerk dies without leaving a will, his possessions must be ceded to the treasury of the crusade.[6]

The second part of the *De Recuperatione*, is privately addressed to Philippe IV on matters of special interest to him. These include the insurance of the subordination of the Church by the creation of more French cardinals,[7] the aggrandisement of France at the expense of the Empire,[8]

---

[1] ib., 1–97. [2] ib., 97–130.
[3] ib., Cap. XIII. Cf. Delaville Le Roulx, *France*, I, 50
[4] ib., Cap. XI; Langlois, 17–18.
[5] ib., 13–15. [6] Delaville Le Roulx, *France* I, 51.
[7] *De Recuperatione* (ed. Langlois), 98 et seq. [8] ib., 104 et seq.

and a bold criticism of the royal domestic policy.[1]   One
point of great interest from the standpoint of the crusade
is Dubois' suggestion that the King should exert every
possible effort to establish an Eastern Empire for one of
his sons,[2] while he may himself remain at home to watch over
the wider interests of France.   Later, Dubois again deals
with this subject at some length in a separate document.[3]
The new kingdom may incorporate the whole of the Near
East, not excluding Egypt,[4] whose conquest he considers
to be an easy matter owing to the vulnerability of its coast.
Finally, it is interesting to note that Dubois, probably under
the influence of Ramon Lull his contemporary, expounds
the importance of the study of Eastern languages and
advises the establishment of schools in the Holy Land
where Latin may be taught to maintain the use of the
Roman rite among future settlers, and also Greek and
Arabic so as to facilitate a movement for the conversion of
both schismatic and Saracen to Catholicism.[5]

Another adviser of the same class as Pierre Dubois, was
Guillaume de Nogaret, the trusted servant and close friend
of the King of France.   It is true that only one solitary
memoir is known to have been written by Nogaret, and
that it is much shorter than the *De Recuperatione* of Dubois.
Nevertheless, it seems to be a document of unusual importance.   Owing to the special place held by Nogaret in the
royal administration, one may safely assume that his memoir
is a genuine expression of Philippe's real intentions in regard
to the crusade.   Nogaret[6] was secretary to Philippe IV
and became 'vice-chancellor' of France in 1307.   He died

---

[1] *De Recuperatione*, 118 et seq.

[2] ib., 107 et seq.; Delaville Le Roulx, *France*, I, 53–4.

[3] *Opinio cujusdam suadentis regi Francie ut regnum Jerosolimitanum et Cipri
pro altero filiorum suorum ac de invasione regni Egipti*, appended by Langlois
to the *De Recuperatione* 131–40.   The document was formerly believed to
be anonymous, but reference to Dubois' other tracts (cf. 137) establishes the
authenticity of his authorship of it.

[4] ib., 135–6, and 138–9.

[5] *De Recuperatione*, Cap. XXXVII; cf. Langlois, 47.   In addition to the
works cited in the above references, see also Boutaric, in *Comptes rendus de
l'Acad. des inscript.*, VIII, 84–106; Renan, in *Hist. Litt.* XXVI, 491 et seq;
and Hauréau, in *Journal des savants*, 117 et seq.

[6] Villani, op. cit., 347, describes Nogaret as 'a wise and crafty cleric'.

in 1313, after taking an active part in the King's contest with Boniface VIII and in the affair of the Templars.[1]

In 1310, the year of the summoning of the Council of Vienne, Nogaret prepared his memoir[2] on the project of crusade and submitted it to Pope Clement V, probably with the approval or rather connivance of King Philippe, judging from the nature of the vast subsidies which he requested from the Church. The memoir begins with an attack on the Order of the Templars.[3] Nogaret then indicates how impossible it is for the King of France to undertake the crusade without raising large levies from Church property.[4] The importance of this statement, as Nogaret's report betrays more clearly at a later stage, was that it assumed the financing of the King at the expense of the Church, for Philippe IV, despite the expansion of his influence and of his revenue, was continually hard pressed for funds. As regards the 'passagium' itself, Guillaume suggests fixing a suitable date, before which the whole of the necessary subsidies must be raised and all the preparations completed in ships, arms, horses, and other equipment for the expedition.[5] Another important consideration is the establishment of peace among Catholic princes; and Nogaret proposes that those who break it should receive the curse of Holy Church. United action is essential in the face of the enormous difficulties which confront the crusaders. The power of the enemy must not be scorned or slighted, for the Saracens are highly trained in feats of arms, and they possess timber and war

[1] Dupuy, *Hist. du différend, passim*; Renan, in *Hist. Litt.*, XXVII, 359 et seq.; R. Holzmann, *Wilhelm von Nogaret* (Freiburg, 1898), *passim*; N. Valois, in BEC, XL, 397 et seq.; Ch. Molinier, *Annales du Midi*, 1901, 136–8; D. Vaissete, *Hist. de Languedoc* (New Ed.), X, note 11. Cf. Molinier (Sources), III, 195–6, no. 2870.

[2] Ed. Boutaric, in *Notices et extraits*, XX, ii, 199–205. Title: Que sunt adventenda pro passagio ultramarino et que sunt petenda a Papa pro persecutione negocii; Domini G. de Nogareto.

[3] ib., 199.

[4] Ib.; 'quod dominus rex Francie . . . assumat prosequcionem ipsius negocii cum Ecclesia Dei et ejus subsidio magno et valido, sine quo rex ipse commode complere onus ipsum non posset'. The same idea is expressed later; ib., 201.

[5] ib., 199–200; 'et expense necessarie procurentur et colligantur'.

material supplied to them by 'falsis catholicis' who also
carry children for sale to be brought up in the discipline
of Mamlūk warriors.[1]

Nogaret then reverts to the crucial question of finance.
He emphasizes that the legitimate home of the crusade
treasury is the Kingdom of France.[2]   The possible sources
of income for this treasury are multiple.   At the head of
his list, Nogaret urges the confiscation of the movable and
all the revenues accruing from the immovable possessions
of the Templars for the cause of the crusade.[3]   He further
suggests that the revenue and expenses of the Order
of St. John of Jerusalem and of all the other Orders of
Chivalry should be accurately assessed and the balance
entrusted to the new treasury for the maintenance of the
crusade.[4]   This ordinance, he adds, must be enforced in
regard to all cathedral and parochial churches, abbeys and
priories, and all manner of benefices [5] in the whole of
Christendom.   In all cases, the assessment must be made,
not on the basis of the old tithe, but on the net value of
the property.[6]   When, in the course of these inquiries, it
is found that property is unrightfully held by any of these
bodies, it must be confiscated as a whole for the cause.[7]

When these preliminary but essential measures have
been taken, the Pope may grant the usual indulgence to
the crusaders; and Tatar and other Oriental nations may
be invited to send aid to the Holy Land.[8]   The Greeks
may be forced or persuaded to join the movement; and the
cities of Venice, Genoa, Pisa and others must not obstruct
the way by their lust for gain, but provide assistance in

---

[1] Ed. Boutaric, in *Notices et extraits*, XX, ii, 200; 'et eis parvos infantes
vendentibus, ex quibus Sarraceni homines armorum nutriunt qui appellantur
Turqui'.

[2] ib., 202; '. . . quosque legitime in premissis expendantur in regno
Francie, apud personas et loca quas Ecclesia dominusque rex duxerint
eligendas'.

[3] ib., 'omnia bona Templariorum ipsorum mobilia, et fructus et redditus
immobilium, ubique terrarum, dicto negocio deputentur et ad ipsum integre
convertantur'.

[4] ib., 202–3.   [5] ib., 203–4.

[6] ib., 203.   'Vires autem ecclesiarum ipsarum estimentur non secundum
antiquam decimam sed secundum quod vere valent; et omnia tradantur ut
supra.'   [7] ib., 204.   [8] ib., 204–5.

honour of God.[1] Nogaret concludes with a plea that all, not only Kings and Catholic princes, but barons and nobles, members of universities and even the lower classes should help to ensure the success of the crusade by furnishing the necessary aids, each according to his means.[2]

The memoirs of both Dubois and Nogaret were written by men whose skill in the diplomatic sphere is well known. The first sketched a scheme of general reform and the second dwelt on the use of certain sources of revenue, while both wrote to glorify their king and country. On the practical side of the campaign, their schemes are imperfect. If the crusade were to be taken seriously, the advice of men who knew the East and were experienced in Oriental warfare would become indispensable. Such men were not lacking in that age, and their views were freely communicated to Pope and King. Four men of action who tendered advice on the plan of campaign are worthy of special mention. These are Jacques de Molay, Grand Master of the Templars, Foulques de Villaret, Grand Master of the Knights Hospitallers, Henri II, King of Cyprus and Benito Zaccharia, Admiral of the French navy.

Both Grand Masters were at the Avignonese court when, in 1307, Clement V asked their opinion on the project of crusade. During the same year, Jacques de Molay submitted his report [3] to the Pope. He begins by denouncing the idea of a preliminary or minor expedition [4] as wasteful and futile, since the fall of 'Akka and the other remaining outposts in the Holy Land had left no Christian garrison on which a handful of men could depend in time of pressure. Even if the crusaders choose to land within the confines of Christian Armenia, the fate of the expeditionary force will be sealed unless it is numerically capable of stemming the overwhelming tide of Egyptian forces.

[1] ib., 205.   [2] ib.

[3] Baluze, *Vit. Pap. Aven.* (ed. Mollat), III, 145 et seq.; Boutaric, Clément, Philippe le Bel et les Templiers, in *Rev. des. Questions Historiques*, 6e année (1872), XI, 17; Delaville Le Roulx, *France*, I, 55, note 2.

[4] This is the 'passagium parvum' to precede the 'passagium generale'—a current view at the time; *vide infra* Burcard and Marino Sanudo. A minor expedition, according to Molay, could only be 'damnosum et vituperosum'.

Moreover, landing in Armenia as a possible base for operations against the Saracens is objectionable even in the case of a 'passagium generale' for three main reasons—first, the climatic conditions of that country which are trying to men from the West; second, the difference between Western and Armenian tactics; third, the doubtful loyalty of the natives in regard to the Franks.[1]   To ensure victory for the Christians, an army of 12,000 to 15,000 mounted men-at-arms and an infantry numbering 40,000 to 50,000 is necessary.   This estimate is based on Sultan Baibars' statement that he can resist 30,000 Tatars, but, in the face of half this number of Christian soldiers, he will retire.[2]   Evidently the Sultan was referring here to the mounted force alone, as the Tatar hordes always fought on horseback.   Molay then suggests that there should be no difficulty in raising these armies from the Kingdoms of France, England, Germany, Sicily, Aragon and Castile; and the collaboration of the maritime republics of Italy is needed for the transport of troops by the sea route.   The author recommends the use of a larger type of vessel in preference to the ordinary galley for reasons of economy, provided that a fleet of ten armed galleys has been sent in advance to clear the Eastern waters of the Mediterranean from the enemy and to seize all the Christian craft guilty of trade intercourse with Egypt.   The host would be well advised to land in Cyprus for a short period to recover from the journey by sea before taking the final offensive against the Mamlūks in the Holy Land.

About four years later (1311), while the General Council of the Church was in session at Vienne to consider among other things the project of a crusade, Foulques de Villaret,[3] Grand Master of Rhodes, wrote to Philippe le Bel ex-

---

[1] Baluze (Mollat), op. cit., 147. 'Si Franci essent in Armenia et indigerent refugio, Armeni non receptarent eos in aliquo castro vel fortalitia sua, quia semper dubitaverunt et dubitant ne Franci auferant eis terram.' Cf. Delaville Le Roulx, *France*, I, 56, note 2.

[2] Baluze, op. cit., 146, 148.

[3] Became Grand Master on 3 November 1305, was deposed in 1319 and died 1 September 1327.   Delaville Le Roulx (Hospitaliers, 1100–1310), 408, and (Hospitaliers, 1310–1421), 1–27.

pressing [1] his willingness to take an active part in the great enterprise. This letter is not concerned with the manner in which a crusade should be conducted, but is an official document to assure the King that the Order of St. John of Jerusalem is definitely making its preparations to enrol in the forthcoming expedition against the Saracens. To prove his good faith in this matter the Grand Master of the Hospital informs the King that orders have been given for the construction of seven galleys in Catalonia, three at Narbonne, sixteen at Marseilles, twelve at Genoa in addition to several large vessels of which one is already stationed in Genoese waters, four at Pisa and six at Venice. Moreover, the Hospitallers have fully equipped five armed galleys at Genoa and two at Venice ready to set sail in or before the spring of 1311 on the proposed 'passagium'.[2] Further, horses have been purchased in Spain and other countries as well as provisions in Sicily, Apulia, Provence and Catalonia;[3] and also armaments are being manufactured in considerable quantities, and men, mounted and dismounted, levied as far as the means of the Brotherhood allow. The Order and its Master, Foulques concludes, are waiting on the good pleasure and the command of the King.[4]

[1] This is given in the form of a letter dated Pisa, 27 January 1311; edited by Delaville Le Roulx in *France en Orient* II, 3–6.

[2] Delaville Le Roulx, op. cit., II, 5. 'Facimus nempe, princeps serenissime, in Catalonia galeas septem, Narbone tres, Massilie sexdecim, Janue duodecim, et navem unam ultra aliam magnam quam ibidem emimus, Pisis quatuor, Venetiis sex fabricari et fieri, et, ultra has, Janue de presenti armari quinque et Venetiis duas destinandas ad partes predictas in proximo vernali tempore, vel antea si possibile fuerit.'

[3] ib. 'In nundinis partium Yspaniarum et alibi quam plures equos emi fecimus, et in diversis partibus Sicilie, Apulie, Provincie et Catalonie, carnes salsas, vinum, oleum, caseos, legumina, aliaque victualia, et arma et biscoctum fieri in non modica quantitate, multosque armorum homines equites et pedites retinuimus, modo quo potuimus meliori; &c.'

[4] ib., 6. Explicit,—'Valeat in eternum regia magnificentia, nos et ordinem suscipiens, ad cuncta sua beneplacita et mandata.' The docility of the Hospitallers illustrated by this document as compared with the independence of the Templars in regard to the King of France may be one of the reasons for which the former Order was preserved and the latter abolished. It must be remembered that Molay's report of 1307 (*vide supra*) was submitted to Pope Clement V and not to King Philippe IV.

Meanwhile, Henri II de Lusignan, King of Cyprus (1285–1324), and nominally King of Jerusalem, dispatched two envoys to submit his views on the crusade to Pope Clement V and the Council.[1]   Henri II and his representatives are not concerned with the details of the preparations for the crusade.   As a man of action, whose kingdom lies within reach of Egyptian and Turk, he is chiefly concerned with the general strategy of the campaign.   The King and his representatives are nevertheless aware of the importance of the preparations which must be executed on a large scale.[2]   For the immediate purpose of weakening the military strength of the Sultan and the Saracens, the maritime blockade of Egypt, Syria and other Muslim territories will be found a very effective instrument.   A number of galleys may at once be equipped in order to capture the evil and treacherous Christians who carry new Mamlūks to reinforce the Egyptian army as well as war material and provisions to the enemy.[3]   An essential condition for the success of this fleet in its mission is its independence of the communes of Venice, Pisa, Genoa and all the other maritime powers of Italy whose loyalty to the cause of Christianity against Islam the King regards with unmistakable suspicion,[4] for he fears that they may take advantage of any connection with the navy of the crusade to enhance their own impious interests in Egyptian commerce.   If these restrictions are observed strictly for two or three years, the maritime power of Egypt will be abolished and her resources depleted.   In the meantime, it will be

---

[1] This document, 'Informatio ex parte nunciorum regis Cypri pro subsidio Terre Sancte et passagio, Consilium regis Cypri pro passagio faciendo', is edited by Mas Latrie in *Hist. de Chypre*, II, Ière partie—Documents, 118–25.

The King's nuncios were Jacobus de Casiatis and Symon de Carmadino. The first was Canon of Ancona. ib., 118.

[2] ib., 119, § 1.

[3] ib.; '. . . debeat premitti aliqua quantitas galearum, que capiant malos et falsos Christianos, qui dictis Sarracenis portant homines armorum, scilicet Mamolucos, lignamina, ferrum, picem, victualia et alias merces necessarias eis'.   Furthermore, the author says (op. cit., 120, § 4): 'Et sententie, precepta et alia de facto sunt necessaria ad compellendos Christianos perfidos, ne per suas fraudes seu potentias portent Sarracenis vetita supradicta.'

[4] ib., 119, § 2.

advisable to instal a band of knights and arbalesters (who are capable of resisting the Saracen bowmen) in the Christian ships, for these may cause considerable damage to the coastal towns of the enemy and strike terror into their hearts,[1] until the time is ripe for the 'passagium'. Henri prefers the sea route to Cyprus for the crusaders, and there they and their horses may land for a period of recuperation and may afterwards sail direct to Egypt and not to Armenia, Syria or elsewhere.[2] Here he follows the example of St. Louis as distinct from the advice of Marino Sanudo,[3] and Prince Hayton[4] of Armenia, who suggest that Armenia may be regarded as a suitable base. The King of Cyprus, on the other hand, regards a landing in Armenia with grave misgivings. The strategy which involves the use of that country as a base for operations against Syria and Egypt involves incalculable perils to the host. Armenia is a much-harassed and weakened land and its people are apt to flee to the mountains in search of safety. Moreover, the journey to Cairo by way of Ghazza is a long one, lasting twenty days, and the way through Syria is obstructed by desert and mountain as well as fortified castles.[5] The direct descent on Egypt has, on the contrary, numerous advantages. The journey by sea from Cyprus to the Egyptian coast is short and direct, lasting only five or six days. Landing will present no serious difficulty, especially as the Sultan will be left in the dark concerning the destination of the Christian troops. The Muslim contingents of Syria will be unable to leave their posts and come to the succour of their master in Egypt for fear of Tatar incursions, which are not infrequent against the Asiatic possessions of the Mamlūks. Further, Egypt is a country where provisions are much more plentiful

---

[1] ib., 121, § 7. 'Item videtur dicto regi et suis, quod cum dictis galeis debeat premitti aliqua quantitas militum, quorum major pars sit balistariorum, qui resistere et opponi possint arcubus Sarracenorum. Qui milites statutis temporibus per galeas predictas veherentur per maritima loca, et multa vastarent, essentque Sarracenis ad terrores et dampna . . . facienda usque ad passagii adventum, . . .'

[2] ib., 122, § 9. 'Et postmodum de Cypro transire directe in Egyptum, et non in Armeniam, nec Syriam nec alibi.'

[3] Bongars, II, 36; also Chapter VI below.

[4] *vide infra*; cf. *Nicopolis* 22–3.   [5] Mas Latrie, op. cit., 122–3, § 9.

than in Syria.   When the Christian invasion of Egypt is
crowned with success, it will be easy to conquer Syria.
The Western host can reach that country by sea in four
or five days, and, without hope of rescue from a fallen
Egypt, Syria will offer no resistance.[1]   While fighting is
in progress, however, the supply of new men, horses and
war materials must continue to reinforce the old by way
of Cyprus.[2]   Henri II's report ends with some useful
information on the armed strength of Egypt.   The Sultan's forces, he says, may be reckoned as 60,000 horsemen,
of whom only 20,000 are 'good knights', 20,000 are of a
mediocre type, and the rest are unworthy[3] of serious
consideration.   The strength of the Mamlūks has, however,
been much reduced by the attacks of the Tatars and by the
internal troubles of Egypt herself.   It is reported that
the Sultan has killed most of his own amīrs.[4]   The enemy
has, indeed, a large infantry, but this is badly armed with
nothing more than the bow and arrow for defence and it
can hardly withstand the action of Christian balistae,
which are much feared by the Saracens.[5]

Henri's memoir was safely deposited in the hands of the
Pope and probably reached the court of Philippe le Bel,
but without any immediate results.   Yet its importance in
fourteenth-century history cannot be exaggerated; for the
policy outlined by Henri II de Lusignan was almost exactly
that followed by Pierre I of the same house in his famous
crusade of 1365 against Alexandria.[6]

At approximately the same date as the report of the King
of Cyprus, another[7] of a different nature was submitted
to Pope Clement V by Benito Zaccaria on the same sub-

---

[1] Mas Latrie, op. cit., 123–4, § 10.   [2] ib., 124, § 11.   [3] ib., 124, § 12.

[4] ib., 124–5, § 12.   'Et iste soldanus, qui ad presens est, multos et quasi
majores suos admiratos occidit.'   This reference is evidently to the third
reign of Sultan al-Naṣir (1310–41) who displayed much vindictiveness
in regard to the party of amīrs who had previously deposed him; cf. Weil
(*Abbasidenchalifat*), I, 299 et seq.; Muir (*Mamelukes*), 66–8; Lane-Poole
(*Egypt*), 306–7.

[5] ib., op. cit., 125, § 12.   'Quia Sarraceni potissime timent balistas
Christianorum, nec audent eos etiam cum suis arcubus expectare.'

[6] *vide infra*, Cap. XIV.

[7] Mas Latrie, op. cit., 129, summarizes Zaccaria's report.

ject. A Genoese by origin, Zaccharia was brought up in the great tradition of seamanship of that republic. He had experienced maritime warfare in the Levant and became master of Ṭarābulus (Tripolis) in Syria for a period.[1] It is believed that he visited Cyprus early in his career and even made the acquaintance of King Henri II de Lusignan.[2] During the first decade of the fourteenth century, he became 'admiral general' of the French fleet.[3] His fame on the sea was recorded by Burcard in the *Directorium*.[4] Here he is mentioned as the 'late Benito Zaccharia', and we may thus assume that he died before 1332. His views are not actuated by political considerations, and he dwells simply on the practical aspects of the 'passage'. He details the numbers of galleys to be raised in addition to the thirteen belonging to the King of France, then harboured at Rouen, la Rochelle, la Réole and Calais; and he gives an estimate of the hire of the Mediterranean craft, the cost of every man's upkeep on the sea and all other necessary expenses. He recommends the advance payment of four months' wages to all men engaged for service in the East to allow them to buy their armour and to avoid confusion and delay at a time when it is imperative to attack the enemy.[5]

The reign of Philippe le Bel was an age of violent activity in regard to the Church. The events leading to

---

[1] Sylv. de Sacy, *Chrestom. arabe* II, 540 (wrongly quoted by Mas Latrie as 42); *Notices et extraits*, XI, 107; Reinaud, *Chroniques arabes*, 566. Cf. Mas Latrie, loc. cit., note 1.

[2] A document dated 17 May 1292 refers to the annulment of a convention between Zaccharia and Henri II, but no further details are given. *Liber Jurium* (Turin Archives), fo. 133 vo; cf. Mas Latrie, l.c.

[3] Mas Latrie, l.c. 'Beneet Zachar amiraus généraus du très excellentime roy de France.'

[4] Reiffenberg, *Mon. pour servir à L'hist. des provinces de Namur, &c.*, IV, 281. Burcard refers to a battle with the Turks 'par messire Martin Zacharie, citoyen de Jennes, homme industrieux, preu, vaillant, noble et loyal, qui, moy présent, obtint pluseurs victoires et maint triumphe des Turcz et fu nepveu de feu messire Bénédic Zacharie, duquel, en fait de mer, vit encoire une glorieuse renommée . . .'

[5] Mas Latrie, l.c. 'Quar à venir por les soudées et à l'attendre et au retorner se gaste grant temps, que couste grant argent, et l'offense qui se feroit ne se fait.'

the Babylonish Captivity and the suppression of the Templars shocked the medieval mind, while the Council of Vienne kept Western Christendom busy with conjecture as to the great issues at stake. Yet the passing of the ill-fated Kingdom of Jerusalem had left an indelible mark on the imagination of the older generations who had witnessed or heard of the succession of disasters in the Holy Land with intense alarm. In spite of all the distracting influence resulting from fluctuations in the fortune of the Church and religious organizations, men continued to clamour for action to redeem the heritage of Christ in the East, and much effort was consecrated to the promotion of the crusade. With mixed motives, laymen such as Pierre Dubois, Guillaume de Nogaret and others formulated their schemes for holy war and urged popes and kings to take the initiative in this matter. Clergy of high standing, too, could not remain passive towards one of the burning questions of the moment, and a number of them came forward with advice and definite plans for the recovery of the land of promise, then in the hands of unbelievers. Prominent among these were Prince Hayton, Guillaume Adam and Guillaume Durant 'le Jeune' who figured among the propagandists of the day and left worthy records of their views on the fulfilment of the crusade.

Hayton (or Hethoum), an Armenian prince of the family of Lampron Count of Gorigos, had had a chequered career in his native land.[1] After assisting in the hopeless defence of Armenia against the successive and ruinous expeditions of the Egyptian Sultans, he appears to have retired to Cyprus about the years 1305–6 in the company of the Armenian King Hethoum. There he renounced the world and took the vows of a Praemonstrant, and in 1307 journeyed to the West and became prior of the convent of his Order in the neighbourhood of Poitiers. At the request of Pope Clement V in the same year, Hayton wrote his *Flos Historiarum Terre Orientis* [2]—a work of great

---

[1] For Hayton and his work see *Nicopolis*, 20–3; Delaville Le Roulx, *France*, I, 64–70.

[2] For numerous MSS., editions and versions see *Nicopolis*, 166, notes 3 and 4; also Röhricht, *Bibl. Geogr. Palaest.*, 65–7.

repute in medieval Europe. Although its title suggests only a history of the East, the *Flos* is essentially a propagandist work of the highest order. Hayton's birth and upbringing in the midst of the turmoil of warfare in the East and his adventures and experience with the armies of both Mamlūks and Tatars lent a well-deserved weight to the force of his argument on the project for crusade.

The author begins his work with a history of the Asiatic peoples including the Tatars from the time of Christ to his own day.[1] Then he exhorts all Christian princes to save the Holy Land and eventually his own native country. In order to acquaint them with their adversary, Hayton describes the army of Egypt and the tactics of the Sultan. Afterwards he enumerates the sources of prosperity and of adversity in the Mamlūk Empire. The former include the strength of character of the Sultan, long truces with the Tatars, abundant crops, security of trade routes, and peace with the Nubians in the south of Egypt and the Bedouins of the Eastern desert as well as the Turkmen settlements in Egypt and Syria. The latter consist of faction and unrest in the Mamlūk state, failure of the periodic Nile inundation, Nubian and Bedouin war with Egypt and the possible sterility of Syria as a result of Tatar devastations or natural causes. If the crusade were undertaken during the lean years of Egypt, the victory of the host would be certain.

Hayton, in common with Burcard[2] and Marino Sanudo[3] and contrary to the views expounded by Jacques de Molay, upholds the theory of a double 'passagium'. The preliminary expedition or 'premier voiage' may be undertaken by a fleet of ten galleys carrying a thousand knights and three thousand infantry with a valiant 'ambassador' in command. Hayton advocates landing first in Cyprus and then in Armenia, and urges that an alliance should be

---

[1] The *Flos* is analysed with full references to the French version by Falcon in *Nicopolis*, 20–3 and 166–8, notes 3–21. Only the gist is given here without the notes in order to avoid repetition. The reader may refer to these in *Nicopolis*.

[2] *vide infra*, Cap. V.   [3] *vide infra*, Cap. VI.

concluded with the Tatars, who can intercept the eastern trade with Mamlūk territories and deplete their garrison in the north of Syria by attacking the provinces situated on the border of the Western Mongol Empire. In the meantime the crusaders may successfully surprise the depleted garrison of Aleppo and proceed direct to Ṭarābulus (Tripolis) where 40,000 skilled Eastern Christian archers will undoubtedly reinforce their lines and ensure the victory for them.

In dealing with the 'voiage general', Hayton reviews the three possible routes—the Barbary route about which he confesses ignorance and suggests consultation with other experts,[1] the land route across Europe and Asia Minor, and the sea route to Cyprus and the Holy Land. Hayton prefers the last route for the final 'passagium' and prescribes a period of repose in Cyprus until Michaelmas (29 September) in order to avoid the excessive summer heat on the Asiatic mainland, to be followed by the voyage to the friendly city of Tarsus in Armenia and to the vulnerable port of Antioch in Syria with every hope of success in the great undertaking.[2]

Another propagandist who, like Hayton, had a con-

[1] This is fully treated by Burcard (Cap. V), Ramon Lull (Cap. IV) and Philippe de Mézières (Cap. VII).

[2] Delaville Le Roulx, *France*, I, 67–8 and notes; Schefer, 'Devise des chemins de Babyloine,' in AOL, II, 89–107. Strictly speaking, Antioch was regarded as a port in so far as it was accessible from the sea by the Orontes, and the real harbour was Port St. Simeon at the river mouth. The course of the campaign itself as delineated by Hayton starts from the district of the Portelle on the outskirts of Armenia across the Iron Bridge (Jisr al-Ḥadīd) which spanned the Orontes (Nahr al-Asī) to the castles in the neighbourhood of Darbesac (Trapasa according to Sanudo, Arabic Darb al-Sūq at entrance of Bailān Pass), Gaston (Baghrās at southern outlet of Bailān Pass), Hareme (Harain, Haaran, Haaram, the Arabic Qal'at Harim on the road between Antioch and Aleppo), Dargons (Dragon, Derkoush south of Antioch), Coursaut (the ancient Coracesium, then known as Alaia) and finally to Ḥamah by one of three routes: first by Lavdicea (al-Ladhiqiya) and Margab (Markab); second along the Orontes through Femie (Ancient Apamea, Arabic Afamiya) and Caesarea (Shaizar); third by la Marre (Ma'arrat al Nu'man), Sernim (Sarmīn) and Meguaret Mesrin (Ma'arrat Miṣrain). The crusaders may then march on Damascus by way of Baalbek. When Damascus succumbs the rest is easy, Jerusalem will offer no resistance, and the road will be open to Ghazzah, and along the coast by Ṭarābulus and 'Akka to Egypt.

siderable knowledge of the East and its affairs, was Guillaume Adam. He was born about 1275 somewhere in
Languedoc and studied theology at Condom in 1302.
Soon afterwards, he became a Dominican friar and was
selected by Pope Clement V in the course of 1305 for
missionary work in the East. He went to Constantinople
and thence travelled through Asia Minor to Syria. This
was a journey of great importance for his work on the
crusade; and when he was in the West during the first half
of 1313—a year in which crusading aspirations had not
abated—Adam appears to have made use of his newly
acquired knowledge in writing the *De modo Sarracenos
extirpandi*.[1] When this was completed,[2] he embarked on
another and more extensive journey to the Mongol Khanate
of Persia, preached the Gospel in India, then sailed to Aden
and penetrated into parts of the Ethiopian territory in
East Africa. About the years 1316–17, he returned to
Avignon, but only for a short time, as Pope John XXII[3]
decided to create a new see at the town of Sultaniah (1 April
1318) with Franco di Perugia as first archbishop and
Guillaume Adam as one of his suffragan bishops. In 1318
he was again on his way to Persia, and in 1322 back in
Avignon where the Pope promoted him to the archbishopric
of Sultaniah in succession to Franco di Perugia who had
resigned that See. Adam was also nominated to conduct
a mission for union with the Catholic Church at the court
of King Leo V of Armenia (31 May 1323), but it is
doubtful whether he took any part in this matter, as he

---

[1] Ed. Ch. Kohler, in *Rec. des Hist. Crois. Doc. armén.*, II.

[2] ib., Introduction—clxxxi et seq., and *De Modo*—521 et seq.; *Hist. Litt.*,
XXXV, 277–8, 282, where the composition of the work is placed before
May 1318. As it was dedicated to 'Raymundus de Fargis, gallus, nepos ex
sorore ab eodem Clemente V, diaconus cardinalis S. Mariae Novae' who died
about 1314–15 (cf. Magnocavallo, 75–7), it may be assumed that the *De
Modo* belonged to the Council of Vienne group of works in Philippe's
reign.

[3] Bull published from Vatican Register LXVII, fo. 318–19, by P. Conrad
Eubel in *Festschrift zum elfhundertjährigen Jubiläum des deutschen Camp
Santo in Rom* (Freiburg, 1897), 191–5; cf. *Hist. Litt.*, XXXV, 278, note 6.
Other bulls concerning Adam's life are edited by Ch. Kohler in ROL, X
(1903–4), 17 et seq.

was still to be found at Avignon on 26 October 1324,
the date of his transfer to the Archbishopric of Antivari,
though he was not consecrated by the Pope till 18 January
1325. He must have left for his new see very soon afterwards, for he is reported once more in 1329 to have made
his way from Antivari to Avignon and later to Narbonne,
where he arrived on 25 January 1337. Then he was
enjoined by Pope Benedict XII to return to his see which
he had abandoned for eight years. Adam remained at
Antivari until his death in 1341.

In some respects, the *De Modo*[1] offers remarkable
similarity of ideas to those of Hayton's *Flos*[2] and Burcard's
Directorium.[3] It also contains new plans. In the first place,
Guillaume discusses the chief sources of the wealth of
Egypt. That country, he says, owes its prosperity to the
support of neighbouring nations who provide Egyptian
emporia with articles of Eastern trade and to the com-
plicity of 'false Christians' who carry slaves and war
material to Egypt, contrary to the rules of the maritime
blockade. Of the latter, he particularizes the Catalans,
Venetians, Pisans and especially the Genoese as guilty of
breach of faith in this respect. The Byzantine Emperor
also furnishes the Sultan with the wheat necessary for the
maintenance of his army. The most effective weapon for
the weakening of Egypt is an attempt to isolate her, first, by a
rigorous enforcement of the blockade and the excommunication of all Christians who venture to trade with the Sultan; second, by the conversion of the Greeks to Catholicism
and by the ultimate conquest of the Empire of Constantinople; and third, by the deflection of trade to the Asiatic
route through the Persian Gulf and up the Euphrates to
the Christian ports of Armenia. He emphasizes the
necessity of intercepting the slave trade between Egypt
and the Mongols of the Russian steppes north of the
Black Sea, and also of blocking the Indian trade by the
novel method of equipping a Christian fleet in the Indian

---

[1] Ed. Kohler, in *Rec. Hist. Crois.*, l.c., and analysed by Delaville Le Roulx,
France, I, 70–7. See also H. Omont, in *Hist. Litt.*, XXXV, 280–2; and
Magnocavallo, 75–7.

[2] *vide supra*, 62.   [3] *vide* Cap. V.

Ocean to arrest Eastern commerce with Egypt by way of Aden. One may search in vain for this idea in works by other propagandists. This possibility must have dawned upon Guillaume Adam while he was travelling in the Indian Ocean and in the Arabian Sea to Aden and the Ethiopian regions of East Africa. This was indeed his chief legacy, one which the Portuguese merchants utilized during the latter part of the fifteenth century and afterwards. Another means urged by Guillaume for the depletion of the resources of Egypt, is the prohibition of pilgrimage to the Holy Places, since the pilgrim traffic is heavily taxed and yields much profit to the Sultan.

When these preparatory measures have been taken, the invasion of Egypt and all her provinces becomes an easy matter, for the Saracens are not redoubtable warriors. In common with Burcard, he mentions that Muslims have a prophecy that the end of their power will be precipitated by a Frankish monarch. To increase their difficulties, however, the Christians may conclude an alliance with the Mongol Khans of Persia who are favourably disposed to collaboration against their rivals in Egypt.

The author prefers the land route by way of Hungary and Bulgaria for the 'passagium generale'. This will enable the crusaders to conquer the Empire of Constantinople and sub-due the Turks of Asia Minor on their way to the Holy Land. This is precisely the route which the crusaders of 1396 followed as far as Nicopolis.[1] The only difference is that Jean de Bourgogne and his European army thought of saving, instead of conquering, Byzantium which was under siege by Bayezid I and the Ottomans at the time of the disastrous crusade. Except for a divergence on matters of detail, the same idea as to the best route and as to the con-quest of Constantinople and of Turkey in Asia was reiterated and extended less than thirty years later in Burcard's *Directorium* addressed to Philippe VI de Valois, but without avail, for the King discountenanced this scheme and his Council rejected it.

The third of the propagandists holding high office in the Church and at the same time enjoying the confidence of the

[1] *Nicopolis*, 50 et seq. and 178 et seq.; cf. *infra*, Cap. XVIII.

King of France was Guillaume Durant [1] 'le Jeune', Bishop of Mende (1297–1328). Though remaining somewhat passive in regard to the contest between Boniface VIII and Philippe IV, Durant appears to have taken an active part in the King's business after the establishment of the papacy at Avignon.[2] In 1308 he participated in the inquest on the case of the Templars, and in 1311 he became a member of the commission which examined their accounts. In compliance with the King's wishes, he searched for the defects of the Order with great thoroughness, and Philippe had to appoint a special military escort to ensure the Bishop's safety. When the Council of Vienne was summoned in 1310, Guillaume wrote an important treatise entitled *De modo celebrandi Concilii Generalis*,[3] in which he urged church reform and explained the ways by which this, in his opinion, might be successfully realized. At the end of Philippe's reign, an assembly of prelates and barons was summoned in Paris in January 1313 to consider the project for a crusade, and Guillaume Durant was invited to it by a special royal brief dated 30 December 1312. It was probably on this occasion that he wrote his *Informacio brevis super hiis que viderentur ex nunc fore providenda quantum ad passagium, divina favente gracia faciendum.*[4]

---

[1] Often confused with his uncle, a former bishop of Mende bearing the same name and distinguished as the 'Speculator'. This confusion dates from an early period in the Middle Ages. In the MSS. 168 of the Hôpital Saint-Nicholas de Cues, 1687 of the Bibl. Maz., 786 of Troyes and 300 of Tours, the *De modo celebrandi Concilii Generalis* is wrongly ascribed to the 'Speculator'. Bossuet, *Défense de la déclaration de l'Assemblée Générale de France de* 1682 (Amsterdam, 1745), I, 63, makes the same mistake. Cf. *Hist. Litt.*, XXXV, 3, notes 3 and 4.

[2] Life of Durant by Paul Viollet, in *Hist. Litt.*, XXXV, 1–64.

[3] ib., 79–129.

[4] ib., 129–34. The original Latin text of the *Informacio* may be found in the B.N. MS. Lat. 7470, fo. 117–23, among other works on the project for crusade compiled about 1330 by various hands. The title is abridged in the *Catalogue de l'ancien fonds*, IV, 363 (Paris, 1741) as follows:

'Informatio brevis de passagio futuro.'

A French version is also extant in MS., Bibl. Ste. Geneviève, 1654, fo. 139–143, dating from the fourteenth century. Incipit: 'Ci commence une information briez sus les choses qui samblent des ore estre à pourveoir quant

Durant's memoir is composed of twenty-six proposals and recommendations for the promotion of a successful crusade. It behoves the Pope and the King of France, he says, to suppress all internal warfare and unrest among the princes and barons of Christendom before bringing the forces of the West into action against those of the East. In common with most of the contemporary propagandists, he strongly upholds the papal ban on trade with the Saracens and the promulgation of the maritime blockade in order to impoverish and weaken Egypt before the decisive stroke was dealt by the 'passagium generale'. Durant appears to be in favour of the sea route, for he speaks at length of the fleet of galleys and transports. This should be gratuitously placed at the disposal, not only of the crusading men-at-arms, but also of the members of the church hierarchy who would agree to stay with the lay elements of the host for one year in the land beyond the sea. Durant's stress on the ecclesiastical aspect of the crusade seems to distinguish his propaganda from that of others. The task of the Church in the field appears to him to be one of capital importance, as the priests and friars may offer a laudable example for the armed forces and preach, exhort and counsel [1] them in time of need. The Bishop deprecates all the evil acts of impious crusaders whose duty it is to amend their lives. On the other hand, it would be a grave error to regard the dispatch of undesirable persons to the Holy Land as a punishment and to tamper with their lands and their privileges during their absence. On the contrary, the rights of all must be preserved intact. Crusaders of every description must be allowed to retain their lands and benefices, their jurisdictions, their revenues and all their normal privileges in common with the rest of the members of their classes who prefer to stay at home. The enforce-

au passage à faire par la grâce de Dieu.' See Ch. Kohler, *Cat. des MSS. de la Bibl. Ste. Geneviève*, I, 117 (Paris, 1893). Cf. *Hist. Litt.*, XXXV, 129–30.

[1] Cf. *Hist. Litt.* XXXIV, 499 and XXXV, 132; 'licet multe ex dictis personis non essent ad arma, nichilominus tamen vite exemplo, predicationis et exhortationis verbo, orationis et devotionis studio, consilio et ex comitiva, quam multi secum ducerent, valde proficere possent, et multi sequerenter eosdem'.

ment of this rule is the only way to banish one element of the lack of enthusiasm for the crusade.[1]

The captain of every branch of crusaders must be well informed as to the number of his followers, both mounted and afoot, and he must provide for them for a whole year. Active negotiations should be carried on with the Genoese, the Pisans, the Venetians and all the other maritime powers for the supply of the necessary fleet; and provisions and engines of war must be secured in good time. Meanwhile, the army is advised to take military exercise and utilize all leisure moments in reading the works of such authors as Vegetius. It is preferable, Durant suggests, that every man should be supplied with a horse; but as horses are not sufficiently numerous in the Kingdom of France to meet the requirements of all the crusaders, these must be sought abroad.

The author then digresses to discussion of legal and social reform; but he soon reverts to the crusade and concludes by urging that missionary work among both schismatics and Saracens should be undertaken in conjunction with the armed expedition. This work may be carried out by volunteers, both ecclesiastical and secular. Here, Durant betrays the influence of Ramon Lull with whom he must have been in close connexion during the meeting of the Council of Vienne.[2]

Even after the death of Philippe le Bel in 1314, Guillaume Durant persisted in upholding the cause of the Holy Land with varying fortunes during the reigns of his friend's successors to the throne of France—Louis X le Hutin, Philippe V le Long, Charles IV le Bel, and Philippe VI de Valois. In 1329 he was chosen by John XXII and Philippe de Valois for an Eastern mission, the terms of which unfortunately are unknown to us, though it was evidently in connexion with the project for crusade. It happened that, at the time, four galleys were in readiness to sail to the Levant with Marie, a French lady who was to be betrothed to the Crown Prince of Cyprus, Guy de Lusignan. She was accompanied by the Latin Patriarch

[1] Cf. *Hist. Litt.*, XXXV, 132; Delaville Le Roulx, *France*, I, 82.
[2] ib., XXXV, 132-4.

of Jerusalem and two French knights. The Bishop of
Mende left with them, probably in the month of August,
though his embassy was not related to the coming marriage.
Afterwards the Bishop and the Patriarch went to Egypt.
The Bishop died after his return to Cyprus in July 1330
and was buried in the Cistercian Church of St. Mary at
Nicosia [1] within two days' journey of the Holy Places,
whose cause he had cherished throughout his career.

In order to present a complete sketch of the propagandist
literature of the age of Philippe le Bel, we have to retrace
our steps to the first decade of the reign. In 1295, a
certain Galvano de Levanti wrote a work called *Liber Sancti
Passagii Christicolarum contra Saracenos pro Recuperatione
Terrae Sanctae* [2] which he dedicated to Philippe IV of France.

Little is known about the author's life beyond the fact
that he was a Genoese physician attached to the court of the
Pope. [3] The treatise itself must have been composed between the fall of 'Akka in 1291 and the publication of the
bull *Clericis laicos* [4] in 1296, after which the tension between Philippe IV and Boniface VIII took a dangerous
turn. The motives which prompted its dedication to the
French monarch are difficult to explain. Perhaps he was
induced to this procedure by the attitude which Philippe
assumed as the future leader of the crusade.

The book consists of an introduction and two parts. In
the introduction, Galvano gives a brief description of the
contents of the work and says that he had received the
inspiration for writing it from the game of chess. He
meant to apply the rules of this game to the establishment of
concord among the princes of the West in a united policy
to invade the East. The first book has little or nothing to
do with the crusade. It is merely a discussion on the
government of princes based on the game of chess. The

---

[1] ib., XXXV, 58 et seq.

[2] B.N. MS. Lat. 669 nouv. acquisit., in fourteenth-century hand on parchment. Extracts with introduction edited by Ch. Kohler in ROL, 6e. année
(1898), nos. 3–4, 333–69.

[3] Kohler, op. cit., 333, 352–3.

[4] This bull forbade the laity of whatever rank to tax the clergy on pain
of excommunication.

second part [1] was presumably intended to be relevant to the
possibilities of crusade.   Of the original sixteen chapters of
this division, only six can be traced, but these are sufficient
to allow an estimate of the work.   The discourse as a
whole is neither geographical, nor historical nor scientific,
but a rhetorical sermon of mystic type lacking evidence
that the author had any first-hand knowledge of the Holy
Land and the affairs of the East.   The character of
Galvano and his writings is best illustrated by a quotation
from another [2] tract where he says—'I do not weep the fall
of Acre or of Tyre and the other towns of Syria; I am not
moved at the captivity of a vile multitude; but I deplore the
fall of an illustrious soul, a temple in which Jesus Christ has
lived. . . .'   The lamentation over the possible misdeeds of
the inhabitants of 'Akka and Ṣūr (Tyre) may serve as an
appropriate illustration of the general feeling of Western
Christians towards the capture of these towns by the
Saracens, and is indeed in keeping with the reproachful
attitude of Thaddeo of Naples.[3]   In the latter part of the
extract quoted, however, the mystic in Galvano emerges
once more and takes the reader nowhere.   A treatise of this
kind could not have had much influence on the material ideas
of Philippe le Bel.   The author, however, refers to a map of
Palestine, which he enclosed with his *Liber*.   If he did so,
the loss, not of the remaining ten chapters of the second part
of the book, but of the map alone is to be regretted.[4]

Notwithstanding the defects of such a work as Galvano's,
the reign of Philippe le Bel was one of the richest ages in
systematic propaganda for the crusade.   It must be remembered that the career and work of Ramon Lull,[5] treated
elsewhere separately owing to its importance, belonged
chiefly to this reign.   Yet in the midst of all this extraordinary activity of theorists whom Philippe encouraged
from the beginning to the end of his reign, and in spite of

---

[1] Kohler, op. cit., 348. 'Tractatus secundus de neophyta persuasione
christicolis ad passagium sanctum.'

[2] *Thesaurus religiose paupertatis*; B.N. MS. Lat. 3181, fo. 45; cf. Kohler,
op. cit., 348 and note 1.

[3] *vide supra*, Cap. II.   [4] Kohler, op. cit., 349.

[5] *vide infra*, Cap. IV.

his posing as the champion of the Holy Land for nearly thirty years, the King's real intentions are shrouded in mystery. Perhaps Nogaret's Memoir devising some of the most ingenious methods for financing his royal master from Church revenues under cover of fictitious crusades was the truest expression of the mind of Philippe le Bel.

CHAPTER IV

RAMON LULL

Propaganda for Crusade and Missionary work. Petitions to Popes.
Liber de Fine and *Liber de Acquisitione Terre Sancte*. Tunis and Cyprus.
Council of Vienne. *Disputatii*. Bugia and martyrdom

BORN in 1232 and stoned to death on the North African
coast in the neighbourhood of Bugia in 1315 or 1316, Lull
lived in a period of decline and fall of the Christian outposts in Syria. He shared with his contemporaries the
bitterness of their feelings at the news of the fall of 'Akka,
the last important stronghold of the crusaders in the Holy
Land. It is indeed possible that the spiritual crisis [1]
through which he passed in the years 1291–2 was closely
associated with this disastrous event in the history of the
Latins in the Levant, although there seems to be no concrete evidence in the original sources to confirm or confute
this suggestion.

After his conversion from a profligate life to penitence
and to the service of God in 1263, Lull spent ten years in
the study of philosophy and in learning Arabic from a
Moorish slave. During the rest of his life,[2] Lull's activity
knew no bounds. He wrote more books than any author
before or after him.[3] He travelled to the intellectual

---

[1] Peers, 235–9.

[2] ib., 19–25. Barber divides Lull's career as follows:
   (1) Illumination of a worldling, 19 et seq.
   (2) Maker of Books, 33 et seq.
   (3) Foreign missionary, 46 et seq.
Although this classification helps to clarify Lull's many-sided activity, it is
defective in two ways: first, the three sections overlap in Lull's actual life;
second, other aspects of Lull's career are of necessity overlooked. Barber's
classification is probably based on the contemporary life of Ramon Lull
(trans. Peers, 5).

[3] Perroquet, in his *Apologie*, 364–90, ascribes to Lull the authorship of
some 4,000 books, of which he has traced 488. Zwemer reproduces the

centres of Europe to lecture to the doctors of many nations. He interviewed Popes and made his way to the sittings of Church Councils. He travelled to the East. He preached the Gospel of Christ to Muhammadans, and only the crown of martyrdom extinguished his zeal for the task he had set himself to accomplish.

The idea underlying Lull's works and all his career seems to have been one of unity. In the realm of knowledge, like Roger Bacon, he was one of the earliest pioneers to conceive all sciences as branches of the same tree, and this he exemplified in his *Arbor Scientiae*.[1] In the world around him, Lull yearned to bring all nations, whether schismatic Christians, Tatars or Muslims to the fold of the Roman Catholic Church. To achieve this aim, he devoted most of his energy, first to promote an active crusade, and second to establish a missionary system under the patronage of the Church in order that all men might be won in a peaceful manner by appeal to reason.

Delaville Le Roulx[2] assumes that Lull, realizing the futility of the use of force in the conflict between the East and the West, gave up the idea of the crusade as entirely hopeless and tried to win the Saracens by reason and instruction. Another[3] author adopts a similar view and tries to prove that Lull aimed at a crusade, not of the sword, but of love, and that the unification of all military orders was based on the root idea of creating one large 'order of spiritual knights'. Neander, the great Church historian,

Acta Sanctorum (T. VII, 640–9) list of 321 books and adds 20 on magic published under Lull's name. Barber's list is a smaller one consisting of 282 extant and 16 lost. Peers, 435–41, has compiled a good index to the works of Lull (genuine and apocryphal) dealt with in his monograph. These include 328 entries. Although Lull was the most prolific of all medieval writers, it is difficult to conceive that Perroquet's contention has any basis of truth. There is also the possibility of interpolation of anonymous works in Lull's; but a discussion on this matter is outside the scope of our work. The genuineness of the tracts analysed below is, however, beyond doubt.

[1] Peers, 269–72.

[2] *France en Orient*, I, 28. 'Écartant de son plan les tentatives dangereuses et impuissantes dont ses contemporains rêvaient la réalisation, il (Lull) repousse l'emploi de la force et songe à reconquérir la Palestine par le raisonnement et l'instruction.'

[3] Zwemer (who is himself a missionary), 52–3, 65, 76.

implies a similar conception of Lull whose 'attention was directed particularly to the Saracens, whom it had been in vain attempted to subdue entirely in the Crusades by the power of the sword'.[1]   Although Ramon Lull is truly regarded as a mystic philosopher and writers are often tempted not to interpret his words literally, a closer examination of his works and his career reveals that he had a genuine and earnest desire to promote an armed crusade against the Saracens.

It is true that during an early period, Lull's efforts were centred on missionary plans.   But in the year 1294, between 13 November and 10 December, he appeared at Naples with a 'Petitio Raymundi pro conversione infidelium ad Coelestinum V'.[2]   The first aim of the petition was indeed to persuade Celestine V to adopt a new missionary policy,[3] especially among the Tatars who, he fears, might be won by either Saracen or Jew and thus become a very grave menace to Christendom.   Nevertheless, his appeal ends with an outstanding statement on the project for crusade.   Not only the Holy Land, he says, but also Muslim territories in general must be invaded by force of arms.[4]   On 13 December 1294, however, Celestine V relinquished the papal tiara to become a hermit and thus Lull's petition came to nothing.   Soon after the election of Boniface VIII (1294–1303), he followed the new Pontiff to Rome in 1295 and succeeded in having an audience with him.   It was probably at this time that he submitted to Boniface the 'Petitio pro recuperatione Terrae Sanctae et pro conversione infidelium',[5] where he puts forward the same main proposals as in the preceding petition.   He begins by indicating the numerical superiority of the unbelievers to the Christians.[6]   It is essential that the Church

---

[1] *Memorials of Christian Life* (Bohn, 1852), includes an account of 'Raimund Lull', 520–38.   The passage quoted is on p. 523.

[2] Golubovich, III, 373 et seq.; also Salzinger, t. VI.   Cf. Peers, 251–5.

[3] *vide infra.*

[4] cf. Peers, 253; 'et hoc per vim armorum'.

[5] Munich MS., Cod. Lat. 10565, ff. 84 vo–85 vo; *vide infra*, Appendix I. *Hist. Litt.*, XXIX, 541–2.   Cf. Gottron, 19; Peers, 256, note 1.

[6] Munich MS., fo. 84 vo.   'Et cum infideles sint multo plures quam Christiani &c.'

should win them and their lands to the true faith, first, by the study of their languages and preaching [1] the word of God in their midst; and second, by an armed crusade [2] against the Saracens. A Church tithe [3] devoted to the furtherance of this plan would ensure its success. Regarding the Greeks and other schismatics, disputation might be held on the basis of authorities [4] and of pure reason, to prove their error.

In April 1305,[5] he wrote the *Liber de Fine*,[6] a work of importance and interest for the historian of the crusade. It consists of a prologue and three divisions in which Lull formulates his plans and shows the necessity for peaceful conversion as well as the use of arms against the Saracens. He begins the Prologue [7] by a lament for the state of the world in which the Christians are but few and the infidels are many. The numbers of the latter are increasing and their territories are being extended by the usurpation of territories which are by right Christian. To remedy this evil the author has addressed himself to popes, cardinals and kings, and further has written many books of which this is the last since he can do no more than he has already accomplished.[8]

These proposals he again submits to the authorities—

[1] *vide infra*, Appendix I.　　　　　　[2] ib., *vide infra*, Appendix I.

[3] ib., *vide infra*, Appendix I.

[4] ib., 'disputando per authoritates et rationes necessarias'.

[5] Peers, 316. Gottron, 98.

[6] Libellus de Fine, in quo traditur modus et doctrina, quo possunt omnes infideles ad fidei Catholicae veritatem breviter reduci et Terra Sancta e(x) manibus infidelium recuperari. Gottron, 64 et seq. *Hist. Litt.*, XXIX, 377. A. R. Pasqual, *Vida del Beato Raymundo Lulio* (2 vols., Palma, 1890), II, 112; *Vindiciae Lullianae* (4 vols., Avignon, 1778), I, 248. Ll. Riber, *Vida i Actes del reverant . . . Ramon Lull* (Palma, 1916), 194–207. Cf. Peers, 316–19 and 316, n. 2. Reference here is made to Gottron's edition and selections.

[7] Gottron, 65–7. 'Cum mundus in malo statu diu permanserit et adhuc timendum sit de peiori, eo quia pauci sunt Christiani, et tamen multi sunt Infideles, quia conantur cotidie, ut ipsos destruant Christianos et, multiplicando se, eorum terras capiunt et usurpant, &c.' (65); thus runs the Incipit of the Prologue.

[8] ib., 66. 'Et quia feci multos libros contra homines infideles . . . quoniam in isto negocio facile plus non possum, ex eo quia quasi solus sum in tractando et neminem quodammodo invenio, qui me iuvet.'

Church and lay—as a final act, in the hope that decisive action may be taken to bring the whole world into the enclosure of the Catholic faith.[1]

The first division of the book, *De disputatione infidelium*,[2] contains his arguments against the Saracens, the Jews, the Schismatics (Jacobite and Nestorian), and the Tatars or pagans. In the introduction he points out the necessity of establishing four [3] monasteries for the teaching of Oriental languages to enable the missionary worker to argue with the diverse peoples in their own tongues and avoid the interpreter's misunderstanding.[4] Now is the time to start the good work before death comes, for a thousand years and more of Christianity have already elapsed and no better plan has yet evolved.[5] This is the 'gladium spirituale' of Christ. Yet there is another sword, the 'gladium corporale'.[6]

The theory of the two swords which must be used together leads the author naturally to the second division of his book, *De modo bellandi*.[7] This is a propagandist document of practical value, offering ample proof that Lull was not merely an idle visionary. In the first chapter [8] of the present division he deals with matters, which though not entirely new or original, remain to be considered as reforms. The leader of the crusade—'dominus bellator rex'—elected by the Pope and cardinals, should be a man of royal blood [9] and his successors must also be sons of kings. All the

---

[1] Gottron, 66. 'Set propono finaliter domino papae et aliis quibusdam principibus seu rectoribus fidei Christiane mittere istum librum, in quo libro continetur materia, per quam possent mediante, si vellent gratia Ihesu Christi ad bonum statum reducere universum et ad unum ovile Catholicum adunire.'

[2] ib., 67–73.   [3] ib., 67–8.

[4] ib., 69; 'quia interpretes non apprehendunt virtutem fidei christiane, neque sufficienciam vocabulorum nostre fidei ipsi habent'.

[5] ib., 69. Exhorting the Pope and prelates, he says: 'Incipite pro deo, incipite! Nam mors venit, et mille anni iam sunt preteriti seu elapsi, in quibus (melius) negocium istum inceptum non fuit.'

[6] ib., 73.   [7] ib., 73–91.

[8] ib., 73–7. 'De electione.'

[9] ib., 73–4. 'Dominus papa et domini cardinales eligant et ordinent unam nobilem ordinem, qui ordo milicie nominetur.' Later, he continues, '. . . quod uno bellatore regis filio ab hoc seculo transmigrato alius similiter regis filius loco illius eligatur, et hoc fiat ab uno in alium successive'.

military [1] orders are to be unified under this king. Further, the Pope and Cardinals should concede a Church tithe for the purpose of the recovery of the Holy Land.[2] Two parts of the revenue accruing from this levy should be used to furnish necessities for the army, and the third for the sustenance of the Brothers employed as tithe-collectors.[3] The clergy of all sees and abbacies should be instructed to dispose the minds of the people to the cause of the crusade. Secular knights and burgesses who might join the new Order 'cum suis propriis sumptibus seu expensis' would be subject to the 'Bellator Rex'; and many are those who are prepared to shed their blood for the Lord.[4]

As to the Rule [5] of the Order, Lull is contented with some meagre suggestions. The knights are to have a black habit for penitence with a red cross for humility and triumph, and as a mark of sorrow all have to wear their beards long.[6] The 'Bellator Rex' is to have a council for consultation and advice on all matters of moment.[7]

The points [8] at which war can be waged against the Saracens for the re-conquest of the Holy Land are five in number. Here Lull appears to treat the subject of the possible routes leading to Syria and Palestine. First, the land route through the Greek Empire, Turkey and Armenia to Syria is dangerous, long and expensive.[9] The second route is by way of the 'island' of Rosetta [10] in the neighbour-

---

[1] ib., 74. 'Ulterius dominus papa cum dominis cardinalibus precipiat atque velit et faciat de ordine Templi et milicie Hospitalis et Alamanorum et de Hucles et Calatrava, et de omnibus aliis penitus militum ordinibus, quicumque et ubicumque sint, unum ordinem, de milicia nominatum, hunc videlicet supradictum.'

[2] ib., 74. 'Et ideo dominus papa et domini cardinales concedant decimam ecclesie quoad presens ad recuperandum terram sanctam.'

[3] ib., 75; 'due partes ad necessitatem sui exercitus faciendae et de parte tercia vivant fratres, qui loca custodient et redditus colligent et servabunt'.

[4] ib., 75–6.   [5] ib., 77–80. 'De regula.'

[6] ib., 77.   [7] ib., 77–8.

[8] ib., 80–1. 'De loco.'

[9] ib., 80. 'Sed ista via est valde gravis seu difficilis et nimis longa et nimis requirit de exercitu et expensis, et sic in principio laudabilis non est multum.'

[10] ib. 'Secundus modus est ire ad quandam insulam, que Raycet appellatur, que est prope Alexandriam situata.' Raycet is identified as Rosetta, Arabic Rashīd; see my article on 'Rosetta' in EI.

hood of Alexandria. The knights can easily seize that
'island' which will serve as a base from which they may
sally against the mainland and in whose waters the Christian
galleys can be safely harboured. Nevertheless, this route
also is both long and costly. Third is the sea route to
Cyprus and Armenia. This again is too long and requires
sea and land fighters. Moreover, neither of these countries
contains sufficient material for re-victualling.[1] Fourth is
the route to Tunis which has already proved to be a failure
by St. Louis's recent experiment.[2] The fifth and most
suitable of the fields in which the crusaders can meet the
Saracens with better results are Almeria, Malaga and
Granada, all of which are situated in Andalusia.[3] The
kingdom of Granada is in the peculiar position of being
surrounded on all sides by the sea and by the kingdoms
of Castile and Aragon, and it is therefore difficult for
other Saracens to lend it assistance. Further, Spain is a
fertile country, has horses in abundance and is within
reasonable reach of the Christian powers. With a small
army, the 'Bellator Rex' can complete the invasion of Spain,
castle by castle and town by town by easy stages. Once
Andalusia is entirely in the hands of the crusaders, they
have only to cross the narrow sea to fight the Berbers in
their own country, starting with the subjugation of the
'Kingdom of Cepte', then moving by stages towards Tunis.[4]

[1] Grotton, l.c. '. . . quia per Chypre et Herminiam non possent sufficere
victualia neque equi'.
[2] ib., 81. 'Et ad hoc experimentum satis probabile datum fuit, quando
sanctus Ludovicus, rex Francie, transfretavit.'
[3] ib., 80. 'Quintus locus est Yspania, videlicet in Andalicia, ubi est
Almaria, Malica et Granada. Hic est locus amenissimus et laudabilis plus
quam alter, &c.'
[4] ib. 'Et sic Andalicia adquisita bellator (rex) cum suo exercitu ampliato
ad maiorem Barbariam poterit ultra ire, primo videlicet ad regnum Cepte,
quoniam de mare nisi per septem miliaria illud distat; . . . post versus
fruntariamaliam, et sic de singulis usque Tunicum &c.'
'Cepte' may be identified as Sabta or Ceuta, in Morocco on the strait
of Gibraltar at 35° 54′ N.–5° 18′ W., 10 miles south of Gibraltar. In Lull's
time it was situated within the realm of the Marinids of Fez. Tunis was then
under the Ḥafṣid dynasty. The kingdom of Tlemcen under the 'Abdal-
Wadis between Fez and Tunis seems to be completely overlooked in Lull's
plan.

Lull curiously ends with a very short passage in which he implies that after these conquests, the capture of the Holy Land and of Egypt will follow in due course.

In the fourth [1] section of the *Liber de Fine*, he lists twelve advantages which the Christians may have over the Saracens if they adopt his plan. The first six lie in the effects of the military kingship and order stationed on the Muslim frontiers ready for continued action while the Christian galleys cut off all hope of succour coming from the Saracens beyond the sea. The remaining six points include useful remarks about the machinery of war employed by the Christian host, the superiority of their balistae over the Saracen bow, the abundance of hard timber suitable for the manufacture of such implements as lances and spears, in Catalonia, Aragon and Castile; the sufficiency of provisions and the existence of iron. On the other hand, the Saracens are favoured by three factors which their opponents do not enjoy. First, they have discipline which they strictly observe; second, they possess the Turkish bow, noted for its excellence; and third, they practise the art of the 'genetour' in their warfare. [2] The remedy, however, is quite simple. Lull proposes a system of dividing the army into units—'unus dominus supra decem et alius supra centum et alius supra mille et alius supra X millia, et sic usque ad ipsum mille millia ascendendo'. [3] Order, too, must be strictly enforced under pain of severe penalties, [4] the 'bellator rex' may train his knights in the art of the

---

[1] ib., 81–5. 'De modo bellandi.'

[2] ib., 84. 'E contrario Sarraceni contra Christianos habent avantagia sólum tria. Unum est propter capdelacionem sive regimen, quod observant, aliud propter arcus Turcios sive Turchos, aliud propter atzagayas et artem quam habent genetarium ad bellandum.'

The art of the 'genetour', that is hovering on horseback on the wings of the hostile forces and making lightning attacks with javelins until they break their formation, was ultimately adopted by the Spanish from the Moors in later medieval warfare. Examples of this practice may be found in the history of the battles of Navarette (1367) and Aljubarotta (1385) in Spain. See Oman (*Art of War*), II, 179–95.

[3] ib., 84. This bears some similarity to the Mamlūk system where we find amīrs or muqaddims of ten, a hundred, a thousand and so on.

[4] ib., 84–5. 'Et si quis talem ordinationem discapdelaret, esset punitus crudeliter per dominum bellatorem.'

'genetour' and may also introduce the Turkish bow for use in his army.

The fifth section—*De admirallia* [1]—of this division is one of exceptional value owing to the practical hints which it offers. Some of these even anticipate the manner in which the crusades of the fourteenth century were to be conducted. The 'bellator rex' appoints a member of his order—a knight—to the post of admiral whose duty it is to control the fleet and all the maritime operations against the Saracens and to intercept traffic with them carried on by false Christians contrary to the ordinances of Holy Church. The galleys must carry a hundred mounted knights, a hundred 'ballistrarii equitantes', fifty men armed with balistae and a thousand foot equipped to ensure a successful landing in hostile territory and a successful battle with two thousand horsemen or even more. This host of the Cross can destroy all the coastal towns and settlements of the enemy.[2]   The lord admiral with a strong ship and four armed galleys may capture the island of Rhodes, which has a good harbour, and also Malta.[3]   Both islands will furnish excellent bases for ensuring that no commercial intercourse is carried on between the Christians and Alexandria and Syria,[4] on pain of excommunication of the culprit and confiscation of his goods. The Indian trade can be maintained by Christians outside Egypt while the blockade persists. Starved in this way, the Sultan will easily succumb to Christian arms [5] within six years.

---

[1] Gottron, 85–7.

[2] ib., 85. 'Et sic possunt destruere terra marique omnia blada, villas, castra, bona, animalia et capere Sarracenos.'

[3] ib., 86. 'Ulterius dominus admirallus unam navem habeat valde magnam et galeas quatuor seu taridas bene munitas seu paratas et capiat unam insulam, que vocatur Rodes, in qua est bonus portus, sicut vidi, et eciam aliam, que dicitur Mauta. . . .'

[4] ib. 'Et eciam sic prohibitum et vetatum, quod nullus Christianus ausus fuerit in Alexandriam vel Suriam mercimonia ire emptum, et esset excommunicatus, quicumque prohibitum pertransiret, et eorum bona, qui hoc presumeret, caperentur.'

[5] ib., 87. 'Et sicut Soldanus et tota sua patria esset pauper. Et Christiani sicut Januenses et etiam Catalini assumerent ire emptum species Abaldach et Indiam et sic extra terram Soldanam. Et sic terra Egyptiaca et Babilonica essent afflicta taliter a sex annis, quod per Christianos faciliter (posset) capi.'

In the sixth section [1] *De predicacione*, Lull indicates the
necessity of having in the Order certain skilled preachers
and teachers of the ways of salvation. Men, conversant
with law, medicine and surgery may attend to the material
requirements of the brotherhood, and care for the sick and
the wounded. It behoves all the clerks of the order to learn
Arabic and study in particular the work which al-Kindī [2]
composed in order to disprove the religion of Muhammad.
This will also enable them to understand the secret war
correspondence of the unbelievers and carry out successful
disputations with captives, who may then be granted freedom to go back to their native lands and convert their
co-religionists.[3]

So far, Lull has dealt in the *Liber de Fine* with the administrative, military and religious aspects of the state of the
'ordo bellatoris', that is, the kingship, the fighting knights
and the preaching brethren of the new order. He seems,
however, to be of the opinion that, to ensure its full success,
the organization must be self-supporting. With this end
in view, he consecrates the seventh [4] and last section of the
second division to projects for the creation of several other

[1] ib., 87–9.

[2] ib., 88, '. . . et probent eis (captives) quod Macometus non fuit verus
profeta, quod si bene velint avertere, facile multum est ad probandum per
unum librum, qui vocatur Alchindi et per alium, qui Teliff nominatur, et per
alium quem fecimus de gentili'. Gottron, 88 note, identifies 'Alchindi' as
the famous Arab philosopher Abu Yūsuf Ya'qūb b. Isḥāq. The context,
however, points to 'Abd-al-Masīḥ b. Isḥāq, an Arab Christian who lived in
the time of the Abbasid Caliph al-M'amūn and wrote an Apology to prove
the truth of Christianity and refute Islam. The complete text of this tract
was published by A. Tien (Turkish Mission Aid Society, London, 1880)
and translated into English by W. Muir (London, 1882). Lull's reference
to this apology is a concrete proof of his erudition, if we bear in mind that the
full text of the Apology was revealed only as late as the end of the last century.

[3] ib., 88. 'Et bonam eciam, quod religiosi clerici de ordine bellatoris
habeat scienciam ad loquendum, legendum et intelligendum linguam
Arabicam . . . ut legere, scribere et intelligere sciant literas bellatoris et
secreta, . . . et cum captivatibus disputare . . . et postea dominus bellator
rex illos liberet et det illis expensas cum pulchra facie et iocunda et mittat eos
regibus Sarracenis et aliis principibus . . . ut eis manifestent et demonstrent,
nos quid credimus de beatissima trinitate . . . et erunt materia conversionis
Infidelium et divulgacionis nostre fidei sacrosancte.'

[4] ib., 89–91. 'De mechanicis.'

departments, humble but indispensable. He mentions three classes of people under the heading 'De mechanicis.' The 'preceptores',[1] brothers skilled in the mechanical arts, direct the concrete activities of the crusading machine. They are to be assisted by the 'secundarii preceptores', under whose direct supervision and at the bottom of the ladder is the labourer class which comprises Saracens and Christians alike. A 'preceptor maior' presides over all departmental 'preceptores'.[2] Some preceptors will be in charge of the supplies, the exchequer, the commerce, the iron, the timber and the building and war materials. Others will look after the fields and the live stock. A budget showing both income and expenditure must be drawn up and submitted each year for the approval of the Council[3] of the Order. In this wise, the temporal and spiritual requirements of the brotherhood will be fulfilled, and its members will stand united and without fear of insubordination.[4]

In the third and final division of the *Liber*, Lull analyses his *Ars generale*, and towards the end of it he complains of the rebuffs that his plans have sustained and of the disappointment and sorrow which fill his old age.[5] Nevertheless, he continues to travel, preach and write urging popes, kings and all good Catholics to take up the Cross. In March 1309, he completes another work of a purely

---

[1] Gottron, 89. '. . . bellator rex de suo ordine habeat preceptores, qui sciant artes mechanicas et serviles, et ea, que sunt in tali exercitu necessaria, gubernare. Et illi tales fratres eiusdem ordinis mechanicos habeant, qui sint secundarii preceptores, sub quibus sint servi mechanici, Sarraceni et Christiani aliqui, qui pro denariis laborabunt.'

[2] ib., 91. 'Unus preceptor maior sit super omnes alios preceptores, qui exploratores fideles habeat et secretos, qui de fidelitate subditorum inquirant et eciam preceptorum.'

[3] ib., 91. 'Et quod thesaurarius reddat computum consiliariis bellatoris, et consiliarii postea domino bellatori in tantum, quod (dominus) bellator rex sciat quantum habet in redditibus annualim, et quantum expendidit illo anno.'

[4] ib., 91. 'Per talem vero ordinacionem potest exercitus in bonis temporalibus et spiritualibus habundare et stare in concordia et quiete.'

[5] ib., 92. 'Propter (predictam) utilitatem, quam video in predictis langueo at vivo in tristicia et dolore, et vado per mundum universum. Et qui me impedit, audiat, si mentales aures habeat, quantum contra bonum publicum hic consistit.' Cf. Peers, 319, where a different punctuation of this passage is adopted.

propagandist nature in the hope that the first Avignonese Pope Clement V may be attracted by the views expressed in it. This is the *Liber de acquisitione Terrae Sanctae*,[1] in which he incorporates the main thesis of the *Liber de Fine* and re-presents it with a slight modification in arrangement.[2] Though his plan to attack the Moors in Spain and the Berbers in North Africa stands, he adds a totally different proposal in his first division of this book. A detachment of crusaders, after seizing Constantinople,[3] may proceed through Asia Minor and recover the Holy Land from the Mamlūks. Meanwhile the Christian fleet sailing from Antioch may harass Alexandria, Damietta and Rosetta.[4] With the loss of his Asiatic possessions as well as the important coastal towns of Egypt, the Sultan will become powerless and surrender all his empire to the Christians. The third [5] division of the work is by no means as new as it sounds from its title. Here the author only recapitulates some of his already well-known views and occasionally supports them with further examples.

We next meet Lull at the Council of Vienne [6] in 1311.

---

[1] Munich MS. Lat. 10565, ff. 89 ro–96 vo. See also Longpré, in *Criterion* (Barcelona, 1927), III, 166–78. Cf. *Hist. Litt.*, XXIX, 342; Peers, 339, 426 (no. 78*a*); Gottron, 40.

[2] Munich MS. f. 90 ro. 'Dividitur iste liber in tres divisiones quarum: Ia. de modo bellandi, . . . 2a vero de modo praedicandi, 3a autem de exemplis.' He submits his work to the 'patri sanctissimo Domino Clementi quinto et Dominis Cardinalibus reverendissimis omnibus ut librum istum recipiant.'

[3] ib., f. 91 ro. 'Per acquisitionem Constantinopolis potest terra sancta acquiri bono modo et faciliter.'

[4] ib. 'Acquisita Suria populata et munita Soldanus non posset ipsam recuperare . . . et sic finaliter Alexandria perderetur et Damieta et Insula quae Raxet nominatur et per consequens totum regnum Aegipti.'

[5] ib., ff. 95 ro–96 ro. 'De exemplis.'

[6] A papal bull dated 12 August 1308 summoned a General Council to meet at Vienne in October 1310; but this was postponed for one year. The main purpose of the Council was to consider the affair of the Templars, but many other subjects of interest were also discussed. Sollerius, *Acta Sanct.*, VII, 395; *Contemporary Life* (Trans. Peers), 43–5; *Vita* II, *Acta Sanct.*, VII, 617. J. Loserth (*Gesch. des spätern Mittelalters*), 237–43; Lavisse, II, 2nd pt., 175–291; Peers, 350–62; Gottron, 42–5; Boutaric, Clément V, Ph. le Bel et les Templiers, *Rev. des Questions historiques*, X (1871), 301–42 and XI (1872), 5, 40.

Here he realizes his primary ambition by obtaining an audience and addresses the convened prelates on his views for reform, views formulated in a petition [1] containing eight articles or 'Ordinationes' for the 'exaltatio sanctae fidei Catholice et bonus status totius universis'.[2]   In the first 'ordinatio' he presses the Council to establish three colleges in Rome, Paris and another [3] suitable city where philosophy, theology and Oriental languages may be taught for missionary purposes.   In the second, he urges the unification of the diverse military orders in one efficient body capable of attacking Berber and Saracen by sea and land. In the third, he suggests that the Church should earmark a tithe for these preaching and fighting organizations.[4]   The remaining 'Ordinationes' deal with reforms outside the scope of the present work such as the extirpation of Averroism, the abolition of plurality of livings and of unnecessary luxury among the clergy, and other matters of religious, social and educational interest.

In the third and last sitting of the Council, it was decided that, for the propagation of the faith among unbelievers, chairs should be created for the study of Oriental languages (Hebrew, Arabic and 'Chaldee') at Rome and in the universities of Paris, Oxford, Bologna and Salamanca.   Professors were to be appointed by the Pope in Rome, the King of France in Paris, and in the remaining universities by their respective prelates and chapters.[5]

Though serious consideration of Lull's plea for a crusade was either neglected or indefinitely postponed, his efforts for missionary work were not utterly disregarded; and the father of Oriental studies in Europe must have had some satisfaction from the Council's decision.   His life was, indeed, primarily that of a preacher in many fields and of an author who aimed at the systematization of all missionary

---

[1] Petitio Raymundi in Consilio generali ad acquirendam Terram Sanctam, Munich MS. ff. 86 ro–88 vo.   Cf. Pasqual (*Life*, op. cit.), II, 191 et seq.; *Hist. Litt.*, XXIX, 340–1.

[2] Munich MS., fo. 87 ro.

[3] ib., 'unum Romae aliud Parisiis tertium in selecta civitate'.

[4] ib., f. 87 vo.

[5] Landon, II, 271–2.

ideas by writing a complete series of disputations [1] with non-Catholic Christians, Tatars and Muslims. As regards the Schismatics, progress was afoot, since the Byzantine Emperor had displayed leanings to Rome. In the Far East, a new Catholic See was about to be established at Khan Bāliq. Yet the effort to draw Muhammadans to Christianity was both negligible and abortive. Indeed, Islam seemed to be gaining ground, while Christians remained indifferent. In this field the call for work was pressing, and it was here that Ramon was determined [2] to act, and to act indeed at the risk of his own life since a wave of intolerance had swept over the world of Islam during this period as a reaction to the successive attacks from Christendom.

It would, however, be erroneous to assume, as some authors do, that Lull was the first missionary to Islam.[3] If we overlook the work done in Persia [4] and in the Middle East, the first of Lull's precursors was St. Francis [5] of Assisi, who accompanied the crusaders of Innocent III to Damietta in 1219. The Latins had recently established themselves in Constantinople after the Fourth Crusade and the Greek schismatics seemingly had little religious independence in Europe and were subject to the jurisdiction of Rome. The idea of bringing the Saracens as well within

---

[1] These disputations appear in the Salzinger ed., vols. II and IV. *Disputatio Latini et Graeci* (II, 4 et seq.); *Disputatio Latini et Nestorini* (II, 8 et seq.); *Disputatio Latini et Jacobini* (II, 24 et seq.); *Liber super Psalmum Quicunque vult sive Liber Tartari et Christiani*, and *Disputatio Fidelis et Infidelis* in vol. IV. For disputations with Saracens, see following note.

[2] In addition to the *Disputatio Latini et Saraceni* (*vide supra* note), Lull wrote two books on Islam: (1) *De Fide Saracenorum* (Salzinger, T. II, 73 et seq.); (2) *Disputatio Raymundi Christiani et Hamar Saraceni* (*vide infra*).

[3] For example, Zwemer.

[4] *vide infra*, Cap. X.

[5] *Acta Sanctorum* October T. XIII, 212 e. 'Primo quidem S. Clara ejusque sodales in Assisiatensi monasterio S. Damiani sedem habentes, ad exemplum S. Francisci, non nisi eleemosynis acceptis victum compararunt; sed, dum ille anno 1219 in Oriente doctrinam Christianam exponebat &c.'
Biographie Universelle (Michaud, nouv. éd., Paris, 1856), XIV, 642, art. on François d'Assise; Baillet, *Vies des Saints*, Oct., 99–132; Michaud, *Croisades*, III, 457–9; Maclear, *Missions in Mid. Ages*, 351–3, and *Apostles of Med. Europe*, 271–3. See also footnote on the Anonymous Continuation of William of Tyre (*Rec. des hist. des crois.*, *Hist. occident.*, Paris, 1859), II, 348.

the pale of the Catholic Church must have appealed to the founder of the Minorite Order. While the crusaders lingered in the region of Damietta, he fearlessly took the hazardous step of crossing from their camp to that of al-Malik al-Kāmil Nāṣir-al-Dīn Muhammad. Francis invited him to adopt the faith of Christ and began to preach the Gospel in his presence. The Sultan, perhaps in admiration of the monk's extraordinary courage and in respect for his profound conviction, generously returned him unhurt to the Christian camp, and Francis thus missed the crown of martyrdom.

The second precursor of Ramon Lull in missionary effort among the Muslims was André de Longjumeau whose career is treated at length in another chapter.[1] Longjumeau was one of St. Louis' trusted servants, who shared his aspirations not only in regard to the armed crusade but also to the evangelization of both Tatar and Muslim nations.[2] Longjumeau's extraordinary activities in the Near, Middle and Far East offer ample illustration of his great interest in these matters. Before taking the Cross again at the end of his life, St. Louis dreamed of preaching the Gospel in North Africa. For this purpose he dispatched Brother [3] André before 1270 to resume his missionary work among the Muslims of that region with the sanction of their king al-Mustanṣir, who did not share his subjects' intolerance. Longjumeau had had many previous connexions with the Muslims in Syria and in Persia, and had

---

[1] *vide infra*, Cap. X.

[2] The Dominican Confessor of St. Louis, Geoffroy de Beaulieu, says in connexion with the King's expedition to Tunis: '. . . dicebat: Pro Deo studeamus, quomodo fides catholica possit apud Tunicium praedicari et plantari. O quis esset idoneus, ut mitteretur ibi ad Praedicandum! Et nominabat quemdam fratrem ordinis Praedicatorum, qui alias illic iverat, et regi Tunicii notus erat.' *Rec. des Hist.*, XX, 23; ef. Pelliot, 221. Guill. de Nangis (*Rec. des Hist.*, XX, 460–1) reproduces the same statement almost literally.

[3] 'Après que le roy ot enseignié ses commandemens à Philippe sons fils, la maladie le commença forment à grever . . . Moult se demenoit le roy qui pourroit preschier la foy crestienne en Tunes, et disoit que bien le pourroit faire frère André de Longjumel, pour ce que il savoit une partie du langage de Tunes: car aucunes fois avoit iceluy frère André preschié à Tunes par le commandement le roy le Tunes, qui moult l'aimoit . . .' *Grandes chroniques*, IV, 426–7; ef, Pelliot, 221.

a fair knowledge of Arabic.   How far he met with any
success on his new mission, is extremely difficult to judge.
It is, however, known that he had returned to the West
before 1270 and that he did not accompany St. Louis in his
last crusade, probably owing to his advanced years.[1]   As he
had returned from China in 1251 and gone from Cyprus to
France with the King, it is probable that he spent some time
between 1252 and 1269 in discussion with the Berbers of
North Africa.

Although Lull was not the first to work among the
Muhammadans, he certainly did more than any of his predecessors and contemporaries to promote and systematize
work in this field.   His missionary career began almost
immediately after his conversion with the study of Arabic
and with the preaching of Christianity to the Muslims
who had survived the Christian conquest in Majorca,[2] and
though the result of his teaching may have been meagre,
all the Moors left under Christian rule were destined to
forcible conversion.   Lull's effort to promote the study of
Oriental languages has already been noted.   In 1276, under
the patronage of King James of Majorca he founded the
College of Miramer, perhaps the first in the West for the
study of Arabic; and John XXI gave him and his college
the papal benediction in the same year.[3]   This was only a
slight anticipation of the forthcoming results of Lull's persuasive action at the Council of Vienne.[4]   He himself must
have been an accomplished Arabic scholar, for he did not
only speak that language freely but also wrote and translated
some of his works into it.[5]

Lull's burning zeal for a missionary crusade among the
Muslims was not confined to idle propaganda from a secure
distance, for on three occasions he thrust himself into
the midst of the Berbers and argued with their *imāms* on
the truth of his faith and the falsehood of theirs.   In 1292

---

[1] Pelliot, 221–2.

[2] Lecoy de la Marche, *Relations politique de la France avec le Royaume de
Majorque*, I, 73.

[3] Peers, 128–35.   [4] *vide supra*, 86.

[5] He translated for example, his own *Ars inventiva veritatis* into Arabic.
Peers, 225.

he sailed from Genoa to Tunis [1] despite an illness from which he seems to have recovered as soon as the craft had sailed with a sure prospect of reaching Muhammadan soil. At Tunis his preaching was regarded as blasphemous and the penalty for this was death. The Hafṣid Caliph, however, magnanimously changed the verdict of death into exile, and Lull was dragged from his cell under a shower of stones through the streets of the town to a Genoese boat ready to sail. His life was narrowly saved from the infuriated crowds, but his mind remained intent on return to save their souls.

Before his second African mission, rumours circulated in the West that the 'Great Khan' of the Tatars had invaded Syria. He therefore hastened to Cyprus,[2] whence he might interview the 'Great Khan' and convert him and his hordes to Christianity. The news of the invasion was not utterly without foundation. In the year 1299, a Mamlūk Amīr named Kipchak and a detachment of 500 horsemen were sent by Sultan Lājīn of Egypt for the defence of Syria against an impending Mongol invasion. Realizing the smallness of their number and the consequences of defeat, these Mamlūks changed sides and fled to the court of Ghazan, the Mongol Khan of Persia. The invasion came during the second reign of Nāṣir when Ghazan with an army numbering 100,000 routed the Egyptians at Salamia north of Ḥimṣ on 23 December 1299 and reached the gates of Damascus. This city promised to surrender on condition of immunity. Ghazan sanctioned the request and an edict was read from the pulpit of the Great Mosque that protection was to be accorded to all, not excluding either Christian or Jew, and promising also good government for Egypt when this should become a Mongol province.[3] Satisfied with this result, Ghazan withdrew to Persia in February 1300, after threatening an early return to chastise any one who dared to repudiate allegiance to him. It was at this juncture that Lull arrived in Syria to find the

---

[1] Sollerius, in *Acta Sanctorum*, VII, 592 et seq.; contemporary *Life*, 17 et seq.; Peers, 240–5; Perroquet, 16 et seq.

[2] Sollerius, op. cit., 592; contemporary *Life*, 30–2; Peers, 304–6.

[3] Weil, *Abbasidenchalifat*, I, 211 et seq.; Muir, *Mamelukes*, 51–5.

Tatars gone beyond his reach. So he entreated the King of Cyprus to help him to preach to 'certain heretics' [1] and to visit the 'Soldan of Babylon and the King of Syria and of Egypt'.[2] But 'good' King Henri II de Lusignan [3] remained unmoved by Lull's entreaties, and the would-be missionary to Egypt journeyed back to Genoa and then to Paris to petition the professors and bachelors of the University to formulate the arguments most suitable for the conversion of heathens [4]—a modest beginning of the *Disputatio Raymundi Christiani et Hamar Saraceni*[5] which he was soon afterwards to write during his period of captivity in the land of the Berbers.

In 1307 he became restless and boarded a ship destined for the town of Bugia [6] in Algeria. This was his second North African mission.[7] Its importance was increased by the fact that the Berbers of Bugia admitted the principle of disputation in search for truth in matters of faith. Thus enabled to come into personal contact with learned Muslims, he was able to gauge the depth of their argument and the objections they raised against Christianity; and on this basis he accomplished the definitive redaction of his *Disputatio*. The Qāḍī (judge) [8] of the town appointed a time and place for the discussion, but no compromise was reached and Ramon was thrown into prison for six months partly pending

---

[1] Contemporary *Life*, 31. In a note on the same page, the Latin life specifies these heretics 'videlicet, Jacobinos, Nestorinos, Momminas'.

[2] ib., 31.

[3] ib.; Makhairas (ed. Dawkins) §§ 41 cts. et seq., and Genealogy, no. 25.

[4] 'De Convenientia Fidei et Intellectus in Objecto.' Ct. Peers, 324 and note 4.

[5] Salzinger, T. IV.

[6] In Arabic Bijāya, situated about 100 miles east of Alger. There are several descriptions of it in the Arabic sources. See Yaqūt: *Mu'jam al Buldān*, I, 495–6; al-Dimashqī, *Kitāb Nukhbat al-Dahr* (Text), 235; al-Bakrī, *Description de l'Afrique Septentrionale* (Trans. de Slane), 166–7; Piri Re'īs, Cap. 85; article 'Bougie' in EI. Bijāya was founded in A.H. 457 by al-Nāṣir b. 'Ilnās b. Ḥammād b. Zīrī b. Manād b. Bulukkīn on the site of an ancient Berber village and has an excellent harbour.

[7] Sollerius, op. cit., 594; contemporary *Life*, 33–9; Peers, 325–33.

[8] Described as Bishop by a contemporary chronicler—'Antistes sive Episcopus civitatis', and by another as 'Episcopus famosus in philosophia' Cf. Peers, 326 note 1. Lull himself describes the Muslim *literati* who came to argue with him while in prison as 'episcopi Saracenorum'. *Disputatio*, I, 46.

his trial for abuse of Muhammadanism and partly to protect him from the angry mob. It was during his incarceration that he formulated his opinions in the famous *Disputatio* with Hamar [1] the Saracen.

This work consists of a prologue and three parts.[2] The first and second parts are of theological, the third of historical value. 'Hamar' puts forward seven essential conditions and eleven attributes of Deity.[3] The 'postulate' of the Saracen is that none of these aforesaid qualities is either 'substantial' or 'accidental', and it is thus argued that Holy Trinity and Divine Incarnation are impossible.[4] He then takes up each of the eighteen conditions and attributes and treats it separately with the object of proving the oneness of God and the falsehood of Christian premises. He concludes by offering his adversary women and wealth, if only he becomes a Muslim. In response, Lull begins with the offer of eternal life if Hamar accepts his religion,[5] and then proceeds in the same manner by taking each of the eighteen points as a basis of proof for both Trinity and Incarnation. Then he concludes the controversy with a statement of forty points or 'signa' to prove that the Jewish religion is good in so far as it forms the basis of Christianity, that Christianity is better because it is more complete, but that the Law of Muhhamad is false and erroneous.[6] These forty 'signa' consist of the ten commandments, seven sacraments, seven virtues, seven deadly sins and nine Church ordinances. In the third part of the *Disputatio*, he says that the basis of this discussion has been reason and not authority. Then he proceeds with the story of his release from prison and his exile, his shipwreck within ten miles of Pisa and the loss of all his books and chattels at sea, and of the recording of his controversy with Hamar while in that city. In conclusion,

---

[1] It is difficult to find the exact equivalent of this name in Arabic. Three suggestions are possible: 'Umar, 'Ammār or 'Amru. Considering the Berber dialect of Arabic, the last, generally pronounced 'Amar, seems the nearest approach to Lull's 'Hamar'.

[2] Salzinger, T. IV, Pt. I. De Positione et Disputatione Saraceni. pp. 2–12. Pt. II. De Positione et Disputatione Christiani, pp. 12–46. Pt. III. De Ordinatione vel de Fine Libris, pp. 46–7.

[3] ib., 2.   [4] ib., 2.   [5] ib., 12.   [6] ib., 34.

he reverts to the subject of his projected crusade and of missionary work. Christianity is in great peril between Islam and the Tatar, he cries again. The Muslim by the kind of reasoning described above and by promise of worldly riches is winning many weak-minded or faithless Christian renegades.[1] A third part of the Sultan's army is Christian by origin, and one-third of the Tatars has embraced Islam.[2] The time is ripe for action on the part of the Christians and the remedies are three in number. First, is the establishment of 'four or five monasteries'[3] for the teaching of the languages of the unbelievers and for specialization in missionary work; second, is the unification of all military orders; and third, is the setting aside of a Church tithe for this cause. Of these remedies, he says, he has spoken at length in the *Liber de Fine* which the King of Aragon sent to the Pope with the promise of 'his person, his land, his army and his treasure' for fighting the Saracen.[4]

In 1315, Lull had attained his eighty-third year; yet his spirit remained undaunted by his failure, twice in succession, to convert the Saracens. For the third and last time, we see him in North Africa. Armed with a letter of protection from King James II of Aragon to 'Miralmomonin Bujahie Zacharie, King of Tunis, son of Almir Abhalabbar, son of the Almirs',[5] he is allowed to lead a quiet life in Tunis, preaching the Gospel in secret and giving the public no cause for suspicion or animosity, and so friendly is the

---

[1] Salzinger, T. IV, Pt. I., 34–46.

[2] ib., 46. After pointing out the triple division of the land of the Tatars— first the country of the Great Khan where Prester John was king in the East, and second 'Cotay' in the North (*sic*)—Lull says: 'Tertius Imperator est Dominus Persiae usque in Indiam, et vocatur Carbenda, et ipse et omnes sui milites sunt facti Saraceni; et hoc fuit factum tempore Casani sui fratris.'

[3] ib., 47; 'quatuor vel quinque monasteria, in quibus Religiosi et Saeculares literati et devoti et ferventes mori propter DEUM addiscerent Idiomata Infidelium, et deinde irent ad praedicandum Evangelia per universum mundum, ut praeceptum est'.

[4] ib., 47; 'de hac materia largius sum locutus in Libro de Fine, quem Dominus Papa habet, quem Dominus Rex Aragonia misit ad eum, qui in Monte Pessulano obtulit suam Personam, suam terram, suam militam, suam thesauram, ad pugnandum contra Saracenos omni tempore, &c.'.

[5] Letter dated at Lleida on 5 Nov. 1314. For Eng. trans. see Peers, 369.

atmosphere in which he teaches that one of his books written at this date is dedicated to the Mufti of Tunis.[1] Then suddenly he takes the western road to Bugia.

More than twenty years before he had expressed his determination to persevere in the missionary cause 'till death, if the Lord permits it'.[2]   On another occasion he wrote that he had 'very great fear of dying a natural death'.[3] In his peaceful life at Tunis, he must have had time to brood over the idea of martyrdom and he must have been drawn to it by an irresistible force from within.   At Bugia, he had his wish fulfilled.   On his arrival at that town either late in 1315 or early in 1316,[4] he was recognized and a furious mob stoned him to death on the beach.   Two Genoese merchants dragged his body to their ship and carried it to Palma where it was interred in the old church of San Francisco.

[1] *Liber de majori fine intellectus amoris et honoris.   Hist. Litt.*, XXIX, 300; cf. Peers, 370–1.

[2] Cf. Zwemer, 64.   [3] Cf. Peers, 371.

[4] On the problem of chronology, cf. Peers, 372–5.

CHAPTER V

BURCARD

Philippe VI de Valois and the Crusade. Burcard.[1] 'Directorium.'
Expedition against Turkey. End of the project for 'passagium generale'

THE fall of 'Akka, the progress of the Egyptians in
Armenia, and the real menace of the Turks to Eastern
Europe—these events seem to have created an atmosphere of alarm and of shame at many courts of Europe
and were perhaps most acutely felt at the Papal curia and
the court of France. Pope after pope had therefore
attempted to promote the march of Latin Christianity against
the East; and the French Kings, who came to the throne
during the early decades of the fourteenth century, pledged
themselves to take up the Cross and save the Holy Land.
Philippe VI de Valois (1328–50) was no exception; and
Pope John XXII, seeing the King's zeal, hastened to publish two bulls, the first dated 16 June 1330 authorizing
him to levy a tithe for two years in view of the intended
'passagium', and the second dated 5 December 1331 granting him and his companions the indulgences usual on
the occasion of the crusade.[2] Meanwhile Philippe started

---

[1] Better known in French literature as Brochart, Brochard and Brocard; in
Latin Brocardus, Brochardus and Burchardus. He is sometimes wrongly
mentioned as Richard; Reiffenberg's preface to the Chevalier au Cygne, in
Mon. pour servir à l'hist. des provinces de Namur, &c., IV, clx et seq. A.
Stewart and R. Conder, in publishing the earlier description of the Holy
Land (1280) by this author's namesake in the Palestine Pilgrims' Text
Society (London, 1896), spell Burchard, which is nearer to the original
Burcard adopted in the present study.

[2] Delaville Le Roulx, France, I, 86–7 and notes; Mas Latrie (Hist. de
Chypre), III, 726. The two bulls are in MS. in Paris, B.N. fr. 4425, f. 282
(16 June 1330); and Arch. Nat., P. 2289, f. 692 and B.N. fr. 4425, f. 8
(5 December 1331). The Pope issued further bulls—'Leticie nobis multae',
'Terra sancta redemptoris', 'Pridem carissimus', 'Ad liberandam terram' and
'Ad terram sanctam',—dated 26 July 1333 extending the privileges accorded

his preparations for the coming expedition. He negotiated with the Venetians for the transport of his contingents to the Holy Land;[1] and measures were taken for the supply of provisions from France, Naples and Sicily, from Crete and from Greece.[2] The King and the French chivalry finally took the Cross at Melun, on 25 July 1332.[3] It was in these circumstances that the advice of men who knew the East was tendered to the King. Guy de Vigevano of Pavia, the physician of Queen Jeanne de Bourgogne, prepared a memoir[4] on the armaments to be recommended for the expedition, their construction and their use. Still longer, and not less important than Guy's memoir, was the *Directorium ad Philippum regem*[5] (*Franciae*), a remarkable work on the whole project of crusade submitted by Burcard.

Little is known of the life and career of this crusading propagandist beyond a few rather disconnected events. So scanty, indeed, is the material about him, that he has often

the King to the various classes, secular and clerical, who might participate in the crusade. Arch. Nat., J. 453, J. 454 nos. 2–6; J. 455 nos. 16–17; B.N. Lat. 12814, f. 225–7. He also promised the same indulgences to the Queen; Arch. Nat. J. 455, no. 8.

[1] The Doge dispatched three representatives of Venice to advise the King on this matter. These were Giovanni Bellegno, Blaise Zeno, and Marino Morosini. The Republic of St. Mark placed at the disposal of Philippe VI a fleet sufficient for the transport of an army of 5,000 knights, with their horses, 1,000 squires and sergeants, and moreover offered 4,000 of her own seamen for six months' service at her own expense. Mas Latrie (*Commerce et expéditions*), 97–101.

[2] Delaville Le Roulx, I, 88.

[3] Boislisle (*Projet de Croisade &c.*), 236 et seq.

[4] B.N. MS. Lat. 11015; cf. Delaville Le Roulx, I, 89 and note 3.

[5] Several MSS. of the original Latin text of this work are known to exist; Oxford, Magd. 43 and 2184; B.N. Lat. 5138 and 5990; Bâle, I, 28; Brussels, Bibl. Roy. 9178; Vatican, Reg. Chr. 603; Vienna, Nat.-Bibl. 536. For MSS. of the contemporary French version (1333) by Jean de Vignay, a Hospitaller of Altopasso, see B.M. Roy. 19 D. I; Munich, fr. 491. For later French translation (1455) by J. Miélot of Lille for Philippe le Bon, Duke of Burgundy, see B.N. fr. 5593 and 9087; Arsenal, 4798; Brussels, Bibl. Roy. 9095. Cf. Delaville Le Roulx, I, 90, note. Fragments of the Latin text appear as anonymous in Quétif, Ord. Praed., I, 571–4. Cf. Molinier (*Sources*), no. 3549 in IV, 109–10; Röhricht, *Bibl. Geogr. Pal.*, 74–6; Delaville Le Roulx, I, 90, note; Reiffenberg, clx et seq. Miélot's trans., edited by Reiffenberg in an appendix to the *Chevalier au Cygne*, op. cit., 226–312, is adopted here for reference.

been confused with Burcard of Mount Sion.[1] The career
of the latter seems to belong exclusively to the thirteenth
century, and after visiting Egypt, Syria, Armenia and
Cilicea about 1232, he settled for ten years in the monastery
of Mount Sion in Jerusalem and wrote his famous guide
to pilgrims to the Holy Land [2] in 1280. Our Burcard,
on the other hand, seems to have lived mainly, and certainly
wrote, in the fourteenth century. Further, his *Directorium*
is sometimes ascribed to Guillaume Adam on the ground
of similarity of style and ideas to the latter's work entitled
De modo Sarracenos extirpandi.[3] In the *Histoire Littéraire
de France*, Henri Omont [4] expresses grave doubt as to this
identification, though he treats the *Directorium* in the section
on Guillaume Adam. Both authors were Dominicans and
both travelled in the East. Moreover, none of the original
Latin manuscripts of the work bears the name of the
author; and the only direct evidence as to the authenticity
of Burcard's work appears in the fifteenth-century French
translation by Jean Miélot, whose statements have recently
been rejected as false. It would appear, however, from
internal evidence, that Burcard's authorship is genuine.
Guillaume Adam is said to have been appointed by Pope
John XXII as one of the delegates commissioned to undertake the task of bringing Armenia within the pale of
Catholicism (31 May 1323). Adam could not have gone
on this mission, for he was still at Avignon till 26
October 1324—the date of his transference from the
Archbishopric of Sultaniah to the See of Antivari.[5] On
the other hand, it is perfectly clear from the *Directorium*
that its author played a prominent part in the conversion

[1] Reiffenberg, clxi, and note 2.

[2] *Descriptio Terrae Sanctae.* For list of MSS. and editions, see Röhricht,
op. cit., 56–60. Burcard of Mount Sion's Guide is translated into English
by A. Stewart with geographical notes by C. R. Conder, op. cit., *vide supra*,
95 note 1. Marino Sanudo appears to have made use of this early work;
cf. Stewart's preface.

[3] See under Guillaume Adam in Chapter III.

[4] XXXV, 283. 'Jusqu'à plus ample informé, il faut se résoudre à ignorer
le nom du rédacteur du Directorium ad passagium faciendum.'

[5] *Hist. Litt.*, XXXV, 279. Cf. Kohler, in ROL, X (1903–4), 21
et seq.

of the Armenians and that he was present at King Leo's court on this solemn occasion.[1] This is a direct proof that Guillaume was not the author; and there is no reason for divergence from the traditional view based on Jean Miélot's statement. Burcard was fully qualified to write the *Directorium*. His travels and experiences in the East were of unusual value for the accomplishment of this work. On the other hand, it would be an error to overestimate the immediate effects of his plan on the projected crusade of Philippe VI. As will be shown after the analysis of the *Directorium*, Burcard's knowledge of Oriental affairs was seriously marred by his blind zeal for Catholicism in regard to the Christians of the East. His crusade was chiefly directed against these at a time when the union of the churches was in view and when Saracen activity demanded a united front.

Burcard travelled to the Near East about 1308. He stayed there for a period of more than twenty-four years, during which he preached Christianity according to the Catholic [2] creed and acted for the Papacy in bringing the Armenians to the Roman profession.[3] After his return to Europe, the projected crusade of Philippe de Valois was public knowledge, and Burcard at once started the

---

[1] The author describes himself as one of the architects of this union with Rome, 'desquelles union, j'ai esté promoteur, ouvrier et exécuteur'. See full extract in note below; Reiffenberg, 296.

[2] Burcard refers in the Prologue to 'les choses . . . que j'ay veues et expérimentées par l'espace de xxiiij ans et plus que j'ay demouré en la terre des mescréans pour y preschier la foy catholique'. Reiffenberg, 228.

[3] Reiffenberg, clxiii; Delaville Le Roulx, op. cit., 89–90; Molinier, op. cit., 109. A number of Armenian Synods were convened during this period at Sîs and Adana, and these renounced the old beliefs of their Church in favour of union with Rome as their aim was to draw crusading help from the West; but many still adhered to the old Armenian rite and elected Sarkîs, Bishop of Jerusalem, as anti-Catholicos in defiance of the pro-Roman Catholicos, Constantin III, who was finally excommunicated as a heretic in 1311. The Egyptian Sultan supported Sarkîs and the schismatic Armenians. V. Langlois (*Numismatique de l'Arménie au moyen-âge*, Paris, 1855), 59; Iorga (*Arménie*), 137; J. Issaverdens (*Armenia and Armenians*, vol. II, Ecclesiastical History, Venice, 1875), 190–1; E. F. K. Fortescue (*Armenian Church*, London, 1872), 28–9. For Armenian religious dogma, see J.-A. Gatteyrias, *L'Arménie et les arméniens* (Paris, 1882), 121–9; Morgan, *Hist. du peuple armén.*, 314–16.

preparation of the *Directorium* [1] which he dedicated to the King in 1332. He divided it into two large sections—the first containing a discussion on such preliminary matters as the urgent need for a crusade, the supply of provisions to the army and the possible routes which the expedition might adopt, while the second dealt with the actual plan of campaign.

According to the modes and conventions of writing in that age, Burcard begins his work with a prologue,[2] in which he indicates the joy of all on hearing the news of the King's decision to champion the cause of Christ and, like a new Maccabeus, fight His battle and recover the land of promise. As a 'poure mendiant', the author of the *Advis directif* is unable to serve his sovereign lord in chariots and on horseback, and he can only offer good council in his treatise to ensure victory for the 'passage d'oultre-mer'.

The first book opens with the motives [3] of the crusade. Four in number, these are the example of the King's predecessors, the spread of the Catholic faith, the saving of many Christians from perdition and the recovery of the Holy Land. He states that the world is divided into three large parts, that is, Europe, Asia and Africa, peopled by Christians, Tatars, Saracens and a multitude of Greek, Nestorian and Jacobite schismatics. The conversion to Catholicism of the Greeks, Nestorians and Jacobites is sufficient incentive for the crusade.[4] Yet, another potent motive is the duty of saving the land of the prophets and of promise, the natural heritage of Christians.[5]

---

[1] According to Miélot's trans. of 1455, the French title is 'Advis directif pour le passage d'outre-mer'. Reiffenberg, 227.

[2] Reiffenberg, 228–9.   [3] ib., 232–9.

[4] ib., 239. 'Et, quant à nostre propos, il souffist avoir motif pour faire ledict passage, que une si grande multitude de pueple soit ostée de ses erreurs, et réduite à la cognoissance de vérité de la foy, ainsi que autresfois ilz ont esté réduitz, comme nous lisons, lorsque la vérité et la bonne doctrine de la foy flourissoient ès parties de Orient.'

[5] ib., 239–41. He claims the Holy Land as 'désignée une partie de nostre heritage, qui a esté désirée des sains prophètes, et promise et donnée à eulx et à nous', but now it is in the hands of the 'adversaires de la croix, . . . vaisseaulx de Lucifer, &c.'.

The preparations for the crusade should be inaugurated
by general prayer in all the churches of Christendom.
Men must amend their lives and purify their souls from
the taint of sin.[1] They should also abide by the rules
of discipline and the canons of chivalry. Here Burcard
quotes Vegetius for the benefit of his readers.[2] Further,
peace and unity must be established among all the nations
of the West. Without these elementary precautions,
neither prowess nor skill in the art of war would be of
any avail. He notes the hostilities between the Kings of
Aragon and Sicily, and between the Genoese and the
Catalans.[3] Excellent soldiers, they have deflected their
efforts from encountering their common enemy to the
ruination of each other's fortunes. Turning to the matter
of provisions,[4] he advises the King to order a search for
these, not only in France, but also in the countries beyond
the sea where much may be obtained in abundance at a
lower cost. Once these preparations are complete with all
the material and instruments of war,[5] the King can deal
with the republics of Venice and Genoa for the conveyance
of all supplies from the West to the territories of Romania [6]
by way of the sea. The Venetians are in possession of
Crete, Negropontis and more than twenty other islands
in the Archipelago; and the Genoese hold the fortified
city of Pera near Constantinople as well as the colony of
Caffa on the north coast of the Black Sea in the empire
of the Tatars. Their nautical experience and knowledge of those regions as well as their maritime power

[1] Reiffenberg, 242–5.

[2] ib., 245–7.   [3] ib., 247–8.

[4] ib., 248. Burcard makes a statement of interest on account of the list of
provisions which it includes: 'Ledit passage a aussi mestier de habundante
foison de vivres, et non mie seulement d'un lieu, ains de diverses régions,
comme sont fromment, vin, wile, farine, léguns, orges, frommages et chars
salées.'

[5] ib., 249. The author specifies the following: 'armeures, vivres, engins,
tentes, grandes et petites, grosses arbalestes et autres avec les garnissemens
nécessaires à toutes ces choses, instrumens à fossier, miner, fraper et pour
abatre et craventer les fundemens et les murs des chasteaulx et des cités, quand
il sera besoing et nécessité le requerra'.

[6] ib., 'l'empire de Rommenie', against which, as will be shown below, most
of his plan is directed.

will be of much profit.[1]   Before sailing, however, it is
essential to equip ten or twelve galleys to guard the waters
of Syria and Romania against any hostile action by false
Christians or unbelieving Saracens.   The island of Cyprus
will provide suitable headquarters for this fleet.   Burcard
entertains fears that some Christians, in their thirst for gain,
may cede some of the crusaders' cargo to the Sultan who
owns no vessels and has no materials or engines of war in
his own lands.   He also supports the maritime blockade
of Muslim countries and makes a special appeal to the
High Pontiff to renew his ban on trade with Alexandria,
Damietta and other Saracen markets.[2]

Burcard then deals at considerable length with the
important matter of the routes to the East.[3]   Of these he
enumerates the four principal ones.   First is the African
or Barbary[4] route, mentioned only once before by Ramon
Lull,[5] and detailed by Philippe de Mézières[6] at a later
date.   Burcard positively decides against this route which
bristles with difficulties.   The distance from Gibraltar
(Jubalthar) to 'Akka (Achon), situated within two days'
journey from Jerusalem, is 3,500 miles; and even if
the crusaders sail direct to Tunis (Thunes), this will result
in the saving of only a hundred miles.   After landing at
either Gibraltar or Tunis, the army of the Cross will have
to reckon with the strongly fortified castles and the impregnable cities of the Muslim Kingdoms of North Africa.
If they accomplish this difficult task, which is doubtful,
they will still have many days' journey across the Libyan
desert, which is so barren that no living creature can survive
in it.   Even if they overcome these hardships and safely
descend into the fertile valley of the Nile, the Sultan of
Egypt will muster all his forces to inflict a crushing defeat
upon them.   The author asserts emphatically that there is
no hope of a successful crusade by this route, and he cannot
see any justification for St. Louis' previous venture against
Tunis.

The second is the sea route,[7] which has often been

[1] ib., 249–50.   [2] ib., 250–1.   [3] ib., 251–68.
[4] ib., 251–2.   [5] *vide supra*, 80.   [6] *vide infra*, 147.
[7] ib., 252–3.

favoured by crusaders and is regularly adopted by pilgrims
to the Holy Places.   In following this route the fleet may
sail from Aigues-Mortes, Marseilles or Nice to Cyprus
where a council of war may be held to decide on immediate
operations, thence to Egypt or Syria.   This route is unsuit-
able for the French and Germans who are not accustomed
to the sea with its tempests and sickness as well as the
insipid food, bad water and lack of room on board the
ships.   The horses will be much weakened by the want
of exercise and loss of sleep on account of the unsettlement
of the sea and the smallness of the space allotted to them.
Many will even perish on the way.   Other objections are
the sudden change of climate from cold to hot which has
an adverse effect on man and horse, the loss of time by
enforced delay in Cyprus during the winter season, the
unnecessary expense entailed by this sojourn, and the
effects of idleness on the morality of the soldiers.   While
in Cyprus, St. Louis lost 250 counts, barons, knights and
other nobles.   Burcard cannot venture to recommend this
route with all its inconveniences and difficulties.

The third route [1] by way of Italy may be pursued in three
directions—either round the north coast of the Adriatic
by the towns of Aquileia [2] (Acquilée) and Capodistria [3]
(Ystrie) to Dalmatia (Dalmace), Serbia (Rassie) and the
Empire of Constantinople; or to Brindisi (Brandis), and
across the Adriatic to Durazzo [4] (Duras) and through
Albania and Blachia [5] to Byzantine territory; or to Otranto [6]

[1] Reiffenberg, 253–5.

[2] Ancient town at the head of the Adriatic near the river Natisone about six
miles from the sea.   It was founded by the Romans in 181 B.C. as a north-
west frontier fortress and connected with Genoa by the Via Postumia.

[3] Istria or Histria is the peninsula at the north-west corner of the Adriatic.
Its medieval capital was Capodistria or Justinopolis near the site of the modern
Trieste.

[4] Ancient Epidamnus and Dyrrachium; Albanian Durresi; Turkish and
Slavonic Drach.   Situated on the gulf of Durazzo about fifty miles south of
Scutari on the coast of the Adriatic, the city of Durazzo is the seat of an
Orthodox Greek metropolitan and a Roman Catholic archbishop.

[5] Province of the Kingdom of Thessalonica on the Aegean, north of the
Duchy of Athens.

[6] On the Italian coast at the outlet of the Adriatic to the Mediterranean,
Otranto was the nearest Italian city to the Balkans.

(Ydronte), the island of Corfu, Achaia, Blachia and Byzantium. After examination of these three ways, he chooses
Thessalonica [1] as the first objective before the final march
against Constantinople. The Aquileian and Istrian route
seems to him to be the most commendable. There will be
no sea to cross and no need for carrying provisions, as the
crusaders will proceed through fertile countries partly
obedient to the See of Rome. Lands inhabited by schismatic [2] nations will easily and by force of arms yield a
spacious road for the crusade. This is the historic route
followed by the Romans, the French and the Germans who
came to help or to chastise the Eastern Empire.

Fourth,[3] is the route through Germany, Hungary and
Bulgaria leading to Constantinople. It had been adopted
by the princes and nobles of France, Germany, Languedoc,
Guienne and Bretagne as well as by 'Peter the Hermit' and
his followers. It is both good and easy. The author then
specifies in one chapter [4] the distribution of crusaders
among the various routes. Rejecting the African route
as impossible, he selects for the King and the main
army the land route through Germany and Hungary
to the Balkans. A minority of men accustomed to the
sea may sail on the galleys and transports conveying
provisions by the Mediterranean. The contingents from
the south of France and Italy will find it more expedient
to travel by the Italian routes of Brindisi and Otranto.
Thessalonica, in all cases, will be the general rendezvous.

As regards regions outside the confines of Catholic
Christendom, Burcard makes a special plea to the King to
avoid the conclusion of alliances with the schismatic princes
of Serbia and Constantinople.[5] On the contrary, it will
be 'lawful and honest' to invade the territories of these
faithless and hateful heretics who have consistently refused

---

[1] The modern Salonica.

[2] Reiffenberg, 254. Speaking of these, Burcard says: 'Et quant est de leur
vaillance et hardiesse de résister, je n'en fay nulle mention néant plus que
de femmes; et s'ilz vouloient empeschier nostre saint voyage, nous ferions
légièrement par feu et par l'espée ung chemin grant et large' in the manner
which will be described below.

[3] ib., 255.   [4] ib., 255–8.   [5] ib., 259 et seq.

submission to Rome. He then enumerates the reasons [1] for which the destruction of the empire of the Greeks must be regarded as one of the essential objects of the campaign. Burcard's argument for this procedure betrays his uncompromising fanaticism and thirst for revenge on the Greeks who had destroyed the Latin Empire of Constantinople. The treasonable basis of the empire of the Palaeologi, the uncertainty of their rightful descent, their disorderly life, and the pitiful treatment of their subjects justify a spirited attack on their realm. The Greeks have lost their learning and their faith since their departure from the true creed. Their lands are so depopulated and their arms so enfeebled that the Latins will meet with no difficulty in the elimination of the vestiges of their power and influence. This will not only bring the Eastern Church to the Catholic fold, but also ensure the supply of provisions, furnish safe harbours for ships, and offer strong bases for offensive operations against the Saracens and for defensive measures in case of unforeseen retreat.[2] After the conquest of Constantinople, ordinances [3] must be enacted to ensure the good faith of the Greeks in their conversion to Catholicism. Men of doubtful loyalty to the new order must be tried in secular courts and punished as heretics. Others who openly defy the Latin Church must be exiled. Those who remain must cede one child from every family to be brought up in the guardianship of Holy Church and trained in the manners and customs of the Latins. All books containing doctrinal errors must be burnt. To clear their conscience and prove their loyalty, all citizens should assemble in the Cathedral of St. Sophia where they may publicly do homage and truly submit to the lordship of the French. The new Church must be completely purged of the vicious observances of the old.

At the end of the first book, Burcard digresses to the subject of Serbia (Rassie) [4] to demonstrate the facility with which that country may be surprised and annexed to the proposed Frankish empire of Constantinople. He gives an interesting description of the country as he saw

---

[1] Reiffenberg, 269 et seq.   [2] ib., 284–7.   [3] ib., 288–91.
[4] He speaks of the 'Roy de Rassie' on pages 266–8.

it at the opening of the fourteenth century. This Kingdom, he says, has no castles in the Western sense; and its
fortifications have neither moats nor outer walls.[1] All
habitations, even those of the King and nobles, are wooden
constructions, except in the coastal towns owned by Latins.[2]
The land is rich in natural products and has five gold and
silver mines. Whoever conquers this country will have a
precious jewel of permanent value.[3] Further, the existence
in it of two Catholic nations—the Albanians and the Latins
—is another strong reason why the crusaders should appropriate it to the West. The Latins have six [4] cities and the
Albanians four,[5] all of which form one see of the Latin
Metropolitan of Antivari. The Albanians are in a majority
and can put in the field an army of 15,000 horsemen, if
only they find the French willing to save them from the
misery to which the Slavonic race has reduced them. In
reality, concludes Burcard, a thousand French knights and
five or six thousand foot together with the aforementioned
Albanian army can win without difficulty the whole Kingdom of Serbia.[6]

As far as the end of his first book, Burcard's crusade is
directed solely against the Eastern Church, the Byzantine
Empire and the Orthodox Kingdom of Serbia. In the
second book he deals with aspects of holy war on Asiatic
soil. He begins with a series of warnings.[7] The King
should have no confidence in the Armenians. It is true
that they have renounced their old errors and united themselves with the Church of Rome by word of mouth and in

---

[1] Reiffenberg, 293. 'Ce royaume n'a comme aulz lieux ne fors ne garnis
ou se bien pou non; . . . et y sont les fortz sans fossez et sans nulz murs.'

[2] ib., 293–4. 'Les édifices et palais, tant du roy comme des autres nobles,
sont de palis et de boys: ne je n'y véys oncques palais ne maison de pierre ne
terre, se non ès citéz des Latins qui sont sur la marine.'

[3] ib., 294. 'Quiconques dont aura ce royaume, il aura vraiement j joyel
gracieux et plaisant et moult precieux en tout ce siècle.'

[4] ib.—These are 'Anthibaire', 'Cathare', 'Dulcedine', 'Suacinense',
'Scutary' and 'Drivate', which may be identified as Antivari, Cattaro, Dol-
cigno or Dulcino in Upper Albania, Siwans or Soans which is now unknown,
Scutari and Drivastum or Drivaste which is the seat of a Latin bishop.

[5] ib.—'Polat le majour', 'Polat le minour', 'Sabbate' and 'Albanie'; i.e.
Pulati, St. Saba and Albanopolis.

[6] ib., 295.   [7] ib., 295 et seq.

writing, and Burcard himself had been one of the preaching friars delegated by Pope John XXII to obtain the necessary guarantees of their good faith; but the errors of heresy have been so deeply rooted in the souls of both clergy and common people that their conversion may only be a superficial one, actuated by fear of their oppressors, the Saracens on one side and the Turks on the other.[1]

The King, moreover, should trust neither the children of the mixed marriages between Latins, Greeks and Georgians,[2] whose promises are deceptive and habits detestable, nor the Syrians [3] whose main aim in life is the accumulation of riches and honours by foul means and breach of faith. To this category of unreliable peoples and tribes Burcard adds the newly converted Muslims, the Assassins, and the issue of marriages between Greeks and Turks.[4] The first combine the vices of a doubly vicious parentage, the second accept baptism chiefly to ameliorate their social and financial condition without any

[1] Reiffenberg, 296. Burcard's statements on the conversion of Armenia may justly be regarded as an original document of great value. He says that 'ilz sont très-mauvais hérétiques et envelopéz en moult d'erreurs, tant le clergié comme le menu pueple; . . . et jà soit ce que seulement les Arménins de la basse Arménie, que on appelloit jadis Scilicie, aient fait une union avec l'église de Romme et aient exprimé par parole et par escript la confession de la foy; desquelles union et confession j'ai esté promoteur, ouvrier et exécuteur, et déléguié j des frères prescheurs que monseigneur Jehan, pape xxij^e y envoya pour ceste cause espécialement entre autre choses encoires, toutefois est ce pueple obstiné en grans choses'. He then compares the Armenians with the leopard and the wolf who cannot change their habits and the Ethiopian who cannot change his skin. 'En vérité', he continues, 'les Arménins tiennent ceste manière de fère, car quant ils sont pressez de la puissance des Turcz ou traveilliez des tributz et invasions des Sarrazins, il viennent souvent et accourent vers l'église de Romme.' In the first passage, Burcard must have had in mind the settlement of 6 January 1199 (?) whereby, in the name of Emperor Henry VI, Cardinal Conrad of Wittelsbach Archbishop of Mayence conferred kingship on Leo I in return for his adherence to the Church of Rome. At first Leo styled himself 'King by the grace of the Holy Roman Emperor', a phrase which he later changed into 'King by the grace of God.' Morgan, *Hist. du peuple arménien*, 193–5.

[2] ib., 298. These are called 'Gasmulins', in Latin 'Gasimulis'. In the rubrics (ib., 233), they are curiously called 'Turquemans' and in Latin 'Basmuli'.

[3] ib., 298.

[4] ib., 233, 299. 'Murtans' or 'Murtez'—Latin 'Murtati'.

real understanding of their new religion and obligations, and the third harbour an unusual thirst for blood.[1]

With these warnings in mind, the King and the Christian host may cross the Bosphorus [2] and take the field against the Turks in Asia Minor. This is the only water passage in the way of the crusaders, and its narrowness will minimize the peril to which they are exposed in crossing it.[3] A great advantage of the march through Asia Minor is the elimination of the danger of attack from the rear by the Turks. The severe reverses which were experienced by the Kings of France and England after landing at 'Akka and Ṭarābulus, till recently in Christian hands, had proved the unwisdom of their general strategy. While fighting the Sultan of Egypt they had also to deal with the Turks who came to help their co-religionists. If the Turks are taken separately, the task of conquering them will be an easy one, since the chance of any succour coming to them from Egypt is remote.[4]

On the subject of the Tatars, Burcard appears to conclude that they would be inclined to lend their assistance to the crusading host. They have invaded Persia and abolished the caliphate of Baghdad (Baudas). In recent years, the 'grant Cachan' [5] (Grand Khan or Khaqan) had routed the forces of Egypt, killed 11,000 of the Sultan's army, and overrun Syria to the gates of Damascus. This irreparable loss to the Mamlūks is bound to make the Christian conquest of the Holy Land a very light task. The Tatars may also reinforce the King's army. It is known that when St. Louis was in Cyprus, Mongol ambassadors hastened to offer him the services of their master; and there is no reason why the proffered aid and alliance should not be forthcoming on the present occasion.

---

[1] ib., 300–1; 'les mauditz Assasins . . . ont soif du sang humain, tuent ung innocent pour certain pris, et ne tiennent compte de la salut de l'omme. Ilz se transfigurent aussi en angèle de lumière, comme fait le diable, quant ilz ensieuvent les gestes, la langue, les meurs, les fais de diverses nations et gens de particulières personnes; et eulx, ainsi couvers de peaulx de brebis, meurent ainçois que on les congnoisse'.

[2] ib., 233, 301. 'Helespont', 'Bofforus', 'Bosforus', and 'Bras de Saint-George' or 'Jorge' are variations in the text.

[3] ib., 302.   [4] ib., 303–4.   [5] ib., 304–5.

In their progress through eastern territories, the crusaders have nothing to fear as to an abundant supply of provisions. Ships will convey these by the Mediterranean. Moreover, when the King of France invades Serbia and the Byzantine Empire, as suggested in this memoir, the newly annexed provinces will furnish much that may be needed, while Turkey is an earthly paradise where fresh vegetables grow in profusion.[1]   Turkey, Burcard adds, can be easily conquered for a number of reasons. The malice of the Turkish race and its perversity and sin will stand against it, while the Lord abides with His host. In the Old Testament history, it is revealed that God never abandoned His people to their enemies except when He wished to punish them for their sins and excesses. [2]   The Turks are a factious nation in more than one way, and the one tribe persecutes, despoils and kills another.[3]   They have no chivalry, and their armies consist of emancipated slaves or disloyal Greeks. Moreover, they are ignorant of the art of war and devoid of prowess. They have no armour to protect them except a leather hauberk, and no weapons other than the Turkish bow. Every one among them has, indeed, his own horse, but this is so lean and feeble that it cannot sustain the shock of the heavily armoured horse of the Christian knight. Their tactics are based on taking no firm stand in the field for valiant combat hand to hand, but on hovering round the enemy, running backward and forward.[4]   'And to conclude briefly,' says Burcard, 'after the Greeks and the Egyptians (Babilonians), they are the most vile nation of the East in feats of arms.' [5]

The Saracens have a prophecy that their sect will be exterminated by a King of France.   When the holy father,

---

[1] Reiffenberg, 306–7.

[2] ib., 308. 'Je ne leus oncques en quelque hystoire du Viel Testament que Nostre Seigneur baillast oncques son pueple en la main de ses ennemis, senon pour péchié.'

[3] ib. 'Les Turcz sont dévisez entre eulx en moult de manières, et l'un persécute l'autre, le despoulle et le occist.'

[4] ib., 309–10. On the advantages of the Turkish arrow, horse and general tactics, see *Nicopolis*, 78–81 and notes.

[5] ib., 310. 'Et pour briefment conclurre, après les Grecz et Babilioniens ilz sont la plus vile nation de tout Orient en fais d'armes.'

Pope Clement, preached the crusade and the news reached the East, their hearts were chilled with fear.[1] Speaking 'en vray et expert jugement', Burcard assures the King that the host of France alone is capable of dealing with Turk, Egyptian, Tatar, Indian and Arab. The sovereign lord Philippe, the new David, will march onward, overwhelmed with honours and triumphs to the very gates of Jerusalem.[2]

Notwithstanding his prolonged residence in the East, Burcard seems to have misconceived or misconstrued many of its most important aspects. The *Directorium*, taken as a whole, falls short of the practical merits of the works of several other propagandists. It can hardly be classed in the same category as Marino Sanudo's *Secreta Fidelium Crucis*. The author, in his preference for the land route across Europe to the direct sea route by the Mediterranean, is reactionary. The example of 'Peter the Hermit' could provide no justification for a blind march from one end of the continent to another in the vain hope of reaching Syria. The hordes that followed that eleventh-century legendary figure suffered incredible hardships and never reached their destination. Burcard's contention that the land route was short and inexpensive had no foundation in reality. It was long and exhausting to man and beast. It was also costly because it meant a long time on the march and consequently a great consumption of provisions. It engendered indiscipline and the spirit of revolt among leaders and followers. Moreover, the princes of countries on the way to the East would raise objections to the passage of the

---

[1] ib., 310; 'les Sarrasins . . . ont trouvé une prophécie que, au temps présent, leur abhominable et orde secte doit estre destruite et déffaite par ung prince de France. . . . Et quant nostre sainct père le pape Clément commanda le passage d'oultre-mer, et que les nouvelles en vindrent jusques à ceulx de Perse, une si grande fréeur et paour leur navra les cuers, comme s'ilz eussent jà eu à leur dos les espées des François.' This statement is not without foundation, though Burcard may have misunderstood or misrepresented the original version of it to suit the circumstances of his memoir. In present-day Egypt, I have occasionally heard a curious legend current among Muslim country people that the end of the world comes after the complete Christianization of all nations. Guilaume d'Adam, V, 73, mentions a similar prophecy; *vide supra*.

[2] ib., 311–12.

host through their realms, since past experience had shown that even the soldiers of the Cross were apt to commit acts of pillage in friendly territories. In his proposed attack on the Byzantine Empire, Burcard only renewed the sad memories of the Fourth Crusade and the miserable end of the Latin Empire of Constantinople at a time when Greek emperors were more than ever open to an understanding with Rome and were even prepared to join their forces with those of the West in one fellowship against the Turk, their common enemy. An untimely attack of this type would only embitter the feelings and widen the gap between the Christian East and the Christian West. Burcard's relentless onslaught on all the Christian communities of the Orient without discrimination between Orthodox and Catholic, as has already been shown in the case of Armenia, would seem to these nations anything but Christian. Still more serious is the unusual levity with which he regards the strength of the Turks and the Egyptians. He appears to be unmindful of the recent sorrowful events in Syria, and future history was to reveal the superiority of Turkish tactics to the antiquated traditional methods of war in the West.

A memoir of this kind, sometimes reactionary and sometimes revolutionary, must have been regarded at the court of France with suspicion as to the wisdom of its contents. King Philippe VI believed in neither the land route nor the attack on the Byzantine Empire, and he had no intention of undertaking either of these projects. He referred Burcard's work to his council for consideration. It was examined with care, and a written report [1] in which the councillors embodied their decisions was submitted to the King. They unanimously rejected the land route and advised their master to journey by sea in the same manner as St. Louis, his predecessor. One modification, however, seemed to them necessary. The galleys carrying the crusaders would do well to sail from Nice along the southern European coast, calling at Genoa, Pisa and Rome on the way to Naples, for three reasons—first, to avoid

[1] An eighteenth-century copy of the report is preserved in the Arch. Nat. (P. 2289, 703–12). This is edited by Delaville Le Roulx, *France*, II, 7–11.

the perils of the high sea; second, to hold meetings with
the assemblies of the towns of Lombardy, Tuscany and
the Roman province so as to procure further levies
from Italy; and third, to perform the pilgrimage to the
holy shrines of the Apostles and Saints in 'Rome la
Grande' and thus make an auspicious beginning to a pious
crusade.   At Naples, the King could consult his uncle,
King Robert of Anjou, for further advice on the 'passage'.
As regards the proposed invasion of the lands of Serbia
(Rassie), the Empire of Constantinople and Asia Minor,
for which many reasons were urged in the *Directorium*, the
King's intention to forgo any such adventures as these
would appear all the wiser in view of the more urgent task
of concentrating all the forces of Latin Christendom to
ensure the recovery of the Holy Land.   Thus the royal
council rejected Burcard's project in its entirety.

While Philippe de Valois was vigorously preparing for
his great undertaking,[1] Venice saw in the crusade an opportunity to further her own interests in the Levant.[2]   The
rapid spread of the Turks endangered her Eastern trade,
and the Republic of St. Mark therefore aimed at the
formation of an anti-Turkish league by winning the Knights
of Rhodes, the Emperor of Constantinople and the rest
of the powers further west to the new cause.   In 1334
the Doge dispatched to France two new envoys, Giovanni
Gradenigo and Andrea Basegio, with instructions to exert
every possible effort to bring Philippe VI within the
League.[3]   A meeting of the Kings of France and Cyprus,
the representatives of the Knights Hospitallers and the envoys of Venice was held in the presence of Pope John XXII,
and all signed a treaty [4] which witnessed to the triumph
of Venetian policy.   It was agreed that the new league
should undertake two expeditions against the Turks.   In

---

[1] For Froissart's account of this project for crusade, see ed. Kervyn, II,
339–47.

[2] Delaville Le Roulx, *France*, I, 99.

[3] For Venetian manœuvring in this respect, see correspondence in Mas
Latrie, *Commerce et expéditions*, 101, and *Nouvelles preuves de l'hist. de
Chypre* (BEC, XXXIV), 65.

[4] Mas Latrie, *Commerce et expéditions*, 104–9.

the first place a flotilla of forty galleys [1] should meet in May
1334 at Negropontis and embark on a preliminary campaign, chiefly to clear the sea of all Turkish warships
which might threaten the safety of the transports of the
forthcoming crusade. In the second place, the 'passagium
generale' should follow in 1335. It was stipulated that
a force consisting of eight hundred men-at-arms, and a
fleet composed of thirty-two armed galleys and thirty-two
transports should be brought together by the confederates
in readiness for the general 'passagium'.[2] Even the King
of Sicily and the Emperor of Constantinople were supposed
to contribute to the crusade, and in the case of their failure
to do so, the League counted on Genoa and Pisa to supply
the shortage. The duration of the campaign was fixed at
five months, and the King of France expressed his willingness to prolong it by another month in case of necessity.[3]

In the meantime, the final arrangements for the sailing
of the first flotilla were made by the appointment of Jean
de Chepoy as admiral of the Franco-papal, and Pietro Zeno
of the Venetian sections of the grouped galleys. The Pope
granted them the indulgences usual in the circumstances
of holy war, and the naval detachments converged in the
waters of Negropontis at the appointed time. The nascent
Turkish navy, led by the Amīr Iakhshi, had shown some
activity round the coast of Greece; and at this time two
hundred armed Turkish barges were stationed in the gulf
of Volo (Demetrius) in Thessaly. At the beginning of
September 1334 news reached Iakhshi that a strong Chris-

---

[1] The Hospitallers furnished ten galleys, Venice ten, Cyprus six, the
Papacy together with France eight, and the Empire of Constantinople six.
Delaville Le Roulx (*Hospitaliers, 1310–1421*), 88.

[2] The contributions of the powers were as follows:

(*a*) France—400 mounted men-at-arms and 16 transports.
(*b*) Knights of Rhodes—200 men-at-arms, 6 galleys and 8 transports.
(*c*) Cyprus—100 men-at-arms, 6 galleys and 4 transports.
(*d*) Venice—10 galleys.
(*e*) Sicily—4 galleys and 4 transports.
(*f*) Constantinople—6 galleys and the remaining men-at-arms.

Mas Latrie (*Commerce et expéditions*), 104–9; Romanin (*Storia docu-
mentata di Venezia*, 10 vols., Venice, 1853–61), III, 112–15; Delaville Le
Roulx, *France*, I, 100 and note 3.

[3] Mas Latrie, l.c.; Delaville Le Roulx, op. cit., I, 100.

tian fleet had destroyed a Turkish flotilla at Kassandra and
that it was already on the way for a decisive naval battle
with his own. Iakhshi fled from Thessaly to Asia Minor,
followed by the confederates' galleys at full speed. On
8 September, an encounter between the hostile forces became
inevitable, the Turks sustained a heavy loss of barges at sea,
and on 14 September fifty more were destroyed. Finally, the
Christians completed the Turkish disaster by seizing the remainder of their fleet in the gulf of Izmir (Smyrna). A
landing was forced on Asiatic soil, the town fortress was burnt,
and the crusaders returned in triumph to their native lands.[1]

The success of this preliminary campaign inspired
Philippe VI and his crusaders with confidence in the great
possibilities awaiting the 'passagium generale' of 1335.
While preparations for sailing were afoot at Aigues-Mortes,
Marseilles and other ports of Languedoc, the Kings of
France, Bohemia and Navarre were discussing the details
of the campaign at Villeneuve-lès-Avignon. In Rhodes,
the Grand-Prior of France had accumulated the necessary
provisions for the French sojourn on that island. The
fleets of Venice and the Hospitallers were in readiness at
Crete. Yet suddenly the plan for a crusade collapsed at
a moment when all preparations were complete. When
the King was at Marseilles inspecting his fleet in readiness
to set sail, news reached him of an impending invasion from
England, and he had to return with all haste to Paris in
order to muster his forces for home defence. The outbreak of the Hundred Years' War was imminent, and even
Benedict XII who succeeded John XXII in 1334 wrote
to warn Philippe VI against the European discord which
the King's absence would help seriously to aggravate. The
prospect of a crusade had vanished, and neither Burcard's
plans nor Philippe's intentions came to fruition.[2]

[1] C. de la Roncière (*Hist. de la marine fr.*, Paris, 1899), I, 233–7; C. de la
Roncière and L. Dorez (*Lettres inédites et mémoires de Marino Sanudo
l'Ancien*, in BEC, LVI, 1885), 23–5; cf. Delaville Le Roulx (*Hospitaliers*,
1310–1421), 89–90.

[2] Froissart (ed. Kervyn), II, 260–1; Lot (*Projets de croisade sous Charles le
Bel et Philippe de Valois*, BEC, 1859), 509; Guillaume de Nangis (ed.
Géraud), II, 134 et seq.; Delaville Le Roulx, *France*, I, 101–2; Morgan
Hist. du peuple arménien, 217; Coville (*Hist. de Fr.*, ed. E. Lavisse), IV, i, 12.

CHAPTER VI

MARINO SANUDO

New Orientation in Crusade: Economic Warfare. *Sanudo's Life and Work. Secreta Fidelium Crucis. Epistolae*

WHATEVER the historical causes of the early crusades may have been, they were pre-eminently acts of devotion. They were holy wars fought for the salvation of the Holy Land from the yoke of an unbelieving usurper. Even so late as the thirteenth century, St. Louis undertook his expeditions against Egypt and Tunis for reasons of piety. In the Later Middle Ages the controversy between East and West began to have a new and different meaning. Devotion to the old cause, though still the ostensible pretext for waging holy war, was then mingled with many worldly interests. The Italian citizen, whether in Venice, Genoa or elsewhere, had lost or almost lost his medieval religious scruples in view of his material gains from trade. This is best exemplified by the famous Venetian saying which is often quoted—'Siamo Veneziani, poi Christiani'.

One of the outstanding results of the influx of crusaders and pilgrims to the East was the development of the maritime power of the Italian republics, notably Venice and Genoa. European knowledge of Oriental countries had also grown, and with it commercial intercourse received an impetus which increased in momentum during the late thirteenth and the early fourteenth centuries. As Western Kings became more and more engrossed in the internal and constitutional struggles of their own realms, the Italian republics flourished to an almost incredible degree on the Eastern trade. The towns of Egypt and Syria developed into vast emporia where most of the European nations had their special hostelries (funduqs) and

warehouses (Khans),[1] their special representatives and
consuls.[2]   Most of the Indian products poured [3] into the
empire of the Mamlūks, and the Venetians, Genoese,
Florentines, Pisans, Catalans and at a later date the French
had no alternative but to come to the subject lands
of the Sultan for the purchase or the exchange of goods.
The revenue accruing to Egypt from these transactions
filled the Egyptian treasury with gold and enabled its rulers
to increase their armaments and reinforce their battalions
with enormous numbers of slaves (mamlūks).   The tex-
ture of Levantine politics was becoming more interwoven
with commerce than ever before in the Middle Ages.   The
welfare, not only of Egypt, but also of the Christian republics of Italy and many other European states largely
depended upon these economic activities, and good-will
between the two sides was a necessary condition for the

[1] These two kinds of establishments were closely connected.   For the
etymology of the word funduq, funduk, fondaco or fundicum, see Heyd, II,
490, note 7; for its organization, see I, 152 and II, 430 et seq.   For funduqs
in Syrian towns, see same, I, 150, 152 and II, 462–3.   In Alexandria at the
end of the Middle Ages, funduqs were to be found for Genoa, Florence,
Naples, Ancona, Palermo, Ragusa, Cyprus, Barcelona (Catalans), Marseilles,
Montpellier, Narbonne, Greece, N. Africa and the Tatars, II, 432 et seq.
The Pisans and the Venetians had funduqs in both Cairo and Alexandria, I,
393 et seq., 411 et seq., and II, 431 et seq.

[2] Venice had consuls in Cairo, Alexandria and Damietta; the Knights of
St. John in Alexandria and Damietta; and the rest (see previous note) in
Alexandria.   'Akka seems to have had a larger number of consuls than any
other town in Syria; for Pisa, Amalfi, Ancona, Genoa, Marseilles and Mont-
pellier were represented in it.   Other states had consuls in Jerusalem,
Damascus, Ṣūr, Ṭarābulus, Beirūt and Aleppo.   For details cf. Heyd's index.
II, 751–2 and his article on 'Les Consulats établis en Terre Sainte au Moyen-
Âge pour la Protection des Pèlerins', in AOL, II, C iii, 355–63.

[3] The Indian trade was carried by one of two routes: first, to Aden, the
Red Sea and Egypt; second, to the Persian Gulf; then up the Euphrates to
Syria.   Heyd, I, 7 et seq., 378 et seq., and II, 58 et seq., 75 et seq., 436 et
seq.   The land route across Asia direct to Christian markets was much too
expensive and only suitable for light and valuable articles.   Merchants therefore had to resort to the Egyptian and Syrian termini for their chief requirements.   The attempt to avoid these by deflecting the course of trade to the
Christian seaports of Armenia, though carried out with some success at first,
ended in complete disaster, for the Egyptians invaded Armenia and levelled
its towns to the ground.   For details see chapter XIX on Counter-
Crusades.

interchange of articles of trade. The economic factor thus became a vital force which governed the movements of the crusaders. Venice and Genoa alone possessed galleys sufficient for the transport of the Christian armies to the Eastern battlefields and without their co-operation the failure of any enterprise against Egypt was ensured. Crusades and commerce thus became two inseparable problems. This is the new orientation [1] in the history of the holy war. All popes, kings and nobles who promoted the cause of the Cross against Islam found themselves confronted with that difficulty. Piety alone became helpless in the face of economic motives and interests. A crusade, in the event of success, must not entail any serious danger to the prospect of trade, otherwise its fate was sealed. From the early decades of the fourteenth century, all wise statesmen in Europe began to realize the gravity of this situation and perhaps no contemporary was more aware of the new circumstances than Marino Sanudo.[2] The whole of his career and all his works and correspondence revolved round an attempt at compromise between the new and growing factors and the older forces in a world of change. An earnest propagandist for the crusade, he never lost sight of commerce.

Sanudo was born in Venice at the beginning of 1270.[3] His father Marco Sanudo of the Torsello family, was a Venetian noble and a nephew of Doge Enrico Dandolo of Fourth Crusade fame. After the fall of Constantinople to the Latins, Marco [4] equipped eight galleys and invaded the Aegean Islands which were soon to become the Duchy

---

[1] Strictly speaking, precedents had occurred before this time; but the movement became marked only in the fourteenth century.

[2] Known as Marino Sanudo 'Il Vecchio' (the elder) to distinguish him from Marino Sanudo 'the younger' who wrote the famous Diarii (1496–1533) of Venetian history as it was recounted to him by his relative Marco II Sanudo, Duke of Naxos.

[3] Magnocavallo, 22. Delaville Le Roulx, France, I, 32, states that Marino was born about 1260; and Bréhier (Croisades), 189, confuses Marco with Marino Sanudo.

[4] Daru, I, 344–6; Gibbon (ed. Bury), VI, 417; Finlay (ed. Tozer), IV, 276 et seq.; Heyd, I, 274 et seq.; Hodgson (Early Venice), 623–5; Miller (Latin Orient), 68–9; Carew Hazlitt, I, 313–14.

of Naxos.[1] Marco was created first Duke of Naxos and suzerain to all other lords of the islands which he had conquered, owing homage himself only to the Latin Emperor of Constantinople and at the same time retaining his citizenship of Venice where he was appointed judge, then elected member of the 'magnum consilium' of the Republic.[2] During his early career of adventure, he was once seized by the Greeks of Nicaea and taken captive before their master. Marco I is said to have impressed the Emperor with his courage, sagacity and manly beauty so much that his captor married him to one of his daughters and gave him back his freedom.[3] Whether Marino was a descendant of this Greek princess,[4] is at present unknown. Nevertheless, one must assume that the admixture of Byzantine blood in the ducal dynasty of Naxos imparted such knowledge of the East as would have been otherwise extremely difficult to acquire. He thus combined the insight of the merchant princes with a large understanding of the nations beyond the sea. He further enriched his store of learning and experience by extensive travels in the area of the Levant [5]—in Italy, Greece, Armenia, Syria and Egypt. In 1286 he lived in the Venetian quarter of 'Akka

[1] Under Byzantine rule known as 'Dodecanesos' or Twelve Islands including Naxos, Paros, Antiparos, Melos, Cythnos, Delos, Syros, Siphnos, Sicinos, Ios, Cimlos and Policandro or Pholegandros. Heyd, Hodgkin and Miller, ll.cit.; also Finlay, IV, 277, note 2 by Tozer. The Sanudi retained the Duchy until 1383 when it was ceded to the Crispi, another Venetian family; then it was seized by the Gozzadini of Bologna in 1566 and remained in their hands until the Turkish invasion of 1617. Tenos, however, remained Venetian until it was ceded to the Sultan by the terms of the Peace of Passarovitz in 1718. Miller, op. cit., 68–9, 170.

[2] Mention of these appointments is made in two documents dated 1305 and 1306. *Libri Commemoriali*, I, doc. 248 and 280; cf. Magnocavallo, 82.

[3] Miller, op. cit., 163–4; Hodgson, op. cit., 424, note 1.

[4] The inscription on the tombstone of Marco and his wife reads: 'Sepultura D. Marci Sanudo Torsello et D. Mariae uxoris ejus et heredum de confinio S. Severi. In qua requiescit Joannes Ferate eorum filius. Cujus anima requiescat in pace. Amen. Orate pro eo.' Cf. Carew Hazlitt, II, 660, note 1.

[5] When presenting his *Secreta Fidelium* to Pope John XXII on 24 September 1321, he mentioned that 'vicibus multis extiteram in Alexandriam et Ancon; . . . in Romania vero maiorem partem temporis meae vitae peregi'. Cf. Magnocavallo, 24, 25–9.

for some time.[1]   In 1289, he sailed from Venice to Negropontis and he was still to be found on that Island in 1296.
Two years after, he was 'familiaris et domicellus' of Cardinal
Richard of Saint-Eustache who died in 1313 or 1314.   He
seems to have visited Rhodes where he made the acquaintance of Foulque de Villaret, the Grand Master of the
Hospital, between 1309 and 1311.[2]   In the following year
he was at Chiarenza in the Duchy of Achaia; and on his
return to Venice, he started a European tour.   He reached
Bruges and then journeyed south to Avignon where he
presented two copies of his *Secreta Fidelium* to John XXII
on 24 September 1321, the Pope appointing a committee[3] to examine the work and report on it.   Sanudo's
next halt was at Venice; but he soon took the road to
Naples, where he tried to capture King Robert II's attention in 1332, and afterwards gave advice to various European princes on projects for crusade, but all without
avail.

It is difficult to reconstruct the whole of Marino's life
in all its details.   Yet it is easy to judge from the scanty
material here assembled that he was a great traveller and
that he spared no possible effort to promote the crusade
according to his ideas and ideals.   His knowledge of Greek
and Latin enabled him to draw freely upon the learned
works of his medieval predecessors.   Evidence is not lack-

---

[1] A good summary of Marino's movements appears in Molinier (*Sources*),
no. 3092 (III, 240–1); Aubrey Stewart's preface to trans. of Sanudo, v–viii.

[2] Molinier, III, 242, places the journey to Rhodes after 1312, but Sanudo
refers to his acquaintance with Villaret between 1309 and 1311 in the Istoria
di Romania; cf. Hopf, 167 and Magnocavallo, 82–3.   Sanudo, referring to
his own work and travels (Bongars, II, 3), says that 'cum eosdem executioni
mandarem, quinquies trasfretaverim ultra mare quandoque in Cyprum,
quandoque Alexandriam, quandoque in Rodum'.

[3] Bongars, II, 1 et seq.; cf. Carew Hazlitt, II, 662–3.   The committee
consisted of 'Fra Benito di Asti, of the Order of the Preachers, Vicar of
Armenia; Fra Jacopo de Cammerino, a bearded Minorite, who had come to
the See on behalf of his brethren of Persia; Fra Matteo of Cyprus and Fra
Paolino of Venice'.   The Committee seems to have been in agreement on the
plan as a whole, and criticized only minor details such as the penalties proposed by Sanudo against those who broke the regulations as to the boycott
of trade with Egypt.   F. Kunstmann, *Studien über Marino Sanudo den
Älteren* (Munich, 1855), 39; cf. Delaville Le Roulx, *France*, I, 35.

ing in his books, to show that, besides his continual use
of the Bible and Bible history, he had used the histories of
Jacques de Vitry,[1] Guillaume de Tyr,[2] Vincent de Beauvais[3] and others.[4] He was also well informed in the contemporary affairs of the world around him, since he had
access to the best society of his age—the society of Popes,
Kings, Doges and nobles. Besides a collection of letters[5]
and his Testament,[6] Sanudo compiled a work called *Istoria
di Romania*[7] which he finished about 1328. His greatest
contribution was, however, the *Secreta Fidelium Crucis*,[8]
sometimes known as the *Conditiones Terrae Sanctae*. As
this work was started in or just after 1306[9] and finished

[1] Bishop of 'Akka in 1216 or 1217; participated in the Fifth Crusade;
became Cardinal-Bishop of Tusculum in 1228; died in 1240; author of
Historia Orientalis seu Hierosolymitana to 1193, in Bongars, I; for various
editions see Molinier (Sources) no. 2384, p. 50.

[2] Born in Latin Kingdom of Jerusalem about 1130; knew Greek and Latin,
probably also Arabic, Hebrew and Persian; became Archbishop of Tyre and
Chancellor of the Kingdom and was sent on several embassies to Rome and
Constantinople. His lost *Gesta Orientalium Principum* is said to have been
based on the Arabic chronicle of Sa'īd ibn al-Baṭrīq (ob. 940), Patriarch of
Alexandria. Probably poisoned in Rome at an unknown date. For editions
of his chronicle of the Crusades, see Molinier, nos. 2187, II, 303–4; also
Chevalier and Potthast.

[3] Dominican friar, studied in Paris, in favour with St. Louis, sub-prior of
the Convent of Beauvais; often styled bishop, but erroneously; died about
1264; best known as author of the *Speculum Historiale*, see Molinier, no.
2524, III, 93–4, also Chevalier and Potthast.

[4] Molinier, III, 243.

[5] Bongars, II, 289–306; Kunstmann (*Studien über Marino Sanudo* . . .
in München. Akad, Abhandlungen hist., 1855, VII), 753–819; L. Dorez
et de la Roncière, in BEC, LVI, 21–34; Magnocavallo, 106 et. seq.

[6] Magnocavallo, 150–4.

[7] Eighteenth-century Italian trans., ed. K. Hopf, *Chroniques gréco-romanes*
(Berlin, 1873), 99–170; see also Mas Latrie, in BEC, XXXIV, 47–8.

[8] The full title of the book in Bongars is *Liber secretorum fidelium Crucis qui
est tam pro conservatione fidelium, quam pro conversione et consumptione infidelium: quanquam etiam propter acquierendam et tenendam Terram Sanctam et
alias multas terras in bono statu pacifico et quieto*. There is only the Bongars
edition of 1611, and no other seems to be forthcoming in spite·of the unusual
importance of this work. For the MSS., see Simonsfeld, *Neues Archiv.*,
VII, 45–72; Magnocavallo, in *Rendiconti dell'Instituto Lombardo*, II, 31
(1898), 1113–1127; Kohler, in ROL, V, 27–32; Röhricht, *Bibl. Geogr.
Palaest.*, 67–8.

[9] Molinier, op. cit., 242.

as late as 1321,[1] it must have taken him about fifteen years before the completion of its last redaction. With long deliberation, industry and wide travels to collect all necessary data, Sanudo produced a document of outstanding merit. In the three main divisions of his book, he dealt with what he regarded as the three natural stages of a successful crusade. It was necessary to throttle and weaken Egypt economically at first. When this was achieved, the invasion of Mamlūk territory might follow without difficulty as the second normal stage. In the third and final section he showed the means and ways by which the conquest could be sustained and the Holy Land preserved in the hands of the faithful.

To start a crusade with a land expedition, meant only suicide. The armed forces of Egypt were far beyond the power of a Western contingent to subdue. Recent history had taught Marino Sanudo that lesson. If Egypt were to be conquered, its resources must first be depleted; and this the nations of the West could perform without any serious danger, much expense or heavy loss of life. The lands of the Sultan produced no gold or silver. They depended for it upon the Christians who bought the Indian pepper, spices and such other goods as were imported by way of Aden and carried to Alexandria.[2] If trade with Egypt were to be stopped for a time, it would mean the economic ruin of that country and the impoverishment of its rulers. It was the duty of the Holy Pontiff, therefore, to bring together a fleet to enforce the prohibition of intercourse with Egypt.[3] Ten galleys would be sufficient, and these could be raised without difficulty—one from Zaccharia of Genoa, the reigning prince merchant in Chios, another from Guillelmo Sanudo of Naxos together with the Ghisi, a third from the Patriarch of Constantinople, two from the

---

[1] Date of presentation to John XXII, *vide supra*, 118.

[2] Bongars, II, 23. Sanudo specifies two routes, the one by Baldach (i.e. Baghdad) and Thorisius (i.e. Tauriz or Tibriz) for goods of light weight and high value, and the other for 'Alia vero mercimonia gravioris ponderis et minoris praetii, ut piper, cinziber . . . per viam Haaden in Alexandriam in maiore quantitate'. The bulk of the latter, however, ensured the Sultan's profits. Cf. Macpherson, *Annals of Commerce*, I, 490 et seq.

[3] ibid., II., 30–1.

Hospitallers, a sixth from the Archbishop of Crete and the remaining four from the King of Cyprus and his clergy and nobility.[1]   For the guidance of the admiral of the fleet, the author described the Levant, and particularly Egypt, marking the mouths of the Damietta and Rosetta branches of the Nile for special vigilance.[2]   This fleet was to have other uses which included the interception of the frequent embassies from the Greek Emperor to Egypt and above all the Sultan's embassies to the Tatars[3] of the Crimea who continually reinforced his armies with large numbers of Mamlūks.   Two or three years of this blockade would prepare the way for the first and preliminary land 'passagium' which Sanudo considered in the second division of the *Secreta*.

The leader of the host must be a diligent and God-fearing man who, in the interest of Christendom, should enjoy the goodwill and friendship of the Venetians[4] in order that he might profit by their advice and help. After the appointment of the leader, came the preaching of the crusade.   In order to secure general response in large numbers,[5] this should be performed by the High Pontiff himself.   The crusaders would profit by alliance with the Christians of Nubia who were ready to invade Egypt from the South, and by a pact with the Tatars who might descend on Syria.[6]   But Egypt remained the root

[1] Cf. Magnocavallo, 85.

[2] Bongars, II, 25. 'Et habet hoc flumen iv ramos magnos: unus ramus Tenex nominatur, qui est versus desertum de Gazara; secundus est Damiatiae, tertius Strioni, quartus Raxeti qui est versus Alexandriam.   De quibus supra-dictis ramis, duo sunt principaliores et maiores: scilicet Damiatae et Raxeti.'

[3] ib., 32–3. 'Sic etiam Ambaxiatae . . . quibus Imperator Graecorum et Soldanus Babyloniae . . . poterunt faciliter impedire: . . . leuiter intercipi poterunt legationibus . . . praedictus Soldanus Imperatorem Tartarum.'

[4] ib., 35: 'unus homo diligens timens Deum, bonae famae, . . . qui sit pro utilitate boni communis christianitatis, et plus diligat illud quam proprium; habeatque benevolentiam et amicitiam Venetorum, ut possit cum illis facere facta sua, et in eis consilium et auxilium invenire.'   Like all his compatriots, Sanudo seems to have kept the interests and superiority of Venice in view. Delaville Le Roulx, I, 35, quotes the saying—'Siamo Veneziani, poi Christiani', in connexion with Sanudo.

[5] ib., 'gens valida in magno numero'.

[6] ib., 36.   Cf. chapters on Eastern Christians and on Tatars.

of the whole trouble.   Once the root was removed,[1] the
rest would be easy.   The preliminary or 'parvum passagium' should consist of 15,000 foot and 300 knights.
These would be sufficient for the occupation of Egypt.
Larger numbers would entail more expense as well as confusion and possible defeat.[2]   Sanudo insisted on starting
operations in Egypt and objected to the land route across
Europe and Asia Minor to the Holy Land.   The diversity
of countries and the difficulty of obtaining provisions were
decisive factors against it.   Nor should the crusading army
land in the unhappy country of the Armenians, whose
prosperity had been almost wiped out by the Sultan's
ravages, nor even go to Cyprus, for St. Louis had not
profited by so doing in the middle of the thirteenth century.[3]   Hostilities must be started on the soil of Egypt
and following the 'exempla Venetae nationis', the crusaders
must first establish themselves on the coast and then extend
their colonizing operations piecemeal over the mainland.[4]
Further, a detachment of 5,000 foot and 150 knights could
periodically take to the sea between the months of April
and October to stop the approach of alien galleys for trade
with the inhabitants of Egypt.[5]   These operations, Sanudo
concluded, were to be merely the herald of the 'passagium
generale' which, consisting of 50,000 foot and 2,000 horse,
could land at Rosetta[6] and complete the Christian invasion,
so auspiciously begun by the 'parvum passagium'.   With
the downfall of the Mamlūks in Egypt, the military
supremacy of Islam would be undermined and all the
remaining Muhammadan countries would surrender to the
host of Christ without difficulty.

The author ends his book with a world history composed
on biblical lines,[7] together with various considerations on

[1] Bongars, II, 'extirpata radice' is the phrase used by Sanudo.

[2] ib., 36–7.

[3] ib., 39.   The reasons for Sanudo's preference for Egypt are: 'Primo,
quia terra Aegypti est sanior quam Cyprensis; et meliores aquae habentur
ibi, et multitudo piscium innumerosa in subuentione populi.   Secundo, quia
si deberet antea exercitus ad Cyprensem Insulam declinare, et inde ad partes
Aegypti maritimas procedere, antequam posset adaggredi inimicos, poterit per
viam rectam partes acquisiuisse praefatas.'

[4] ib., 51.   [5] ib., 81–3.   [6] ib., 90–1.   [7] ib., 98 et seq.

the history of the early crusades and the Kingdom of Jerusalem.[1] He reviews the geography and topography of the Holy Land for the benefit of devout pilgrims.[2] Although primarily concerned with the crusade, the *Liber Secretorum Fidelium Crucis* is a work of exceptional value for the student of the history of commerce, of medieval economics as well as navigation, geography and cartography. In all these spheres his attempt at accuracy and fullness makes Marino Sanudo a pioneer of scientific geography and economics. Some even regard the *Secreta* as the origin of all statistical studies.[3] The mass of material with which Sanudo provides the historian of commerce [4] is unequalled elsewhere in the Middle Ages. His geography is rendered all the more valuable by a series of comprehensive maps.[5] His description of the waters of the Levant and of the various forms of galleys, old and new, reveals an extraordinary and original knowledge of the nautical and naval conditions of the time. His aim was to furnish the Christian admirals with a detailed guide-book for manning ships and for the itineraries of the various fleets.

The first function of sea power must be the enforcement of the boycott of commerce which, though mainly directed against Egypt, must encompass the whole field of Islamic countries including the Kingdoms of Tunis and Granada as well as the rising Turkish Sultanate in Asia Minor.[6] In order, however, to meet the urgent trade requirements of the West which were then available only in the markets

---

[1] ib., 140 et seq.   [2] ib., 243 et seq.

[3] For example, Marco Foscarini; cf. Molmonti (trans. Brown), I, 138.

[4] Heyd (Commerce), II, *passim*; *vide* Index.

[5] These are: (*a*) Mappa Mundi; (*b*) The Levant; (*c*) The Holy Land; (*d*) Plan of Jerusalem; (*e*) Plan of 'Akka. Of these maps, (*b*), (*c*) and (*d*) are reproduced in Aubrey Stewart's trans. of Sanudo, Bk. III, Pt. XIV, published in the Palestine Pilgrims' Text Society. For Sanudo as geographer and cartographer, see Lelewel (*Géogr. du moyen âge*), II, 19–34; Röhricht, *Zeitsch. des deutschen Palaestino-Vereins*, XXI (1898), 84–128; Magnocavallo, *La carta de mari Mediterraneo di Marin Sanudo, il Vecchio* Bulletino della Soc. geogr. Ital., Rome, 1902); Fulin, in *Archivio Veneto*, XXII, 49–51 and 52–62. There is also an older account by Daru, VI, 288 et seq.

[6] Bongars, II, 27–9.

of Egypt, the author suggested two methods. In the firs
place, the necessity for the products of Egypt itself migh
be avoided by a policy which should aim at producing thes
or their substitutes in territories under Christian rule in
the Mediterranean. Some of these articles, such as cotton
which was grown in Egypt on a small scale, could be obtained from Cyprus, Rhodes, Crete, Sicily and Malta as wel
as the countries of Armenia and Romania 'in bona quantitate'.[1] Perhaps the only exception to this rule was flax
(Cassia fistula), sold in abundance (*in magna quantitate*) a
the khans of Alexandria and Damietta and nowhere else
outside Egypt.[2] In the second place, indispensable item
imported from India through Egypt might successfully be
deflected to the friendly Mongol Khanate of Persia and
overland to Christian Armenia [3] whose defence agains
Turkish and Egyptian incursions he supported vigorousl
and on every possible occasion.

Marino Sanudo was not content to formulate his theorie
in the *Secreta* and then to leave them at the mercy of com
mittees. Throughout the whole of his life, he was an
active propagandist and no mere theorist. From th
beginning, he supported the bull of Nicholas IV [4] for
bidding trade with the infidels; and Clement V's bull o
1308 for the same purpose was probably issued on th
advice of Sanudo [5] as well as of Jacques de Molay, Grand
Master of the Temple.[6] When submitting the *Secreta* t
John XXII at Avignon on 24 September 1321, the autho
expressed the wish that the committee appointed to examin
his work should be trustworthy and the Pope assured him
thereof.[7] Two years passed and no action was forthcoming
Sanudo therefore wrote a letter dated December 1323 t
the High Pontiff reminding him of the book previousl
presented to his holiness.[8] In 1325 he wrote a circula

---

[1] Bongars, II, 24, 33; cf. Heyd, II, 611–14.

[2] ib., II, 24–5; cf. Heyd, II, 602–3.

[3] ib., II, 23.   [4] *vide supra*, Cap. II.

[5] Heyd, II, 27; Hodgson (*Venice*, 1204–1400), 321.

[6] *vide supra*, 55.

[7] Bongars, II, 1; cf. Carew Hazlitt, II, 663.

[8] Epistola i, in Bongars, II, 289–90, dates the letter in 1324; Kunstman
736, and Magnocavallo, 108, correct this to 1323.

letter [1] to a number of cardinals for the same object; and
in 1326 he issued another to a number of important but
unnamed [2] persons lamenting the neglect of his plan and
depicting the miserable state to which Armenia was then
reduced.   In the same year he wrote to several people of
high standing (also unnamed) recommending his *Librum
et mappas mundi*.[3]   Between 1328 and 1330, he wrote to
Ingramo Archbishop of Capua, to Pietro de la Via, nephew
of the Pope, and to various cardinals, urging prompt consideration of his views.[4]   Outside the Church, too, he did
not remain passive.   His visit to King Robert II of Sicily
has already been mentioned.   In 1332, he also sent his
Secreta to Philippe VI of the House of Valois, who had been
elected by the Pope 'Capitaneus-Generalis illustrissimus
passagii Dei et Terrae Sanctae'.[5]   There is decisive
evidence that he submitted his book to the King of England, probably Edward II, as well as to a large number of
French nobles.   In a letter dated in or before 1326 to
Ferry IV, Duke of Lorraine (1312–28), known as 'Le
Lutteur', he says,[6] 'That book I have presented to our Lord
the Pontiff, to the Kings of France, England and Sicily,
to the Cardinals and many other Prelates, to the Count of
Hanover, and to several of the French Counts (including
one Comte de Clermont); and seeing that your progenitors
. . . bestirred themselves in the affairs of the Holy Land
. . . I send you with these presents the Prologue, Rubrics
and Chapters of the aforesaid book, and some other matters.
I am ready to transmit to you the whole work, with the
maps of the world, should you express a desire to possess
it.'[7]   In 1326, he wrote to King Leo of Armenia reporting on his visits to the Pope, many cardinals, the King of
France and many French nobles, and assured him that he
was doing his utmost to obtain the necessary help for his

[1] ib., ii, in Bongars, II, 290–1.   [2] ib., 297–8.
[3] ib., 304–7.   [4] ib., xx and xxi.   ib., 312–16.
[5] ib., iv, Kunstmann, op. cit., 790 et seq.   Cf. Magnocavallo, 131; and
Hodgson, op. cit., 325 and note 1.
[6] Bouillet, *Atlas d'histoire et de géographie* (Paris, 1872), Table 45,
pp. 472–3.
[7] Ep. xiv, in Bongars, II, 303.   For English version quoted here, see
Carew Hazlitt, II, 662.

much-harassed kingdom.[1]   In 1324 and 1326, he dispatched two letters to the Greek Emperor Andronikos II
Palaeologos (1280–1328) to the same effect in regard to
the holy war against the Turks and further advised him to
unite the Greek Church with the Latin in all sincerity.[2]
Among the nobles of France to whom Sanudo wrote asking
for support of his plan, Louis, who was created first Duke
of Bourbon in 1327 and died in 1341,[3] is worthy of special
mention, for it was this Louis' grandson, Le Bon Duc
Louis II (1356–1400), who ultimately took the Cross and
headed the Barbary Expedition of 1390.[4]

During the whole of his career, Sanudo 'the elder' never
lost sight of the possibilities of economic warfare in projects for crusade as the most effective weapon for asserting
Western authority over the East.   It is true that the origin
of his ideas may be traced to the action of Nicholas IV,[5]
and it is indeed difficult not to associate that Pope's attempt
at a blockade of Egypt with Sanudo's advice.   At his
death, probably a little after 1343, however, he could justly
pride himself that neither his predecessors nor any of his
contemporary propagandists had done more than he had
to elaborate and popularize this comparatively novel method
of undermining the strength of Islam and of conquering
both the Holy Land and Egypt.   He carried his argument

---

[1] Ep. vi, Bongars, II, 298–9. Cf. Iorga (*Arménie*), 129.   In the short
fourteenth-century French memoir (Bongars, II, 5–6) which Sanudo probably submitted with his work to the Kings of France and England, special
mention is made of Armenia, 'Car trop seroit grand dommage et grande honte
à toute Chrestienté, si celle terre se perdoit.'   The memoir begins thus,
'Ramenbranze à la Royale Maiesté faite humblement et deuotement par
Marin Sanud, dict Torxel, de Venise, lequel vous présenta les livres et les
mappe-mondes, pour conquerre et tenir la terre Saincte, et les terres circostans
icelle.   Et dict que ce seroit plus légère chose à vostre haulte Maiesté d'auoir
la Seigneurie du monde, et gagner Paradis, que ne fu à Alexandre, qui fu Sire
du monde: en suivant l'ordonnance et la manière que cy après s'ensuit.'

[2] ib., vii and xii, Bongars, II, 299, 301.   In the French introductory
memoir to the *Secreta* (p. 5), Sanudo says: 'Ie ne doubte pas, avec l'ayde de
Dieu, que le Roy Robert, le Roy Frédéric de Secille, et l'empereur de Constantinoble, seront obéissants à vous en toutes choses, qui seront raisonnables.'

[3] Bouillet, op. cit., Table 25, pp. 434–5. Sanudo's letter dated 1334
appears in Kunstmann, op. cit., 808–13.

[4] *vide infra*, Cap. XVII.   [5] *vide supra*, Cap. II.

in the *Secreta Fidelium Crucis* to its furthest logical extent,
and thus made it extremely difficult for those in power to
bring forward any reasonable objection to the application
of his plan.   The result was the declaration of that much-
desired trade war on Egypt.   As will be shown at a later
stage in this study, the blockade was doomed to failure.
Sanudo and his supporters had miscalculated the limitation
of the human element and the force of the geographical
factors governing a campaign of this kind.   Venice, Genoa
and the other republics depending on commerce for their
well-being were not prepared to sacrifice their desire for gain
beyond a certain term; and the flow of trade was bound
in time to resume the channels drawn by nature as against
those devised by man.   Even Sanudo's logic and long fore-
thought could not alter the fate of an unnatural blockade.

CHAPTER VII

PIERRE DE THOMAS AND PHILIPPE DE MÉZIÈRES

Pierre de Thomas: early life; propagandist and crusader; Patriarch of Constantinople and Apostolic Legate of East; Sack of Alexandria; Death and Legacy.   Philippe de Mézières: early life; connexions with Pierre de Thomas and Pierre I de Lusignan; propagandist, ambassador and crusader.   Diplomatic Correspondence; *Vita S. Petri Thomasii*; *Nova Religio Passionis*; *Songe du vieil Pèlerin*; *Oratio Tragedica*; *Epistre au Roy Richart*; *Epistre lamentable et consolatoire*

THE distinctive feature of the history of the crusade during the first three or four decades of the fourteenth century is the abundance of propagandists who exhorted all good Catholics to uphold the cause of holy war.   Pilgrims, missionaries, statesmen, churchmen and men of action submitted various plans for projects of crusade to those in authority including Popes, Kings and Councils.   In these documents, preparations, routes and possibilities of successful campaigns in the Levant were discussed in great detail. The labours and enthusiasm of the theorists of this era were at last rewarded when the West embarked on a number of expeditions against the East in the remaining part of the century.   As a result, propagandist literature passed through a period of marked decline; and the reason is not far to seek, for men's minds turned to action instead of the exhortation of others to do what was regarded as their sacred duty to save the heritage of Christ.   Nevertheless, it would be an error to assume that this period was quite devoid of the propagandist activity which filled the opening years of the century.   It now, however, took a different form, and the early tracts and treatises on the crusade, were now supplanted by diplomatic correspondence and negotiations for immediate action.   The new tendency may best be illustrated by the careers of

PHILIPPE DE MÉZIÈRES SUBMITTING HIS EPISTLE
TO RICHARD II. MS. ROYAL 20 B. VI., Fol. 2 ro.

BANNER OF THE CHIVALRY OF THE PASSION
MS. ROYAL 20 B. VI., Fol. 36 vo.

Pierre de Thomas [1] and Philippe de Mézières—two men who, by their dominating personality and influence, contributed more to the promotion of crusades than probably any of their contemporaries. It was not until the end of the century that Philippe de Mézières, in his advanced years and in retirement, reverted to the old method of furnishing others with books on the crusade.

Pierre de Thomas [2] was born of humble parents [3] at the

[1] Sometimes called Pierre Thomas (cf. Iorga's *Mézières*, also Wadding, *passim*), which is misleading, as Thomas or more accurately Salignac de Thomas is Pierre's birthplace and has only that to do with his name. Another misconception is that he became a Saint. Though public opinion in Cyprus after his death regarded him as such, he was never actually canonized by the Church of Rome. Officially he is recognized only as 'Blessed'. *Vide infra.*

[2] The sources for Pierre's biography are:

(*a*) *Vita S. Petri Thomasii*, written by Philippe de Mézières, a work of an apologetic nature; but owing to the scarcity of materials on Pierre's life, it has to be regarded as the chief source. See *Acta Sanctorum* under 29 January —Jan. III, 605 et seq.

(*b*) Mézières' Correspondence, Arsenal MS. 499 D, fo. 134 ro.–163 ro. Cf. H. Martin, *Cat. des MSS. de la Bibl. de l'Arsenal*, I, 348–50; and Iorga, *Collection de Lettres de Philippe de Mézières*, in *Rev. Hist.*, XLIX (1892), 39–57 and 306–22.

(*c*) Bulls in Reynaldus. See also B.N. Suarez MS. 21 for Urban V's bull; cf. AOL, I, 257 et seq. (*Dépouillement de Suarez.*)

(*d*) Mas Latrie, *Hist. de Chypre*, II, 253 et seq., 281 et seq., and III, 744 et seq.

(*e*) Guillaume de Machaut, 'Prise d'Alexandrie', lines 3508 et seq.

Secondary authorities:—

(*a*) L'Abbé Parraud, *Vie de Saint Pierre Thomas*. Avignon, 1895.

(*b*) *Lives* by Daniel a Virgine Maria and Luke Wadding, in *Speculum Carmelitarum* II, 171–95 and 199–213 respectively.

(*c*) Iorga, *Philippe de Mézières* &c., 131 et seq., *passim–vide* Index.

(*d*) Mas Latrie, *Patriarches Latins de Constantinople*, in ROL, 3ᵉ année (1895), no. 3, 439–40.

(*e*) Golubovich, *Bibl. Bio-bibl. della Terra Santa*, V, 77–80, 95–6, 200–2.

(*f*) General works of reference on the Catholic hierarchy such as Gams, Eubel and Carolus a Sancto Paulo. See also Molinier (*Sources*), IV, nos. 3556–7.

The biography of Pierre de Thomas is a suitable subject for a monograph.

[3] *Vita*, 611; 'de parentela inferiore'. They were poor serfs engaged in raising cattle; cf. Iorga (*Mézières*), 132.

village of Salignac de Thomas [1] in the diocese of Sarlat.
The date of his birth is not precisely known, but it may
safely be assumed that it was in the late thirteenth century.
After studying the trivium in Agen at an early stage in his
career while living exclusively on alms, Pierre left for Lec-
toure and Condom for the completion of his studies.   He
impressed the prior of the Convent of Sainte-Marie-du-
Carmel with his genius.   He was thus welcomed by
the Carmelite brotherhood when he expressed his wish
to take their habit.   His fellow friars then rewarded his
zeal for learning by sending him first to Bordeaux for one
year, then to Paris.   Afterwards he was nominated to a
lectureship at Cahors, where he began to establish a reputation for eloquence, ability and piety.   Abundant charity,
however, made it possible for him to resign his new post
and return to the French capital.   This time, in Paris, he
graduated in theology and, what was even more important,
he made the acquaintance of the Cardinal of Périgord who
furnished him with sufficient funds to lengthen the term
of his studies until he had obtained the degree of Doctor
'in sacra pagina'. [2]   His fame and popularity began to
spread with great rapidity.   People were so moved by his
preaching that one sermon resulted in gifts amounting to
a thousand florins for a convent at Avignon. [3]   Popes and
prelates saw in him a very promising instrument for the
execution of the foreign policy of the Curia.   He was
considered by Clement VI (1342–52) as a suitable candidate for the bishopric of Badajoz in Spain, [4] but after
Clement's death, his successor Innocent VI (1352–62)
selected Pierre for important embassies to the courts of
King Lewis of Apulia and Queen Joanna his consort, of

---

[1] In the valley of the Dordogne in the south-west of France, in the Duchy
of Aquitaine.   In the *Vita*, ib., Mézières says that Pierre came from 'Lingua-
Occidentana (i.e. Languedoc), Ducatu Aquitaniae, Petragorensi provincia,
villa quae dicitur Salimosa de Thomas, diocesis Sarlatensis'.

[2] *Vita*, 612–13; Iorga, op. cit., 132–4; Mas Latrie (*Patriarches Latins de
Constantinople*), 439; cf. Wadding, l.c.

[3] *Vita*, l.c.; Iorga, 134.

[4] According to Gams, 11, he would have been appointed to this bishopric
in 1346.   Cf. Mas Latrie, l.c.

the schismatic emperor of Serbia,[1] and of the Holy Roman Emperor Charles IV, meanwhile appointing him Bishop of Patti and Lipari in Sicily.[2] Pierre de Thomas then travelled through Italy, Hungary, 'Slavonia' and Serbia, and, defying the perils of the road and the danger of shipwreck, he ultimately sailed to Nicosia in Cyprus.[3] On his way through Venice he participated in the work of arbitration and reconciliation begun by Bongiovanni, Bishop of Fermo, between the Republic of St. Mark and the King of Hungary.[4]

In the course of 1357, while in Cyprus, Pierre decided to realize his ambition of going on a pilgrimage to the Holy Places. King Hugh de Lusignan warned him of the risk he was undertaking by a hazardous journey to Saracen territory at a time when preparations for the crusade were actually on foot. The dauntless Carmelite had no fear of the enemy and alone made his way to the Church of the Resurrection, preached to a Christian congregation on Mount Sion and returned to Famagusta unharmed, probably in the year 1360. Innocent VI, who appreciated Pierre's courage, appointed him Bishop of Coron in the Morea in 1359, then Archbishop of Crete in 1361 and Latin Patriarch of Constantinople in the following year.[5]

During his peregrinations in the East, Pierre became so well acquainted with its affairs and problems that the Pope selected him for the delicate mission of converting the Greeks to Catholicism. The Byzantine Emperor at the time, John V Palaeologos (1341–91), was pressed by the Turks on all sides and was less reluctant than his predecessors to submit to the authority of Rome in the hope that he might thereby receive material aid from the Latins to save his tottering realm. He thus welcomed the papal nuncio, listened patiently to his arguments for the union

---

[1] In the *Vita*, 613, Mézières notes that the King of Serbia also called himself Emperor of Bulgaria—'Rex Raciae, qui modo se vocaverit Bulgariae Imperator.'

[2] ib.; Letters of Introduction dated 1354 in Reynaldus, XXV, 607 et seq.; Mas Latrie, op. cit., 440; Iorga, op. cit., 134–5.

[3] *Vita*, 613–15.   [4] ib., 613–16.

[5] ib., 617 et seq.; Iorga, op. cit., 138–9; Mas Latrie, l.c. Golubovich, V, 79, believes the date of the pilgrimage to be 1360.

of the Eastern and the Western Churches and even betrayed
signs of willingness to accept the Roman creed.   It is
difficult to gauge the depth of the Emperor's conviction
in this matter; but consideration of similar episodes in the
later history of the Empire before its final downfall in 1453
may help to clarify judgment in the matter.   Realizing that
all was at stake, emperor after emperor, in desperation, went
to Rome feigning conversion to Catholicism in the vain
hope that the West might be roused to save what was left
of his moribund empire.   On this occasion, Mézières tells
us that Emperor John V was prepared to depose the schismatic and hostile Patriarch and have a Catholic elected in
his place.[1]   Nevertheless, it is clear that Pierre's mission
came to no fruition in spite of the tempting proposition
of peace between the Churches and union against the
Muslim Turk.[2]   Notwithstanding his failure, Pierre's diligence, wisdom and virtues were universally recognized,
and the High Pontiff appointed him special Apostolic
Legate of the whole East with a triple duty—first, to
preach and promote the crusade against infidels, second,
to persist in his work of drawing all schismatics to the
See of Rome, and third, to purge Crete of the taint of
heresy.[3]

Pierre began at once to discharge his new duties as
Roman Legate without fear or favour.   Crete was his first
objective.   The people of that island, including many of

---

[1] *Vita*, 616. 'Sed Imperatore civitatem Constantinopolim adveniente, et
Domino Fratre Petro continue sibi praedicante et docente, ipse Imperator
factus est verus Catholicus, et obediens Ecclesiae Romanae. . . .   Juravit
etiam promittere servare, et facere observari pro posse, quae ad sanctam
Ecclesiam Romanam pertinent: necnon Patriarcham Graecum perfidum, et
unitatis Ecclesiae inimicum promisit deponi, et unum alium Catholicum eligi
debere.'

[2] ib., 617; '. . . devotione et unitate Ecclesiae Romanae, et laetantes
animabantur contra Turcos ad sustinendum bella Dei in pace Ecclesiae'.

[3] Mas Latrie, l.c., fixes the date of this legacy as 1364, and Suarez (in
AOL, I, 284), refers to a bull dated 6 July 1364 and issued by Urban V
(1362–70) by which Pierre became Patriarch and Apostolic Legate, but
Mézières in the *Vita*, 618, says that this appointment was made by Clement
VI.   The bull nominating Pierre Legate is dated 11 May 1359. *Bullarum
Carmelitarum*, I, 64–8; Reynaldus, *ad ann.* 1359, no. 19; cf. Iorga (*Mézières*),
140 and note 4.

its nobles, had come under the influence of heretical teachings. The Legate sailed from Cyprus to Candia, and in the name of the Church ordered the Venetian Governor to seize all suspects and punish them without mercy. It happened that the most powerful leader of the heretical sect was a kinsman of the Governor's wife, and this complicated matters and led to delay in the execution of the Legate's orders. Pierre was not the man to be intimidated by any form of hostility or indifference to his plans. He declared the whole island under interdict. Churches were closed and bells ceased to ring, while heretics became outlaws. This proved to be an effective weapon, for all but the leader repented their sins and were readily pardoned. The leader, in spite of his relationship with the Governor's family, was seized, tried and burnt to death.[1]

In Cyprus the Legate's fiery zeal for the conversion of the Orthodox inhabitants to Catholicism was unlimited. He argued with their priests in vain, however, and on one occasion, a Greek mob was roused to the use of force. Pierre's life became endangered in the ensuing scuffle and only the appearance of the King's brother, the admiral, with an armed detachment saved him with great difficulty from the infuriated crowds. Efforts for a peaceful conversion having failed, the Legate tried to persuade the civil authorities in the Island to torture the Orthodox inhabitants until they renounced their faith; but the King, who explained that the Greeks outnumbered the Latins, rejected this brutal method of satisfying Pierre's ardour.[2]

In regard to the crusade against Muhammadans, the Legate never ceased throughout his career, and especially after his memorable pilgrimage, trying to kindle enthusiasm for the holy war. He used his diplomatic skill and renowned eloquence in the service of a cause which appealed to his imagination and piety. It was indeed largely due to his energy that the successive expeditions of Pierre I

---

[1] *Vita*, 619; Hackett, 128–9.
[2] This episode occurred in December 1359. *Vita*, 620 et seq.; Makhairas's *Chronicle* (ed. Dawkins), I, 89–91 and II, 94–5; Amadi, 409; Bustron, 258; Mas Latrie (Machaut), 281 note; ib. (*Hist. de Chypre*), II, 253, 281; Hackett, 130–1.

de Lusignan against the Turks in Asia Minor and the
Mamlūks in Egypt were made possible.   Until his death,
Pierre de Thomas was chosen by the Pope to promote most
of the crusades of the period.   Both Clement VI and
Urban V had a very high opinion of his loyalty and ability;
and the latter Pope, after the appointment of Cardinal
Talleyrand de Périgord, Bishop of Limoges, to preach the
holy war on one occasion, soon relegated the trust to Pierre
de Thomas,[1] who was not merely a preacher of the cause,
but also an active crusader ready to fight with all his fellow
Christians in God's battle against the unbelievers.   His
greatest contribution was probably the part he played in the
Sack of Alexandria in 1365.[2]   Prior to this date, he was one
of the three great agents—Pierre I de Lusignan, Pierre de
Thomas and Philippe de Mézières—who engineered this
crusade and assisted in the mobilization of the forces from
many countries of Latin Christendom for the expedition
against Egypt.[3]   As the fleet anchored in the old port [4] of
Alexandria, Philippe de Mézières says that his saintly hero [5]
became impatient for action and, longing for martyrdom,
prompted the King to order the immediate landing of the
crusaders to attack the hostile Saracens who had gathered
on the shore and waited for the ensuing battle, uttering
fierce war-cries.   In passing, however, it must be noted
that the Arabic contemporary manuscript [6] dealing with
these events states definitely that this crowd consisted only of
the harmless citizens of Alexandria who went to witness an
unusual sight with no idea of the misery and desolation
which lay in store for them and their homes.   Mézières,
who stood by the side of the Legate, calmed his fervour
and informed him that the moment had not yet come for
the attack, and Pierre was stricken with indescribable grief
at what seemed to him to be an undue delay and a loss of
time and opportunity.   When, at last, disembarkation was
decreed at the dawn of the following day, this 'athleta

---

[1] Date of change 8 June 1364 (f. Iorga, *Mézières*), 204 and note 8.
[2] *vide infra*, Cap. XV.   [3] Iorga (*Mézières*), 6, 204 *passim*.
[4] The old port is situated on the western side of the ancient lighthouse.
[5] *Vita*, 639 et seq.; Hackett, 129–30; Iorga, 283, 291, 295.
[6] *vide infra*, Cap. XV for details.

Christi', clad in full armour as all the other knights, stood on part of a galley jutting out over the water, crucifix in hand, exposed to the arrows of the enemy, to bless the host of God. While fighting was in progress, he refused to make use of a proffered shield in spite of his faithful companion's advice. Finally, as men were preparing to evacuate their posts after the pillage of the city, the Legate exhorted them to take a firm stand and retain their conquest. At this juncture, Guillaume de Machaut pays the 'Saint' a strong tribute in his poem.[1]

When the glorious expedition came to this speedy end, Pierre was the first to write to both Pope and Emperor to inform them of the success of the host of Christ.[2] Soon after his return, however, his feeble frame began to give way under the weight of past tribulation and triumph. He fell ill and died at Famagusta on 6 January 1366,[3] and a wound which he had received at Alexandria hastened the end. In his testament, he prayed that he might be buried at the entrance of a choir where all could tread on his remains. In Cyprus, he was at once recognized as one of the Saints of the Island;[4] and even his Greek enemies who

---

[1] '*Prise d'Alexandrie*', lines 3508–19:

> De Coustantinoble, là mis
> Avoit li papes & tramis
> Com legat, le bon patriarche;
> N'est plus preudomme, que je sache.
> Si que très bien les sermonna
> Et moustré en son sermon a
> Comment messires saint Thomas
> De bien faire onques ne fu las,
> Mais fu en Ynde la majour,
> Pour l'amour de Nostre Signour,
> Et y mourut piteusement
> Pour bien faire et non autrement.

[2] *Vita*, 631–2; Arsenal MS. 499, fo. 134, 'Quedam scriptura in summa breviter recollecta de laudabili et devota intencione victoriosissimi et christianissimi regis Petri di Lizingniaco. XV. regis latini Ierusalem, et Cypri regis, a iuventute sua; de capcione Sathalie; de via ipsius ad dominum papam Urbanum de passagio indicto; quomodo dictus rex personaliter invitavit ad passagium imperatorem romanum et quasi omnes principes occidentales; et de capcione Alexandrie.' Cf. Martin (*Cat. des MSS. de la Bibl. de L'Arsenal*), I, 348 Iorga (*Collection de Lettres*), 43 note 3.

[3] ib., 632 et seq.; Hackett, 133–4.   [4] ib., *passim*; Hackett, 432.

hated him during his lifetime and reviled his bigotry, did reverence to him after his death. Tradition began to weave miracles round his tomb, and he was long remembered in the island alike by Catholic, Schismatic, Jew and Saracen for his fearless attempt to alleviate the sufferings of all at Famagusta when it was once stricken by the plague.[1]

Pierre de Thomas left a legacy of his cherished ideals of the crusade in the person of his closest friend and admirer, Philippe de Mézières. From his early youth Mézières had fallen under the spell of this holy man who exercised the greatest influence on his mind during years of close companionship until death parted them. It was in the tragic circumstances of the plague at Famagusta that the two first met, and from that moment Philippe spoke of Pierre as his 'Father in God'. The two had consecrated their lives to the crusade, and this link in common strengthened the ties of their friendship. In his sermon [2] at the Légate's funeral, Philippe refers to the letters exchanged between them day and night, and to the spiritual and mystic conversations by which the master guided his disciple, and he likens their friendship to that of the Apostles Paul and Barnabas [3] without the differences of the latter two. Quoting Pierre's own words, Philippe states that their bodies were separate, but their souls were united. Now, alone, he is 'tossed up and down like the locust' (*excussus sum sicut locustae*).[4] Their lives had indeed been so closely connected that it would be difficult to dissociate the chief events of the last decade in the Legate's biography from the Chancellor's activities. When the Legate's influence disappeared early in 1366, Mézières became the great executor of his master's wishes and ideals for nearly half a century.

Philippe de Mézières was therefore the spiritual successor of Pierre de Thomas. A dreamer [5] and a mystic pilgrim,

---

[1] *Vita*, 622–3; Hackett, 133; Iorga, 128–9.

[2] Arsenal MS. 499, fo. 137 ro.–138 vo.; 'Planctus D. Philippi de Maseriis pro morte S. Petri Thamasii.' C. Iorga, *Mézières*, 129–31 and *Collection de Lettres*, 44–5.

[3] Planctus, fo. 137 vo. [4] Cf. Psalms, 109, v. 23.

[5] cf. the 'songes' and the 'somnia' which Philippe wrote after his retirement.

he was also a vital force in all the affairs of the Levant while his Chancellorship of the Kingdom of Cyprus lasted. He was born in 1326 or 1327 of a minor noble family in the province of Picardy.[1] He had his early education at Amiens, and in 1345 began his active career of service under Lucchino Visconti [2] in Lombardy, then at the court of André King of Naples until the assassination of the latter in 1346. Mézières thereupon left Naples, journeyed to Castille and back to France where he stayed only for a short time before embarking on his Eastern travels. He is reported to have been present at a battle in the neighbour-hood of Smyrna in the same year [3] and he was knighted on this occasion. Afterwards, he left Humbert, the Dauphin de Viennois, leader of the expedition, and went on a pil-grimage to the Holy Land. On his way to Jerusalem the young knight conceived the idea of a new order of chivalry, the 'Nova Religio Passionis Jhesu Christi', as the solid basis of a successful crusade for the salvation of the Holy Places from Saracen dominion. This plan became his chief concern throughout his career, and even after his retire-ment it occupied a central place in most of his works. After his visit to Palestine, he sailed to Cyprus where he

---

[1] Prior to Iorga's studies there had been much conjecture as to the origin of Philippe de Mézières.

First, he was regarded as a Sicilian by—
    (a) Vossius: *De historicis latinis* (Leiden, 1651).
    (b) Antonio Teisserio: *Catalogus auctorum* (Geneva, 1686).
    (c) Poitevin: *Apparatus sacer*. (III, 181. Ed. Venice).
    (d) Mira: *Bibliografia siculana*,—according to Mongitore (*Biblioteca sicula*), and this may be traced back to Maraccio (*Biblioteca Mariana*, Rome, 1648).

Second, there existed the view that he was Venetian: this was based on the Latin form Manserius, thus confused with the Venetian family of Masserii. This view was supported by Oudin, then by Ap. Zeno (*Giornale de' Litterati*, IX, 154).

In the 'Planctus' delivered by Mézières at the funeral of Pierre de Thomas, he reveals his identity in the following words, 'Sed ego quid autem te picardus miles infimus et publicanus et cancellarius indignissimus', which leave no room for doubt as to his Picard origin. Arsenal MS. 499, fo. 137 vo; cf. Iorga, *Collection de Lettres*, 45 and *Mézières*, 9–11.

[2] Brother and successor of Galeazzo I of Milan (ob. 1328), Lucchino died of the Plague in 1349.

[3] Iorga (*Mézières*), 54–5.

tried in vain to convert King Hugh IV de Lusignan (1324–
59) to his views.   In the meantime he made the acquaintance of Pierre de Lusignan, the future King of Cyprus.
This proved to be one of the great turning-points in
Philippe's life, for as soon as Pierre I (1359–69) was
crowned, he appointed his old friend as Chancellor of the
Kingdom, a post which Mézières retained until the assassination of his sovereign.   During the interval between his
meeting with Hugh IV and the accession of Pierre I,
Philippe spent most of his time preaching the crusade in
Aragon and France, participating in the wars of 1354
in Normandy under the command of Arnoul d'Audrehem,
Marshal of France and probably in the companies organized
by Bertrand du Guesclin, though the details of his activities
in these wars are obscure and incomplete.[1]   The importance of his career as active propagandist, diplomatist and
crusader became pronounced only when he was summoned
by Pierre I to Cyprus.   It was then that he met Pierre de
Thomas, and afterwards accompanied the King on his
European journeys of 1363–4 in search of men and money
for the crusade.[2]   At the courts of the maritime republics
of Italy, at Avignon, and in the capitals of Western Kingdoms, he was the principal assistant of Pierre I in his
extensive negotiations.   Even outside the King's mission
he became a force in European politics.   Perhaps the most
notable service he rendered to the establishment of peace
in the West was undertaken in conjunction with Pierre de
Thomas in 1364, when the two ambassadors mediated with
a great measure of success in the scandalous dispute
and imminent war between Bernabo Visconti of Milan and
the Church.[3]   The main outcome of the journey, however,
was the crusade against Alexandria in 1365, and reference
has already been made to him in connexion with the part
played by Pierre de Thomas during the attack.   Early in
1366 he lost the Legate, his spiritual father.   Afterwards

[1] Iorga (*Mézières*), 95–6.

[2] Froissart (ed. Kervyn), VI, 373–6, 378–96; Iorga, 144 et seq.

[3] Diplomatic correspondence on the dispute, in *Mézières*, Arsenal MS.
499, fo. 144 vo et seq.   Cf. Iorga, *Coll. de Lettres*, 306 et seq., and
Mézières, 210 et seq.

he left Cyprus in the hope of raising further assistance for a new crusade. It was during his absence that another heavy blow befell him in the assassination of Pierre I de Lusignan in January 1369. This was the culmination of his bereavement and the end of his career in Cyprus. The nobility of the island discountenanced his return to office and he was forced to retire from public life. As a result Mézières ceased to be an active crusader and became a simple propagandist for the holy war. He played for a time some part in French affairs. In May 1373, Charles V of France appointed him a member of the Council of the Kingdom and tutor to his son, the future Charles VI. Later he was involved in the polemics of the Great Schism of the Church. As a member of the court of France, he found it hard to keep out of a controversy for which the King was in great measure responsible, and ultimately his sympathies went with Clement VII as against Urban VI.

In September 1380, Philippe saw another monarch pass away in the person of Charles V le Sage. It was then that he decided to retire completely from public life and spend the remainder of his days within the walls of the Convent of the Celestines in Paris. After a career abounding in triumph and defeat, he thus settled down to write or to dictate his reminiscences, and to become a propagandist for the crusade. This period of his life was one of extraordinary activity in the sphere of writing. In five-and-twenty years he left a literary heritage of the greatest value, and the hero of the crusade turned to be one of the most prolific authors of the age. Prior to the date of his retirement, indeed, he had written the life of his friend and spiritual father—the *Vita S. Petri Thomasii*[1] (1366). As soon as he entered the Celestine convent, he dictated to the monks his diplomatic correspondence[2] and short discourses dating from 1366. During the years 1384–96 he continued to record, perfect and expand his views[3]

---

[1] *Acta Sanctorum*, 29 January. *Vide supra*, 129 note 2.
[2] Arsenal MS. 499. *Vide supra*, l.c.
[3] The chief works written during this period are: *Nova Religio Passionis* (Bodleian MSS. Ashmole 813 and 865, and Bibl. Mazarine MS. 1943; and Arsenal 2251; cf. Iorga, *Mézières*, vii, and Molinier, in AOL, I, 338);

on the prospect of a successful crusade in the light of his experience in the East and the knowledge that he had acquired of its affairs. After the disaster to the Western chivalry at Nicopolis, he spent 1397 writing a comprehensive treatise [1] in which he formulated once and for all his ideas and advice on this matter. Thenceforward to his death (29 May 1405), he appears to have relinquished his long struggle for a great cause.

Mézières's contribution to the stock of ideas germane to our subject was the conception of a new religious Order of Chivalry which should supersede all others and if possible incorporate them. The older Orders had failed to accomplish their chief aim—the salvation of the Holy Land and its retention in the hands of Christians. Their failure could be ascribed to a dual weakness— faction amongst the leaders and insubordination in the ranks.[2] It was hopeless to try and remedy old and deeply rooted vices. In order to eliminate the vices of existing Orders, Latin Christendom must build on an entirely new foundation. This, Philippe de Mézières supplied to his contemporaries in the form of the 'Militia Passionis Jhesu Christi'. The original conception of this organization goes far back into his career. As a youth of hardly twenty-one years of age, while on his way to the Holy

Somnium Viridarii (Latin, B.M. MS. 19 C. IV, B.N. MSS. 3180 C and 3459 A, Vienna Nationalbibl. 2652 including fragments only; French, *Songe du Verger*, B.N. MSS. fr. 537, 1066, 9195, 12442, 24290, 24291 and nouv. acq. fr. 1048; Turin, R. Bibl. M. VI 7; for early editions, see Iorga, *Mézières*, vii–viii); *Songe du vieil Pèlerin* (Arsenal MSS. 2682 and 2683; B.N. MSS. 9200, 9201 and 22542; Vienna Nationalbibl. 2251); *Oratio tragedica* (Bibl. Mazarine, 1651); *Épistre au Roy Richart* (B.M. Royal B IV). It is hoped that the last manuscript, transcribed by the writer, will be published in the near future in Paris or Brussels.

The inclusion of the *Somnium* in the above list is made with the strictest reservation, as its ascription to Mézières by Iorga is almost certainly erroneous. For the literature of the subject, see G. W. Coopland, *An Unpublished Work of John of Legnano—The Somnium of* 1372, in Nuovi Studi Medievali, T. II, fasc. I, 65 et seq., and the latest attempt at verification of the author of the *Somnium* by A. Coville, *Évrart de Trèmaugon et le Songe du Verger* (Paris, 1933), 24 et seq.

[1] *Épistre lamentable et consolatoire* (Brussels MS., Bibl. de Bourg. 10486; major part published by Kervyn in Froissart, XVI).

[2] *Nicopolis*, 27.

Places, after assisting at the battle of Smyrna, to which reference has been made, he received this inspiration; and for nearly the whole of the subsequent four decades of his life, he made every effort to build up the new Order of the Passion and codify its Rule. The first redaction of this seems to have been made in 1367–8, the second in 1384, and the third as late as 1395.[1] Meanwhile, Mézières seized all opportunities to further the interests of this new body at the courts of the Popes and Kings of Western Europe and to commend it to all the leading people of his time.[2] He also left ample material in the Rule of the Lord's Passion for the interpretation of the main conception and for a historical evaluation of the organization itself.[3]

In the 'prefacio seu compendium',[4] Mézières explains the chief object of his Order in terms characteristic of his mind, mystical yet practical at one and the same time. This Order, he says, is designed to offer mankind an image of perfection (*summa perfectio*) so that all may purify their actions from vices and shape their lives on its model. Further, it is intended not only for the conquest, but also for the retention of the Holy Land in the hands of the Christians.[5] The preface ends with a mystic eulogy in

[1] The Mazarine MS. includes the first and second redactions, and the Arsenal and Bodleian MSS. the third, *vide supra*, note; cf. Molinier, *Description de deux MSS.*, in AOL, I, 338 et seq., and Iorga, l.c.

[2] Molinier, op. cit., 362–4; and *Nicopolis*, Appendix II, 133–5, including lists of members of the Order of the Passion.

[3] *Nicopolis*, Appendix II (see preceding note); and Appendix III, 136–8, contains the rubrics of the Rule from the earlier Bodleian MS. Ashmole 813.

[4] Mazarine MS., fo. 1–15 cf. Molinier, 339 et seq.

[5] The full list of motives for the creation of the new Order as detailed by Mézières is:

(*a*) Amendment of life.

(*b*) Revival of the Cult of the Passion of Our Lord, now abandoned.

(*c*) Effective aid to the Eastern Christians in view of the forthcoming conquest of the Holy Land.

(*d*) The retention of the Holy Land after completing its invasion.

(*e*) The spreading of the Christian faith among other distant nations.

(*f*) The ending of the Schism in the Church of Rome and the war between England and France.

Mazarine MS., fo. 17 vo et seq., and Bodleian MS., fo. 4 ro et seq. Cf. Molinier, op. cit., 341–2, and *Nicopolis*, 136–7.

which the author adopts the Virgin Mary as the supreme protectress (*singularissima advocata*) of his Order.

Mézières recognizes the principal vows of the older military organizations. On the other hand, he modifies and adapts some of them so as to meet the circumstances of Eastern life which he had experienced for many years during his early career in Cyprus.

Obedience and discipline must be strictly and relentlessly enforced. The rule of poverty must also be observed, and all the revenues accruing from the temporal acquisitions of the Order should be devoted to the cause of the Holy Land. Celibacy, however, might be modified to conjugal fidelity in the interests of the morality of the Chivalry in Eastern climes.[1] Philippe then deals with the actual organization of the central and local government of the Chivalry. As a former great official of the Kingdom of Cyprus, he was naturally competent to handle this matter with skill and knowledge of the requirements of an efficient state planted in the land beyond the sea, yet abiding by the Western medieval conceptions of governance. At the head of the Order, he suggests the election of a prince of royal blood, who should employ twelve[2] ministers to manage the various departments of his state. Similarly, under the supervision of a central 'bureaucracy', every province should be ruled by a governor who would in turn be assisted by twelve persons holding offices corresponding to those of the central state. A patriarch and a number of archbishops, bishops, deans and priests should attend to spiritual welfare. Mézières then treats at great length various matters, to-day of purely archaeological interest, such as the habits and vestments of the various classes of the hierarchy of the Order, its arms and banners, and even supplies the reader with illuminated designs to illustrate his description of all these details.

The practical application and the historical development of the rules of the Order offer some points of interest.

[1] *Nicopolis*, 27–8.
[2] Molinier, op. cit., I, 340. These twelve are the constable, chancellor, marshal, admiral, treasurer, 'provisor' (presumably for educational purposes), 'procurator' (or attorney-general), 'moderator', judge and two consuls.

From the outset, Mézières naturally chose Pierre I de Lusignan as supreme patron of the organization. After the tragic end of Pierre's reign and the chancellor's retirement from Cyprus, he continued his efforts to promote the acceptance of the Order in the West. In the course of the year 1385, he initiated four Knights of the Passion, or, as he calls them, four 'evangelists'.[1] With unflagging energy he succeeded in attracting to membership further persons of high standing in various countries of Europe. Though the list of names which he compiled in 1395 is not particularly extensive in numbers, it is very impressive in regard to the variety and quality of its contents. Men from France, England, Germany, Spain, Aragon, Gascony, Navarre, Scotland and Lombardy, and prelates of the Church had either enlisted or promised their support. These included such influential people as the 'Good Duke', Louis de Bourbon, the Marshal Boucicaut and the Admiral Jean de Vienne in France, the Duke of York, the Count of Rutland and Hugh Despenser in England, and the Duke of Milan. Benedict XIII expressed his desire to possess a copy of Mézières's work on the Chivalry of the Passion.[2] When, in the same year (1395), Philippe was instructed to write his epistle to Richard II, treated later in this chapter, he seized this opportunity to recommend his Order to the King and the nobles of England.

Neither his advanced years nor his seclusion hindered the veteran champion of the crusade from promoting the cause of Christianity whenever an opportunity presented itself. As tutor of the young Charles VI he sought every means to influence his pupil's mind and convert him to

---

[1] Molinier, op. cit., I, 362; *Nicopolis*, 133. These four were Robert the Hermit 'messaige de Dieu et de monseigneur saint Jaque aux roys de France et d'Engleterre sur le fait de la paix des II roys et sur le fait de l'union de l'Église et du saint passage d'Oultremer', Jean de Blezi 'seigneur de Mauvilly, de Bourgoingne, chambellan du Roy et chevetaine de Paris', Louis de Giac 'de Limosin, chambellan et grant eschançon du Roy', and Otto de Granson 'de la terre de Savoye, chevalier d'onneur du roy d'Engleterre et du duc de Lencastre'.

[2] ib., op. cit., I, 364; *Nicopolis*, 135. 'Le Pape Benedic, qui de son propre mouvement a voulu avoir le livre de la chevalerie.'

his crusading ideals.   In 1389,[1] he wrote the *Songe du
vieil Pèlerin*, a lengthy moral allegory, to guide the King
in the ways of righteousness and of good governance.
In this work Mézières gives his advice through the mouth
of 'Queen Truth' (*la Reine Vérité*); and here he uses his
classical and medieval learning and experience in the East,
and expresses his opinions on the settlement of the war
with England and his ideas on the crusade.   It is a work
of considerable bulk and the confusion of its varied contents
is a serious defect which faces the reader of the *Songe*.
In spite of all its shortcomings, this little-known [2] work
ranks among the most important of the age.   In his quest
of comprehensiveness, the author did not overlook the
project for crusade which the King might possibly lead
to the Holy Land [3] on his coming of age   A whole chapter
of the *Songe* is therefore given to a detailed exposition of
the practical preparations for the 'passage d'oultremer'.
The first condition of an Eastern triumph is the establishment of the King's peace with his brother of England.
Union between the forces of this 'desert' of France and
of England is imperative for success in a war for the
land of promise.[4]   Cyprus, once abounding in wealth in
the days of the 'Vieil Pèlerin' and the valiant King Pierre I
de Lusignan—the victor of the battles of Alexandria in
Egypt, of Adalia in Turkey, of Baras in Armenia, and of
Tortosa and Tripoli in Syria—is now divided between the

---

[1] Iorga, *Mézières*, viii and 468.

[2] A full transcription of the B.N. MS. fr. 22542, made by Dr. G. W. Coopland (Liverpool), has been kindly lent for use in connexion with the present
study.

[3] *Songe* (B.N. MS. fr. 22542), Lib. III, fo. 327 vo.   Here Mézières urges
the King 'd'aler une foys vers Orient à la sainte cité de Hierusalem . . . de
édifier de nouvel les sains lieux de la dicte cité de la Terre Sainte'.

[4] ib., III, 311 vo.   'Et ce qui sera accordé pour les paix soit tenu ferme-
ment.   Ce faisant, Beau Filz, Dieu mandera la rose du ciel et la gracieuse
manne qui sera de telle vertu que les pères des enfans d'Israel, c'est assavoir
la plus grande partie des diz pères qui en cestui désert de France et d'Angleterre faisant la guerre et espandant le sang de leurs frères crestiens. . . . Et
leurs enfans avecques toy, Beau Filz, jeune duc du peuple, avecques Calif
appellé à présent le roy d'Angleterre yront en la terre de promission.   Et
rechaptant à l'espée la sainte cité de Hierusalem et la sainte terre à confusion
des ennemis de la foy et exaltacion de la croix vous demourra en possession.'

powers of avarice and tyranny, and is therefore incapable
of upholding the cause of the Cross;[1] and the Kings of
the West must depend on their own arms for a fruitful
campaign in the Levant.

Philippe suggests one measure which cannot be traced
in any other work of propaganda. For practical purposes
and with the consent of the Pope, he contends, the King
may elect a valiant, learned, prudent and loyal person with
considerable experience in the conditions of the foreign
territories of the East, so that he may be dispatched to
the Sultan of Egypt with royal messages and presents.[2]
This ambassador is to be instructed to approach the Sultan
and his court and explain that the King of France is willing
to re-establish that policy of peace and friendship which his
ancestors in the time of Charlemagne had pursued before
him. The ambassador may further be authorized to
remain in the East and comfort and rally the Eastern
Christians in Syria, reporting meanwhile to the King
on the state of that country through the agency of western
merchants trading in those regions. Another ambassador
can be sent to the Turks for the same purpose.[3] It is
difficult to define with precision what exactly Mézières
hoped for from these permanent embassies. We may, how-

---

[1] *Songe*, III, 331 vo. 'Chippre, qui ou temps du Vieil Pèlerin pour l'abon-
dance de la marchandise estoit si riche en personnes et biens que le trèsvaillant
roy Pierre de Lysignen de son royaume, par sa vaillance et prouesse à ses
despens . . . print en bataille Alixandre en Egypte, Sathalie en Turquie,
Baras en Arménie, Tourtoige et Triple en Surie. . . . Mais à présent pour
lu dit royaume de Chippre, par l'oppression tyrannique et avarice inhumaine
. . . la marchandise est perie et les habitans . . . devenus sauvaiges. . . .'

[2] ib., III, 334 vo–335 ro. 'Encores . . . en poursuivant la pratique par
le consent du Vycaire de mon Père, tu manderas un vaillant escuer qui saiche
parler latin, saige preudomme et loyal et bien expert des condicions des
estranges pays du Souldan . . .; sa messagerie sera telle . . . que tu as treuvé
ès anciennes croniques royalles que ton grant père . . . Charlemaine, en son
temps ot grant amitié avecques le Souldan . . . il dira que tu as bonne
voulenté moralle avecques le Souldan ensuivant en cestui cas. . , . Et le dit
escuer un temps demourra en Surie et renconfortera de ta part saigement
lesdiz Crestiens en les exortant à sainte pacience, et te rescripiant souvent par
les marchans de l'estat de par delà.'

[3] ib., III, 335 ro. 'Et par ceste manière tu manderas ung autre semblable
aux seigneurs de Turquie.'

ever, assume that he wished to mitigate the sufferings of
the Eastern Christians and fathom the strength of the
enemy with whose arms the Latins would have to cope
at the appropriate time.

In common with Hayton, Guillaume Adam and Burcard,
he refers to the encouraging fact that the Sultan and his
Council are informed by the court astrologers that the law
of Muhammad will come to a speedy destruction.   If the
French and the English and all other Christians amend
their lives, 'the Sultan may of his own free will and without
bloodshed cede the Holy Land and all other possessions
having to do with the exaltation of the Christian faith'.[1]

Nevertheless, Mézières does not give up the idea of
active preparations for the 'saint passage d'oultremer'.   He
continues to reaffirm the importance of peace between
England and France and the end of the Schism in the
Church.[2]   All extravagant and demoralizing habits must
be renounced.   The King should suppress feasts, jousts,
vain assemblies, gambling and all disorderly practices on
pain of royal wrath and a fine to be devoted to the cost of
preparations for holy war.[3]   It is expedient that a council
of three prudent men of the 'tiers-état' should be elected
in every 'baillage' to settle local disputes and restrain the
avarice of some of the King's officers, while others may be
appointed for raising men and money for the great enterprise.[4]

The next important matter with which Philippe deals
at length is the problem of the routes to be pursued by

[1] *Songe*, III, 335 ro; 'le Souldan et son grant conseil sont informez par leurs
astrologiens que la loy de Mahommet briefment doit estre destruicte et si
doubtent fort en ce cas de ta royale magesté, par aventure se à ton pourchaz
les François et Anglois et autres Crestiens aucunement voulassent amander
leurs vies telle grace de mon père pourroit advenir que sans espandre sang
humain, par la bonne volunté du Souldan la Terre Sainte te seroit rendue et
autres biens touchans à l'exaltacion de la foy crestienne'.

[2] ib., III, 336 ro.

[3] ib., III, 337 ro ; 'que toutes grans festes, joustes, et vaines assemblées, et
noces trop sumptueuses du tout en tout soient condempnées et sus grans
peines, c'est assavoir de l'indignacion royalle et de certaine somme qui sera
convertie à la préparacion du dit saint passage. . . .   Encores il fault con-
dempner (le) jeu des dez dont maulx viennent.'

[4] ib., III, 337 vo–338 ro.

the crusaders.   He does not seem to uphold the concentration of all forces in one and the same direction, although
the Holy Land remains the common goal.   Various routes
suit various nations, and in all directions much may be
achieved for the promotion of the Christian cause.   The
Germans and the Hungarians can travel direct by the
land route and recover the Empire of Constantinople and
the Kingdoms of 'Thrace' and Bulgaria for Catholicism[1]
and cast out the Turks from Europe.   The Prussians
and Lithuanians may traverse Russia and its adjoining territories to join the Germans at Constantinople and assist in
suppressing the power of the Turks.[2]   The contingents of
Aragon, Spain, Portugal and Navarre must, on the other
hand, follow the African route and invade the Kingdoms of
Granada, 'Belle Marie',[3] Tlemsen, Morocco and Tunis.[4]
Meanwhile, Charles VI and his 'brother' of England
accompanied by the Scotch and Irish, the contingents of
Hainault, Holland and Zealand, the Liégois, the people
of Lorraine, the Savoyards, the Barrois and other levies
from the land beyond the Rhine together with the forces of
'Gaul', Lombardy, Tuscany, Apulia and Italy may take the
sea route to Egypt and Syria, allowing a section of the army
to disembark in Armenia and Turkey.[5]

[1] ib., III, 338 ro ; 'le roy de Hongrie et de Behaigne & l'empereur . . . des
Alemans alassent tout droite par terre en Constantinoble en recouvrant à la foy
catholique . . . le royaume de Trasse, de Boulgayre et l'empire de Constantinoble en reprenant les Turcqs et les faire passer le braz Saint George'.

[2] ib.   'Et les seigneurs de Prusse avecques le roy de Layto . . . passeront
parmy le royaume de Russye et des pays d'entour en venant vers Constantinoble, et se adjousteront avec les Alemans pour reprimer la puissance des Turcs.'

[3] Iorga (*Mézières*), 207 note 6, 470, and 477 note 7, reads from other
versions 'Belle Marine' or Benemarin which apparently means the Banu
Marin (known as Merinids in Western literature) who ruled Morocco from
the middle of the thirteenth to the middle of the fifteenth century.

[4] ib.   'Et de l'autre part le roy d'Aragon, d'Espaigne, de Portingal et de
Navarre doient aller à la conqueste du royaume de Grenade et passer oultre
ou royaume de Belle Marie, de Tremesan, de Maroch, et de Thunes.'

[5] ib., III, 338 ro et vo.   'Encores tu, . . . accompaigné de ton frère
d'Angleterre, des Escoz, des Yrlandoys, Hennuiers, Hollandoys et Zeloys,
et des Liégois, des Lorrains, Savoyens, et Barrois, de ceulx deçà le Rhin, et de
la chevalerie du royaume de Gaule et de la puissance de Lombardie, de
Toscane, de Puille et d'Ytalie pourra passer par mer en Egypte et en Surie,
et une partie en Arménie et en Turquie.'

It is expedient that the maritime republics of Venice
and Genoa should be asked by the King to supply the
necessary fleet without which no men-at-arms can cross
the sea.[1] The port of embarkation, whether Venice,
Brindisi or Naples, must be fixed beforehand; and Mézières
suggests that the King should use craft of middle size,
especially the 'taforesse' [2] and the 'nef moyenne' in preference to the ordinary armed galley, for reasons of speed,
efficiency and economy. The 'taforesse' carries from sixteen to twenty horses, sails in shallow waters as far as the
landing ground, and has a large gateway in the stern, so
that mounted men-at-arms can gallop from the ship direct
to battle without delay, and when repelled by the enemy
they may ride back to their quarters and retire to the sea
without danger of being harassed.[3] The armed galley
carries only twenty-five men-at-arms and thirty to sixty
arbalesters, whereas the 'nef moyenne' is capable of accommodating a hundred or two hundred men-at-arms, eighty to
a hundred horses and arbalesters 'without number'—all at
the cost of three or four hundred florins while the monthly
upkeep of an ordinary galley may be estimated at 1,400 to
1,500 florins.[4] Mézières, however, concludes this 'point'
by explaining to the King that there is no need for him to
discard completely the armed galley and other types of

[1] *Songe*, III, 338 vo. 'Encores . . . tu doyes requerre . . . Venise . . . et
Gennes . . . sans l'aide de lesquelx si grant armée de gens d'armes bonnement
ne pourroit passer.'

[2] *vide infra*, 343 note 4.

[3] *Songe*, III, 338 vo. 'Tafforesse est un vaisseau de mer qui va à vingt ou à
trente advirons et porte de XVI à XX chevaulx. Et a le dit vaisseau une
grant porte en la poupe et ne lui fault que deux ou troys paulmes d'eaux.
Et tous les fois que la dicte tafforesse en terre doit arriver contre les ennemis
les gens d'armes seront montez sus les chevaulx dedans le vaisseau . . . et
yront courre souldainement sus leurs ennemis. Et s'ilz sont chaciez ilz
rentreront tout à cheval dedans la taforesse malgré leurs ennemis et tantost se
retrayront en mer.'

[4] ib., III, 339 ro. 'Car aujourduy une galée armée couste le moys
mil et iiii^c florins . . . une galée raisonnablement ne portera que xxv
hommes d'armes et xxx arbalestiers de commun cours, et une nef moyenne
portera C ou ii^c hommes d'armes et iiii^{xx} ou cent chevaulx et arbalestiers
sans nombre et pour tout le voyage ne coustera que trois ou quatre cens
florins.'

ea-craft, for a number of these will be useful for the 'saint
passage'.[1]

It is important that the dates of sailing should be precisely
defined within the most favourable season of the year.
After the preparations for the expedition are completed,
the crusaders may set out in June, but not later than July.
This, the author asserts, will enable the hosts of God to
land on Eastern soil at the beginning of winter in September or October.   Realizing how impossible it is for
the chivalry of the West, clad in full armour, to fight in
the excessive heat of Egypt and Syria, Philippe advises that
landing in summer should be avoided as fatal.[2]   Moreover, arriving in the winter, they may gradually become
accustomed to the heat and thus the danger of mortality
in the following summer may be lessened.

In the remainder of this chapter of the *Songe*, Philippe
touches two points of importance without his usual extended
treatment.   First, in connexion with the possibility of
congestion of the cavalry on board ship, he advises the
King to ordain the reservation of one section of the transport for sailing in the 'second passage';[3] but he does not
specify a 'passagium generale' and a 'passagium parvum'.
In the second place, to avoid scandal, prudent women must
accompany their husbands.[4]   With the second, he deals,
as has already been shown, in the *Nova Religio Passionis*;
and of the first he says more in his *Epistle to Richard II*.[5]

---

[1] ib., III, 338 ro et vo.

[2] ib. 'Encores, Beau Filz, il est expédient que le terme de passage soit
tellement ordonné et que toutes choses soient si prestes que sans nulle faulte
tu doyes entrer en mer ou moys de juing ou au plus tart de juillet, c'est
assavoir pour aler en la terre d'orient qui est chaulde à l'entrée de l'iver; c'est
assavoir estre là en septembre ou au plus tart en octobre, car si la chevalerie de
Dieu d'occident qui est froide région se trouvoit en Egypte ou en Surie à
l'entrée de l'esté . . . il mourront sans nombre.' This is one of the few
passages having direct bearing on the fatal effect of the Eastern summer heat
on the Western knight.

[3] ib., III, 339 vo.

[4] ib., III, 339 vo–340 ro. 'Encores il est expédient . . . que tu doys
mener . . . la royne . . . et les autres princes, barons et chevaliers, auxi
chacun sa femme, c'est assavoir pour retranchier l'occasion et la matière de
toute villaine luxure . . . par deffaulte des preudes femmes.'

[5] *vide infra*, 150–2.

It is noteworthy that Mézières does not make any reference to his new Order of the Chivalry of the Passion in this chapter of the *Songe*. But he soon reverts to the old theme in the *Oratio tragedica* written in the course of the years 1389–90. There is little new material in the *Oratio*. In the Prologue,[1] he urges the interests of his Order. Knights, he says, employ their time and energy for varying purposes. Some lead a solitary life and others dedicate themselves for public service, but the most worthy of all are those who defend the Church and the Cross—those who fight the Saracen usurper of the holy city of Jerusalem. In his old age, Mézières regrets, he cannot place himself in any of these categories of chivalry. All that is left him now is the ardent desire to promote the cause of the Order of the Passion for the peace of his soul. As in a dream, he then reviews his past life from the time of his departure from the castle of Mézières to his retirement to the Convent of the Celestines in Paris. This is an autobiography of his triumphs and his disillusions, both mystic and full of grief.

In 1390 he had watched the Barbary expedition and the return of the Duke of Bourbon without any decisive achievement. In 1395, during the interval of peace between England and France, Hungary was menaced by the Turks and Constantinople was a beleagured city. Men throughout Europe began once more to discuss universal action against a dangerous enemy. The King of France called upon Philippe to write to the King of England in support of peace in Europe and holy war in the East. This was a golden opportunity for the 'vieil solitaire', as Mézières then called himself, to introduce his ideas to the court of England. Mézières had the contemporary taste for allegories, and it was in this form that he wrote his *Epistle to Richard II*.[2] He pleads

---

[1] Mazarine MS. 1651, fo. 129 ro. 'Prologus in oracione tragedica seu declamatoria Passionis Domini nostri Christi.' Cf. Iorga, *Mézières*, 471 et seq.

[2] B.M. MS. 20 BVI, fo. 2 ro. 'Une poure et simple épistre d'un vieil solitaire des Célestins de Paris adressant à trèsexcellent et trèspuissant très debonnaire catholique et très deuost prince, Richart par la grace de Dieu Roy

with the King in the Prologue [1] to his work for patience
in hearing good advice. The epistle itself consists of
nine 'matères' or chapters.[2] Here he drives home his
main ideas of peace between England and France and
of peace in the Church as a necessary preliminary measure
to a successful crusade. The peace between the two
'brethren' may be sealed by the Anglo-French marriage
alliance, and the crusade may be carried to a successful
issue if the chivalry of the West adopt his plan of the
'Militia Passionis'. In the central 'matère' [3] of the
Epistle where Mézières considers the 'saint passage
d'oultre mer', he invents a parable of two kings and an
aged knight. The two kings—the 'roy vigilant' and the
'roy malauisé'—represent the Sultan of Egypt and the
titular King of Jerusalem; and the 'vieil cheualier' is
Philippe himself. The second king has been defeated by
the first and is now suffering the indignity of exile [4] as a
penalty for maladministration, injustice and military in-

d'Angleterre &c. Pour aucune confirmacion tele quele de la vraye paix et
amour fraternelle du dit Roy d'Angleterre, et de Charles par la grace de Dieu
Roy de France.'

[1] ib., fo. 2 vo–5 ro, including prologue and rubrics.

[2] The substance of the nine chapters may be summed up as follows:
 (i) Peace between England and France. Fo. 5 ro–23 ro.
 (ii) End of Schism. Fo. 23 ro–28 ro.
 (iii) The Crusade. Fo. 28 ro–38 ro.
 (iv) The Anglo-French match. Fo. 38 vo–49 ro.
 (v) Condemnation of war among princes. Fo. 49 vo–54 vo.
 (vi–ix) Enlargement on peace discussion. Fo. 54 ro, 58 vo, 62 ro,
73 ro–83 vo respectively.
A short official letter from Charles VI to Richard II dated 25 May 1395
sent with Robert the Hermit and evidently coming from Mézières's pen covers:
 (i) Charles's congratulations to Richard on his victories in Ireland.
 (ii) Peace between England and France.
 (iii) The projected crusade.
 (iv) Evangelization of East.
 (v) Request for a reply with French envoy. The reply praises peace
efforts, but it says nothing on the crusade.
 Froissart (ed. Kervyn), XV, 388–91; Iorga, 479–82; *Nicopolis*, 30–2 and
171 note 63.

[3] Cap. iii of Epistle, fo. 28 ro et seq.

[4] ib., fo. 28 vo. 'Le Roy vigilant estant en la maistre cité de son anemi
qu'il auait acquise fist iij choses solempnelles en aprobacion de sa victoire.
Premièrement toutes les banières armes et enseingnes du Roy malauisé il fist

discipline in his legitimate heritage. Then the 'vieil cheualier' who has never ceased to blow his trumpet in order to rouse the Kings of Latin Christendom during the past forty years, appears on the scene of exile. Mézières seizes the occasion to present to the King of England his plan of the new Chivalry of the Passion as the only 'médecine préparative' for the salvation of the Holy Land from the usurping infidel. The new Order is also intended to purify the West from all the evils which now prevail in it. It must include the Knights and men-at-arms of Catholic countries in one large and holy fellowship. This having been achieved, the new body will proceed to a preparatory campaign [1] which corresponds to the 'passagium parvum' treated by other propagandists. Then the 'passagium generale' may follow under the leadership of the kings of England and France with every assurance of success in the conquest of the Holy Land. As a natural corollary, missionary work can be undertaken without serious impediment and Catholicism will be spread throughout the East.[2] Robert the Hermit, says Mézières in conclusion, and such distinguished Englishmen [3] as the Earl of Huntingdon, the Duke of York and Sir John Harleston who have promised to support the new organization, can furnish the King with other details concerning the Chivalry of the Passion of Jesus Christ. After the invasion of Turkey, Egypt and Syria which abound in 'riches and delectables', the two kings will hold their own realms as of small account, for these are cold and frozen, full of pride and avarice.[4]

ardoir et destruire publiquement. Secondement au son de ses trompes royales il fist banir du dit roiaume son anemi le roy malauisé. Et tiercement il retint tous les hommes du dit royaume en seruage.'

[1] *Songe*, fo. 34 vo–35 ro; 'le vieil solitaire présente au Roy d'Angleterre une nouvelle cheualerie de crucifix qui doit estre mandée oultremer deuant les ij Roys qui par la grace de dieu feront le saint passage'. Cf. fo. 36 vo.

[2] ib., 36 vo. The principal duty of the 'Militia Passionis' after the conquest of the Holy Land is 'pour multiplier la sainte foy catholique ès parties d'orient'.

[3] See *Nicopolis*, 47 and 173 notes 86–9.

[4] ib., fo. 81 vo–82 ro. 'Et que plus est quant par la grace de dieu vous aures conquesté turquie egypte et surie, qui sont remplis de toutes manières

Mézières's plea for peace between England and France could not have been entirely ignored by Richard II as the events of the period testify; but it is doubtful whether the King gave any attention to a plan which implied the incorporation of the armies of all Christian countries into a single body. Nevertheless, the Crusade of Nicopolis was, as many of the early crusades, undertaken by the chivalry of many countries with England strongly represented. It ended in a disaster which shocked Europe. Mézières, in spite of his advanced years, set out to analyse the causes of the Christian defeat in the last of his great literary achievements. In 1397 he sent a lengthy epistle [1] lamenting the failure of Western chivalry, to console the Duke of Burgundy whose son had led the crusaders, and to prescribe for the last time the remedies which he regarded as most effective to avert a similar disgrace in future. The campaign had failed because the army was lacking in good government and in the essential rules of discipline, obedience and justice.[2] Pride, covetousness and luxury— the three daughters of Lucifer—had, instead, filled the hearts of the leaders and even penetrated the ranks of the followers. The 'Militia Passionis', if adopted in the West, would eliminate these vices. This new Order of Chivalry, he continues, would include three estates [3]—the Kings, the nobility and the bourgeoisie, and the common people, corresponding to the leaders of the host, the mounted men-at-arms, and the infantry. The three classes would further be knit together into a large and homogeneous unit

de richesses et de delices . . . vous feres pou de compte de vos royaumes d'occident qui sont et frois et engelez et à orgueil et à auarice et à luxure souuentefois enclins et dédiés.'

[1] Épistre lamentable et consolatoire sur le fait de la disconfiture lacrimable du noble et vaillant roy de Honguerie par les Turcs devant la ville de Nicopoli en l'empire de Boulguerie adreçant à très-puissant, vaillant et très-sage prince royal, Phelipe de France, duc de Bourgoingne, &c., la dicte épistre aussi adreçant en substance et non pas en sa forme à très-excellens princes et roys de France, d'Angleterre, de Behaigne et de Honguerie en espécial, et par consé-quent à tous les roys, princes, barons, chevaliers et communes de la crestianté catholique, de par un vieil solitaire des Célestins de Paris, qui pour ses très-grans péchiés n'est pas digne d'estre nommé. Relevant parts ed. Kervyn in Froissart, XVI, 444–525; see Bodl. MS. Ashmole 342; cf. *Nicopolis*, 124–5.

[2] Kervyn, XVI, 452 et seq.　　　　　　[3] ib., XVI, 467 et seq.

governed by the new Rule of the Passion. Mézières exhorted the Duke of Burgundy, the Kings of England and France, and all good Catholics to avenge [1] the slaughter of the Christian host by the Turks at Nicopolis. He discussed the possible routes for the crusaders on the lines pursued in the *Songe*. The Epistle ends with a vision in which Jean de Blaisy, one of the first four 'evangelists' of the Passion, who probably perished at Nicopolis, appeared to Philippe in his cell and told him a parable in support of the new Chivalry.[2] But manners had changed and the time for Orders of Chivalry was over, and Mézières was but a visionary whose aspirations belonged to a past age, a propagandist battling against the nascent factors in fifteenth-century history.[3]

[1] Kervyn, XVI, 458.   [2] ib., XVI, 513–25.

[3] Realizing his failure in his mission, Mézières, as has been stated, calls himself continually, in the days of his retirement, a dreamer, a solitary and a hermit, and in the *Epistle to Richard II*, fo. 36 no., he calls himself 'vieil abortif'.

CHAPTER VIII

PILGRIMS AND PROPAGANDISTS IN THE FOURTEENTH CENTURY

Pilgrimages and conditions of medieval travel. Pilgrims, preachers and propagandists. Ricoldo de Monte-Croce. Wilhelm von Boldensele. Jean de Bourgogne ('Mandeville'). Giacomo di Verona. Ludolph von Suchem. Pietro di Penna. Lionardo di Niccolò Frescobaldi. Niccolò di Marthono. Thomas Brigg and Thomas Swinburne. Ogier VIII d'Anglure. Noble Pilgrims from France, England, Italy, Germany and East Central Europe. Anonymous Travels. Conclusion

PILGRIMAGES and crusades were closely associated during the Middle Ages. The argument that the second were born of the first, is not utterly without foundation, for both were acts of piety and penitence, and moreover the pilgrims of the eleventh century carried back with them tales of Christian suffering and of desecration of Holy Places by the fanatic Saljūq conquerors who had departed from the tolerant policy of the early Caliphs. Thus the armed crusader took the place of the presumably defenceless pilgrim in the prolonged contest between the East and the West over the possession of the Holy Land. With the complete downfall of the Latin Kingdom of Jerusalem, at the end of the thirteenth century, however, there was a reversion to the old way of pilgrimage to Jerusalem, then in alien hands. The number of pilgrims, indeed, increased during the fourteenth century to such an extent that the maritime Republic of Saint Mark found it a paying proposition to establish a semi-regular service for the pilgrim traffic to the Holy Places beyond the sea.[1]

[1] See for example *Pièces relatives au passage à Venise de pèlerins de Terre Sainte* in AOL, II, 237–49; R. Röhricht, *Deutsche Pilgerreisen*, 6–13, 43–7 and 49–52.

Although the motives of pilgrims included the love of travel and adventure in distant countries, religious devotion remained at the root of their enterprise. A pilgrimage [1] was generally regarded as a solemn occasion by the royal administration and by the Church. After verifying the genuineness of the pilgrim's intentions, the King's officers furnished him with a writ to prove the identity of the bearer and to commend him to the good offices of all men,[2] while the Church authorities solemnly blessed his staff and wallet (or 'burdon' and 'scrip') as well as his red-crossed white or grey garment. Barefoot (the pilgrim

---

[1] Useful and interesting chapters on medieval pilgrimages may be found in Jusserand, *English Wayfaring Life* (8th edition), 338–403; Salzman, *English Life in the Middle Ages*, 274–82; Cutts, *Scenes and Characters of the Middle Ages*, 137–94; Abram, *English Life and Manners in the Middle Ages*, 248–59; articles on Pilgrimage in *Catholic Encyclopedia*, *Encyclopedia Britannica* and other standard reference works. See also Sivry et Champagnac, *Dictionnaire des pèlerinages* (Paris, 1859). In the *Pageant of the Birth, Life and Death of Richard Beauchamp Earl of Warwick*, 1389–1439 (ed. Viscount Dillon and H. St. John Hope, London, 1914), plate IX, there is a good illustration of the Earl's sailing to Jerusalem on pilgrimage. Many of the medieval pilgrimage records have been translated into English and published by the Palestine Pilgrims' Text Society. The *Zeitschrift des deutschen Palaestina-Vereins* (ZDPV), 1876, &c.; Röhricht, *Deutsche Pilgerreisen* (*vide infra*, notes); and Röhricht and Meisner, *Deutsche Pilgerreisen nach d. heil. Lande* (Berlin, 1880),—include a full record of known German pilgrimages. See also T. Wright, *Early Travels in Palestine* (Bohn, London, 1848); H. Michélant and G. Raynaud, *Itinéraires à Jérusalem . . . au XIᵉ, XIIᵉ and XIIIᵉ siècles* (Geneva, 1882); R. Röhricht, *Bibl. Geogr. Palaest.*; B. de Khitrowo, *Itinéraires russes en Orient* (Soc. Or. Lat., Geneva, 1889). For early pilgrimages, see P. Geyer, *Itinera hierosolymitana saec.*, IV–VIII (Vienna, 1898); T. Toller and A. Molinier, *Itin. hierosolym. et descr. Terrae Sanctae* (Geneva, 1879–85); also good article by C. Jenkins on Christian Pilgrimages, A.D. 500–800, in *Travel and Travellers in the Middle Ages*, 39–69, including many useful references. The Hakluyt Society, the Early English Text Society, the Camden Society and the Broadway Travellers' Series include a number of pilgrims' records in their publications.

[2] Statutes 5 Ric. II st. 1, C. 2; 12 Ric. II, cap. 7; 13 Ric. II, 1, C. 20; also Ordonnance of Charles VI dated February 27, 1399, in *Recueil d'Isambert*, VI, 843; Sivry et Champagnac, in Migne, *Encyclopédie théologique*, XLIII–XLIV, contains ample illustration of restrictions on pilgrimages; cf. Jusserand, op. cit., 361–2. These restrictions in England and France were intended as a check on vagabondage among villeins. Although the examples here quoted belong to the contemporary reigns of Richard II and Charles VI, they were probably not without precedent.

being generally [1] denied the relative comfort of travelling
on horseback or in a medieval wagon) and without any
weapons for protection, he started his arduous journey
across Europe, battling with the dangers of the road and
exposed to the inclemency of the weather.   After the termination of the first or overland stage, the pilgrim was
huddled with crowds of others in a small rickety craft
bound for Syria.   Here he suffered a discomfort of
accommodation unimaginable to the modern traveller.
Moreover, the medieval ship remained at the mercy of the
waves from the time of sailing to that of anchoring at its
destination, and the risk of foundering in gales at sea was
a real peril in those days.   The Mediterranean was infested
with pirates, both Christian and Saracen, ready to prey
upon any unarmed victim.   Those who survived this
second stage would then proceed to the Holy Places either
on foot or riding donkeys,[2] paying heavy tolls and taxes
on the way at every town, bridge or castle, and often facing
the indignity of being reviled as infidels by the Muhammadan inhabitants.   And all these miseries and sufferings
had to be faced once more on the return journey.
There is no wonder that those whom fortune and fortitude
enabled to plod their way back home in safety appeared
to their fellow-countrymen with a halo of sanctity.   Vil-
lagers and townsfolk alike clustered round the holy traveller
to inquire about the places beyond the sea, and pulpit

[1] For the medieval 'poste' system in which horses for hire by pilgrims were
specially branded to eliminate the temptation of quitting the normal road leading to a shrine in order to appropriate the animal, see Karkeek, *Chaucer's
Schipman* (Appendix) and his *Barge and the Maudelayne*, in the Chaucer
Society Essays (1884); cf. Jusserand, op. cit., 348 and note.   The main point
is, of course, that the use of horses was allowed in some cases.

[2] The use of the donkey in the Holy Land may be explained in three
ways:
(*a*) Christians were generally not permitted to travel on horseback in
equality with Muslims.
(*b*) Christians' preference for following the example of our Lord's entrance
into Jerusalem on Palm Sunday riding an ass.
(*c*) The idea of humility attached to donkey riding as against travelling on
horseback appealed to the pious frame of mind of the pilgrim.   Those who
have seen the excellent donkeys of Egypt and Syria, however, may choose to
discount the association of humility with the use of these animals.

accommodation was provided in churchyard, common and market-place for publication of news of the Holy Land.[1] Tales of wonder and affliction were told, and exhortations for saving the oppressed heritage of Christ from a usurping miscreant fervently made, and both preacher and congregation were often moved to tears.

It is indeed difficult to define with accuracy the magnitude of the propagandist work accomplished by pilgrims and palmers in an age when prevailing illiteracy made it impossible for all of them to put on record their memoirs of pilgrimages to the Holy Land and of the sermons delivered on their return therefrom. At the same time, it would require more than a chapter to present a full survey of the material left by the few who were capable of imparting their experience and knowledge in writing. A glimpse of their efforts will, however, reveal the important place which the pilgrim held in the annals of propaganda for the crusade. It is essential to bear in mind that pilgrims came from all parts of Christendom— from England, France, Germany, Italy, Spain and even Russia, and there were in addition members of the Eastern Churches, whether Orthodox, Monophysite or Nestorian. Roman Catholics naturally formed one large 'international' fellowship with Latin as a convenient medium for the exchange of speeches and sermons, and the Orthodox another fellowship probably with Greek as a means of expression, while all shared the same aspirations at the various places of Christ's birth, passion, burial and resurrection.   If, however, we remember that men like Burcard, Guillaume Adam, Pierre de Thomas, Philippe de Mézières and others, treated separately owing to their special place in this study, were pre-eminently pilgrims, we may realize the importance of the pilgrim class of propagandists.

At the opening of the fourteenth century, Ricoldo de Monte-Croce,[2] a pilgrim and an author of some worth, consecrated his life to work in the East. Born about

---

[1] G. R. Owst, *Preaching in Medieval England*, 56, 61 and 199.

[2] Introduction by R. Röhricht to *Lettres de Ricoldo de Monte-Croce*, in AOL, II (Documents), 258–63.   For MSS., editions and translations of Ricoldo's works, see Röhricht, *Bibl. Geogr. Palaest.*, 61–2.

1242 at Monte-Croce in the neighbourhood of Florence, he joined the Dominican Order at the Convent of S. Maria Novella at Florence in 1267, became Master of Arts at the Convent of St. Catherine at Pisa in 1272, lived through the period of that painful exodus of the Latins from Syria in 1291, reappeared on the scene at Florence in 1301, and in the same year travelled to the Curia to present the Pope with a work entitled *Confutatio Alcorani*. He died on 31 October 1320 after having lived in the East for a considerable period. The nature of his activities is revealed by a general survey of his various works. First, he composed an *Itinerarium* [1] as a guide to pilgrims and crusaders. Second, he wrote a *Confutatio Alcorani*,[2] a *Libellus contra nationes orientales*, and a *Libellus contra errores Judaeorum* [3] as bases of theological discussion with Schismatics, Jews and Muhammadans with a view to the conversion of the whole world to Catholicism by force of argument and of reason. Third, he issued a series of letters known as *Epistolae ad ecclesiam triumphantem*,[4] which are, strictly speaking, not letters but reflections written in the East (data in Oriente). The author lived in

---

[1] Laurent, *Quatuor peregr. Medii aevi* (Leipzig, 1873), 101–41; French trans. in 1351 by Lelong mentioned by Quétif and Échard (*Script. ordin. praedicat.*), I, 504*b*; by Fineschi (*Memorie istoriche degli uomini illustri di S. Maria Novella di Firenze*, Florence, 1790), 311; and edited by Louis de Backer, in *L'Extrême-Orient au Moyen Âge* (Paris, 1877), 256–334; see also Tobler, *Bibliogr. geogr. Palestinae*, 30–1; cf. Röhricht, *Lettres*, 259, note 7.

[2] First ed. Seville 1500; trans. and reprinted in various languages, cf. Tobler, 31; Fineschi, 324; Quétif and Échard, l.c.

[3] The two *Libelli* appear to be still in MS. at S. Maria Novella; cf. Fineschi, 311 and 324, and Röhricht, l.c. note 9.

[4] Vatican MS. 5717, includes the *Epistolae* among the following works:

    (i)   Albertus Aquensis, *Hist. Hierosolym.*, ff. 1 ro–198 vo.
    (ii)   Guill. Tripolitanus, fo. 210 vo–218 vo.
    (iii)   Jacob. Vitriacensis, *Hist. Hierosolym.*, lib I, ff. 219 ro–249 ro.
    (iv)   Ricoldus, *Epistolae*, ff. 249 vo–267 ro.
    (v)   Ricoldus, *Contra legem Sarracenorum*, ff. 268 ro–300 ro.
    (vi)   Marco Polo, ff. 301 ro–376 vo.
    (vii) *Epistola presb. Johannis ad Fridericum*, II, f. 377 ro et vo.
    (viii) Eugenius, *Decretum de Reductione Armenorum*, ff. 378 ro–382 ro.
    (ix)   Poggius, *De varietate fortunae*, ff. 382 ro–397 vo.
    (x)   Ludolphus de Suchen, ff. 401 ro–443 vo.
    Cf.   Röhricht, l.c., note 11; *Epistolae*, op. cit., 264–96.

the midst of the enemies of the faith and preached the word of God under the most precarious conditions. He witnessed scenes of Church desecration [1] and saw the Christians either forced to abjure their faith or carried into slavery at the point of the sword.[2] These atrocities were not the will of God. They were wrought by the sins of the Christians whose duty it was to redeem themselves and end Saracen iniquities. He himself did his utmost in several ways. He tried to save sacred relics from the Churches and monasteries which were pillaged by the Muslims after the fall of Latin Christianity in Syria. He bought from Muslim merchants a number of sacred ornaments, breviaries and most precious of all, St. Gregory's 'Moralia'.[3] Second, he settled in Baghdad for some years studying the Qur'ān and the principal works of the Islamic faith [4] in order to complete the *Confutation* and the *Libels*. It was here that he wrote most of his works including the *Epistles*. Third, he preached to Saracens in Arabic and waited for the crown of martyrdom in vain, for the Muslims for some reason refrained from imposing the usual penalty of death on him for the abuse of their religion.

Next in chronological order, we hear of a German Dominican, a certain Wilhelm von Boldensele [5] (alias Otto

---

[1] *Epistola*, III, in AOL, II, Doc., 278–9. 'Scis enim Domina (Maria Magdalena), quia pulcram ecclesiam tuam quam in honorem tuum edificaverunt christiani in Magdalon stabulatam inveni a Sarracenis et quasi vile stabulum animalium brutorum, pulcram eciam ecclesiam quam christiani edificaverunt tibi in Bethania, ubi Ihesus amor divinus flevit et fratrem tuum Lazarum de monumento vocavit, ipsam inquam ecclesiam stercoratam et stabulum animalium brutorum inveni.' Examples of desecration and of transformation of churches into mosques are cited in the other epistles in connexion with his visits to the various Holy Places.

[2] *Epistola*, II, op. cit., 272. Here, he laments in a spirited passage the unholy violence to which holy women from Syrian convents were subjected by the Saracens—'virgines consecrate sint sclave et concubine Sarracenorum et Sarracenos filios generent Sarracenis, &c.'. See also *Epistola*, III, 279.

[3] *Epistola*, II, 271–2 and III, 279–80.

[4] *Itinerarium*, 131, 133–4, 139; cf. Röhricht, in AOL, II, Doc., 263.

[5] Various forms extant: Bolunzele, Boldensleeve, Boldensel, Bouledeselle and Baldesel. *Ambassades europeénnes en Chine*, in *Nouvelles annales des voyages* (4ᵉ année, Décembre), 257–309; Comte de la Borde, *Comment. géogr. sur l'Exode et les Nombres* (Paris, 1841), xii–xlii; *Bull. de l'Académie roy. de Bruxelles*, XI, no. 3.

von Neuhaus [1]), who left his Convent at Minden and took the road to Rome. There he managed to obtain absolution for a pilgrimage to the Holy Land in 1333, probably through the intercession of Cardinal Élie de Talleyrand,[2] who requested Wilhelm to write a description of the Holy Land for him to be used in connexion with the crusade which he had been appointed to preach by Pope Benedict XII and in which he was replaced by Pierre de Thomas. Wilhelm made an extensive tour of the Levant in which he visited Greece, Rhodes and Cyprus as well as the important cities of the Holy Land and of Egypt including Jaffa, 'Akka, Ghazza, Damascus, Jerusalem and Cairo. He also made a pilgrimage to the monastery of St. Catherine on Mount Sinai, and while in Lebanon received the assurances of the Maronites that they would fight with the Western Christians in the next crusade against the Mamlūks. As a result of his travels he wrote in 1336 the book entitled *Hodoeporicon ad Terram Sanctam*.[3] Boldensele seems to have reached Baghdad in the course of his peregrinations but the bulk of his work is devoted to the description of Jerusalem and other Christian Holy Places.

A pilgrim of a different type was Jean de Bourgogne, better known as 'Sir John de Mandeville'.[4] He was

---

[1] R. Röhricht (*Deutsche Pilgerreisen nach den Heiligen Lande*, Innsbruck, 1900), 89; ib., *Bibl. Geogr. Palaest.*, 73–4; Grotefend, in *Zeitschr. d. historisch. Vereins für Niedersachsen*, 1852 (1855), 209–26, 231 f.

[2] Born in 1301; became bishop of Limoges in 1329, and cardinal in 1331. Reiffenberg (Appendix to *Chevalier au Cygne*), 276 et seq., note. *Vide supra*, Cap. VII (Pierre de Thomas).

[3] Published in Canisius, *Lectiones Antiquae*, ed. J. Basnage (Antwerp, 1725), VI, 338–57; also Grotefend, *Itinerarius Guilielmi de Boldensele*, in *Zeitschr. d. hist. Vereins für Niedersachsen* (Hanover, 1855), 236–86. German trans. Jäck, Taschenbibl., II, 109–62; extracts in Röhricht and Meisner, 465–6, and Röhricht (Gotha ed. 1889), 102.   French trans., Jehan de St. Denys, *L'hystoire merveilleuse de Tartarie* (Paris, 1529), lxvi–lxxvii.   English extracts in Cobham, *Excerpta Cypria*, 15–16.

[4] *Mandeville's Travels*, trans. from the French of Jean d'Outremeuse, ed. P. Hamelius (2 vols., in Early Eng. Text Soc., Original Series, 153–4, London, 1919–23), II, 3; and *Early Travels in Palestine*, ed. Th. Wright, 129, where Jean describes himself as 'I, John Maundeville, knight, . . . born in England, in the town of Saint Albans'.   There is no contemporary evidence to show the existence of a knight bearing the name Jehan de Mandeville, although Mangeuilain occurs in Yorkshire (16 Hen. I; Roll. Soc., XV,

essentially a traveller and a collector of others' accounts of their travels which he incorporated in his own work. Although the authenticity and originality of his work have recently been contested, there is no reason to believe that he did not reach the Levant and make his way to Egypt and the Holy Land. His knowledge of these regions seems to provide ample illustration of the genuineness of this part of his book. Jean further states that he 'passed through Tartary, Persia, Eremeny (Armenia), the Little and the Great; through Libya, Chaldea, and a great part of Ethiopia; through Amazonia, India the Less, and the Greater . . . and throughout many other isles that are about India'.[1] In his descriptions of the remote parts of Africa and of the Middle and Far East which he certainly did not visit, he drew freely upon ancient writers such as Solinus and Pliny,[2] and upon his medieval predecessors and contemporaries including Vincent of Beauvais, Oderic of Pordenone, Prince Hayton of Armenia, Boldensele and probably Guillaume Adam.[3] Even if the doubts of modern

---

40), and the family of the Bishop of Nevers was known as 'de Mandevilain' which is regarded as a place-name from Magneville or Mandeville. Jean has been identified as 'Jean d'Outremeuse' or 'Jean de Bourgogne, dit à la barbe' or 'ad Barbam', a naturalist and physician, native of Liège. Like his name, his English origin has been suspected; and although St. Albans possesses a sapphire ring, and Canterbury a crystal orb, gifts from one Mandeville, some even suggest that these could have been sent from Liège and 'Mandeville' might have never seen England. On Mandeville's original name, his life, work and sources, see E. W. B. Nicholson, in the Academy, 12 April 1884; *Bull. de l'Institut archéologique liégoise*, IV (1860), 171; A. Bovenschen, *Die Quellen für Reisebeschreibung des Johann von Mandeville* (Berlin, 1888), revised in *Unterschungen uber Johann von Mandeville*, in *Zeitschrift der Gesellschaft für Erdkunde zu Berlin*, XXIII, pts. 3 and 4 (nos. 135–6); J. Vogels, *Handschriftliche über die englische Version Mandeville's* (Crefeld, 1891); G. Kurth, *Étude critique sur Jean d'Outremeuse*, in memoirs of Brussels Academy (Hayez, 1910); Hamelius, op. cit., II, introduction and notes. G. F. Warner in his edition in the Roxburghe Club and his article 'Mandeville' in DNB; article 'Mandeville' by E. W. B. Nicholson and H. Yale in *Encyc. Brit.*; Jusserand, op. cit., 392–3, note 2; *Nicopolis*, 25 and 169 note 30. For list of MSS., ed. and trans., see Röhricht, *Bibl. Geogr.*, 79–85.

[1] Hamelius, I (text), 3; Wright, 129.

[2] ib., II, 19–21, 25, 29, 32–3 (introduction and notes); Wright's Introduction, xxvi.

[3] Bovenschen, op. cit.; see also Chapters III and IX.

scholarship as to the authenticity of Jean's story of his travels are extended to his possible visits to the Holy Places, the author's aim in the compilation of his work is clearly put forward in the Prologue. The Holy Land, 'made moist with the precious blood of our Lord Jesus Christ', he says, 'is the same land that our Lord promised us in heritage. . . . Wherefore every good Christian man, that is of power, and hath whereof (*sic*), should labour with all his strength to conquer our right heritage, and drive out all unbelieving men. For we are called Christian men, after Christ our Father. And if we be right children of Christ, we ought to claim the heritage that our Father left us, and take it out of heathen men's hands'.[1] Jean's work is therefore paramountly a work of propaganda. The author, moreover, writes for the 'solace and comfort' of 'men desiring to hear speak of the Holy Land', as a long time had elapsed without a 'general passage or voyage over the sea'.[2] The causes to which he ascribes this failure to undertake a new crusade are significant; for 'now pride, covetousness and envy have so inflamed the hearts of worldly lords that they are busier to disinherit their neighbours than to claim their right heritage aforesaid. And the common people, that would put their bodies and their goods to conquer our heritage, may not do it without the lords.' Then he exhorts the leaders of Christendom to exterminate all these evils and unite all their forces into one godly host of crusaders. If they act in this wise, Jean confidently believes that 'within a little time our heritage aforesaid should be recovered and put in the hands of the right heirs of Jesus Christ'.[3] He is anxious that all men should be acquainted with his thesis; and to achieve this purpose he has 'put this book out of Latin into French, and translated it again out of French into English'.[4]

Jean de Bourgogne begins the actual work with some descriptions of the land route 'from the west side of the world' through Almaine (Germany) and Hungary to 'the

---

[1] Hamelius, I, 2; Wright, 128. [2] ib., I, 3; Wright, 128–9.
[3] id., l.c.; Wright, 128. [4] ib., I, 4; Wright, 129.

land of the Bougres' (Bulgaria) and Constantinople.[1]
This reminds us of the route followed by the crusaders
of Nicopolis who never reached their contemplated destination. From Constantinople he shows that there are two
routes to Jerusalem—first across the 'Brace of St. George'
(Bosphorus) and Turkey (Asia Minor) towards the city
of 'Nice' (Nicaea) by land; and second by sea to Rhodes,
Cyprus and 'the haven of Tyre, which is now called Sur'.[2]
Jean does not, however, completely lose sight of the route
from Western Europe through France, Burgundy and
Lombardy with embarkation at Genoa or Venice for
'Babylon' (Cairo).[3] For the benefit of both pilgrims and
crusaders, he devotes some attention to the roads leading to Jerusalem from the Syrian coastal towns and from
Cairo by way of the 'Mountain of St. Catherine' in Sinai.
For the crusader, in particular, he gives an estimate of the
armed forces of the Mamlūks. The Sultan, he says, 'can
lead out of Egypt more than 20,000 men-at-arms; and
out of Syria, and Turkey, and other countries that he
holds, he may raise more than 50,000. And all these
are at his wages; and they are always ready, beside the
people of his country, who are without number. And
each of them has six florins by the year; but he is expected
to keep three horses and a camel.' [4] He describes the
coast of Egypt as being exceptionally well fortified and its
rockiness makes it the more dangerous. Alexandria, he
says, is indeed 'a very strong city; but it has no water
except what is brought by conduit from the Nile, which
enters into their cisterns; and if any one stopped the water
from them they could not hold out a siege.' [5] The author
refers to the Eastern Christians of the Greek and Nestorian
churches in a few short passages, but he says nothing about
the possibility of their support for a Latin crusade.[6] He
further devotes a chapter [7] to the manners, customs and
religion of the Saracens. The chief interest of this section

---

[1] Hamelius, I, 6; Wright, 129–30.
[2] ib., I, 13–20; Wright, 137–43.
[3] ib., I, 35; Wright, 155.
[4] ib., I, 23; Wright, 146.
[5] ib., I, 29; Wright, 150–1.
[6] ib., I, 80–1; Wright, 188–9.
[7] ib., I, 84–92; Wright, 194–200.

lies in the fact that it is one of the few descriptions of Islam in the literature of medieval Europe, where legend is intermingled with some truth. The rest of the book, apart from a detailed description of Holy Places, deals with the countries of the Middle and Far East which Jean had never seen and the accounts of which he had derived from other travellers' works. Here, it may be remarked that ' plagiarism', a practice neither discredited nor discountenanced in the Middle Ages, was practised freely by this author.

Contemporary with Jean de Bourgogne was Giacomo di Verona, an Augustinian monk who left Verona with a number of companions (of whose names we have no record) on 7 May 1335 to perform a pilgrimage to the Holy Places which he described in his *Liber Peregrinationis*.[1] On 7 June Giacomo arrived at Otranto where he held a successful disputation with the Jews of that town; and on 24 June he reached Crete which he mistook for Malta when he marked its coast as the place where St. Paul had been shipwrecked on his way to Rome.[2] Six days later (30 June) he landed at Famagusta, a principal port of Cyprus. On the same day he reported the arrival of a fleet from Lajazzo carrying thousands of Armenian fugitives, whose lands had been seized and homes destroyed by the Sultan.[3] The sight of their misery roused him to an indictment of the indifference of the powers of the West to the sad lot of their fellow-Christians in the East. He noticed that since the fall of 'Akka in 1291, the women of Cyprus had remained in mourning. At Nicosia he preached in the presence of King Hugh IV de Lusignan. Finally, he again set sail on 21 July, arriving at Jaffa on 30 July, and at Jerusalem on 5 August. At this point of his narrative, he describes the Holy Places [4] and enumer-

---

[1] Ed. R. Röhricht, in ROL, 3ᵉ année (1895), no. ii, 155–302 (Editor's Introduction, 155–62; Author's 'Proemium' or Introduction, 163–71; Text of the *Liber*, 171–302. Ib., *Bibl. Geogr.*, 85; Golubovich, III, 21–4.

[2] *Liber*, 171–83; includes the account of the journey from Verona to Jerusalem.

[3] ib., 171; cf. Weil, *Abbasidenchalifat*, II, 335 et seq.; Petermann, *Beiträge zur Gesch. der Kreuzzüge aus armenischen Quellen*, 180.

[4] ib., 183 et seq.

ates the fortified towns and villages which were once the pride of the Cross under Latin Rule. He departed from Jerusalem to Mount Sinai by way of Ghazza [1]—a route which appears to have been unknown to previous travellers from the West and which cannot be traced in the sources prior to Giacomo's *Liber Peregrinationis*. After visiting the Monastery of St. Catherine, he continued his journey through Egypt and reached Cairo on 30 September. Here he describes the wonders of the Egyptian capital and gives an account of the Sultan's army. Cairo, he says, has a wonderful and impregnable citadel with strong walls and large towers accommodating a regular militia of 20,000 horse [2] according to the estimate of Christian merchants in those parts. This militia consists of Saracen, Turkish, Greek and Christian slaves who have been made to abjure their faith, and every soldier possesses a horse, though the horses are small.[3] They are badly armed. They have a steel helmet but no coat of mail, and their chief weapon is the bow.[4] The tombs of the Mamlūks in the neighbourhood of the city attract his attention as objects of beauty the like of which he has never seen in the whole of Christendom.[5] In a modest attempt to give

---

[1] *Liber*, 225 et seq.

[2] Cf. estimate of Jean de Bourgogne. *Vide supra*, 164.

[3] For importance of light steed in Eastern tactics and warfare, see *Nicopolis*, 79.

[4] *Liber*, 239; 'et habet (soldanus) in civitate (Cayrum) castrum mirabile et (in) expugnabile cum muris, turribus et edificiis magnis, et in castro habet magnam miliciam Saracenorum, Turchorum, Grecorum, Christianorum, qui negaverunt fidem Cristi, et habet multos sclavos, . . . Magna milicia est, et computata fuit per mercatores nostros cristianos xx milia equitum; omnes habentes arcus et equos parvos, videlicet roncinos et palafredos; nullum autem dextrarium vidi ibi, et omnes equestres erant male armati, quod in capite portant unum capellum parvum de ferro et aliqui habebant corracias, aliqui vero non, sed armaturas de coreis, et nullus habet brachia armata propter arcum, neque crura et tibias portant munitas, quia habent breves strepas, et dum volunt jacere cum arcu, elevant se super pedes in sellis et sic jaciunt sagittas'.

[5] ib., 240; 'cimiteria magna, ubi sunt sepulchra Saracenorum, et sunt ibi mirabiles sepulture de lapidibus marmoribus, porfiricis et alabastro et aliis nobilibus lapidibus nobiliter et mirabiliter edificatis et deauratis, que non vidi in tota cristianitate tales magnificas sepulturas'.

a geographical description of Egypt and the Nile, he notes that the river is the normal means of communication between Cairo and Alexandria.[1]   Unfortunately, he does not give any account of the latter city; but he pays Damietta a visit as it happens to be near the land route which he has resolved to follow back to Ghazza.   The harbour of Damietta, like those of Jaffa, 'Akka and Ṣūr, has been blocked by huge boulders so as to render its water unnavigable for Christian fleets intending to attack Egypt and Syria at those points.   Giacomo writes a special chapter[2] on Islam and the manners and customs of the Muhammadans. This includes some interesting remarks.   Although he describes Islam as an 'abominable' faith,[3] he appears to have adopted a less severe attitude towards Muslims. These, he asserts, have departed from the primitive tenets of their religion and are now well disposed towards Christianity.   Moreover, the disgraceful conduct of the Sultan and his amīrs (admirati), who indulge in unnatural vice,[4] has turned the sympathy of the people from the rule of Islam to Christianity.   The author's motives in these statements are clear enough; for, by depreciating the enemy and exposing his weakness, he may persuade Christians to inaugurate a new 'passagium' for the recovery of the Holy Land.   Curiously, in subsequent chapters, Giacomo unwittingly contradicts his own argument by accounts of incidents in the course of his travels.   On his return to Jerusalem,[5] he was forced to leave within three days of his arrival owing to a rising wave of fanaticism among the Muslim inhabitants and he took the road to Nazareth,[6] but again met with hostility towards Christians. He then left for Damascus by a little frequented road to

---

[1] ib., 241; 'per quem fluvium (Nilum) omnia de Alexandria ad Kayrum in navibus portantur'.

[2] ib., 259–64.

[3] ib., 264; 'lege et gestis Mahomet, qui sunt abhominabilia apud Deum et apud homines'.

[4] ib.   Referring to these misdeeds, he says, 'quam tamen aliqui Saraceni detestantur et de tali lege trufantur, ut ego audivi a pluribus; et si contingerit passagium fieri, multi ad Cristi fidem converterentur et illas horrendas leges pocius abbominabiles penitus derelinquerent'.

[5] ib., 251–9.   [6] ib., 264–86.

avoid encounters with Muslims.   In the Syrian capital
he saw an Armenian embassy which had come to beg
for peace with the Sultan; then he went to Baalbek, Saida
(Sidon), Ṣūr (Tyre), 'Akka and finally to Beirūt,[1] whence
he sailed for his native town.   He arrived at Verona in
October 1335.[2]

The *Liber Peregrinationis* is essentially a work of propaganda [3] for the crusade and a guide to pilgrims.   The
accurate dates of departures and arrivals provided by the
author are of value in defining the length of time taken
by medieval travellers between the various stations on the
way to the East.   It is true that there is little new material
in this respect, but Giacomo's evidence helps to confirm
or confute previous and later information on this subject.
Though he appears to have made some use of the works
of Ricoldo de Monte-Croce [4] and of Philippe de Savoy,[5]
the chief merit of Giacomo's account is its originality.

In spite of the popularity of the pilgrims' guides during
the fourteenth century, those of German origin do not
appear to have enjoyed a particularly wide circulation,
judging from the scarcity of early manuscripts thereof.
Moreover, Germans who took the trouble to record their
travels are few and, saving Schiltberger's great classic,
these never attained any considerable degree of excellence
and interest in medieval times.   Besides Boldensele, only
one other fourteenth-century pilgrim from Germany took
the trouble to present an account of some importance of his
travels in the Levant, and even this did not make the widespread appeal [6] commanded by works originating in other
countries, notably France and Italy.   Ludolph von Suchem
or Sudheim, who sojourned in the East for an uninterrupted
period of five years between 1336 and 1341, composed

---

[1] *Liber*, 286–96.   [2] ib., 296–302.

[3] ib., 302.   Besides the material in the text, the Explicit of the *Liber* is
clear on this matter: 'Quam Terre Sancte acquisicionem celeriter suo populo
prestet ille Jhesus Cristus, qui est Dei filius benedictus in secula seculorum.
Amen!'

[4] *vide supra*, 158–60.

[5] Röhricht's Introduction to the *Liber*, 160.

[6] G. A. Neumann, Introduction to edition of Latin text of *Ludolphus de
Sudheim*, in AOL, II, Documents, 327.

his *Description of the Holy Land and the Way Thither*[1] in 1350 and dedicated it to Baldwin von Steinfurt, Bishop of Paderborn (1340–61). This bishop, it is suggested, may have been a companion of Suchem in his Oriental travels. The *Description* was first written in Middle High German and afterwards translated into Latin,[2] and, judging from the text in the Archives de l'Orient Latin, appears to consist of two distinct books— first *De Itinere Terre Sancte*,[3] and second *Descriptio Terrae Sancte*.[4]   Both works include much and varied material of some import; but, having been written nearly ten years after the completion of Suchem's Oriental journey, they are not free from flaws, for, as Ludolph himself says, he was writing 'according to my humble understanding and genius and weakness of my memory'. Further, he continues, 'let no one suppose that I have beheld with my eyes each several one of the things which I intend to put in this book, but that I have extracted some of them from ancient books of history, and that some I have heard from the lips of truthful men'.[5]   This candid and honest recognition of his debt to others confirms the great possibility of Ludolph's use of Hayton's *Flos*, and Monte-Croce's *Epistolae*, and Boldensele's *Hodoeporicon*.[6]

The *De Itinere* begins with a short but comprehensive review of all the routes to the East. Suchem mentions the land route through Hungary and Bulgaria to the Empire of Constantinople, continuing either by land through Turkey after crossing the Hellespont or by sea to Rhodes, Cyprus and the Holy Land.[7] He does not lose sight of the long sea route[8] from Marseilles or Venice;

---

[1] Eng. Trans. by A. Stewart in the Palestine Pilgrims' Text Society (London, 1895).   For edition of Latin text, see following notes.   References are made to both as specified in notes.   List of MSS., &c., in Röhricht, *Bibl. Geogr.*, 76–9 extracts and notes in Golubovich, III, 24 et seq.

[2] Neumann, op. cit., II, Doc., 326   [3] ib., 329–37.

[4] ib., 337–76.   [5] Stewart, 2.

[6] Neumann's Introduction, op. cit., II, Documents, 324.   *Vide supra*, analysis of works of Hayton, Monte-Croce and Boldensele.

[7] Neumann, op. cit., II, Doc., 329–30.

[8] In this connexion he speaks of the perils of the sea: (i) The 'gulph', i.e. squalls caused by irregularities in the height of the coast.   (ii) The 'grup',

and he also refers to the North African land route from Spain which he regards as perilous to Christian travellers.[1]

The *Descriptio* consists of two large parts. The first, *De Situ Locorum Terrae Sanctae*,[2] deals specifically with what may be inferred from its title, namely, the enumeration and description of the Holy Places, one by one in detail. The second, *Descriptio Geographica et Ethnographica*,[3] is a motley geographical, historical and social compendium including much that is of interest in regard to the Holy Land and the East in general with chapters on the Eastern Christians and on the Saracens. Besides the Latins, he says, other Christian sects consist of Greeks, Syrians, Indians, Nubians, Armenians, Georgians, Nestorians, Jacobites, Maronites, Copts, 'Ysini' and 'Maronini'.[4] He gives a brief definition of the beliefs peculiar to each sect of this comprehensive and impressive list; but his statements are often incorrect and at times mere imagination. He appropriates the Nubians[5] to the Latin Church, whereas in point of fact they were members of the Holy Orthodox Church of Alexandria. The Indians, he says, are 'quasi Latini', but do not recognize the authority of the Pope.[6] Of the 'Ysini' and 'Maronini', little is known beyond Ludolph's description of them as Nestorians

---

when two winds meet. (iii) The 'shoal'. (iv) The 'fish', sometimes large enough to endanger safety of ships. (v) The 'pirates', not infrequent in this period. Stewart, 13–17 cf. *Nicopolis*, 26 and 170 note 40.

[1] Neumann, op. cit, II, Documents, 330. 'Illi vero qui de Hyspania volunt ire per terram, transeunt per mare angustum de Balthar; de quo contra solem transeunt ad regnum (Marrochie) et ad alia regna Africe, donec venient ad Allexandriam. Deinde vadunt ad Terram Sanctam. Sed hec via est christianis periculosa propter calores et barbaros.'

[2] ib., 337–62.

[3] ib., 362–76; consisting of the following chapters: I. De Montibus. II. De Incolis. III. De Indumentis. IV. De Fructibus. V. De Presulibus. VI. De Sectis Christianorum. VII. Distinctior Iudeorum Declaratio. VIII. De Sarracenis. IX. De Morte Machumeti.

[4] ib., 367.

[5] ib., 368. 'Nubiani tenent se totaliter ad ritum Latinorum.'

[6] ib. 'Indi habent se quasi Latini; sed Pape non obediunt, sed suo patriarche et eorum episcopis, &c.' He evidently means the Syrian Church which owed its origin to St. Thomas the Apostle by tradition. *Vide infra*, Cap. X.

—the former being inhabitants of Egypt.[1] In referring to the Armenians, he rightly notes that they are continually harassed by the Saracens. Speaking of Islam, he traces its origin to the legend that when Sergius, a monk of the Benedictine Order, failed to obtain honours in Rome, he departed to Arabia and dictated al-Qur'ān (Alterianum) to Muhammad [2] (Magometus, Machometus) in A.D. 620. Ludolph then, in one of the rare medieval accounts of Islam, briefly describes the new religion.[3] He devotes one paragraph to the fall of Baghdad at the hands of the united forces of the King of Armenia and the Tatar Emperor.[4] In another, he speaks of the authority of Saracen 'bishops' or Qadis,[5] and concludes with a fictitious tale of Muhammad's death in Mekka (Mocha) and the accession of Abu-Bakr (Ebubekr) in whose reign Jerusalem was conquered by the Muslims and of 'Umar (Omardus) who destroyed the Temple in the Holy City.[6]

Beyond descriptions of the routes leading to the Holy Land, Ludolph says comparatively little about the crusade, for he evidently had in mind the pilgrim rather than the crusader. Nevertheless, we may note a few pertinent remarks on the subject of the crusade. He ascribes, for instance, the loss of 'Akka to the factious quarrels among Christians.[7] He gives a good description of the city of Alexandria, the scene of the crusade of 1365. 'Alexandria,' he says, 'is the first seaside city of Egypt, and one of the best of the Soldan's cities. On one side it stands on the Nile, the river of Paradise, which falls into the sea close by it, and its other side is on the sea. This city is exceeding beauteous and strong, and is fenced about with lofty towers and walls which seem impregnable. . . . In this city the Soldan keeps mercenary soldiers and his body-guard, who guard the city and the harbour. . . . The city appears to the human eye to be impregnable, and yet it could be easily taken.' [8] Ludolph's prevision was proved true a score of years after he had written his book.

Ludolph von Suchem's *Itinerary* to and *Description* of

[1] ib., 369–70.   [2] ib., 371–2.   [3] ib., 372–3.
[4] ib., 373.   [5] ib., 373–4.   [6] ib., 375–6.
[7] Stewart, 54–61.   [8] ib., 45–6.

the Holy Places appear to have been used by Pietro di Penna in the redaction of his *Libellus de Locis Ultramarinis*.[1] Little is known about Pietro's life, not even the date at which his *Libellus* was written. Some say he lived in the thirteenth and others in the fifteenth century; but the editor of the *Libellus* considers that Pietro must have lived and composed all his works in the fourteenth century.[2] He was a preaching friar probably in the Dominican monastery of the small Calabrian town of Penna. Judging by a list of his works,[3] his chief interest was in the Holy Land and in the confutation of the beliefs of the Muslims and Jews. Besides Ludolph's work, he seems to have been acquainted with and to have freely drawn upon Jacques de Vitry's *Historia Hierosolymitana*,[4] the anonymous *Histoire des Rois de Jérusalem*,[5] and the *Epitome Bellorum*.[6] His studies are far from original, and it is highly doubtful whether he had been to the Holy Land.

The *Libellus* consists of three distinct sections. He explains in the Prologue [7] the circumstances leading to the composition of this work. Having decided to perform a pilgrimage to the Holy Land, he says, he was stricken with sea-sickness on the way and detained at the 'island' of Myra.[8] There, he probably abandoned his original

---

[1] Ed. Ch. Kohler, in ROL, IX (1902), nos. 3–4, 313–83.

[2] Editor's Introduction, 313–28.

[3] ib. Besides the *Libellus*, he wrote:

(*a*) *Liber contra Judaeos.*

(*b*) *Tractatus contra Alchoranum.*

(*c*) *Tractatus de notitia Verbi Incarnati.*

(*d*) *Liber XXII Capitulis absolutus, vias docens quibus comprehendi potest Terra Sancta et videri quare deperdita fuerit et qualiter recuperari potest.*

For lists of MSS. of these works, see Kohler's Introduction to the *Libellus*.

[4] Ed. Bongars, in *Gesta Dei*, I.

[5] Ed. Ch. Kohler, in ROL, V (1897), 213–53.

[6] Ed. Canisius, in *Lectiones antiquae* (1st ed., 1601), VI, 251–93; also ed. Basnage (1725), IV, 426–46.

[7] Kohler, op. cit., 330–1.

[8] Modern Dembre, the ancient town of Lycia, situated a short distance inland between the rivers Myrus and Arcadus. Its fame began in the Christian era when St. Paul landed there in A.D. 61 and St. Nicholas of Patara became its bishop in the third century. Myra was made capital of Lycia in the reign of Theodosius II, and as such it was besieged in 808 by Caliph Harūn-al-Rashīd.

plan, that is, if the journey was begun at all. In the second place, he writes an abridged history of the Kingdom of Jerusalem from its foundation to the beginning of the thirteenth century (1208), preceded by a survey of the period prior to the Arab Conquest of the Holy City [1] in the seventh century. In the third place, he attempts a description of Syria, Palestine and some parts of Lower Egypt, with special reference to the places revered by Christians.[2] Here, Pietro's personal references [3] are scarce, and when made they are so confused and uncertain that the reader may rightly begin to entertain considerable doubt as to their authenticity. Whatever the real value of the *Libellus* as a source may be, the fact remains that it was intended as a work of propaganda for the crusade. The author introduced the Holy Land to the reader to the best of his abilities. Whether his pilgrimage was imaginary or real, he deliberately wrote to rouse the fervour of all good Christians to reconquer the heritage of Christ from its unbelieving masters.[4]

Pilgrimages from the Italian republics were abundant during the Later Middle Ages owing to their commercial relations with and peculiar privileges in the Levant. In addition to the numerous 'Italian' travellers treated in this and other chapters, two fourteenth-century pilgrims claim some attention—Lionardo di Niccolò Frescobaldi, and Niccolò di Marthono. Both have left written accounts of their travels.

Lionardo was a member of the ancient and noble family of the Frescobaldi in Florence. He was employed by the

---

[1] Kohler., 332 et seq.   [2] ib., 345–83.

[3] ib., 320–1, includes list of these passages. Kohler suggests that Pietro's sources for the description of the Holy Land included the *Enarratio locorum T. S.* of Eugesippus-Fretellus, the *De Situ Urbis Jerusalem*, the *Libellus de Locis Sanctis* of the 'pseudo-Theodoricus', and the travels of Philippus Savonerius and Johannes de Warzburg, and of Olivier the Scholastic (ed. Hoogeweg, 3–24), Burcard of Mount Sion (*vide supra*, Cap. V), Odoric of Pordenone (*vide infra*, Cap. X), and Ludolph von Suchem.

[4] *Libellus*, 331; '. . . et videlicet quilibet fidelis christianus et devotus hec audiens ad istius terre amorem accendatur et propter ipsius liberacionem animam et rem non formidet (applicare), quam nobis Pater in excelsis in hereditate dimisit, &c.'.

Republic in a number of high offices and diplomatic missions. In 1385 he was nominated Podesta of the Città del Castello (Bologna). In 1390 he was delegated by the Florentines to supervise the submission of Montepulciano which had capitulated to Florence. Finally, he became ambassador of the Republic at the Roman Curia in 1398 during the pontificate [1] of Boniface IX (1389–1404). Before the conferment of these honours and promotions upon him, desirous of performing a pious pilgrimage to the Holy Places, he left Florence on 10 August 1384 for Venice [2] where he joined a group of other pilgrims consisting of many Frenchmen and a few Venetians [3] and some of his own townsfolk. Hitherto, the normal route followed by pilgrims had been the sea route to Rhodes or Cyprus and thence direct to the Holy Places. Those who intended visiting Egypt travelled either by land across Sinai or sailed to one of the Egyptian coastal towns, especially Damietta, the nearest port to Syria, and made the return to the West by way of Alexandria. Frescobaldi undertook his journey in the reverse direction by sailing from Venice to Alexandria,[4] where he stayed at the Venetian 'funduq' (*fondaco*) of the Contarini. Here he met representatives of many Italian, French and Catalan cities [5] and of other Christian nations.[6] The pilgrims then hired a barge and sailed evidently by the canal connecting Alexandria with the Rosetta branch of the Nile and thence proceeded upstream to Cairo. In the capital, he noticed that there were few Latins and many Greeks, Nubians, Georgians, Ethiopians and Armenians.[7] Several features appear to have struck him as worthy of special note in Egypt—the prosperity of Alexandria as a trade

---

[1] Introduction to the *Viaggio di Lionardo di Niccolò Frescobaldi in Egitto e in Terra Santa*, ed. G. Manzi (Parma, 1845), ix. For MSS., ed. and trans., see Röhricht, *Bibl. Geogr.*, 91.

[2] Viaggio, 49.

[3] ib., 51; 'molti pellegrini Franceschi e alquanti Viniziani'.

[4] ib., 51 et seq.

[5] ib., 57–8.

[6] ib., 62; 'molte generazioni di Cristiani'.

[7] ib., 73; 'Christiani Latini, di questi ha pochi, Greci, Nubini, Georgiani, Tiopiani, Ermini'.

emporium,[1] the river traffic,[2] and the size of Cairo.[3] Yet, most of all, the manner in which the inhabitants of Egypt moved about town and country without carrying arms,[4] contrary to the Western practice, attracted his special attention and aroused his wonder. This state of internal security in Egypt contrasted favourably with the uncertainty of the roads in many countries of the West during this period. Frescobaldi's visit to Egypt ended with his sojourn in Cairo, for travel beyond that point was closed to foreigners who might penetrate the closely guarded secret route of the Indian trade through Upper Egypt. He then joined the caravan to Mount Sinai where he called at the Monastery of St. Catherine on the way to the Holy Places, and finally sailed back from Beirūt to Venice by way of Cyprus and Crete.[5]

Niccolò di Marthono belonged to a social grade different from that of Lionardo Frescobaldi. He was an obscure notary of the little Italian town of Carinola near Calvi in the Campagna. Having resolved to perform a pilgrimage to the Holy Places, he set sail from Gaeta on 17 June 1394. Except for his choice of Venice as his starting-point, he seems to have followed almost exactly the same route as Frescobaldi, landing at Alexandria, then travelling to Cairo, Mount Sinai and the Holy Land, and returning by way of Cyprus. His vocation was that of the pen and not of the sword. He was small of stature and inexperienced in affairs of war and in seafaring. Thus in his simple diary—*Liber Peregrinationis ad Loca Sancta*[6] —he speaks more of the perils of the sea and the road than of wild schemes for action against Egypt. In naïve style, he records his personal observations and tells the reader that he looked everywhere for the four-legged serpents in the waters of the Nile without avail. On the other hand,

---

[1] ib., 63.   [2] ib., 69.

[3] ib., 70. 'Il Cairo e Babilonia si è una grandissima città di lunghezza di miglia dieciotto o più, e larga circa a otto miglia.'

[4] ib., 73–4.   [5] ib., 133.

[6] Ed. L. le Grand, in ROL, 3e année (1895), no. 4, 566–669. See also C. Enlart, *Notes sur le voyage de Nicolas de Martoni en Chypre*, in ROL, 4e année (1896), no. 4, 423–32; Cobham, *Excerpta Cypria*, 22–8; Golubovich, V, 305–9; Röhricht, *Bibl. Geogr.*, 94.

he saw many of these in the desert, but they were very much smaller than he had been led to expect. On his return to his native town of Carinola, to his great grief, he found that his wife had died and that her death had been hastened by her growing fears and anxiety for his safety. On the whole, his diary contains no deliberate exhortation for the crusade. His pilgrimage was an act of pure devotion.[1]

English pilgrims, too, were quite numerous, although the written accounts of their journeys are meagre and compare rather badly with those by men of other nations during the period under review. One explanation may be that travel was a more usual matter in England whose medieval empire covered most of the British Isles and vast territories in France. Multitudes of Englishmen were continually crossing the sea either to Ireland, Flanders or Gascony in the same manner as the Italian merchants and mariners sailed to and fro across the Mediterranean in search of goods and markets; if we overlook the activities of the clergy and the limited class of secular explorers such as Marco Polo[2] and great theorists such as Marino Sanudo,[3] we can find very few written accounts of pilgrimages by the Italian sailors and business men who paid frequent visits to other countries. The same seems to apply to the English men of action. They devoted little time to the art of writing; and when they did so, their accounts were curt and business-like. A notable example of this may be found in Thomas Brigg's *Itinerarium in Terram Sanctam Domini Thomae de Swynburne.*[4] Little can be said about Brigg beyond the conjecture that he was either a squire or a chaplain attached to the train of Thomas Swinburne on his pilgrimage to the Holy Land.[5] Thomas

---

[1] *Liber*, 668, concludes with the following naïve verses which explain the author's sole motive:

> 'Finito scripto isto,
> Sit laus et gloria Christo,
> Qui scripsit hoc opus
> In paradiso reservetur locus.'

[2] *vide infra*, Cap. X.   [3] *vide supra*, Cap. VI.

[4] Ed. comte Riant, in AOL, II, Documents, 380–8; Röhricht, op. cit., 94.

[5] Riant, 378.

Swinburne,[1] on the other hand, was a personage of some importance in his time.   On 14 October 1390, Richard II appointed him Chastellain of Guisnes for two years as from 8 February 1391, though he actually remained in that office until 8 November 1393.[2]   While retaining his title of Chastellain of Guisnes, he received permission from the King to perform the pilgrimage in 1392.   After his return from the East, Swinburne became Mayor of Bordeaux on 8 March 1402,[3] then Chastellain of Fronsac on 1 March 1408.[4]   In the meantime, he appears also to have been one of the English ambassadors at Calais for the settlement of Flemish affairs [5] in 1404; and in the following year was entrusted with the admiralty of the English fleet at Bordeaux in addition to his mayoralty of the city.[6]

Swinburne, accompanied by Brigg, left Guisnes on 6 August 1392, arrived at Venice on 1 September, and sailed with a group of other pilgrims from Germany and Bohemia on the following day.[7]   They landed at Alexandria on 20 October, and after staying there for ten days sailed up the Nile on 29 October arriving at Cairo on 3 November.[8] In the Egyptian capital, he saw among other wonderful things Pharaoh's famous granaries (*granaria famosa*), that is, the pyramids of Giza, the elephants and the giraffes. He also visited the Coptic Church of Our Lady underneath whose altar was the cave where She and the Child Jesus

---

[1] ib., 380.   Thomas is believed to have been one of the early members of the family of the Swinburnes of whom the best known modern representative is the poet Algernon Charles Swinburne.

[2] French Rolls, 14 Ric. II, m. 8 and 15; 15 Ric. II, m. 10; and 17 Ric. II, m. 13; cf. Riant, op. cit., 379 and notes 8 and 9.

[3] Vascon Rolls, 6 Hen. IV, m. 5; cf. Riant, l.c., note 10.

[4] Vascon Rolls, 10 Hen. IV, m. 6; cf. Riant, l.c., note 11.

[5] F. C. Hingeston, *Roy. and Hist. Letters during the Reign of Henry IV* (Rolls Series, 1860), I, 230, 304, 314, 332, 348, 392; cf. Riant, l.c., note 12. It is interesting to note that among the ambassadors was one William de Lisle, an English knight 'de camera regis', who appears to have performed the pilgrimage to the Holy Places; Hingeston, I, 379 and French Rolls, 16 Ric. II, m. 8, cf. Riant, l.c., notes 15 and 16.

[6] Trokelowe, *Annales Henrici IV*, 415; cf. Riant, l.c., note 13.

[7] *Itin.*, 380.

[8] ib., 380–1.   The length of the journey is estimated by Brigg as 'quatuor dietas'.

took refuge in Old Cairo.[1]   The pilgrims then took the
road to Mount Sinai on 8 November and stayed at the
Monastery of St. Catherine from 19 to 22 of the same
month.   For the rest, the *Itinerarium* is but an enumeration of Holy Places and dates of arrivals and departures
on the road from Ghazza (Gaza) to Beirūt [2] with little new
material.   Finally, they sailed to the West by way of Rhodes
on 15 January 1393.   The work closes with an interesting account of the expenses of the journey including the
cost of passage by sea and travel by land, the prices of provisions, the custom duties and the interpreters' fees,[3] all
of which are worthy of special study.

In France, the most important record of late fourteenth-
century pilgrimages came from the pen of Ogier VIII
seigneur d'Anglure, who visited the Holy Land and Egypt
during the period of the Crusade of Nicopolis.   Widespread interest was displayed in his pilgrimage from an
early date and his work has been edited several times.[4]
Ogier's accurate statements and personal observations, in
spite of the failures and gaps in his diary, amply justify this
interest.   The dates and often the hours of his arrivals and
departures are given with precision.   The description of
Holy Places, towns and the manner of his peregrinations is
provided in simple, terse and realistic style.   It is a lamentable feature, however, that he overlooked matters which
evidently caused him no special concern such as the minor
expenses at the various stages of his journey.   Fortunately,
a number of Italian travellers and the English Thomas
Brigg gave sufficient attention to this aspect of medieval
travel.

Ogier VIII was descended from a minor noble family of

---

[1] *Itin.*, 381–2.

[2] ib., 383–6.   They reached Ghazza (Gaza) on 3 December, Hebron on
7, Bethlehem on 8, Jerusalem on 9 and left on 17 coming to Damascus on 25
and Beirūt on 3 January 1393 where had to wait for twelve days for a ship
bound for the West.   There is no indication of the route beyond Rhodes.

[3] ib., 387–8.

[4] First edition in 1621, 2nd in 1858, and 3rd in 1878 by F. Bonnardot and
A. Longnon under the title *Le Saint Voyage de Jhérusalem du Seigneur
d'Anglure* in the 'Société des anciens textes français', to which reference is
made in this study.   For MSS. and ed., see Röhricht, *Bibl. Geogr.*, 92–3.

crusaders and warriors, originally of the ancient house of Saint-Chéron (Sanctus Caraunus) in the village of Perthois.[1] Ogier de Saint-Chéron, first seigneur d'Anglure, took the Cross in 1190 in the company of comte Henri II de Champagne, afterwards King of Jerusalem, who went to the Holy Land with his uncles the Kings of France and England.[2]   This was the campaign intended for the recovery of the holy city from Ṣalaḥ-al-Dīn,[3] and Ogier stayed in the East for several years.   His successors participated in the wars of the French Kings.   Ogier VI fought at Poitiers (1356) and shared the captivity of Jean le Bon in England, and Ogier VII served in most of the wars of Charles VI and notably in the war against England in Flanders (1383).[4]   Ogier VIII, on the other hand, appears to have enjoyed a more peaceful career than his predecessors.   Born about 1360, he succeeded to the seigneurie d'Anglure on his father's death on 25 October 1383, and he himself died at an unknown date in the year 1412.[5] Before the end of his life, however, he resolved to perform a devout pilgrimage to the Holy Places.   He started, presumably with a number of other French pilgrims, from the Château d'Anglure on 16 July 1395.   He defines the object of the journey as a pilgrimage to the Holy Sepulchre in Jerusalem, to the Monastery of St. Catherine in Mount Sinai, and to the early hermitages of St. Anthony and St. Paul in the Egyptian desert.[6]

The course of the pilgrims' itinerary is interesting. From Anglure, they went to Châlons-sur-Saône, traversed

---

[1] East of Anglure in the Valley of the Blaise.   *Saint Voyage*, Introduction, xxx.

[2] D'Arbois de Jubainville, *Hist. des ducs et des comtes de Champagne*, IV, 568; cf. *Saint Voyage*, Introduction, xxxi note 2.

[3] It is interesting to note that from that time, the eldest son in the family of Ogier was named 'Saladin'.   An exception to this rule is, however, known in the person of Ogier VIII, the name of his second brother, Jean dit Saladin, instead of his own, continuing this proud tradition.   *Saint Voyage*, Introduction, xxxi, xliv, xlix.

[4] ib., xxix, xli–xliii.   [5] ib., xlv–li.

[6] ib., 1; 'pour aller ou saint voyage du Saint Sepulcre en la saincte cité de Jhérusalem, et pour aller à Saincte Katherine du monlt de Synaÿ ès désers d'Arrabe, ou gist la plus grant partie du corps de ladicte saincte Katherine, et pour aler à Saint Anthoine et Saint Pol, premier hermite ès désers d'Égipte'.

Burgundy, la Bresse and Savoy, and descended into the
plains of north Italy by the paths of Mont Cenis, evidently
on horseback as far as Pavia [1] which they reached on 31
July.   There they hired a barge and two days after their
arrival, they sailed down the River Po to Cremona, Ferrara
and Venice, completing this stage on 9 August.   Instead
of continuing the journey by sea without delay, they lingered
for about three weeks during which they visited the churches
of Venice and Padua.   On 29 August they set sail on board
a Venetian galley and journeyed along the eastern coast of
the Adriatic past the Venetian town of Pola,[2] then to the
island of Corfu, and the city of Modon [3] on the south coast
of the Morea, and finally came to Rhodes on 19 September
and saw the beauty of its capital and the fortifications of
the Knights Hospitallers.[4]   On the following day they
embarked direct for the Holy Land and anchored in the
waters of Beirūt on 28 September.[5]   A sojourn of about
three weeks in Syria and Palestine was sufficient for the
pilgrims to visit the Holy Places.   Little new material of
outstanding interest can be found in Ogier's account of
these visits.   He enumerates towns, churches and relics
with frequent reference to their Biblical associations.   He
also saw the tombs of Godefroy de Bouillon and of Baldwin
King of Jerusalem in a little chapel at the foot of Mount
Ascalon,[6] reminiscent of the early crusades and early
triumphs of Christians in the Holy Land.   In the valley of
the Jordan the travellers were domiciled in a special hostel
newly built by the Sultan for pilgrims and strangers.[7]
In the chapter on Jerusalem, Ogier betrays his hostility to
the vile Saracens who held the city.[8]   Finally, at Ghazza,

---

[1] *Saint Voyage*, 1–2.   Ogier refers to the sale of the pilgrims'
horses at Pavia—'Illec vendismes nos chevaulx et y sejournasmes deux
jours.'

[2] On the coast of the peninsula of Capodistria, the ancient Justinopolis.

[3] Another Venetian maritime colony.   The pilgrims were there on 16
September; *Saint Voyage*, 8.

[4] ib., 8–10.   [5] ib., 10.

[6] ib., 26.

[7] ib., 35–6, 39; 'ung hauberge que le Soudam y fait faire tout neuf pour
harberger les pèlerins et autres gens estranges'.

[8] ib., 40; 'Jhérusalem . . . ordement et vilment tenue des Sarrazins'.

the pilgrims decided to make their preparations [1] for the
desert journey to Mount Sinai on the way to Egypt.   They
left Ghazza on 24 October and arrived at the Monastery
of St. Catherine on 6 November.[2]   There were springs on
the route, but they could not camp anywhere near them
because 10,000 Saracen pilgrims returning from Mekka
were occupying the place and 60,000 more were to arrive.[3]
At a stone throw from the chapel of the monastery of St.
Catherine he noticed, probably to his horror, the existence
of a mosque which was frequented by Saracen pilgrims
travelling to Mekka by way of Mount Sinai.[4]

Ogier and his companions resumed their journey on 10
November and arrived at al-Matariya (Moiteria) in the
outskirts of Cairo on 20th, but they did not actually enter
the Egyptian capital until the 22nd of the same month.[5]
It is worthy of note that Ogier's account becomes much
more interesting outside the Holy Land.   He describes
Cairo as a large and marvellous city inhabited by Saracens,
and he reports the existence of 12,000 mosques and 40,000
'cabaretz' for the sale of cooked meat in the capital.   He
further mentions the beautiful fountains in all parts, the
strong and noble citadel, the spacious open squares, the
Sultan's six elephants and many other wonderful things.[6]
Of the ancient Coptic churches, he curiously has little to
tell us, and this little in a confused manner.   He speaks
of one church of St. Martin of the Armenians in 'Babiloine',
of other churches of St. Mary 'de la Bosve' and 'Nostre
Dame en la Coulmpne'.   He mentions a brother of the
King of Armenia who was Patriarch of the Jacobite
Christians (Yaccopites).[7]   He visits 'Pharaoh's granaries', [8]
and he finally sails up the Nile on 25 November on his way
to the nearest point of the caravan traffic to the ancient monasteries of St. Anthony and St. Paul.[9]   The extraordinary

---

[1] ib., 44.   The preparations included 'de biscuit, d'asnes, de harnois, de
chievres qui portent eaue, de paveillons'.

[2] ib., 44, 46.   [3] ib., 45.

[4] ib., 51; 'devant celledicte église, au get d'un pois, a un muscat de Sarrazins
. . . et ainsi font les autres Sarrazins qui oudit mont de Sinaÿ vont en
pèlerinage'.

[5] ib., 53, 56, 58.   [6] ib., 58–63.
[7] ib., 63–5.   [8] ib., 65–8.   [9] ib., 68.

value of this part of his work is that it proves definitely
that the rule of debarring foreigners from travelling anywhere beyond Cairo in Upper Egypt so as to preserve the
secrecy of the Indian trade route was not strictly observed in
the case of genuine and honest pilgrims.   The journey up
the Nile and across the Arabian desert lasted until 2 December.[1]   The unique fourteenth-century description of both
great Coptic abbeys is one of the highest interest, but it is
outside the scope of this study to enter upon a detailed analysis of it.   The first of these abbeys, he notes, was even more
beautiful than the monastery of St. Catherine.   Its inhabitants numbered a hundred monks—most holy, good-living,
charitable, benign and self-denying Christian Jacobites.
The pilgrims marched along the Red Sea to the Abbey of St.
Paul in that vicinity and found there sixty monks of the same
habit, rite and piety as the brotherhood of St. Anthony.[2]
After visiting the hermitages of the two Saints, the pilgrims
retraced their way to Cairo on 4 December.   Ogier remarks
that this road was not as safe as that leading to the monastery of St. Catherine's owing to the ferocity of the Bedouins
who attacked all strangers, and one Pierre de Morqueline,
a knight of Picardy, had to be taken aboard on the Nile
with an arrow wound which he had sustained in a scuffle with
these tribes.[3]   They reached 'Babiloine' on 8 December
and continued the river journey with a guard of six Genoese
merchants to Foa and Alexandria, where they arrived on
13th of the same month, while their belongings were carried
by the Sultan's camels overland.   Here they visited the
church of St. Mark, the patron of the Venetians.   This
city abounded in Christians of many 'nations'—French,
Venetian, Genoese, Castilian, Aragonese, Cypriot, Neapolitan, Cretan, Narbonnaise, and others from Ancona and
Marseilles [4]—who had 'funduqs' (*fondiques*) for merchants
and pilgrims.   Ogier's band was lodged in the Narbonnaise 'funduq'.   He was specially attracted by its spacious
gardens, the beauty of its gates and the strength of its
fortifications.[5]

---

[1] *Saint Voyage*, 69.
[2] ib., 70–4.
[3] ib., 74–5.
[4] ib., 78.
[5] ib., 78–9.

At last, the party sailed from Egypt on 21 and landed at Limassol in Cyprus on 26 December, and then travelled on horseback to the court of Nicosia where they enjoyed royal hospitality till 3 January 1396.[1] To their grief, however, the comte de Sarrebruck, Ogier's stepfather, fell ill and died at Nicosia where he was buried in the church of the Franciscans.[2] Sailing again from Limassol (22 January), they visited the islands of Castellorizzo [3] and Rhodes,[4] and called at Ragusa on the sea route to Venice [5] where they met Henri de Bar and Enguerrand de Coucy on their way to join the crusaders of Nicopolis at Buda.[6] In connexion with his return visit to the Republic of St. Mark, Ogier makes an important statement bearing upon the maritime services organized by the Venetians. Special sections of their fleet were equipped for sailings in various directions—five galleys for the Holy Land, three for Flanders, four for Constantinople; and eight guarded the Venetian waters as far as Modon.[7] The rest of the journey was undertaken overland to Padua, Vicenza, Verona, Milan, Lake Maggiore, the district of Lausanne, the County and Duchy of Burgundy, Champagne and finally to the Chateau d'Anglure. This stage lasted from 29 May to 22 June 1396.[8]

Ogier d'Anglure was only one of numerous pilgrims of noble origin who flocked to the Holy Land from many countries of Europe during the latter half of the fourteenth century. Others from France include three great crusaders—Jean II le Maingre, dit Boucicaut, Marshal of France, and the comtes d'Eu and de la Marche; while England is represented by Henry Bolingbroke and the Duke of Norfolk, and Italy by Thomas III Marquis of Saluces, Francesco Petrarca the poet, Giovanni Francesco

---

[1] ib., 79–84; Mas Latrie, *Hist. de Chypre*, II, 430–2; *Excerpta Cypria*, 28–9.

[2] ib., 84–8.

[3] ib., 89–90. Chastel Rouge or Château Roux known in the Arabic chronicles as Qashṭīl al-Rūj. *Vide infra*, 288 note 2.

[4] ib., 91–5.   [5] ib., 95–8.   [6] ib., 98; *Nicopolis*, 52–3.

[7] ib., 99. Ogier, 98, also speaks of the walled 'Archenal' in Venice, capable of holding ninety galleys, old and new, in dry docks.

[8] ib., 98–102.

lord of Mantona and Niccolò III Marquis of Este and lord of Modena, Reggio and Parma.[1] Among the representatives of Germany in this movement we may find many names of the highest nobility of the time including Count Rudolf von Sargans and Dukes Otto IV von Brandenburg-Landeshut and Stephan and Friedrich von Bayern; Duke Albrecht IV of Austria and Duke Wenzel of Pomerania were among the notable pilgrims from Central and Northern Europe.[2]

Numerous pilgrims from Eastern Europe, too, have left accounts of their journeys. These include Stephen of Novogorod[3] (circa 1350), Ignatius of Smolensk[4] (1389–1405), and the Archimandrite Grethenios of the Convent of the Holy Virgin in Moscow[5] (circa 1400).

No account of the pilgrimages of the age, however, can be complete without reference to the numerous anonymous pilgrims[6] of the century. Two tracts, probably dating from early in the fourteenth century and of unknown authorship have much in common without being identical—the Via ad Terram Sanctam, and the Memoria Terre Sancte.[7] Both deal with three main subjects which have direct bearing

---

[1] Lucy T. Smith, Expeditions to Prussia and the Holy Land by Henry Earl of Derby in 1390–91 and 1392–93 (Camden Society, 1894); El viaggio al santo Sepolcro . . . el qual fece . . . Niccolò da Este con altri gentiluomini suoi compagni, in Miscellanea di opusculi inediti et rari dei secoli XIV e XV, I, 106–64 (Turin, 1861); Riant, Pièces, in AOL, II (Documents), 237–49; Delaville Le Roulx, France, I, 160; Nicopolis, 36–7; N. Iorga, Thomas II Marquis de Saluces (Saint-Denis, 1893); Röhricht, Bibl. Geogr., 89–90, 94.

[2] R. Röhricht, Deutsche Pilgerreisen, 93–100.

[3] Mme B. de Khitrowo, Itinéraires russes en Orient, i, 116–25; cf. J. Martinov, Récit sur les lieux saints de Jérusalem, traduit d'un texte slavon, in AOL, II (Documents), 389–93.

[4] De Khitrowo., 129–57; Röhricht, Bibl. Geogr., 93–4.

[5] De Khitrowo, 167–91; Röhricht, op. cit., 102. Other Eastern European pilgrims in the fifteenth century are Friar Epiphanos (circa 1416), Deacon Zosimos (1419–21), a merchant named Basil (1465–66) and several others who went as far as Constantinople and Mount Athos. De Khitrowo, 195 et seq.

[6] vide infra, Appendix II.

[7] Ch. Kohler, Deux projets de croisade en Terre-Sainte, in ROL, X (1903–4), 406–57; Nicopolis, 23–4 and 168 notes 22–4, where a short analysis of the first projet is made from the Bodleian tract in the Ashmole MS. 342, ff. 1–6.

upon the project for crusade—the most suitable season
for an Eastern expedition, the best port for the landing
of the host of God on the other side of the Mediterranean,
and the most expeditious course for a campaign in Egypt
and the Holy Land.   The end of the summer is chosen
by the anonymous writers as the best season for the 'voyage'
beyond the sea for reasons similar to those already discussed in a previous chapter.[1]   Next, Alexandria, Damietta, 'Akka and Ṭarābulus in Mamlūk territory,
Lajazzo in Christian Armenia, and the ports of the Latin
Kingdom of Cyprus are all possible points for the disembarkation of troops.   On the other hand, it was held
that an attempt on Alexandria might be perilous, while
Damietta was in ruins and the harbours of 'Akka and
Ṭarābulus were insufficient for holding a fleet of considerable magnitude.   Cyprus was also regarded as un-
suitable, judging from the bitter experience of St. Louis,
King of France, and his lamentable failure in Egypt.
Lajazzo seemed, therefore, to be the most hopeful base
from which the crusaders might proceed in a southerly
direction towards Jerusalem by way of Antioch and
Damascus.   Then a description of the route from Ghazza
to Cairo is detailed in view of an invasion of Egypt after
the recovery of Jerusalem.   A third example of anonymous pilgrimages is left by a Frenchman [2] who travelled
to the Holy Land in 1383.   Like the other two, his
is a short memoir; and unlike them, it contains little
propagandist material for the crusade.   The slight interest
offered by this journal is limited to the series of dates [3]
of arrivals and departures, nevertheless incomplete, and
to the details of the custom duties and tolls exacted from
the pilgrim at the Holy Places.[4]   These details of expenses,

[1] *vide* Cap. VII, Philippe de Mézières, *Songe du Vieil Pèlerin.*

[2] Ed. H. Omont, in ROL, 3ᵉ année (1895), no. 3, 457–9.

[3] ib., 457.   These are: Beirūt on 18 February 1383, Damascus on 23,
Ṭabariya (Tiberius) on 26, Nazareth and district on 27, Jenina on 28, and
Sebastiya (the ancient Samaria) and Nablus on 1 March 1383.   After this
the record stops, as the pilgrim was probably in great haste to reach Jerusalem.

[4] ib., 457–9.   The author grumbles at some forced payments, for instance
(457), at Jenina he says,—'et si me fist on paier par force ix. derans, je
ne sçay pour quoy'.

together with those furnished by Thomas Brigg, deserve the attention of the medieval economist and the historian of commerce in the Levant during the Later Middle Ages.

Fourteenth-century pilgrims, high and low, returned to their homes with the cherished memories of the great heritage of Christ. They imparted their aspirations for a recovery of the Holy Land to their neighbours and fellow-countrymen either in their memoirs or by word of mouth. It is difficult to exaggerate the effect of their propaganda in an age of faith. Their labours were not undertaken in vain. The numerous crusading expeditions against Turkey and Egypt, though mainly resulting in ephemeral successes, were the outcome of the strenuous efforts exerted by propagandists for a cause which was ultimately rendered abortive by factors and circumstances beyond the control of zealous individuals. Europe was becoming engrossed in its own religious, social and political troubles, and the prospect of a universal crusade in the earlier sense of the term became more and more remote every day. This new orientation in the politics of Latin Christendom, as will be amply illustrated in the following chapter, was intensified during the fifteenth century when the crusade became a memory—a ghost of the past.

CHAPTER IX

PILGRIMS AND PROPAGANDISTS IN THE FIFTEENTH CENTURY

New Orientation in fifteenth-century propaganda. Court of Burgundy: Ghillebert de Lannoy, Bertrandon de la Broquière and Jean Germain. Emanuele Piloti and Pope Eugenius IV. Independent pilgrims: Pero Tafur, William Wey and Felix Faber. Pius II and the Crusade after the Fall of Constantinople

PROPAGANDIST literature reached its high-water mark during the fourteenth century. Of enormous bulk, it was generally characterized by a marked sense of devotion and genuine enthusiasm for the salvation of the Holy Land. It would, however, be a grave error to contend that all fourteenth-century pilgrims, travellers and propagandists were entirely free from those extraneous motives of the love of travel and adventure, the quest of trade and material gain, and the work of diplomatic and military reconnaissance in the East, which prevailed during a later period. The occasional deprecation of pilgrimages on the ground of resultant waste of money in lands subject to the Saracens, the opposition of the Italian merchants to a cause which they considered as ruinous to their Oriental markets, and the growing influence of missionary activities as a peaceful substitute for armed expeditions into Muhammadan countries—all these were factors existing long before the beginning of the fifteenth century. Many thinkers of the fourteenth century, moreover, looked upon projects for crusade with open disfavour. Gower,[1] in the *Confessio Amantis*, rejects the idea of killing a Saracen as contrary to the teaching of Christ; for

> A Sarazin if I sle schal
> I sle the Soule forth withal,
> And that was never Christe's lore.

---

[1] Gower's Works (ed. Macaulay), vol. II, *Confessio Amantis*, Lib. IV, ii. 1674–81, 346; cf. *Nicopolis*, 122 and 199 note 14.

Langland, too, holds a similar view and speaks benignly of Muslims whose religion is not wholly unlike Christianity. Their greatest sin is that they were misled by the Prophet Muhammad who became an apostate and established a new sect on his failure to be elected pope.[1]   Honoré Bonet, though admitting the right of the Pope to preach the crusade, argues that war against unbelievers is unjust for two reasons.   In the first place, God has given them their blessings and 'why should Christians take these from them?'   In the second place the Scriptures explicitly ordain that Holy Baptism should not be enforced upon unbelievers, 'but we must leave them in their free will that God has given them'.[2]   The greatest of the fourteenth-century anti-crusaders was John Wyclif, who opposed wars of conquest in general as mere acts of brigandage and robbery.   A 'croyserie' raised by one section of God's 'Heerde' to kill another is the 'lore of Antichrist', and a papal bull which grants indulgences for the crusade makes no martyrs of those who fall in battle, for the Pope himself is 'Antichrist, that by ypocrisie reversis Jesus Christ in his false lyvying'.[3]   If the arguments of Gower, Langland,

---

[1] *Piers Plowman* (ed. Skeat), Text B, Passus XV, lines 386 et seq.; cf. *Nicopolis*, 122 and 199 notes 15–17.   Langland tells the popular medieval legend of Muhammad and the Dove, also to be found in Vincent of Beauvais' *Speculum historiale*, Lib. XXIII, cap. 40.   The Prophet is said to have trained a dove to pick corn from his ear and informed his congregation that he thus received a message from Heaven.   Reference to medieval accounts of Muhammadanism has continually been made in the preceding chapters.   Other accounts may be found in the following works: *Roman de Mahomet* (en vers du XIIIe s.) par Alexandre Du Pont, et *Livre de la loi au Sarrazin* (en prose du XIVe s.), ed. Reinaud & Michel (Paris, 1831); *Romancero de Champagne*, ed. Tarbé (Reims, 1863), T. III, Pt. 3, 'Chants légendaires et historiques' (420–1550); *Roman de Renart Contrefait* by Le Clerc de Troyes (Reims, 1851) in Tarbé's *Proverbes champenois avant le XVIe s.*; Robert, *Fables inédites des XIIe–XIVe s.* (Paris, 1825), I, cxlv; Le Roulx de Lincy, *Livre des légendes* (Paris, 1836), I, 52–3; Dante (Cary's trans., London, 1884), Hell, 142–3.   For a special study of this subject, see A. d'Ancona, *Leggenda di Maometto in Occidente*, in *Giorn. stor. della litterat. ital.*, XIII (1890), 199–281; and E. Doutté, *Mahomet Cardinal* (Châlons-sur-Marne, 1899).

[2] *Arbre des batailles* (*circa* 1387), cf. *Nicopolis*, 123 and 199 note 18.

[3] *Tracts and Treatises of John de Wycliffe* (ed. R. Vaughan), 70 and 74; *Select English Works of John Wyclif*, ed. T. Arnold, I, 367 and III, 140-1; cf. *Nicopolis*, 123–4 and 199–200 notes 19–21.

Bonet and Wyclif were symptoms of an impending change in the crusading outlook, European thought was drifting fast from the original conception of the crusade. The Hildebrandine system of the Popes had ceased for ever to be a reality and the Great Schism had shaken the foundations of the authority of the medieval Church, while the spirit of the new 'national royalism' was becoming more and more incapable of realizing the old idea of universal action which was the basis of any effective crusade. Devoted pilgrims, indeed, continued to go to the Holy Land in considerable numbers during the fifteenth century; but these included some who were merely diplomatic envoys sent to inquire into the causes which had rendered the Saracens so formidable a menace to Christendom. This is the new orientation in the history of the crusades. The war with Muhammadans was no more a purely Asiatic affair. The Turkish advance in Europe had changed the battleground between East and West, and the crusade became a defensive rather than an offensive war. The battle of Nicopolis in 1396 may justly be regarded as the end of one chapter and the beginning of another in the history of the crusade and propaganda therefor in the West. It was not merely a defeat of Sigismund and the European contingents who came to his help, but also a humiliation of the strong house of Burgundy, not to be forgotten by their Dukes for several decades. It sealed the fate of the Empire of Constantinople, although its final extinction was postponed until 1453. It confirmed the settlement of the Ottomans in Europe and opened the road for their advance at a later date to Buda and Vienna. Europe was therefore in no small danger; and projects, diplomatic and otherwise, to save the rest of Christendom from falling a prey to the Turk were continually formulated at the Burgundian court and the papal curia.

The leading propagandists of the early fifteenth century came from Burgundy, whose dukes ruled over some of the richest provinces in Europe. So great was the reputation of the Burgundian court for wealth and power, that envoys from the distressed territories passed by royal and imperial courts on their way to the Duke as the leading prince in the West. To him appeal might be made for effective help. The anachronistic tendency of the Dukes to look back rather than forward appears to have been accentuated in the person of Charles le Téméraire, who, in other days, might have made a magnificent leader of the crusade. The interest of the Burgundian Dukes in plans for crusade remained unabated until they became deeply involved in their struggle with that enemy of the old order, Louis XI. The reign of Philippe le Bon [1] saw the last ducal attempt to revive the crusade. It was chiefly due to his influence and at his expense that Ghillebert de Lannoy and Bertrandon de la Brocquière were dispatched to gauge the strength and weakness of the Muslim invader; and both left extensive accounts of their reconnaissance in the land beyond the sea.

Messire Ghillebert de Lannoy, seigneur de Santes, de Villerval, de Tronchiennes, de Beaumont et de Wahégnies, traveller, diplomat and moralist, was born in 1386 of a noble family.[2] At the early age of thirteen (1399), he participated in the futile expedition of the comte de Saint-Pol to England against Henry of Lancaster and in favour of Richard II. As esquire to the Seneschal of Hainault, Jean de Warchin,[3] he followed his master on his first pilgrimage to the Holy Places in 1401. The pilgrims started in April, sailed from Genoa [4] to Palestine, visited the Monastery of St. Catherine in Mount Sinai, and in Cairo met the Coptic Patriarch of the Orthodox Church of Alexandria.[5] Among other countries they visited the

[1] I. D. Hintzen, *Kruistochplannen van Philips den Goede* (Rotterdam, 1918); G. Doutrepont, *Épitre à la maison de Bourgogne sur la croisade turque projetée par Philippe le Bon* (1464), in *Analectes pour servir à l'histoire ecclésiastique de la Belgique*, XXXVI (1906).

[2] *Œuvres de Ghillebert de Lannoy, Voyageur, Diplomate et Moraliste*, ed. by Ch. Potvin with notes and map by J. C. Houzeau, Louvain, 1878; for life of Lannoy, see introduction, xi–xxxiii.

For an English translation of the *Travels and Embassies* see *Archælogia* (1821), XX, 381–444.

[3] Potvin, op. cit., Introduction, xii.

[4] ib., 11.

[5] ib. 'Fusmes aussy au Kaire et en Babilonne où nous véismes le patriarche d'Inde.'

Empire of Constantinople, Rhodes, Cyprus and Turkey. The whole journey lasted two years.[1]

Lannoy's account of his first pilgrimage is very short and provides no new materials. It appears, however, to have left an indelible impression on his youthful imagination, for, in his mature age, he always cherished the idea of undertaking another pilgrimage. In 1420 an opportunity presented itself to him for the realization of his ambition. At the request of the Kings of England and France and of Philippe le Bon as principal patron,[2] Lannoy embarked on his second journey to the East in the following year. The result of this political pilgrimage is embodied in his *Voyages et ambassades*, the text of which may conveniently be considered in three sections. The first[3] traces the journey by land and sea to the Holy Land. Here Ghillebert says that, eight in number,[4] the party proceeded on 4 May 1421 overland across Germany, Prussia, Poland and Russia to the Genoese colony of Caffa on the coast of the Crimea. Thence they sailed to Constantinople where they were received by the Emperor Manuel and his son, to whom they presented the gifts of the King of England and letters conveying news of the establishment of peace between England and France.[5] Lannoy urged the union of the Eastern Churches with Rome, for which purpose he joined the ambassadors of the Pope who had arrived at the imperial court before him.[6] The pilgrims then sailed to Rhodes, Candia in Crete, and finally to Alexan-

---

[1] ib., 11–12.

[2] ib., 51. 'Ce temps pendant, emprins le voyaige de Jhérusalem par terre, à la requeste du roy d'Angleterre et du roy de France et de monseigneur le duc Phillippe, principal esmouveur'.

[3] ib., 51–71.

[4] ib., 51–2. 'L'an mille quatre cens vingt et ung, le quatrième jour de may, me party de l'Escluse, moy huitième, c'est à sçavoir: moy, le Gallois Dubois, Colart le bastard de Marquette, le bastard de Lannoy, Jehan de la Roe, Aggregy de Hem, le roy d'armes d'Arthois et Copin de Poucque.'

[5] ib., 65. 'Ouquel lieu de Constantinoble je trouvay le viel empereur Manuel et le jeune empereur son filz, auxquelz empereurs présentay les joyaux du roy de Angleterre, enssamble les lettres de la paix de France et d'Angleterre.'

[6] ib., 65; 'de avanchier l'union d'entre les esglises Rommaines et Grégeoises, . . . avecq les ambaxadeurs du Pape, qui lors y estoient pour ceste cause'.

dria.[1]   The journey was resumed by land to Rosetta and
by the Nile to Cairo, where he visited the Coptic Patriarch,
who presented him, as ambassador of the King of France,
with a phial of sacred balm.[2]   In Cairo Lannoy purchased
the necessary provisions and hired camels and donkeys for
the seven days' journey to the Monastery of St. Catherine.[3]
Instead of going to the Holy Land, he returned to Cairo
and sailed up the Nile for two days to the Church of St.
George, whence he crossed the Arabian desert to the
Monasteries of St. Anthony and St. Paul.[4]   Afterwards,
he sailed downstream to Damietta, passed by sea to the Holy
Land and finally returned to Venice by way of Rhodes.[5]

The second [6] part of his work consists of a bare enumeration of holy places and relics and of the traditions and
legends associated with them.   The third [7] and most important part embodies, for the benefit of crusaders, the result
of Lannoy's reconnaissance in Egypt and Syria.   It begins
with a lengthy description of his visit to Alexandria and its
two harbours, the old and the new.   Even on a clear day,
this city could be seen from the sea at a distance of only
twenty to twenty-five miles owing to its construction on a low
and flat plain.   Within the walls, two towers stood on
prominent heights—the one commanding the city itself
with its two harbours and the other the road to Cairo.[8]
The new harbour was open to Christian sea-craft, while
the old was exclusively reserved for the use of Muslims.

---

[1] Potvin, 67–8.

[2] ib., 68; 'et fus devers le patriarche d'Inde, lequel me présenta, comme
ambaxadeur du roy de France, une fyole de fin balme, de la vigne où il croist,
dont il est en partie seigneur'.

[3] ib., 68–9.

[4] ib., 69–70; '. . . remontey sur cameulx et m'en alay à Saint-Anthoine des
désers, où il y a deux journées de chemin, qui sont cinq journées du Kaire.
Saint-Anthoine est une abbaye de moines jacobitains, cristians circoncis, dont
il y a cincquante.   Et est chastel situé sur une fontaine saillant d'une roche,
et y a beau gardin de palmes et plusieurs autres arbres et fruis . . . et alay à
Saint-Pol des désers, le premier hermite, qui est situé en lieu bas entre mon-
taignes sur une fontaine saillant de roche, et est le chastel fort et abbaye de
jacobitains, subgectz à ceulz de Saint-Anthoine, et y a ung gardin de
palmiers.'

[5] ib., 71.

[6] ib., 73–97.

[7] ib., 99–162.

[8] ib., 100.

It was by way of the latter, however, that the fleet of
Pierre I de Lusignan had steered its way towards the
city walls sixty years before Lannoy's [1] visit. Harbours,
walls, gates, garrisons, gardens, houses and streets—on
all those he writes in his description of Alexandria. He
records the existence of numerous Christian merchants in
the city, especially Venetians, Genoese and Catalans with
their large and beautiful funduqs in which they were in-
terned every night at sunset and on Fridays for two or
three hours at midday during the Muslim prayer-time.[2]
There are also dormitories for the merchants of Ancona,
Naples, Marseilles, Palermo and Constantinople; but these
are now empty.[3] The author then gives a brief description of Rosetta and of the course of the Nile to Cairo.[4]
Of the capital of Egypt, he says that it is a great town
full of people and merchants from all parts of the world.[5]
On the mountain at the outskirts of the town stands a
large and strong citadel which is the Sultan's residence.
The town walls, though complete, are apt to pass unnoticed
owing to the overflow of houses to the districts on the
outer side of them.[6]

The next chapter of the *Voyages* is one of unusual importance, as here Lannoy analyses the condition of the

---

[1] ib., 101–2. 'Item, dedens le viel port, n'ose entrer nulle navire de
Cristiens, ne nul Cristiens, par dedens la ville, ne par dehors, ne l'ose ap-
prouchier depuis environ soixante ans, qui fut l'an vingt et deux, ouquel an le
roy Pierre de Cyppre la print par ce lieu là, pourquoy on peut ymaginer que
ce lieu là est le plus avantaigieux.' He describes the old harbour by report
and not by observation as shallow and unfit for large vessels. This also
explains the use of the 'taforesse' in Pierre I's crusade. Cf. Cap. XV.

[2] ib., 109–10. 'Item y a pluisieurs marchans Cristiens dedans la ville qui
là demeurent, en espécial Vénissiens, Gênenois et Catelans, qui y ont leurs
fontêques, comme maisons grandes et belles, et les enferme on là dedens et
tous les Cristiens, chascune nuyt de haulte heure, et, les matins, les laissent
les Sarrasins dehors de bonne heure, et pareillement sont enferméz tous les
vendredis de l'an, deux ou trois heures le jour, c'est à sçavoir à midy quant ils
font leur grant oroison.'

[3] ib., 110. 'Et y a autres couchiers d'Ancône, de Naples, de Marseille, de
Palermes et de Constantinoble, mais à présent n'y a nulz marchans.'

[4] ib., 110–13.

[5] ib., 114. 'Elle est moult plaine de poeuple et très marchande. Et y a
marchans de Inde et de toutes les parties du monde.'

[6] ib., 114–15.

Egyptian state, the Sultan's power, and the system of
recruitment for the Mamlūk army.[1]   As a European who
had been accustomed to fifteenth-century factions in France
and Burgundy and who had participated in the wars between Burgundians and Armagnacs, Lannoy seems to
have been at once overcome with wonder at the centrali-
zation of all power in Egypt and Syria in the hands of the
Sultan, the one supreme ruler of both countries.   The
chapter opens thus: 'It is to be understood that in all
the lands of Egypt, of Syria and of "Sayette",[2] commonly
there is but one lord, that is to say a Sultan of Babylon
who dominates[3] all.'   This monarch is not elected from
the ranks of the natives who are too feeble to guard the
country.   He is always a Mamlūk amīr who, by his common sense, wisdom and good governance, has advanced
himself and acquired power and supporters.[4]   Nevertheless,
it often happens that in his lifetime, a strong Sultan
aims at the establishment of dynastic hereditary rights by
forcing his son upon the amīrs as rightful successor to the
throne.   This is a serious danger to the strength of Egypt,
for it is then that factions are fostered by aspiring amīrs
who covet the sultanate for themselves.   After their
master's death, these aspirants often seize the new youthful
head of the Mamlūk state, imprison him and finally put
an end to his life by means of strangling or poison in
secret.[5]   During Lannoy's sojourn in Syria, he witnessed
the accession of as many as five of these rulers.

[1] Potvin, 117 et seq. 'Cy s'ensieuvent les conditions et natures des Soudans
de Babilonne, de leurs admiraulz et esclaves et des Sarrasins d'Égipte; de
la nature des païs de Égipte et de Surie.'

[2] 'Sayette' may be interpreted as 'Ṣaʿīd', i.e. Upper Egypt, thus reserving
the use of the word 'Egypt' for Lower Egypt or the Delta where foreigners
were allowed to travel, whereas Upper Egypt was closed to them in view
of the Indian trade route whose secret the Egyptians preserved exclusively
for themselves.

[3] Œuvres de Lannoy, 117.   'Il est à sçavoir que en tout le païs d'Égipte, de
Surie et de Sayette, communement il n'y a que ung seigneur, c'est à sçavoir
ung soudan de Babilonne qui domine sur tout.'

[4] ib.; 'admiral esclave qui, par le sens, vaillance et grant gouvernement de
lui, se sçaura tellement advanchier qu'il aura acquis puissance et amis. . . .'

[5] ib., 118; 'sy advient il trop peu souvent que icelui filz puist, après le
soudan, venir à la seignourie, ainchois est prins et mis en prison perpétuelle ou

The military forces of the Sultan stationed in Cairo are approximately ten thousand Mamlūk horsemen (*esclaves*) who serve as his permanent bodyguard. These start their career as slaves recruited from foreign nations such as the Tatars, Turks, Bulgarians, Hungarians, Slavonians, Wallachians, Russians and Greeks, without discrimination as between Christian and non-Christian races.[1] These Mamlūks are ranked as amīrs of ten lances, of twenty, of fifty and of a hundred, and may advance in this scale to the amīrate of Jerusalem, Damascus, Cairo and other state offices. The sultan provides them with women, horses and robes as well as a good military education and promotion in return for their services to him in time of war. When marching to battle, the Mamlūks are always mounted; and their equipment includes breast-plates covered with silk, small helmets, bows and arrows, swords, maces and drums. The beating of the drum serves the double purpose of calling men to their post and of scaring the enemy's horse.[2] Though slaves, the Mamlūks enjoy many privileges denied to the natives of the land who are debarred from military service and are confined to the menial labour of the soil.[3] These latter are without arms. The Arabs living in the Egyptian desert are, on the other hand, a source of mischief to the state and often wage war with its rulers.[4] Finally, he refers to the Copts who are scattered in large numbers in Egyptian towns up and down the country.[5]

estranglé couvertement ou empoisonné par aucun d'iceulz admiraulz. Et est icelle seignourie très périlleuse et très muable.'

[1] ib. 'Et est à sçavoir que iceulz esclaves sont d'estranges nacions comme de Tartarie, de Turquie, de Bourguerie, de Honguerie, d'Esclavonnie, de Wallasquie, de Russie et de Grèce, tant de païs cristiens comme d'autres.'

[2] ib., 119–20. 'Item, quant iceulz esclaves vont en guerre, ils sont tousjours de cheval, armez seullement de cuirasses meschantes, couvertes de soye, et une ronde petite huvette en la teste, et chascun l'arcq et les flesches, l'espée, la mache et le tambour pour eulz rassambler comme trompettes, et aussy quant ilz voient leurs ennemis en bataille, ilz sonnent tous à une fois iceulz tambours pour espoventer les chevaulz d'iceulz.'

[3] ib., 119.   [4] ib., 120.

[5] ib., 121. 'Item, est à sçavoir qu'en tout le païs d'Égipte, en bonnes villes ou aux champs, il y a grant quantité de Cristiens desquelz fay peu de mencion pour ce que peu de prouffit pourroient faire aux Cristiens servans à la matière.'

Lannoy then points out that the natives of Syria and especially the nomadic Turkmens in the north do not suffer the same hard lot as the Egyptians. They possess horses and arms for their own defence and are skilled in the art of war.[1] The author, reverting to Egypt, gives a lengthy description of the Nile with its periodic inundation,[2] and ends his account with the interesting remark that 'Prester John' who lives in the uplands of the source of the river refrains from the diversion of its course from Egypt only for the sake of the large number of Christians who still inhabit that country.[3] Hence, the Sultan never allows Christians to pass to India by way of the Red Sea or the Nile for fear that they may persuade 'Prester John,' who is frequently at war with him, to deflect the river from Egypt or commit any other mischievous acts.[4]

After an account of other Egyptian towns and of Lake Manzalah, Lannoy begins his report on Syria with Jaffa, once a prosperous and fortified town, but now poor and dilapidated. It has, however, retained something of its former importance owing to the influx of Christian pilgrims to it as the nearest coastal town to Jerusalem. It lies on a naturally fortified site on a high mountain.[5] On the road from Jaffa to Jerusalem, the traveller passes by Ramleh (Rames), a strong town of some size with orchards of fruit trees.[6] Jerusalem itself is not invulnerable. Its walls are low and there are only two small castles—one inside and the other outside the walls—for purposes of defence. The surrounding country is mountainous, poor and lacking in water.[7] An account of the coastal towns of 'Akka,[8] Ṣūr[9] and Beirūt[10] is given, and the inland city

---

[1] Potvin, 121–5.   [2] ib., 125–30.

[3] ib., 130; 'mais le prestre Jehan bien le feroit et lui donneroit autre cours, s'il vouloit, mais il le laisse pour la grant quantité des Cristiens qui habitent en Égipte, lesquelz pour sa cause morroient de faim'.

[4] ib. 'Item, est à sçavoir que le Soudan ne laisse nul Cristien passer en Inde par la mer rouge, ne par la rivière du Nyl, vers le prestre Jehan, pour la paour . . . que ceste rivière lui soit ostée, ou autre chose à lui contraire, car les Cristiens et le prestre Jehan de par delà lui font souvent guerre.'

[5] ib., 139–40.   [6] ib., 141.

[7] ib., 141–3.   [8] ib., 144–7.   [9] ib., 147–51.

[10] ib., 155–8.

f Damascus ¹ is briefly described.   The report concludes
ith the description of Gallipoli,² the key town which links
he European and Asiatic possessions of the Turks.   Lan-
oy remarks that he who possesses the castle and harbour
f Gallipoli can intercept the passage of the Turks from the
ne continent to the other and so cut them off from hopes
f conquest in Greece.³   Lannoy returned to the West
n the year 1423, and travelled to London to report to the
oung Henry VI (1422–61) and to the King's Council.⁴

The other important fifteenth-century embassy sent to
he East by Philippe le Bon was that of Bertrandon de
a Broquière, the Duke's first esquire, counsellor and
hamberlain.   Throughout his career, he seems to have
istinguished himself as the trusted ambassador of Philippe
n many occasions notably at the courts of France and
England.⁵   At the end of the year 1432, he was selected
y the Duke for a 'certain long and secret voyage' which
as been identified as his Eastern embassy.⁶   The purpose

¹ ib., 158–9.   ² ib., 160–1.
³ ib., 161.   'Et qui auroit ledit chastel et port, les Turcs n'auroient nul
cëur passaige plus de l'un à l'autre et seroit leurs pays qu'ilz ont en Grèce
omme perdu et deffect.'
⁴ ib., 161–2.   Lannoy also returned to the King a golden clock 'que je
levoie présenter de par le dit roy son père, au grant Turcq'.   He does not
xplain why the clock was not presented to the Sultan.   Henry VI granted
im 300 nobles and his expenses.
   In Burgundy, Lannoy was later created a knight of the Order of the Golden
Fleece as stated in his own memoirs, 166—'L'an vingt et neuf, publia mon-
eigneur le duc Philippe de Bourgongne son ordre de la thoison, où il me fist
honneur de moy eslire l'un des vingt et cincq.'
⁵ For details of Bertrandon's European embassies, see Ch. Schefer's intro-
luction to the edition of *Le Voyage d'Outremer de Bertrandon de la Broquière*,
n *Recueil de voyages et de documents pour servir à l'histoire de la géographie de-*
uis le XIIIe jusqu'à la fin du XVIe siècle, XII (Paris, 1892), xvi et seq.   An
English version of La Broquière's work appears in Th. Wright's *Early Travels
in Palestine* (London, 1848).   See also Röhricht, *Bibl. Geogr. Palaest.*
108.
⁶ Schefer, op. cit., introduction, xvii, quotes the *Compte de Jehan Abonnel
du 1ᵉʳ janvier au 31 décembre* 1432, fo. 50: 'à Bertrandon de la Broquière,
premier escuier tranchant de monseigneur, la somme de deux cens livres du
prix de XL gros, monnoie de Flandres la livre, laquelle icelluy seigneur luy a
donnée de grâce espéciale pour luy aidier à soy habillier et aller plus honneste-
ment en certain lointain voyaige secret auquel il le envoie de présent, comme il
appert par mandement de mondit seigneur'.

of la Broquière's book is clearly put forward at the outse
of the first chapter, 'to induce and attract the hearts o
noble men who wish to see the world' [1] and to furnish th
necessary knowledge of the land beyond the sea for th
benefit of 'any Christian king or prince willing to under
take the conquest of Jerusalem and to lead a large arm
thereto by land'.[2] To accomplish this task, he travelle
overland to Venice and then sailed on 8 May 1433 by on
of two Venetian galleys carrying pilgrims to the Hol
Land.[3] Touching at the ports of Parenzo, Pola (Polle)
Zara (Jarre), Sebenico (Sebenich) and Modon (Moudon
as well as the islands of Corfu, Rhodes and Cyprus
Bertrandon finally landed at Jaffa.[4] Thence he proceede
like Lannoy by the normal pilgrim route direct to Jerusalem
by way of Ramleh (Rames). Inside the Church of th
Resurrection he meets Abyssinians, Armenians and Jacob
ites; and notes that of all the Christians in the Holy Land
the Franks are the object of the worst oppression.[5]

Bertrandon and nine others then pay a hurried visit to
the Monastery of St. Catherine and return to Jerusalem
without going further into Egypt, so that there is n
parallel in his work to the excellent report which Lannoy
submitted to Duke Philippe on the state of that country.
La Broquière's mission, indeed, seems to have been confined
to Muslim territories in the Near East other than Egypt;
and this he executed with an observant eye. He gives a
full description of Jaffa, 'Akka, Ṣūr, Beirūt, Damascus and
Aleppo, and he describes the land routes which connect

[1] Schefer, op. cit., 1. 'Pour induyre et attraire les cueurs des nobles
hommes qui désirent véoir du monde, par commandement et ordonnance de
trèshault, . . . Philippe, &c.'.

[2] ib., 2; 'affin que si aucun roy ou prince crestien voulloit entreprendre la
conqueste de Ihérusalem et y mener grosse armée par terre, ou aulcun noble
homme y voulsist aller ou revenir, qu'il peust sçavoir les villes, cités, &c.'.

[3] ib., 4–5. On the way to Venice, la Broquière digressed from the direct
route and visited Pope Eugenius IV in Rome which he left on 25 March.

[4] ib., 7–9.

[5] ib., 12. 'Et dedans l'esglise dudict Sainct Sepulcre a aussi bien d'autres
manières de Crestiens comme Abeçins qui sont de la terre du prestre Jehan,
Jaccobites, Herménins et Crestiens de la saincture. Et de tous ceulx cy les
Francz sont plus subjectz que nulz des autres.'

[6] ib., 14–25.

the Syrian cities.   Damascus in particular strikes him as
an exceptionally wealthy and populous town, second to
none but Cairo in the Sultan's realm.[1]   He records the
existence there of numerous Christian merchants; and as
is the case in such Egyptian towns as Cairo and Alexandria
these Christians are locked up at sunset and allowed to
re-open their warehouses only after sunrise.[2]   Among
the French merchants of Damascus, he meets the merchant
adventurer Jacques Cœur, not yet of 'grant autorité' in
France.[3]   He also sees a Genoese merchant called 'Gentil
Emperial' who, he is told, is commissioned by the Sultan
to undertake the purchase of slaves from Caffa for the
reinforcement of the Mamlūk army[4]—a degrading trade
which the Italian merchants and especially the Genoese
practice, notwithstanding the papal appeals and bulls
prohibiting it on pain of excommunication.

La Broquière then leaves for Armenia, where he meets
Genoese merchants and Cypriot ambassadors,[5] and continues his work of reconnaissance in this country for sixteen
days.[6]   Finally, he passes into Qaramania and crosses the
whole of Asia Minor to Brusa (Bourse).[7]   Here he becomes acquainted with two Christians, one of whom is a
Genoese [8] who takes him as a guest for ten days in a Florentine hostel.   During this period he visits the town at

[1] ib., 38. 'Damas est la milleure ville que le Souldan ait, excepté le Caire,
et m'a l'en dit que en ceste ville se trouvent bien cent mille hommes.'

[2] ib. 'Elle (Damas) est aussy moult riche et bien marchande et où les
Chrestiens sont fort haïs, selon qu'il me sambloit; car il y a gens commis à
fermer les portes de tous les marchans, tantost que le soleil est couchié, et
reviennent ouvrir lendemain quant bon leur samble.'   Cf. Lannoy and other
travellers of the period.

[3] ib., 32. 'Et quand nous fusmes venus à Damas, nous y trouvasmes
plusieurs marchans françois, vénissiens, genévois, florentins et catelans, entre
lesquels y avoit ung françois nommé Jacques Cueur qui, depuis, a heu grant
auctorité en France et a esté argentier du Roy, etc.'

[4] ib., 68 and note 1.   Cf. *ante*.

[5] ib., 104 et seq.

[6] ib., 115. 'Je chevaulchay bien seize journées au long de son pays lequel
marchist sur la Perse du costé devers northost comme on me dist.'

[7] ib., 115 et seq.

[8] ib., 131. 'Parvezin de Barut' and 'Espignolins de Jennes'.   The latter
was probably a member of the well-known Genoese family of the Spinola.

his leisure.[1] Brusa is a great town and trade centre, the
best of all in Ottoman possession. It is well situated at
the foot of a mountain, and a river runs through it.[2] It is
here that Turkish rulers are interred.[3] Besides possessing
a silk, jewel and pearl trade which is almost totally monopolized by Europeans, Brusa contains a large hall for the sale
of Christian slaves, both men and women, and the sight
of them arouses Bertrandon's sympathy and sorrow.[4] At
last he crosses the Bosphorus to the Genoese colony of
Pera [5] (Pere). Here he meets Benedetto Folco da Froli,
the ambassador of the Duke of Milan, Francesco Sforza,
who had sent him to the court of the Grand Turk with a
double mission—to urge peace between Murad II
(1421–51) and Sigismund of Hungary (1368–1437); and
to incite the Turks to wrest Salonica from the hands of
the Venetians.[6] As a result of his prolonged stay in these
regions, Bertrandon comes to the painful conclusion that

[1] Schefer; 'etmefist mener à l'ostel d'ung Florentin, là où je logay moy et mon
cheval et fu l'espace de dix jours et visetay la ville de Bourse bien à mon aise'.
It is interesting to note the reference to his horse which occurs fairly frequently in the account of the journey in Asia Minor and Turkey. Evidently
the use of the horse by Christians was forbidden only in Muslim Egypt and
Syria.

[2] ib., 132–3.

[3] ib., 133 and note 2. 'Et est ceste ville où les seigneurs de la Turquie se
enterrent.' The first six Sultans from Othman I to Murad II—La
Broquière's contemporary—were all buried in a green coloured edifice
(Yechil Jami'), in Brusa. Cf. Parvillée, *Architecture et décoration turques
au XV*^e *siècle*, Paris, 1874; and Evliya Effendi, *Narrations of Travel*, pt.
III, 7.

[4] ib., 135. 'Et sy y véis vendre des Chrestiens, hommes et femmes, dans
une halle moult haulte, qui est une chose piteuse à véoir et les assiet on sur les
bancz. Et ceulx qui les veulent achepter ne voient que le visaige, les mains et
un pou des bras des femmes.'

[5] ib., 140.

[6] ib., 141–2. 'Je trouvay en ceste dicte ville de Pere ung ambaxadeur que
le duc de Milan envoioit devers le Grant Turc et l'appelloit on Messire
Benedic de Fourlino, . . . pour trouver ung appaisement entre l'empereur
Sigemond . . . et entre le Grant Turc . . . Et me dist ledit Messire Benedic
qu'il avoit esté cause de faire perdre Salonique aux Venissiens pour leur faire
dommage et la faire gaignier au Turc; de quoy il fist grant dommaige. Car
j'en veys depuis des gens de celle ville renier la foi de Jhesucrist et prendre la
loy de Mahommet que les Turcs tiennent.' Cf. *Documente diplomatici
Milanesi*, II, 242 and III, 49.

he Turks are more friendly to the Latins than are their
own co-religionists the Greeks.[1]   He finds Constantinople
a mere shadow of past glory, a derelict city in a land completely overpowered by the Turks.   The Emperor, he
says, has to pay an annual tribute of 10,000 ducats to
the Sultan to save his tottering stronghold of Constantinople from final collapse, and he must return any
Christian slaves who escape to that city to their Turkish
masters.[2]   On the other hand, he records the Emperor's
heroic statement that he would rather die in the defence
of Constantinople than surrender his heritage.[3]

La Broquière left Byzantium on 23 January[4] 1433
together with Benedetto Folco da Froli for the Sultan's
court at Adrianople.   In his progress through the country
and during his sojourn at the Turkish European capital,
he was able to observe and put on record much valuable
information regarding the state and power of the Ottomans.
Besides giving us an intimate portrait of Murad's person[5]
and some interesting details about his administration, he
estimates the Sultan's revenues at two and a half million
ducats and his armed power at 120,000 strong.[6]   Before
leaving Adrianople on 12 March, La Broquière saw, much
to his sorrow, a group of Christian slaves brought in chains
for sale.[7]   After this he wandered in Macedonia, Bulgaria,
Serbia, Albania and Bosnia, visiting many important towns
including Sofia and Belgrade, and making inquiries as to
the condition of the Christian inhabitants in the Balkan
countries which had succumbed to the Turk.[8]

[1] ib., 149. 'Car autant que j'ai hanté lesditz Grecz et que m'a peu
touchier et que j'ai eu affaire entre eulx, j'ai plus trouvé d'amitié aux Turcz et
m'y fieroye plus que auxditz Grecz.   Car, comme il m'a peu sambler, ilz ne
aiment point les Crestiens obéyssans à l'église de Romme.'

[2] ib., 164–5. 'L'Empereur de Constantinoble est en grande subjection
du Grant Turc, car il me fut dict qu'il luy paye tous les ans X^m ducatz de
tribut seulement pour le corps de la ville. . . .   Et, se d'aventure, aucun
esclave crestien eschappoit de la maison des Turcz et s'en venoit à Constantinoble, il fauldroit que l'Empereur ou ses gens le rendissent au Turc.'

[3] ib., 151.   [4] ib., 167.   [5] ib., 181–2.
[6] ib., 182.

[7] ib., 199. 'Je véys mener des Crestiens enchainez vendre, et demandoient
l'aumosne avant la ville, qui est grant pitié à véoir les maux qu'ilz portent.'

[8] ib., 199–216.

Before the end of his work, La Broquière reverts to the important subject of the military strength of the Turks, their implements of war and their tactics in battle with some analysis of the causes which had led to the disaster of the Christian host at Nicopolis. The Ottomans, he says, are men of medium size and middle strength, all wearing beards. The common saying that a man is as strong as a Turk is without real foundation in truth, for a Turk compares badly in this respect with a Christian. Nevertheless, they are a diligent and frugal race.[1] They clothe themselves in such a way as to be able to fold up their flowing robes for free movement in case of emergency.[2] Further, they wear no heavy armour and load their light horses [3] with no weighty equipment which may hamper the swiftness of their march from one point to another; and hence in time of war they can cover three days' march or even more in one night.[4] On festive days as in the case of celebrations connected with the conversion of a Greek, their war apparel reminds the author of the paintings of the time of Julius Caesar.[5] Their armour consists of the bow and quiver (*l'arc et le tarquais*), the sword, the mace [6] (*mache*) and a wooden guard (*pavais de boys*) for covering themselves while shooting arrows on horseback. Their best quality in warfare is obedience; and it is mainly this, asserts Bertrandon, that explains their achievements and conquests. The discomfiture of the combined forces of Sigismund of Hungary and John of Burgundy in spite of their great

[1] Schefer, 217.

[2] ib., 218; 'ilz envelopent toutes leurs robes par dessoubz qu'elles ne les empeschent point en fait de leur guerre ou au chemin, quant ilz ont affaire, et s'en habillent trèsbien'.

[3] ib., 218. 'Ilz ont de moult bons chevaulx qui sont grans coureurs et longuement et les tiennent fort maigres, &c.'

[4] ib., 219–21. After a description of the light horse equipment, La Broquière says: 'Ils sont legierement armez et, en une nuyt, ilz font autant de chemin ou plus qu'ilz feront en trois jours, en alant ainsi qu'ilz vont.' This is, of course, the quality which made Bayezid I acquire the nickname of 'Yilderim', i.e. Lightning.

[5] ib., 219; 'et sont de la façon que on voit en peintures du temps de Julle César &c.'.

[6] ib., 221; 'une mache grosse sur le rond, de plusieurs quarrés à court manche qui est un perilleux baston &c.'.

forts at the battle of Nicopolis may be ascribed to the
lind obedience of the Turks to those in command as
gainst faction among the Christians.[1] La Broquière
nalyses their tactics in battle fully and with care and
ccuracy. The occupation of a fortified position, the
mbush in thickly wooded lands, the use of the arrow and
he light cavalry to harass the flanks of the enemy at the
istance of a bowshot, the division of the army and the
rrangement of the troops in special battalions to cope
vith the disposition of the hostile forces, the feigning of
ight to draw their foe into a deadly trap—all these
natters are treated by the author, and all go far to explain
he course of events that won the day for the Turks at
Nicopolis.[2]

The rest of the work is devoted to Bertrandon's return
ourney overland through Serbia, Hungary, Austria,
Bavaria, Switzerland and Burgundy. On arrival in his
native land, he reported to his master Duke Philippe who
vas at the time staying at the Abbey [3] of Ponthières in the
Côte d'Or. He presented him with his Eastern garments
and a Qur'ān which the chaplain of the Venetian Consul at
Damascus had rendered into Latin. This, the Duke gave
to Jean Germain, Bishop of Châlons-sur-Saône and Chancellor of the Order of the Golden Fleece.[4] The journey
was ended before 16 March 1439; for it is known that an

---

[1] ib., 221-2. 'Ilz sont gens trèsobéissans à leur seigneur et n'est nul si
grant soit il que, pour sa vie, osast trespasser son commandement. Et je croy
que c'est une des choses qui luy a fait faire de plus grandes exécutions et
conquestes. . . . Et mesme, quant ilz desconfirent l'empereur Sigemond et
Monsieur le duc Jehan que Dieu veuille pardonner, ilz firent la diligence telle
que j'ay dit cy devant.'

[2] ib., 222-31. Nicopolis, 66–97.

[3] Voyage, 260 and note 4.

[4] ib., 260-1; also introduction, lxxv. It was probably on the basis of this
gift of 'l'Alkoran et les fais de Mahomet que le chappelain du consul des
Venissiens à Damas m'avoit baillés par escript en latin' that Bishop Jean
Germain wrote his three works entitled:

(a) Adversus Mahometanos et infideles.

(b) Adversus Turcarum Alcoranum.

(c) De Saracenorum legis falsitate tractatus.

For Jean Germain's Discourse on the project of crusade submitted to
Charles VII, vide infra.

appeal for assistance against the Turks by Jean Torzelo—
an envoy of the Emperor of Constantinople—was submitte
on that date to the Duke and handed to La Broquière fo
examination and report on the matter.[1]

In conformity with the Duke's command, La Broquièr
wrote a concise report expressing his opinion on the projec
of an expedition against the Ottoman Turks, but, probabl
contrary to the Duke's expectation, it discountenanced suc.
action. In spite of this advice, however, Philippe was no
disposed to depart from his original and much-cherishec
plan of the crusade. For him it was not merely a piou
scheme, but also a means for asserting his power anc
prestige by leading a host of God derived from many coun
tries of Latin Christendom. As late as 1452, only ;
few months before the downfall of Constantinople in th
following year (21 April 1453), he appointed Bishop Jear
Germain and others [2] to proceed to the French court to ex
hort Charles VII to make common cause with Philippe fo

---

[1] The story of this appeal is told by Waleran de Warvin in the *Cronique*
d'Engleterre, ed. by Mlle Dupont, II, 34–5. The text of the appeal itsel
and La Broquière's remarks on the project are appended by Schéfer to th
Voyage d'Outremer, 263–6 and 267–74. See also introductory remarks by
Schéfer to Jean Germain's *Discourse* in ROL, 3ᵉ année (1895), no. 2, pp
305–7.

Jean de Torzelo is described as 'chevallier, serviteur et chambellan de
l'empereur de Constantinoble' who came to Florence and dispatched the
appeal to the Duke with one Andria de Pellazago, a Florentine. In hi
report on Torzelo's appeal, La Broquière seems to make it clear that the
conquest of Turkey is by no means an easy matter and that the recovery o
the Holy Land by the land route is impracticable. The difficulty of in
flicting a defeat upon the Turks is enhanced by their speedy movement
and by their complete submission to the command of the Sultan in war
fare. As regards 'la conqueste de la Terre Sancte de quoy Messire Jehar
Torzelo met en son advis qui se feroit ung mois par apprez, il me samble
que la chose n'est pas si légière à faire, au moins par terre. . . . Au regart de
la mer, je m'en rapporte à ceulx qui cognoissent mieulx la chose qu'il ne faict.
Voyage d'Outremer, 273–4.

[2] Schefer in ROL, 3ᵉ année (1895), no. 2, pp. 311–12. Other
ambassadors were Andrieu, seigneur d'Humières and Nicolas Lejaul,
maître de requêtes de l'hôtel. The Duke also simultaneously sent
Jean de Croy, seigneur de Chimay, Jacques de Lalaing, knight of the
Toison d'Or, and L'abbé d'Everlode for the same purpose to the papal
court.

the crusade. It was on this occasion that Jean Germain wrote his *Discours du Voyage d'Oultremer* which he addressed to the King.[1] After a preamble of conventional sort, the author [2] quotes St. Augustine's *Civitas Dei* (Lib. XIX) on the three political forms of government to which the world is entrusted (*ad regimen monasticum, yconomicum et politicum*) in the midst of which the Church has been planted for the preservation of peace throughout Christendom. This divine peace had kept the world for Jesus Christ until the appearance of the religion of Muhammad seven hundred years before Germain's time.[3] It is true that the 'Empire of Rome, that of Constantinople, the kingdoms of France, Castile, Spain, England, Sicily, Dacia, Denmark, Hungary, Bohemia, Scotland, Cyprus and Germany are to-day by the grace of God subject to Jesus Christ'.[4] On the other hand, continues the Bishop, Granada is a Muhammadan stronghold within the confines of Christendom, Africa is no more Christian, and Egypt and Syria belong to Muhammad while Tartary remains idolatrous.[5] The author then reminds the King of France of the noble efforts of the early crusaders from Godefroy de Bouillon to St. Louis for the recovery of the Holy Land.[6] Nowadays, the Sultan prides himself on being the lord of all Christians, to whose humiliation, and 'as a sign of his presumption, he would not suffer the Cordeliers of Mount Sion to perform divine service in a loud voice in the Church of the Holy Sepulchre', while the prayers of Muhammad are said within the precincts of that holy shrine.[7] Moreover, not content with the

---

[1] *Le Discours du Voyage d'Oultremer au très victorieux roi Charles VII prononcé en* 1452 *par Jean Germain, Evêque de Chalon*; ed Ch. Schéfer, in ROL, op. cit., 314–42, with introduction, 303–14.

[2] ib., 314–15.   [3] ib., 316–17.   [4] ib., 3 7.

[5] ib., 317–21.   [6] ib., 322–5.

[7] ib., 326; 'il (le sultan) se vante d'estre seigneur des chrestiens et les reppute ses hommes cerfz de quelque estat qu'ilz soient, en tant qu'il leur peut acroistre et diminuer tribut, qui est chose qui doit ferir bien le cueur de tous nobles hommes. Et, en signe de sa presumpcion, il ne seuffre aux frères Cordeliers du mont de Syon faire le divin service à haulte voix en l'église du Saint Sepulcre, et fait chanter le sabat ("salat", i.e. prayers; or "Sabbath", i.e. the weekly prayers of a Muhammadan community on Friday) de son Mahomet en la terre de l'église dudit Saint Sepulcre.'

despoliation of the Christians in Syria twenty-six years ago, he had invaded the Latin Kingdom of Cyprus and carried its King into captivity, exacted a heavy ransom from him, and now holds him as tributary.[1]   Seven years ago he had attacked Rhodes, and shortly afterwards had seized the island of Castellorizzo which belonged to the Knights Hospitallers.[2]   Only three years ago he had exiled the Coptic Patriarch from Cairo; and as a result of this atrocious act, the Ethiopian Emperor and his Christian subjects have continually waged war against the oppressor.[3]   In Europe itself, the Ottomans have conquered the territories of the Empire of Constantinople and Greece; and the princes of Bosnia, Wallachia and Serbia have become his tributaries, though all of them by right owe homage to the King of Hungary.[4]   This new Muslim empire has spread over the whole of the Balkan Peninsula, and Turkish raids have been carried even into Hungary for the last twenty years, and if the Christians remain as passive as they are at present, the city of Constantinople itself will ultimately succumb to the Turks and their conquests may be pursued as far as Rome.[5]   Surely this march of events is in itself a heavy reproach to the conscience of Christendom which

[1] *Discours*, l.c. 'Derechef, non content d'avoir foulé la chrestienté en la Surye, depuis vingt six ans en ça, envahy le royaume de Cypre, prins le roy en bataille, l'a tenu son prisonnier, et délivré par finance, et le tient aujourdui son tributaire.'

[2] ib. 'Et jà, depuis sept ans en ça, s'a traveillé de prandre l'isle et cité de Roddes, et, environ six ans, fist par ses admiraulx assaillir et prandre le chastel Rouge, qui appartenoit au maistre de Roddes, l'a fait abatre et mené prisonniers les souldoiers d'icellui en Surye.'

[3] ib. 'Et, depuis trois ans, a fait chasser hors du Cayre le Patriarche des Indes, subget de prebstre Jehan, et tous ses subgectz chrestiens, dont s'est meue guerre entre ledit prebstre Jehan et ledit souldan.'

[4] ib., 327. 'D'autre part, le Turcq, non content de ses limites, a conquis l'empire de Constantinoble, . . . a gaigné la Grece jusques en Hongrie et fait tributaires le Roy de Bosnie, les seigneurs des deux Walachies, grande et petite, le dispot de Rasse, tous liges hommes du roy de Hongrie.'

[5] ib., 327–8. 'Et n'a cessé, depuis vingt ans en ça, fouler les royaumes de Hongrie par courses. . . . Et, se Dieu et les princes chrestiens n'y pourvoient et il continue ses conquestes, comme il a fait depuis quatre vingt ans en ça, il se fera empereur de Constantinoble et pourra legièrement assez venir jusques à Romme, où il trouvera nacion assez encline à mal faire, et se intitulera empereur d'Orient et d'Occident.'

as deserted the princes of Eastern Europe to a grim fate
t the hands of Muslim conquerors.[1]

Jean Germain then prescribes the remedies for these
vils. The lords of Damascus, he says, have no love for
he Sultan of 'Babilon'. This is proved by their recent
•ehaviour in allying themselves with Timur against him,
nd they will do their master harm whenever this is pos-
ible.[2] Meanwhile the Greek and other Balkan nations
re only subject to the Turk by force of arms. The
)ttoman Sultan has an unnatural mastery over alien races.[3]
'action in the Empire of Egypt and the instability of the
)ttoman hold over the Balkan states are factors which
/ill facilitate the task of Western Christianity in the
:ast. As to the cleavage of the Church between Orient
nd Occident, Pope Eugenius IV has healed it at the
Council of Florence (1439). This brings within the
ale of the Roman Church the Empires of Constantinople
nd of Trebizond, the Armenians, the 'Jacobites of
:thiopia', Russia, and 'Prester John of India'; and
united front comprising all manners and divisions of
Christians has been created to face the enemy.[4] At present,
oo,ooo combatants from Armenia and 50,ooo from
Georgia can march on Syria without delay, while the con-
ingents of the West invade the dominions of the Turks
n Europe on their way to the East.[5] The *Discours* ends
/ith a personal exhortation to Charles 'the Victorious'
/hom the author describes as the 'new David', the 'new
Constantine' and the 'new Charlemagne', to relieve the
Catholic faith by new conquests which will be associated
/ith his name in memoirs, chronicles and histories for all
ime.[6] But the 'victorious' monarch was much too busy
n the work of consolidating his conquests from the English

---

[1] ib., 328; 'et, au grant reprouche de la chrestienté, mettra en telle necessité
:s princes d'icelle, qu'il fauldra qu'ilz vivent tributaires soubz luy(le souldan)'.

[2] ib., 328–9; 'le souldan de Babilonne n'est mye bien avecques les seigneurs
e Damas, pour ce qu'il leur a osté leur seigneurie, et, sont communement
liez avecques le Tanbollan de Perse. Et luy porteroient voulentiers dom-
ıage.'

[3] ib., 330. 'Aussi le Turcq n'est mye seigneur naturel de la Grece, ains
stranger et la tient comme tirant, par force . . .'

[4] ib.　　　　　　[5] ib., 331 et seq.　　　　　　[6] ib., 342.

in France to pay any serious attention to these supplications on behalf of the Holy Land; and neither the weight of Philippe's influence nor the eloquence of Jean Germain's rhetoric produced the desired effect on the King's mind.

While these negotiations, consultations and exhortations were in progress at the courts of Burgundy and France, a propagandist document of high value came from a totally different quarter. Emanuele Piloti, a native of Crete with long experience in the various countries of the Near East, addressed a long work to Pope Eugenius IV advising him on the most effective manner of conducting a crusade for the recovery of the Holy Land from Muslim hands. At the time of the composition of his tract, he appears to have lived in Muhammadan countries for a period of thirty-five years.[2] Piloti was a practical man of affairs with considerable acumen and power of observation. After a term as consul in Alexandria to the Genoese Republic, he entered the service of the Venetians, and on one occasion at the news of a Genoese landing in Alexandria fled from the city.[3] In 1408, he mediated for the Venetian merchants at the court of the Sultan in Cairo.[4] From his youth, he could recall the humiliation of the host of Christendom by the Ottomans at Nicopolis.[5] Of the Christian captives seized by the Turks on that occasion, two

---

[1] Emanuelis Piloti Cratensis (*sic*) de modo, progressu, ordine ac diligent providentia habendis in passagio christianorum pro conquesta Terrae sanctae cujus rei gloriam Deus asseret sanctissimo pontifici maximo, Eugenio quarto ut simul confundat infideles Occidentis, tractatus. Ed. Le Baron de Reiffenberg, *Monument pour servir à l'histoire de Namur* &c., IV (Brussels, 1846) 312–419. Emanuele declares that he wrote first in Latin and his work was then translated in 1441 into French. This bears clear marks of the Italian spoken by some of the Latins of the Near East during this period. Reiffenberg, in the introduction, clxxvi, suggests that the reverse is more probable and that the Latin translation was possibly made by another.

[2] ib., 313.   [3] ib., 395.   [4] ib., 400–2.

[5] ib., 408. 'O seigneurs crestiens il me recorde de mon temps que, en l'an mille IIJ^c LXXXXVIJ la bonne mémoire de la illustre impereur de Romains et le illustre prince et duc de Bourgogne, avecques très-grant puissance et très-grant suit de crestiens, alant contre poyens, et entrèrent dessus Turquie, là où ilz furent rompus et mal traictiés, et prins une très-grande quantité de crestiens et furent fais poyens.'

The year of the battle of Nicopolis is erroneously given by the author. For exact date, *vide infra*, Cap. XVIII.

hundred slaves were sent by the Ottoman conqueror as a
present to the Sultan of Egypt; and Piloti saw them and
spoke to them in the Citadel of Cairo, and he says that all
had been forced to renounce their faith.[1]   In later years, he
witnessed and recorded the downfall of the Latin Kingdom
of Cyprus in the year 1427 [2] and the capture of King Janus
and 6,000 Cypriot men and women of position.[3]   Piloti
could not remain silent after watching these stirring events.
Thus he wrote his *De modo, progressu, ordine ac diligenti
providentia habendis in passagio christianorum pro conquesta
Terrae sanctae*, a work in which he utilized his prolonged
experience in the East for the benefit of prospective
crusaders.   The author is a man of affairs and shows
himself incapable of conveying his ideas in good style.
Yet much valuable material can with patience be sifted
from his statements; and in spite of the confusion prevailing throughout his account, his main theme is quite
intelligible.

The leader of the crusade, Piloti insists, needs four [4]
preliminary conditions to ensure his success.   He must be
surrounded by wise, prudent and practical men of the
world, capable of giving him sound advice at all times.
The leader himself must be a man of large wealth.   Further,
his followers should be desirous to achieve glory and fame
for their master, whose authority and prestige must also
be accepted by the kings and princes of the Christian world.

---

[1] ib., 412; '. . . aulcuns Turs manda à donner deux cens de leurs esclaves
crestiens qui furent prins au souldain du Caire; lesquelx estoyent de toute
nation crestienne de François et d'Italiens, et tous furent fais tornez estre
moyens.   Lesquelx je lez vis tous dedans le chateau du Caire, et si parla
(*sic*) avecque eulx, et tous estoyent josnes, beaulx et tous eslus.'

[2] This date as well as others quoted in the text may cause confusion as to the
original date of the redaction of the *tractatus* which is recorded at the opening
as 1420.   The explanation is that Piloti started writing in 1420 and finished
some years later.   Cf. Reiffenberg, clxxvi.

[3] *De modo*, op. cit., 386.   'Et depuis, que fust en l'an MCCCC et XXVJ,
l'armée du souldain print l'isole de Cipre et le roy en personne, avecques
ammes vj^m, dames, damoiselles, seigneurs de toutes réputations, et tous furent
menés au Cayre avecques grant charge et vitupère de la foy crestienne; pour
quoy quasi toutes celles ammes devindrent paganes.'   For details of this
expedition, *vide infra*, Cap. XIX.

[4] ib., 317–18.

When these preliminary conditions are fulfilled then the crusade may be undertaken with a strong possibility of success. As to the course which the host of God may follow, Piloti makes it perfectly clear that the expedition should first be directed against Egypt and not the Holy Land. The only way to reduce the Sultan's power to impotence and to annihilate the religion of Muhammad as a prelude to the recovery of the Holy Land, and the propagation of the faith of Christ, is none other than the occupation of Cairo.[1] This city is the largest in the whole world and its inhabitants are numberless.[2] In prosperity, too, it exceeds all others.[3] To seize Cairo, however, the crusaders must conquer Alexandria; for without this Mediterranean port, he argues, Cairo and the whole of Egypt cannot[4] 'live'. Piloti describes the road from Alexandria to Cairo for the guidance of the crusaders.[5] Two great weaknesses in the Sultan's rule will facilitate the task of the Christian invaders—first, his bad government which has led to the depopulation of Alexandria,[6] and second, the practice of butchering his amīrs on the grounds of suspicion of treachery.[7] Later in the work, the author gives an estimate of the Sultan's forces which the crusaders will have to encounter. These consist of 7,000 to 8,000 mounted slaves (Mamlūks), 10,000 to 15,000 camels and mules for transport of equipment and provisions accompanied by 2,000 horse, and last but not least the Sultan himself with the rest of his men

---

[1] *De modo*, 325. [2] ib.

[3] ib., 326–7. The author enumerates many of its resources.

[4] ib., 327; 'laquelle (Alexandrie) se peut réputer certainement, sans contraire, estre l'entrée et l'issue du Cayre et de tout l'Égypte; sans laquelle ville d'Alexandrie ledit Cayre avecques tout l'Égypte ne porroit vivre'.

[5] ib., 346–8. Later he enumerates the conditions for the conquest and retention of Alexandria. These include unity of action already mentioned by Piloti in regard to the whole crusade and the avoidance of scandalous quarrels by entrusting the government of the city to one man. Ib., 365–6.

[6] ib., 351–2. 'Par la mal seignorie et mavais governe que lez seigneurs du Cayre ont fait et font en celluy pays, Alexandrie, qui est la bouche et la clef de leur estat est déshabitée et habandonnée, &c.'

[7] ib., 407. 'La coustume du souldain du Caire si est de faire boucherie de sez armiraulx . . . pour la grant doubte qu'il a de eulx que par trahiment ne li lièvent sa seignerie (*sic*), comme aultre fois il est entrevenus.'

whose numbers Piloti unfortunately leaves undefined. One feature of the march of the Egyptian army is the departure of the transport and equipment with its vanguard of 2,000 cavalry one day ahead of the remaining forces. Next follows a middle detachment of 2,000 horsemen, and then the rearguard comes with the Sultan himself in command.[1]

The sum-total of Piloti's argument is that the crusaders should aim first at the occupation of Alexandria and Cairo. When these great cities are reduced to Christian domination, the Sultan will be so much enfeebled that the conquest of the Holy Land will follow without difficulty. It is interesting to notice that Piloti, in contrast to the narrow bigotry of some of his former fellow-propagandists such as Burcard, adopts an enlightened and benevolent attitude towards the Muslim races who may succumb to the arms of the Cross. The crusade is not regarded by him as a war of revenge with the aim of the extermination of unbelievers. On the contrary, it is a means towards the assimilation of Saracen men and women into the following of Christ, not by 'disgust or displeasure', but by 'honour and courtesy'.[2] The people of Egypt are by nature pure and without malice, and owing to their credulity they will believe in the doctrines of Muhammad until God reveals the truth to them. Under gentle treatment, their spirit and heart will soften, and they will perceive the love and charity which are the characteristics of Christianity. When Cairo —'the Rome of pagans'—is converted, all other 'pagans' will ultimately follow its example and the light will spread throughout the world.[3]

Although intended as a propagandist document, the *De modo* is also an important source for fifteenth-century history of commerce in the Levant, and it may justly be regarded as the complement to Marino Sanudo's *Secreta fidelium crucis* [4] in this particular sphere. In his old age,

---

[1] ib., 417.

[2] ib., 392; 'mais certainement est de commettre et ordener que à lez personnes, c'est assavoir dez Sarrasins, aussi bien hommes comme femmes, ne soit fait aulcune guaste (It.: *guasto*) ne desplaisir, mais honneur et courtosie'.

[3] ib.   [4] *vide supra*, Cap. V.

Piloti retired from Alexandria to live in the city of Florence, whence he urged Pope Eugenius IV, both by writing
and by word of mouth, to adopt the plan put forward in
his *De modo*.[1]

To assume, however, that all fifteenth-century propaganda was the work of inspired diplomats and astute trade
representatives would be a serious error. Independent
pilgrims of the fourteenth-century type still existed in the
fifteenth, though their numbers became smaller and their
devotion was not unmixed with the simple love of travel
in distant lands. Three notable examples may be quoted
here to illustrate this aspect of late medieval pilgrimages.
First, we have Pero Tafur, a Spaniard; second, William
Wey an Englishman; and third, Felix Faber, a German [2]
—all of whom have left important records of their travels
in the Near East.

Born in Cordova about 1410,[3] Pero Tafur undertook
his travels and adventures in the East and performed his
pilgrimage to the Holy Places between the years 1435
and 1439. Sailing from Malaga, he reaches Genoa in
December[4] 1435. Then he travels to Venice where he
finds no pilgrims' ship available, and so takes the road to
Rome in order to utilize the time of his forced delay by
visiting the shrines of the holy fathers.[5] Afterwards, he
makes his way back through Italy by Viterbo, Perugia,
Assisi, Gubbio, Rimini and Ravenna to Venice.[6] Thence he
sails to Jaffa, calling *en route* at Parenzo, Zara, Ragusa,
Corfu, Modon, Crete and Rhodes.[7] In Jerusalem and its
neighbourhood, he is not content with visiting Christian holy
places, but bribes a Portuguese renegade with the sum
of two ducats to escort him in Moorish disguise through
the Mosque of 'Umar, which he calls the ancient Temple
of Solomon.[8] His original plan—to proceed direct to the

---

[1] *De modo*, 382; cf. Reiffenberg's introduction, clxxix.

[2] For MSS. and editions of works by these pilgrims, see Röhricht, op. cit.,
110, 116, 130–1. Special editions used here are specified in notes. Cf.
Appendix II.

[3] Pero Tafur, *Travels and Adventures*, trans. and ed. by M. Letts, in the
Broadway Travellers' Series; introduction, 2 and text, 72.

[4] ib., 21–6.   [5] ib., 27–43.   [6] ib., 44–7.

[7] ib., 48–53.   [8] ib., 54–62.

Monastery of St. Catherine—is altered when he misses
the caravan destined for Mount Sinai.[1]   Hence he sails
from Jaffa to Beirūt, and after visiting the place where,
according to tradition, St. George slew the dragon, he
departs again to 'the ancient city of Famagusta, which the
Genoese had captured when they took the King of Cyprus
and carried him to Genoa with his wife'.[2]   He goes to
Nicosia where the Sultan's safe-conduct for travelling to
Egypt is obtained for him; and therefrom leaves for
Damietta and Cairo by sea [3] and river.   In connexion with
his stay in Cairo which lasted for one month,[4] Pero Tafur
gives a lively description of some of the scenes of daily
life in that city and the wonders that he saw in Egypt,
including the 'Granaries of Joseph' and the Sultan's
elephants.[5]   He records the existence in that country of
a sect of people of whom 'some go about wearing horns,
others bedaubed with honey and feathered, and others
carrying poles with lanterns and lights hanging from
them; others have bows and arrows drawn ready to shoot,
and thus in diverse manners go about, saying, that they
are persecutors of Christians.' [6]   Finally, the Sultan grants
him leave to go to Mount Sinai, orders one of the court
interpreters to accompany him to his destination, and gives
him three camels for the journey across the desert which,
according to Tafur's estimate,[7] requires fifteen days.   He
confuses the Coptic Patriarch with the Greek when he
asserts that the 'Patriarch of Alexandria' lives at the Monastery of St. Catherine and that he 'elects the Patriarch who
is sent to Greater India to Prester John'.[8]   But probably
the most interesting event during his sojourn in Mount
Sinai is the curious coincidence of Niccolò de' Conti's
arrival from the Far East with goods of all description
including 'spices, pearls, precious stones and gold, per-
fumes, and linen, and parrots, and cats from India, with
many other things, which they distribute throughout the
world'.   The camels loaded with these goods are so
numerous 'that I cannot give an account of them, as I do

[1] ib., 62.   [2] ib., 64   [3] ib., 66, 71,
[4] ib., 77.   [5] ib., 78.   [6] ib., 71.
[7] ib., 81–2.   [8] ib., 83.

not wish to appear to speak extravagantly'.[1] Pero tell
Niccolò of his desire to travel to the Far East; but the
Venetian gentleman who with his wife and children had
been forced to apostatize by the Sultan's officers at Mekka,
succeeds in dissuading the Spanish nobleman from carrying out this hazardous plan.[2] The two travellers return
to Cairo together. Thence Pero Tafur starts his homeward journey by a circuitous route through Alexandria,
Damietta, Cyprus, Rhodes, Chios, Pera, Constantinople,
Adrianople, Trebizond, Caffa and finally by sea to Venice.
In speaking of Adrianople, he gives an interesting description of Sultan Murad II (1421–51) and the Turks. He
describes the Sultan as 'a discreet person, grave in his
looks' and 'so handsomely attended that I never saw the
like'. He estimates his army at 600,000 men, all mounted
'on very small and lank horses'.[4] Both the Sultan and his
men live continually in camp outside the city. Their
fighting outfit consists of 'an iron staff, and a tambourine
with their bows and quivers'.[5] The crusading movement
which was then in preparation against the Turks justifies
a little further consideration of Pero Tafur's impression of
this race. 'The Turks have a vast dominion,' he says,
'but the country is very sterile and sparsely populated and
mountainous. Greece, which they occupy, is a flat and

---

[1] Pero Tafur, 83. Niccolò de' Conti may justly claim the title of the Marco
Polo of the fifteenth century. Of noble Venetian origin, he turned to the Venetian practice of trade in the Levant at an early age. In Alexandria and Cairo,
he lost all; and he decided to join the court of Timur, in whose train he was
taken to very many parts of Asia. Further, he is known to have been in
Hindustan, Ceylon, Sumatra and Java. After amassing much wealth, he
returned to Cairo by the Red Sea and reached Venice in 1444. He appealed
to the Pope to absolve him from his apostacy at Mekka. The Pope bade
him recount the story of his adventures to Poggio Bracciolini, the papal
secretary, who recorded them in Latin. The text of Bracciolini was published in 1723, and an English translation of it appeared under the title
India in the Fifteenth Century in the Hakluyt Society publications in
1857.

[2] Pero Tafur, 84–6. The story of Niccolò de' Conti is continued in
Chapter X, 87–95.

[3] ib., 102 et seq.   [4] ib., 126.

[5] ib., 127. Further details as to Turkish horses on p. 128; cf. *Nicopolis*,
79–80 and 188 notes 83–4.

fruitful land, although now it is depopulated by war, for the Greeks bear the whole burden of the struggle, and the Turks are ruthless and treat them with great cruelty. Indeed, it is difficult to believe how so great an army can be provisioned. The Turks are a noble and truthful people. They live in their country like nobles, as well in their expenditure as in their action and food and sports, in which latter there is much gambling. They are very merry and benevolent, and of good conversation, so much so that in those parts, when one speaks of virtue, it is sufficient to say that any one is like a Turk.' [1]   After seeing for himself 'the person, household and estate of the Grand Turk', Tafur returns to Constantinople, and visits John IV Emperor of Trebizond in his diminished capital on the south coast of the Black Sea and the Genoese colony of Caffa planted on the north side in the Tatar Khanate of Russia.[2]   The restless traveller was, however, not content with his peregrinations beyond the sea. After reaching Venice he wanders in north Italy, Austria, the Rhineland and the Low Countries before returning once more to the Republic of St. Mark, whence he sails on his homeward journey, visiting *en route* amongst other places the Moorish town of Tunis.[3]

Another pilgrim of the same century as Pero Tafur, is William Wey, Fellow of Eton College. In spite of the fact that his work has long been in print, it has passed almost unnoticed by successive generations of historians since its publication.[4]   About the author himself little is known beyond the possibility of his Devonshire origin, his graduation as Bachelor of Divinity, his appointment as Fellow of Exeter College, Oxford, and his transfer to Eton College, newly founded by Henry VI on 11 October 1442.[5]   It was during the tenure of this last fellowship that William performed his first pilgrimage to the shrine

---

[1] Pero Tafur, 128.

[2] ib., 129–37 and 244 note 1; cf. W. Miller, in E.H.R. (1923), 409.

[3] Pero Tafur, 231–4.

[4] *The Itineraries of William Wey, Fellow of Eton College,* published from the Bodleian Manuscript for the Roxburghe Club, London, 1857.

[5] ib., Introduction, i–ii.

of St. James of Compostella in Spain in [1] 1456. On 11 August 1457, he received royal licence [2] to travel to the East, and accordingly went on his first pilgrimage to Jerusalem in 1458 and his second in 1462. At an unknown date he seems to have resigned his fellowship to take up holy orders. He lived as an inmate of Edyngdon Monastery in Wiltshire for a period, and since Eton College and her sister college at Cambridge were specially founded for secular priests, William Wey presumably must have vacated his post at Eton. [3] The last of his pilgrimages was probably undertaken at the advanced age of seventy. [4]

Although Wey's narrative offers no special contribution to the existing body of knowledge as to either length and stages of the voyage or the description of the holy places, it possesses several noteworthy features. It opens with an exposition of some practical matters which must have been a great source of anxiety, particularly to pilgrims of modest means. These include the rates of exchange [5] in

---

[1] *The Itineraries of William Wey*, iii. William Wey's name appears in the books of Eton College as Fellow attesting the admission of one Richard Hopton on 10 May 1453 and of John Gegur on 7 November 1453 to Fellowships of his College.

[2] This royal brief, edited in the introduction to the *Itineraries*, iii–iv, is worthy of quoting *in extenso* as a good example of special licences granted to English pilgrims: 'Trusty and well-beloved we grete you wele, and, forasmuche as we understonde that our well-beloved clerc Maister William Wey, oon of youre Felawes, entendeth in brief time by the grace of God to passe over the See on peregrinance, as to Rome, to Jerusalem, and to other Holy Places, and so humbly hath he soughte us to graunt unto hym our especial licence so to doo: Wee, having tendre consideration unto his blessed purpos and entent, have licensied hym to execute his said peregrinage, and wol that at suche tyme as he shall retourne unto our College that he be accepted there as a Felawe of the same, in like Wyse and Fourme as he now standeth therein, and that the yerely pension with other Deutes growing unto hym during his said peregrinace within our said College, be observed oonly and kept to his propre use unto his said Retournynge. And that this considering our License graunted unto hym and his good entent be doon, any statute or ordeynance made to the contrarie notwithstanding. Yeven under our Signet at our Castell of Kenelworth, the xith day of August.'
'To our trusty and well-beloved the Provost and Felawes of oure College Roial of our Lady of Eton.' Though the year is not mentioned in the letter, inquiry into the preceding and succeeding entries establishes this as 1457.

[3] *The Itineraries of William Wey*, iv–v.   [4] ib., v.   [5] ib., 1–3.

the countries to be traversed between England and the
Holy Land, and the food (*preuysyoun*) [1] prices in the different
parts—two subjects of special interest to the medieval
economist. 'Kepe all thes thynges afore wryt,' Wey
advises the pilgrim, 'and ye schal, w^t the grace of God,
well spede yn yowre jorney to goo and com to the plesure
of God, and encrese of yowre blys, the whyche Jhesus
gravnt yow'.[2]   Then follows a versified account of his
journey, in English,[3] which he probably composed to help
travellers to memorize the outstanding points about the
various places on either side of the Mediterranean.   The
author subsequently includes a plan in an itinerary in which
he describes the holy cities with their sacred relics and
monuments, and he also defines the approximate periods
necessary for the accomplishment of visits to all places of
interest to the pious traveller.[4]   Also he tabulates ten
motives for a pilgrimage to the Holy Land as an act of
devotion for the redemption of sins.   Having completed his
introductory notices, the author then gives the actual story of
the two pilgrimages which he had undertaken in succession.
In the first of his journeyings, he made one of 197 pilgrims
who sailed in two galleys on 18 May 1458 and reached Jaffa
on 18 June, thus taking one month by sea from Venice to the
Holy Land.   Finally, he arrived at Jerusalem six days later,
having been detained on board the galley until the 21st
of that month.   He spent several days in the Holy City
and neighbouring towns, and left for Jaffa on 2 July on
his way back to the West.[5]   He concluded his account of
the first pilgrimage with an interesting list of the distances
between the various towns of Belgium, Germany and Italy
at which Englishmen were normally bound to call on their
way to Syria,[6] which may be of considerable use to the
historical geographer of Europe in the Later Middle Ages
and of no slight help in the reconstruction of the trade
routes of the time.   In the story of his second journey
in 1462, Wey mentions historical events which took
place on the Continent during his progress.   He states
that he was twice forced to deflect the course of his route

[1] ib., 4–7.   [2] ib., 7.   [3] ib., 8, 18.
[4] ib., 19–25.   [5] ib., 56–79.   [6] ib., 79–81.

—first, at Aix-la-Chapelle on account of a war between two Rhineland bishops,[1] and second, at Basel because of the hostilities then in progress between Pope Pius II and Frederick III, Duke of Austria.[2]   On 22 April he arrived at Venice, and here he stayed until 26 May.   During this period, he saw the magnificence and wealth of the Republic of St. Mark demonstrated in the ceremonies connected with the vigil and feast of St. Mark [3] on 24–25 April, the death of Doge Pascale Malpiero on 3 May and his funeral after lying in state for three days at the ducal palace,[4] the election of his successor Chistoforo Moro, and the festivities of the wedding of the Republic to the sea.[5] On the way to the Holy Land, good news reached his ship on 27 June at Axtis concerning a crushing defeat sustained by the Turks with a loss of some 30,000 in Wallachia as well as bad news of the Turkish occupation of the Morea.[6] The pilgrims made their way through the waters of Rhodes and Cyprus, and finally dropped anchor at Jaffa on 16 July, after spending about six weeks on the high seas.[7]   This time he found Syria seething with civil disturbances as a result of fierce rivalries among the Mamlūk amīrs; and he could not therefore go much farther than Jerusalem.[8] On the return journey, he heard the alarming news which had reached Candia from Constantinople that a 'Turkish' fleet of 300 galleys and other sea-craft had been fitted out for an assault on Rhodes.[9]   Towards the end of his account of the second pilgrimage, William Wey appends a Greek vocabulary[10] for the use of other pilgrims in obtaining the daily necessities of life.   The words are transliterated into Latin characters and the vocabulary as a whole proves that the author was no Greek scholar.

---

[1] *The Itineraries of William Wey*, 82.   [2] ib., 82–3.   [3] ib., 83–4.
[4] ib., 85–6.   [5] ib., 86 et seq.   [6] ib., 93.
[7] ib., 94–5.
[8] ib., 96 et seq. 'Erat eciam eo tempore guerra inter duos soldanos, scilicet Babilonie et Damasci, pro dominio et regimine Terre Sancte et quis eorum ibi regnaret' (99).
[9] ib., 101–2. 'Item quinto die Septembris venimus Cande, ubi dictum erat per virum venientem a Constantinopoli, quod Turcus erat in mare cum tricentis navibus, galeis, grypis et fustis versus Rodys, quo tamen ivit nescimus.'
[10] ib., 102–16.

The work is enriched with a large map of the Holy Land [1] of special interest in the study of medieval cartography.

Perhaps the most elaborate, if not the most important record of a fifteenth-century pilgrimage is Brother Felix Faber's *Evagatorium*.[2] Faber twice undertook the journey to the Holy Places between the years 1480 and 1484. On his return from the second pilgrimage, he settled down at his Dominican Convent at Ulm to describe his wanderings with such fidelity as we may expect from fifteenth-century standards.   What he had seen, he described in great detail; and what he had not seen, he outlined in accordance with 'trustworthy' reports or by copying from pilgrims of a preceding age, notably Germans such as Ludolf von Suchem and Burcard.[3] He therefore presents us with a full and almost complete picture of the Holy Places in the latter decades of the fifteenth century. Naturally, the reader cannot hope for striking new discoveries in the realm of holy relics and holy monuments, which had been fully explored by Faber's pious predecessors.   On the other hand, some of the author's reports, though secondary to the main object of his work, deal with such aspects of his travels and of life in the East as may be of use to prepare other pilgrims' minds for what they might have to face in their undertaking.   These subsidiary hints to pilgrims are historical documents of value, since they furnish the modern writer with a real and lively picture of the conditions of the society of that age.

From the outset of the *Evagatorium* the reader is introduced, in an atmosphere of intense gravity, to the great risks incurred in a pilgrimage to lands very remote in those days and lying beyond the sea.   Nevertheless, with

---

[1] The map is reproduced in a separate volume with a special introduction. William Wey's own explanatory remarks about his map appear in the first volume, 128 et seq.

[2] *Fratris Felicis Fabri Evagatorium in Terrae Sanctae, Arabiae et Egypti Peregrinationem*, ed. C. D. Hassler, 3 vols., Stuttgart, 1843–9, in Bibliothek des literarischen Vereins in Stuttgart.   English translation of sections on the Holy Land by Aubrey Stewart in the Palestine Pilgrims' Text Society, 2 vols., in 4 pts., London, 1892–3.   Reference here is made to the original complete Latin text unless otherwise specified.

[3] *vide supra*, 95, 168.

typical medieval devotion to his faith, Felix Faber is urged
from within to start the journey. He consults Count
Eberhard the Elder of Wurtemburg who declines to give
him specific advice on so unusual a wandering.[1] Then
he goes to an aged knight who had twice made the pilgrimage and to a sister of well-known holiness in a neighbouring
convent, in search of further counsel and inspiration.
These last two give him every encouragement to fulfil his
intention.[2] He therefore writes to a friend in Rome who
obtains for him the necessary licence from Pope Sixtus IV
and a safe-conduct from Leonardo de Mansuetis, General
of the Dominican Order.[3] Early in the morning of 14 April
1480, he receives the pilgrim's blessing, kisses and embraces
all the brethren of his convent, starts with one Master
Ludwig and a servant, all on horseback, from Ulm to
Memmingen where, by previous appointment, they are
joined by Lord Apollinaris [4] von Stein with his son and a
number of men-at-arms.[5] Thence the company proceeds
across the Alps to Venice to take ship for the Holy Land.

The account of Faber's first pilgrimage is much shorter
than that of his second. A noteworthy feature in it is
the frequency of his reference to the Turks. Just as the
pilgrims were ready to set sail, bad news came to the
Republic of St. Mark. Muhammad II was besieging the
island of Rhodes and the Aegean and Eastern Mediterranean swarmed with Turkish craft so that it had become very
dangerous for pilgrims to cross the sea.[6] The German
pilgrims met and petitioned the Venetian Senate for a safe-
conduct to save their galley from Turkish attack. They
received the reply that the galley itself, by virtue of its
Venetian provenance, was the safest surety in accordance
with solemn treaty obligations between Venice and Turkey.

---

[1] *Evagatorium*, I, 26–7   [2] ib., I, 27.   [3] ib., I, 27–8.
[4] ib., I, 28; 'Dominus Hypolithus vel Apollinaris, vel Pupillus de Lapide.'
[5] ib., I, 29.   It is interesting to notice that the pilgrims travelled on horseback (*ascendimus equos*) and that they also were guarded *en route* by armed men
(*cum multis armigeris*).
[6] ib., I, 32.   'Machumetus magnus, insulam Rhodum obsideret classe
magna per mare, et armato exercitu equitum et peditum per terram, et totum
mare Aegaeum, Carpaticum, et Maleum infestum haberet, et possibile non
esset hoc anno transducere peregrines in Terram Sanctam.'

Notwithstanding this definite assurance, the rest of the journey across the sea reads like a tale of terror. Wherever they cast anchor—at Modon, Candia in Crete and Limasol in Cyprus—rumours of merciless ravages added to their anxiety and their sense of impending calamity. Finally,[1] on sighting the coast of the Holy Land near Jaffa, all praised God for a safe passage and all chanted the 'Te Deum laudamus'.[2] In Jerusalem, Faber met two English pilgrims who intended to travel to the Monastery of St. Catherine in Sinai; but as they spoke neither German nor Latin, he preferred to postpone this part of the journey until his return to the East as he had resolved to perform a second pilgrimage.[3]

It was during this second journey in 1483–4 that Faber travelled far and wide in Egypt and Syria. The story of this pilgrimage is indeed so full of interest that it would be impossible in anything but a special monograph to deal with its varied aspects. There are five outward requirements for a pilgrim—thus Felix begins the account of his journeys—first, a flowing grey robe bearing a red cross with a monk's cowl sewn to the tunic unless the pilgrim is a member of a religious order whose rule directs otherwise; second, a black or grey hat with a red cross on the front; third, a long beard and a face drawn with the weight of suffering and danger; fourth, a scrip on the shoulders containing the slender provisions necessary for his sustenance; and fifth, when overseas, an ass with a Saracen driver as a substitute for the pilgrim's staff of Christian countries.[4] With a party of German pilgrims, Faber crossed the Brenner Pass, sailed to Jaffa from Venice, visited Jerusalem and many other places in the Holy Land, the Monastery of St. Catherine, and finally sailed back to Europe after calling at the capital of Egypt. He describes Venice as the famous, great, rich and noble mistress of the Medit-

---

[1] ib., I, 39 et seq. An interesting reference to the military equipment for the defence of the pilgrims' galley in case of attack by the Turks is made by Faber. This includes cannons, spears, lances, shields and bucklers, catapults, and bows, stones and darts (*bombardas, cuspides, lanceas, scuta et clypeos, balistas et arcus, lapides et jacula*). Ib., I, 40.

[2] ib., I, 41.   [3] ib., I, 41–2.   [4] ib., I, 65.

erranean, standing on a wonderful site in the midst of waters with lofty towers, great churches, splendid houses and palatial abodes.[1] He gives the details of the contract which the party concluded with the captain of the galley for their conveyance to the Holy Land, providing for all emergencies, even of death on board.[2] Then, in the form of a diary, he records with considerable accuracy the events of the pilgrimage day by day in a manner unknown in contemporary works of this kind. Taken as a whole, Faber's work is a lively human document abounding in items of interest, both general and special.

In a preliminary section, Felix enumerates the perils of the sea of which, except for foundering, the most serious and the least known from the writings of previous travellers is the peril of the perfect calm of wind and water. As a result of this abnormal quiet on the sea, the ship becomes stationary, the food putrid, the water and wine undrinkable, and insects of all descriptions spring into life to add to the melancholy and discomfort of the passengers in the foul air of the vessel.[3] Faber then describes the galley itself, the laws by which it is governed, the celebration of divine service on board, the pastimes of pilgrims while at sea, the manner of taking their meals, their sleeping accommodation, and finally enumerates some precautions against sickness of the body and weakening of the spirit.[4] After a full description of the route to Jaffa and the landing of these pilgrims, the author writes a very detailed account of the Holy Places, particularly those in and around Jerusalem. Although the Saracens are blamed for rough and inconsiderate handling of pilgrims on several occasions, Faber does not omit the mention of some incidents which help to explain the strength of the Mamlūk administration

[1] *Evagatorium*, I, 83.   [2] ib., I, 89–91.

[3] ib., I, 114–17. 'Quando enim nulli flant venti, et mare sine motu est, et navis fixa subsistit, tunc omnia in navi marceseunt, et putrescunt, et muscida fiunt, aquae foetidae, vinum inutile, carnes etiam desiccatae ad fumum vermiculis plenae, tunc subito generantur infinitae muscae, culices, pulices, pediculi, vermes, mures, et glires, et omnes homines in navi redduntur pigri, somnolenti, caloribus squalidi, passionibus tristitiae, irae, invidiae impatientes et caeteris indispositionibus gravati' (116).

[4] ib., I, 122 et seq.

and justice.   A Muslim merchant who had fraudulently sold worthless objects describing them as jewels to a Christian knight was flogged and forced to return the price to the victim.[1]   Faber's Saracen attendant, in spite of his fierce and cruel look, was friendly, kind and obliging to his master throughout the pilgrimage.[2]   On the outward journey to Mount Sinai, the pilgrims were allowed to take a hot bath in common with the Saracens without discrimination [3] between faithful and infidel.   At Ghazza, they saw an army of the Sultan including Christian renegades from Hungary, Sicily and Catalonia.   A Mamlūk of Hungarian origin came to the pilgrims to see whether there were any of his countrymen among them, and on finding one, he joined in their celebrations, drank wine with them in secret, and took some of the Christian visitors to view the Saracen camp and the army stables.   Thus they saw with wonder and admiration the army's equipment and beautiful horses.[4]

In the course of his account, Faber devotes two long chapters to the early history of Christianity in Jerusalem and to the Christian re-conquest of the Holy City by the nations of the West, chiefly drawn from Vincent de Beauvais' *Speculum Historiale* and Antonius's *Chronicon*.[5]   At the outset of the first chapter, he makes a very important statement which indicates the real attitude of the Western Christians towards the Holy Land after the fall of Constantinople.   'At this present day,' he says, 'the Christians would care little about the Saracen bearing rule in Jerusalem, provided only that we were allowed freedom to pass in and out of the temple of our Lord's Sepulchre without fear,

---

[1] ib., I, 201–2.   [2] ib., I., 207.
[3] ib., II, 368.   [4] ib., II, 371–3.
[5] This is probably the *Chronicon sive Summa historialis ab O.C.*–1437 by Antonius, Archbishop of Florence, who died in 1459.   Edited several times at Venice and Nuremberg during Faber's lifetime.   First Venetian ed. in 4 vols., 1474–9, and first Nuremberg ed. by Ant. Koburger in 3 vols., 1484— the year of Faber's return from the East.   Cf. Potthast, *Bibl. Hist. Medii Aevi*, 146.   Faber's sources also include the works of St. Augustine, St. Jerome, St. Thomas Aquinas, Albertus Magnus, Josephus, Eusebius, Orosius, Diodorus Siculus, Burcard and others.   *Evagatorium*, II, 120, 167, 173, 184, 200, 225, 256, 335, 347, 381, 448, 470–3; III, 61, 65, 83, 90, 105, 125, 128, 132, 160, 186–96, 247–51, 263, 271, 275, 305, 333, 342, 359, 33.

and without vexatious and extortionate payments.'[1] The crusades seem to him a matter of past history, which he narrates at some length in the second of the two afore-mentioned chapters.[2] The exodus of the Latins from the Holy Land and the final loss of Jerusalem, in Faber's opinion, were sealed by a noteworthy event. Gazan (Cazanus), the 'good Christian Emperor of the Tartars' occupied the holy city at the close of the thirteenth century and offered it to the prelates and princes of the West; but not one of them lifted a hand in response to that Emperor's offer. 'So, through this ingratitude, the Holy Land has been so utterly lost to us that now no one so much as thinks about recovering it, unless it should please God to work some miracle to that end.'[3] At the end of this chapter, Faber surveys the nations represented in the holy city and gives a brief account of their creeds and general characteristics.[4] These appear under separate headings including Saracens, Greeks, Syrian Christians, Jacobites, Abyssinians, Nestorians, Armenians, Georgians, Maronites, Turcomans, Bedouins, Assassins, Muhamma-dans, Mamlūks, Jews, and Latin Christians. His account of Muhammadanism, though not withholding blame, is fairer and much less influenced by legend than those of his predecessors. The Greeks cherish so great a hatred to-wards the Church of Rome that they have surrendered almost the whole of Greece to the Turks rather than submit to the Latins. The Syrian Christians are treacherous to Latin and Greek, effeminate and unfit for war. The Abyssinians are so much feared by the Saracens that they are allowed to travel unmolested in all parts of Muslim countries. The Mamlūks, chiefly renegade Christians, are

---

[1] *Evagatorium*, II, 233. 'Hodie Christiani parum curarent, quod Sarraceni dominarentur in Jerusalem, dummodo in templum nostrum dominici sepulchri pateret nobis libere ingressus et egressus sine timere, sine vexationibus et exactionibus.' Cf. A. Stewart, II, i, 262.

[2] ib., II, 249 et seq.

[3] ib., II, 318. 'Unde propter istam ingratitudinem alienata est terra sancta a nobis adeo, ut non sit amplius quasi cogitatus de rehabendo eam, nec est amplius via, nisi Deus aliquo miraculo velit operari ad hoc.' Cf. A Stewart, II, 377.

[4] ib., II, 323–8.

loathed by Saracen and Christian whom they govern by force of arms. The Latin Christians consist of a number of Minorite friars living in the church and monastery of Mount Sion. 'These alone,' Faber says, 'long with all their hearts for Christian princes to come and subject all the country to the authority of the Church of Rome, which may He grant Who reigneth for ever and ever '[1] But this was only an ideal which the author recognized as impossible of realization at that time.

Having thus completed their travels in the Holy Land, the pilgrims purchased all they needed for their visit to the Monastery of St. Catherine on their way to Alexandria, whence they would travel home by sea. The journey to Alexandria usually lasted forty-six days, of which twenty-five were spent in crossing the wilderness of Mount Sinai by caravan. After a short stay at the Convent, they took the road to Cairo, 'the greatest town in the whole world' whose antiquity and size Faber describes in a special chapter.[2] Finally, the pilgrims sailed downstream by the Rosetta branch of the Nile in the direction of Alexandria. This city, says Faber, was most favourably situated for purposes of commerce. It had two distinct harbours—one for the ships of the Christians and another for those of the infidels.[3] Within the walls, two towers were constructed on two artificial heights for the watch against the intrusion of armed enemy galleys into Egyptian waters. The governor of the city, a man of military ability and prudence, was kept in close contact with the authorities in the interior of the country by means of carrier-pigeons. These precautions were actuated by fear of a Christian invasion based on the

---

[1] ib., II, 328. 'Hi soli totis praecordiis optant, ut christiani principes veniant et Romanae ecclesiae et imperio omnia subjiciant, quod ille concedat, qui sine termino regnat.'

[2] ib., III, 78–83. 'Descriptio vel circumscriptio illius maximae urbis totius mundi, Cairi et Babyloniae novae, quae alias dicitur Babylonia Aegypti. Et implicantur multa in hac circumscriptione de Sarracenorum vita, et moribus et ritibus.'

[3] ib., III, 175–6. 'Civitas haec est commodissime sita ad celebranda commercia, portus habens duos disjunctos. . . .

'Portus anterior est pro navibus Christianorum suscipiendis, posterior vero pro navibus infidelium.'

memory of the expedition of Pierre de Lusignan which had
left the city in a state of ruin and desolation.[1]   Apart from
a description of Egypt, mainly drawn from ancient geographers, the rest of the *Evagatorium* consists of a detailed
account of the return journey by the traditional sea and
land routes to the Dominican convent at Faber's native
town of Ulm.

The sum-total of Faber's more relevant statements on
the subject of the crusade is that the Holy Land had
definitely passed from Christian to Saracen hands with
little hope of its recovery for Latin rule.   What he regarded
as a reasonable demand from the Sultan was confined to
the safe-conduct and freedom of Christian pilgrims to visit
the Holy Places.   This was the new orientation in the long-
standing contest between the East and the West, and
there is good reason to believe that most of Faber's contemporaries thought in this way.   On the other hand, the
memory of the successive disasters that had befallen the
Latins in their Eastern expeditions was too recent to be
lightly forgotten.   The rapid progress of the Muslim Turk
in Europe itself staggered all Christians, and the downfall
of Constantinople in 1453 profoundly moved them.   However violent the temper of Catholics might have been against
Eastern orthodoxy, Rome could not gaze upon such a
calamity as the extermination of the Empire of Constantinople without alarm as to the fate of the countries border-
ing on the newly acquired Ottoman territories and partly
or wholly subject to papal obedience.   The idea of the
crusade therefore underwent a significant change.   Originally an offensive war for the recovery of the Holy Land
from the Egyptians, it became a defensive struggle to
save Europe from the Turks.   This may be illustrated
by the propagandist activity of Pius II who appears to have

---

[1] *Evagatorium*, III, 178–9. 'Anno etiam Domini 1230 (*sic*) Petrus,
Cypri regis frater (*sic*), natione Gallicus, classe instructa cum Catalonis et
Gallicis eam invasit, dirupit et combussit, et ditissima spolia reportavit, nec
postea convaluit, unde hodie est civitas quodammodo desolata, et in dies
domus super domum cadit, et miserabiles ruinae sunt in ea, nam praeter
muscheas et domus Mamaloccorum, regentium, et fonticos mercatorum paene
deserta est, nec in domibus adhuc stantibus sunt habitatores.'

embraced the cause of the crusade some years before his accession in 1458 and who employed all his eloquence and diplomatic skill, especially during the last years of his pontificate to bring the forces of Europe into unison against their common enemy. He died at Ancona in 1464, a martyr to the cause of the crusade which he failed to lead against the Turks.[1]

Years before his pre-eminence in the Catholic hierarchy, Aeneas Sylvius, as papal nuncio to Germany, had displayed a singular interest in the crusade. Writing at Neustadt on 25 November 1448, he complains to Pope Nicholas V [2] (1447–55) of the discord and selfishness prevailing among the leaders of the Christian states, a fact which explains the crushing defeats inflicted by the Turks on the countries of Eastern Europe. At the Diets of Ratisbon [3] on 23 April 1454, of Frankfurt [4] on 28 September 1454, and of Neustadt [5]

[1] For Pius and the crusades, see Campano, *Vita Pii*, II, in *Muratori*, III, pt. ii, 974 *passim*; Sanudo, *Vitae Ducum Venetorum*, in *Muratori*, XXII, 1174; *Cronica di Bologna*, in *Muratori*, 732–3; Iorga, *Notes et extraits*, 4ᵉ serie, 175 et seq., Platina, *Lives of Popes*, II, 261–75; Gregorovius, *Stadt Rom* (German ed., 1908), VII, 194–208; C. M. Ady, *Pius II*, 304–39; C. N. di Camugliano, *Chronicle of a Florentine Family*, 264–77; Creighton, *Hist. of Papacy*, III, 311; Pastor, *Hist. of Popes*, III, 253 et seq.; L. Fumi, *Pio II e la pace di Oriento*, in *Studi e documenti di storia* (Rome, 1885), VI, 249 *passim*; Finlay, *Greece* (ed. Tozer), IV, 414–15; Bury's *Gibbon*, VII, 206–7; Milman, *Latin Christianity*, VII, 467–70; Robertson, *Christian Church*, VIII, 180–85; Daru, *Venise*, II, 567 et seq.; Barante, *Ducs de Bourgogne*, V, 120 et seq.

[2] Iorga, *Notes et extraits*, 4ᵉ série, 41–2. Iorga inadvertently makes Aeneas Sylvius report to Nicholas II instead of Nicholas V.

[3] ib., 90–1.

[4] ib., 101–2. In this Diet it was stipulated that, pending action in the following summer, the King of Hungary should conclude no treaty with the Turks, but instead should muster all his forces in readiness. In the meantime the Emperor, the Electors, the King of Bohemia and the Duke of Burgundy would meet at Neustadt to consider matters of detail, while the Pope was implored to exert every possible effort to win over Aragon, Venice, Genoa and the other Italian republics as well as the kingdom of France to the cause against the 'sevientem hostem fidei, magnum colubrem, dyabolicum hominem Machometum'.

[5] ib., 111–13. Discussions continued until April, but no definite decision was reached. It was not until 1460 (ib., 175–6) that a preliminary plan was adopted for a crusade which should be 'erlich . . ., nutzlich und fruchpar'.

on 24 February 1455, the papal envoy was one of the architects of projects for crusades considered by these assemblies.   After his election as Pope, Aeneas Sylvius, as Pius II, received many Eastern embassies, both genuine and false, and gave them much attention and hospitality. Perhaps the most impressive occasion was the flight of Thomas Palaeologos from the Morea to Rome with the head of St. Andrew in 1461.   The fugitive was granted an allowance, and the sacred relic was deposited in St. Peter's Cathedral with all the medieval pomp and honour due to saints and martyrs until it was finally removed to the special chapel built and consecrated for St. Andrew by Pius himself.[1]

The propagandist ideas of the Pope may be presented in two different categories.   In the first place, he aimed at the conversion of the Turks; but instead of following in the footsteps of Ramon Lull and the other great exponents of missionary work among Muslims, he naïvely adopted the primitive and hopeless method of writing an eloquent epistle in 1461 to Muhammad II in which he was conjured to stand forth as Constantine and Clovis and repudiate his errors by adopting the Christian faith.[2]   This way was, of course, foredoomed.   In the second place, failing the way of peace, the Pope resorted to the way of action.   He used his influence in an attempt to persuade all Christian states to contribute towards the manning of a fleet and the recruiting of an army for a crusade against the Turks. The negotiations which preceded this abortive project only served to prove the duplicity of the Italian republics and the meaninglessness of the promises of other Catholic states. At the outset, the situation seemed promising enough to

---

[1] *Pii Secundi . . . Commentarii Rerum memorabilium*; ed. J. Gobbelino and F. Bandino-Piccolomineo, Frankfurt, 1614.   Cf. C. M. Ady, *Pius II*, 310–13.   The Chapel of St. Andrew was demolished in the clearing operations for the construction of the new Basilica of St. Peter; but a statue of St. Andrew still indicates the spot where the head was preserved.

[2] Epistola no. 396, in *Pius's Opera*, 872 et eq.   This is a masterpiece of rhetoric and erudition in which Pius attempts to prove the superiority of the Christian religion and civilization.   Iorga (op. cit., 4ᵉ série, 126–7)—has edited an apocryphal letter written in Middle High German from Muhammad II to Pius II.

encourage the Pope in his design.   The Doge of Venice,
Prospero Malpiero, an advocate of peace with the Turks,
died in 1462 and was succeeded by Christoforo Moro.[1]   In
the same year alum mines were discovered by Giovanni
de Castro in the Tolfa mountains in the neighbourhood of
Civita-Vecchia, which added a new and considerable source
to papal revenues, while the Turkish mines in Asia Minor
suffered a serious blow.[2]   In the following year, the dissensions between the Emperor Frederick III and Matthias
Corvinus came to a happy end, and Hungary was thus free
to conclude its alliance with Venice against the Turks.   In
1463, too, a Burgundian embassy arrived in Rome to
inform the Pope that the Duke would be ready to lead an
army of 6,000 men to the East during the spring.[3]   Everything appeared to augur well for the crusade, and the Pope
published the Bull Ezechielis [4] (October 1463) preaching
holy war while he negotiated for the contributions of other
Italian Republics to the great cause.   Yet all this was
mirage.   When the time came for action, the European
princes found numerous pretexts in the internal troubles
of their own countries to justify their delay, or their absten-
tion from the crusade.   On account of their contiguity
to Turkish dominion, Hungary and Venice were the
only states to respond somewhat favourably to the papal
appeal.   The Duke of Burgundy, on the other hand, sent a
message to inform the Pope that he had to postpone his
promised Eastern expedition for another year and blamed
Louis XI for this decision.   The Italian republics were
more interested in courting the friendship of the Turks and
acquiring favourable trade terms from them than in uncertain expeditions which might involve their fleets and their
commerce in ruin.   Moreover, their jealousies and inter-
necine scheming were too strong to be curbed even

---

[1] Daru, l.c.; Hazlitt, *Venetian Republic*, II, 124–7; L. M. Bagg, *Crises in Venetian Hist.*, 120 et seq.

[2] The income accruing from the alum trade to the Sultan was estimated at 300,000 ducats per annum, and the Pope exhorted Christian countries to assist in deflecting this trade to Rome.   Reynaldus, *ad ann.* 1463, no 86 (7 April); *Commentarii*, vii, 185–6.   Cf. Ady, op. cit., 317–18.

[3] *Commentarii*, xii, 332.

[4] *Opera*, Ep. 412; *Commentarii*, xii, 344; cf. Ady, 323 n.1.

by papal oratory and intervention. Their contributions were far from sufficient to ensure the success of an expedition against a strong enemy; and the Pope had to fall back upon his own resources and construct a fleet of galleys of his own at Ancona.[1] To furnish the Princes of Europe with an example which they might follow, he himself took the Cross in St. Peter's on 18 July 1464.[2] He was then a sick man, incapable, not only of leading the crusade, but also of travelling to the port of embarkation. Nevertheless, he insisted on being carried, sometimes in a barge on the Tiber, and sometimes in a litter on the Ancona road, only to die at his destination on 14 August of the same year.[3] The disorderly recruits assembled at Ancona from many countries began to retrace their steps homeward, and the rulers of the Italian republics must have sighed with relief. The new project of crusade was buried with its author, and the states of Italy were left to pursue an egotistical policy which ultimately led them to the road of ruin. Paul II (1464–71), who succeeded to the Papal throne, though upholding the idea of the crusade in principle, lagged far behind his predecessor in enthusiasm for action. It appears that he gave the funds raised by Pius II for the crusade, to Venice and Hungary to be used in combating the Turks; and the idea of a papal crusade was only momentarily resuscitated at the Curia during the pontificate of Innocent VIII (1484–92) on the occasion of the flight of Bayezid II's brother, Djem, to the West.[4] This project, too, did not materialize, and Venice and Hungary were left alone to stem the rising tide of Turkish hostility to Christendom. The age of universal action and even of genuine propaganda for a crusade had gone by the end of the fifteenth century; and men like Felix Faber only wished to be allowed to perform their pilgrimage to holy places in peace, while others turned their thoughts to their own defence against the Ottoman menace nearer home.

[1] Sanudo, op. cit., in *Muratori*, XXII, 1178.
[2] Ady, 330.   [3] ib., 334–9.
[4] Robertson, *Hist. of Christian Church*, VIII, 231–3.

PART III
THE EAST AND THE CRUSADE

EUROPE AND THE TATARS[1]

Nestorian Church in Far East. Missions under Innocent VI: Giovanni de Plano Carpine and Ascelline. Embassies of Louis IX: André de Longjumeau and Guillaume de Rubruck. The Polos and Cathay. Establishment and extinction of the Roman Church in China: Giovanni de Monte Corvino. The Society of the Pilgrim Friars in the Middle East and Central Asia. Odoric of Pordenone and Giovanni dei Marignolli. Timur and the West. Failure of crusading alliances between Europe and the Tatars

THE field of the crusade during the later medieval period extended far beyond the confines of Syria and Palestine. The West looked to the Far and Middle East for assistance in its struggle with the Muslim powers of the Near East. The papal policy had three aims: first, it was hoped to bring the Tatars of the Khanates of Cambaluc [2] and Persia within the fold of the Roman Catholic Church, and thus secure a triumph for the Cross even greater than the conversion of the Magyars during the eleventh century; second, to eliminate by this means the growing danger of the new scourge of God whose ravages had twice caused consternation throughout Europe in the years 1222–3 and 1241–2, that is, within living memory at the beginning of the fourteenth century; [3] third, to obtain, at what was thought an auspicious moment, united action between the Latins and

[1] Tatar or Mongol is adopted here instead of the familiar but corrupt 'Tartar'.

[2] In Arabic sources Khan-Bāliq, the modern Peking.

[3] Matthew of Paris makes abundant reference to the impending Tatar menace and to the exchange of embassies between Europe and the Far East. *Chronica Majora et Additamenta*, and *Historia Anglorum*. *Vide* indices.

The first of the two campaigns reached the River Don and led to the settlement of the Kipchak Turks in the Southern Russian steppes, while the second was conducted further into Poland, Moravia and Hungary, thus reaching the confines of Germany, but without leaving any permanent Mongol settlement in these regions. Cahun, *Mongols*, 279, 243 et seq.

the Mongols to crush the Mamlūk empire between them. The idea of a crusade in which both forces might be brought to co-operate in saving the Holy Land from Muslim domination, though probably not a new one,[1] appears to have received increased consideration during the period under review.   The Pope had sent several missions and St. Louis had dispatched two embassies in order to promote Christianity at the court of the Great Khan, but though their preaching was heard with sympathy their plans never materialized.

For a fair estimate of the hopes based on the possibilities of such a union between the West and the Far East, it is necessary to summarize the origin and growth of pre-Latin Christianity among the Tatars and in China.[2]

Although Matteo Ricci[3] and other Jesuit missionaries, on their arrival in China late in the fifteenth century, searched for Christians in vain, Christianity had not been unknown in the Far East during the Early Middle Ages.[4] Tradition ascribes the foundation of a Christian Church in China to the Apostle St. Thomas.   The *Breviarium Chaldanicum*[5] states that 'by St. Thomas the Chinese also with

---

[1] G. F. Hudson (p. 135), though unfortunately giving no authorities in support of his assumption, suggests that the Byzantine embassies to China in the seventh century should be regarded as representing the first attempt at an alliance of this kind against Islam.   The absence of reference to the sources in Hudson's interesting study is unfortunate.

[2] In the Mongol empire, Christians were known as *tarsa*—a word used by Persian historians—and *ärkägün*, in Chinese ye-li-k'o-wen. Cordier, 62; cf. Pelliot, *T'oung Pao*, 1914, p. 636. Moule, 216–18. Although the subject of pre-Latin Christianity in the Far East has been much elucidated by numerous modern researches (*vide infra*, especially footnotes), it was not unknown to such early scholars as Claude Visdelou, Bishop of Claudiopolis (*c.* 1718); see d'Herbélot, Bibliothèque Orientale, (The Hague, 1779), IV, 369 et seq.—*Monument de la Religion Chrétienne, trouvé par hazard dans la ville de Si-Ngan-fu, métropole de la province de Xensi en Chine.*

[3] Biography of Matteo Ricci in D. Jenks, *Six Great Missionaries of the Sixteenth and Seventeenth Centuries* (London, 1930), 80–110; much more important is the monograph by Henri Bernard, *Matteo Ricci's Scientific Contribution to China*, Eng. trans. E. C. Werner (Peiping, 1935).

[4] Moule, 1 et seq., quotes Father Ricci at length.

[5] Ed. P. Badjan (3 vols., Paris, 1886), III, 476 and 478. Cf. Moule, 11 and 26. The Syrian Church in South India has been associated with the name of St. Thomas, its founder, according to tradition, until the present

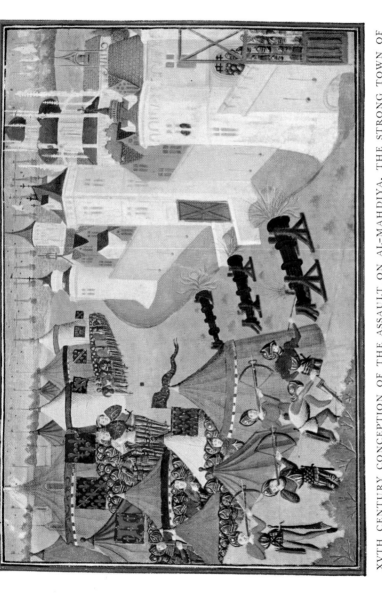

XVTH CENTURY CONCEPTION OF THE ASSAULT ON AL-MAHDIYA, THE STRONG TOWN OF AFRIQUE. (M. CLXVII, P. 401.) MS. HARL. 4379, FOL. 83 VO.

the Ethiopians have turned to the truth', that 'St. Thomas has flown and gone to the Kingdom of the Height among the Chinese', and that the 'Indians and Chinese . . . bring worship in commemoration of Thomas to thy name, our Saviour'. This is no place to discuss the historical value of these statements; but it is certain from internal evidence that the Nestorian Church had been established in China as early as the seventh century. A slab of stone [1] bearing Christian inscriptions in the Chinese language, found several feet beneath the surface of the earth near the city of Chou-Chih to the west or south-west of Hai-an in Shensi (Shan-hsi), is believed to date from the T'ang [2] period and is probably connected with a church [3] built in that district in 638. T'si Tsung, known as the 'polished emperor', received with honour in 635 a certain A-lo-pen, a Persian monk of high virtue who 'carried the true Scriptures'. The Emperor read his books and commanded that they should be made known throughout his realm.[4] Three years later (638), a decree was published ordering the local officials of the I-ning quarter to build a monastery for this holy man and twenty regular monks.[5]

During the subsequent centuries, the number of Christians in those regions appears to have multiplied. This is clear from contemporary materials, both Chinese and Syriac, which are, moreover, confirmed from Arabic sources. Moule [6] has mentioned some of the Arab authors who made statements to this effect. These include Abu Zaid [7]

day. Tradition, too, associates his name with China, as is shown by the words of Ebedjesus 'et Sinensium' and of Amru's 'et ulteriores Sinas' when both enumerate the parts evangelized by the Saint.

[1] Moule, 27–35. For tradition of St. Thomas, see also Cordier's *Notes on Yule's Marco Polo*, 116–18.

[2] The T'ang Dynasty reigned in China from 618 to 907 A.D.

[3] Moule, 32.

[4] ib., 28–9. Cf. Havret, *La stèle chrétienne* (in Variétés sinologiques, 1895, &c.), 22–4; Parker, *A Thousand Years of the Tartars*, 142.

[5] Moule, 65 and 66.   [6] ib., 75–7.

[7] E. Renaudot, *Anciennes relations des Indes et de la Chine, Seconde relation ou discours d'Abouzeid el Hacen Sirafien*, 45, 50 and 51. Cf. Moule, 76–7 note 97. Like Hakluyt and Purchas, Abu Zaid had never seen China, but collated other people's travels. Renaudot's first Relation is an edition of the travels of a certain Sulaiman, and the second is Abu Zaid's corrections and

(A.H. 304/A.D. 916), and Abu'l-Faraj [1] (c. A.H. 377/A.D. 987). Another Arab traveller, apparently unknown to the historians of the medieval church in China despite his importance, is also worthy of special attention. Abu Dulaf,[2] a poet at the court of the Samanid Naṣr II b. Aḥmad of Bokẖāra (A.H. 301–31/A.D. 913–42), was enjoined by his master in 942 to accompany a Chinese embassy back to its native country. Later he wrote an interesting account of his travels [3] in which he recorded that he had met Christians and seen churches in several towns in China.[4]

additions to the first. See also Reinaud, *Relation des voyages* (Paris, 1845), xv, 63 (text), 64 (trans.); G. Ferrand, *Relations de voyages et textes géographiques arabes, persans et turks relatifs à l'Extrême-Orient*, I, 82–9.

[1] *Kitāb al-Fihrist*, edited by G. Flügel (2 vols., Leipzig, 1871–2) and G. Ferrand, op. cit., I, 118 et seq. For Christians in China, see Flügel, I, 349 and Ferrand, I, 129.

[2] Full name, Abu Dulaf Misʿar b. Muhalhal. See short biography by C. Brockelmann in EI, III, 519–20; also Yāqūt's *Dictionary*, I, 89–90.

[3] See Yāqūt's famous geographical *Dictionary*, ed. Wüstenfeld, III, 444 et seq.; published separately by the same editor from a Qazwīnī text in *Zeitschrift für vergleichende Erkunde* (Magdeburg, 1842), II, 205–18; then collated from both Yāqūt and Qazwīnī by K. von Schölzer, Berlin, 1845; see also Ferrand, op. cit., 89–90; Ferrand in the same work made a French trans. of Abu Dulaf from the Yāqūt text, 210 et seq. The most important study on Abu Dulaf is probably J. Marquart's *Das Itinerar des Misʿar ben al-Muhalhil nach der chinesischen Hauptstadt*, in *Oesteuropäische und ostasiatische Streifzüge* (Leipzig, 1903), 74–95.

Although our references are made to the version of Abu Dulaf's account of China in Yāqūt's *Dictionary*, it must be noted that this is incomplete. Abu Dulaf's original and complete work has recently been discovered in the unique Meshhed MS. of Aḥmad b. Muḥammad b. al-Faqīh's *Kitāb Akhbār al-Buldān* in the Mausoleum of Imām Riẓa library. Photographs of this MS. are now preserved in the Staatsbibliothek in Berlin (MS. Simulata Or. 48), ff. 175 ro et seq. Abu Dulaf's work consists of two epistles (*Risālahs*). The first (ff. 175 ro–183 vo.) is incorporated *in extenso* by Yāqūt under al-Ṣīn (China), but the second (ff. 183 vo.–196 vo.) is quoted only in part and under various headings by him. The whole of Abu Dulaf's *Risālahs* are now in preparation for publication in the Oriental Seminary of the University of Bonn. Cf. P. Kahle, *Islamische Quellen zum chinesischen Porzellan*, in ZDMG, Band 88 (1934), 43–5.

[4] Abu Dulaf found Christians in China and Central Asia among the tribes of 'Jikl' (Yāqūt, III, 446 and Ferrand, I, 211), 'Tubbat' (Yāqūt, III, 447 and Ferrand, I, 213) and 'Khītān' (Yāqūt, III, 450 and Ferrand, I, 218) and also in the town of 'al-Ṣaimūr' (Yāqūt, III, 453–4 and Ferrand, I, 223).

The door of China was therefore not closed to Christians. The reason is not far to seek; for China that we are now apt (perhaps with some exaggeration) to regard as the example of discord and uncertainty, was, except on a limited number of occasions, a haven of peace and security for the foreigner during the Middle Ages. Ibn Baṭṭūṭa,[1] who travelled in the fourteenth century, provides us with a graphic description of a system by which foreign travellers were escorted from one government 'funduq'[2] (hostelry) to the next, from whose warden the escort had to procure a diploma testifying to the safe arrival of the guests. 'The land of China,' he says, 'is the most secure of all lands and the best at present for the traveller. A person can journey alone (in China) for nine months with vast treasure for which he need harbour no fear.'[3]

Protected by this 'Pax Tartarica',[4] the Nestorian priest, the Muhammadan traveller, the Western merchant and the Catholic missionary moved freely throughout the territories under Mongol rule. First on the scene was the Nestorian, then followed the Muslim Arab and finally the Western Christian. The works of the Latins who visited China, the diplomatic correspondence exchanged between the Pope and Kings of France on the one side and the Mongol Khans on the other, and the records of the missionary work and acts of heroism by the heralds of Roman Catholicism—all these have recently been brought to light. Christianity is indeed reported to have suffered twice complete obliteration in China, in A.D. 980[5] and in A.D. 1368, with the downfall of the Mongol dynasty.[6] Nevertheless, there is sufficient

---

[1] *Voyages* (Defrémery and Sanguinetti), IV, 267–8. Compare with Pegolotti's *Libro di Divisamenti di Paesi* written between 1335 and 1343 from which Hudson (156) quotes an interesting passage to the effect that the route to China across the central Asian steppes was 'perfectly safe, whether by day or by night'. Extracts from Pegolotti in Yule's *Cathay and the Way Thither*, III, 137–73.

[2] Through Arabic, this word passed into European language as fondaco, fondachi, fontechi. See previous chapters.

[3] Ibn Baṭṭūṭa, op. cit., IV, 267.

[4] For the use of this term, see Hudson, 134, 156 and 159.

[5] Abu'l-Faraj, l.c. Cf. Moule, 75–6.

[6] Moule's chronological table, 271.

evidence that numerous conversions were made during
the thirteenth and fourteenth centuries, and that the Great
Khans were not unfavourably disposed to the adoption of
Christianity [1] as their state religion and to union with
Europe in its fight against Islam.

The earliest exchange of embassies dates from the middle
of the thirteenth century. This took place between Pope
Innocent IV [2] and the Great Khan Güyük. In 1245,
during the meeting of the Council of Lyons, the Holy
Pontiff sent two ambassadors with letters inviting the Great
Khan and the people of 'Tartary' to join the Church and
take up the cause of Christendom. One of these ambas-
sadors, Lorenzo of Portugal, was appointed to go to the
Tatar court by way of Armenia and Persia, but it is doubtful
whether he went further than Lajazzo.[3] The other, a
Franciscan, Giovanni de Plano Carpini,[4] left Lyons on 16
April 1245 and took the northern route to Kiev [5] where he

---

[1] For short account of Christianity among the Mongols, see W. Barthold,
Turkestan down to the Mongol Invasion (Revised ed. and trans. by H. A. R.
Gibb, London, 1928), 387–90.

[2] The origin of this movement may, however, be traced as far back as the
pontificate of Gregory IX (1227–41) who is said to have dispatched the first
Franciscan mission to Baghdad in 1233. In the same year, the same Pope
issued the following seven bulls for missionary work in Mesopotamia, Asia
Minor, Syria, Egypt, Georgia and Morocco: (i) *Animarum salutem* (24
March, data fratribus Minoribus presbyteris in terras Saracenorum proficiscentibus); (ii) *Cum messis multa* (8 April, data fratribus Ord. Min. in
terras Georgianorum, Saracenorum et aliorum infidelium proficiscentibus);
(iii) *Animarum salutem* (6 May); (iv) *Cum messis multa* (17 May); (v) *Pro
zelo fidei* (17 May); (vi) *Animarum salutem* (31 May); (vii) *Cum messis
multa* (10 June). Sbaralea, *Bullar., an. cit.*; Eubel, Epitome, nos. 102, 104,
107–8; Golubovich, II, 300–1.

In 1244 Innocent IV (1243–54) issued two similar bulls—*Pro zelo
christianae fidei* and *Animarum salutem*—for missionaries in the East. Golubovich, II, 315.

Little is known of these early missions as compared with that of 1245, the
documents of which are brought together by Golubovich, II, 317.

[3] Golubovich, II, 319–24; Pelliot, *Mongols et Papauté*, 5–7.

[4] Carpini's mission was 'ad Tartaros et nationes alias Orientis', a phrase
which points to the possibility that the envoy may have had other letters to
other 'nations' of the East; Carpini, ed. Beazley, p. 43; Pelliot, 7 note 1.
Further material on Carpini may be found in Golubovich, II, 318–19;
Howorth, I, 162 et seq.; III, 350 and 533; IV, 93–5.

[5] For routes in Asia, see article by Miss Eileen Power in *Travel and*

arrived on 3 February 1246.[1] He finally reached the
imperial camp of Sira-Ordo in Mongolia within half a day's
journey of Qaraqorum on 22 July 1246[2] and witnessed the
coronation of Güyük on 15 August.[3] He remained the
guest of honour at the new Khan's court till 13 November
1246. At the end of 1247, the envoy had returned to
Innocent with Güyük's reply,[4] which, though non-com-
mittal, was neither forbidding nor even unfriendly.

Materials concerning Plano Carpini's mission are abundant in the Papal Registers and in the chronicles of Mathew of Paris and Vincent of Beauvais, in addition to the ambassador's own account of his travels. The details of Lorenzo's journey are, on the other hand, very scanty. There
was, however, a third [5] and little-known embassy from the
same Pope Innocent IV. During the sitting of the Council
of Lyons, he dispatched a certain Ascelline,[6] a Dominican
Friar of Lombard origin, with three [7] members of his Order
to deliver papal letters to the Great Khan or his representative. On their way, they seem to have been joined [8] by two
more brothers—André de Longjumeau [9] and Guichard of
Cremona.[10] It is very probable that Ascelline's letters were
similar in all respects to those entrusted to Giovanni de

Travellers in the Middle Ages, 124–58; Beazley, *Dawn of Modern Geography*,
III, 309–99; M. B. Charlesworth, *Trade Routes of the Roman Empire* (Cambridge, 1924), 99–109; Heyd, *Histoire du commerce*, II, 221 et seq.

[1] 'Secunda die post festum Purificationis Dominae nostrae.' Pelliot, 8
note 1.

[2] Carpini, ed. Beazley, 99, 'in die Beatae Mariae Magdalenae'.

[3] ib., 100. 'In die Assumptionis Dominae nostrae.'

[4] This document is extant in the original Tatar tongue, in Persian and in
Latin. Pelliot, op. cit., 11–28.

[5] ib., 66–139; P. Mortier, *Histoire des maîtres généraux de l'Ordre des
Frères Précheurs*, I (1903), 383–4; Howorth, III, 72–6.

[6] He appears in the sources under various names, Ansellimus, Anselmus,
Azelino, Anzelin, Ezzelino, Ascelinus, Azelinus, and Ezelino. Pelliot, 87–94,
discusses these forms and adopts Vincent of Beauvais' spelling of Ascellines or
Ascelen. This is also the form adopted by Giovanni de Plano Carpini, 74
and 107.

[7] Alberic, Alexander and Simon de Saint-Quentin. Pelliot, 67.

[8] ib., 94.

[9] Famous in connexion with St. Louis' embassy to the Tatars. *Vide infra.*

[10] Guichard discontinued the voyage at Tiflis where he stayed at the
Convent of his Order. Pelliot, 97.

Plano Carpini and addressed to the Great Khan and the
nations of the East.[1]   Ascelline started his journey from
Lyons in March on July [2] 1245 and was joined by his other
companions on the way to Tiflis.   Thence the company
proceeded through Armenia, Georgia, Syria and Persia to
the camp of Baiju, the Great Khan's lieutenant in Western
Asia—'in territorio Sitiens castri',[3] arriving there probably
during May 1247 and staying till late in July of the same
year.   At first, the outlook for the ambassadors was rather
unpromising.   Arriving without presents and with letters
implying papal superiority, the Dominicans moreover, refused to pay the Tatar homage of kneeling three times before
Baiju whom they thus prejudiced against themselves.[4]   Some
of the army chiefs spoke of inflicting the penalty of death on
them for their arrogance.   The situation was saved only by
the timely advent of a messenger from the Great Khan
instructing Baiju to adopt a friendly attitude towards the
Western ambassadors, who were thereupon returned safely
and with letters similar in intent to those carried by Plano
Carpini from Güyük.   The interesting feature in this
diplomatic exchange is that Baiju sent two envoys with the
Pope's representatives.   These were Aï-beg and Sargis—
the first name evidently of Turkish origin and the second
probably that of a Nestorian Christian.[5]   The Tatar's
motive was to spy on the strength of the Western nations
and of the Pope.   The embassy took the road to 'Akka.
We next meet them in Lyons [6] where they stayed at the
papal court till the death of the Emperor Frederick II on
19 December 1250 and the return of the Holy Pontiff to
Rome.   Innocent IV held several meetings with them to

---

[1] Pelliot, 74–5.   [2] ib., 96–7.
[3] Baiju's reply to the papal letters; ib., 102–3.   On the authority of
Barbier de Meynard, *Dictionnaire historique de la Perse*, 334, Pelliot, op. cit.
104–5, identifies 'Sitiens' as Saisaban, Saisawan or Saisian; see also Yāqūt',
Geographical Dictionary (ed. Wüstenfeld), III, 215.
[4] ib., 111 et seq.
[5] ib., 131.
[6] Matthew of Paris records their arrival in the summer of 1248; *Chronica
Majora* (ed. Luard), V, 37–8, and *Historia Anglorum* (ed. Madden), III
38–9.   Cf. *Mon. Germ. Hist.*, XXVIII, 301–2; Rémusat, *Mémoires*, 1e *Mém.*
426; and Pelliot, 134.

inquire as to the disposition of their people towards conversion to Christianity and co-operation with the West. He then sent them home with valuable presents and with letters courting Tatar alliance and goodwill.[1]

André de Longjumeau [2] reappeared on the scene in connexion with the first of the two embassies sent by Louis IX to the Mongol Emperor. The King had already taken the Cross in 1241, and the crusade was preached in France until he sailed from Aigues-Mortes on 28 August 1248. He landed at Limassol in Cyprus on 17 September and established his headquarters at Nicosia with King Henri I of the house of Lusignan until the expedition sailed to Damietta on 13 May 1249.[3] It was between these two dates that negotiations were resumed with the Tatar Khan Äljigidäi,[4] who had taken the initiative by dispatching two envoys— David and Marcus [5]—with a letter to St. Louis as soon as the news of his crusading project reached the East. This letter is a document of great importance.[6] First, it is 'missi a rege terre chan verba Elchelthay' to 'Regi magno, propugnatori strenuo orbis, gladio christianitatis etc., filio regis Francie' [7]—in other words from monarch to monarch and from equal to equal, with all due reverence and without arrogance. Second, the Tatar seeks the benefit of co-

---

[1] Pelliot, 134–5.

[2] The third and last fascicule of Pelliot's study, *Mongols et Papauté*, 141–222 contains a detailed reconstruction of Longjumeau's career.

[3] ib., 150–1; Wallon, *St. Louis* (Paris, 1875), I, 277.

[4] Äljigidäi is known in the Western sources as Elchalchai, Elgigaday, Elchelchai, Elchalcai, Elcheltay, Ercalthay, Eschartay and Achatay. Pelliot, op. cit., 154; Golubovich, III, 356.

[5] Vincent of Beauvais (xxxii, 91), 'Sabeldin Musfat David'; Guillaume de Nangis (*Recueil des historiens*, XX, 360), 'Sabeldin Mouffath David;' Mathew of Paris (*Chron. Majora*, VI, 146), 'Saphadin Mephat-Davi'; *Annales S. Rudberti Salisbury* (*Mon. Ger. Hist.*, IX, 790), 'Salbotum Monfat sive Monfath David'; *Grandes chroniques de France* (IV, 295), 'David, Marc et Olphac' and sometimes only 'Marc et Alphac'. The first of these ambassadors may be identified as Saif-al-Dīn Muẓaffar Da'ūd (i.e. the-sword-of-the faith the-Victorious David), an Arabic name of a Nestorian Christian probably from the region of Mosul. Marcus is the name of another Nestorian who might have been in Mongol service. *Vide* Pelliot, op. cit., 152–4.

[6] The best edition of this letter appears in Pelliot, 161–5.

[7] ib., 161–2.

operation with the French and offers to do everything in his power to free all Christians from servitude 'in honore et reverentia et nullus tangat possessiones eorum'.[1] Third, the letter makes a statement which betrays the hand of an Eastern [2] Christian scribe, that in the law of God, there is no difference amongst 'all who worship the Cross' whether they be Latins, Greeks, Armenians, Nestorians or Jacobites.[3] The letter was a great diplomatic achievement on the part of the Mongols. The downfall of the Caliphate of Baghdad at their hands was contemplated and it was essential for the establishment of their power at the ancient Muslim capital to keep the Egyptians busy in another field while Islam remained at their mercy in the Middle East. In this, they succeeded, and the history of St. Louis' crusade against Egypt is a vindication of their wise policy.

On the other hand, the French king treated the Mongol [4] representatives with honour and respect, took them to attend Mass with him, and finally granted them leave to return to their master on 27 January 1249. With them he sent another embassy of three Dominican brothers—André and Guillaume de Longjumeau and Jean de Carcassonne. As the first of these had just returned from the East after valuable experience with the Tatars, he was appointed 'capitaneus et magister' of the mission.[5] The pious St. Louis was more concerned with the salvation of the souls of the Mongols than with their possible use as allies in his crusading plans.

[1] Pelliot, 163.

[2] It is interesting to note that several passages of the letter read like Arabic or Persian, e.g. the 'centum milia salutem' in the incipit, the recurring 'Domino concedente' (the Arabic Inshallah), and the explicit 'Datum in finibus Muharram'.

[3] ib., 163; Reynaldus, ad ann. 1248 no. 35; Golubovich, II, 389. 'Ita precipit quod in lege Dei non sit differentia inter latinum et graecum et armenicum (et) nestorinum et iacobinum, et omnes qui adorunt crucem.'

[4] Cahun, 391; *Nicopolis*, 168 note 20.

[5] Pelliot, 176 et seq. Rockhill (*Journey of Rubruck*), xxix, though uncertain about the third member of the mission, states that they were further reinforced with four laymen of whom one 'maistre Jehans Goderiche' appears to be an Englishman.

The new embassy sailed from Cyprus to Antioch,[1] travelled inland to Mosul[2] and Tauriz (Tabriz), and finally arrived at Äljigidäi's camp in the heart of Persia. Unfortunately, the Great Khan Güyük had died and Äljigidäi would not undertake the full responsibility of deciding the new line of policy in regard to co-operation with St. Louis. The ambassadors had no alternative other than to proceed further east to the imperial court where Q'ul-qaimiš occupied the throne for the brief period before both he and Äljigidäi were killed by Mongka. Gifts were exchanged and credentials were presented, but the intrigue that followed Güyük's death again prevented decisive action. Longjumeau and his companions ultimately returned to the Levant by way of Aleppo in 1251[3] without securing either Tatar conversion to Christianity or Tatar co-operation in the crusade. However, they related to the King the vast possibilities for missionary work in Mongolia, possibilities which made strong appeal to the saintly king.

On Longjumeau's return, Louis IX dispatched another embassy composed of Guillaume de Rubruck and another friar, Bartolomeo da Cremona.[4] Rubruck recorded the experiences of his Eastern adventure in the form of a *Diary*[5] which he dedicated to St. Louis. This work has been unanimously recognized by Far Eastern scholars as a source of unusual importance for the conditions of travel in medieval Asia and for the Tatar races in that age. But, besides this, the historian can find there much that is relevant to missionary activities in Mongolia and to the subject of co-operation between East and West for an effective crusade.

Starting from Caesarea in 1252, Rubruck and his com-

---

[1] Joinville (ed. Wailly), 168.   [2] Pelliot, 191.

[3] ib., 208 et seq., Rockhill, xxxiii, 119, 136; Joinville (ed Wailly), 175.

[4] They were accompanied by one Nicholas, Rubruck's servant. Purchas, XI, 9.

[5] For MSS., editions and translations, see Beazley and Rockhill. A complete English version appears by Samuel Purchas. His *Pilgrimes*, XI, 5–149, to which reference is chiefly made in this chapter. Rubruck or Rubruquis was a Franciscan of Flemish origin. For a general account of his journey, see Howorth, I, 215–16, 540–1, and IV, 94–5; *Travel and Travellers in the Middle Ages*, 129–32; Baker, 35; Hudson, 147–8. Pelliot, 208–22, refers briefly to Rubruck, and Moule not at all.

panions went to Constantinople, then sailed to Soldaia in
the Crimea and marched to the camp of Batu in the Russian
steppes and to the court of Mongka Khan in Mongolia.[1]
On their way, they visited the Alan [2] tribes, who professed
the Catholic faith, but only in name, since they had no
shepherd to guide them and teach them the tenets of their
religion. 'Then instructed I them as well as I could and
strengthened them in the faith,' [3] says Rubruck. In the
cities of the Eastern mountains of Adia, Rubruck found, not
only idolators, but also Nestorians, Catholics and even Saracens living side by side in perfect harmony.[4] Within a bowshot of the imperial court, the ambassadors rejoiced to find a
chapel with 'an Altar very well furnished, for there in a
Golden cloth were Images of Christ and the blessed Virgin
and Saint John Baptist and two Angels, the lineaments of
their bodies and garments distinguished with Pearls, and a
great silver Cross having precious stones in the corners, and
the middle thereof, and many other Embroiderings; and a
Candle burning with Oil before the Altar, having eight
Lights'.[5] Inside the chapel, they met an Armenian monk
who had come only one month before them, and he said
that 'he was a Hermit of the Territory of Hierusalem'.[6]
After joining in singing Ave Regina Coelorum and in
prayer, the Armenian advised them to tell Mongka Khan
that if he became a Christian, the whole world would be

[1] Purchas (Rubruck), XI, 9 et seq. On arrival in the Crimea, the
ambassadors were received with honour by Sartokh, son of Batu Khan;
Golubovich, II, 388.

[2] Alan tribes, Alaian or Alani. Cf. Moule, 140, 141, 196, 208, 252, 254,
258, 260–4; Howorth, I, 128, 138, 314. According to Bratianu, *Commerce
génois dans la Mer Noire au XIIIe siècle* (Paris, 1929), 116, 215, 280, 283,
the Alani seem to have entered into the service of the Byzantine princes and
participated in their broils for a time towards the end of the thirteenth, and
the opening of the fourteenth century.

[3] Purchas, XI, 29.

[4] ib., 59 et seq.

[5] ib., 74–5. For another description of a Cross brought by an Armenian
from Jerusalem, see p. 91. This was made of silver and weighed 'foure
markes', had precious stones in the corners and the middle, but lacked
the 'Image of our Saviour (because the Armenians and the Nestorians are
ashamed that Christ should appear nailed to the Cross)'.

[6] ib., 75.

obedient to him. Rubruck's answer to this suggestion was that he would willingly persuade the Emperor to turn Christian, 'For I came for this purpose, to preach thus unto all'; but he could not promise him that the French and the Pope would pay him tribute.[1]

On Christmas Day, the Great Khan granted the ambassadors an audience, and because it was Christmas they sang at his gate the hymn:

> 'A solis ortus cardine,
> Et usque Terrae limitem,
> Christum canamus Principem,
> Natum Maria Virgine.' [2]

On this occasion, however, Rubruck's oration was of no avail, for the Emperor had not recovered from the previous night's jubilation and heavy drinking. During a second meeting, they sang 'Veni Sancte Spiritus' in his presence and after listening to the Nestorian's argument in praise of his creed as against all others, the Great Khan departed, leaving his queen to distribute gifts to the monks.[3] It is interesting to note that the tutor of Mongka's eldest son was a Nestorian called David.[4] The Eastern Christians appear to have been much in favour at the imperial court. On one occasion an Armenian fled to the Great Khan to complain that a church in his native land had been destroyed by the Saracens, and the Tatar ordered that it should be rebuilt at his expense from the tribute paid by Persia and Greater Armenia.[5] Rubruck does not conceal his bitter hatred of the Greek and Nestorian schismatics in Mongolia, although he indirectly testifies to their activity in that field. He tells us, for instance, that the Nestorians 'baptized in the Vigil of Easter more than threescore persons very orderly', and that all Christians rejoiced at this triumph.[6] It is more than doubtful whether he himself achieved any measure of success in converting others or even in impressing the Great

---

[1] ib., l. c.   [2] ib., 77.   [3] ib., 87.

[4] ib., 90. Rubruck describes David as 'a very Drunkard', but his verdict is not to be accepted without reservations, for David was a 'loathsome schismatic'.

[5] ib., 91. The cost amounted to 200 jascots or 2,000 marks.

[6] ib., 107.

Khan with the sanctity of his mission.   One day Rubruck
and his companions were curtly dismissed with the words,
—'Chan knows well enough that you have no message unto
him, but you came to pray for him, as many other Priests
do.'¹   Discouraged and unsuccessful in his mission,
Rubruck left his companion Bartolomeo da Cremona to
continue preaching to the Tatars, and he himself retraced
his steps to the West in July 1254.   At the end of his
Journal, he informs King Louis IX that Turkey was full of
Christians and that the occupants of its throne were impotent children.²   This explains his preference for the land
route to Constantinople and through Turkey and Armenia,
which he recommends to the crusaders.   He advises the
King and the host of the Cross to adopt the simple ways
of living practised by the Tatars, and 'they might win
the whole world'.³   Finally, realizing the failure of his
mission to the Tatars, he implores that 'our Sovereign Lord
the Pope would honourably send a Bishop, and answer
their follies'.⁴

Hitherto no Latin traveller had ever gone beyond the
Khanates of Persia and Mongolia into the interior of
China itself.   This was achieved for the first time in
history by two Venetian merchants, Niccolò and Maffeo
Polo.   The two brothers, led on in their quest for trade,
penetrated further and further into Cathay until they reached
the court of Qublai Khan about 1265.   On their return to
Europe some four years later, they visited Pope Gregory X
and informed him that Qublai asked for Christian missionaries to preach their religion in his realm.⁵   At the end of

¹ Purchas, 117.   ² ib., 147–8.   ³ ib., 148–9.
⁴ ib., 149.   For the establishment of a Catholic hierarchy in China, see
below in the account of Giovanni di Monte Corvino.
⁵ H. Yule, *Book of Ser Marco Polo*, I, 13–14; cf. Publ. de la Soc. de l'Or.
Lat., *Itinéraires français, XIᵉ–XIIIᵉ S., Voyages en Syrie de Nicolo, Maffeo et
Marco Polo*, ed. Michelant et Raymond (Geneva, 1883), 207–8; Moule, 129,
The purport of the letter from Qublai Khan was that 'He begged that the
Pope would send as many as an hundred persons of our Christian faith;
intelligent men, acquainted with the Seven Arts, well qualified to enter into
controversy, and able clearly to prove by force of argument to idolators and
other kinds of folk, that the Law of Christ was best, and that all other religions
were false and naught, and that if they would prove this, he and all under him

1271, the Holy Pontiff responded by appointing two Dominican [1] friars to accompany the merchants and open up this new field for missionary work. He supplied them with letters to the Emperor of China; but the Dominicans, intimidated by the ravages of a Mamlūk invasion of 'Armenia',[2] discontinued the journey at Lajazzo. Fortunately, the Polo brothers had taken with them this time Niccolò's young son, Marco Polo, who stayed in China for seventeen years and afterwards wrote a complete account of his adventures.[3]

Marco found on his arrival that Nestorian Christianity had long been ahead of him in these regions as explained at the opening of this chapter. The Saracens, too, had reached the court of Qublai Khan with the mission of Islam.[4] In an attempt to define the Tatar's conception of different religions, Marco puts the following words in the mouth of Qublai: 'The Christians say their God is Jesus Christ, the Saracens Mahomet, the Jews Moses, the idolators Sogomoni Borcan, . . . and I do honour and reverence to all four.' . . . 'But by that which the Great Kaan showed,' continues Marco, 'he holds the Christian faith for the most true and good, because he says that it does not command a thing which is not full of goodness and holiness.' [5] The writer then blames the Pope for his failure

would become Christians and the Church's liegemen.' Finally, he charged his envoys to bring back to him some 'Oil of the Lamp which burns on the Sepulchre of our Lord at Jerusalem.'

[1] These were Niccolò of Vicenza and William of Tripoli. Yule, 22.

[2] The reigning Sultan in Egypt at this time was the first Bahrite Mamlūk, Baibars (1260–77), a strong ruler who inflicted several crushing defeats on the Christians in Syria. Weil (*Abbasidenchalifats*), I, 61 et seq.; Muir (*Mamelukes*), 24–6.

[3] For a full bibliography of Marco Polo, see Yule's introduction and Cordier's *Notes and Addenda*, 137–43. Moule, 128–43, has brought together most of the relevant extracts from Polo's work bearing on the subject of Christians in China. Howorth, I and IV *passim*, also includes much useful material, *vide* indices.

[4] Moule, 131, 137, 138, 141.

[5] ib., 135–6 The Khan, in abhorrence of the manner of Christ's death, prohibited the carrying of the Cross which he regarded as a brutal reminder of His crucifixion.

to comply with the Khan's request to send Christian
preachers to his realm; for this, he assures us, would have
resulted in the conversion of the whole of China.[1]   The
way had already been paved for the spread of Christianity
in that country.   There were Kings in Cathay who, with
most of their subjects, professed the faith of the Cross.[2]
To argue with the Tatars on religion, was not Marco's
vocation.   After remaining in China from 1275 to 1292 in
the service of the Great Khan as army chief, governor of
provinces and towns, counsellor and ambassador, he returned to the West by the sea route round the east and
south coasts of Asia to Persia, whence he proceeded to
Venice in 1295 by way of Tabriz, Trebizond and Constantinople.[3]

The true and worthy successor of Marco Polo was
Giovanni de Monte Corvino, a man whose singular heroism,
extraordinary career and genuine self-denial mark him as
the great founder of the Roman Catholic Church in China
and the father of Latin missionaries in the Far East.   By
his contemporaries and later historians, he would have
passed unnoticed, had not one of his letters reached the
West after he had been working and preaching single-
handed for years in Cathay.   Of his life, little is known
beyond what can be derived from a few papal letters and
Corvino's own correspondence.[4]   Born in the first half of
the thirteenth century, Monte Corvino is believed to have
been a 'soldier, judge and teacher . . . and then became

[1] Moule, 137.

[2] Yule, I, 248 et seq.; Cordier's *Notes*, 62.

[3] Baker, 46 et seq.   Book III of the text of Marco Polo contains all the
details of the journey.   On this occasion Marco was travelling as the Great
Khan's ambassador in the train of a bride for the Khan of Persia.

[4] The letters were first discovered by Luke Wadding who published them
in the *Annales Minorum, an.* 1305; some appear in Reynaldus, *Annal. eccles.,
an. cit.*; Golubovich, II, 131–7, and III, 86–95.   Moule, 168–213, has
rendered them into English from a contemporary MS. (B.N., fonds latin
5006) and compiled a good bibliography of the subject, 213–15.   Reference
is made here to Moule unless otherwise specified.

Additional material for Giovanni's life may be found in *The Book of the
Estate of the Great Kaan*, probably written by John of Cora, Archbishop of
Sultaniah, about 1300; Moule, 249–51.

See also Howorth, I, 315, 544, 556; L. E. Browne, 105–6.

a most learned and well-informed Minor Friar'.[1]   In 1280 or thereabouts, the Minister General of the Franciscans selected him for missionary work in the East.   Accordingly he travelled first to Persia where he settled until about 1288. He then returned to Rome in the following year bearing a letter from Arghūn,[2] prince of the Western Khanate of the Mongol Empire in Asia.   In this important document, the Il-Khan commits himself to undertake an expedition against the Mamlūks in the Holy Land during the spring of 1290, seize Jerusalem and deliver it to the King of France. Whether there was any active response from the French monarch, is extremely doubtful, but Nicholas IV [3] on the other hand hastened to prepare three letters dated at Pieta in July 1289 and allowed Monte Corvino to deliver one of them to Qublai Khan, another to Arghūn, and a third to Mar Jabalaha, Patriarch of the Nestorians.   In the first letter,[4] the Pope expresses his gratification at the news of the Tatar's 'great love towards our person and the Roman Church and also towards the nation and people of the Latins'. He commends the bearer of the letter and his companions to the Emperor's kindness and asks him to listen to their teaching.   The second letter,[5] sent to Arghūn for the same

---

[1] Moule, 166–7.   Cf. Wadding (2nd ed.), IV, 345 and V, 194, as well as VI, 94; Van den Wyngaert, Jean de Mont Corvin, 7 n., and Sinica Franciscana, I, 345; *Font. Rer. Bohem.* (1882), III, 495; Marignolli (in Moule), 255.

[2] Text in Bonaparte, Planche XIV, no. 1, p. 10; Kotwicz, no. 4, p. 11. The letter is addressed to 'Irad Barans', i.e. Il Re di Francia which may be explained by influence of Genoa and Venice whose trade extended to Persia.   It is difficult to say whether the two above-mentioned letters are identical, since Kotwicz's text refers to an envoy—the archer 'Muskeril'— and includes no reference to John.   Innocent IV's letter (Moule, 169) refers to Arghūn's messenger, but not to his letter, which was, of course, addressed to the French King.   For purely historical purposes, the main point in the two letters is the *rapprochement* between Mongol and Christian.   Howorth, III, 350–2, refers to a letter from Arghūn to Philippe le Bel and to a letter from the Pope to Arghūn, III, 349.

[3] Golubovich, II, 432–42, 477–9; Chabot, in ROL, II, 568 et seq.; Mosheim (*Hist. Eccles. Tart.*), 97, 105; Heyd, II, 110–11, 218–19. Nicholas is stated to have sent letters in 1289 and 1291 to a Pisan merchant named Jolus or Ozolus who had been in Persia to congratulate him and commend to him the Franciscan missionaries in those regions.

[4] Moule, 168–9.   [5] ib., 169–70.

purpose as the first, includes an interesting additional statement concerning the Eastern Churches.   The Holy Pontiff
refers here to the Khan's 'great love towards us and the
Roman Church and also towards other Churches of Christians'.   It would appear that Innocent's motive for this
was rather diplomatic than considerate and sympathetic towards the schismatic churches.   This would naturally apply
to the third letter,[1] in which he urges Mar Jabalaha 'to
accept our special introduction for the same brother and his
companions and treat them with kindness and favour that,
fortified with such and so great protection, they may be able
to conduct themselves in their ministry more profitably and
conveniently, and more effectively to carry on the work of
Jesus Christ'.

Brother Giovanni at once proceeded to Tabriz in Persia
where he must have handed the second and third letters to
Arghūn and Mar Jabalaha.   Then he and his companions
sailed across the Indian Ocean to Malabar.   There they
stayed in the ancient church of St. Thomas the Apostle for
thirteen months, and there Niccolò of Pestoia died and was
buried.   After baptizing about a hundred people at various
points on his journey, Giovanni again took the sea route in
the reverse direction to Marco Polo's voyage, ultimately
reaching the region of Cathay [2] alone; and there the Great
Khan received him with kindness but was 'too old in idolatry'
to forsake it.   Giovanni settled[3] in Khan Bāliq and resumed
his missionary work with patience and assiduity.   It is said
that he built a fine church with a campanile containing three
bells and baptized as many as 6,000 persons.   He also tried
to save 'King George' [4] from the perfidious errors of the
Nestorians'.   In this connexion he says that 'If I had had

---

[1] Moule, 170–1.   [2] ib., letter no. 5, 171–6.

[3] ib., 173.   Monte Corvino led a solitary life in his new quarters until a
German brother from the province of Cologne came to him in the second year
after his arrival.   Little is known about this German, but he may have carried
some of Giovanni's news to the West.

[4] King George is also mentioned by Marco Polo as holding the Province of
'Tednuc' under the suzerainty of the Great Khan.   Yule, I, 284 et seq.;
Cordier's *Notes*, 62; Pelliot, *T'oung Pao* (1914), 632 et seq., and *Journ. As.*
(1912), 595–6.

two or three other comrades to help me perhaps the Emperor
the Kaan too would have been baptized.' [1]

To Giovanni, thus completely detached from Europe and
with no wish to desert his flock, a faint hope of communicating with the West suddenly presented itself when a
Mongol envoy from Persia to the court of Khan Bāliq was
about to return to his quarters. Giovanni gave him a letter
addressed to the Vicar of the Franciscans in the Crimea and
asked him to use every possible means to convey it to its
destination. Fortunately, in about two years' time the
wonderful news reached Rome, and Pope Clement V
responded to the appeal from the Far East by immediately
appointing Brother Giovanni 'Archbishop and Patriarch of
the Whole East'.[2] Further, he dispatched seven other
brothers as bishops to assist him [3] in the newly created see,
and empowered him to ordain and appoint other pastors as
might appear to him necessary for the maintenance of the
Roman Church in Cathay.[4] Of the seven brothers only
three [5] reached China in 1313 and they were later reinforced
by another three [6] of whose fate little is known. Those
who survived the journey were treated with favour by the
Great Khan who granted all Christian missionaries liberal
allowances [7] and gave them full freedom to pursue their good
work amongst his subjects. Nevertheless, the Latin settlement was doomed to dwindle rapidly and without hope of

[1] Moule, 174.   [2] ib., letter no. 8, 182.

[3] ib., 167–8, 183. These were Andrea of Perugia, Peregrine of Castello,
Niccolò of Apulia, Guillaume de France ('Franchya sive de Villa longa aut
Villanova'), Pietro of Castello, Andrutius of Assisi and one brother Gerard.
Guillaume de France received letters of introduction from Edward II dated
Dover, 22 May 1313; cf. Patent Rolls, 6 Ed. II, pt. ii., membrane 1.

[4] Moule, 183–8. Papal letters and licences.

[5] ib., 168. These were Andrea, Peregrine and Gerard.

[6] ib. Pietro of Florence and Brothers Jerome and Thomas. The first
was made Bishop on 20 December 1310, and the remaining two on 19
February 1311; cf. Wadding, op. cit., VI, 267–9.

[7] Moule, 192. A letter from Bishop Andrea of Zaitūn states that the
Latin missionaries obtained 'Alafa' from the Emperor for food and clothing
for eight persons. He defines 'alafa' as the allowance which the Emperor
pays to 'messengers of magnates, ambassadors, warriors and artificers . . .
and to jugglers, paupers and . . . persons of various classes. And these payments surpass the income and expenditure of several Latin Kings.'

recovery. In a letter dated January 1326, Brother Andrea says: 'All the Bishops made suffragans of the See of Khan Bāliq by the Lord Pope Clement are departed in peace to the Lord. I alone remain.' [1] Archbishop Giovanni himself met his end in 1328,[2] and the last of his successors, a Franciscan, Giacomo of Florence, was murdered in some unknown place in the heart of Asia [3] in 1362. Thus the Roman Church in medieval China seems to have become extinct.

Contemporary with the Franciscan brotherhood of Giovanni di Monte Corvino in China, we also hear of some missionary activities in the Middle East and Central Asia by a 'Society [4] of Pilgrim Friars' which was affiliated to the Preaching Order of St. Dominic. It is a well-known fact that the Friars went with the crusaders for the evangelization of the Levant. With the extermination of the Latin Kingdom of Jerusalem in Syria, they began to look for other fields of work and generally they followed the trade routes further East. The Dominicans established their new foundations in the region of the Black Sea where the Genoese influence was strong. In the fourteenth century, the 'Society of Pilgrim Friars' was already in possession of convents at Pera near Constantinople, in the Island of Chios in the Aegean, at Caffa in the Crimea and Trebizond in Asia Minor.[5] From these centres, their missionaries proceeded to the East into Persia and Turkestan. Christianity of the Nestorian type was still a living institution at that time in Persia, and Nestorians and Latins appear to have lived side by side in complete harmony as may be understood from the papal letters to Mar Jabalaha III, Patriarch of the Nestorians, already quoted in the preceding pages. In 1314, Franco di Perugia founded the first Latin

---

[1] Moule, 195; Golubovich, III, 305–8.

[2] Moule, 196. A letter dated 11 July 1336, refers to 'John, a valiant, holy, and capable man, who, however, died eight years ago'. See also Golubovich, III, 96.

[3] Moule, 197; Golubovich, V, 92.

[4] P. R. Lorentz, *Les Missions Dominicaines en Orient au XIVᵉ siècle et la Société des Frères Pérégrinants pour le Christ*, in Archivium Fratrum Praedicatorum (Paris and Rome, 1932), II, 1–83.

[5] ib., 2, 6 et seq.

convent in those regions, and in 1318 he became first Roman Archbishop of Sultaniah [1] with Guillaume Adam, author of *De Modo Sarracenos Extirpandi* (analysed elsewhere in this study [2]) as one of his suffragan bishops. Among the Turks of Transoxania, on the other hand, the Dominican missionaries had to face a different situation. Christianity, which had once flourished in those regions, weakened almost to the point of extinction before or just at the outbreak of the early crusades, while Islam gained most of the lost ground. [3] At the time of the advent of the Friars of the 'Society of Pilgrims' in Turkestan just before the year 1329, there was little prospect of any outstanding achievement for them in the midst of a strongly Muhammadan population. Nevertheless, Äljigidäi, the Mongol sovereign of this territory, received them well and sent them back with an encouraging message to Rome. Pope John XXII (1316–34) responded by the creation of a new Latin bishopric at Samarqand, subject to the Metropolitan see of Sultaniah. Thomas Mancasole of Piacenza [4] was nominated first bishop and left for Samarqand in the spring of 1330. Nothing more was heard of him or his mission. [5] The relations between the West and both Mongols and Turks in Central Asia were thus suddenly arrested until the reign of Timur saw a temporary revival of the exchange of diplo-

---

[1] ib., 36 et seq.   [2] *vide supra*, Cap. III.

[3] Barthold, *Zur Gesch. des Christentums* in *Mittel Asien* (Tübingen and Leipzig, 1901), based mainly on Jāme' al-Tawārīkh of Rashīd al-Dīn (1247–1318); ib., Turkestan (ed. Gibb), 254–6; ib., articles, 'Turkistan' and 'Turks' in *Encyc. of Islam*, IV; Pelliot, *Chrétiens d'Asie Centrale et d'Extrême-Orient*, in *T'oung Pao*, XV (1914), 623–44; also Chavannes et Pelliot, in *Journal Asiatique*, XI, I, 269; L. E. Browne, *Eclipse of Christianity in Asia*, 137 et seq.

It is interesting to note, however, that Nestorian Christians under Mongol rule in China and Central Asia were usually described as Turks (Moule, 139 n. 19, 216–17), but this cannot be regarded as a convincing proof of the survival of Christianity in any considerable measure among the Turkish tribes during the fourteenth century.

[4] Golubovich, III, 356. The bull dated Avignon 21 August 1329 says: 'Ioannes XXII universis christianis in imperio Elgigaday et terris Chorasan, Turquestan et Industan Minoris Indiae constitutis, commendat Thomam Mancasole (Ord. Praed.) episcopum Semiscantensem.'

[5] Lorentz, op. cit., 46.

matic embassies between the court of Samarqand and the
courts of Castile and France.[1]

Of the remaining Latin adventures in Asia during the
first half of the fourteenth century, two more are worthy of
mention. The first is associated with Oderic of Pordenone
and the second with Giovanni de' Marignolli; and both
these men left clear and useful accounts of their travels.

Friar Oderic [2] was born in 1274 and died in 1331. He
began his travels in 1316 when he took the route to China
by way of Constantinople, Tabriz, Baghdad, Ormuz, then
by sea to Malabar, Ceylon, Madras, and calling at Sumatra
and Java, finally reached 'Cartan' [3] (Zaitūn) and 'Tai-tu' or
Khan Bāliq.[4] In this town he stayed for three years and
saw Archbishop Giovanni towards the end of the latter's
life.[5] Afterwards he returned to Avignon in 1330 by the
land route through Tibet, Afghanistan and along the south
coast of the Caspian Sea.

In 1338,[6] the Yuan (Mongol) emperor of Khan Bāliq
sent an embassy consisting of 'Andrew the Frank with fifteen
companions . . . to ask the Pope himself to send us his
blessing and always to make mention of us in his holy
prayers, and to accept our commendation of our servants
the Alans [7] who are his Christian sons'. The message
continues—'Also let him bring to us . . . horses and other
wonderful things.' [8] The Pope complied with the Tatar's

---

[1] See end of this chapter.

[2] Ed. H. Cordier; also Laurent, *Quatuor Peregrinationes* (Leipzig, 1873)
142–58; contemporary life in *T'oung Pao* (1921), 275–90; relevant extracts
in Moule, 241–9. See also Yule, *Cathay*, I, 29–41; Golubovich, III, 374–
93; Angelo de Gubernatis, *Storia dei Viaggiatori Italiani* (Livorno, 1875),
138–42; Kunstmann, in *Hist. Polit. Blätter*, XXXVIII, 507 et seq.
Neumann, in *Osterreich. Zeitschr. für kath. Theologie*, 1872, 6 et seq. Appears in Röhricht, *Bibl. Geogr. Palaest.*, 69–71, as Odericus de Foro Julii

[3] Oderic (ed. Cordier), 263. Cartan, Catham, and Catan are also used.
For full list of various names of Zaitūn, see Cordier's note on Oderic, 274.
Moule, 241, uses 'Kaitun'. Howorth, I, 304–5, 557, refers to Oderic's
travels and work.

[4] Moule, 246.　　　　　[5] ib., 196, 246–7.

[6] Letters dated at Khān Bāliq, 11 July 1336 (ib., 254), and the journey
takes approximately two years.

[7] *vide supra*, 244 note 2 on Alani.

[8] Extract from letter carried by envoys. Moule, 252.

request and also sent four missionaries to preach the Gospel in the Emperor's realm. Giovanni de' Marignolli, one of the four, left a complete record of this new mission. Starting from Avignon in the same year,[1] they travelled to Constantinople, and thence sailed to Caffa [2] in the Crimea where the Genoese merchants had a long-established settlement for carrying on trade with the Tatars. Following the inland route from Caffa, the ambassadors visited the Alan tribes on their way to Khan Bāliq. They stayed for three years in this capital enjoying the lavish hospitality of the Great Khan and the company of the last medieval archbishop in China.[3] Afterwards they returned by the sea route to India and Persia, and arrived at Avignon in 1353.[4]

During the latter half of the fourteenth century, Cathay became once again as remote as it had been in the days before Marco Polo and Giovanni de Monte Corvino, and the hopes of union of West and Far East against Islam became more and more faint with the passage of time. The revolution of 1368 had swept Mongol power from China, and with it disappeared that benevolent attitude which the Great Khan had adopted towards the missionary religions of the East and of the West as a counterweight to the conservatism of the Confucian doctrines of the Chinese people. Missionaries alike of Christianity, of Islam, and of Buddhism were henceforward to be met with indiscriminate ill-treatment. Yet the propagandists of our period continued to pray for peaceful penetration of heathen territories by means of missionary work and insisted on dreaming of union with the Tatars for the extermination of Islam. Ample illustration of this has been made in the

---

[1] Departure recorded by Wadding, op. cit., VII, 258 and VIII, 87, and return to Avignon in 1353; cf. Moule, 251. Marignolli (ib., 254) says that Benedict XII sent him with Giovanni of Florence, Bishop of Bisignano, and others, to the ruler of the Tatars, and that they left Avignon in December 1338.

Marignolli's *Itinerarium* appears in Dobner, *Mon. hist. Bohem.* (Prague, 1768), XI, 113 et seq.; Golubovich, IV, 257–309; Yule, *Cathay*, II, 309–94; Angelo de Gubernatis, *Viaggiatori Italiani*, 142–61; cf. Röhricht, *Bibl. Geogr. Palaest.*, 87.

[2] Heyd, II, 158 et seq., 185 et seq., 225 et seq., 368 et seq.

[3] Moule, 257–9.   [4] *vide supra*, note 1.

preceding chapters, especially in connexion with Ramon
Lull and Marino Sanudo.

It is difficult, however, to estimate the degree of seriousness in the attitude taken by the Pope and the Western
Kings in regard to this matter.   Kotwicz [1] has published
a letter which increases the historian's scepticism.   In 1305,
Oeldjeitu Khan wrote to the King of France blaming him
for his prolonged forgetfulness of the amicable relations of
their ancestors and urging the renewal of a policy of united
action.   Although the letter was written a comparatively
short time after the fall of 'Akka [2] which had caused a painful
reaction throughout Christendom, there was no practical
sign of response to the Tatar request.   The hope of union
was finally extinguished when the Mongols passed over to
Islam.   At the close of the thirteenth century, Ghazan [3]
and his chiefs and councillors declared Muhammadanism
to be their state religion.   One must, however, guard
against overestimating the effect which this link between
Mongol and Mamlūk had in the sphere of politics and
expansion.   The Mongols still retained their old hatred to
their new co-religionists, Mamlūk and Turk alike.   The
whole career of Timur, his ravages in Syria and Asia Minor
which culminated in the great triumph of Angora [4] in July
1402, and the crushing defeat of Bayezid I are strong testimony to this hostility.   In contrast to his attitude towards
the Muslim potentates of Egypt and Turkey, he seems to
have remained friendly with the Christian powers in Europe.
He once attempted a *rapprochement* with France by writing
to Charles VI [5]—'the most serene, most victorious King and

---

[1] Kotwicz, 33–5.   Letter to 'Iridūwerens', i.e. il re di Francia; *vide supra*,
note.

[2] *vide supra*, Cap. II.

[3] Ghazan became Muslim on 16 June 1295; Howorth, III, 383–4.   This
seemingly contradicts Oeldjeitu's policy (*vide supra*); but as will be seen below,
the adoption of Islam did not lead to an immediate and drastic reversal in the
attitude of the Mongols towards other Muhammadan princes over whom they
claimed full suzerainty.

[4] Gibbons, 251 et seq.   The authorities differ as to the date of the battle
of Angora, but all agree in placing it between 20 and 28 July; see Gibbons,
251 note 1.

[5] Sylvestre de Sacy, *Mém. sur une correspondance inéd. entre Tamerlan et*

Sultan, the King of the French and many other nations, the friend of the Most-High, the very beneficent monarch of the world, who has emerged triumphant from very great wars'.   After the fall of Bayezid on the field of Angora, Timur found two Castilian ambassadors [1] in the Sultan's train.   The victor sent them back to their master, Henry III, unhurt and laden with presents; and shortly afterwards, he dispatched an envoy of his own, a certain 'Chagatay noble called Hajji Muhammad' to the said King of Castile with letters and gifts as a mark of amity.[2]   In return for this compliment and courtesy, Henry III sent to the court of Samarqand, an embassy, since made famous by Clavijo's admirable account [3] of his travels in the Tatar realm between 1403 and 1406.   Timur received the ambassadors with great honour, and, in the course of an inquiry as to the health of their master affectionately asked, 'How is it with my son your King?   How goes it with him?   Is his health good?' [4]   When the envoys asked his permission to leave Samarqand, to quote Clavijo's own words, 'he told us he regarded in affection (the King of Spain) now as his very own son'.[5]   These expressions may have been merely the usual course of Oriental compliments, but the friendly tone underlying them is unmistakable.   Yet the historian may search in vain for any concrete plans of alliance with the

---

... *Charles VI*, Extrait du Moniteur no. 226 (1812), 7–8. De Sacy believes that the title quoted here is an interpolation by the bearer who wanted to commend himself to the King of France, as the title of Sultan was strictly reserved to Muslim rulers.   This contention seems doubtful as applied to that early period, for Ibn Baṭṭūṭa describes, for example, the Byzantine Emperor as Sultan; Defréméry et Sanguinetti, IV, 58.

[1] Clavijo, 24–5. These were Payo de Sotomayor and Herman Sanchez de Plazuelos.

[2] ib., 25. In note 3 on p. 340, the editor adds that of the Christian women slaves in Bayezid's camp, Timur found two of noble origin, Maria and Angelina.   The first was a Greek and the second was a granddaughter of the King of Hungary.   These also Timur sent back with the Spanish ambassadors to their King who dowered them and married them to two of his nobility.

[3] Howorth, II (Division I), 264; Guy Le Strange's introduction to Clavijo, 1–21, and notes, 339 et seq.; Bouvat, *Empire Mongol*, 63–6; Cahun, *Hist. de l'Asie*, 498–99.

[4] Clavijo., 221.

[5] ib., 227; according to Guy Le Strange's translation.

Mongols for the recovery of the Holy Land at the time when Timur himself had penetrated into Syria and inflicted heavy defeats on the Mamlūk Sultan at Aleppo and Damascus [1] in 1401. This irreparable loss of time and chance ultimately led to the total estrangement of the Mongols from an active alliance with the West in a crusade to save the Holy Land.

In justice to the homeland of Clavijo, however, it is worthy of note that the possibility of an alliance with the Mongols remained a feature of Spanish policy until the beginning of modern history. The proof may appear at first to belong to the realm of legend rather than the world of facts. At the close of the fifteenth century, Ferdinand and Isabella embarked on a crusade against the tottering Muslim kingdom of Granada which finally surrendered to them on 2 January 1492. To carry their crusade still further to a successful issue inside and outside the Iberian Peninsula, the Catholic monarchs first decreed the expulsion of Jews from Spain on 30 March of the same year, and second, they are said to have granted Christopher Columbus their permission to sail to India and the Kingdom of the 'Great Khan' by a new western route, and at their own expense manned a fleet for his use on this expedition. The real motive of the second of the two projects, long overshadowed by the spectacular discovery of the New World, is best expressed in the text of the *Journal* ascribed to Columbus himself and preserved by Las Casas in the following extract:

And immediately afterwards (i.e. after the conquest of Granada), in this same month (January), in consequence of information which I had given Your Highnesses (Ferdinand and Isabella) on the subject of India and the Prince who is called the 'Great Khan', which, in our Roman, means 'the King of Kings'—namely, that many times he and his predecessors had sent ambassadors to Rome to seek doctors of our holy faith, to the end that they should teach it in India, and that never has the Holy Father been able so to do, so that accordingly so many peoples were being lost, through falling into idolatry and receiving sects of perdition among them;

Your Highnesses, as good Christian and Catholic princes, devout and propagators of the Christian faith, as well as enemies of the sect of Mahomet

---

[1] Weil, *Abbasidenchalifat*, II, 83 et seq.; Muir, *Mamelukes*, 122–3; Bouvat, op. cit., 52 et seq.; Cahun, op. cit., 492 et seq.

and of all idolatries and heresies, conceived the plan of sending me, Christopher Columbus, to this country of the Indies, there to see the princes, the peoples, the territory, their disposition and all things else, and the way in which one might proceed to convert these regions to our holy faith.[1]

Can we argue from these statements that the aim of both Columbus and his two royal benefactors was to bring the Tatar and the Latin into effective action against the Muhammadan—the enemy of the faith of Christ? If so, this may well be regarded as the last medieval attempt to unite the West with the Far East by means of winning the latter to the fold of Roman Catholicism; and in this respect, the holy enterprise was a complete failure, for the New World stood in the way and cut short the fulfilment of pious hopes and aspirations. Interest in the Far East grew slighter as the Old World became engrossed in its transoceanic exploits, discoveries and the promise of riches untold.

[1] B. de Las Casas, *Historia de las Indias*, in Coleccion de Documentos inéditos para la Hist. de España (Madrid, 1875–6), LXII, 262; cf. Bertrand and Petrie, *Hist. of Spain*, 237–9.
The conception of an Indian journey, however, appears from official documents and Oriental sources to have originated after the first journey of Columbus. Kahle, *Die verschollene Columbus-Karte von* 1513 (Berlin and Leipzig, 1933); cf. Geographical Review (New York, 1933), XXIII, 621–38. Without disputing this, it is certain that the idea of combined action with the Far East in the crusade against Islam was not alien to Columbus and his contemporaries.

CHAPTER XI

THE CRUSADE AND EASTERN CHRISTENDOM

Propagandists and Eastern Christians. Union with Rome—making and breaking. The Greeks: Councils of Lyons and Ferrara-Florence; Ottoman Conquest and the schism. The Armenians: unions, revolts and schisms. The Georgians: Greek, Mongol and Turkish influences. The Nestorians: Latin missionaries and after. The Copts: persecution; Abyssinian and Aragonese mediation; union with Rome and schism. The Ethiopians: relations with Copts; projects for Crusade

THE majority of the late medieval propagandists made frequent references to the Eastern Christians as possible allies or enemies in the crusade; [1] and some of these references are elaborate though inaccurate. The struggle between East and West had its repercussions on Oriental Christendom in varying degrees according to geographical and political circumstances. The Greeks and the rest of the Balkan races became an easy prey to the rising tide of Ottoman conquest in Europe. The Georgians fell under the Mongol, and afterwards the Turkish yoke. The Armenians were the object of Egyptian attack, and their kingdom passed first to Egypt and then to Turkey. The Nestorians alone remained sufficiently remote from the scene of strife until the Latin missionaries brought them into direct contact with the West. In Egypt, the Copts suffered as Western pressure became acute. They were within reach of an oppressor who spared neither their lives nor their property. The West intervened on their behalf on a few occasions in time of peace with some slight and ephemeral results; but it was the Ethiopians who remained throughout the Middle Ages the most ardent supporters of this enduring race which kept alive one of the most ancient forms of the Christian religion. Sometimes, the

---

[1] *vide supra*, especially Burcard (Cap. V) and Felix Faber (Cap. IX).

emperors of Ethiopia tried to intimidate the Mamlūk
sultans, and sometimes they actually negotiated with the
West for a conjoint crusade against Egypt.

The attention of the West, however, seems to have been
centred mainly on winning the Greeks to the Church of
Rome as a preliminary measure to a successful crusade.
Two great landmarks may help to define the opening and
the closing of the period of attempts to bring the Byzantine
Empire within the fold of Catholicism—the Council of
Lyons in 1274 and the Council of Florence in 1439.
Between the dates of these two councils, a series of diplomatic and ecclesiastical *rapprochements* took place, but any
success that they had was temporary and due to the increasing pressure of the Ottoman invader on the empire.   The
whole movement ended in complete failure, and the breach
between the East and the West gaped as widely as ever
in the past.

The Council of Lyons (1274) was convoked by Pope
Gregory X to deal with three important matters of universal
interest—the reform of the Church in the West, the
reunion with the East, and the recovery of the Holy Land.
The Greek Emperor, Michael VIII, felt his position
insecure, for he had lately destroyed the Latin Empire of
Constantinople and was afraid of retaliation from the West;
hence, to avert this danger, he negotiated with the Pope
on the subject of the reunion of the Churches.   Charles
of Anjou, King of Naples and Sicily, having concluded the
treaty of Viterbo (1267) by which Baldwin II surrendered to
him his imperial claim in the East, was now trying to form an
alliance with the Greek Despot of Epirus with the object
of a joint assault on Constantinople.   To foil the would-
be aggressor, Michael succeeded in convincing some of his
clergy of the benefits to be gained from a union with Rome
and finally dispatched Germanus III, a former Greek
Patriarch of Constantinople, Theophanes, Archbishop of
Nicaea, George Acropolita, the Grand Logothete, and two
nobles of the imperial court to represent him at Lyons.
The Latins had also prepared for the occasion by summoning St. Thomas Aquinas, the prince of the theo-
logians of the age, who came to the Council armed with

his book, *Contra Errores Graecorum*. Discussion, however, was found unnecessary when it was revealed that the Greek envoys carried with them a solemn written pledge from the Emperor declaring his submission to the Pope. Finally, in the fourth session of the Council (6 July), George Acropolita publicly abjured the Schism and recognized the authority of the Roman See. The Bulgarians and the Serbians had also sent similar letters of submission. The occasion was solemnized by the chanting of 'Te Deum Laudamus' and the recital of the 'Credo'. The envoys sang them in Greek, twice repeating the 'filioque' [1] clause in the Creed to impress the Catholic clergy by the sincerity of their conversion. The Pope subsequently arranged a truce between Charles of Anjou and Michael VIII on 1 May 1275.[2]

The union of the two Churches, however, was more apparent than real; for though Michael had scored a diplomatic triumph to ensure the safety of his empire from the Angevin peril, the Orthodox clergy and the Greek people, on the other hand, had neither forgotten their old hatred for the Latins and Catholicism, nor had they forgiven them the horrors of the Fourth Crusade. Doubtful of the good faith of the Greeks, Pope after Pope demanded some guarantee from the Eastern Church to ensure Greek submission to Rome. The open breach ultimately came in July 1281, when Martin IV excommunicated the Emperor, entered into alliance with Charles of Anjou and the Republic of St. Mark, the old enemies of Byzantium, and preached a crusade against the Empire. Nevertheless, Michael

---

[1] See below note on Council of Florence and Bull 'Laetentur Coeli'; also A. Fortescue, *Orthodox Eastern Church*, 372–84, and R. C. Jenkins, *Last Crusader or Life and Times of Cardinal Julian*, Appendix C, 396–401.

[2] Mansi, *Collectio conciliorum*, XXIV, 39 et seq.; Hefele, *Conciliengesch.* (2nd ed.), VI, 119 et seq.; Reynaldus, *Annal. ecclesiast.*, ann. 1273 et 1274 *passim*; Potthast, *Regesta pontif.*, nos. 20527, 20630–1, 20760; C. Chapman, *Michel Paléologue* (Paris, 1926), 113–24; Kidd, *Churches of Eastern Christendom*, 263–71; Vasiliev, *Emp. Byz.*, II, 267–78; Norden, *Papsttum und Byzanz*, 399–536; Gibbon (ed. Bury), VI, 474–6; Finlay (ed. Tozer), V, 128–9; Hirsch-Gereuth, *Kreuzzügsidee nach den Kreuzzügen*, 37–88; A. Fortescue, *Orthodox Eastern Church*, 204–8; Blanc, *Hist. ecclés.* (Paris, 1860), II, 109–11.

was fortunate enough to defeat the combined forces of the
Latins at Belgrade, and, to add to the troubles of the allies,
he subsidized the rebels of the Sicilian Vespers, which culminated in the massacre of the supporters of the house of
Anjou in southern Italy on the eve of 30 March 1282.[1]

When Michael died in December 1282, his diplomacy
had been successful in putting an end to the danger of a
Latin invasion, and the Empire enjoyed a period of comparative peace during the reign of his successor, Andronikos
II (1282–1328). So confident were the Greeks at the
time, that they did not hesitate publicly to renounce the
union with Rome, and their Emperor was therefore excommunicated in 1307 by Clement V. If the menace from
the West had been finally averted, a more calamitous
one remained in store for the Empire. The Ottoman
Turks began their conquest of Asia Minor during this
reign, and though momentarily checked by the help of
the Catalan Grand Company,[2] it was resumed with greater
vigour in the reign of his successor, Andronikos III
(1328–41). The Turks reached the waters of the Bosphorus in 1338, and their sudden appearance in this region
caused consternation among the Greeks who had lost their
Asiatic possessions and the Venetians whose trade was in
jeopardy. In the face of a common enemy, the Emperor
and the Venetians together with the Knights Hospitallers
entered into a league with the crusading kings of France
and Naples. Although the success of the league activities
was slight, if not negligible, the alliance gave concrete
evidence as to the reversal of the policy of Andronikos II
which had resulted in the complete alienation of the Greeks

---

[1] Mansi, XXIV, 105; Potthast, nos. 21465, 21478 and 21815; Reynaldus,
ann. 1281 no. 25; Tafel and Thomas, *Urkunden*, III, 289; Marino Sanudo,
Historia di Romania, in Hopf's *Chronique gréco-romanes* (Berlin, 1873),
122 et seq.; *Arch. Stor. It.*, XXII, 380–1; Pachymeres, in CSBH (ed. Bonn),
324 et seq., 461 et seq.; Fleury, *Hist. ecclés.*, XVIII, 252 et seq.; Kidd,
270–1; Chapman, 113–45; Vasiliev, II, 274–8; Norden, 537 et seq.; Gibbon
(ed. Bury), VI, 476; E. Pears, *Destruction of Greek Empire*, 22–36; Du
Cange, *Emp. de Constantinople*, II, 1–26, 323–6.

[2] Schlumberger, *Expédition des 'Almugavares' ou Routiers Catalans en
Orient*, 1302–11 (Paris, 1924); L. Nicolau d'Olwer, *Expansio de Catalunya
en la Mediterrània Oriental*, 49–102.

from Rome.   In fact, a new policy had already been fostered by the marriage alliances which Andronikos III
concluded with Western princes.   Agnes, the Emperor's
first wife, was a daughter of Henry Duke of Brunswick-
Grubenhagen.   When she died (1324), Andronikos chose
another Latin wife (1326), Anne, daughter of Amedeo V
Duke of Savoy, the father of the future crusader of 1363–6,
Duke Amedeo VI.   In 1339, Barlaam,[1] a Greek uniate
monk from Calabria, visited Constantinople.   He was well
received by the Emperor who secretly nominated him as
his emissary to the curia at Avignon and charged him with
the delicate task of negotiating the reunion of the Churches
with Benedict XIII (1334–42).   Barlaam, however, wished
to prepare the way for a more enduring union by means
of persuasion.   In this he failed and was condemned by
the Greek Synod.   The prophet of peace then retired to
Calabria and Andronikos III himself died in 1341.

The following reign was one of civil war between the
usurper John Kantakuzenos (1347–54) and his own son-
in-law, the young Emperor John V (1341–91).   This was
the period in which the Turks inaugurated their career of
conquest in Europe, and to which reference has already
been made.[2]   Kantakuzenos, who had given his own young
daughter Theodora in marriage to the sexagenarian Sultan
Orkhan, nevertheless wished to demonstrate that he was
not pro-Ottoman and sent a Byzantine embassy to the West
to assert his willingness to open hostilities with the Turks,
if only the European powers would support him with more
men in return for the union of the Churches.   Judging,
however, by past events, the West had its misgivings as
to the genuineness of the Emperor's offer, and hence its
procrastination in response, for it was not until three years
later that Clement VI (1342–52) dispatched two Preaching

---

[1] Barlaam's works in MPG, CLI, 1255 et seq.   On Barlaam himself, see
Petrarch, *Epistolae de rebus familiaribus* (ed. Fracassetti, Florence, 1863),
xviii and xxiv, and *Variorum Epistol.*, xxv; Boccacio, *Genealogiae deorum*
(Paris, 1511), f. cxii vo.; Vasiliev, II, 423–7; A. Fortescue, *Uniate Eastern
Churches*, 108 and n. 4; Krumbacher, *Gesch. d. Byz. Lit.*, 100 et seq.;
Kidd, 273–6.
[2] *vide supra*, Cap. I.

Friars to negotiate the union. On their arrival at Constantinople, they found that their imperial host, who had given the initiative to the proceeding, insisted that only an Oecumenical Council could settle the re-union. The Pope explained that such a Council in the circumstances of Europe at the time was impossible to convene. The Hundred Years' War was raging between England and France, and Cressy had just been fought in 1346. The Kingdoms of Hungary and Naples were in a state of war in which the papacy itself was to some degree entangled. Cola di Rienzi, who had stirred up so much trouble in Rome, still lived in Apulia and was about to leave for Prague to try and persuade Charles, King of the Romans, to invade the papal possessions in Italy. Above all, Europe was still suffering the effects of the Black Death. The negotiations in Constantinople therefore failed, and ultimately Kantakuzenos abdicated his imperial crown in 1354 and retired to a Greek monastery.[1]

John V, who now resumed the throne as John VI, found himself incapable of arresting the rapid Ottoman expansion in Europe under Murad I (1359–89), and in turn looked to Western Europe for relief. He went himself to Rome, solemnly professed Catholicism and accepted the primacy of the Pope (1369–70), but no material aid was forthcoming. He took the road to Venice where, instead of obtaining help and comfort, he suffered the indignity of detention for debt and was only released when his son Manuel arrived with money. The policy of union was nevertheless continued by Manuel II (1391–1425), who, after the defeat of the European crusaders at Nicopolis [2] (1396), visited the courts of the West in 1399–1400,[3] sent an embassy to Pope Martin V (1417–31) at the Council of Constance in 1418, and another to the European courts when Murad II (1421–51) set siege to Constantinople in

---

[1] Vasiliev, II, 298–315; Kidd, 278–83; Dichl., *Emp. Byz.*, 194–211, reviews the causes of Byzantine decadence in this period; Pears, *Destruction of Gr. Emp.*, 52–108; Gibbon (ed. Bury), VII, 27 et seq.; Finlay (ed. Tozer), III, 436 et seq.; Gibbons, *Foundations of Ottoman Emp.*, 91 et seq.; *Nicopolis*, 1–8 and notes.

[2] *vide infra*, Cap. XVIII.   [3] *vide supra*, Cap. I.

1422. On his death-bed, however, Manuel advised his son and successor, John VIII (1425–48) to continue the negotiations, but to insist on an Oecumenical Council and defer any final decision, for 'the pride of the Latins and the obstinacy of the Greeks will never agree'. Although the relatively peaceful beginning of John's reign enabled him for a time to carry out his father's will and postpone a final decision in regard to the matter of union, Ottoman pressure was soon renewed with such vigour that the unhappy Emperor had no choice but to court favour with the West and acquiesce in bringing the Eastern Schism to a definitive settlement at any cost in the vain hope of securing the necessary aid to save Constantinople.[1]

The Council of Basle, convoked in 1431, had been in session since that date when an imperial delegation arrived on 12 July 1434. It was well received by Pope Eugenius IV and by the Council, as both were ready to negotiate the union. After a protracted discussion as to the meeting-place of the Council which was to consider the conflict of the Churches, the Pope obtained a decision for Ferrara where the delegates opened the first session on 8 January 1438, the Council being translated to Florence [2] on 26 February 1439. Emperor John VIII himself together with Joseph II, Greek Patriarch of Constantinople, and twenty-one other Greek prelates including Isidore, Metropolitan of Russia, and a

---

[1] Phrantzes (Emperor Manuel's secretary, ob. 1477), in MPG, CLVI, 784; Fleury, XXI, 484; Finlay (ed. Tozer), III, 491, where John VIII is called John VI; Kidd, 280–5; Vasiliev, II, 315–36; Pears, 109–20.

[2] For the history of the Council of Ferrara-Florence, see Mansi, op. cit., vol. XXXI *passim*; Hefele, op. cit., VII, 681 et seq.; Sylvester Syropoulos, *Vera historia unionis non verae* (Lat. trans. R. Creyghton, The Hague, 1660); Ceccioni, *Studi storici sul concilio di Firenze* (Florence, 1869); Platina, *Lives of Popes*, II, 221–5; Gorski, *Hist. of Council of Florence* (trans. from Russian by B. Popoff and ed. by J. M. Neale, London, 1861); Pastor, *Hist. of Popes*, I, 315 et seq.; Creighton, *Hist. of Papacy*, II, 173 et seq.; Norden, op. cit., 712 et seq.; Flick, *Decline of Med. Church*, II, 198–202; Fortescue, *Orthodox Eastern Church*, 208–20; Kidd, 285–90; Pears, 123–28; Gregorovius, *Stadt Rom*, VII, 66–71; Gieseler, *Eccles. Hist.*, III, 411–14; Robertson, *Hist. of Christian Church*, VIII, 94–109; Blanc, *Hist. ecclés.*, II, 167–70; Jenkins, op. cit., 269 et seq. Although the last book is entitled *The Last Crusader*, it is largely a study of Cardinal Julian's projects of church reform submitted to the Councils of Basle and Ferrara-Florence.

large number of Greek clergy were present at the meetings of the Council. The problems raised at Ferrara and amicably settled at Florence included the acceptance by the Greeks of the Latin doctrine of the 'Procession of the Holy Ghost' by the insertion of the 'filioque' clause into the Nicene Creed, the use of leavened or unleavened bread in the celebration of the Eucharist, the two views [1] of purgatory, and finally the recognition of the authority of the Roman See and the primacy of the Pope, 'saving the privileges and rights of the Eastern Patriarchs'. The decree embodying all these agreements was issued by Eugenius IV on 6 July 1439, in the form of a bull—'Laetentur Coeli'.[2]   In return for the re-union of the Churches, the Pope concluded a treaty with the Emperor by which he undertook to send the Greeks back to their homes in comfort, to reinforce the defence of Constantinople from his own treasury with two galleys and 300 men every year and, in the event of imminent danger, to supply the city with twenty galleys for six months or ten for one year, and finally to use his influence at the courts of Western Europe in reviving the crusade against the Muslim Turks.[3]   The Pope indeed tried to carry out the first part of his share in the bargain by sending the two galleys with 300 men; but the measure of success he might achieve in regard to the promise of another crusade [4] remained doubtful.   The Greek people, on the other hand, do not appear to have given the delegates a warm reception. They showed their hostility when Metrophanes II (1440–3), the new Patriarch under the Catholic regime, rose to give his benediction, by turning away from him in order that they might not be tainted with Latinism.   In 1443, the Greek Patriarchs of Alexandria, Antioch and Jerusalem issued an encyclical renouncing the agreements of Florence and

---

[1] The one view implied that those who died truly penitent in the Lord were purified by the pains of purgatory, and the other that they also derived comfort from the sacrifice of the Mass and the acts of piety and prayers of the faithful on earth.

[2] Mansi, XXXI, 1025–34; cf. Kidd, 508 note 110.   The bull formulates the decisions of the Council on the outstanding points of difference between the East and the West.

[3] Flick, *Decline of Med. Church*, II, 201.   [4] *vide infra*, Cap. XIX.

accusing the Patriarch of Constantinople of heresy and the betrayal of his trust.[1]   The situation was drifting every day from bad to worse, and the end of the ancient Empire was near at hand.

The failure of all the efforts exerted for an enduring union between Constantinople and Rome from the Council of Lyons (1274) to the Council of Ferrara and Florence (1438–9) was a foregone conclusion which could not have surprised even contemporaries.   The reasons are numerous; but perhaps the most decisive of all, was the fact that the union from beginning to end arose, not from religious conviction or anxiety for the peace of the Churches of God, but from fear—fear of the horrors of another Latin invasion at the close of the thirteenth century, and fear of extermination by the Turks during the remaining years of the shrinking Byzantine Empire.   Union was therefore a matter of diplomacy and not of faith.   It was imposed on the people and clergy of Greece by the Emperor and a handful of supporters, but never struck root outside the imperial court.   The old hatred which was intensified by the destructive policy of the Latins in their wars with Greece could not be overridden even by the influence of the Emperor himself, and the union was thus foredoomed and a forlorn hope.

As to the rest of the Orthodox Churches in the Balkan Peninsula, namely the Churches of Bulgaria and Serbia, their history in the Later Middle Ages may be regarded as bound up with that of the Patriarchate of Constantinople. At the Council of Lyons (1274), their representatives were present and they endorsed the union of the East and the West which was concluded between Pope Gregory X and the Greek Patriarch Germanus III.[2]   Then came a period of confusion owing to the wars of the Bulgarians and the Serbians each wishful of aggrandizement at the expense of the other or at the expense of the Greeks, until the Ottoman invader destroyed the independence of all.[3]   The final

---

[1] Phrantzes, Lib. II, Cap. 17; Ducas, Cap. 31; Chalkokondylas (in CSHB, ed. Bonn), 291 et seq.; cf. Gibbon. (ed. Bury), VII, 134–8.

[2] *vide supra*; Kidd, op. cit., 270.

[3] For further details, see Kidd, 319–42.

establishment of the Turk in Constantinople resulted in the strengthening of the authority of the Greek Church over her fellow-members under Ottoman rule. The Turks knew only one master in the person of the Sultan, and they naturally applied this conception to the government of the Churches within their territories. The re-established autonomy of the Patriarchate of Constantinople ensured the end of all ideas of re-union, and the Turks themselves would not have tolerated any revival of such ideas.

In Armenia, however, Rome was favoured by different circumstances. The Latins were regarded during the anxious period of the Egyptian invasion as possible protectors, and the Armenians did not harbour the same bitter feeling against the Catholics as the Greeks. The historical basis for that hatred in Greece did not exist in Armenia, although it would be a serious error to assume that the Armenians acquiesced in the ecclesiastical sovereignty of Rome without reservations or restrictions. Moreover, the last Armenian dynasty had from an early date its affinities with the West owing to frequent inter-marriage with the Latins, especially the Lusignans in Cyprus.[1] Finally, it must be remembered that Armenia gave birth to one of the greatest propagandists for the crusade in the Later Middle Ages, Prince Hayton, whose work has been considered in the preceding pages.[2]

Reference has already been made to the Armenian Synods convened at Sîs and Adana during the early part of the fourteenth century [3] and to the ultimate recognition of the

---

[1] Iorga, *Arménie*, 122, 124. For early crusades and Armenia, see Ter-Grigorian Iskenderian, *Kreuzfahrer und ihre Beziehungen zu den armenischen Nachbarfürsten bis zum Untergange der Grafschaft Edessa, nach armenischen Quellen* (Diss., Berlin, 1915).

[2] *vide supra*, Cap. III.

[3] The first important attempt to unite Armenia with Rome in this period took place at the Council of Sîs in 1308, where the Armenians accepted the view of the two distinct natures of Christ. This led to serious rioting among the people ending in the murder of King Leo IV and his guardian Prince Hayton. Morgan, *Hist. du peuple arménien*, 214–16; J. Issaverdens, *Armenia and Armenians*, II, *Eccles. Hist.*, 188–90; Iorga, 134–7; Fortescue, *Orthodox Eastern Church*, 215; Schlumberger, *Arméniens au moyen âge*, in *Récits de Byzance et des croisades*, II, 105–11.

Roman creed by many Armenian prelates in 1323 through
the labours of a Catholic mission of which Burcard appears
to have been a principal member.[1]   Despite the fanatical
adherence of the Armenians to their Monophysite beliefs,
Catholic propaganda continued with greater vigour as the
country increasingly became the scene of Mamlūk ravages.
In the year 1327, during the pontificate of Jacob II,
Patriarch of Sîs, an Armenian named John, who had studied
the Latin language and had been converted to Catholicism
by one Bartholomew, Latin Bishop of Adharbaijān,[2] started
to preach in favour of Rome and won over enough supporters to force the deposition of the Patriarch.   Later,
John founded a new preaching brotherhood called the
Order of Unionists which he based on the Dominican
model.[3]   Meanwhile, Pope Clement VI (1342–52) offered
the Armenians an annuity of 12,000 gold crowns and one
thousand knights [4] to assist in the defence of the country,
if the Schism were brought to an end.   A council was
convoked at Sîs to consider the union, but the result did
not satisfy the Pope.   Hence an exchange of embassies
and correspondence took place between Avignon and
Sîs, in which a certain friar, Daniel of Tabriz, played a
prominent part.[5]   Then followed a period in which the
Black Death disconnected the two capitals, and the country
remained divided between unionist and schismatic until its
collapse before the Egyptian arms in 1373.   Next we hear
of four Armenian delegates at the Council of Ferrara-
Florence in 1439; and in November of the same year, Pope
Eugenius IV published the *Decretum pro Armenis* and the
Bull 'Exultate Deo' issued for the instruction of the
Armenians in the holy sacraments according to the Catholic
rite and to announce the union of the Churches.[6]   Yet
subsequent events proved clearly that the coming of the
Armenians within the pale of Catholicism was very much

[1] *vide supra*, Cap. V.

[2] Issaverdens, op. cit., 192.   [3] ib., 193–4.

[4] *Hist. des Crois., Documents arméniens*, I, 707; cf. Iorga, 141.

[5] Golubovich, IV, 333–62; Gay, *Clément VI et les affaires d'Orient*,
132–50.

[6] Mansi, op. cit., XXXI, 1047–60; Kidd, 299; A. Fortescue, op. cit., 215;
Issaverdens, 201–2.

a matter of form and was without reality to the people as a whole. After the invasion of their country by the Turks and the fall of Constantinople, Muhammad II took Joachim, the Armenian Bishop of Brusa, with him to his new capital and, following the Greek precedent, nominated him head of the Armenian Church with a considerable measure of civil jurisdiction over his people. That the Armenians ultimately drifted from Catholicism, is proved beyond doubt by the outline of the creed and ceremonies of the Armenian Church submitted by Abgar and Alexander the Armenians to Pope Pius IV (1560–5) in Rome on 8 November 1564.[1]

The nearest Christian Asians to the Armenians were the Georgians, who inhabited the rough country lying between the Black Sea and the Caspian, north-west of Greater Armenia and in close proximity to the Greek Empire of Trebizond. Although not overlooked by the propagandists of this period, they contributed little to the crusade in the Later Middle Ages, and it would therefore be irrelevant to devote to their history more than a few general remarks. From an early date the Georgians seem to have fallen under Byzantine influence and retained their Christianity in the Greek Orthodox form until the collapse of the Eastern Empire. In the fourteenth century they became vassals of the Mongol Empire in Persia and at a later date submitted to the conquering arm of the Turks. Their remoteness from the field of the crusade, their indifference towards the Roman Catholic Church, and above all the supremacy of the Mongol and the Turk in succession made their collaboration with the Latin irrealizable.[2]

Of all the Eastern Christians in Asia, the Nestorians geographically covered the widest field, thanks to their missionary activity long antecedent to the advent of the Latins. As has already been shown, their influence

---

[1] An English trans. of this declaration appears in Issaverdens, 215–21. For this period in general, see—ib., 202 et seq.; Adeney, *Greek and Eastern Churches*, 547–9; Kidd, 434; E. F. K. Fortescue, *Armenian Church*, 20–33.

[2] On the Georgian Church, see W. E. D. Allen, *Hist. of Georgian People* (London, 1932), 266–74.

extended from Persia to Cathay and India.[1] At the
beginning of the fourteenth century, the Nestorian Patriarch had twenty-five metropolitans and about 250 bishops
in his hierarchy.[2] They were highly favoured at the courts
of the Mongol Emperors until these either adopted Islam
as a state religion or gave way to the rising local dynasties
—both pagan and Muhammadan—in the Far and Middle
East. At the outset they were not unfriendly with the
Latins as has been noted in the chapter on 'Europe and
the Tatars'. Prolonged contact, however, exposed variance
on matters of doctrine with resultant hostility. The
earliest example of these clashes was the discussion held
between Guillaume de Rubruck and the Nestorian priests
in the presence of the Grand Khan Mongka (circa 1352).
The attitude of one party to the other did not improve the
prospects of Christianity among the Tatars and as a natural
corollary, it adversely affected the projects of religious and
military union with Catholic Europe for a decisive battle
against Egypt.

The people least mentioned in the contemporary sources
of the West and most neglected in the modern histories
of the crusade are the Jacobite Christians within the Mamlūk Empire itself. These consisted mainly of the Coptic
community of Egypt.[3] The crusades, as is revealed by

[1] vide supra, Cap. X.

[2] Chabot, Hist. de Mar Jabalah III, in ROL, I, 566 et seq., and II,
73 et seq., 235 et seq.; cf. Kidd, 422: L. E. Browne, Eclipse of Christianity in
Asia, 93–108.

[3] On the history of the Coptic Church and people during the Later Middle
Ages, see 'De Patriarchatu Alexandrino' in Le Quien's Oriens Christianus, II,
329–68; J. M. Neale, Hist. of Holy Eastern Church (2 vols., London, 1847),
II, 310 et seq.; E. L. Butcher, Hist. of Church of Egypt (2 vols., London,
1897), II, 173 et seq.; Kidd, op. cit., 443–6 and notes. G. Wiet's article
'Kibt' in EI, II, 990–1003, is invaluable for bibliographical purposes and the
sources of Coptic history. Unfortunately, like T. W. Arnold's Preaching
of Islam (3rd ed., London, 1935, reprinted from 2nd revised ed.) this
learned article was written to sustain a thesis and has the characteristic defects
of such work. From the wide range of materials available, covering as it
does many centuries, it is possible by a selection of documents, influenced
consciously or otherwise by the initial hypothesis, to arrive at conclusions
which cannot be accepted as in accordance with the evidence as a whole.
M. Wiet's attitude to his subject is modified in his chapter on the Copts in the

the Arabic chronicles of the time, both published and un-published, reacted unfavourably upon the fortunes of these oppressed sons of ancient Egypt, despite their avowed neutrality in war and their virtual inability to render any support to the combatants on either side. When the Mamlūks sustained a defeat before the arms of Western Europe, they at once turned to the easiest way of retaliation by avenging themselves upon the defenceless Copts at home, as in the year 1365 after the sack of Alexandria.[1] In fact the history of the Copts presents little more than a series of persecutions; and the wonder, as some impartial and understanding writers [2] declare, is not that the progress of their religious thought has been retarded or suppressed, but that the Coptic Church has had the tenacity to survive in a sea of violence until modern times. Under the rule of Rome, they suffered the same sad lot as other Christians; and under Byzantium, they were harshly treated by the Melkite Greeks who supported the theocracy of the Emperor of Constantinople against the local autonomy of the Patriarchs. Then came Islam which gave them a short period of respite under the early Caliphs who continued the enlightened and tolerant attitude of the great 'Umar I. This, however, soon gave way to a policy of sporadic

---

Précis de l'hist. d'Égypte (Cairo, 1932), II, 267–9, which is, however, too general in character to be of serious importance. J. M. Neale also reviewed the early writings on the Coptic Church in his *History*, I, vii–xiii. It is essential to note that the sources of Coptic history, with some slight additions, may invariably be regarded as including most of the useful material for the history of the Abyssinian Church. A definitive history of the Coptic Church, calling as it does for an intimate knowledge of the Arabic and Coptic languages and the cultures they express, still remains to be written.

[1] *vide infra*, Cap. XV.

[2] The Church historian, B. J. Kidd (op. cit., 443, 445), says 'the marvel is, not that instances of apostasy were many, but that generation after generation stood firm when by turning Mohammedan any Christian could escape'; and in connexion with the apostasy of the Bishop of Sandafah in the persecution which took place during the patriarchate of Cyril III (1235–50), the same author adds, 'It is no small credit to the loyalty of the Coptic episcopate that this is the first and only known instance of a bishop apostatising.' Similar examples of constancy can be found in E. L. Butcher's *History of the Church of Egypt* (2 vols., London, 1897), and M. Fowler's *Christian Egypt* (London, 1901). Innumerable travellers of many ages, too, have paid tribute to the loyalty of the Copts.

persecution which, under the new regime, threatened the
Coptic Church with extermination.   It would be a serious
error to say that all the Muhammadan rulers of Egypt
pursued the same vindictive and relentless way of persecution.   Exceptions existed, especially during the Fatimid
period.   Although still theoretically enjoying the privilege
of protection and a measure of religious liberty accorded
to all dhimmi (people of the Covenant [1]) subjects, the Copts
in fact suffered on occasion much misery and oppression
from Mamlūk rule.   Destruction of their churches and
drastic action against their depleted numbers continued
to recur in the Later Middle Ages.   Apart from the
innumerable isolated cases of violence, the records show
that dismissals from office and persecutions of varying
intensity took place in the years 1279, 1283, 1301, 1321,
1354, 1365, 1419, 1422 and 1447.[2]   These were some-

---

[1] On the 'alleged' Covenant of 'Umar, its nature and some authentic
treaties between the early Muslims and dhimmi subjects, see A. S. Tritton,
Caliphs and their Non-Muslim Subjects (Oxford, 1930), 5–17; T. W. Arnold,
Preaching of Islam, 57 et seq.; Golubovich, *Biblioteca bio-bibliografica della
Terra Santa*, IV, 88 et seq., M. Hamidullah, *Corpus ou traités et lettres
diplomatiques de l'Islam à l'époque du Prophète et des caliphes orthodoxes*
(Paris, 1935).   On the treatment of dhimmis in the Later Middle Ages,
see the following two Fatwas (juridical consultations):

   (*a*) Bélin, *Fétouâ relatif à la condition des Zimmis*, in JA IVe série, T.
XVIII (1851), 417–516.

   (*b*) A. S. Atiya, *An Unpublished XIVth Century Fatwa on the Status of
Foreigners in Mamlūk Egypt and Syria*, in *Festschrift P. Kahle* (Leiden, 1935),
55–68.

   The first of these was written in A.H. 759/A.D. 1357–8, and the second on
25 Ṣafar A.H. 754/1 April 1353.   Though chiefly touching status of
foreigners, the second deals also with Ahl al-Dhimma.   Short notice on
dhimmis may be found in Nuwairi's *Ilmām* (Berlin MS., Ahlwardt 9815,
vol. II, fo. 223 vo).

   [2] *Patrologia Orientalis*, XVII, 777; Ibn Faḍl-Allah, *Ta'rīf*, 63; Qalqa-
shandī, VIII, 36; Maqrīzī, *Khiṭaṭ* (Bulaq), II, 42, 75, 85, 90, 237, 391,
497–8, 507; Quatremère, *Sultans mamelouks*, I *a*, 231 and II *a*, 8 and *b*, 133,
179, 213; ib., *Mém.*, II, 223–5, 242, 247, 261–2, 288; Abul-Maḥāsin b.
Taghrī Bardī (ed. Popper), VI, 398–400, 450, 456, 464, 468, 559, 665, 718,
724, 819–20, 823 and VII, 160, 269, 272, 277, 587; cf Wiet's art. *Kibt*,
in El, III, 996 Sakhāwī, *Dhail al-Sulūk*, 36, 123–4, 180–1.

   Other unpublished references to ill-treatment and persecution may be
found in the following MSS.: al-'Umarī, *Masālik*, Aya-Sofia MS., Section 16,
vol. III, ff. 673, 691, and Paris MS., fonds arabe 2328, ff. 135 vo, 145 ro,

times instances of mob fury and sometimes deliberate acts
by the Sultans themselves. The Copts were the only
section of society fitted for the management of state finance
and were employed by the rulers of Egypt in this department of government. Individuals who rose to positions of
wealth and authority were, however, liable to be dismissed
from office and deprived of their property at the caprice of
their alien Mamlūk master, who, it must be noted, had no
regard for the native of the country—Copt and Muslim
alike. The result was paralysis of the machinery of the
state and the rulers had to resort again to the disliked, but
necessary, Copt. Subsequently the same vicious circle
recurred, and the crusade only aggravated Mamlūk feeling
towards their Christian subjects. The only benefit, and
that a slight one, which they reaped from time to time was
the outcome of direct negotiations on their behalf from three
quarters. In the first place, the Emperor of Constantinople,[1] though himself harassed by the Ottoman Turks,
sent ambassadors to the Mamlūk court with gifts and
requested the Sultan to treat the Christians in his dominion
with leniency. It is very probable that the Emperor's
mediation was only on behalf of the Melkite Greeks who

148 vo; Nuwairi, *Nihāyat al-Arab*, Vat. MS. 741, ff. 64 vo, 98 ro, and
Leiden MS. V 19 Gol., ff. 5 vo, 122 vo; Ibn Duqmāq, *Nuzhat al-Anām*,
Gotha MS. 1571, f. 1 ro ib., *al-Jauhar*, Bodl. MS. Digby Or. 28, f. 161 ro;
al-Salāmī, *Mukhtaṣar*, Cairo MS. Hist. 1435, f. 77 ro; Dhahabī, *al-'Ibar*,
B.M. MS. Or. 6428, f. 133 vo; Maqrīzī, *Sulūk*, Cambridge MS. Qq 276
(vol. I), ff. 186 ro, 193 vo, 201 ro; ib., Bodl. MS. Marsh 260 (vol. II, non-
foliated), *ann.* A.H. 767; ib. Gotha MS. Pertsch 1620 (vol. IV), ff. 26
vo, 49 vo, 106 vo.

For fear of any misunderstanding as to the view here put forward, it is
essential to note that this harsh treatment of the Copts was not altogether
due to religious prejudice. The native Muslims of Egypt often fared as
badly as the Copts at the hands of the foreign ruling class of Mamlūks, and
the word 'Fellāh' (Egyptian farmer) implied much contempt throughout the
Mamlūk and even the Turkish periods until recent times. Further, cases of
abuse of judges, usually native Muslim graduates of al-Azhar University,
were without number. It is needless to say that both Coptic and Muslim
natives in the smaller villages of Egypt lived for centuries together in complete
harmony irrespective of religious differences, while instances of mob fury
were almost invariably confined to the larger towns.

[1] Examples may be found in the chronicle of al-Nuwairī, Vat. MS. 741,
f. 42 vo (A.H. 710), 57 ro (A.H. 712).

were and still are a minority among the Christians in Egypt.
In the second place, at the end of the thirteenth and the
beginning of the fourteenth century, the Kings of Aragon
sent a number of letters to the Mamlūk Sultans recommending to them all Christians in their realm and urging
the reopening of closed churches in Egypt and the Holy
Land.   The Sultans' replies show that they did not remain
utterly deaf to these requests, although the result of their
response to Aragonese appeals was slight and ephemeral.[1]
In the third place, the Negus of Ethiopia, in his mountain
strongholds at the source of the Blue Nile, was the most
ardent supporter and protector of the Coptic race.   From
the first half of the fourth century, when Frumentius the
Copt converted the Emperor of Ethiopia and his people
to Orthodox Christianity, the Abyssinians and the Copts
had continued in close touch.   The Church of Aksum [2]
was, as it still is, a branch of the Holy Eastern Church of
Alexandria.   Since the consecration of Frumentius by
Athanasius (*circa* A.D. 330), the Patriarchs of Alexandria
have nominated the Metropolitan Archbishops of Abyssinia
who have always been Copts until the present day.   This
strong religious connexion between the two races may help
to explain the great sympathy which the Ethiopian Emperors had for the Copts throughout the Later Middle
Ages.   To obtain relief for their fellows in Egypt, the
Emperors adopted one or other of four ways—first, they
threatened retaliation against their Abyssinian Muhammadan subjects if the Sultans would not put an end to
their odious treatment of Christians; [3] second, they themselves threatened to obstruct the course of the Blue
Nile and deflect the inundation water from Egypt, and

---

[1] See analysis of letters from Aragon and Mamlūk replies in Appendix III.
The Mamlūk correspondence, discovered in the Archivio de la Corona de
Aragon in Barcelona, by the author, is here revealed for the first time; and
it is hoped to publish extracts from the original Arabic texts in a separate
article.

[2] The fate in these latter days of Aksum, for sixteen centuries the seat of
Orthodox Christianity in Ethiopia, calls for no comment here.

[3] Examples of this may be found in Maqrīzī, Sulūk, vol. IV, Gotha MS.
Pertsch 1620, f. 26 vo (Rabīʿ II A.H. 822/March A.D. 1419); Sakhāwī, op.
cit., 71–2 (Rajab A.H. 847/November A.D. 1443).

so turn that country into a barren desert; [1] third, they sent
embassies to the Sultans' court with presents to induce an
amicable settlement; [2] and fourth, they negotiated for alliance
with Western Europe for a well-timed crusade during
which the Ethiopians might descend from their heights
into Nubia [3] and Upper Egypt while the host of the West
invaded Lower Egypt from the Mediterranean. [4] Of these
different ways, the second and the fourth came to nothing,
while the way of retaliation appears to have intensified the
Coptic persecutions, and amicable negotiations brought
only temporary relief.

As to the attitude of the Coptic Churches of Alexandria
and of Aksum towards the papal attempts to re-unite all
churches of East and West, it is extremely difficult to
find any traces of real intercourse between the two parties
before the Council of Ferrara-Florence (1438–9). To
this Council, it is well known that the Coptic Patriarch
Johannes XI (1427–53) delegated his namesake Johannes,
Abbot of St. Anthony, [5] and that the Emperor of Ethiopia

---

[1] Sakhāwī, 67 et seq. This possibility is referred to by Philippe de Mézières,
Songe du vieil pèlerin, B.N. MS. fr. 22542, I, f. 44 ro 2. Cf. *Nicopolis*,
167 note 17*a*.

[2] Maqrīzī, op. cit., ff. 136 vo–137 ro (Jumāda I A.H. 841/Oct. A.D. 1437);
Sakhāwī, 67 et seq.

[3] It is interesting to note that the Nubians passed to Islam only during the
Later Middle Ages. Before that time, Nubia was one of the great fields of the
Coptic missionary, and Christian churches and relics have recently been
excavated in those regions. Budge, *Nubia and Abyssinia*, I, 103 et seq.;
F. Ll. Griffith, *Christian Documents from Nubia*, British Academy tract
(1928), 30 pp.; *Nicopolis*, 167–8, note 17 § 2.

[4] Maqrīzī, op. cit., ff. 87 vo–88 ro; Ibn Taghrī Bardī, *al-Nujūm*, (ed.
Popper), VI, 637–40. Both authors speak of a Persian merchant called
Nūr-al-Dīn 'Alī al-Tabrīzī, who, although a Muslim, executed a mission of
rapprochement between the Negus (al-Ḥaṭā) and the Kings of the 'Franks'
in order to unite their forces for a crusade against Egypt. He was
finally betrayed by one of his Muslim slaves, seized by the Sultan of
Egypt, summarily tried and hanged on 24 Jumada I A.H. 832/1 March
1429.

Projects of union were, however, contemplated as early as the reign of
King Weden Ar'ād (1299–1314) who sent an envoy to the curia of Clement V
at Avignon. Budge, *Abyssinia*, I, 287–8.

[5] Neale, II, 336; Butcher, II, 230–1; Kidd, 445. In Blanc, *Hist. eccles.*,
II, 169, 'Andrew envoy of the Jacobites of Egypt.'

Zara' Ya'qūb [1] (1434–68), nominated Nicodemus, Prior of the Abyssinian Convent in Jerusalem, and another Ethiopian to accompany the Abbot for the conclusion of the peace between the Churches. Union was accomplished, and Pope Eugenius IV published a *Decretum pro Jacobitis* [2] of which Johannes appears as one of the signatories. Without resorting to the same squabbles as the Greeks over their re-union with Rome, the Copts ignored the papal decree owing to its extravagant claims, and no one thought of reviving the idea of effectively bringing the Churches together once more. After the Turkish Conquest of Egypt in 1517, the Ottoman viceroys of Egypt followed the same policy towards the Coptic Patriarchate as that of their masters towards the Greek and Armenian Patriarchates in Constantinople, and any communion with Rome was thus discouraged during the new era. [3]   In Abyssinia, as an immediate result of the union, two Catholics were sent to Aksum. We know that one of these was a Venetian, Francesco de Branco Leon, and that his argument for Catholicism was confounded by an Ethiopian priest named George in the King's presence. [4]   This meant the end of movement for union with Rome on the part of Ethiopia.

The main result of all these abortive attempts of the papacy to take advantage of the miserable state of the Christians of the East and impose its full authority upon them was the alienation of the Oriental Churches from Rome. The failure of projects for re-union of the East and the West undoubtedly contributed to the ultimate collapse of the whole idea of the crusade. [5]

[1] Budge, *Hist. of Ethiopia*, I, 304–12.

[2] Mansi, op. cit., XXXI B, 1734–43.

[3] It is, however, wrong to assume that in Egypt under Turkish rule the breach with Rome was absolutely complete. Correspondence was exchanged between Rome and Alexandria, perhaps secretly, during the pontificate of Clement VIII, for an attempt towards re-union. V. Buri, *Unione della Chiesa Copta con Roma sotto Clemente VIII*, in *Orientalia Christiana*, XXIII 2, no. 12.

[4] Neale, l.c.

[5] Additional material on the Greek union may be found in O. Halecki, Empereur di Byzance (Travaux historiques de la Soc. des Sciences et des Lettres de Varsovie, VIII, 1930).

PART IV
THE CRUSADES

CHAPTER XII

PRELUDES

Charles de Valois: project for crusade against Eastern Empire.   Knights Hospitallers: conquest of Rhodes.   Papal League: occupation and loss of Smyrna

THE history of the crusade in the Later Middle Ages may be divided into three fairly distinct periods, each containing a series of events which bear the same general marks, and each following the other as a natural corollary. The first, extending from the beginning to approximately the middle of the fourteenth century, was an age of active propaganda and of minor preludes to the great battles of the West in the East. These preludes were only the immediate results of the prolific output of theorists whose work has been analysed in the foregoing pages. The second, covering the rest of the century, was an age of crusades, of which the capture of Alexandria (1365), the Barbary expedition (1390) and the crusade of Nicopolis (1396) were notable examples. They all failed miserably to settle the centuries old dispute with Muhammadanism by force of arms, whether in Egypt, in North Africa or in Turkey; and this demonstration of the incapacity of the West appears to have imbued the mind of Islam with contempt for what was regarded as the inferiority of the Christians and encouraged it to pursue its victories by counter-attack. This gave rise to the third phase of the crusade which came in the fifteenth century and turned the balance in favour of the counter-crusades of Egypt against the Christian outposts in the Levant, and of the Ottomans in Eastern Europe. The defence of Byzantium in 1453, though partly undertaken by a number of small fighting units from the West, could hardly be called a crusade, for it did not possess that quality of co-operation among all the peoples of Christendom for the recovery of the Holy Land which was the essence of holy war. The battles of Hungary and Venice were styled as crusades; but in reality they were little more than defen-

sive struggles.   Some of the European monarchs, such as
Francis I [1] of France, formulated a belated sixteenth-century
plan for a crusade which never materialized, and his sincerity
in this respect becomes very doubtful when we recall that it
was he who negotiated the capitulations with Turkey and
that he courted the alliance of Suleiman the Magnificent
against his own co-religionist the Emperor Charles V.[2]

The crusade, though it had been a movement of the past
for many years before the beginning of the sixteenth century, had been a vital force in the politics of Europe in the
fourteenth.   The extinction of the kingdom of Jerusalem
in the Holy Land with the capture of 'Akka in 1291 by the
Muslims of Egypt and the even earlier collapse of the Latin
Empire of Constantinople at the hands of the schismatic
Palaeologi in 1261, had left their marks on the minds of
princes, popes, and common people as the Middle Ages
drew to a close.   Large-scale attempts to heal the still-
bleeding wounds of Christendom were, indeed, not forthcoming in the near future; but the clamour of propagandists
and the popularity of the holy cause, intermingled with personal interests and love of adventure, produced a series of
minor expeditions, the outcome of which was sometimes
nullified by overpowering circumstances and sometimes
justified by a small conquest of relatively enduring value
as a nucleus and a base for further and more extensive projects.   The first of this series was directed, not against the
Muslims in the Holy Land, but against the Greek Empire
of Constantinople.   Reference has been made to the abortive attempt of Charles of Anjou, King of Naples and Sicily,
to embark on a crusade against Byzantium in the seventies
of the thirteenth century.   This was foiled by the diplomatic skill of Michael VIII Palaeologos at the Council of
Lyons in 1274 and the part he played in the Sicilian Vespers
in 1282.[3]   The subsequent failure of the agreement for the
union of the churches reached at Lyons, however, revived

---

[1] vide infra, Cap. XIX, for belated projects of crusade.

[2] De la Jonquière, Empire Ottoman, I, 157–65.

[3] vide supra, Cap. XI. Also Vasiliev, Emp. Byz., II, 270 et seq.; Finlay
(ed. Tozer), III, 353 and IV, 205; Du Cange, Emp. de Constantinople (ed.
Buchon), II, 18 et seq.
This was not Charles's first crusade. He had been previously with St. Louis

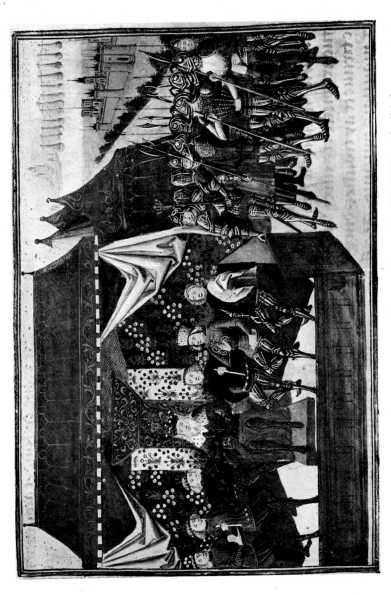

THE KING OF HUNGARY IN COUNCIL (M. ccvi, p. 436).   MS. HARL. 4380, Fol. 84.

he project of Charles of Anjou in other hands.   It is signi-
icant at this juncture to note that the crusade at the end of
he thirteenth and the beginning of the fourteenth centuries
mplied war against both Saracen and Greek.   A concrete
eminder in Europe of the loss of Constantinople was given
»y the dispossessed titular Latin Emperors of the East who
oamed homeless in the West.   Philippe de Courtenay,
vho married Beatrice, daughter of Charles of Anjou, King
·f Naples, was the second [1] of these emperors without
mpire.   On his death in 1301, he left one daughter,
Catherine de Courtenay.   Numerous suitors came to ask
he hand of the sole heiress of imperial claims.   Foremost
mong these was the Greek Emperor Andronikos II (1282–
328) who wished to unite her in marriage to his own son
Michael IX Palaeologos and thus settle the dispute between
he West and the East on the rights of succession to his
hrone.   This might have been an ideal union from the
Greek point of view, but Catherine refused and Michael
imself died during his father's own lifetime in 1320. [2]
econd, Frederick of Aragon, the brother of Jaime II, who
laimed the kingdom of Sicily from the house of Anjou con-
~ary to the will of the Pope, tried to win Catherine's hand,
ut without avail. [3]   The third suitor came from France in the
erson of Charles de Valois, the King's brother.   He was
upported by the formidable Philippe le Bel and the match
·ceived the blessing of the Pope and the approval of Cather-
1e's uncle, Charles of Anjou, who pledged himself to oppose
ny union with the Aragonese dynasty on account of its usur-
ation of his kingdom. [4]   It was stipulated by the Pope and

his North African expedition of 1270, and after the death of the French
ing, it was he who concluded peace with the King of Tunis; and Villani
Troniche Fiorentine, various editions, Lib. VII, Cap. 38; cf. Selfe and
Vicksteed, 250) says that many people accused Charles of purely selfish
otives in treating with the Saracens.

[1] The first of these was Baldwin II, who succeeded to the imperial throne
the age of eleven but was superseded by Jean de Brienne as emperor-elect
r life (1231–7).   Baldwin then resumed the empire till his exile from
·onstantinople in 1261.   He died in 1273.

[2] Du Cange, op. cit., 28–9.

[3] Villani, Lib. VIII, Cap. 42; Du Cange, II, 37–8.

[4] Du Cange, II, 39 et seq.

the Angevin King that prior to the conquest of Constantinople, the Latin armies should purge Naples of the Aragonese peril.   The marriage took place on 18 January 1301, and Catherine subsequently resigned her imperial claims to her husband.   The new Emperor then marched in the direction of Naples to fulfil his first promise, but his troops became so depleted by sickness on the way that he had to abandon his original plan and to approach Frederick of Aragon for peace which was concluded by the treaty of Caltabellota on 31 August 1302.[1]   This left Frederick master of Naples with the condition that Charles de Valois should have the right to embark his troops from that port if he chose to proceed to the East by sea.   Moreover, Frederick promised to reinforce Charles's Eastern expedition with a fleet numbering from fifteen to twenty galleys together with a detachment of two hundred men for a period of four months at his own expense, in addition to ten more galleys and four hundred horses if these were necessary, and he also undertook not to negotiate any alliances with the Greek Emperor.[2]   In his actual failure to carry out his first enterprise, Charles de Valois thus seemingly won a new supporter to his second.   An agreement of this kind, born of fear and uncertainty on both sides and not based on common interest or sympathy, was bound to collapse.   By virtue of his origin, Frederick upheld the policy of his native country in giving support to the 'Almugavares', better known as the Catalan Grand Company of adventurers in Greece under the command of Roger de Flor, who entered the service of Andronikos II in 1302–3.[3]

On the other hand, Charles de Valois continued to pursue his own project against the Empire.   After his return to France, he dispatched Thibaut de Cépoy to treat with the Venetians and explore the route for the coming crusade. Cépoy concluded the desired treaty with the Doge Pietro

[1] Muntaner (ed. Buchon), 413; Mas Latrie, in BEC, XXXIV (1873), 4

[2] Du Cange, II, 44–6.

[3] Schlumberger, *Expédition des 'Almugavares'*, 20 *passim*; Finlay (ed. Tozer), III, 391–3.   Moreover, it appears that Frederick was actually intriguing with the Greeks to frustrate Charles's plan, as revealed by Philippe le Bel's correspondence; Boutaric, in *Not. et Extr.* (Paris, 1861), 83–4; c Delaville Le Roulx, *France*, I, 45 note 2.

Gradenigo on 27 December 1306, whereby Valois should furnish the men and Venice the fleet, and the expenses of the campaign should be defrayed equally by the two parties. The place and time of the departure of the combined forces were fixed as Brindisi in March 1307 [1] respectively. Charles found it impossible to fulfil this last obligation as it gave him less time to complete his preparations than he expected. Meanwhile the death of the Empress Catherine de Courtenay in 1308 further added to his difficulties and at least momentarily complicated matters for him. During this delay another treaty of alliance against Andronikos II was concluded with Uroš, King of Serbia, on 27 March 1308; [2] and Pope Clement V granted Charles the usual tithe towards the cost of the crusade. Meanwhile, Cépoy proceeded to the Archipelago to court further allies. In Negropontis, he approached the Catalan Grand Company with this purpose in view. The Almugavares were a band of adventurers levied from the poorer class of proud and reckless Spanish nobility, without any principle or definite policy other than their own aggrandizement and enrichment, and they were therefore ready to lend support to anyone who paid them well. They had served the Emperor of Constantinople, and now they were prepared to fight against him. Cépoy remained in their midst and became entangled in their intrigues. At last, he realized the hopelessness of his plight and returned to France in 1309. [3] The history of the rest of this project is one of continued postponements on the part of Charles. Although he was the originator and main agent, it seemed more and more doubtful whether he really intended to fulfil this enterprise. The Venetians made their preparations in good time and waited impatiently until Charles wrote to Clement V in February 1309 asking him to mediate for another postponement, making new

---

[1] Daru, *Venise* (1821), VII, 236; Du Cange, op. cit., II, 101–2, 346; Buchon, *Recherches et matériaux pour servir à une hist. de la domination française etc. dans . . . l'empire grec.* (Paris, 1840), I, 48–9; Carew Hazlitt, *Venice*, I, 489.

[2] In BEC, XXIV, 115–18; cf. Delaville Le Roulx, op. cit., I, 46 note 1.

[3] Muntaner (ed. Buchon), 467 et seq., Du Cange, II, 137 et seq.; Schlumberger, *Almugavares*, 233 et seq.

excuses for his delay and asking for more contributions towards the extraordinary expenses of the war.[1] Uroš, too, waited for the host of France until his death in 1310; and Charles kept whatever provisions he had accumulated in Venice for some years, but without leading the armies for whose use they were intended.[2] With the lapse of time the whole project became a shadow and was ultimately forsaken. Valois' plan, which thus came to nothing, was not an isolated example of these attempts to reconquer Constantinople for the Latins. It had a predecessor in the abortive expedition of Charles of Anjou, and a successor in the unrealized 'passagium generale' (1335) of Philippe VI, King of France, both of which have been treated elsewhere.[3]

Though these three elaborate projects to wreck the Eastern Empire never came to fruition, a group of adventurers, few in number and uncontrolled by any great Western leader, managed to wrest part of the Archipelago from the Emperor's realm. Their conquests included the island of Rhodes, destined to become the great stronghold of the Knights of St. John of Jerusalem and, in conjunction with its sister island of Cyprus under the Lusignan dynasty, to make history for the later medieval crusade.

Since the expulsion of the Latins from 'Akka in the year 1291, the Knights Hospitallers, who had been housed in part of the fortifications of that city, were stranded and homeless except for the temporary refuge accorded to them by Henri II de Lusignan (1285–1324) in the town of Limassol,[4] on the south coast of the island of Cyprus. Here they stayed for approximately sixteen years, a period during which the Order recovered from the heavy blow which it had sustained in 1291. The Knights were further strengthened by the active reform of their rule, notably under

---

[1] For the accounts relating to the expedition, see B.N. MS., fonds Baluze, 394, 696; Moranvillé, in BEC (1890), 60–81; cf. Schlumberger, 233 note. See also Du Cange, 352–6.

[2] Mas Latrie, *Commerce et expéditions*, 62 et seq.

[3] *vide supra*, Cap. V.

[4] Limisso in the works of Vertot and Delaville Le Roulx; otherwise Limazim, Limasol, Lemeso, Limeçon and, in the Arabic chronicles, ḥiṣn al-Lamsūn (fortress of the Lamsūn).

their Grand Master, Guillaume de Villaret [1] (1296–1304),
and by the abolition of the Templars, half of whose tempor-
alities were passed to the Hospitallers [2] (1312). During the
reign of Guillaume's successor and nephew, Foulques de
Villaret (1305–19), the crusade was being seriously considered at the Council of Vienne (1308) and the court of
Philippe le Bel, and Foulques submitted for their consideration a memoir which has been analysed elsewhere in this
study.[3] Yet far more important than these deliberations was
the conquest of Rhodes which had remained up to that time
a part of the empire of Andronikos II. The Hospitallers
were reluctant to prolong their subordinate position in
Cyprus under the Lusignans; and in 1306 the occasion
presented itself for them to regain the full freedom they had
hitherto sought in vain. Strangely, this came about through
an ignoble alliance with a mysterious Genoese corsair
named Vignolo de' Vignoli, who, disregarding the Cypriot
laws forbidding shelter to piratical bands, landèd on the
south coast of the island to suggest to the Grand Master
participation in this scheme. Villaret welcomed the idea,
and the pirate and the Grand Master finally met on 27 May [4]
1306, off the coast of Limassol and concluded a treaty conceding one-third of the island to Vignolo and two-thirds to
the knights if the project succeeded. Vignolo was also
promised other smaller islands which might be invaded by
the combined forces as well as full jurisdiction in his territory
except in serious cases involving loss of life or mutilation.[5]
Of the said islands of the Archipelago, Lango and Leros

---

[1] Vertot, *Chevaliers de Malte*, II, 26–54; Delaville Le Roulx, *Hospitaliers
en Terre Sainte et à Chypre*, 251–66.

[2] See letter dated 2 March 1312, from Philippe le Bel to Clement V
communicating royal approval with reservation as to the decision of the
Council of Vienne on the disposal of the property of the Order of the Temple
in G. Lizérand, *Dossier de l'affaire des Templiers* (Paris, 1923), 196–203.

[3] *vide supra*, Cap. III.

[4] *Gestes des Chiprois*, 319 et seq.; Amadi, *Chroniques*, 254–9; Bustron,
Chronique de l'île de Chypre, 141–3; cf. Delaville Le Roulx, op. cit., 272–3.

In the *Gestes des Chiprois*, Foulque de Villaret is described as 'large et
courtois et moult libéral, et fu de si bon portement en sa baillie'.

[5] The whole treaty appears in a footnote in Delaville Le Roulx, op. cit.,
274–6, note 2.

were already in Vignolo's possession together with one
hamlet in Rhodes, which he held by special permission of
Andronikos II.   The Genoese pirate insisted on retaining this grant and asked for another village probably to
be used for refuge in case of emergency.   Villaret acceded
to all these terms and afterwards seems to have sailed to
Western Europe to negotiate the project for crusade with
the Papacy at Avignon.[1]

On 23 June 1306, a small fleet of two galleys and four
smaller craft sailed from Limassol carrying thirty-five
knights, six native horsemen and a detachment of five hundred foot.   These were joined by two more Genoese
galleys off the west coast of Cyprus near the cape of St.
Piphani.   The fleet then went to the small island of
Castellorizzo [2] near the shores of Asia Minor, while
Vignolo himself paid a flying visit to Rhodes to test the
disposition of its inhabitants.   Vignolo and the army
of the Hospital were re-united at the island of Guilla
and finally landed near the city of Rhodes, only to find
its inhabitants stubbornly determined to resist them.
On 20 September, the knights surprised and seized the fort
of Pheraclos or Faraclo on the east coast of the island facing
Anatolia; and on the 25th they tried to enter the fort of
Rhodes itself, but in vain.   On 11 November, the castle of
Filermo [3] succumbed, not to their arms but to betrayal
from within.   This castle lay to the west of the city of
Rhodes and proved invulnerable, until the gates were
opened to the enemy by treacherous hands.   Advance
beyond Filermo, however, by direct assault on the walls
was regarded as hopeless.   It was therefore decided to
lay siege to the town and starve it into surrender.   The
beleaguered citizens appear to have been amply provisioned
for the occasion and their supplies must have constantly

---

[1] ib., 276, 279, 280.   Delaville Le Roulx fixes the date of Villaret's return
from the West as 1310; but he continually refers to him as if he were present
in the Rhodian expedition.   If we believe him as to that date, it must be
assumed that the actual siege and capture of the island took place during the
Grand Master's absence in the West.

[2] Kastellorizo, Castellorizzo, Castel Rosso, Castellorosso, Chastelroux, or
Château Rouge, known in the Arabic sources as Qashṭīl al-Rūj.

[3] Amadi, 257–8.

been replenished. Hence the siege dragged on for two years. During this time, the knights tried the way of diplomacy with the Emperor Andronikos II, and offered to rule the island under his suzerainty and even furnish his army with three hundred of their number for war against Muhammadans, if he would order the citizens of Rhodes to give up the town. This was refused by the Emperor in April 1308. The Knights were not prepared to abandon the hope of victory and filled all gaps to prevent any provisions filtering into the town. So when Andronikos dispatched a laden Genoese ship, the blockade was too stringent and too alert and the vessel was ultimately blown by a strong gale to Famagusta in Cyprus. There it was seized by one Pierre le Jaune, a knight of that island, and immediately taken by him to the besiegers. To save his life, the commander, who was a native of Rhodes, offered to mediate between his fellow-citizens and the knights. The Rhodians, it was revealed, were ready to surrender if their lives were spared and their property respected. The knights agreed, and the city opened its gates to them on 15 August.[1]

Whilst in Europe, Foulque de Villaret seems to have secured the Pope's blessing for the enterprise against Rhodes and he was further authorized to nominate a Latin archbishop for the island when it was conquered.[2] On his return to the East, he found the island in the hands of his fellow-knights; and the Order finally transferred its residence from Limassol to the city of Rhodes which it soon turned into one of the best-fortified strongholds in the Levant. This acquisition seems to have impressed the contemporary world so much that the whole of Europe

---

[1] Baluze, *Vit. Pap. Aven.* (ed. Mollat), I, 68, 99, 'in festo assumptionis beate Marie Virginis'; Jourdain the Minorite, in Muratori, *Antiquitates Italicae*, IV, 1031. These, however, place that date under the year 1310, contrary to the authority of Amadi (*Chroniques*, 254-9) who furnishes us with the most valuable information on the whole campaign. It seems unlikely that the siege of Rhodes lasted four years, and there is no special reason to discount Amadi's statements which are our best source. Villani (Lib. VIII, Cap. 104), too, reports the fall of Rhodes in 1308. For further considerations on the chronology of the campaign, see Delaville Le Roulx, op. cit., 278-9.   [2] Vertot, op. cit., II, 67.

then began to recognize the Order of St. John of Jerusalem as the Knights of Rhodes. The geographical situation of the island on the border-line between the Aegean and the Mediterranean, combined with its nearness to the Asiatic mainland, made it a centre for trade comparable to the markets of Cyprus. Moreover, its position within easy reach of the rapidly dwindling Christian Kingdom of Armenia enabled the Knights to offer the poor Armenians some help, although the Mamlūk conquerors were too strong in this particular *terrain* even for the Hospitallers' proved valour. On the other hand, their proximity to the Asiatic shores made them a thorn in the side of the advancing Turkish Empire. Most of the crusaders of the Later Middle Ages counted Rhodes as one of their principal stations. From Rhodes, Egypt and Syria could be approached either direct or by way of Cyprus without difficulty; but Asia Minor was much nearer, and this fact may help to explain that the next crusading enterprise resulted in the capture of Smyrna.

Strictly speaking, the conquest of Rhodes was not a crusade, but an adventure and an act of aggression against the Byzantine Empire. On the other hand, the expedition against the Turks which culminated in the fall of Smyrna may be regarded as a real crusade in which the Papacy was directly involved. Further, it marked the new orientation in the course of the movement of holy war. Although the popes, kings and nations of the West had freely discussed the project of attacking the Saracens since the fall of 'Akka in 1291, their schemes had materialized only in part and that at the expense of the schismatic Greeks, and no enterprise of worth was undertaken against the Muhammadans until 1343-4. These years mark the attempt of Byzantium and the West to act together against their common foe; and from that time, the crusades aimed both at the invasion of Muslim territories and also at the defence of the Empire.

The town of Smyrna or Izmīr,[1] in the province of

---

[1] Originally a Greek town, it was ceded to the Genoese by Michael VIII Palaeologos after his recovery of Constantinople by the treaty of Nymphaeum (13 March 1261) and lost by these to the Turks in 1300. Manfroni, *Relazioni*, 791 et seq. Heyd, I, 429; Bratiani, *Commerce génois*, 81-2.

Aidīn,[1] situated on a large and deep bay at the foot of a
fortified hill, furnished the Turks with an ideal haven from
which their craft sallied into the Aegean to seize ships
from the Christian trading fleets and to raid the towns
on the islands of the Archipelago and the coast of the
European mainland, without discrimination between Greeks
and Latins. The Turkish navy was, indeed, as yet far
from being sufficiently strong to meet the armed fleets
of the West in battle on the high seas.[2] Nevertheless,
it was becoming, even at that early stage in its history, a
serious menace to defenceless ships laden with goods sailing
between the Black Sea and the merchant republics of southern Europe. This is the crucial factor behind the eagerness of the Venetians to lend their maritime support to the
impending attack on the coasts of Asia Minor. Pope
Clement VI, however, treated the whole matter as a crusade
against Islam. His activities in promoting the movement
were multiple. His aim was, failing to persuade the Kings
of England and France to put an end to the Hundred
Years' War and assist in the cause of the Cross, to bring
together as many smaller powers as possible into a holy
league to attack the Turks. The Kingdom of Cyprus and
the Knights of Rhodes, holding the furthest Latin outposts
in the East and more exposed to the danger than the West,
were always ready to participate in any crusade which might
ensure their own security. In both, Clement had useful
allies on whose response he could rely; but without ships,

---

[1] In this period, Aidīn was, of course, not an Ottoman province. It belonged to the dynasty of Aidīn-oghlu, Amīrs (or Sultans) of Ephesus (Aya-
soluk), founded about 1300. The expedition now under consideration was
therefore not directly against the Ottomans alone, but against the Turks
in general.

[2] As quoted above, there was not yet an Ottoman navy. In his *Tuḥfat
al-Kibār fī Asfār al-Biḥār*, Ḥājji Khalīfa states 'that before the time of the
late Sultan Mohammed, the Ottomans had not ventured to undertake naval
expeditions, or to engage with the European nations'. See J. Mitchell's
trans. *Hist. of the Maritime Wars of the Turks*, 12. The Sultan named in
this passage is Muhammad II. The same author asserts that the need for a
Turkish navy was felt during the unsuccessful siege of Constantinople by
Murad II. At this stage, however, we have to distinguish between the
'Turkish', which is a wider term, and the 'Ottoman' navy.

their goodwill had little value, and the Pope therefore turned to the maritime republics in northern Italy. On 19 July 1342, he wrote a letter to Cardinal Guillelmo Curti appointing him papal legate with the dual rôle of peacemaker in Lombardy and negotiator with Venice for armed aid against the Turks.[1] The Pope also wrote a letter to the Doge and dispatched it by Enrico d'Asti, Bishop of Negropontis and Latin Patriarch of Constantinople.[2] The Venetian Senate, in their usual cautious way, approached the matter by inquiring as to the nature of the aid which they were to provide and by reiterating the view previously communicated to Pope John XXII that a fleet of forty galleys each carrying 200 men, and fifty transports,[3] with 120 oarsmen and 20 mounted men-at-arms on board each, would be insufficient to face Turkish strength. Twenty-five galleys, which was probably the number suggested by the holy see, the Venetians considered hopeless. They were, however, prepared to contribute a quarter of the armed galleys for the expedition, that is, from six to ten units, and recommended that the fleet should be stationed in the Archipelago for three years. The Pope sent a tardy reply to the Venetian memoir in August [4] 1343 in which he ordered the formation of the league, and the news from the East that 'Umar Bey, Amīr of Aidīn and master of Smyrna, had equipped a fleet of 250 or 300 barges to raid the coastal towns of Europe and participate in the civil war in Greece,[5] aroused the Venetians to immediate action. A fleet of twenty galleys was raised. The Pope and the King of Cyprus contributed four, the Knights of Rhodes six and Venice

---

[1] Reynaldus, *ad. ann.* 1342, no. 17; cf. Gay, *Clément VI et les affaires d'Orient*, 32–3.

[2] *Commemoriali*, IV, no. 22.

[3] 'Usserii' or 'hussiers' were mainly vessels for horse transport. De la Roncière, *Hist. de la marine franç.*, I, 251; cf. Gay, op. cit., 34.

[4] Golubovich, II, 195; a digest of other bulls issued by Clement VI in connexion with the expedition and extracted from the Venetian *Commemoriali* appears in the same work, II, 194–6.

[5] Reynaldus, *ad. ann.* 1343, no. 2; Kantakuzenos (ed. Bonn), III, § 56, 344 et seq.; Nicephoras Gregoras (ed. Bonn), XII, § 7, 597 and XIII, § 10, 672; cf. Gay, 35.

and its vassal states in the Archipelago the rest. On 16 September, Clement VI placed a Genoese, Martino Zaccharia, in command of his own galleys and appointed the Latin Patriarch, Enrico d'Asti, as head of the coalition fleet, with strict orders not to allow the forces to be deflected from their planned course of action.[1]

Zaccharia and the papal galleys reached Negropontis and found waiting Pietro Zeno, commander of the Venetian fleet. The campaign seems to have been popular with the Latins in the Archipelago, as they must have voluntarily contributed to the Christian fleet, the number of whose galleys exceeded all expectations. One Byzantine historian estimates it at twenty-four [2] galleys, and another at twenty-seven.[3] The primary object was to crush the growing menace of the Turkish principality of Aidīn and its naval aggression in the Archipelago and suppress Turkish piracy in the Aegean. Smyrna appeared to be the centre of mischief, and on its way thither the coalition fleet was forced into skirmishes with the enemy of which little is known. It is said that a naval battle took place on Ascension Day, 1344, in which the Turks lost fifty ships.[4] Early in the summer of the same year, letters reached Avignon from the Latin Patriarch and the Grand Master of the Hospital indicating the signal courage of the Venetians and Pietro Zeno and reporting a victory of their fleet.[5] Martino Zaccharia, formerly lord of Chios and expelled from it by the Byzantine Emperor, tried to persuade the leaders of the expedition to re-occupy the island for him and use it as a base, as it was situated just outside the Bay of Smyrna. This proposal was refused on two grounds—first, it did not fall within the original plan of the expedition; and second, it would strain relations with the Emperor whom the Pope hoped to draw within the league.[6] The fleet then crossed

---

[1] Gay, 36–7.   [2] Kantakuzenos (ed. Bonn), III, § 68, 42.

[3] Nicephoras Gregoras (ed. Bonn), XIII, § 13, 689.

[4] *Hist. Cortusiorum*, in Muratori (*Rer. It. Script.*), XII, 914.

[5] Letters dated 3 June, 25 July and 12 August 1344. *Reg. Vat. Clement.*, VI, 138, nos. 43, 162, 163 and 213; *Reg. Vat.* (*de negotiis Tartarorum et aliorum infidelium*), 62, ff. 57 vo, 59; cf. Gay, 39 and note 4.

[6] The Pope's letter rejecting Zaccharia's scheme is dated 18 September; Reynaldus, *ad ann.* 1344, no. 2. This confirmed the Patriarch's decision.

the bay to the port of Smyrna, and after setting most
of the Turkish craft harboured there on fire, the Christian
host landed safely on the narrow strip of land skirting the
coast at the foot of the hill which was crowned by a castle
on the site of the ancient Acropolis.   In spite of the precariousness of their position, the invaders remained masters
of the harbour and finally seized the town itself on the
hillside and the Muslims among its inhabitants were
massacred [1] on 28 October 1344.   Nevertheless, it is
to be noted that the highest fort on the hill was too difficult to approach and remained in Turkish hands during
the whole period of the Latin occupation of the city.
This easy capture of Smyrna by the Latins despite its
natural strength, needs some explanation.   In the first
place, the town was inadequately defended at the time,
and 'Umar Bey's absence [2] with the bulk of his army
must have depleted its garrison to the point of insecurity.
In the second place, the contemporary accounts indicate
that the main stronghold on the hilltop was too far removed
from the centre of the town and that there were no strong
walls, in the Western sense, surrounding the lower quarters.   In the third place, its inhabitants were mainly
Christian merchants who were not disposed to assist in the
defence.   In the fourth place, it would be an error to
magnify the military strength of the petty amīrs who had an
unstable hold on their segregated amīrates in Asia Minor
and who, further, fought against one another.   Collaboration
among them and control by a centralized state from above
were not among the features of their government.   That
the consolidation of the Ottoman power in Asia Minor
during the sultanate of Orkhan and even later did not exist,
is a thesis which appears to be proved beyond doubt. [3]   It
will be shown a little later in this study that some of the
Muslim amīrs on the southern coast of Asia Minor were so

---

[1] Daru, *Venise*, I, 598.

[2] Ibn Baṭṭūṭa, II, 311–12, states that 'Umar Bey was ultimately killed in
leading one of the attacks on the invaders, although it is difficult to define
which of these attacks was really meant by the Arab traveller.

[3] This is H. A. Gibbons's thesis in Appendix B to his *Foundation of the
Ottoman Empire*, 277–302.

much afraid of being absorbed by their formidable neighbour of Qaraman that they preferred to become tributaries
to the Christian King of Cyprus.   Of these factors, however, the first was probably the most decisive in the capture
of the town, and the fourth in its retention in Christian
hands.   When 'Umar Bey arrived, he found it impossible
to recover his lost dominion; and only the hordes of the
invincible Timur were capable of clearing the Christians
from it when, after the battle of Angora on 20 July 1402,
they swept over the whole peninsula.

A summary of the history of Smyrna [1] between the dates
of its fall into the hands of the Latins and its sack by the
Tatars is both interesting and relevant.   The Christian
occupation of the city was accompanied by the destruction
of the Turkish ships anchored in the bay.   This certainly
crushed the strength of the nascent navy of the Turks; but
on land they remained masters of the situation, especially as
the highest fort overlooking the town was still in their hands.
Behind Smyrna, the Turks waited and watched for an opportunity to avenge themselves upon the Latins.   Meanwhile,
the coalition troops, whose numbers were far from being
large enough to cope with the enemy, were enticed by their
first success into the vain hope of carrying their triumph still
further, and on 17 January 1345 sallied inland from their
coastal shelter to break through the siege and destroy the
siege machinery.   This foolhardy attempt resulted in a
battle in which three leaders—the Latin Patriarch, the
Genoese Zaccharia and the Venetian Zeno—lost their lives,
while the rest of the Christians scrambled back for safety
within the town.[2]   The Turks seem to have taken no

---

[1] Delaville Le Roulx, *Hospitaliers à Rhodes*, 95 *passim*; ib., *Occupation
chrétienne à Smyrne* (1344–1402), in *Florilegium ou Rec. de travaux d'érudition dédiés à M. le Marquis Melchior de Vogüé* (Paris, 1909), 178–86; ib., same
article in *Mélanges sur l'Ordre de S. Jean de Jérusalem* (Paris, 1910); Gay,
op. cit., 55–7; Gibbons, *Foundations of Ottoman Emp.*, 185, 258–60, 283,
299–300.

[2] Two versions are extant: (*a*) that the Christians were surprised while
attending Mass in a church outside the town; (*b*) that after Mass, the legate
delivered his sermon and then led his congregation to the field of battle.   *Hist.
Cortus.*, in Muratori, *Rer. It. Scrip.*, XII, 914; *Vite de' Duchi di Venezia*, in
ib., XXII, 610; Muratori, *Antiquitates Italicae*, III, 361 et seq.; Joannes

advantage of their victory, and one chronicler asserts that the Christians inflicted a defeat upon them a little later and thus atoned for their recent humiliation.[1] However this may be, the death of the captains of the league gave rise to a certain amount of confusion in the ranks and the Pope hastened to appoint their successors. The Archbishop of Crete became vice-legate and a Genoese, Conrad Picamiglio,, commander of the fleet, while a Hospitaller, Jean de Biandra, the prior of his Order in Lombardy, became captain-general of the league.[2] The choice of a Knight of St. John as the permanent head of the expedition was well-advised in order to avert the possibility of Italian betrayal of trust for material gain and trade privileges with the Turks as might happen if a Genoese or a Venetian were appointed to this dignity, and also on account of the nearness of Rhodes, which would facilitate the problem of defence whenever necessary. Besides, the Hospitallers were the only party willing to furnish the town with a permanent garrison, while the Venetians and the Cypriots were not disposed to sustain the heavy expenditure involved in the maintenance of a standing army [3] in that part of Asia Minor. The following period was therefore one of skirmishes, threats and attempts to conclude a treaty be-

Vitoduranus, *Chron. a Friderico II*, in *Arch. für schweizerische Gesch.*, XI, 225, and Golubovich, II, 149; Kantakuzenos, III, § 95, 582. Cf. Gay, 56–7; Iorga, *Mézières*, 43; Delaville Le Roulx, *Hospitaliers à Rhodes*, 95; ib., *France*, I, 104.

[1] Vitoduranus, l.c.; Gay, 57.

[2] Chevalier, *Choix de documents . . . sur le Dauphiné*, doc. XXXI, 105–6, where Jean de Biandra is mistaken for 'Jacobi de Preoliis'; see Bosio, *Istoria della religione di S. Giovanni Gierosolimitano*, II, 69, and Delaville Le Roulx, *Hospitaliers à Rhodes*, 96 note 1; in Daru, *Venise*, I, 597, 'Jean de Biadra'. Iorga, *Mézières*, 45, adopts the wrong name in accordance with the document published by Chevalier.

[3] The cost of keeping each knight in Smyrna amounted to 100 florins, and the normal garrison was 120 knights which brought the estimate of the total expense up to 12,000 florins, apart from the unforeseen items. The papacy contributed 3,000, which was the equivalent of the tithe on ecclesiastical benefices in Cyprus. Bull 'Inter ceteras solicitudines' (*Reg. Vat.* 266 f. 51); cf. Bosio, op. cit., II, 118 and Delaville Le Roulx, *Hospitaliers à Rhodes*, 185–6. See also *Reg. Vat.* 144, f. 84; *Commemoriali*, IV, f. 173, no. 178; Predelli, *Libri Commemoriali*, II, 148, no. 352; cf. Delaville Le Roulx, op. cit., III, 285.

tween the Turks and the Hospitallers fixing their relations
on a stable basis.   A projected treaty to save bloodshed was
contemplated in January 1348; but this was rejected by the
Pope.[1]   Another siege was thus begun, and the Turks
fared badly this time, for their general 'Umar Bey was
mortally wounded while conducting operations.   Negotiations were renewed by 'Umar's brother, Khiḍr Bey,
Amīr of Ephesus, who offered concessions to the Christians
in order to free his own hands for action elsewhere.   He
promised to surrender half the customs duties in the whole
of his principality, to give protection to Christians and allow
their bishops to build churches without impediment, to concede to the consuls of Cyprus, Rhodes and Venice the right
of jurisdiction over their nationals in his domain, to
disarm or destroy the remainder of his fleet, to suppress
Turkish piracy in return for its suppression on the side of
the Christians, to grant the ships of the league members free
access to all ports in his subject territories, and to restore
fugitive slaves to their Christian masters or pay indemnity
for them.[2]   The treaty was prepared on 10 April 1348, but
the reluctant Pope Clement VI limited his ratification of it
to the acceptance of a mere truce lasting until 25 December
1350.   Venice and Cyprus ultimately withdrew from
Smyrna, and the Pope dissolved the league on 8 September
1350.[3]   This left the Hospitallers as sole guardians of the
town.   In spite of the frequency of alarming reports as to
the fate of the Anatolian garrison, the situation remained
unchanged during the next few decades.[4]   The amīrs of

---

[1] The negotiators of the first treaty were Barthélemy 'de Tomariis', vicar
of the French legate in Crete and Dragonet de Joyeuse, brother of the
Hospital.   The terms included the destruction of the town fortifications in
return for trade privileges in Turkey.   Gay, 86–7; Delaville Le Roulx,
op. cit., 108–9.
[2] Mas Latrie, *Commerce et expéditions*, 112 et seq.; Tafel and Thomas,
Diplomatarium Veneto-Levantinum, IV, 313 et seq.; Heyd, *Commerce*, I, 543;
Gay, 87–93; Delaville Le Roulx, op. cit., 108–12.
[3] Bull 'Licet dudum carissimus'; *Reg. Vat.*, 145, f. 55; cf. Delaville Le
Roulx, op. cit., 112.
[4] It is interesting to note that even the Hospitallers were reluctant to undertake alone the heavy burden of the defence of Smyrna and that once in 1374
Gregory XI had to impose the government of the town upon them on pain of

Aidīn were losing their former strength and the Ottomans were busy invading new territories and consolidating old ones in Europe. They had no immediate interest in mustering their Asiatic forces and deflecting the course of their European conquest in order to invest the solitary Christian town of Smyrna which was bound sooner or later to succumb to their arms. Perhaps the most anxious time for the Hospitallers was inaugurated by Bayezid I in 1390 after his annexation of the principality of Aidīn from its lawful, but feeble amīr, 'Isa Bey. The Sultan then thought of clearing all foreign influence from Aidīn and actually besieged Smyrna in the following years,[1] but sickness and plague depleted the number of his army, and he was further occupied by the imminent invasion of his realm in Europe. The town had another period of respite. After the disaster which befell Western chivalry at Nicopolis in 1396, it was thought that the victor might direct his armies against Smyrna. He preferred, however, to expand in Greece and to besiege the much more important city of Constantine until fate called upon him to encounter his more redoubtable enemy—Timur the Tatar, in 1402.

The appearance of the Mongols in these regions meant the end of all independent units in Asia Minor. After the battle of Angora was fought in July 1402 and Bayezid became the captive of a master who knew no mercy, Timur sent envoys to Smyrna asking the Hospitallers to submit to him and either profess Islam or pay tribute. Otherwise their doom would be sealed and their town levelled to the ground. Smyrna had twice been visited during 1402 by the admiral of the Hospitallers, Buffilo Panizati, who inspected the preparations for the defence, and the garrison had been raised to two hundred knights whose upkeep weighed heavily on the finances of the Order. In these seemingly reassuring circumstances, Inigo d'Alfara,[2] who

excommunication. Delaville Le Roulx, *Hospitaliers à Rhodes*, 185. The Grand Master at the time was Robert de Juilly.

[1] Bosio, op. cit., II, 143 et seq.; Gibbons, 185, 283; Delaville Le Roulx, op. cit., 222–4.

[2] Delaville Le Roulx, op. cit., 284. It is also known that some attempt was made at the beginning of 1402 to revive the league against the 'Turks'; Iorga, *Not. et extr.*, 1e série, 115 (16 February).

was in command of the garrison, rejected Timur's offer
outright. This meant the end of their day. The Mongol
hordes poured round Smyrna on 2 December 1402.
Timur himself and his princes, including Muhammad
Sultan, Miran Shah, Abu-Bakr, Jihan Shah, and Malik
Shah with their innumerable armies laid siege to the town.
All communications with the outer world were cut, even the
entrance of the harbour was closely guarded to arrest the
passage of provisions from that direction. Siege machines
were constructed and the onslaught was conducted with
unusual vigour. It has been remarked that the weakest
side of Tatar warfare was siegecraft.[1] The fury of their
thirteenth-century ravages in Europe left the majority of
the strongly fortified towns intact. Yet the details of the
attack on Smyrna reveal a skill in conducting a siege, at
least during this period, that calls for some revision of current opinion. Colossal wheeled structures were speedily
made and rolled into the ditch close to the walls to house
200 men at a time. From these ladders emerged for climb-
ing to the ramparts for hand-to-hand fighting. Moreover,
mounds were piled up, and from their summit arrows with
Greek fire were shot to the centre of the town. Great
masses of beams and blocks were set alight by the fortifications to weaken the structure of the walls and help in creating
a breach.[2] Perhaps the main factor in the tragedy was the
overwhelming numbers of the Tatars and the cheapness of
human life among them. The knights performed marvels
of valour; but what could a few do in the face of an army
whose size exceeded their fears beyond wildest conjecture?
In approximately fifteen days the town fell, its inhabitants
were massacred, and its fortifications completely destroyed.
As the defence was collapsing and the Tatars pouring within
the walls, ships with reinforcements appeared on the horizon.
The Tatars floated some severed heads towards them,
and they soon retraced their way to safety. The last great
Christian outpost (if Byzantine Trebizond and Genoese
Phocea be excepted) on the Asiatic mainland was thus

[1] Oman, *Art of War*, II, 333.
[2] Sharaf-al-Dīn (see following note), extensively quoted by Vertot, II,
295–300.

extinguished, and the peninsula which was momentarily under Tatar suzerainty soon reverted to the Turks in general and ultimately to the preponderant influence of the Ottomans.[1]

[1] On the Tatars and Smyrna, see Ibn 'Arabshah, 'Aja'ib al-Maqdūr (Leiden, 1636), 161–2; Sharaf-al-Dīn 'Alī ('Timur's secretary, wrongly identified as ibn 'Arabshah by Muralt, *Chronographia Byzantina*), Kitabi fātiḥ Nameh Amīr Timur (a life of T.), Fr. trans. *Petis de la Croix* (*Hist. de Timourbec*, 4 vols., Paris, 1722), IV, 47 et seq.; Ducas, *Hist. Byz.* (ed. Bonn), 73 et seq.; Chalkokondylas (ed. Bonn), II, 161; Theodoric of Niem, *Historiae de Schismate* (Basle, 1566), Lib. II, Cap. 38; Vertot, II, 293 et seq.; Bosio, II, 157; Heyd., II, 267; Delaville Le Roulx, op. cit., 285–6; Gibbons, 259.

CHAPTER XIII

THE CRUSADE OF HUMBERT II DE VIENNOIS

Origin of the crusade. Character of the Dauphin. Negotiations and preparations. Apocryphal letter on a battle at Smyrna. Preparations and itinerary. Aims of campaign. Negotiations; second battle of Imbros and Truce. Retirement of Humbert and end of his career

THE success of the crusaders at Smyrna may not, to the reader, stand out with any great distinction in the long perspective of the struggle between East and West; but it impressed the contemporary observer out of all proportion to its concrete results. More than a century had passed without a resounding triumph of the crusading policy in the Levant. On the contrary, Egyptian rule had been spreading in Syria at the expense of the few remaining Latin outposts which spoke of past glory. Moreover, a new enemy, as redoubtable as the Egyptians, had appeared in a field which bordered on the Christian countries of Trebizond, Georgia and Armenia in Asia, and was rapidly engulfing whole Christian principalities in Europe. This was the great menace of the Ottomans, who had crossed the Hellespont and were to stay and absorb many kingdoms in Europe. The horizon was thick with clouds and the future seemed without promise; and men expressed the view that the disasters of Christendom were the inevitable consequence of the sins of the age, while, with some lack of logic, they made plans for the conquest of the infidel. When this came with the invasion of Smyrna, it threw the whole of Latin Christendom into ecstasy. The tide had begun to turn, the humiliation of 'Akka was redeemed, and the birth of a new era in the history of the crusade was at last within view. The Pope ordained that processions should be held in cities to commemorate the great victory of the host of God.[1]   He wrote to the Doge of Venice congratulating him as one of the promoters of the crusade and asking him to persist in a policy so gratifying.[2]   Other letters which were issued by the Pontiff bear witness to a supreme effort to bring all hostilities in Europe to a happy end and to direct all combatants against Islam.   He urged Edward III of England to stop the invasion of France and as a good son of holy church thus facilitate the recruit-ment of men for holy war.[3]   He defended the crusade at the court of Philippe VI de Valois.   The Pope urged that, unless prompt action was taken to break the Turks, they might soon attack the King's nephew, Robert of Tarentum, and ultimately march to Naples.[4]   Further, Philippe's ardour for the crusade had been proved ten years earlier,[5] and the time was ripe for a new resolution. The crusading fever became high, and men waited for another Godefroy de Bouillon to appear on the scene and carry the sword and the Cross throughout the East. Noblemen arrived at the curia of Avignon to ask for the crusaders' indulgences and for permission to sail to Smyrna.[6]   It was at this juncture that Humbert II, Dauphin de Viennois, decided to share the same privilege in the service of the holy cause.[7]

Humbert II, Baron of Faucigni since 1328, succeeded his brother Guiges VIII in the Dauphiné in 1333.   Be-tween those two dates, he was absent in Hungary, where the Queen of France, Clémence of Hungary, had be-queathed her territories to him.   In 1332, he travelled to Naples and married Marie de Beaux, daughter of Bertrand Count of Andrie and niece of King Robert.   In 1335, the Holy Roman Emperor Lewis of Bavaria offered him the title of King of Vienne in return for his support, but Humbert

---

[1] Iorga, *Mézières*, 43.

[2] *Commem.*, IV, no. 174 (II, p. 149); cf. Iorga, l.c.

[3] Reynaldus, *ad ann.* 1345, nos. 1 and 2; 'Dat. Avin. XV kal. Aprilis, anno III.'   Also no. 9; 'Datum Avin. XV kal. Aprilis, anno III.'

[4] ib., *ad ann.* 1345, nos. 3 and 4.   'Datum apud Villamnovam Avinionensis diocoesis V id. Maii, anno III.'

[5] *vide supra*, Cap. VI.

[6] Bosio, op. cit., 43; cf. Iorga, l.c.

[7] *Vit. Pap. Aven.* (ed. Mollat), I, 255, 265, 282, 293.

declined to accept this honour until Lewis himself had settled his differences with the Roman See and received his own crown from the Pope.[1] Then his elevation to kingship would also have to be approved by the Church. As the quarrel between the Papacy and the Empire continued, this plan came to nothing. In the same year, however, he acquired the lands of the Bishop of Geneva who ceded them to the Dauphin to escape from the troubles stirred up against him by the Comte de Génévois. In 1337, he further succeeded to Guillaume de Vienne, seigneur de St. Georges, in his ancient but doubtful claims over the County of Vienne, and thus consolidated his own territories in the Dauphiné. In 1340, he transferred the seat of his government to Grenoble; and in 1342, he founded a Dominican Convent for eighty nuns in the neighbourhood of that town. It was during the following year that the Dauphin, who was without an heir,[2] decided to concede his hereditary feudal rights to Philippe, duc d'Orleans, and later to Jean, duc de Normandie before they should finally return to the King of France.[3] These are some of the events in Humbert's career up to the time when he was preparing to lead the Christian host against the Muhammadans.

Historians [4] seem to be unanimous in suspecting the

---

[1] Lewis IV of Bavaria was crowned in Rome on 17 January 1328, by Sciarra Colonna, Prefect of the city, and three other representatives of the popular party in defiance of Pope John XXII who subsequently excommunicated the new Emperor and his supporters. It was probably these events that inspired the theories of Marsiglio di Padua and Jean de Jandun attacking papal authority and supporting that of the Emperor. Lewis remained in excommunication during the pontificates of Benedict XII and Clement V. When Lewis wished to settle his differences with the latter, the Pope required that the Emperor should declare that his Empire was a fief granted to him by the Church. The Diets of Frankfort in 1338 and 1339, however, solemnly rejected the papal demand, and the breach between the two remained until the death of Lewis in October 1347. Bryce, *Holy Roman Emp.*, 217–24.

[2] His only son and successor had died in an accident during the year 1335, and since that time he had had no other legitimate children.

[3] *Art de vérifier les dates* (1 vol. ed., Paris, 1770), 763. *Vide infra.*

[4] Cf. Delaville Le Roulx, *France*, I, 105 and *Hospitaliers à Rhodes*, 97; Iorga, *Mézières*, 45 et seq.; Gay, *Clément VI et les affaires d'Orient*, 62 et seq.; Faure, *Le Dauphin Humbert II à Venise et en Orient*, in *Mélanges d'Archéologie et d'Hist. publiés par l'École Fr. de Rome*, XXVII (1907), 509–62.

genuineness of the Dauphin's motives in taking the Cross. His vanity and his love of adventure, it has often been suggested, were at the root of his attempt to lead a crusade and achieve universal fame; and the confusion of his ideas and the weakness of his character ensured his ultimate failure. The meagre results of his crusade have led critics to judge his motives over-harshly. When motives and results of Humbert's life are treated separately, as they should be, a more benevolent attitude towards him than has hitherto been held, becomes both expedient and correct.

The Dauphin was an unhappy man. He had lost his only son in an accident (1335) and was thus left without an heir of his own blood to his demesnes. His wife's health, too, was failing,[1] although she survived long enough to accompany him in his adventure.[2] He sought consolation in the service of God, and the idea of the crusade attracted his devotion. He appears to have been impulsive, and his interests, like a pendulum, swung from one extreme to another. As a youth, he lived in comfort and ease, and occupied his time in the chivalrous games and jousts common to the age.[3] He quarrelled with many and incurred the wrath of the Church by his contest with the Archbishop of Vienne. So furious were the two contestants against one another that only the Pope could save the situation, and Clement VI rescued the Dauphin from excommunication imposed upon him by the Archbishop.[4] Now he wished to atone for his past sins by placing himself

---

[1] Delaville Le Roulx, *France*, I, 105; Iorga, op. cit., 49.

[2] *vide infra.*

[3] Gay, op. cit., 62, note 2, suggests that Humbert was the object of one of Petrarch's letters (*Lit. famil.*, ed Francassetti, III, 10) addressed to an anonymous prince reproaching him for an inglorious life of opulence and sloth in spite of his youth, strength and valour. Matteo Villani, Lib. 1, § 26 (in Muratori, RIS, XIV, 31) describes the Dauphin in the following words: 'Era in que' dì il Dalfino di Vienna huomo molle e di poca virtú, e fermezza.'

[4] Chevalier, *Choix de documents hist. inéd. sur le Dauphiné*, no. 12, 48–53; Valbonnais, *Histoire des Dauphins de la troisième race* (2 vols., Geneva, 1721), I, 314 et seq., II, 426, where the latter author, according to Chevalier (op. cit., 52) used all documents extant on the subject in a register 'Processus causae Viennae pro parte Dalphini 1340' which existed at that time. See also de Pétigny, *Notice sur Jacques Brunier, chancelier d'Humbert II*, in BEC (1839–40), I, 263.

and his fortune at the disposal of holy church.   The beginning of this change in his career may be traced to the period
of the establishment of a new order of chivalry, the Order of
St. Catherine, which he undoubtedly inspired and endowed
for the celebration of religious offices on that Saint's day and
for the defence of the Dauphiné, with the motto—'Pour
mieux valoir'.[1] The exact date of the foundation of the Order
is uncertain; but it may safely be placed in the thirties of
the fourteenth century.[2]   The foundation of new orders
of chivalry was not infrequent in this period.[3]   Yet it is
hard to dissociate them from the idea of holy war which
had given rise to them in the past.   At first, in January
1345, the Dauphin conceived the idea of fighting the
Moors in Spain;[4] but the good news of the capture of
Smyrna, which reached Europe in December 1345,[5] and
caused so much rejoicing, was followed by the alarming
report of the death of the three principal leaders of that crusade including the Latin Patriarch Enrico d'Asti in a
subsequent skirmish with the forces of the Turkish 'Umar
Bey outside the walls of the town.[6]   This determined the
Dauphin to take up arms in defence of the endangered
Christian conquest in Asia Minor, instead of going to Spain.
It is strange that Humbert's biographers make little comment on these points which seem to elucidate some aspects
of his character and his intention to wage war with the
infidels.   If he was so vain and self-seeking as he is
now generally painted, how can we account for the unusual sacrifice of disposing of all his fiefs?   It is true
that he had no children; but if he had no real intention to
make good his crusade, he would have had to provide for

---

[1] Chevalier, op. cit., no. 6, 35–9, a document containing the rule of the new
Order founded at La Côte-Saint-André and showing that it was a different
order from the twelfth-century one bearing the same name in Helyot, *Hist.
des ordres relig.* (ed. Migne), I, 710–12.

[2] Chevalier, 39 note 1.   [3] *vide supra*, Cap. I.

[4] Valbonnais, *Mém. pour l'hist du Dauphiné* (Paris, 1711), no. 200; cf.
Gay, 62.

[5] This is confirmed by a bull dated 23 December 1345, in which the
victory is known to be mentioned for the first time.   Gay, 41–2, and Delaville Le Roulx, op. cit., 95.

[6] *vide supra*, Cap. XII.

his return to the West.   He was indeed hard-pressed for
money; but even in this case, he could have pawned part
of his numerous demesnes instead of disposing of all.   The
clue to his behaviour is his zeal for the service of God,
and this is sufficient to vindicate his much-abused memory.
His failure to realize his hopes is a totally different matter.

In pursuance of the aim to which he had devoted himself,
the Dauphin sent an ambassador, Guillaume de Royn,[1] to
Avignon with the request that the Pope might nominate
him 'Captain-General of the crusade against the Turks and
the unfaithful to the Holy Church of Rome'.[2]   In return
for this, Humbert would hold himself bound to equip at
his own expense three hundred men-at-arms, a thousand
arbalesters and five galleys for the expedition.   He suggested St. John the Baptist's Day (24 June 1345) for the
embarkation of his army, if the Holy See would make a
speedy response to his request.   Yet the College of Cardinals hesitated at first to give their full and unconditional
support to this plan, and the Pope delayed his verdict.
This has been taken as a point against Humbert and
ascribed to the suspicion of the Holy See as to his political
and military capacity to lead the crusade.   Again, this
judgment appears to have been founded on events which
had not yet taken place.   The cause of the delay was
probably the elaborate and slow procedure of the curia
rather than mistrust and lack of enthusiasm at Avignon.
The Pope had confidence in him as an admirable head of a
holy expedition on account of his personality, the nobility
of his origin, the power with which he was endowed,
and his marked virtues.[3]   Finally, Humbert came to
the Pope to plead for himself, and his case was not met
with disfavour.   On 23 May, he concluded an agreement with three citizens of Marseilles to equip four

---

[1] Valbonnais, op. cit., no. 204; Gay, 62; Faure, 513.

[2] In a charter of 2 September 1345 (Roman, in AOL, I, 538), the Dauphin
styles himself as 'Humbertus, dalphinus Viennensis, Sancte Sedis Apostolice
capitaneus generalis et dux exercitus christianorum contra Turcos'.   Cf.
Gay, 62 and Iorga, 45—'Capitaine général du saint voyage contre les Turcs et
contre les non-féaux à l'Église de Rome.'

[3] Cf. Iorga, 46 note 2.   'Personam tuam, generis nobilitate praeclaram,
potentia praeditam, virtutibus insignitam.'

armed galleys, each capable of carrying two hundred
men, for the campaign.[1] Three days later, he received
the Cross and the banner of the Church of Rome from
Clement VI's own hand together with the plenary absolution granted on these occasions, and he was appointed
'Captain-General' of the crusade.[2] The schedule of the
journey to the East was then drawn up with precision.
Humbert was enjoined to sail no later than 2 August, and
his arrival at Negropontis was fixed about the middle of
October. It was stipulated that his army should include
at least one hundred men-at-arms, maintained and specially
well-equipped at his own expense, and that he and his
followers should remain in the East for the duration of the
papal league with Cyprus, Rhodes and Venice. These
terms were unanimously approved, and active preparations
were started. When it was revealed that the equipment
of the fleet could not be achieved before 2 August, the
Pope willingly granted an extension until 2 September.[3]
In the meantime Humbert dispatched a representative, one
Nicolas d'Astribort, to the Republic of St. Mark to hire
transports for him;[4] and the Holy Pontiff wrote to the
Doge announcing the crusade and asking him to facilitate
the fulfilment of Humbert's requirements.[5] Other letters
were also issued from the curia to the Italian cities of
Genoa, Pisa, Florence, Perugia, Siena, Ancona, Milan,
Verona and Bologna urging them to contribute towards
the expedition.[6]

At this point, keeping to the chronological order of the
crusade, it seems desirable to give some consideration to
a document which has received much comment from
medieval historians. This is an apocryphal letter dated
1345 and addressed by King Hugh IV of Cyprus to Queen
Joanna of Naples.[7] The King refers to a battle which took

---

[1] Gay, 63.

[2] ib., l.c.; Valbonnais, op. cit., no. 207; ib., *Hist.*, II, 511; Iorga, 46.

[3] *Reg. Vat.*, 169, nos. 2 and 3; Reynaldus, *ad ann.* 1345, no. 6; cf. Gay, 63.

[4] Tafel and Thomas, *Dipl. Ven.-Lev.*, I, no. 250; cf. Gay, 63–4.

[5] Iorga, *Mézières*, 46.

[6] Letters dated 18 July 1345. Müller, *Documenti delle citta toscane
coll'Oriente*, 116; (*Reg. Vat.*, 139, nos. 135–43; cf. Gay, 64, note 5).

[7] An old French version of this letter was first published by Michelet in

place between the crusaders and the Turks at a place
situated between Smyrna and Altoluogo (Altum Locum,
probably Ephesus) on St. John the Baptist's Day (24 June)
1345. The Turks numbered 200,000, and the crusaders
only 12,000. The battle had long raged between the two
sides, but the overwhelming numerical superiority of the
former and the exhaustion of the latter led to despair among
the Christians who prayed for aid from Heaven. Suddenly
the miracle happened when a mounted person with a flowing beard, riding a white horse and carrying a white banner
with a red Cross [1] appeared on the field to give the Christians comfort and encouragement. This decided the issue
of the fray. The Turks were routed, and their dead
amounted to 70,000.[2] After this victory, the Christian
survivors inquired as to the identity of that celestial
Knight. Before he disappeared, he answered them with
the words—'Ego sum qui dixi; Ecce agnus Dei, ecce qui
tollit peccata mundi'.[3]

Some historians have tried hard to prove that this
legendary episode had some basis in reality, and their
attention has been unduly fixed on a battle fought by
Humbert the Dauphin in Asia Minor.[4] This view, however, is disproved by the facts of the case itself. In the
first place, this imaginary battle was supposed to have
occurred on St. John the Baptist's Day which was fixed
for the departure of the Dauphin from Marseilles, and even
this was postponed to 2 September by papal dispensation
owing to delay in the preparations.[5] Humbert could

1837 in a note to his *Hist. de Fr.*, III, 190. The earlier original Latin text
was edited by Iorga in 1895, in ROL, 3ᵉ année, no. 1, 27–31.

Commentaries on it are made by de Pétigny, in BEC (1839–40), I, 263
Delaville Le Roulx, *France*, I, 107; Iorga, *Mézières*, 51 et seq.; Gay, 66–70.

[1] Iorga, in ROL, 29. 'Et subito apparuit unus, sedens super equum
album, habens vexillum album, in quo crux erat coloris rubei, mira rubedine
insignita, excellens super omnem illam multitudinem.'

[2] ib., 30–1. In the French version the Turkish losses were 73,000, the
Christian 3,052; cf. Michelet, l.c.

[3] Iorga, op. cit., 30. In the French version (cf. Michelet, l.c.) is added
the phrase 'Celui de cui aujourd'huy vous celebrez la feste', i.e. St. John the
Baptist.

[4] Cf. commentaries of de Pétigny, Delaville Le Roulx and Iorga. *Vide
supra*, 307 n. 7.   [5] *vide supra*, 306.

therefore hardly be associated with this. In the second place, the year 1345 was one of defeat rather than triumph for the host at Smyrna, owing to the death of three Christian leaders in a skirmish outside the walls of the town.[1] So it seems quite clear that the whole tale has no historical basis and the letter itself is a mere fabrication. This is confirmed by the fact that Hugh de Lusignan himself never took part in the military operations at Smyrna. The truth is probably that the letter was written by an unknown hand to kindle the enthusiasm of men in favour of the Dauphin's crusade.[2] Beyond this, the document appears to have no great significance for the history of either the crusade or the kingdom of Cyprus.

As regards the course of Humbert's itinerary to the East, it is almost certain that he sailed from Marseilles at the end of August 1345;[3] and on 2 September from his galley, *The Holy Cross*, at a small island near Marseilles, he issued an order for 130 florins to be spent on the purchase of jewels destined for Berlionete, the future wife of Bardon de Bardonnèche. The Dauphin was accompanied by his mother, his wife, Marie de Beaux,[4] and a considerable number of knights and priests.[5] A few days later, he landed at Genoa. An account of his passage through this republic was written by Georgio Stella in the *Annales*

---

[1] *vide supra*, Cap. XII.

[2] This view is adopted by Gay (op. cit., 67) who indicates the existence of wandering poor priests such as Venturius of Bergamo who devoted his efforts at the time to propagandist work. Further, apocryphal letters were not unusual during this period. Gay (ib., 172-4) has published another one supposed to have been sent by 'Umar Bey (Morbasimus), Amīr of Aidīn to Clement VI.

[3] Valbonnais, *Mém.*, nos. 219-20; Roman, *Charte de départ du Dauphin Humbert II*, in AOL, 537-8; Gay, 64. Roman fixes the actual departure from Marseilles on 2 September, the date of the charter, although this includes no direct reference to Marseilles. Iorga (*Mézières*, 47) puts the date as the beginning of August without any reason assigned.

[4] Stella (*vide infra*, note), 1085.

[5] Names of these appear in a document published by Chevalier (*Choix de documents*, no. 28, 96-9), where they are classified under 'Milites', 'Religiosi', 'Carmelites', 'Seculares', 'Scutiferi', 'Poterii', and a number of gentlemen and ladies in waiting. Their numbers were respectively 63, 16, 6, 16, 50, 20 and 17, giving a total of 188.

Genuenses where it is stated that the object of the journey was Jerusalem.[1] The Dauphin then marched to Pisa, Florence, Bologna and finally to Venice.[2] His army was reinforced by new levies from the towns of Lombardy and the Tuscan republics, although it is difficult to fix their number. Humbert was particularly well received by the citizens of Bologna, and after his departure, throughout the winter of 1345–6, bands of warriors from that city followed him to join the expedition.[3] He arrived at Venice on 24 October 1345,[4] where the Republic of St. Mark gave him a flattering reception, but offered no galleys. On 15 November, a letter from the curia at Avignon in reply to a message from the Dauphin, granted him papal assent to the request to postpone his arrival at Negropontis until Christmas.[5] Meanwhile, the Captain-General dispatched the new Latin Archbishop of Mytilene to submit further details of the campaign to Clement VI who extended the period of the grant of tithe on ecclesiastical benefices to five years instead of three in order to ensure the duration and success of the expedition.[6] At last Humbert sailed to the island of Cephalonia where he had previously arranged to meet the rest of his host.[7] The Pope was finally informed, on 30 April 1346, of the entry of the crusading fleet into the waters of Negropontis; and he sent back the ambassador, Bartholomew 'de Thomariis'[8] with a number of letters relating to the crusade and addressed to Humbert, to

---

[1] In Muratori, RIS, XVII, 1086. Gay (op. cit., 64) suggests that the Genoese chronicler's assertion that the crusade was intended for Jerusalem might prove that the Dauphin did not wish to reveal his plan to that republic. On the other hand, the mention of Jerusalem as the object of the expedition may be quite genuine. Crusaders continued to dream of saving it, and in all probability the Dauphin entertained hopes of fulfilling this task himself.

[2] Gay, 64, 67.

[3] *Chronica di Bologna*, in Muratori, RIS, XVIII, 393 et seq.

[4] Delaville Le Roulx, *Hospitaliers à Rhodes*, 97; Gay, 68, also places his arrival in October; but Iorga, *Mézières*, 50, thinks that the date was 12 September which is evidently too early.

[5] Valbonnais, *Mém.*, no. 221. Gay, 68; Delaville Le Roulx, *Hospitaliers à Rhodes*, 97.

[6] Valbonnais, *Hist.*, 528 (Preuves); Gay, 68–9.

[7] Chevalier, *Choix de documents*, no. 29, 99–104.

[8] Canon of the church of Smyrna and vicar to Archbishop Francesco.

Francesco, Archbishop of Candia (Crete), who succeeded the Patriarch Enrico d'Asti as vice-legate, to King Hugh IV de Lusignan, to the Grand Master of Rhodes [1] and to the Dowager-Empress Anne of Constantinople.[2]

The chief aims of this crusade, as may be deduced from its origins, were three—first, to strengthen the papal league with Venice, Rhodes and Cyprus; second, to relieve Smyrna from Turkish pressure; and third, to assist the Genoese in saving their colony of Caffa in the Crimea, then invested by the Tatars.[3] According to one source,[4] it is said that soon after his arrival in the Archipelago, Humbert engaged the Turks in a naval battle in February 1346, and that twenty-six vessels of the hostile fleet foundered at sea. If this report were true, it would have been an auspicious beginning for the crusade, and other successes might have been expected from the Dauphin. Whatever the facts, the subsequent history of the campaign was one of inactivity. The Captain-General's reluctance to take any decision without papal ratification hindered the advance of the host, and valuable opportunities were wasted by futile and prolonged negotiations for doubtful alliances and truces.

The first of these negotiations was with the Catalans in the Duchy of Athens and with the Dowager-Empress of Constantinople. The Catalans attracted Humbert as possible allies. They had been under sentence of excommunication for some time, and he offered to mediate on their behalf at Avignon if they promised to join his army.[5] This plan apparently did not materialize. In the meantime Niccolò Pisano, commander of the Venetian galleys, with one companion, went to the court of the Dowager-Empress Anne in the hope of persuading her to cede, at least temporarily, the island of Chios to the crusaders as a base for their operations. Mention has been made

---

[1] The Grand Master Hélion de Villeneuve was already dead by 7 or 27 May 1346; but the election of his successor, Dieudonné de Gozon, was not ratified by the Pope until 28 June. Delaville Le Roulx, *Hospitaliers à Rhodes*, 98–101.

[2] *Reg. Vat.* 140, nos. 123 et seq.; cf. Gay, 69 and note 4.

[3] Heÿd, II, 195–6.

[4] Istorie Pistolesi, in Muratori, RIS, XI, 514; cf. Gay, 70 note 1.

[5] Gregorovius, *Stadt Athen*, II, 133–4.

of the papal letter commending the crusaders to her. For the time being, tension between the Eastern and Western Christians was not high, and the Turkish menace might have brought the Latin ambassadors and the court of Constantinople to an understanding, had it not been for the destructive war waged by the Genoese who wished to take advantage of the weakness of the Empire and annex Chios to their own republic.[1] This brings us to the second stage, that of negotiations with the Genoese, who had little faith in the outcome of the Dauphin's crusade and hated the league on account of the membership of the Venetians. They therefore hastened to dispatch to the East a fleet of thirty galleys under the command of Simone Vignosi. The pretext was the defence of Caffa, but the deeper cause was suspicion of Humbert's aim at Chios which the Genoese coveted for their trade interests. Their fleet dropped anchor at Negropontis early in June 1346.[2] The Dauphin, whose fleet numbered only twenty-six, at once conceived the idea of uniting the two into one naval unit. He tempted Vignosi with a large sum of money in return for his alliance or at least his neutrality; but the wily Genoese refused, as he had his own designs in the Archipelago. After pillaging some of the Dauphin's equipment,[3] he hurriedly set sail from Negropontis; and, to foil the crusaders' plan, Vignosi proceeded in the direction of Chios to present himself to its inhabitants as a well-meaning friend who wished to protect them against Humbert and the hateful Latins. Remembering former experiences, however, the Greeks declined the proffered services and Vignosi revealed the true nature of his intentions by setting siege to their capital in June 1346. The Empire was incapable of sending relief, and Chios, after three months' stubborn resistance, fell to the invaders in September 1346.[4] Vignosi resolved to pursue his conquests as

---

[1] Gay, 70–1.

[2] Stella, *Annal. Gen.*, 1086 et seq.; Gay, 71–2; Heyd, I, 491–2.

[3] The Genoese booty included 'horses, jewels, equipment and other objects'. De Pétigny, op. cit., 284; Heyd, I, 493; Gay, 72.

[4] Nicephoras Gregoras, in MPG, CXLVIII, Lib. XV, Cap. VI, 1006; Kantakuzenos, in MPG, CLIII, Lib. III, Cap. XCV, 1270; Stella, 1086–9;

far as Lesbos (Mytilene) and Tenedos, but his ambitions
were frustrated by the reluctance of his followers.[1]   Nevertheless, the original plan of the league was anticipated by
the alert action of the Genoese.   There was little left for
the Dauphin but to approach the Turks for a settlement.
This constitutes the third and last stage in the efforts of
the coalition under his leadership.   The crusaders sailed
direct to Smyrna where they increased the number of its
garrison to several thousands.[2]   That a few skirmishes
took place between Turks and Latins outside the town,
can be inferred from vague remarks gleaned from Philippe
de Mézières' work on the Chivalry of the Passion.[3]
Tidings reached Grenoble of a battle in which Humbert
defeated the Turks near Smyrna in the course of 1346.
The losses on both sides were considerable.[4]   It is doubtful
whether the Dauphin's war demoralized or even intimidated
the Turks, who still retained their possession of the castle
overlooking the town.[5]   There were other obstacles to
the extension of hostilities—first, the heat of the summer,
second, the Western tradition of fighting in full medieval
armour which was incompatible with the climatic conditions of the East, third, sickness which was spreading in
the ranks, and fourth, the heavy cost of supplying a large
army with provisions which had to be imported by sea from

Lib. Jur. reipubl. Gen., in *Mon. Hist. Patr.*, II, 558–72; C. Pagano,
Dell'imprese e del dominio dei Genovesi nella Grecia, 271–85; Heyd, I, 492;
Gay, 72–3.

[1] Stella, 1090; Heyd, I, 493.

[2] Gay, 74, estimates the joint forces in Smyrna after the coming of the
Dauphin at 15,000 and calls it a 'small army'.   There is evidently some
exaggeration in this estimate; and if we remember that the Knights of Rhodes
had grumbled at having to keep three hundred in the garrison, it becomes clear
that an army of that size could not be called a small force.

[3] Arsenal MS. 2251, ff. 12 vo–13 vo; cf. Iorga, *Mézières*, 54–5;
Gay, 73.

[4] Valbonnais, *Hist.*, II, 621; Gay, 73–4.

[5] The Turks were only biding their time to recover Smyrna.   Even after
their defeat at the naval battle of Imbros (*vide infra*) and the conclusion of
peace with the Latins, they were reported in a letter dated 7 October 1350,
from Andrea Dandolo, Doge of Venice, to the Commune of Perugia, to be
preparing for another assault on the town.   *Arch. Stor. It.*, T. XVI, Pt. II,
536.

Rhodes and Cyprus. Humbert himself fell ill and wrote to the Pope urging a truce and proposing negotiations with the Turks. Clement VI advised the Captain-General to confer with the other members of the League on the terms offered and then communicate any decisions reached for his ratification. These instructions were dated 28 November 1346.[1] The difficulties of supply and the expense incurred thereby, together with the partial withdrawal of the Venetians proved a decisive factor in the dissolution of the League. In reality the whole burden of the defence of Smyrna ultimately devolved on the Hospitallers, and the history of this phase of the struggle has been outlined in the previous chapter.

With the approach of the winter, the petty hostilities in progress were finally suspended except for the defence of the town; and Humbert and his nobles sailed to Rhodes. On 29 January 1347, the Dauphin is known to have made his last will and testament in the capital of that island.[2] A little later, his wife, Marie de Beaux, who had long been suffering from illness, died, and the news of her death reached Grenoble on 1 May 1347.[3] Originally, Humbert had intended to crown his Oriental journey by a pilgrimage to Jerusalem, but later changed his mind and decided to retrace his steps to France. The reason for this change of plan is unknown. The Pope absolved him from his vow to remain in the East for the duration of the Holy League, or at least for the fixed period of three years.[4] In all, Humbert's expedition had lasted less than two years. He arrived at Venice in June, and lingered in North Italy for about two months, during which he concluded an alliance with Giovanni and Lucchino Visconti in Milan on 19 August 1347. Then he crossed the Alps between Saluces and Briançon and went direct to the Dauphiné, even before

[1] Gay, 74–5.
[2] This was witnessed by the Grand Master of the Hospital, Dieudonné de Gozon, and the Venetian Admiral, Pancrace Giustiniani. Valbonnais, Mém., no. 236; Gay, 77.
[3] Valbonnais, Mém., no. 603; Gay, 78.
[4] Gay, 78 (Reg. Vat., 140, no. 1070).

visiting Avignon.[1] After his return, the maritime forces
of the League seem to have played a more active part than
before his departure. A naval battle at the island of
Imbros was fought and the Turks were reported to have
lost a fleet of considerable size. In spite of the continuation of the negotiations with the Amīr of Aidīn for a truce,
the Turks, at least up to that time, did not seem genuinely
willing to give the Christians a permanent peace. In the
spring of 1347, they landed an army in Imbros with
the intention of occupying the island. The confederates, now depending almost exclusively on the Hospitallers, dispatched a fleet composed of the galleys of the
Order under the command of Pierre d'Arnal de Peres
Tortes, Prior of Catalonia,[2] who besieged the invaders and
finally burnt more than a hundred units of their fleet.[3]
The date of this victory may be placed in May and Pope
Clement's letter of congratulation to the Grand Master of
Rhodes, Dieudonné de Gozon, was dated 24 June 1347.[4]
This was undoubtedly the greatest Christian triumph
against the Turks since the capture of Smyrna on 28 February 1344. It had, indeed, no positive result; but, on
the other hand, it forced the Turks to accept the *status quo*
at Smyrna and offer more privileges to the Christians in
Asia Minor and led to the peace of 10 April 1348 which
was concluded with 'Umar's successor Khiḍr Bey.[5] The
only improvements in the situation in the East between
those dates were due to the efforts of the Hospitallers
and not to the elaborate preparations of the Dauphin.
He had, in fact, failed completely to achieve any of the

[1] id., l.c. (*Reg. Vat.*, 141, nos. 1073–82, 1287; *Reg.*, 141, nos. 64, 350);
de Pétigny, 263. Humbert was regarded by the house of Saluces, through
whose territory he must have passed, as their protector against the en-
croachments of the house of Savoy; Iorga, *Thomas III Marquis de
Saluces*, 35.

A document dated November (?) 1347 (Chevalier, *Choix*, no. 35, 119–20),
reports the presence of the Dauphin at Avignon with a number of knights and
priests, most of whom were crusaders. An ordinance dated 17 December
1347 (ib., no. 37, 122–3) was also issued by him at Avignon.

[2] He became Prior of the Order in Catalonia on 10 January 1347 and
was appointed admiral of its fleet on 17 April 1347. Delaville Le Roulx,
Hospitaliers à Rhodes, 108 note 1.

[3] ib., 108.   [4] id., l.c., notes 2 and 3.   [5] *vide supra*, Cap. XII.

three principal aims of his crusade. The papal league became a moribund institution while he was in the Levant, his skirmishes at Smyrna were of little or no military value, and the project for the relief of Caffa came to nothing. Even if the last of these aims had been seriously contemplated, it would have been frustrated by the shameless behaviour of the Genoese under Vignosi's command before sailing from Negropontis. The Dauphin's character, his weakness and indecision, were at the root of the collapse of this crusade. His bereavement by the death of his wife in Rhodes must have added much to the confusion of his ideas and to the despondency from which he had suffered since the loss of his only son. Much valuable time, too, was wasted by the Captain-General in futile negotiations and by his strict fidelity to the papal curia in submitting every detail to the Pope and awaiting definite instructions from him. On the other hand, part of the blame must fall upon the Italians, whether Venetian or Genoese. The Republic of St. Mark had obtained trade privileges from the Turks after the capture of Smyrna. It was these, and not the holy cause professed by Clement VI, that they fought for; and as soon as they realized their primary and personal interests in the war, they wavered in their support to the League. The Genoese attitude became openly hostile to the crusade with the arrival of Vignosi in the Aegean. Their ungodly raid on the fleet of the holy league was made possible only by the good faith of the crusaders. The idea of such an attack could not have entered their minds. In trusting men without conscience and without shame, they were caught unawares.

The rest of the Dauphin's life was as tragic as his past. He had lost his son and his wife, and was left with little hope of perpetuating his dynasty. It was once thought that he would re-marry and resume his old fiefs after his return to the West; but, instead, he renounced the world and abandoned all his demesnes in Languedoc in favour of Charles of France, son of Jean, formerly Duke of Normandy, and heir to the throne. This cession was carried out solemnly in an assembly at Lyons on 16 July 1349, when he invested his successor with the sword of the

Dauphiné and the banner of St. George together with the sceptre and ring of his state.[1]   On the next day, he resigned the leadership of the crusade and took vows as a Dominican.[2] Nothing was left to him but grief and disillusionment, and he sought consolation in serving God.   The futility of his efforts and the failure of his career have embittered all his biographers.   Yet, on reflection, a fair critic would find that Humbert was in part the victim of the perfidy of the Genoese and the egotism of the Venetians.   His shattered life, his profound sorrow and his bereavement while he was still in his thirties [3] must have aroused the sympathy of contemporaries, the Pope included.   Clement VI granted him the honorary title of Latin Patriarch of Alexandria [4] in 1351, in succession to Guillaume de Charnat, Bishop of Paris, who died in 1348.   To the end of his life, however, he continued to style himself as 'late Dauphin de Viennois'.[5]   In 1352, the King of France entrusted him with the administration of the Archbishopric of Rheims.   He took a special interest in missionary work in the East and encouraged the study of Greek in the University of Paris.   On 25 January 1354, he was nominated Bishop of Paris, but did not live to undertake his

---

[1] *Art de vérifier les dates*, 763.   The treaty of abdication made the stipulation that the holder of the Dauphiné should retain the title of Dauphin and rule this province separately in accordance with its ancient customs.   On the other hand, no condition was laid down by Humbert to the effect that only the eldest son of the King should assume the title of Dauphin, although this became the usage in France after the accession of Charles VII to the throne and his cession of the Dauphiné to his heir, the future Louis XI, in 1426.

[2] Matteo Villano, op. cit., 31, suggests that Humbert sold his fiefs and joined the Church, 'sperando in quello di venire Cardinale'.

[3] As he died in 1355 at the age of forty-three (*vide infra*), he must have been only about thirty-seven at this time.

[4] Mas Latrie, *Patriarches Latins d'Alexandrie*, in ROL (1896), 4; Quétif and Echard, *Script. Ord. Praed.*, I, 642; Baluze, *Vit. Pap. Aven.* (ed Mollat), I, 255, 282 (where date is mentioned as 3 January 1351), and 306 (same date confirmed).

[5] Mas Latrie, l.c., quoting Douet d'Arcq (*Collection de sceaux*, II, no. 6278, 453), gives the inscription on Humbert's seal as 'S. secretu Huberti, patriarche Alexandrini, dalfini Vien. antiquioris'.   A document in Chevalier, op. cit., no. 45, 132, dating from 1352, describes him as 'dom. nostri Humberti, sancte ecclesie Alexandrine patriarche, administratoris perpetui ecclesie Remensis, dalphini Viennensis antiquioris'.

duties in his new see. He died on his way to the capital
at the convent of his Order, at Clermont in the Auvergne
on 22 May 1355. He was forty-three years of age at the
time of his death. His remains were laid to rest with the
Dominicans of St Jacques in Paris.[1]

Humbert lived outside his time. In his whole-hearted
devotion to the Church, he belonged to another age. Com-
bining with his religious temperament the militant sense of
chivalry of his rank and upbringing, he appeared as the
ideal crusader. But his reluctance to take decision without
the authorization of the Pope crippled him in action and
spoilt his opportunities; and the Italian lack of scruple
ensured the collapse of his Eastern plans.

[1] *Art de vérifier les dates*, 763–4; Mas Latrie, l.c.; Iorga, *Mézières*, 59;
Gay, l.c.

CHAPTER XIV

THE CRUSADES OF PIERRE I DE LUSIGNAN: ADALIA AND THE WESTERN JOURNEY

Pierre's accession and character. First foothold on Asiatic mainland: Gorigos in Armenia. Capture of Adalia and nominal submission of Tekke, Alaya and Monovgat; friction with the Turks and consequences. Dream of a great crusade. Journey through Europe. Preparations for the capture of Alexandria: influence of Urban V, Pierre de Thomas and Philippe de Mézières; Venice and the fleet; the King and the crusaders in Rhodes

THE accession of Pierre I de Lusignan [1] to the throne of Cyprus after his father's death in 1359 seemed to inaugurate a new era in the history of the later crusade. The movement reached its apogee with the capture and sack of Alexandria during his reign. Afterwards, indeed, frequent attempts were made to break the power of Islam; but all failed and some ended in disaster. Both in character and in training, Pierre I was probably more suited to lead the holy war than any contemporary Latin monarch. Young, virile, chivalrous, pious and full of enthusiasm for the cause, he had an additional incentive to immediate action against Turks and Saracens in the condition of affairs in his island-kingdom.

A legend has been woven around Pierre's birth by his

---

[1] Pierre's father, Hugh IV, married twice. His first wife, Marie d'Ibelin, left an heir to the throne (Guy, Prince of Galilee) who was betrothed to Marie de Bourbon, titular Empress of Constantinople. Guy, however, died in his father's lifetime, leaving one son, prince Hugh, whose mother claimed the crown of Cyprus for him against the rights of Pierre I de Lusignan, the first son of King Hugh IV's second wife, who had already been enthroned as King-designate before his father's death. Makhairas' *Chronicle* (ed. Dawkins), §§ 74, 84, 105, 289 and 395 and notes; Buchon's Chronological Tables, in *Chroniques étrangères relatives aux expéditions françaises pendant le XIIIe siècle*, table 1; *Art de vérifier les dates* (1 vol. ed., Paris, 1770), 389; Bouillet, *Atlas universel d'hist. et de géogr.*, CCXXXV–VI.

biographer Guillaume de Machaut.[1]   The King was born
on the day of St. Denis (9 October), 1329,[2] and all the
'gods' and 'goddesses' of mythology came to bless him.
From his early youth, he was trained in arms, honour and
the love of God.[3]   When he was about twenty years of
age, he had a memorable vision [4] which inspired him
throughout his career and guided all his actions.   During
a sojourn at Mont Sainte-Croix [5] near the town of Larnaca,
the Crucified Jesus appeared to him, and four or five times
directed him to take the Cross and conquer his heritage
and the land that God had promised to the holy fathers.[6]
These words from the lips of the Master inspired him with
fresh courage for his enterprise.[7]   While still Count of
Tripoli, the young heir to the throne of Cyprus founded
the 'Order of the Sword',[8] a new organization of chivalry
for the salvation of souls and the recovery of the Holy

---

[1] *Prise d'Alexandrie* (ed. Mas Latrie), lines 127–246.

[2] ib., ll. 134–6 and p. 277 note 1.

[3] ib., ll. 259 et seq., on the education of the young prince.

[4] ib., ll. 291 et seq.

[5] ib., l. 291, Machaut marks the place of the vision as 'Famagosse', i.e.
Famagusta, which is an error.   Pierre was at the time of the vision in the
Benedictine abbey of Mont Sainte-Croix, in which a Cross with miraculous
power was highly venerated by the inhabitants of Cyprus.   Ib., p. 277,
note 3; *Hist. de Chypre*, II, 213, note 4; 430, note 4, 512, 541 and III, 520;
Ogier VIII d'Anglure (*Saint voyage de Jhérusalem*, 82), while at Nicosia
in Cyprus performed a pilgrimage to the 'Saincte Croix qui . . . est la croix
où le bon Larron fut pendus à la destre de Nostre Seigneur Jhesu Crist'.

[6] Machaut, ll. 306–10, says that Jesus addressed the prince
          'Quatre fois ou v. tire à tire:
          "Fils, entrepren le saint passage,
          "Et conqueste ton heritage,
          "Que Dieus aus sains peres promist,
          "Et où pour toy son corps tout mist".'

[7] ib., ll. 329–32.
               'Il (Pierre) prist ferme conclusion,
               A grant deliberation,
               Par maintes fois en son corage,
               Qu'il entreprenroit le passage.'

[8] ib., ll. 349 et seq.; also pp. 277–8 note 4; Mézières (*Chevalerie de la
Passion*, f. 15 vo), on his return from the Holy Land in 1347, refers to the
existence of the Order of the Sword; cf. Iorga, *Mézières*, 83 note 2.   Mas
Latrie, *Hist. de Chypre*, II, 249–50 note 3, and in BEC, 1ere série, V, 421–2
and note.   Felix Faber (*vide supra*, Cap. IX), refers to the existence of the

Land.   Later, when the conquest of Jerusalem was found to be impossible and Cyprus itself was attacked by the Saracens, the first duty of its members was narrowed down to the defence of the island.   Its arms consisted of a silver sword or dagger with a cross-shaped hilt, an emblem of purity and fortitude; [1] and round the weapon was a ribbon on which was inscribed the motto of the Order—'C'est pour loiauté maintenir'.[2]   Knights of many countries joined the new Order.   Apart from the chivalry of Cyprus, Machaut tells us, its members included nobles from France, Spain, Rome, Lombardy, Germany, England and Sardinia.[3]

The young prince was a great lover of adventure and travel in strange lands.   His father, King Hugh IV, however, had always been reluctant to give his men permission to travel to the West as he feared that they might be attracted by the glamour of its courts and desert the island whose government depended upon the Latin minority.   Nevertheless, at the risk of his father's anger, Pierre made secret preparations, and he and his brother Jean de Lusignan, Prince of Antioch and Constable of Cyprus, accompanied by other knights, boarded a galley and sailed from the island in 1349.[4]   At the news of their departure, the old King became very angry and spared no expense in having the runaways arrested.[5]   Afterwards he imprisoned them at Kerynia for that disobedience, which, according to Makhairas, had filled his heart with grief and ultimately caused his death on 10 October 1359.[6]

Throughout his life, Pierre was greatly influenced by his friends, of whom the closest were Philippe de Mézières

---

Order in the fifteenth century and describes the investiture with the sword or dagger; see A. Stewart's trans., I, 25.   Faber calls it the 'Order of the Kings of Cyprus.'

[1] Machaut, ll. 405–6, 491.   [2] ib., l. 366.   [3] ib., ll. 369–80.

[4] Makhairas, §§ 79–85; Machaut, ll. 513 et seq.; Strambaldi, 33; Amadi, 407.   Other knights who fled with the two princes, Makhairas tells us (§ 79), were Simon de Norès and Pierre de Couches.   The first is identified by Dawkins in a note as being probably Simon Tenouri, who became Marshal of Jerusalem in the reign of Pierre I.

[5] Makhairas (§ 94) says that Hugh IV spent 500,000 besants before he recovered his children.

[6] ib., § 85.

and Pierre de Thomas, whose activities as crusading propagandists have already been treated in a separate chapter.[1] Among the traits which characterized these three heroes were their unbounded zeal for the crusade, their devotion to the Church of Rome and their firm determination to fight the infidels to the last.

The situation of Cyprus made its kings the natural champions of Christianity against Islam. It was the uttermost Latin possession in regions where Muhammadan influence was preponderant, since Armenia's allegiance to Rome was doubtful and the country was on the border of collapse. Unlike Armenia, Cyprus enjoyed much security behind the waters of the Mediterranean owing to the maritime weakness of Egypt at this stage. Its position on the sea route to the Holy Places made it a convenient halting-place for the pilgrim traffic; and in trade, it became a vast warehouse both for the East and the West. Under the Lusignans, it therefore reached a greater degree of prosperity than ever before.[2] Although Pierre placed all the wealth of the island at the disposal of the crusaders, his need for more men and money for the successful conduct of holy war on a large scale was nevertheless considerable. This explains his long journeys to the courts of Europe in attempts to complete his preparations and reinforce his armies with western help.

The circumstances of his accession to the throne, too, must have contributed to the formation of his character and policy towards holy war. Hugh IV's oldest son was not Pierre, but Guy, who married Marie de Bourbon and died in his father's lifetime leaving an infant son Hugh.[3] After his brother's death, Pierre is said to have been crowned as King-designate of Cyprus by Hugh IV himself in order to avoid any future arguments as regards succession. In spite of this precautionary measure, Pierre found in his

---

[1] *vide supra*, Cap. VII.

[2] For commercial importance and prosperity of Cyprus, see Heyd, II, 2–23. Strambaldi, 36, gives some account of this aspect. Makhairas, §§ 92–5, provides a concrete example of the flow of wealth into the island in the story of Lakha the Nestorian which, though evidently much exaggerated, must have contained an element of truth.

[3] *vide supra*, notes.

nephew an antagonist who challenged his right to the throne of Cyprus. Clement VI was at first unwilling to confirm his succession without investigation; and Pierre's embassy to the curia of Avignon had no easy task in convincing the Pope who only accepted the situation with conditions and reservations on behalf of the dispossessed grandson of the deceased Hugh IV.[1] The new King fully understood Clement's enthusiasm for the crusade, and this may have encouraged him to espouse the cause of the Cross in order to add to his prestige at the papal curia. It would, however, be a serious mistake to overrate this personal motive in Pierre's attitude towards war with the Saracens. Undoubtedly it added to his fervour; but, on the other hand, the King's will to take the Cross was actuated mainly by his desire to serve God and his resolution to deliver the Holy Land from the oppressive hand of the infidels. His birth, his education, the state of his kingdom, the traditions of his house, the bent of his mind, and the influence of his close friends and supporters—all these factors collaborated to make of Pierre an ideal crusader; and the genuineness of his feeling for the cause was less unmixed than in the case of any contemporary monarch. He was the real 'athleta Christi'.

From the outset of his reign, Pierre was determined to devote himself to holy war. He wished to ruin the power of Islam in the amīrates of Asia Minor and in Egypt. In pursuit of this aim, he found it necessary to have a base on the Asiatic mainland for his military operations. A valuable opportunity was presented when Leo V, King of Armenia, pressed by the Egyptians on one side and by the Turks on the other, offered to cede Gorigos [2] to Pierre in return for his assistance in the defence of his country. Gorigos

---

[1] Reynaldus, *ad ann.* 1360, no. 15; Strambaldi, 50; Makhairas, §§ 102, 105–8. It was stipulated by Innocent VI on confirming Pierre's right of succession that he should grant his nephew an annual allowance of 50,000 'white' besants of Cyprus.

[2] Makhairas, §§ 112–14; Machaut, ll. 628–40; Strambaldi, 42–3; Amadi, 410–11. Gorigos, Gorhigos, Courc, Curch, Kurk or Curicho was situated on the south coast of Asia Minor near the mouth of the River Saleffi just inside the Armenian border. The Armenian embassy consisted of two Greeks—Michael Psararis and Costas Philistis.

was doomed sooner or later to fall into the hands of the Turks if it remained an Armenian possession, while cession to the Cypriots would not be a serious loss to the Armenians. Leo, therefore, hastened to dispatch a special embassy to the new King soon after his accession in January 1360, to convey to him this decision. The ambassadors were received with honour, their welcome offer was accepted, and on 15 January galleys carrying four companies of archers under the command of an 'English' knight called Robert de Lusignan [1] were dispatched to take possession of Gorigos. On their arrival, the people of the town opened the gates to them and solemnly swore allegiance to Pierre. This was the first foothold of the forces of Cyprus in Asia Minor. The news of this Latin lordship of Gorigos struck fear in the hearts of the neighbouring Turkish Amīrs who rightly thought that the powerful King was only using this as a base for an impending attack upon their dominions. So a Muslim league [2] was formed by Ibrahim Bey, the Grand Qaraman,[3] together with the Amīrs of Alaya,[4] Tekke

[1] Makhairas, § 114. The identity of this 'English' knight remains a mystery. Dulaurier (*Rec. des historiens des croisades, Documents arméniens,* I, 711) says that he was probably a Frenchman from Poitou, and Stubbs (*Seventeen Lectures,* 193) adopts a similar interpretation by calling him an 'Englishman by courtesy' owing to the possibility that his native country might have been part of the continental demesne of the Plantagenets. Cf. Dawkins' notes to Makhairas, II, 99; Iorga, *Mézières,* 124 note 1.

[2] Makhairas, § 116; Strambaldi, 44–5; Amadi, 411.

[3] The Grand Qaraman, and not the Ottoman Sultan, was the most powerful of the Turkish rulers in Asia Minor during the fourteenth century. He was the true successor of the Saljūq Sultans. The decline of his power began in the reign of Bayezid I (1389–1403); but even after the Timurid invasion of Asia Minor, the Grand Qaraman recovered sufficiently to withstand Ottoman aggression until his amīrate was seized by Muhammad II in 1467 and finally annexed to the Ottoman Empire by Bayezid II in 1486. At the time of Pierre's expedition the Qaraman's realm occupied roughly the central part of Asia Minor extending from the slopes of the Taurus to the Mediterranean between the receding confines of Armenia and the gulf of Adalia. Hajji Khalīfa, Jihannuma (Istanbul A.H. 1145), 615 et seq.; Bertrandon de la Broquière, 118–20; Texier, *Descript. d'Asie Mineure,* II, 131. Cf. Gibbons, 165–7, 187–90, 289–90; articles Karaman and Karaman-oghlu by Kramers in EI.

[4] Alaya, Alaia, al-Alaia, Candelor, Kandelore, Quandelore, Escandelour, Scandeloro or Lacandelour is believed to be a corruption of the ancient

including Adalia,[1] and Monovgat or Manavgat.[2]   They
equipped a fleet as large as their means allowed with the
intention of raiding Cyprus and intimidating the ambitious
king whose policy of aggression stood out in contrast to
the peaceful reign of his predecessor, Hugh IV.   Whether
the united fleet of the Turks carried out its contemplated
plan of sailing to Cyprus or not, is difficult to decide.   No
pillage of Cyprus is reported by the chronicles of the time,
and the possibility is that as soon as their activities were
revealed to the King, he started those negotiations and
preparations that led to the capture of Adalia on the south
coast of Asia Minor.

Pierre's first move towards the accomplishment of his aim
was to send an embassy to Rhodes to negotiate a working
alliance with the Hospitallers and procure the four galleys
promised by the Grand Master [3] on occasions of war with
the infidels.   In the meantime, he ordered all his nobles
and his army to stand in readiness for the expedition; and

Coracesium.   Once an Armenian town, it was seized by the Saljūq Sultan
'Alā'-al-Dīn (1219–37).   At the time of Pierre's expedition, it was situated
within the borders of Qaraman on the coast of the gulf of Adalia.   Nevertheless, its amīr negotiated independently with his Turkish neighbour of Tekke
and with the Christian Kingdom of Cyprus, freely changing allegiance
according to the exigencies of the moment.   In the fifteenth century Alaya
sought the help of Cyprus against the Ottomans, but finally lost its independence in 1472.   Makhairas, l.c.; Cuinet, *Turquie d'Asie*, I, 867; Gibbons,
285.

[1] The Amīrate of Tekke extended along the gulf of Adalia and further west
to Menteshe.   Its history is centred round the town of Adalia.   Adalia
appears in the sources as Satalia, Satalie, Attalea, Autaliah, and Antaliah.   The
province of Tekke imparted its name to him who ruled it—Tekke-Bey.
Originally he was only a Saljūq governor, but ultimately declared himself
independent; and, except for the temporary occupation of Adalia by the King
of Cyprus, the amīr retained his autonomy until the whole province was
annexed by the Ottomans in 1450.   Gibbons, 295–6; Spruner-Menke,
Hand-Atlas, Map 88; Cuinet, *Turquie d'Asie*, I, 853 et seq.; articles Adalia
and Teke-Oghlu in EI.

[2] Small amīrate at the mouth of the River Monovgat, the ancient Melas,
midway between Adalia and Alaya, east of Side, very probably within the
confines of Tekke.   See map by Lanckoronski, *Villes de la Pamphylie et de la
Pisidie*, I; Beaufort, *Karamania*, 157; cf. Dawkins' notes to Makhairas, II,
p. 99, § 116.

[3] Roger de Pins (1355–65).   Vertot, II, 204 et seq.; Delaville Le Roulx,
Hospitaliers à Rhodes, 129–47.

a large fleet was manned at Famagusta for their conveyance.
In addition to the four galleys from Rhodes, two were
contributed by the Pope, twelve by private Latin 'pirates'
in search of booty, forty-six by the King, and others by
various lords and barons bringing the total number of craft
to one hundred and nineteen vessels. The host embarked
on Sunday 12 July 1361 at Famagusta.[1] The flagship
was commanded by Pierre himself, the Rhodian squadron
was under the 'Admiral' of the Order,[2] the Genoese seamen led two galleys, and other lords followed, each with
his contingent in his own ships.[3] It is said that the Amīr
of Tekke who was also Lord of Adalia suspected the object
of the campaign as the invasion of his territory and so
wrote several letters to the King in the vain hope of persuading the Christian fleet to advance in another direction.[4]
Notwithstanding his repeated supplications, the host landed
at a small place called Tetramili, close to Adalia, on Tuesday
23 August 1361.[5] Adalia itself, situated on the south
coast of the peninsula at the head of the gulf bearing the
same name, was well fortified and commanded an admirable
position for the export of goods from Asia Minor. Its
capture would be as great a gain to the Christians as the
conquest of Smyrna. Fortunately for the Cypriots, the
Amīr of Tekke and his troops were not stationed within its
fortresses at the time and the garrison was inadequate
to offer any serious resistance to the overwhelming forces
of the enemy. The King and his army, consisting of
mounted men-at-arms as well as detachments of infantry,
marched on it without delay. On 24 August, they invested
the town on every side; and, before nightfall, seeing the
hopelessness of their plight, the inhabitants opened the
gates to the besiegers and surrendered all the fortifications

---

[1] Makhairas, §§ 117–18; Strambaldi, 45–6; Amadi, 411.

[2] According to Bustron, *Chroniques*, 250, this is Jean Forbin, and according
to Amadi, 411, 'Joan Fortin, l'amiraglio'. Ferlino d'Airasca was the titular
admiral at the time, and Delaville Le Roulx, op. cit., 141 note 2, suggests that
the commander of the galleys of the Hospital was therefore one of his
lieutenants.

[3] Makhairas, § 119; Strambaldi, l.c.

[4] Makhairas, § 120.

[5] ib., § 121; Strambaldi, 47, refers to Tramil instead of Tetramili.

to the King in order to avoid bloodshed.[1]   A Christian
detachment consisting of many knights, archers and
crossbowmen, replaced the Turkish, and Pierre appointed
Jacques de Norès, the Turkopolier of Cyprus, as governor of the town and commander of the garrison with
a small fleet of three galleys at his disposal.[2]   On 8 September 1361, the rest of the army resumed the march
to Alaya, the next important town east of Adalia.   Seeing that the outcome of any resistance to the Christians
would be disaster, the Amīr of the town emerged with
a handful of followers to submit to the King, and, as
proof of his good faith, placed the keys of the fortifications
in the hands of the invaders.[3]   Pierre accepted the offer
and having declared his suzerainty over the district, ordered
his men to depart to Ousgat, a place which is difficult to
identify.   The Amīr of Monovgat, who saw that his
Muslim neighbours both on the eastern and western sides
of his territory had submitted to the invaders, hastily
dispatched envoys with presents and an offer of submission,
which Pierre accepted.[4]   At this point the campaign came
to an end.   Apart from the actual occupation of Adalia
by the Christians, the King took no steps to maintain his
suzerainty over Alaya and Monovgat, accepting the
promises of their Amīrs to fulfil their duties to him as their
immediate lord and master.   Events soon proved these
promises to be quite worthless.   In fact, their doubtful
submission to Cyprus may have been actuated, not by fear
of the military superiority of the King, but by diplomatic
expediency.   The smaller amīrates of southern Anatolia,
strewn along the border of the great Muslim principality

---

[1] Makhairas, §§ 121–3; Strambaldi, l.c.; Amadi, 411; Machaut, ll. 641 et
seq., probably to heighten the poetic effect of the fall of Adalia, refers to
(ll. 656–58):

> 'Maint Sarrazin, mainte pucelle,
> Maint Turc & maint enfant perir,
> Par feu, ou par glaive morir.'

[2] Makhairas, § 123; Strambaldi, 48. The Turkopolier was the commander of a battalion of mounted men-at-arms who were not ranked as
knights and were generally mercenaries drawn from the natives of Cyprus.

[3] Makhairas, § 124; Strambaldi, l.c.

[4] Makhairas, § 125; Strambaldi, l.c.; Amadi, 411–12.

of Qaraman, were no doubt apprehensive of being incorporated in the realm of their strong neighbour. It is
quite possible that their nominal surrender to Christian
Cyprus was partly intended as a check to the ambitions
of Qaraman which might lead to the total suppression
of their independence.

The Christian army then retraced its journey to Cyprus.
Some galleys went to Kerynia on the north coast of the
island, others to Famagusta, and the King and his chief
nobles ultimately reached the capital Nicosia late in September 1361, to be received with great honour.[1] As soon
as Pierre had withdrawn from Asia Minor, the Muslim
Amīrs who had suffered by his visitation began to make
plans for an attack on Adalia. A number of sieges,
skirmishes and threats ensued in an attempt to recover their
loss. It would be idle to detail all the events of this protracted contest, since there was frequent repetition of the
same course of events. Perhaps the first important encounter was that of the winter of 1361–2. Adalia was virtually a beleaguered town without hope of obtaining provisions from the surrounding country, and its access to the sea
could not be fully utilized for supplies owing to the climatic
conditions of the season. Both garrison and inhabitants were
starving and the horses had to be fed on citron leaves.[2]
Nevertheless, the Turkopolier held out and drove the enemy
away from the fortifications until relief came in May 1362
with the arrival of four galleys, six transports and six pirate
ships. Jean de Sur, the Admiral of Cyprus, replaced Jacques
de Norès in command, and the reinforced fleet sailed westwards to the fort of Myra on the coast of the Amīrate of
Tekke and burnt it to the ground after seizing its garrison.[3]
In fear of retaliation, the new commander repaired the walls
of Adalia and raised the height of its castle and keep.[4]

Meanwhile, Tekke and Alaya concluded an offensive
alliance whereby the former should invest the town by land

[1] Makhairas, l.c.; Strambaldi, l.c.; Amadi, 412.
[2] Adalia is still famous in the East for an abundance of lemons of unusual
size and sweetness.
[3] Makhairas, §§ 126–8; Strambaldi, 49.
[4] Makhairas, § 132.

and the latter blockade the entrance to its harbour.   Forty-
five thousand men and eight galleys are said to have assisted
in these operations.   The land forces vigorously attacked
the walls, but were repulsed with heavy losses by the use
of stone missiles as well as the crossbow and the longbow.
Finally, the Christians sallied from the town and routed
the Turks while Jean de Brie chased their fleet as far as
Yerakites [1] where their seamen saved their lives by deserting
the ships, and then setting them on fire.[2]   With the collapse
of their efforts at Adalia, the Turks planned a series of
concerted raids on the island of Cyprus itself.   They were
encouraged in this by the news of the King's departure to
the West and of the disastrous effects of a recent plague
and the depopulation of the island and its garrison.[3]   The
leader in these raids was a certain Muhammad Ra'īs who
led the Turkish fleet to the County of Carpas and carried
back many prisoners and much booty to Asia Minor.[4]
The regent of Cyprus immediately seized the Turkish
merchants in the island and sent a fleet under the command
of Francesco Spinola to punish the Turks for this lawlessness.   A battle ensued in which Spinola was drowned; but
the Turkish losses were so heavy that Muhammad Ra'īs
had to flee to Ṭarābulus (Tripoli) in Syria for refuge at the
court of its Muslim Governor.   The Cypriots sought to
seize him by diplomatic means, but failed owing to the
reluctance of the governors to surrender a co-religionist to
the Christians.[5]   It was at this juncture that the Genoese

---

[1] Identified by Dawkins in his notes to Makhairas, II, 106, as probably the
ancient Korakesion in the vicinity of Alaya.

[2] Makhairas, §§ 132–3.

[3] It is said that at Famagusta alone thirty or forty lives were taken every day
by the plague.   The Legate, Pierre de Thomas, held a solemn procession in
the city to implore Heaven to raise the scourge from the island.   Even Turks,
Saracens and Jews were moved to tears, and, barefooted, joined the rest.
Reynaldus, *ad ann.* 1361, no. 9; Hackett, *Church of Cyprus*, 133.

[4] Makhairas, §§ 137–9.   The Turks anchored in Morphou Bay and
landed near Pendaya.

[5] ib., §§ 139–44.   Makhairas names the Mamlūk governor as 'Melek
Emir' believed by Dawkins (*Notes to Makhairas*, II, 108, § 144) to be 'Melek
Bekhna' and later (ib., II, 115, § 159 note 2) identified, on the authority of
Herzsohn (*Überfall Alexandrien's*, 42) as 'Menkeliboga el-Schamsi'
of Damascus, a mamlūk of the all-powerful Yalboghā al-Khaṣṣiki in Egypt.

embarked on their treacherous career against Cyprus and momentarily distracted the Cypriots from fighting the Turks. Adalia, however, remained in their hands until 1373 when in the reign of Pierre II (1369–82) the island was so weakened by the Genoese that it could no longer hold its Asiatic possession in the face of continued Turkish attacks.[1]

After the capture of Adalia by the Cypriots and the nominal submission of Tekke to Pierre I during the second year of his reign, the King's plan of an overwhelming crusade to break the power of Islam became his primary concern. To realize his dream, however, he found it necessary to appeal to the whole of Latin Christendom; and to bring all that was possible of the resources of the West into the field of holy war, he decided to embark on a journey to the courts of Europe and negotiate for effective alliances in person. This journey may be regarded as a landmark, not only in Pierre's career, but also in the history of the later crusade. The King travelled for three years to all the leading courts of Europe in search of supporters and returned to the East with sufficient men and galleys to ensure his capture of Alexandria.

Pierre's departure from Cyprus took place on 24 October 1362.[2] He went first to Rhodes where he was well received by Roger de Pins, Grand Master of the Hospital. His retinue was increased by two more Cypriot nobles from the garrison of Adalia,[3] and the party sailed to Venice,

---

[1] Makhairas, § 368; Gibbons, 298.

[2] Makhairas, § 129; Strambaldi, 50. The King was still at Nicosia on 15 June and 15 September 1362, according to evidence derived from his correspondence with Florentines and with Niccolò Acciajuoli, a Frankish noble in the Achaia. Mas Latrie, *Hist. de Chypre*, II, 236–7 and 239 note; Buchon, *Nouvelles recherches sur la Morée* (1834), II, Pt. 1, 134. By the first of these documents, the Republic of Florence promised ('pro remissione peccatorum christianitatis') to support the King in his attempt to recover the Holy Land ('nostram propriam hereditatem'). The same document refers to the 'captio Sathallie civitatis'. Makhairas, l.c., enumerates the King's companions on this journey as Pierre de Norès, Jean de Gaurelle, Jean de Finio, Nicolas d'Ibelin, Jacques de Norès, 'and many other knights and many of his servants'.

[3] Makhairas, § 131; Strambaldi, 51. According to a message from the King, Pierre de Sur and Jacques Le Petit joined him at Rhodes from Adalia.

arriving there on 5 December 1362.   They stayed in the
Republic until the New Year in order to persuade Lorenzo
Celsi, the enterprising young Doge who had succeeded
the old and calculating Giovanni Delfino in the previous
year, to supply the crusaders with the necessary fleet.[1]
Afterwards, they travelled through Lombardy by way of
Mistra, Padua, Verona, Milan and Pavia to Genoa where
the King remained the whole of February and part of
March 1363, probably to settle the differences between the
Genoese and his people and also to ensure the support
of another great naval power besides Venice.[2]   About the
middle of March, the royal party left the republic of Genoa
for Avignon.   Their arrival at the papal curia is reported
on Ash-Wednesday, 29 March 1363, about six months
after the death of Innocent VI and the accession of Urban
V.[3]   The King's nephew, Hugh de Lusignan, who disputed
his right to the crown, having heard of his uncle's visit to
Avignon, hastened to that city to lay his grievances before
the Pope.   Each of the two parties pleaded his claims
to the throne of Cyprus, and finally Urban confirmed
his predecessor's verdict that Pierre should pay his dispossessed nephew an annuity of fifty thousand besants.[4]
Meanwhile, negotiations for the crusade were proceeding
with the princes who happened to be at Avignon.   Foremost among these was Jean II, King of France, who was

Both chroniclers refer to Innocent VI, the Pope who reigned at the time of the
King's departure.   Innocent, however, died before Pierre's arrival and was
succeeded by Urban V (*vide infra*).

The position of the Hospitallers during this period does not appear to have
commanded much confidence at the curia, and the Grand Master must have
welcomed Pierre as a possible mediator on his behalf at Avignon.   Delaville
Le Roulx, *Hospitaliers à Rhodes*, 142–4.

[1] *Vite de' Duchi*, in Muratori, RIS, XXII, 655, where 1361 is mentioned
by error for 1362; cf. Mas Latrie, op. cit., II, 239 note; Iorga, *Mézières*,
145–7 and notes.

[2] Mas Latrie, II, 239–40 note and 247 doc. dated 1 January 1363;
Stella, in Muratori, RIS, XXVII, 1096; Iorga, op. cit., 150–2.   Pierre was
also the guest of the Visconti in Milan for twelve days from 21 January 1363.

[3] *Vit. Pap. Aven.* (ed. Mollat), I, 396, 400 (Tertia Vita and Quarta Vita
Urbani V).   Innocent died on 12 September and Urban was elected
28–31 October 1362; ib., 249, 383, 394, 398.

[4] Makhairas, § 131; Strambaldi, 51 ('50 millia aspri de Cipro').

noted for his chivalry and piety, and Pierre had no difficulty in winning him over to his cause. When Urban V preached holy war on 14 April and appointed Cardinal Talleyrand de Périgord his legate for this purpose, the two monarchs were the first to take the Cross from his hand, and their example was followed by a multitude of nobles from many countries.[1]

It was an auspicious and encouraging beginning for the crusade thus to win the King of France and the flower of his chivalry to the Cypriot side in addition to the promise of support by the Republic of St. Mark. Pierre's dream, however, extended far beyond these limitations. He wished to bring all the contingents of Europe under the banner of the Cross. From Avignon, he pursued a circuitous route to solicit favour and assistance at the royal courts of most countries of the West. In the summer of 1363, Froissart reports his presence in Flanders, Brabant and Germany.[2] In the Rhineland, he travelled from Basle to Strasbourg (4 July), Mayence (25 July), and Cologne.[3] Thence he crossed the German frontier and in August went to Paris to discuss definite plans for the crusade with Jean II who agreed to join him in March of the following year to commence hostilities against the

---

[1] *Vit. Pap. Aven.* (ed. Mollat), I, 352–3, 384, 386, 400; Machaut, ll. 679 et seq. In the Prima Vita, 352, the King of the Danes Waldemar IV is said to have been present and to have shared the same honour 'ad faciendum generale passagium ultramarinum, et specialiter contra Turcos'. The first part of this statement may be mistaken, as the King of Denmark was engaged in his wars with the Baltic free towns (Iorga, *Mézières*, 162); but the last words are noteworthy as they indicate the original and primary aim of the crusade as against the Turkish amīrates of Asia Minor and not Egypt. It was also on this occasion that Amedeo VI, Count of Savoy, took the Cross; *vide infra*, Cap. XVI. Apart from the nobles of Cyprus who were in Pierre's train, others of France became crusaders. These included Jean d'Artois comte d'Eu, Charles comte de Dammartin, Jean II vicomte de Melun and comte de Tancarville, Arnoul d'Audrehem of noble Artesian origin, Robert de Juilly or Juillac, Grand Prior of France and future Grand Master of the Hospital, and Jean I le Meingre dit Boucicaut, Marshal of France; Delaville Le Roulx, *France*, I, 121–2.

[2] Ed. Kervyn, VI, 375–6. Froissart ante-dates Pierre's visit of 1364 to Bohemia (Behaingne) by placing it in 1363; *vide infra*.

[3] Iorga, *Mézières*, 174–5 and notes.

infidels.[1]   From the French capital, he travelled through north-west France as far as Rouen and Caen to meet Charles, Duke of Normandy, the future Charles V.   Pierre stayed at Caen for approximately one month (13 August– 11 September 1363), but though he received valuable presents he obtained no real response to his exhorta- tions [2] to join the crusade.   After journeying in Brittany, he returned to Calais and crossed the Channel on a visit to the court of Edward III [3] of England.   His presence in London is mentioned by Walsingham [4] and Knighton,[5] and he is known to have taken part in a great tourna- ment held in his honour at Smithfield.[6]   The King of England gave his Cypriot guest many presents, which included a large and beautiful ship named *Catherine*, costing him 12,000 francs and built specially for the pur- pose of an English journey beyond the sea to Jerusalem.[7] Further, Edward III paid all expenses incurred by Pierre on his voyage to and from England.[8]   The travellers then returned to Paris for the Christmas festivities and made their way to Aquitaine to see the Black Prince.[9]

It was probably on his way back from Aquitaine that Pierre heard the alarming news of the death of two of his

[1] Froissart (ed. Kervyn), VI, 378.

[2] *Chron. des quatre Valois* (ed. S. Luce), 128; Mas Latrie, op. cit., II, 248; Iorga, op. cit., 176.

[3] Froissart (ed. Kervyn), VI, 379–80.   David, King of Scotland, was in London at the time.

[4] *Historia Anglicana*, I, 299.   The chronicler also states that during his travels in England, the King of Cyprus was plundered by highwaymen.

[5] *Chronicon*, II, 118.

[6] Mas Latrie, op. cit., II, 247, doc. no. 4; Walsingham, op. cit., I, 296, where the tournament is cited under 1362 instead of 1363.   Iorga, op. cit., 179, says (on the authority of Froissart, ed. Luce, VI, 90) that the King arrived in London on 6 November and was received by the Count of Here- ford, Walter de Maundy, Raoul de Ferrier, Richard de Pembroke, Allan de Booksell, Richard Stury and other knights.   Nevertheless, it would appear that Froissart's date must be wrong in view of the document published by Mas Latrie.

[7] Froissart saw the ship in Sandwich harbour, and he says that Pierre did not take it with him; ed. Kervyn, VI, 385–6.

[8] Froissart, l.c.   Pierre wrote to Celsi, Doge of Venice, from Paris, on 17 February 1364; Mas Latrie, op. cit., II, 240 note, 252–3 note.

[9] Froissart, VI, 286 et seq.

most distinguished and most useful allies in the crusade.
Cardinal Talleyrand de Périgord, the Apostolic Legate for
holy war met his end on 17 January 1364,[1] and Jean le
Bon of France, early in May; and the King of Cyprus
hastened to Paris in order to attend the funeral of his
friend and the coronation of his successor.[2]   After the
traditional anointing of Charles V in the Cathedral of
Rheims, Pierre and his train again took the road to Central
Europe, evidently to negotiate an alliance with the Holy
Roman Emperor and to visit the German princes in the
hope of enlisting their sympathy and their support for the
forthcoming crusade.   The knights and burghers of
Esslingen and Erfurt gave Pierre a great welcome and
many of them espoused his cause.[3]   The Margrave of
Franconia, on the other hand, made it clear to the King
that he could not respond independently to his appeal and
that his duty was to pursue whatever course his suzerain
the Emperor might decide for him.[4]   Pierre's next call
was upon the Duke of Saxony, Rudolf II, a friend and
relative of the Emperor.   Jousts were held and the King
took part in them to the great delight of the Saxon nobles.
He received presents of value from his host; but the Duke
refused to take any decision in relation to the crusade with-

---

[1] *Vit. Pap. Aven.* (ed. Mollat), I, 385.

[2] Froissart (ed. Kervyn), VI, 409 et seq.; Machaut, ll. 731 et seq.   The
funeral of Jean II took place at St. Denis on 7 May and the coronation of
Charles V at Rheims on 19 May 1364; *Chron. de Saint-Denis*, VI, 231, 233;
cf. Mas Latrie, op. cit., II, 240 note under 1364.   Machaut laments Jean's
death and praises him in a passage of allegorical rhetoric (ll. 763 et seq.):

> 'Li roys Jehans, dont Dieus ait l'ame,
> Ot espousé la milleur dame
> Qu'on peust trouver en ce monde.
>
> .   .   .   .
> . . . ce fu ma dame Bonne.'

[3] Machaut, ll. 881 et seq.   Pierre stayed in those regions 'Bien ij. yvers &
un esté' (l. 892).

[4] ib., ll. 897 et seq.   Machaut puts a long statement in the Margrave's
mouth including the following lines (921-4):

> 'Vous alez devers l'empereur
> De Romme, qui est mon signeur,
> Si que à li me conformeray;
> Car ce qu'il fera je feray.'

out first consulting the Emperor and obtaining his sanction. This, however, did not mean a blunt refusal or even indifference to Pierre's supplications, for the Duke offered to accompany him to Prague for further consultation with the Emperor.[1] After nine days of festivities,[2] the two princes left for the imperial capital and were met with cordiality by Charles IV (1347–78) whom Machaut praises very highly.[3] Feasts, the like of which the King had never seen elsewhere, and splendid tournaments, were held for three consecutive weeks.[4] At last, when Pierre disclosed to his august host that the real aim of his visit was to seek 'aid and comfort' for his holy enterprise,[5] Charles suggested holding a conference with the two other central European monarchs of Hungary and Poland at Cracow for mutual decision and united action.[6] At the Polish capital, the Emperor declared himself whole-heartedly for the crusade, and the other kings also strongly supported his view.[7] Before the adjournment of the meeting, a resolution was passed to the effect that special dispatches should be sent to the German princes inviting their collaboration

---

[1] ib., ll. 939 et seq.   [2] ib., ll. 975–8.

[3] ib., ll. 987 et seq.

> 'On ne porroit en nulle terre
> Nul plus sage homme de li querre,
> C'on dit ça & dela les mons
> Que c'est li secons Salemons.' (989–92).

[4] ib., ll. 1122 et seq.   [5] ib., ll. 1204–11.

[6] ib., ll. 1212 et seq. The author of the *Annales S. Crucis Polonicae* (ed. Pertz, *Mon. Germ. Hist.*, XIX, 684) wrongly places the conference in 1363 and further states that the Kings of Hungary, Denmark and Bohemia were present, but that of the *Mon. Poloniae* (II, 630) mentions the princes of Hungary, Cyprus, 'Dacia' and Poland; cf. Iorga, *Mézières*, 195 note.

The fullness of detail in Machaut's description of the itinerary of the Emperor and the King illustrates the importance of the writer's source. From Prague the two princes went

> 'À Bresselau, Liguenisse,
> À Nuistat, à Suedenisse;
> Costen, Calix, Buton, Glagouve
> Passerent, & par Basenouve;
> De là en Cracoe arriverent.' (1272–6).

These towns may be identified as Breslau, Liegnitz, Neustadt, Schweidnitz, Kosten, Kalisz, Beuthen, Glogau, Baranow and Cracow respectively.

[7] Machaut, ll. 1289 et seq.

in the holy war.[1] Jousts were then held to celebrate
the end of a successful journey; and, indeed, it seemed at
the moment that Pierre had realized all his expectations.
It remained for the future, however, to reveal how much
of these great promises was to be carried out when the time
came for action.

Cracow marked the furthest point in the King's itinerary,
and there he decided to return to Venice whence he would
sail back to his native island. As he passed through
Austria, he called upon its Duke in Vienna to preach the
crusade, not without apparent results, and to enjoy more
festivities and receive more precious gifts.[2] The King's
approach to the Adriatic became known in the Republic
of St. Mark on 26 October 1364, when special preparations
were approved for his reception.[3] He made his final entry
into Venice on 11 November 1364.[4] The Doge and the
Venetian nobles welcomed him on his arrival outside the
city.[5] Although the sympathies of Celsi, the new Doge,
were the result of motives wider than those which had
prompted his predecessor Delfino, the enthusiasm of the
Venetians as a whole was no altruistic gesture. The
Cypriot army had proved its usefulness to the Republic
in quelling the Cretan revolt of 1363–4 against Venetian
rule,[6] and it might yet render further services to their
interests in the East. While sojourning in Venice to ensure
the maritime support of the Republic, Pierre also managed
to make peace with the Genoese and thus avert what might

---

[1] Machaut, ll. 1346–52.　　　[2] ib., ll. 1430 et seq.

[3] Document in Verci's *Storia della marca Trivigiana*, XIV, 20; Sanudo,
Vite de' Duchi, in Muratori, RIS, XXII, 775; cf. Mas Latrie, *Hist. de
Chypre*, II, 240 note under 1364.

[4] Machaut, ll. 1536–8.　　　[5] ib., ll. 1542–6.

[6] This is revealed by two letters issued by Pierre: the first, dated London,
24 November 1363, instructed the Regents in Cyprus to assist in the suppression of the rebellion at Candia; the second, dated 17 February 1364,
informed the Doge that he had quelled the rebellion and that he and his
crusading colleagues including the Count of Savoy would not be ready for
the expedition by August and that the Venetians might therefore have ample
time to fit out the necessary fleet. *Libri Commem.* (*Ven. Arch.*), VII,
ff. 31 (27) vo and 40 (36) ro. Among other letters, the first is published
by Mas Latrie, op. cit., II, 251–2. On this rebellion see also Reynaldus,
ad ann. 1364, no. 8.

have precipitated a catastrophe for his crusading plans and even for his realm.[1]   He wrote from Venice on 16 May 1365 to Gabriele Adorno, Doge of Genoa, mentioning his gratification at the conclusion of the treaty and referring to the impending campaign against the infidels.[2]   Towards the end of the following month, the King, his chivalry and all those who had joined him from the various countries of Europe boarded the fleet equipped at Venice and sailed by the usual and much-frequented trade route to the East.[3] Pierre called at Candia, probably to verify the news of the total suppression of the Cretan rebellion and also to have a few days' respite from the agonies of sea-sickness which made it impossible for him to sleep or take any food or drink.[4]

While the King thus journeyed from one end of the Continent to the other, his chief supporters in the crusade— Urban V, Pierre de Thomas, and Philippe de Mézières— exerted every effort to establish peace among belligerent Catholics in the West and direct universal interest towards the cause of the Cross.   On 31 March 1363, the zealous Pope wrote to Jean II le Bon in praise of the capture of Adalia by Pierre de Lusignan, meanwhile stressing the danger which still threatened Christendom from the Turkish side and urging the undertaking of the crusade.[5]   On the same date he sent a special message to the Archbishop of Rheims asking him and his suffragans to offer the usual tithe on ecclesiastical benefices as well as plenary indulgences to all those who would follow the King in his worthy

[1] For treaty (18 April 1365) concluded by Guy de Regnoul de Reggio, Pierre's physician, and Pierre de Thomas, Latin Patriarch of Constantinople, on behalf of Cyprus with Genoa; see Mas Latrie, op. cit., II, 153–66; Reynaldus, ad ann. 1365, no. 18; Makhairas, §§ 153–4; Strambaldi, 60–2.

[2] Mas Latrie, II, 366–7.

[3] ib., II, 240–1 note under 1365. Machaut, l. 1610, wrongly fixes the month of sailing as May. It is known, however, that the privileges of Venetian citizenship were conferred upon the King's Chancellor and companion, Philippe de Mézières, as late as 22 June 1365; Libri Commem., VII, f. 51 (47) vo; cf. Mas Latrie, II, 272–3. On 19 July, news had already reached Pope Urban V of the King's embarkation; Reynaldus, ad ann. 1365, no. 18.

[4] Machaut, ll. 1644 et seq.

[5] Reynaldus, ad ann. 1363, nos. 14–15.

enterprise.[1] He further sent two prayers to be said by way of exhortation to the faithful on this occasion. Another letter of 16 April implored the King of Navarre to make peace with his father-in-law, Jean II, and with the King of Aragon, so that the way might be made clear for hostile action in the East.[2] Letters (25 May) inviting almost the whole of Christendom to participate in the crusade were communicated to the Holy Roman Emperor, to the Kings of England, Hungary and Bohemia, to the Dukes of Luxemburg, Austria, Saxony and Bavaria.[3] Lorenzo Celsi, Doge of Venice, was requested at the same time to equip the necessary galleys for the 'passagium' which, argued the Holy Pontiff, who realized that to the Italian Republic commercial interests were a greater incentive than a sacred cause, would ultimately further the Venetian trade in the Levant.[4] The energy of the Pope did not diminish with the passing of time. In the following year (1364), he seems to have paid special attention to the possibility of enlisting English sympathy for the crusade. Companies of Englishmen were continually fighting on the Continent, particularly in France and Italy, during this period; and to bring them within the field of holy war would be a double service to Christendom. First, it would put an end to their maraudings in Europe and at the same time strengthen the forces against the infidel in the East. On 14 April he wrote to the papal nuncios, Albornoz, Bishop of Sabina and Androin de la Roche, Cardinal of St. Marcellus, recommending to their notice a certain Robert Woodhouse, envoy of the English company at Pisa which desired to join the crusade, and requesting that a subsidy should be raised for them from Italian territory.[5] Three days later, Urban sent two messages to Lorenzo Celsi, Doge of Venice,

---

[1] Reynaldus, *ad ann.* 1363, nos. 16–17.

[2] ib., *ad ann.* 1363, no. 18.

[3] *Vat. Arch.*, L.S. 245, ff. 66 et seq., 127–9, 136, 161–3; cf. Iorga, *Mézières*, 169–70, and notes; Bliss and Twemlow, *Calendar of Papal Registers*, IV, 2.

[4] *Ven. Arch. Libri Commem.*, VII, f. 22 (18) ro.

[5] Bliss and Twemlow, *Calendar of Papal Registers*, IV, 8. Robert Woodhouse was the envoy of the English Company led by Albert Stertz. He returned with a letter of credence and a verbal message.

and Gabriele Adorno, Doge of Genoa, begging them to
supply the company with the necessary ships for their
conveyance to the East and thus rid Italy of their maraudings and greatly help the crusade.[1]   A letter of 20 April
addressed to one Thomas de Ufford, knight, captain of
another English company in Italy, praised his zeal for the
Cross and exhorted his company to follow his good example.[2]
To Queen Joanna of Naples, the Pope recommended
William de la Pole, lord of Castle Ashby, knight, who,
having taken the Cross from his own hands, proposed to
join the crusade at the head of a great number of Englishmen from Tuscany and intended to pass through her realm
on the way to Otranto for embarkation.   The Pope asked
her to supply them with victuals.[3]   A papal bull of 17
May 1364, conferred upon the Captain and the Company
of the English in Italy all the privileges of the crusaders
with plenary indulgences; and another of the 20th allowed
them to choose their confessors and have portable altars.[4]
Moreover, on 24 May, Urban wrote three letters to Aymar
de Pictavia, comte de Valentinois, to Ralph, sire de Louppy-
le-Château and governor of the Dauphiné, and to Amedeo,
Count of Savoy, requesting safe-conduct for Thomas
Beauchamp (Bellocampo), earl of Warwick, and his English
companies on their way to the Holy Land.[5]   On the whole,
Urban V appears to have been aiming at a great revival
of the golden age of the crusade by re-uniting all the faithful
in a final struggle for the liberation of the Holy Places.
His bulls before and after the capture of Alexandria,
bearing directly upon the crusade of Amedeo VI of Savoy,

---

[1] id., l.c.   [2] id., l.c.

[3] id., l.c.   The Pope wrote two other letters addressed to Robert, titular
Latin Emperor of Constantinople, and to the Count of Lecce, to the same
effect. Ib., 9; a letter granting William de la Pole the privileges of
crusaders including plenary indulgence, and another to the same and Thomas
de Ufford commending them and their company to the Bishop of Sabina and
the Cardinal of St. Marcellus.

[4] ib., IV, 8.

[5] ib., IV, 9.   Later in the year (17 November 1364), the Pope wrote to
Beauchamp acknowledging receipt of the earl's messages and commending his
discretion and devotion in taking the Cross and going either to the Holy Land
or to pagan Prussia; ib., IV, 19.

give yet further testimony to his activity as will be shown at a later stage in this study.[1]

The second great ecclesiastical promoter of holy war was Pierre de Thomas, the successor of Cardinal Talleyrand de Périgord, the Apostolic Legate who died before the fulfilment of his task.[2] Pierre's close companion, Philippe de Mézières, chancellor of the Kingdom of Cyprus, also did much to bring the movement to a successful issue.[3] It is impossible here to attempt a complete survey of the diplomatic work achieved by these two heroes of the fourteenth-century crusade; but it will help towards understanding the success of the expedition of 1365 against Alexandria to review the part played by them, especially in Venice, prior to the great event. Philippe's[4] correspondence illustrates his activity in this matter. The Chancellor was at Venice probably early in the year 1364 to negotiate an agreement on the naval equipment of the crusade on behalf of his king. The moment seemed inauspicious for negotiations of this kind, as the Venetians were much perturbed by the rebellion in Crete, and were hardly inclined to listen to any plan likely to rouse the Saracens as well against them. Mézière's difficulty was increased by these untoward circumstances, and the Doge wrote on 28 January 1364 offering galleys for the conveyance of a small contingent of a thousand men on condition that they should go first to Crete to ensure the complete elimination of the spirit of revolt among its inhabitants.[5] Thanks, however, to the persuasive influence of Pierre de Thomas, and still more to the part played by the Cypriot regent in the restoration of calm and order at Candia,[6] Lorenzo Celsi doubled his offer and was now prepared to pay

---

[1] *vide infra*, Cap. XVI.

[2] *vide supra*, Cap. VII.   [3] *vide supra*, l.c.

[4] Arsenal MS. 499; cf. Iorga's article, in *Revue historique*, T. 49 (May–August 1892), 306 et seq.

[5] Mas Latrie, *Hist. de Chypre*, III, 745 note 1; 'scilicet usque medietatem mensis Marcii proximi veniant usque mille equites de gentibus passagii pro eundo ad partes Crete, pro recuperatione insule nostre, et non ultra, quare non habemus navigia parata ad presens pro majori quantitate'.

[6] *vide supra*, reference to Pierre I's letter of 17 February informing the Doge of the end of the rebellion.

half the cost of the equipment.[1]   This was a signal success and a good augury for the expedition.

Crusaders were already in Venice awaiting Pierre's arrival, and some of the more impatient companies went ahead of him to the island of Rhodes, while the government of the Republic was fitting out the main galleys in readiness for the King.   Although the bulk of the army was to embark from the lagoons, it would appear that smaller contingents sailed from Otranto [2] and Genoa.[3]   The contribution of the Genoese, however, should not be over-estimated, or their goodwill over-emphasized.   Machaut, who freely praises the Republic of St. Mark, adopts a reserved attitude in speaking of Genoa on this occasion.[4] The meagreness of the Genoese contribution was probably due to their hatred of the Venetians; and to their own self-interested schemes which at a later stage culminated in the decline of the Kingdom of Cyprus.   The main fleet from Venice together with other naval squadrons converged into the waters of Rhodes, where they were still further reinforced by the Hospitallers' galleys and a large number of Cypriot craft.

Pierre and his retinue set sail from Venice on 27 June 1365; [5] and Urban V wrote on 19 July to bless him and his campaign.[6]   The objective of the expedition remained

---

[1] *Vita S. Petri*, Cap. 7; Mézières' correspondence, cf. Iorga, op. cit., 307–8; Machaut, ll. 1578 et seq.

[2] *vide supra*, 339, papal letters to Queen Joanna and others concerning an English company due to sail from Otranto.

[3] *vide supra*, peace between Cyprus and Genoa concluded by mediation of Pierre de Thomas as a preliminary measure for the safeguarding of the island and for possible aid to the crusaders from that republic.

[4] Machaut, ll. 1592–7.

> 'Je ne dis pas que Genevois
> N'aient la huée & la vois,
> Et tres grant puissance seur mer,
> Ho là! je n'en vueil nuls blasmer!
> Car comparisons hayneuses,
> Sont, ce dit on, & perilleuses.'

[5] *Ven. Arch.*, Misti, Reg. 31, f. 100, where a resolution was taken by the Senate for the final equipment of galleys on 19 June; cf. Iorga, *Mézières*, 277.

[6] Reynaldus, *ad ann.* 1365, no. 18 (XXVI, 113, col. 2).

secret within a closed circle of the King's most trusted
advisers. Even the Republic of St. Mark which had
furnished the bulk of the fleet was left in doubt as to the
ultimate destination and fate of its ships and its seamen.
This was a wise precautionary measure; for the possibility
of an Italian betrayal of the expedition to the enemy in
return for trade privileges was not remote, and Pierre and
his advisers were well aware of this fact.

Before leaving Venice, the King sent a galley to Genoa
to publish the peace with that Republic and probably to
invite more Genoese galleys for collaboration in the crusade.
Accompanied by three more, the galley returned to Cyprus
where again the peace was publicly proclaimed at Nicosia
and Famagusta, and then they went to Rhodes in response
to Pierre's directions.[1]   Another galley was ordered to sail
post-haste to Cyprus bearing commands to the regent from
the King to prepare every available ship and meet him at
Rhodes.[2]   The Cypriot fleet consisted of thirty-three
transports for the horse, ten trading vessels, twenty ships
of a type known as 'dove',[3] besides the armed and other
galleys amounting to one hundred and eight units in
all, ready to set sail from Famagusta under the leadership of Jean de Lusignan, the King's brother and
Regent who appointed Jacques de Norèsthe Turkopolier
as vice-regent on 25 June 1365.[4]   The Cypriot fleet
reached Rhodes on 25 August and was hailed by cries of
joy from the King's men awaiting them.[5]   Besides the
transports obtained from that island, the Grand Master of

---

[1] Makhairas, § 165.   [2] ib., §§ 160–1.

[3] Gr. περιστέριν; Fr. columbel, colombet; It. columba, i.e. ship with a
keel, the nature and description of which are now unknown. Kemna,
Der Begriff 'Schiff', 237; cf. Dawkins notes to Makhairas, II, 113, § 162
note 1.   All these terms, however, seem to be identical with the Arabic
'Hamāmah' (i.e. pigeon, pl. 'Hamā'im'), a type of light ship mentioned in
Arabic historical and geographical literature. De Goeje, Bibliotheca
Geographorum Arabicorum (Leiden, 1870), III, 32; Maqrīzi, Khiṭaṭ (Bulāq
ed.), II, 180; Ibn al-Kindī, Governors and Judges of Egypt (ed. Guest), 263;
cf. H. Kindermann, 'Schiff' im Arabischen (Bonn Dissert., 1934), 24.

[4] Makhairas, § 162.   The Regent, however, fell ill at Aliki on the way
to Rhodes and had to remain in the island; ib., § 163.

[5] ib., § 164.

the Hospital, Raymond Berenger, placed four galleys [1] and a hundred knights led by the Admiral of the Order, Ferlino d'Airasca,[2] at the disposal of the King, who brought with him fifteen galleys from Venice in addition to the sixteen [3] which had sailed first to Genoa before coming to Cyprus and Rhodes.   The total number of the joint naval squadrons was one hundred and sixty-five vessels; and on this estimate, there seems to be no variance among the sources.[4]   Men,

[1] ib., § 167.   Makhairas is explicit on this estimate of these four galleys; but Strambaldi, 66–7, appears to confuse the galleys of the Order with the Venetian and the Genoese ships in his estimate of sixteen which is evidently adopted by the historian of the Order, Delaville Le Roulx, *Hospitaliers à Rhodes*, 152.   It is possible that the chronicler confused these with the royal fleet which numbered sixteen galleys.

[2] As already remarked in a previous note, Ferlino was the titular head of the Hospitallers' navy, and it might be assumed that he was here assisted by other agents.

[3] Makhairas, l.c.

[4] ib., l.c.; Strambaldi, 67; Amadi, 414; Bustron, 262.   The following passage from Amadi illustrates the variety of ships used in the expedition: 'Era galie 33, fuste 6, nave 9, burchi 13 per li cavalli, vasseli XI, et altri navigli XX. che fanno la summa de vele 92.   A Rhodi feceno armer altre galie et navigli che acompagnaron l'armada del re, che erano in summa vele numero 165.'   Machaut, too, gives some interesting particulars in lines 1876 et seq.:

> 'Il y avoit coques & barges,
> Panfiles, naves grans & larges,
> Griparies & tafourées,
> Lins & fyacres & galées,
> Targes à chevaus & huissiers;
> Et si avoit de bons courciers,
> Plus tost courans que nuls chevaus,
> Pour courir les mons & les vaux.'

Perhaps the most interesting of these vessels was the 'Tafourée', known to the Egyptians as 'ṭaifūr' or 'ṭaifūriya' meaning according to Maqqari (II, 89 and 334), plate or marble basin which indicates the shallowness of its hold.   Its importance was outlined by Mézières in the *Songe du vieil pèlerin* (B.N. MS.) fr. 22542, f. 338 vo, col. 1 and 2: 'Taforesse est un vaisseau de mer qui va à vingt ou à trente advirons et porte de XVI à XX chevaulx.   Et a le dit vaisseau une grant porte en la poupe et ne lui fault que deux ou troys paulmes d'eau.'   It was designed for landing men-at-arms on horseback ready for battle and for their retirement to the ships at the close of the fray.   Moreover, whereas the cost of the construction of a galley amounted to 1,400 and 1,500 florins and its upkeep 500, four taforesses could be equipped for the cost of each galley.   Cf. Mas Latrie, op. cit., II, 277 note; *Nicopolis*, 29, 171 note 55; Kindermann, op. cit., 61–2; Defréméry, in J.A., IV, 13 (1869).

material and ships were ready in October 1365 for a great
campaign.   Pierre dispatched the news to his Queen at
Nicosia and sent warning to all Cypriots not to go to the
lands of the Sultan and to those who were already in Muslim
territory to hasten back home.[1]   Finally, the order was
given to the fleet to sail early in the month.   The great
hopes of Pierre de Lusignan, Pierre de Thomas and
Philippe de Mézières were at last approaching realization.
The Turks had been beaten at Smyrna and Adalia.   Now
it was the turn of the Egyptians at Alexandria.

[1] Makhairas, § 168.

CHAPTER XV

THE CRUSADES OF PIERRE I DE LUSIGNAN: CAPTURE AND LOSS OF ALEXANDRIA

Object of the crusade.   Choice of Alexandria and causes.   Arrival, landing and preliminary skirmishes.   The Egyptian system of defence.   Entrance of Christians into city and flight of inhabitants.   Massacre and pillage. Evacuation of city.   Effect of news in Europe.   Negotiations for peace. Raids on Syrian coast.   Results of the Crusade

THE central event in the reign of Pierre I de Lusignan and, indeed, in the whole of the history of the crusade in the fourteenth century, was the capture and loss of Alexandria in 1365.   It is difficult to exaggerate the magnitude of its consequences on the relations between East and West in the Later Middle Ages in general and on those between the realms of Cyprus and Egypt in particular.   The sack of a city as flourishing and as strong as Alexandria naturally produced consternation among Muslims and brought joy to the hearts of Christians.   On the other hand, it embittered the Sultans against the Kings of Cyprus, for whom they held in store a punishment exceeded only by the complete suppression of the Armenian monarchy.

The preparations for the crusade, as has been shown in the previous chapter, were completed in September 1365, and the Christian fleet was anchored at that time in the waters of Rhodes.   The plan of the campaign, though probably drawn up with some precision by the King and his most trusted advisers and companions such as Pierre de Thomas and Philippe de Mézières, remained a closely guarded secret until the crusaders were on the high seas. The King's faith in the Italian units of his contingents was small, and his fear that they might betray his cause by warning the Sultan as to the object of the expedition in

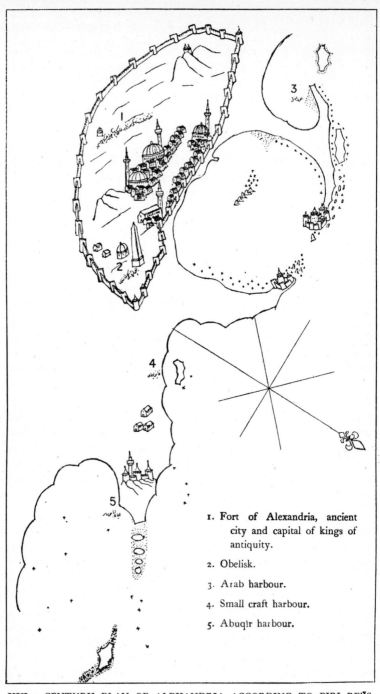

1. Fort of Alexandria, ancient city and capital of kings of antiquity.

2. Obelisk.

3. Arab harbour.

4. Small craft harbour.

5. Abuqir harbour.

XVITH CENTURY PLAN OF ALEXANDRIA ACCORDING TO PIRI RE'IS
(*Berlin MS. Diez A* 57 *fo.* 24d.)

return for lucrative trade privileges made him most reluctant to divulge any information concerning the real destination of the fleet.   The secrecy of Pierre's policy was more
than justified by the instructions which the Republic of
St. Mark had issued to its representatives, and which are
now accessible to us.[1]   The Doge enjoined his admirals
to accompany the crusaders, ostensibly as pious helpers,
but in reality as spies to discover and communicate the
King's designs to him.   Men were left to surmise, however,
and it was rumoured in the ranks that the armies of the
Cross were to be disembarked somewhere on the coast
of Asia Minor or Syria.   Even many of the leaders of the
host who moved in the higher circles remained in the dark,
and the King, the Apostolic Legate and the Chancellor
of Cyprus did not appear to discourage contradictory
rumours as long as the fleet had any contact with the soil
of Rhodes.   Finally, on Saturday, 4 October 1365,[2] the
troops mounted the galleys in readiness for the unknown.
When all had come on board, Pierre de Thomas delivered
a spirited sermon from the royal galley and gave his benediction to the holy enterprise.   Then the thronged gulf
of Rhodes resounded with the voices of men who cried, in
Mézières's words—'Vivat, vivat Petrus Jerusalem et Cypri
rex, contra Saracenos infideles'.[3]   Afterwards, orders were
given to the captains to follow the coast of Asia Minor as
far as the little island of Crambusa.[4]   It was only at this
juncture that the aim of the crusade was officially announced,
and the fleet was at once turned in the direction of Alex-

[1] The instructions are dated Venice, 26–27 June 1365.   For relevant
extracts, see Mas Latrie, *Hist. de Chypre*, III (Documents), 751–2.

[2] Machaut, ll. 2090–2, puts this date as Monday, 28 September, but he is
evidently wrong in this respect.   The 28th was a Sunday, and, further, the
acceptance of this date would upset the chronology of the campaign as
accepted by Machaut himself at a later stage and confirmed by other sources.
Iorga, *Mézières*, 284 n. 5, quotes Machaut's date erroneously as 29 September.   For further considerations on chronology, *vide infra*.

[3] *Vita S. Petri*, in Bolland., AS, III (29 Jan.), 629.

[4] Makhairas, § 171; Machaut, ll. 2101–2; Strambaldi, 67, where it is
mentioned as 'Rauso'; Amadi, 414.   Mézières' *Vita*, l.c., states that 'totum
exercitum versus Turquiam duxit'.   Crambusa is situated off the coast near
Cape Khelidonia and east of Myra in the gulf of Adalia.   Dawkins' notes to
Makhairas, II, 115–16; and Mas Latrie's notes to Machaut, 279–80.

andria.[1] The journey to the Egyptian coast lasted five days during which the galleys were at first tossed and dispersed by the winds and the waves, but the sea quietened down and Alexandria came within view on Thursday, 9 October, at the sixth hour of the day.[2]

---

[1] Machaut, ll. 1962 et seq., ascribes this decision to the advice of Percival de Coulogne before the departure from Rhodes and contends that the King hesitated at first in accepting this view. This seems somewhat doubtful as no other source confirms it and the idea of attacking Alexandria became known only after the fleet had sailed from Rhodes.

[2] Makhairas, l.c.; Machaut, ll. 2194–5 ('jour de la feste St. Denis'); Amadi, 414; Bustron, 262; Mézières' *Vita*, l.c. ('Erat autem dies Jovis et hora quasi sexta'), although this is contradicted by a later passage where the fall of Alexandria on the day following the arrival of the fleet is reported on 10 October, ('Et capta est civitas magna Alexandrie quasi hora nona, die Veneris, Octobris mense, anno sexagesimo quinto, quarta die)'. Mas Latrie suggests that 'decima die' should replace 'quarta die' in accordance with the *Legenda gloriosi patriarche Constantinopolitani sancti fratris Petri Thome*, by Jean de Carmesson, master of theology and 'minister' of the Franciscans in the Holy Land and Cyprus; *Hist. de Chypre*, II, 281 n. 1, 284. Strambaldi, 68, puts the date as 5 October, which is unacceptable. The *Secunda Vita Urbani V* (in Baluze, *Vit. Pap. Aven.*, ed. Mollat, I, 386) gives 11 October 1365.

The best of the Arabic sources leaves no room for doubt as to the date here adopted. *Al-Ilmām* of al-Nuwairī, who was in and fled from Alexandria at the time of the crusade (Berlin MS., Ahlwardt 9815–Wetz. 359, f. 101 vo) places the attack on Friday, 22 Muḥarram A.H. 767. According to the *Wüstenfeld-Mahler'sche Vergleichungs-Tabellen*, the 22 Muḥarram A.H. 767 corresponds to 9 October 1365; but as these tables often vary by a day or two in conversion of dates (see examples in *Nicopolis*, 150 note) and as Friday is explicitly mentioned by Nuwairī as the day of the attack, it may safely be assumed that it coincided with 10 October and that the arrival of the fleet took place on Thursday the 9th. There is, however, much discrepancy in the other Arabic sources. Maqrīzī (Oxford MS., Marsh. 260, non-foliated, *ad ann.* A.H. 767, Sulūk, III) and ibn Qāḍī Shuhba (*Continuation of Dhahabī's Annals*, vol. I, B.N. MS., fonds arabe 1600) fix the arrival on Wednesday, 21 Muḥarram. Ibn Taghrī Bardī (*Nujūm*, ed. Popper, V, pt. I, 194) says Alexandria was taken on Friday, 23 Muḥarram, and in this he is in agreement with ibn Duqmāq (*al-Jowhar*, Oxford MS. Digby Or. 28, f. 167 vo) and Bohtor (*Hist. of Beirūt*, B.N. MS., fonds arabe 1670, f. 13 vo, in margin). Ibn Khaldūn (*al-'Ibar*, V, 454) says the Cypriots cast anchor at Alexandria on 17 Muḥarram; and an anonymous B.M. MS. (Or. 1738, 66 ro) includes a vague reference to the fall of the city about the end of that month. Al-Nuwairī's evidence as an important eye-witness, supported by the independent statements of Western chroniclers, appears to be decisive in fixing 9 October for the arrival of the fleet and 10 for the commencement of hostilities. It is interesting to note that al-Nuwairī (f. 102 ro) mentions that the fleet was

It may be helpful at this stage to interrupt the story in chronological sequence of the events of the capture and loss of Alexandria in order to summarize the immediate causes leading to the choice of that city as the object of the present campaign.   The only contemporary Arabic author who witnessed the invasion gives us a view of the factors which seemed to him and, it must be assumed, also to his fellow-Egyptians as having led to this act of aggression.   Writing only about four or five months after the capture of Alexandria, al-Nuwairī [1] puts forward seven

---

first sighted on Wednesday, 20 Muḥarram (8 October), that is, a day earlier than in the rest of the sources.   This may be explained by the existence of Egyptian scouting vessels as well as watches from the height of observation towers.   Capitanovici (*Eroberung von Alexandria*, 32–7) makes an attempt at a digest of the chronology of the campaign.   On the Arabic side, his knowledge is limited to Maqrīzī and ibn Taghrī Bardī (*Abu'l-Maḥāsin*).

On al-Nuwairī and his work *al-Ilmām*, see following notes.

[1] His full name is Muḥammad b. Qāsim b. Muḥammad al-Nuwairī al-Mālikī al-Iskandarānī.   His work, *al-Ilmām bil-I'lām fīmā jarat bihi al-Aḥkām wal-Umūr al-maqḍiya fī Waq'at al-Iskandariya*, held as anonymous by Ahlwardt (Berlin Catalogue, no. 9815), bears the author's name twice (ff. 120 ro and 169 ro) as al-Nuwairī.   A short biography of him occurs in ibn Ḥajar's *Durar*, IV, 142, no. 375.   See also Ḥājji Khalīfa (ed. Flügel), II, 107, no. 2136; Gildemeister, *Ueber arabisches Schiffwesen*, 431; Herzsohn, *Überfall Alexandrien's*, xii, n. 6; Kahle, *Katastrophe des mittelalterlichen Alexandria*, 154; Atiya, article *Rhodes* in EI, III.

Little is known about al-Nuwairī beyond what he says about himself in his book.   He came to Alexandria at the end of A.H. 737 (July A.D. 1337) on a pilgrimage to its holy shrines; but finding it both prosperous and beautiful, he settled there and worked as a copyist for its wealthy people.   He fled with the fugitives when attacked by the crusaders and returned shortly afterwards to find the streets covered with the carcasses of animals and its great edifices either pillaged or burnt down to the ground.   He began to write *al-Ilmām* in Jumādā II, A.H. 767 (February 1366) and finished it in Dhulḥijja A.H. 775 (May 1374).   Cf. ff. 120 ro–21 ro.

Al-Ilmām consists of three volumes—the first two are in Berlin (Wetz, 359–60) and the third in Cairo (Hist. 1449).   Another MS. dating from the eighth Hijra century exists in India (Bankipore 2335).   A B.M. MS. (Or. 606) includes some extracts from *al-Ilmām*.   Reference here is made to the Berlin and Cairo MSS.

Although originally intended to be a history of the events of 1365 at Alexandria, *al-Ilmām* was enlarged by the addition of much extraneous material, literary and otherwise, which rendered the relevant historical parts of it a small portion, compared with the bulk of the work.   The irrelevant sections are, however, not utterly without use.   The first volume, for ex-

reasons for the descent of the Christians on the city. The
first of these, he contends, was the persecution of the
Eastern Christians, who, in the year 755 (1354/55) during
the reign of Sultan Qalāwūn, were all dismissed from the
government service, forced to wear undignified clothes
to distinguish them from Muslims, and subjected to other
forms of vexatious treatment.[1]   The second was the
Sultan's refusal to grant Pierre's request to be allowed to
follow a Cypriot tradition and receive his crown at Ṣūr
(Tyre).[2]   The third was the lenient treatment of the
Frankish corsairs in the waters of Alexandria, which convinced the Christians that the city was inadequately defended
and would be an easy prey to its attacker.[3]   The fourth,
fifth and sixth include incidents of pillage at Rosetta and
Abuqīr in the neighbourhood of Alexandria which confirmed the King's belief in the defencelessness of the
Egyptian coast.[4]   The seventh was the rising of the mob in
an attempt to massacre the 'Franks' in Alexandria.[5]   Such
were the causes of the impending invasion as visualized by
al-Nuwairī.   In fourteenth-century Europe, on the other
hand, much propaganda had been circulated in order to
excite men's desire to seize that great city for Christendom.[6]
Alexandria was the veritable 'Queen of the Mediterranean'.
Its numerous and wonderful funduqs abounded in spices,
silks and wares of all kinds. Almost all trading countries of
the East and West had representatives and consuls in its busy
marts. Alexandria was the terminus of the Oriental trade
routes and the beginning of the Occidental. The customs derived from the passage of goods through it provided the
Sultan with a source of immense revenues which he used
for his self-aggrandizement at the expense of the neigh-

---

ample, includes considerable information on Arab ships and nautical science
(ff. 123 vo et seq.) which the author must have gathered from Egyptian
sailors in the town; and the third volume contains an account of the Cypriot
attack of 1367 on Ṭarābulus (f. 27 ro et seq., *vide infra*).   M. Ét. Combe is
now preparing a French version of the important sections on Alexandria.

[1] Berlin MS. Wetz. 359, ff. 95 ro et vo.

[2] ib., ff. 94 vo–95 ro.   [3] ib., f. 95 ro et vo.

[4] ib., ff. 95 vo–96 vo.   [5] ib., ff. 96 vo–97 ro.

[6] *vide supra*, e.g. Pitoti and other propagandists in previous chapters in
Part I.

bouring Christian states.   The fall of Alexandria would
necessarily minimize this danger and offer the invader a field
of untold booty.   Moreover, its strategic position was a
unique one.   A Christian monarch in possession of its harbour and fortifications could with a small fleet intercept all
communications between Egypt and the external world.
Further, a well-trained army could sally from this stronghold
into Egypt itself and proceed on the road to Cairo and extin-
guish the empire that had robbed Rome of its heritage in
the Holy Land.   Such considerations as these could not
have escaped the ambitious Pierre I de Lusignan.   If we
believe al-Nuwairī, the King had his spies and accomplices
within the town itself, and these made his path of conquest
an easy one.[1]   At the time of the expedition, the invader
had three distinct advantages over his enemy.   In the first
place, the governor (wālī)[2] of the city, Khalīl ibn Ṣalāḥ-
al-Dīn ibn ʿArrām, was absent on a pilgrimage to Mekka;
secondly, the garrison was depleted and the central administration was unmindful of the need for reinforcing it owing
to the long and undisturbed peace enjoyed by Alexandria;
and thirdly, it was the season of the Nile inundation when
all the Delta was submerged and dispatch of speedy relief
from Cairo was an impossibility.[3]   The internal state of
Egypt, too, was a very unhappy one.   There was no strong
Sultan at the time to lead the people and to weather the
attack on the country.   A boy of hardly eleven years of age,

---

[1] op. cit., f. 106 ro.   Al-Nuwairī asserts that a certain Shams-al-Dīn ibn
Ghurāb, secretary (Kātib) of the Diwan of Alexandria was in Pierre's pay
for that purpose and that his body was later cleft in two and hung on the
Rosetta gate of the city as a penalty for treachery.   In the course of this
story, al-Nuwairī suggests that the King visited the city in the habit of a
merchant before the battle and was shown round it by ibn Ghurāb.   Although this is evidently a legend, the moral of the whole story is that Pierre
must have been aware of the internal weakness of Alexandria; see also f. 98 ro.

[2] After the conquest of Alexandria, its governor was raised to the rank of
'Nā'ib', usually an amīr of a thousand, in order to strengthen its defence.   The
first 'Nā'ib' of Alexandria was Boktomor who succeeded Khalīl b. ʿArrām.
Ibn Taghrī Bardī (al-Nujūm, ed. Popper), V, 195; Ibn Duqmāq (al-Jauhar,
Oxford MS. Digby Or. 28), f. 168 ro.

[3] al-Nuwairī, ff. 100 vo–101 vo.   On f. 1 vo, the author says that
Alexandria had remained unattacked and unimpaired under Muslim rule
since its conquest in the days of ʿAmr.

Sha'bān, had been placed on the throne as a figurehead by Yalbogha, the strongest of the Mamlūk amīrs and a kind of King-maker of the time, who directed the affairs of state without scruple for his own ends. The Mamlūk ruling class was factious and Egypt as a whole groaned under the weight of Yalbogha's exactions, rapacity and cruelty.[1] Whether the leaders of the crusade were informed as to how things stood in the Sultan's realm is difficult to know from the Western sources. The existence of European and Cypriot agents in Alexandria, however, suggests that they were, and a similar conclusion may be inferred from al-Nuwairī's own statements [2] on the Oriental side.

On the other hand, it would be a serious error to exaggerate the ease with which Alexandria might be taken at this moment. The fortifications of the city were famous throughout the West. Its walls were invulnerable, its towers high and solid, and its numerous entrances [3] furnished with gates of strong timber reinforced with steel. The King realized the hardships which he had to face in the ensuing encounter and thus proceeded into the Old Harbour [4] with great caution and patience. Although it

---

[1] Weil, *Abbasidenchalifat*, I, 510 et seq.; Muir, *Mamelukes*, 97 et seq.

According to ibn Taghrī Bardī (ed. Popper, V, 194) and ibn Duqmāq (Oxford MS. Digby Or. 28, f. 167 vo.), the Sultan was at the time at Siriaqos in the Delta.

[2] op. cit., f. 98 ro.

[3] The fourteenth-century gates of Alexandria are a subject of archaeological interest. Al-Nuwairī (op. cit., ff. 37 vo, 105 vo, 106 ro et vo) makes mention of seven of them: Bāb al-Dīwān (Porte de la Douane), Bāb al-Bahr (Porta Maris, Porte de l'Esplanade) and al-Bāb al-Akhdar (i.e. the Green Gate, known also as Bāb al-Gharb or the Gate of the West) on the northern side; Bāb al-Khokha (Gate of Necropolis, Porte des Catacombes, Bāb al-Qarāfa or Cemetery Gate) on the western side; Bāb Rashīd on the eastern side facing Rosetta; and Bāb al-Sidra (Bāb al-'Amūd or Gate of the Pillar—of Pompey, Porte de la Colonne), and Bāb al-Zuhrī on the south side. The last three are usually known as abwāb al-Barr or Land-Gates. There is, however, an ambiguous reference to a certain 'Bāb al-Barr' (fo. 105 vo); but, judging from the general context, this can only be identified as one of the two south gates opening on the Damanhūr and Cairo road. Cf. fifteenth-century Vatican plan of Alexandria; R. Pococke's plan of the remains of the city walls in 1743; Jondet, *Atlas d'Alexandrie*; Kahle, op. cit., 142–3.

[4] Alexandria had (and still has) two harbours divided by a land tongue which connected it with the Pharos Island. This was a real island in

ALEXANDRIA IN THE FIFTEENTH CENTURY
MS. COD. URBIN. 277 IN THE VATICAN.

was possible for him to land on the day of his arrival in the waters of Alexandria (9 October), he preferred to wait until the following morning and was content with sending a reconnaissance boat which returned at full speed under volleys of Saracen arrows.[1]   The galleys were brought together into one solid block floating in the middle of the harbour.   The natives, who at first thought them trading vessels about to bring more wealth and not complete ruin to their town, began to have misgivings as to their fate when they noticed this strange formation in mid-harbour.   Yet, with unusual scepticism they doubted whether such a fleet would be able to land sufficient men to harm a city so strong.[2]   After nightfall, a series of lanterns were lighted along the walls as a precautionary measure against the enemy filtering into the town under cover of darkness. Nevertheless, Christian spies are said to have landed in native garb during the night to ascertain the state of the defence.[3]

On Friday 10 October, from daybreak onwards, large numbers of the inhabitants began to emerge from the town to Pharos Island and to the beach.   Some were spectators, and others vendors.   There was much buying and selling and bargaining [4] in full Oriental fashion, notwithstanding the impending calamity.   They had no experience of wars or sieges at home and in their ignorance they came out of

antiquity, and it retained its original name, although it had long been connected with the mainland.   It is, however, worthy of note that the Arabic word 'jazīra' (island) is often used for peninsula, e.g. Jazīrat al-'Arab, that is, Arabian Peninsula.   The Eastern or New Harbour, now used chiefly by fishermen, was in the Middle Ages reserved for Christian ships, and Bāb al-Baḥr and al-Bāb al-Akhḍar opened in its neighbourhood.   This harbour was known in the fourteenth century as Baḥr al-Silsila, i.e. the Sea of the Chain, probably because its entrance was chained at night to guard Muslim goods and ships against the maraudings of piratical bands.   The Peninsula, now covered with buildings, was at the time of the crusade an open sandy place with but few buildings.   The oldest plans of the city (Vat. MS. Cod. Urb. 277, and the majority of those of Piri Re'īs in the Istanbul and Dresden MSS.) show the walls in direct contiguity with the New Harbour, but a strip of land separates them from Baḥr al-Silsila.   This is significant as will be seen later in regard to the movements of the inhabitants after the invasion of the city.

[1] Al-Nuwairī, op. cit., f. 102 ro.   [2] ib., f. 102 ro et vo.
[3] id., l.c.   [4] ib., f. 102 vo.

their stronghold in the face of death. Later, the feeble
garrison, consisting of a small band of volunteers and a
disorderly corps of Bedouins, joined the new arrivals, presumably with the intention of preventing the disembarkation of the hostile forces. These Arabs had no coats of
mail and their arms merely consisted of their swords and
their javelins.[1] Besides, in the absence of Khalīl b. Ṣalāḥ-
al-Dīn b. ʿArrām on his pilgrimage,[2] the town had no
experienced governor to confine the inhabitants to the walls
and to organize the defence. The acting governor, one
Janghara,[3] was a man of feeble and indecisive character.
In his hands, a situation which was crying for immediate
action, was rapidly deteriorating and drifting towards complete disaster. When a Maghribine merchant, ʿAbdallah
by name, approached him to urge that people should return
to safety within the town, those who owned establishments
outside the walls opposed the suggestion and insisted on
remaining outside to fight for their endangered property.
Janghara gave way to the unwise resolution of these latter.[4]
Perhaps the only laudable measure of defence taken by him,
was the obvious one of barricading the three great portals
of the Green Gate which faced the Old Harbour.[5] While
crowds of natives lined the coast, shouting wildly and
showering insults on the invaders, the first galley began at
the third hour of the day (*hora tertiarum*) to make its way
towards the land.[6] A small corps of Maghribine volunteers with drawn swords waded into the shallow water in
a desperate attempt to intercept the landing and burn the
ship. They called for fire and slings, but no one seemed
to take heed of their request. After much confusion and

---

[1] Al-Nuwairī, f. 103 ro. Al-Nuwairī describes these Arabs as galloping
away on hearing the rejoicing of women, though they were only armed with
sword and javelin. On a previous occasion, he says (f. 100 ro) that 'when
the Franks shot their arrows at them (the Arabs), they flew away like pigeons'.

[2] ib., f. 100 vo.

[3] He was only an amīr of ten.   [4] ib., f. 103 vo.

[5] ib., f. 102 ro. This was done on the day of the battle (10 October).
This gate was filled up with stones and mortar. Afterwards, it was repaired
and opened during the tenure of office of the amīr Sayf-al-Dīn al-Akaz as
governor of Alexandria.

[6] ib., f. 102 vo; *Vita S. Petri*, l.c.; Machaut, ll. 2330 et seq.

delay, fire was rushed to them, but this being of feeble
nature, fell into the water and was extinguished. A
skirmish therefore became inevitable with the unaided
Maghribines. The occupants of the vessel had the advantage of a position in contrast to that of their opponents
who were becoming involved in deep water. Only a
few blows were needed to exterminate this foolhardy
body in its entirety, and the first batch of crusaders came
ashore.[1]   They were followed by those from other galleys,
and other fighters landed, both mounted and dismounted,
all ready for the fray.   Pierre de Thomas, in full armour
and with a Cross in his hand, stood on a lofty bridge projecting from his ship over the water, and blessed the
Christians as they leaped ashore.[2]   The first to land is
said to have been Amé III, comte de Génève, who was
nearly overpowered by a multitude of Saracens, but was
saved by Simon de Norès and Jean du Morf who rushed
to his rescue.[3]   Other knights who distinguished themselves in the landing included Perceval de Coulogne,
Brémont de la Voulte, Hugh de Lusignan, Prince of Galilee,
and even the King himself.[4]   Meanwhile, Ferlino d'Airasca
and the contingent of the Hospital landed unexpectedly
in the New Harbour to the left of the first encounter and
attacked the Egyptians from the rear, and the defence was
thus caught between two fires.[5]   The Arabic chronicler
marks the great speed with which the crusaders forced their
landing in spite of the volleys of arrows and missiles
showered upon them by the defence.[6]   The scene that
followed must have been one of utter disorder and panic.
The vendors and spectators who had miscalculated the
speed of the enemy's disembarkation lingered in their un-
safe quarters until they were suddenly attacked by the
armed bands and many of them were trampled down before
they reached the confines of the city.[7]   The only semi-

[1] Al-Nuwairī, f. 103 vo.   [2] *Vita S. Petri*, l.c.
[3] Machaut, ll. 2258 et seq.   [4] ib., ll. 2294 et seq.
[5] ib., ll. 2499 et seq.
[6] Al-Nuwairī, l.c. This may be explained partly by the use of the
'taforesse'. According to Machaut, ll. 2426 et seq., the number of the disembarked crusaders was about 8,000 besides the Hospitallers who descended
on the eastern coast.   [7] ib., f. 103 vo.

organized resistance was that of the Bedouin corps whose vanguard was composed of infantry and its rear of cavalry.[1] The foot could hardly withstand the shock tactics of the mailed knight, while the arrows of the Christians stung the Muslim horse in the rear and caused a stampede in the lines.[2] Before a pitched battle was even begun, the Egyptian forces were put to flight and the infuriated horses added to the havoc. Janghara himself sustained a painful injury from an enemy arrow during the flight and bitterly repented his rejection of the Maghribine's advice when it was too late.[3] Now it was only a matter of every man trying to save his own life by hurriedly taking refuge within the walls before the final closing of the gates. So numerous were the corpses of the dead at the maritime entrances of the city that the gates were shut with great difficulty.[4] Those who remained outside were massacred. A body of thirty archers in a religious hospice in the cemetery used for the celebration of pious offices were caught on its roof and slaughtered so that their blood flowed into the rain-pipes and was seen with horror, coagulated and dried up at the foot of the building, for days afterwards.[5] The Christians had won the day beyond doubt, but Alexandria remained intact within its walls, since the gates were closed in spite of the efforts of the crusaders to gain a passage through them. It may be noted that Machaut estimates the man-power inside the city at twenty thousand strong and speaks of all manner of artillery being installed on the walls and especially over the gates and in the towers.[6]

At this juncture, the King called off all offensive operations.[7] He wished to give his men a period of repose after the landing skirmish and the pursuit of the routed Arabs, and at the same time ordered the rest of the horses to be disembarked on the 'island' which was then com-

---

[1] Al-Nuwairī, l.c.   [2] ib., ff. 103 vo–104 ro.
[3] ib., f. 105 vo.   [4] Machaut, ll. 2531–5.
[5] Al-Nuwairī, f. 104 ro et vo. The said body of archers was known as that of Qā'at al-Qarāfa, for whom a 'ribāṭ', i.e. Hospice, had been recently built outside the Sea Gate (Bab al-Baḥr) by a pious shaikh named Abu-'Abdallah Muḥammad b. Sallām.
[6] Machaut, ll. 2538 et seq.   [7] ib., ll. 2550–7.

pletely in the crusaders' hands,[1] while the leaders held a council of war to consider the tactics to be followed in the forthcoming siege and encounters.[2]   It was in this council that a group of discontented barons had an opportunity to express their views on the whole campaign.   One of them [3] addressed a plea to the King for the withdrawal of the army from Egypt to save futile Christian bloodshed in a wild adventure.   Alexandria, the speaker contended, was a very strong city, its resources multiple, and its walls insurmountable.   Moreover, it enclosed a large and active garrison, amply supplied with an artillery which they could use with ability and with effect against any assailant.   It was not a question of valour, but of expediency, to avoid an attack whose results appeared so hopeless.   Even if the campaign were carried beyond Alexandria into the country, it would have to be remembered that there were no fortresses on the road to Cairo or even to Jerusalem where the crusaders might take refuge in an emergency.[4]   Other barons listened attentively and then commented upon the speech as the plain truth.[5]   The King, who must have been disheartened at their suggestion of retreat, had to appeal to their sense of honour and loyalty lest they should desert the holy enterprise.[6]   Finally, it was agreed to try to seize the city by storm,[7] and a reward of one thousand gold florins was promised to the first man who should mount the walls, five hundred to the second, and three hundred to the third.[8]

---

[1] ib., ll. 2558 et seq.   [2] ib., ll. 2616 et seq.

[3] ib., l. 2640, where Machaut describes the speaker as 'un amiraut'. Whether this was the admiral of Rhodes or Cyprus is difficult to say with precision.   Iorga, *Mézières*, 294 and note 2, suggests that it was the admiral of the Hospitallers and asserts that both the admirals of Rhodes and Cyprus were among the 'rebels'.   The word 'amiraut', however, is used by Machaut, l. 2699, rather loosely and may be taken for 'baron'.

[4] ib., ll. 2650 et seq.   [5] ib., ll. 2705.
[6] ib., ll. 2706 et seq.   [7] ib., ll. 2738 et seq.
[8] ib., ll. 2752–57.

> 'Avec ce, le crieur cria
> Que le premier qui montera
> Sus les murs, ara sans doubtance
> Mil petis florins de Florence;
> Li secons en ara v[c],
> Li tiers ccc, . . .'

While these deliberations were in progress on the part of the Christians outside the city, Janghara and his men were actively engaged in a final bid to save what was left inside.

In the first place, they concentrated most of their artillery and forces on the section of the wall facing the enemy in the island, between Bāb al-Baḥr (Porta Maris) and the western extremity of the city. In the second place, the acting governor dispatched all the gold and silver in the state treasury to Cairo by the land gate.[1] In the third place, the 'Frankish' consuls and merchants numbering fifty were seized and removed inland as hostages under special guard. At the outset, they were disposed to resist the order for their arrest. As a result, one of them was executed, and the rest preferred to abide by the will of their captors rather than succumb to the same fate as their companion. They were led in chains by one of the land gates into the country in the direction of Damanhūr.[2] Meanwhile, it seems possible that the guards were enjoined to inform the central administration of the critical state of Alexandria and urge the relief army to come at once to its succour. As to the organization of the defence within the city, it is appropriate at this stage to reveal its strength and weakness in the light of the events that followed. The Egyptian concentration was more or less limited to the western part of the north wall beyond Bāb al-Baḥr. Several reasons were advanced in support of this tactical measure. This quarter of the city appeared to be the only vulnerable spot. It faced the 'Island' and the Old Harbour where the Christians and their fleet were stationed, and the strictest vigilance in this direction was imperative.

---

[1] Al-Nuwairī, op. cit., f. 105 vo, recounts the story of saving the treasure. Janghara and a few followers, he says, rode out of the town wading through the sea water to Bāb al-Khokha whereby they re-entered the city to the Treasury. Janghara, who was previously wounded and somewhat disabled by an arrow during the flight (vide supra, 356), could not reach the walls before the closing of the gates and was therefore forced to approach the city by riding to the western gate. Cf. Kahle, op. cit., 147.

[2] Al-Nuwairī, l.c. The guards entrusted with this task were known as 'Jabaliya', i.e. police corps; Kahle, 147. For the land gates, vide supra, 352, n. 3. Damanhūr is, of course, the present capital of the Beḥaira Province west of the Rosetta Branch of the Nile in the Delta.

The rest of the wall was regarded as safe and even un-
approachable by the enemy, since the waters of the New
Harbour on the north side and of the Khalīj (the modern
Maḥmūdiya Canal) on the south side formed two natural
moats which cut the Christian communications with the
parts beyond. One loophole in this system of defence,
however, proved fatal. Shams-al-Dīn ibn Ghurāb, who
was later accused of treachery and of being in Pierre's pay,[1]
supported by another principal official, one Shams-al-Dīn
ibn 'Odhaiba, had decided to close the inner gates of the
custom house for fear that foreign residents might remove
dutiable goods to the city and thus rob the state.[2] As a
result, the wall became inaccessible from these inner gates.
Further, there was a lofty tower [3] in the area lying between
Bāb al-Baḥr (Porta Maris) and Bāb al-Dīwān (Porte de la
Douane); and no porches or side passages connected the
outlying parts of the wall on the two sides of this tower.
Thus the troops defending Bāb al-Baḥr had no quick means
of coming to protect Bāb al-Dīwān in case of an unforeseen
emergency. On the other hand, the latter and undefended
gate was as vulnerable as the former, and, moreover, it was
not as strong as al-Bāb al-Akhḍar (the Green Gate) with
its three massive portals. This proved to be the decisive
factor in the great tragedy.

It is, however, doubtful whether the Christians noticed
all these facts at the outset. Machaut, indeed, tells us
that after the final agreement to take the city by storm,
the King enjoined Perceval de Coulogne straightway to
lead the assault on Bāb al-Dīwān (Porte de la Douane [4]).
Nevertheless, al-Nuwairī, who witnessed the events of the
siege and made a faithful record of all its developments,

---

[1] *vide supra*, 351, n.1.

[2] Al-Nuwairī (Wetz. 359), ff. 105 vo–106 ro. An open and walled space
is to be noticed within the city next to the Porte de la Douane in the Cod. Urb.
(*vide supra*) plan. This was evidently reserved for storage of dutiable goods
and was therefore uninhabited. With the closing of the outlying doors, this
space would furnish the attackers with a completely undefended quarter, once
they began to filter into the city.

[3] It may be inferred from al-Nuwairī's work (Wetz. 360, f. 186 vo) that
this was the Ḍirghām Tower.

[4] Machaut, ll. 2766 et seq.

tells a somewhat different story from that of Machaut.
The Christians, he says, made their first assault, not on
Bāb al-Dīwān, but on Bāb al-Baḥr, which was situated
nearer their quarters on the 'Island'.   On approaching the
wall in this direction, they had a hot reception.   Volleys
of Muslim arrows and showers of stones from their catapults hindered the advance of the crusaders.   The failure
of this attempt was followed by another unsuccessful
device.   A large vessel filled with burning naphtha was
pushed with the points of spears towards Bāb al-Baḥr in
the hope that the flames might reach and devour it, thus
clearing the way for an influx of crusaders into the city
for a hand-to-hand battle.   In this, the spearmen were
again brought to a standstill at a considerable distance by
the watchfulness and activity of the Egyptian archers.
The vessel was deserted on the way and the gate remained
intact.   The Christians lost a few of their number in the
attempt, and the survivors retired to the shore of the
Eastern Harbour.   It was here that these men discovered
the only accessible gap in the defence in that neighbourhood.   Looking up to the wall above Bāb al-Dīwān beyond
the tower to the east as far as the New Harbour, they found,
to their great joy, that it was undefended and that there
was even no moat [1] to impede an attack.   Ladders were
therefore rushed to that empty quarter, and numbers of
crusaders mounted to its battlements, while others burnt
the Porte de la Douane [2] in readiness for the subsequent
onrush of the rest of their companions.   The Muslims on
the other side of the wall, debarred by the tower from
reaching that spot and having no hope of attaining it by
the inner gates of the custom house before the Christians
should arrive, stood helplessly gazing for a period.   When

[1] Al-Nuwairī (Wetz. 360), f. 186 vo, explains the reason why there was
no moat round this part of the wall.   In olden times, the sea had washed its
foot and formed a natural moat to it.   With the passing of time, however,
the sea receded for a distance and the unbroken peace of the city did not raise
the question of digging any moats in that area as a substitute.

[2] According to the *Vita S. Petri*, l.c., the entry of the Christians into
Alexandria took place at midday (*Hora nona*).   Al-Nuwairī, f. 107 vo, says
that the actual pillage and burning inside the city began early in the after-
noon and continued till late on Saturday.

they ultimately realized that the day was lost to them,
they began to evacuate the northern quarters of the city in
a desperate attempt to reach the land gates and save their
lives.[1]

Machaut provides us with some interesting details of
the fighting on the Christian side prior to their triumphant
entry into the town.   A Scottish knight who appears to
have made the assault on the wall lost his life in the attempt.[2]
After the first retreat, the King was the first to mount his
horse, and, with his barons and the Knights Hospitallers,
proceeded to reinforce the defeated lines and to conduct
the siege operations himself.[3]   One sailor discovered that
a mouth of the Khalīj (canal), which conveyed the necessary
fresh water from the Nile into the city and flowed into the
Eastern Harbour underneath the wall near the Porte de La
Douane, was undefended, and so he made his way through
this opening and went up to the ramparts by the staircase
from within.[4]   Meanwhile, an agile squire managed with
difficulty to climb the wall from the outside.[5]   It may be
assumed that these two assisted in the installing of the
ladders for others to join them.   'Avant! signeurs, montez,
montez!' cried the two pioneers to their companions below;
and it was on hearing their voices, according to Machaut,
that confusion began in the Saracen ranks on the other
side of the wall.[6]

The havoc that followed on the flight of the inhabitants
is vividly described by al-Nuwairī who accompanied them.
Some, he says, descended from the walls by means of ropes,
and, in their desperate hurry, a few fell to the ground and
were either disabled or killed.   Others crowded to the
land gates and hastened to take refuge in the neighbouring
towns and villages such as al-Baslaqon and al-Karyūn and
in the fields on the way to Damanhūr.   One merchant,
who put all his savings amounting to six thousand dinars

[1] Al-Nuwairī (Wetz. 359), ff. 105 vo–106 ro.
[2] Machaut, ll. 2828–33.
[3] ib., ll. 2862 et seq.

> 'Li rois estoit sus son cheval,
> Et les freres de l'Ospital
> Environ lui, trestous ensamble.'

[4] ib., ll. 2910–19.   [5] ib., ll. 2920–2.   [6] ib., ll. 2923 et seq.

in a purse and joined the fleeing refugees by the Rosetta Gate dropped the purse in the struggle for life and was unable to stoop to recover it owing to the pressure of human masses in search of safety. Those who escaped with some of their treasures were plundered by the marauding Arabs on the unguarded roads and in the open fields.[1]

At this stage, al-Nuwairī disappears with the refugees from the scene of battle, and we have to look elsewhere for information about subsequent events. Although he tells us that the banners of the Cross were planted high on the walls and the towers, and that there was nothing left for the inhabitants except flight, Machaut gives sufficient details about armed bands that still remained in the central streets and about the fighting which ensued in the heart of the city in spite of its occupation, through the rest of the day and during the night. First we hear of a savage massacre of inhabitants and tardy refugees. Men hid themselves in secret places, in the gardens and even in cisterns. The carnage was so great, that an estimate of more than twenty thousand dead is given by Machaut.[2] It was a massacre unequalled since the days of Pharaoh[3] in Alexandria. While many of the crusaders were busy at their task of exterminating the dwellers in the city, the King and a group of armed knights decided to sally forth from the walls in order to destroy a bridge[4] over the Khalīj (Canal). This was an important strategic point and its occupation would prevent the Sultan's army of relief from investing the city on all sides, and confine the forthcoming fighting to the area which the crusaders had occupied before their entrance into Alexandria[5]

---

[1] Al-Nuwairī, ff. 105 vo, 106 vo, 107 ro.

[2] op. cit., ll. 2950 et seq.

> 'Nos gens queurent de rue en rue,
> Chascuns ocist, mehaingne ou tue.
> Tué en ont plus de xx. mille.'

[3] ib., ll. 2978–9.

> 'N'onques si grant occision
> Ne fu dès le temps Pharaon.'

[4] This bridge appears on the Cod. Urb. (*vide supra*) plan of Alexandria.

[5] Machaut, ll. 2980 et seq.

proper. Moreover, in the course of the day, they had already burnt two of the land gates—Bāb Rashīd and Bāb al-Zuhrī [1]—without thinking of the consequences in the event of the arrival of the Sultan's army from Cairo. Apart from enabling the entrapped citizens to save themselves by walking out of these permanent openings as occasion offered, the burnt gates would necessarily furnish the attackers with two vulnerable loopholes in the defence. The crusaders had no time to construct new gates to replace the old, and Pierre must have realized that the most expedient measure was the destruction of the bridge which connected the Cairo road with those two gates over the Canal. So the small contingent under the personal command of the King marched to one of the land gates on the south,[2] that is, either Bāb al-Zuhrī or Bāb al-Sidra leading to the Cairo road. As soon as they emerged from their stronghold, they were harassed by armed bands of warriors numbering hundreds and thousands [3] who were in ambush in the fields beyond. Hard fighting then took place, and only with great difficulty did the crusaders regain their headquarters without reaching their objective.[4] It is said that Pierre's life was seriously endangered in the last skirmish. On his return to safety, he spent the little that was left of the day in posting guards at the gates and supervising the defence, and at night retired to one of the large towers to rest.[5] This was denied him. Under cover of night, a large body of Saracens forced their way into the city by one of the southern gates,[6] and the King was roused to organize the battle that ensued in the 'Rue

[1] Kahle, 152.

[2] ib., l. 3004, where Machaut calls it 'La porte dou Poivre'. This occurs again a little later; *vide infra.*

[3] ib., ll. 3006–8.

> 'Quant li roys vint enmi les chans,
> Il vit, à milliers & à cens,
> Les Sarrasins par grans tropiaus.'

[4] ib., ll. 3010 et seq.   [5] ib., ll. 3112 et seq.

[6] Machaut, l. 3183, calls it St. Mark's Gate and says that some call it 'La Porte de la Poivre'; *vide supra.* As to the numbers Machaut (ll. 3230–43, 3242) appears to exaggerate in his estimate; he puts the Saracens at 10,000 and the Christians who fought them at 40 or 50 men-at-arms.

de la Poivre'.[1]   In spite of a crushing numerical superiority on the Saracen side, the Christians fought with incredible heroism and cleared the invaders out of the city.[2]   This virtually marked the end of serious fighting and incursions during the remaining period of the occupation of Alexandria.

After the fall and complete subjugation of the city, the King convoked a general council comprising all his barons, men-at-arms, sergeants and even valets, who met on the 'Island'[3] to consider the new situation.   Opinion in this assembly was divided.   The King, Pierre de Thomas and Philippe de Mézières[4] strongly advanced the view that the crusaders should not evacuate the city, but defend their conquest when the Sultan's army eventually came to dispute it with them.   On the other hand, the majority held a completely different view, which was voiced by the Vicomte de Turenne.   It was, he argued, impossible to retain and defend owing to the smallness of the Christian garrison, while the gates were open to an enemy whose overwhelming numbers[5] would seize the crusaders 'in a trap'.[6]   The members of the foreign contingents who

---

[1] Machaut, ll. 3215–16.   [2] ib., ll. 3256 et seq.
[3] ib., ll. 3288 et seq.

> 'Que toute maniere de gent,
> Gens d'armes, vallet et sergent,
> Fussent tuit à une assemblée,
> En une place grant & lée
> Qu'est entre la ville & la mer.'

[4] It is interesting to note that the King had announced in the customs building (Dīwān) his intention to grant Philippe de Mézières one-third of the city of Alexandria, where he could establish and develop his new Order of the Passion. *Chevalerie de la Passion*, ff. 15 vo–18 vo; *Orat. Traged.*, f. 194; cf. Iorga, *Mézières*, 299 and notes 3 and 4.

[5] Machaut, l. 3348; 'v.ᶜ fois v.ᶜ mil hommes' were the vicomte's words.
[6] ib., ll. 3363–6.

> 'Quant li soudans chevauchera:
> Tuit serons pris à la ratiere.
> Si que, sire, en nulle maniere
> Je ne conseille la demeure.'

The author of the *Anonimalle Chronicle*, 51–3, gives a curious episode, perhaps to heighten the dramatic effect of the capture and loss of Alexandria. Three days after the occupation of the city, he says, a scouting detachment of thirty Saracens came in contact with the Christians.   One of that Saracen

wanted booty and not a permanent conquest supported the vicomte with all their power.[1] Even a few of the royal army including Jean de Sur, the admiral of Cyprus, and the King's two brothers were among the malcontents who cried openly for evacuation and flight.[2] It was a hopeless situation. Neither the persuasive influence of the Legate and the Chancellor nor the exhortation of the King was of any avail. The soldiers were determined not to remain on the Egyptian coast longer than was necessary to fill their fleet with booty from Alexandria, and indeed seven days were spent in plunder.

During this short period of Christian occupation, the city was plundered and ruined to an extent hard to realize. It would be idle to make a full inventory of all the objects of art removed, all the warehouses pillaged, and all the funduqs, schools, palaces, mosques and even whole quarters burnt down and destroyed by the host of God. Yet no history of this crusade could be complete without quoting a few notable examples to demonstrate the greatness of perhaps the greatest catastrophe in the annals of Alexandria. Al-Nuwairī, who returned to the city after the crusaders had left it, gives a vivid picture of that staggering scene of disaster. All the gold and silver upon which the invaders could lay their hands, all the light articles made of precious metal or of brass, all the silks, carpets and valuable cloths, were carried to their ships in huge loads. Camels, horses and donkeys were used for the conveyance of the booty, and when their ships were overladen and they had no more use for the beasts of burden, they stabbed them with their swords and lances, and left them dead or dying on the beach until the Muslims burnt their corpses after the recovery of the city.[3] Warehouses without number were set aflame. An eye-witness,

corps galloped to the Christian side and announced himself as an old member of the Knighthood of St. John of Rhodes in captivity in Egypt. He informed them that the Sultan was coming to Alexandria with an army sufficient to surround the Christians and kill every one of them. On hearing this, the chronicler asserts, the crusaders left the city and took to their ships.

[1] ib., ll. 3369 et seq.
[2] *Vita S. Petri*, l.c.; *Oratio Traged.*, f. 194 vo; cf. Iorga, o.c., 301–2.
[3] Al-Nuwairī, ff. 107 ro et seq.

who had watched the crusaders through a crevice in a secret hiding-place, told al-Nuwairī about their method of arson.   Closed doors were covered with black material, and this again with red.   Whether these materials were tar and sulphur, is very difficult to ascertain.   The main point is that when such doors were touched with a flame, they quickly caught fire.   Bands of Christians, we are told, also carried with them rings dipped in oil, tar, pitch and naphtha.   These were fixed on the points of arrows and, set alight, they were shot up to the wooden ceilings of buildings to ensure the complete ruin of the place.[1]   In burning the various buildings, they did not discriminate between what belonged to the Muslim merchants and what was Christian property.   The destroyed funduqs included those of the Catalans, the Genoese and the Marseillais.[2]   Mosques and mausolea were stripped of everything beautiful in them, and all their precious glass lanterns were smashed to pieces.[3]   The houses were combed by small bands of archers who demanded from such inhabitants as still remained all their treasure on pain of death.   In this, they did not spare either Muslim or Christian.   A crippled Coptic lady, the daughter of a priest called Girgis ibn Faḍā'il and the trustee of a Coptic church situated next to her house, managed to save the church property with the greatest of difficulty, but had to surrender all her personal savings in spite of making the sign of the Cross and revealing her faith.[4]   Seventy ships, al-Nuwairī tells us, were laden with booty.   So heavy were these, that much of their contents had to be dropped into the sea near Abuqīr in order to avoid danger of foundering or of tardy progress; and Egyptian divers continued to salvage what they could from the sea for some time later.[5]   Cisterns full of oil, honey and refined butter were broken and their contents covered the roads, and huge quantities of spices were to be found on the sea-shore.[6] The arsenal and munition stores containing sixty thousand

---

[1] Al-Nuwairī, fo. 108 ro.   [2] ib., f. 108 vo.
[3] ib., ff. 105 ro, 108 vo.
[4] ib., Berlin MS. Wetz. 360, ff. 358 vo–359 ro.
[5] ib. (Wetz. 359), f. 109 ro.   [6] ib., 108 vo.

arrows, great numbers of bows, swords, lances, coats of mail, artillery equipment, naphtha and all kinds of war material and engines were, however, saved from pillage and destruction by mere chance. A group of men-at-arms stopped by the gate for a while, but thinking from its appearance that it might be one of the city entrances owing to its exceptionally large size and its proximity to the walls, they decided to leave it untouched.[1] Among the ruined buildings were all the state offices including the Dīwān.[2] Immediately before they decided to leave the crusaders crowned their ruinous work by the burning of the remaining city gates except Bāb al-Sidra.[3] Acts of cruelty of the worst type were committed without scruple and without regard to age or sex. The streets were covered with the corpses of massacred and mutilated men, women and children.[4] The city became a scene of horror, an open grave. Of those who had escaped the sword, the crusaders carried with them about five thousand into captivity. These included, not only Muslim men and women, but also Jews and Eastern Christians.[5] Many of them were presented to the various princes of the West, and only a few returned to their homes after the payment of heavy ransoms and as a result of such prolonged negotiations between the courts of Cyprus and Egypt as will be described later in these pages. The occupation of the city lasted only seven days, yet it is staggering to realize how in a period so short, the hand of ruin could dissipate so vast an accumulation of wealth and prosperity—the outcome of centuries of peace and industry.

On Thursday, 16 October 1365,[6] the disillusioned King

[1] ib., f. 109 vo.   [2] ib., ff. 109 vo–110 ro.

[3] ib., f. 109 vo.   These included the two portals of Bāb al-Baḥr, the three portals of al-Bāb al-Akhḍar and Bāb al-Khokha. *Vide supra*, 352, n. 3.

[4] Incredible examples of the crusaders' cruelty are given by al-Nuwairī. An old man found in al-Khalāṣiya School was thrown to his death from an upper floor; ib., f. 108 vo. Woman and children were slaughtered, and it is even said that infants were torn in two in a kind of tug-of-war, and that boys were dashed to death against stone walls; ib., 117 ro.

[5] ib., f. 110 ro.

[6] Al-Nuwairī, f. 110 ro., and al-Maqrīzī (T. III, Oxford MS., non-foliated, year A.H. 767) give this date correctly as Thursday, 28 Muḥarram. Other

of Cyprus found himself alone with a mere handful of faithful supporters and crusading enthusiasts in Alexandria. The bulk of the army had already deserted their posts and, contented with their share of the pillage, settled down at ease in the ships of the fleet in readiness for setting sail on the first possible occasion. Meanwhile, the vanguard of the Egyptian army from Cairo under the command of Amīr Quṭlobogha al-Manṣūrī [1] was within the precincts of Alexandria. There was nothing left for the miserable remnant of the Christian garrison with Pierre at its head but to vacate their last posts and board the fleet. Then the laden galleys unfurled their sails and at once set sail for Cyprus. Their departure was undisturbed by the enemy who had no ships left and no heart to pursue them on the high seas. As to the cause of the delay in the arrival of the relief army, it has already been noted that the Nile flood swamped the whole of the Delta, the direct roads were impassable, and squadrons had to travel most of the way along the edge of the western desert.[2] Another factor must have contributed to retard the departure of the troops from Cairo. Yalbogha al-Khaṣṣikī, the Atabikī in power at the time of the invasion, was regarded as a hateful usurper by a strong party of Mamlūks in Egypt, and at first he thought that behind the news of the crusade might lurk an insidious plot to undermine his influence in the state.[3] This explains his reluctance to comply with Janghara's request until it was graphically confirmed by the influx of refugees from Alexandria. At this moment, the original governor of the city, Ṣalāḥ-al-Dīn ibn 'Arrām, had just returned from Mekka, and was immediately ordered to proceed to his seat of office ahead of the army. It is said that he was able to supplant the banners of the Cross by those of Egypt on certain parts of the walls on 13 October within view of the invaders, and that he sent a Jew named

sources vary a little. Machaut, l. 3608, says that the troops remained in the fleet for two days after the council and before the order was issued for setting sail. The *Vita S. Petri*, p.c., fixes this on the sixth day of the occupation.

[1] Al-Maqrīzī, op. cit., *ann. cit.* According to ibn Taghrī Bardī, op. cit., V, 195, the commanders of the vanguard included, among other amīrs, Kundok and Khalīl ibn Qawṣūn.

[2] *vide supra*, 351.   [3] Al-Maqrīzī, l.c.

Ya'qūb on the 14th to the King, who was on board ship, to negotiate the exchange of Muslim prisoners with the Franks previously taken to Damanhūr as hostages. After crossing forty ships carrying the fruit of plunder and crowded with captives, Ya'qūb found the King in a tent with openings overlooking the sea. He was dressed in precious robes embroidered with gold and studded with pearls, and he wore a gold crown surmounted by a glittering jewel. He had one monk on his right and another on his left. These, one might conjecture, were Pierre de Thomas and Philippe de Mézières. After hearing the object of his embassy, the King enjoined him to tell his master to procure written messages from the Frankish prisoners to prove that they were still alive and gave him respite until the following morning. This request was impossible to fulfil, as the consuls and merchants in captivity were too far removed in Damanhūr,[1] and the fleet sailed at the appointed time before the transaction came to any fruition.[2] The victors had a hard passage. The sea, calm at first, became perturbed with a violent tempest and the galleys were dispersed in all directions.[3] This was regarded by the Legate and his disciple, Philippe de Mézières, as the first outward sign of divine wrath against those who had taken the Cross and forsaken their obligations.[4] In the end, however, the scattered craft reassembled at the ports of Limassol and Famagusta.[5] The spoils and the army were landed in safety on the island, the King thanked the alien troops for their services and they ultimately departed to their respective countries, letters were dispatched to the Pope and the rulers of the West announcing the triumph of Christ, and a great procession was held at Nicosia to commemorate the event.[6]

---

[1] According to Yaqūt, *Mu'jam al-Buldān* (ed. Wüstenfeld), II, 601, it was a day's journey from Damanhūr to Alexandria. Two days would, therefore, have been necessary for the return journey to bring the captives.

[2] Al-Nuwairī (Wetz. 360), ff. 185 vo–186 ro, on the authority of one al-Sharīf al-Hassani who heard this from Ya'qūb the Jew himself.

[3] Machaut, ll. 3611 et seq.   [4] *Vita S. Petri*, l.c.

[5] Machaut, ll. 3631–3; Makhairas, § 173.

[6] Reynaldus, *ad ann.* 1365, nos. 19–20; Makhairas, §§ 174–5; *Vita*, l.c.; Machaut, ll. 3634 et seq.; Strambaldi, 68–9; Amadi, 415.

The news of the success of the crusade had a mixed reception in Europe. The Pope and the curia at Avignon were much gratified. At the court of France, Charles V, whose father had died as a sworn crusader, was roused to the point of delegating Jean d'Olivier to inform King Pierre that his master had resolved to send a great army to Cyprus in order to complete Pierre's late triumph by finally crushing the power of the miscreants.[1]   Du Guesclin took the Cross in the course of 1356 with the intention of fighting the Muslims either with the noble King of Cyprus or with the crusaders of Spain.[2]   Florimont, sire de Lesparre, and a small contingent in a galley equipped at his own expense, actually reached Cyprus in order to assist in the battles of the faithful against the infidels.[3]   Amedo VI, Count of Savoy, who had already taken the Cross in company with King Pierre from the Pope's hands at Avignon, had completed his preparations to fulfil his vow and was about to sail to the East.[4]   This would have been the most substantial reinforcement to Cyprus had it not been deflected from its original course into another by circumstances outside the King's control.   In one quarter, the news of the capture of Alexandria was badly received and bitterly criticized.   Venice, which cared little for the holy cause and much for its trade interests in the Sultan's dominions, was alarmed on hearing the news and at once charged its diplomatic agents with the difficult task of mending the damage wrought by the crusade.[5]   Its envoys hastened to the Sultan's court to protest against the recent events, to assure the victim of aggression that they had no hand in the matter, and to beg for the re-establishment of peace and amity and the resumption of trade intercourse so beneficial to both parties.   The Sultan refused to come

---

[1] Makhairas, § 175.

[2] Chevalier, *Chron. de Du Guesclin*, I, 65.

[3] Makhairas, § 187; Machaut, ll. 4698–4711; Rabanis, *Notice*, 10–14. Makhairas says that Lesparre changed his mind on arrival at Famagusta and went to fight the King of France on behalf of the King of England.   According to Machaut, he seems to have participated in Pierre's second expedition to Gorigos.   As will be shown, however, he was a member of the crusade of Amedeo of Savoy.

[4] *vide infra*, Cap. XVI.   [5] Makhairas, § 176

to any definite understanding with a Christian nation while
he was still in a state of war with Cyprus. Peace, he
argued, must be made first with the King of that island.[1]
The envoys then sailed to Cyprus and persuaded Pierre
to open negotiations with the Sultan.[2] Exchange of
embassies between the two courts was begun with a view
of arriving at an amicable solution and healing old and
new wounds; but before any treaties were signed or even
the real intentions of the Sultan made known, the Venetians
hurried to the West to announce that peace was concluded
between Cyprus and Egypt.[3] This premature announce-
ment put an end to the preparations on foot in Europe
for the crusade and weakened the position of King Pierre
in his negotiations. As a result, Amedeo of Savoy led
his expedition to Byzantium, and when Pierre sent to
invite him to come with his army to his aid, he informed
the King that the Venetians had given him to understand
that peace was concluded with Egypt and his assistance
was thus unnecessary; he was on his way to fight the Turks
and it was too late then to alter his plan while his help
was urgently needed in the Balkans to save his cousin the
Emperor from captivity in Bulgaria.[4]

The negotiations between Cyprus and Egypt may be
divided into two stages. The first showed some promise
of success in the preliminary talks. The King, who had
dismissed his foreign troops and had no very immediate
prospect of further substantial help from the West, sent
three Catalans to act for him at the Sultan's court. These
were Jean d'Alfonso, a baptized Jew, George Settica and
Paul de Belonia. Armed with presents and credentials,
they proceeded to Alexandria, and thence to Cairo, where
the Sultan received them and asked them as a primary
condition to request their master to return the captives he
had carried off from Egypt.[5] In good faith, Pierre

---

[1] id., l.c.; Machaut, ll. 3798 et seq.
[2] Makhairas, §§ 177–9.   [3] ib., § 183.
[4] id., l.c.; *vide infra*, Cap. XVI.
[5] ib., §§ 182, 184. Al-Nuwairī, Wetz. 360, f. 190 ro et vo, refers to the
coming of Catalan envoys who were taken to the Regent in the midst of active
preparations for retaliation against Cyprus. Although the Western sources

responded by ordering all the remaining prisoners to be brought together on a special galley and sent them to Egypt in the custody of Paul de Belonia.[1] The return of the prisoners marked the end of the first stage in the negotiations and the beginning of the second. Having recovered what he could and having learnt that there was no immediate danger to his realm from Western Europe, the Sultan changed the conciliatory attitude which he had hitherto adopted.[2] For more than four years, futile negotiations continued, now and again interrupted by Cyprian raids on the coasts of Syria and Egypt to intimidate the unwilling Sultan and force him to come to terms. The Mamlūks were only playing for time until their naval preparations were complete. Yalboghā had ordered every carpenter in the realm to be engaged in cutting down trees, especially those on the thickly wooded Syrian mountains near Aleppo, and to proceed diligently with the construction of the fleet, necessary for the conveyance of an avenging army to Cyprus.[3] Whenever the Sultan rejected the proffered terms for the settlement of the dispute, the King resorted to the pillage of the Syrian coast. In November 1366, a large combined fleet of one hundred and sixteen sail, fifty-six galleys and sixty large sailing ships and other craft, was manned for this purpose

continually refer to the Sultan, it should be borne in mind that the chief agent in the negotiations on the Egyptian side, at least during their preliminary stages, was the Atabikī Yalboghā al-Khaṣṣikī, the Regent in power in 1366.

[1] Makhairas, § 184. Belonia was accompanied by Guillaume de Ras; but the latter fell ill and had to retire for treatment at Nicosia. The number of prisoners who were kept in the island could not have been very great, as many of the original 5,000 were presented to Western rulers (*vide supra*). Al-Nuwairī, op. cit., f. 169 vo, gives an example of the extent of these presentations by asserting that the King sent to his 'cousin' (?) in Genoa five hundred. Al-Nuwairī further says that the King favoured the French in this respect as against his own Cypriot nobles, and that this resulted in the plot which ended in his murder. Al-Maqrīzī (vol. III, Oxford MS. Marsh. 260, non-foliated, *ad ann.* 767), however, reports the arrival of a Genoese embassy to return their share of the prisoners, numbering only sixty, and to deny the participation of their republic in the campaign.

[2] Makhairas, § 186.

[3] Al-Nuwairī, Wetz. 360, f. 191 ro, says that Yalboghā actually prepared a fleet of 150 pieces including galleys and transports.

under his own command.   But a violent tempest drove
the units of the fleet far apart, and only Florimont de
Lesparre with fifteen galleys reached Ṭarābulus, ransacked
the town, and returned to Cyprus.[1]   In June 1367, another
embassy to Cairo under the leadership of Jacques de Norès
the Turkopolier returned to Famagusta without achieving
the desired settlement.[2]   So another raid on Ṭarābulus
followed in September.[3]   This time, the fleet, numbering
according to al-Nuwairī's estimate one hundred and fifty
sail including galleys and transports,[4] reached the harbour
of that town intact; but the inhabitants appear to have
been on their guard against these frequent attacks and
ambushed the enemy in a thicket of sugar-cane and reed
situated between the walls and the sea.[5]   As the attackers
were retiring to their fleet in a disorderly manner in twos
and threes, they were surprised by the Saracens and sustained some loss before they had time to consolidate their
lines for defence, and they found much difficulty in regaining
their ships.[6]   They ultimately sailed from Ṭarābulus to
Tortosa, where they pillaged the town and burnt accumulated masses of timber, pitch and tow intended for the construction of galleys for the Sultan.   Other non-inflammable
materials such as iron and nails were dumped into the sea.[7]
Afterwards they halted at Latakia, but they were unable to

[1] Makhairas, §§ 190–1; Machaut, ll. 5832 et seq.

[2] Makhairas, §§ 202–5.

[3] ib., § 210; Machaut, ll. 6748 et seq.

[4] Cairo MS., Hist. 1449, f. 27 vo.

[5] Makhairas, l.c.

[6] id., l.c.   Al-Nuwairī, Cairo MS., ff. 29 vo–30 ro, alleges that the
Christian contingent, numbering about 800, was killed in its entirety, and
that the Muslim losses are said to have been twenty-one dead, or, according
to another report, only four including two Maghribines, one Turkmen and
one native of Ṭarābulus.   The same author says further that the expedition
was composed of Cypriots, Genoese, Venetians, Cretans (Kharāyṭa), Rhodians,
French, Hungarians and other alien troops.   Their total number was
16,000 of whom 1,000 were knights.   The Venetians had thirty sail, the
Genoese twenty, the Rhodians ten and the rest came from Cyprus.   These
details, al-Nuwairī says, were furnished by a Christian captive who went over
to Islam in order to save his life.   See also ibn Qāḍī Shuhba (B.N. MS. fonds
arabe 1600, ff. 197 vo–198 ro), who knew al-Nuwairī's work.

[7] Makhairas, § 211.

land there owing to violent winds and the strength of its harbour fortifications.[1]

The tension between Egypt and Cyprus persisted until the rule of Pierre I de Lusignan came to a tragic end with the King's murder by his rebellious nobles in 1369. His death, however, did not bring about any sudden change in Cypriot policy towards the Sultan. During the first year of the reign of his successor, Pierre II (1369–82), destructive raids continued in much the same way. In June 1369, a flotilla of four galleys under the command of Jean de Morf sailed to the Syrian coast and wrought destruction at the ports of Ṣaidā (Sidon), Boudroum (Botirom, Botiron, Boutron), Tortosa and Latakia.[2] More serious still was a raid on Alexandria in daylight. In less than a month after the previous raids (July 1369), the same ships had been revictualled in Armenia and sailed to Alexandria. There, they sent a message to the governor of the city to ask whether the Sultan would come to terms, and the answer was in the negative. The Christian galleys then forced their way into the Old Harbour and attacked a large Muslim sailing ship from Morocco. Afterwards they sailed to Rosetta, but the strong winds prevented them from landing. So they went to Ṣaidā and Beirūt, fought another battle at the former town, and returned to Cyprus.[3] The recurrence of these unexpected sallies from Cyprus all along the coast of the Mamlūk Empire from Alexandria to Tortosa became more and more disquieting every day. It had been hoped by the Sultan since the disastrous occupation of Alexandria in October 1365, that the Egyptian army might be able to chastise the Cypriots by a serious reprisal on their island. In fact,

---

[1] Makhairas, § 212. Al-Nuwairī, Cairo MS., f. 56vo, says that the Muslims entrapped three galleys in the harbour, and that one was captured and all its crew killed, while the other two were wrecked. Another contradictory account of this event is reported by the same author, ff. 56 vo–57 ro, on the authority of Muḥammad ibn Bahādir al-Karkarī of Alexandria who was at Latakia at that time. Three galleys of the fleet foundered in the violent tempest, he said, and provisions and pillage from Ṭarābulus were recovered from them.

[2] Makhairas, §§ 285–6. For Boudroum, *vide* AOL, I, 298.

[3] Makhairas, §§ 286–8.

al-Maqrīzī [1] reports that as early as 1366, the naval preparations on the Būlāq quay of the Nile were complete for the
projected expedition to Cyprus. A hundred vessels were
ready to set sail, stocked with men [2] and war material.
But the internal state of the country hindered the accomplishment of the project. The character of the regent,
al-Atābikī Yalboghā al-Khāṣṣikī, his greed and his tyranny,
caused his own Mamlūks to rise in arms against him.
There was open revolt and civil war in which the fleet
was used by one faction against another. Yalboghā lost
his life in these troubles; but his disappearance did not
improve matters, since the triumphant Mamlūks formed
an oligarchy of the worst type and conducted the government of the country to suit their ends. The trials of Egypt
did not finish at this point. The country was impoverished
by the loss of trade with the Christians and the state
funds were depleted. Moreover, famine and the plague
made one of their usual visitations to Egypt at this inauspicious moment. The Sultan was the loser by his
obstinate procrastination. The strain arising from all
these unfavourable circumstances ultimately made him curb
his pride and accept the principle of negotiating peace
seriously with Cyprus, and, like a good diplomat, bide
his time until a more suitable occasion came for retaliation
against the island that had given him such grounds for
grievance. It was at this juncture that Genoese [3] and
Venetian [4] delegates appeared at the Cypriot court in

---

[1] *Kitāb al-Sulūk*, III (Oxford MS., *vide supra*), *ad ann.* A.H. 768. See
also al-Jaʿfarī (*Kitāb al-Sālik*, B.N. MS., fonds arabe, 1607, f. 71 ro et vo),
who says that the hundred ships were ready in less than a year. Al-Nuwairī,
Wetz. 360, f. 191 ro) refers to the construction of 150 ships on the Nile by
the Atābikī Yalboghā.

[2] Al-Maqrīzī, op. cit., l.c., where the sailors are distinguished as Maghribine, Turkmen and Upper Egyptian.

[3] Al-Maqrīzī, l.c., reports the coming to Cairo of a Genoese embassy some
time in 1367 to ask for resumption of trade with Alexandria.

[4] The *Libri Commemoriali*, T. VII (Venetian Archives), include much
material showing the amount of pressure exerted by Venice to induce the
papacy to sanction the efforts for peace and the return to the normal course of
trade. At first the Pope showed some reluctance; see bull of Urban V on 25
January 1366, ib., f. 59 (55) vo. On 23 June 1366, Urban wavers in his
decision by conceding to the Signory the right of sending four ships and eight

August 1369 requesting that the Regent should send
envoys to reopen the negotiations for peace with the
Sultan.[1] The path was not a smooth one for the mediators. Numerous embassies were exchanged and many
threats were uttered at various times before a genuine
rapprochement came within view.[2] Finally, the envoys of
the Sultan reached Cyprus on 29 September 1370,[3] and
approximately a week later the peace was proclaimed and
the Christian prisoners in Syria and Egypt regained their
freedom.[4]

Although the atmosphere of hostility between the East
and the West was cleared for the time being, the Egyptians
did not forget the damage done to Alexandria. Cyprus
was regarded as their capital enemy for many generations
yet to come; and at heart the Sultans continued to cherish

galleys for trade; but, on 17 August 1366, a new bull 'Ad perpetuam rei
memoriam' suspends this privilege, ib., ff. 73 (70) ro, 74 (71) vo. Another
bull dated 17 May 1367, allowing Venice to send twelve galleys and four ships
to the lands of the Sultan for the same purpose was again suspended on 28 June
1367; ib., ff. 75 (72) vo, 85 (82) vo. On 8 May 1368, two bulls were
issued to ratify the dispatch of two and six galleys respectively for commerce
in goods not prohibited; ib., f. 99 (96) ro. On 26 July 1369, however, a bull
was issued granting the Doges of Venice and Genoa permission to conclude an
alliance against the Sultan in view of his confiscation of the property of Christian nations and the imprisonment of Christians; ib., f. 119 (114) vo.

Following the publication of these bulls, the Venetians are recorded to have
sent four galleys under Marino Veniero on 24 September 1367, and two others
under Pietro Grimani and Masseo Michele shortly afterwards, four under
Marco Giustiniani on 24 September 1368, and two under Niccolò Loredano
on 20 October 1370; ib., f. 85 (82) vo.

Ib., ff. 111 (108) vo–113 (110) ro. Meanwhile, an alliance was concluded between Venice and Genoa on 28 July 1369, to last until the end of
1370, binding the two republics to provide by August two armed galleys each
in readiness at Rhodes in order to collaborate with the Cypriots in the
blockade of the Sultan's lands until the latter set the Venetian and
Genoese prisoners free. The squadron would appear at Alexandria in
November for this purpose. Neither of the allies would be authorized to
treat with the Sultan alone, on pain of a fine of 20,000 gold florins. Perhaps
this treaty was yet another factor in persuading the Sultan to come to terms.

[1] Makhairas, § 290.   [2] ib., §§ 291–308.   [3] ib., § 306.
[4] ib., § 309; Mas Latrie, *Hist. de Chypre*, II, 347–50. It is difficult to
trace the exact terms of this peace. During the lifetime of Pierre I, a project
of treaty was drawn up by the King in Rome, 19 May 1368; but it was
rejected by the Sultan; Mas Latrie, op. cit., II, 291 et seq.

the idea of inflicting a heavy punishment upon the Lusignan Dynasty and its island kingdom. When the time came several decades later in the early part of the fifteenth century, they struck Cyprus with all their might. Janus de Lusignan, who was carried into captivity to Cairo in 1426, paid dearly for the past glory of his ancestor, Pierre I; and although he was returned to his throne a little later, he virtually became a tributary to Egypt and Cyprus lost its real independence for ever.[1] This was probably the most enduring of the results of the crusade against Alexandria. It is even doubtful whether the immediate results of the campaign were less unhappy. It failed in its chief aim, that is, a permanent land base for the Christians, and it did not solve the problem of the reconquest of the Holy Land—the true heritage of Christ—from the hands of the infidel usurper. It did not weaken the Sultan to the extent contemplated as a preliminary measure towards the abolition of Egyptian independence. It dealt only a local, though indeed very serious, blow to one of the finest cities of the medieval world. If Alexandria had been mutilated by the Christians of the West, it had to be repaired at the cost of the Christians of the East. Indirectly, the Latin warriors of the Cross only plundered the fortunes of their Eastern co-religionists; for, as soon as the campaign came to an end, the Sultan issued a decree whereby all the property of the Christians in Egypt and Syria was confiscated and used to pay for the damage done to Alexandria. The Coptic Patriarch was dragged to the court where he and his community were subjected to all kinds of humiliation and exactions.[2]

The main results of the crusade of 1365 may therefore be summarized in the disablement of Alexandria and the temporary suspension of its trade with the West, in the enrichment of a medley of alien adventurers who participated in the expedition and behaved more like a band of robbers than a holy army for a holy cause, in another persecution of the Eastern Christians resident within the Empire of the Mamlūks, and in a series of counter-crusades

[1] *vide infra*, Cap. XIX on Counter-Crusades.
[2] Al-Maqrīzī, op. cit., *ad ann.* A.H. 767.

which ended with the downfall of the kingdom of the Lusignans. It is noteworthy that this expedition was the last of the serious crusades conducted directly against the Sultan of Egypt. The subsequent campaigns were either intended to crush the power of the Turks, such as that of Amedeo VI of Savoy which was deflected from its normal course to a war with the Bulgarians in 1366, or intended as localized attacks, such as the Crusade of the Good Duke Louis II of Bourbon against al-Mahdiya in 1390. It would, however, be a gross misrepresentation of the truth to contend that the idea of saving the Holy Land had disappeared from Europe. The crusaders of 1396 embarked on their great undertaking with high hopes of reaching Jerusalem. They reached Nicopolis.

CHAPTER XVI

THE CRUSADE OF AMEDEO VI
OF SAVOY

Circumstances leading to Amedeo's Crusade. Negotiations, levies and pre-
parations. Itinerary. Capture of Gallipoli. Campaign in Bulgaria.
Negotiations with the King of Bulgaria and deliverance of the Emperor of
Constantinople. Attempt to unite Churches. Return of the crusaders.
Report to Rome. Results of the Crusade

CONSIDERATION of the circumstances in which the crusade
was undertaken by Count Amedeo VI of Savoy, known as
'Il Conte Verde', may help to clarify the history of its
course and the measure of its success as a holy war against
the Turks. That the propagandist activities in the first
few decades of the fourteenth century came to fruition
several years before Amedeo had thought of defending
the cause of the Cross, has already been proved by the
expedition against Smyrna (1344), the crusade of Humbert II de Viennois (1345–7), and the first of the crusades
of Pierre I de Lusignan resulting in the capture of Adalia
(1361). The fall of Smyrna and Adalia into the hands
of the Christians undoubtedly whetted their appetite
for greater victories in the East and contributed no small
share towards the inauguration of the two contemporary
crusades of Amedeo VI [1] in aid of the Eastern Empire and

---

[1] Amedeo VI, son and successor of Count Aymon of Savoy, was born on
4 January 1334. He came to the throne of Savoy in 1343 under the tutelage
of Amedeo, Count of Geneva. In 1347, he took advantage of the weakness
of Joanna I, Countess of Provence and Queen of Naples, and seized her
possessions in Piedmont. In 1348, he celebrated a three-day tournament in
which he was dressed in green, hence his name 'Il Conte Verde'. In
1353, he waged war with the Dauphiné, then annexed by France, and
invaded parts of it. In the following year at Abrès he defeated Hugues
de Génève who had taken the part of France in the wars of the Dauphiné.
On 5 January 1354 he ceded Faucigni and Gex to France. His marriage

of Pierre de Lusignan against Alexandria. The death of Pope Clement VI at the end of the year 1352, did not put an end to the cause to which he had dedicated most of his life work. During the pontificate of Clement's successor, Innocent VI (1352–62), the papal propaganda for the crusade suffered from the uncertain condition of European politics; but it would be a serious error to assume that interest in the affairs of the East had come to an end. In 1356, Innocent wrote to Lewis the Great, King of Hungary, concerning an expedition against the Serbians who had revolted against papal authority.[1] In the same year he dealt with the problems of Byzantine union with Rome and, consequently, the saving of the Empire from the Turkish invader.[2] In 1361, he again turned to the question of union with the Greeks and of war against the Ottomans, probably at the initiative of the Legate Pierre de Thomas [3] after the fall of Adalia.[4] Clement VI's real successor in regard to the crusade was Urban V (1362–70). The part played by Urban in promoting the expedition to Alexandria has been shown in the previous chapter, and an examination of the bulls issued by him in regard to Amedeo's crusade will be made in the present one. The papacy, therefore, remained a factor in keeping the crusade alive. The personal circumstances of the Count of Savoy, however, were decisive in enlisting his sympathies for the crusade and undoubtedly governed the course of his Eastern expedition. His dynasty had been in blood relationship with the Palaeologi since the marriage of Andronikos III (1328–41) to Anne of Savoy, and John V (1341–91) was a cousin of Amedeo VI. This point will elucidate Amedeo's

to Bonne de Bourbon, sister of Jeanne, wife of the Dauphin Charles who became Charles V, followed the treaty of peace between the two parties. The treaty stipulated for the support of Savoy in favour of France against England. Amedeo then took the Cross, and on his return played a prominent part in Italian affairs. He died a victim of the plague at San Stefano in Apulia on 2 March 1383. *Art de vérifier les dates*, 386.

[1] Reynaldus, *ad ann.* 1356, no. 24. The people of 'Rascia' are described as 'rebelles, schismaticos, infideles, et Catholicae fidei contemptores'.

[2] ib., *ad ann.* 1356, no 32.

[3] *vide supra*, Cap. VII.

[4] Reynaldus, *ad ann.* 1361, nos. 8 and 9.

action on his arrival at Constantinople.   In addition to
these circumstances, two important events both directly and
indirectly helped all projects of crusade during this period.
In the first place, the peace of Brétigny, concluded in 1360
between Jean II le Bon, King of France (1350–64), and
Edward III of England (1327–77), gave Western Europe
a breathing-space from the Hundred Years' War.   On the
other hand, it rendered many of those who participated in
its battles idle and deprived them of the prospect of enrich-
ing themselves by the customary pillages to which fighting
in France easily lent itself.   They were forced then to look
for another field and they found it in the crusade.   In the
second place, the wanderings of Pierre I de Lusignan
over Europe in an attempt to gain supporters for the holy
war naturally produced much enthusiasm in many countries
for this cause.[1]   In fact Amedeo had been a sworn crusader
since 1363 when he and King Pierre took the Cross from
Urban's own hands at Avignon; and his delay in following the King of Cyprus was mainly due to trouble in his
own demesnes.[2]

The history of Amedeo's crusade must therefore be
traced back to its origin in 1363, when Urban V preached
war upon the enemies of the faith.   During that year, the
Holy Pontiff published a number of bulls dated at Avignon
1 April[3] and 5 May[4] by which he granted Amedeo the
financial privileges due to a crusading prince.   These
included the alms, donations, subsidies and tithes accruing
from the County of Savoy and all the territories under his
jurisdiction.   Two points of special interest are revealed
from a close examination of these documents.   First,
Amedeo's expedition was regarded by the Church, not
merely as a minor attempt to relieve the Byzantine Empire,
but chiefly as a 'passagium generale' conducted for the

---

[1] vide supra, Cap. XIV.

[2] Datta, Spedizione in Oriente, 1 et seq., 19 et seq.; Delaville Le Roulx,
France, I, 141.

[3] Archivio di Stato (Turin), Viaggio di Levante, Mazzo J⁰, nos. 1–7;
Bollati di Saint-Pierre, Illustrazione della Spedizione in Oriente di Amedeo
VI, documents nos. VI–XII, 344–67; Datta, Spedizione, 225 et seq.

[4] Viaggio di Levante, Mazzo J⁰, no. 8; Bollati di Saint-Pierre, XIII,
368.

ultimate recovery of the Holy Land.[1]   Second, the King
of France, Jean II le Bon, had expressed the desire to
participate in this crusade, and there is no reason for thinking that he did not preserve his interest in this cause until
the end of his life in 1364.[2]   The original plan was therefore that the campaign should be undertaken by the Kings
of France and Cyprus as well as the Count of Savoy; and
the Pope conferred the usual spiritual indulgences and
privileges equally upon all crusaders.[3]   The death of the
French monarch in 1364, however, confused this plan,
and the attention of the curia was distracted by the capture
of Alexandria in the following year.[4]   There was no further
talk of Amedeo's project until February 1366, when Urban
wrote to John V Palaeologos promising to induce the
Count as well as King Lewis of Hungary and Pierre of
Cyprus to come to the rescue of his empire if he renounced the schism and submitted to Rome 'in sinceritate
cordium'.[5]

In the same year Amedeo took an active part in the final
preparations for the crusade.   On 3 January he placed

---

[1] Bollati di Saint-Pierre, 345—'. . . legantes vel donantes . . . per sex
annos proxime secuturos in memoratis Comitatu et terris pro dicto passagio
et Terre sancte subsidio'; ib., 349, where the crusade is dedicated 'aduersus
Sarracenos, impios detentores Terresancte'; ib., 351, 'pro recuperatione
Terre sancte;' ib., 357, 'ad recuperationem Terre sancte que, proh dolor,
Sarracenis perfidis ancillatur, ac ad defensionem fidelium partium Orientis
&c.'.

[2] ib., 351. 'Carissimus in Christo filius noster Johannes rex Francie
illustris gaudenter accipiens desiderium transfretandi, quod diutius, ut
asseruit, gessit in corde, nuper produxit in lucem; nam ipse ac . . . rex Cipri,
aliique multi nobiles cum eorum potentia pro recuperatione Terre sancte . . .
promiserunt personaliter transfretare ac receperunt de nostris manibus
venerabile signum Crucis.'   Another reference to the two kings and the
crusade may be found in another document of the same date (1 April); ib.,
357.

[3] Datto, 42; Delaville Le Roulx, op. cit., I, 144.

[4] Reynaldus, ad ann. 1364, no. 17; the Pope writes to Charles V, the
new King of France, on the subject of the crusade, but without result.   ib.,
ad ann. 1364, nos. 24–7, dealing with the mission of Pierre de Thomas in
the East, the crusade of Pierre de Lusignan and the union of the Churches.
Ib., ann. 1365, passim, mostly occupied with the capture of Alexandria.

[5] ib., ad ann. 1365, nos. 1–2.   Urban describes Amedeo to John as
'consanguineus tuus'.

the Countess his consort, Bonne de Bourbon, at the head
of his state and ordained that she should receive all revenues
due to him during his absence on crusade against Saracens,
Turks and other infidels.[1]   As to the immediate financing
of the expedition, the Count could hardly rely upon his
own resources.   His mint produced only the meagre sum of
778 Venetian gold ducats every year in ready money and
he could wait no longer for the funds due from the papal
grants to accumulate.   So he came to an agreement with the
bankers of Lyons, whereby he received the advance sum
of 10,000 florins in exchange for his concessions from the
Church.[2]   This and the Count's own revenue, added
together, were obviously but a meagre contribution towards
the fulfilment of a 'passagium generale' or even of a smaller
campaign in the Orient.   Yet Amedeo, in his eagerness to
carry out his solemn vow, used whatever money he was
able to acquire in the hiring of troops and the equipment
of galleys and transport vessels for their conveyance.   Like
most of the crusading armies of the time, Amedeo's followers
were composed of motley groups of fighters with varied
motives.   First came his nobles and vassals who were
bound by medieval custom to serve and support him.
Others were genuine crusaders whose chief concern was
the defence of a holy cause and the glory of the Catholic
faith.   Many, too, must have enlisted in search of adventure in distant fields and strange lands.   The bulk of the
Count's money was, however, spent on paid mercenaries
hired for a fixed term.   Last but not least, we must remember that the temporary stoppage of the Hundred Years'
War after the treaty of Brétigny (1360) threw a considerable multitude of Englishmen and Frenchmen whose sole
vocation was warfare into a state of idleness, incompatible
with their warlike temper and their thirst for booty.   These
must have roamed hither and thither offering their services
to the fighting princes, in whom Italy more than most
countries abounded in the fourteenth century.   Amedeo's
crusade undoubtedly gave them a golden opportunity
which they seized, and so they joined him on his Eastern

[1] Bollati di Saint-Pierre, doc. I, 329–33, and II, 334–5.
[2] Datta, 40–3; Delaville Le Roulx, l.c.

expedition.[1]   The main feature of this army was that almost
all its ranks were paid recruits; even the Count's direct
vassals had the right to some compensation for service
rendered outside the field of duty imposed upon them by
feudal law and custom.   This strained Amedeo's finances
to a degree which will be shown by a short examination of
his accounts at a later stage in this chapter.   Another
feature was that many different nations were represented
in his army—a feature which illustrates an important aspect
of the crusade as a war of the whole of Christendom against
the expanding forces of Muhammadanism.   Italy furnished
him with the main body of the host; but other groups of
no mean size were raised from other countries.   Twenty-
eight German men-at-arms were supplied by the Count's
brother-in-law, Galeazzo Visconti of Milan.   The provenance of this detachment was probably the German company
of Hennequin Borgraten, previously offered by Galeazzo
to the citizens of Pisa for employment in their wars with
Florence in the 'sixties of the century.[2]   An English company, too, under the command of one 'Lebron' and a certain
William joined the crusaders.[3]   France appears to have
contributed an even larger share than either Germany or
England, in the form of a company led by a 'constable'.[4]
A new Order of Chivalry (Chevaliers de l'Annonciade)[5]
was created in Savoy, probably on the occasion of this
crusade; and among the French notables who joined this
brotherhood and took the Cross were Jean de Vienne, the
future admiral of France who lost his life on the field of
Nicopolis in 1396,[6] Hugues de Châlons seigneur d'Arlay[7]

---

[1] Similar circumstances arose in connexion with the Crusade of Nicopolis
(1396) after the conclusion of the peace between Richard II of England and
Charles VI of France (1395). *Vide infra*, Cap. XVIII; *Nicopolis*, 9.

[2] Delaville Le Roulx, *France*, I, 144–5.

[3] Datta, 46 et seq.   [4] id., l.c.

[5] Loray, *Jean de Vienne*, 36 note, proves the foundation of this Order in
1366.   Delaville Le Roulx, op. cit., I, 145, note 2, places its creation in
1362, but he admits the weight of Loray's evidence in support of the argument for 1366 nevertheless.

[6] Bollati di Saint-Pierre, 338; Loray, op. cit., *passim*; *Nicopolis*, 42, 70,
77, 85–6, 92, 115, 129.

[7] Froissart (ed. Kervyn), XX, 533; Delaville Le Roulx, op. cit., I, 146,
note 1.

in Burgundy, Rolland de Vaissy from the Bourbonnais,[1] and Guillaume de Chalamont from the Dombes.[2]   Among the French companions of the Count, moreover, were Étienne de la Baume seigneur de Saint-Denis in Bugey and Chavannes in the Franche-Comté, who became admiral of the crusade, Guillaume de Granson, seigneur de Sainte-Croix in Burgundy,[3] Florimont de Lesparre [4] and Basset [5] from Gascony, and several others.[6]

The majority of these feudal lords were accompanied by a train of followers who swelled the number of the crusading army.   Usually every knight had under his own banner a small company of four to twelve squires.   In some cases, this number reached thirty and even forty men.   The Sire de Basset had ten men-at-arms, fifteen arbalesters and twenty archers in his own galley.   Florimont de Lesparre had thirty,[7] and Hugues and Louis de Châlons about the same number.[8]   These are, however, only illustrations of the strength of Amedeo's army whose total number may be estimated approximately between 1,500 and 1,800 strong without counting the seamen on board the galleys.[9]   The fleet consisted of fifteen galleys—six from Genoa, five from Venice and four from

[1] Delaville Le Roulx, l.c., note 2.

[2] id., l.c., note 3.   [3] id., l.c., note 4.

[4] Bollati di Saint-Pierre, doc. III, 336–7; Datta, 263–5. See also Rabanais, *Notice sur Florimont de Lesparre* (Bordeaux, 1834), for further particulars about his life.

[5] Bollati di Saint-Pierre, 338.

[6] Such as Louis de Châlons from Burgundy, the seigneurs de Saint-Amour and de Varambon from the Bresse, and the seigneurs d'Aix, de Virieu and de Clermont from the Dauphiné.   Bollati di Saint-Pierre, doc. IV, 338–9; Kervyn's *Froissart*, XX, 533; Delaville Le Roulx, op. cit., I, 146–7.

[7] *Viaggio di Levante*, Mazzo II, no. 1; Bollati di Saint-Pierre, doc. III, 336–7.

[8] *Viaggio di Levante*, Mazzo I, no. 1; Bollati di Saint-Pierre, doc. IV, 338–9; Delaville Le Roulx, op. cit., I, 147.

[9] This estimate, given by Delaville Le Roulx (op. cit., I, 147–8), is based on the number of galleys of the crusading fleet and the capacity of each galley. The fleet consisted of fifteen galleys, and, on the authority of Guillaume de Machaut (*Prise d'Alexandrie*, lines 4602–4), a galley carried 25 knights, and as every knight must have had four or five men under his banner, the total number may be placed between 1,500 and 1,875.

Marseilles.[1] The general rendezvous of the three naval squadrons was the Venetian colony of Coron on the south coast of the Morea in the neighbourhood of Modon.

The Count left his territories about the middle of May and arrived at Pavia on the 27th of the same month; and, proceeding by way of Padua, he completed the first stage of his journey by reaching Venice on 11 June 1366.[2] Before sailing, he issued two ordinances in which he detailed the government and order of the fleet, the duties of warriors, and the penalties for breach of the established rules.[3] In spite of the entreaties of Urban V to the Republic of St. Mark, the Venetians did their worst to hamper the expedition of Savoy for fear that it might impair their trade privileges with the Muslims. The Count had to supervise his own preparations and pay heavily for them. In fact the Venetians succeeded in deflecting the whole course of the crusade. Amedeo's original plan was to sail to Cyprus and reinforce the army of Pierre I de Lusignan in its conflict with Egypt. After the capture and loss of Alexandria in 1365, a Venetian galley hastened to the West and spread the false news of a treaty of peace between Cyprus and Egypt. On hearing this, Amedeo changed his route as will be seen from his itinerary.[4] However, the Venetian fleet under the personal command of the Count sailed about 20 June,[5] and reached Pola[6] on the 23rd of that month and Ragusa on 1 July. Then pursuing the normal

---

[1] *Chron. de Sav.*, 303; cf. Iorga (*Mézières*, 334), contrary to Datta's estimate (60–2) of six Venetian, six Genoese and three from Marseilles, adopted by Delaville Le Roulx (I, 148–9).

[2] Datta, 65 et seq.; Delaville Le Roulx, I, 148. At Pavia, Amedeo assisted in the christening ceremonies of Galeazzo's newly born grand-daughter Valentine, the future wife of Louis d'Orléans. Amedeo was her godfather.

[3] Bollati di Saint-Pierre, doc. IV and V, 338–43. These include some interesting details on the maritime rules of the time, e.g. if the captain of a ship proposed to sail by night, he was requested to inform other ships by the sign of lighting two lanterns under the main lantern.

[4] Makhairas's *Chronicle* (ed. Dawkins), I, §§ 175, 183 and 186, pages 154–7, 162–3, 166–7.

[5] Datta, 79 et seq. The exact date is unknown, although it is certain that the fleet was at Pola on 23 June.

[6] On the coast of the Istrian Peninsula, almost opposite Ravenna.

route to the East by way of Corfu and Modon, it ultimately joined the Genoese and French galleys at Coron
on 19 July.[1] At this juncture, Amedeo's progress was
delayed by his mediation in an armed dispute between the
Latin Archbishop of Neopatras, Cardinal Angelo Acciajuoli,
and the titular Latin Empress of Constantinople, Marie de
Bourbon, whose possessions at Zuchio and the castle of
Manolada in the Morea the former wished to seize.[2]
When this had been quickly settled by the Count, the
crusaders resumed their journey, and, passing alongside
of the island of St. George d'Albora, they reached Negropontis on 2 August.[3] Their fleet was arranged in three
squadrons.   The vanguard consisted of the Genoese galleys
entrusted to Étienne de la Baume, the admiral of the
expedition.   The second and central squadron including
the Venetian craft and carrying the army of Savoy was under
the command of the Count himself, assisted by his Marshal,
Guillaume de Montmayeur.   Basset led the third (i.e.
French) squadron, which carried the mixed elements of the
army derived from many countries and sailed in the rear.[4]
In this order, the campaign in the Aegean was begun after
a short halt at Negropontis.

The first object of the crusaders was to attack the Turks
at Gallipoli and thus cut their communications between
Asia and Europe.   Gallipoli was the earliest Ottoman conquest in the Balkans dating from the reigns of Kantakuzenos
in Byzantium and of Orkhan in Asia Minor[5] (c. 1352);
and it remained one of their most vital possessions in the
Peninsula until they consolidated their empire in Europe
by the capture of Constantinople.   At the time of

---

[1] Datta, 85 et seq.; Delaville Le Roulx, I, 149–50.

[2] Morel-Foratio (ed.), *Libro de los Fechos et Conquistas*, 154; *Chron. de Sav.*,
303–4; Delaville Le Roulx, I, 150.

[3] *Chron. de Sav.*, 305; Datta, 89 et seq.

[4] Bollati di Saint-Pierre, doc. V, 340–3; *Chron. de Sav.*, 302–3.   Datta,
85 et seq.; Delaville Le Roulx, I, 149.   The ordinance for the fleet was
originally issued in Venice, but it is difficult to trace its full effect before the
union of the fleet in the Mediterranean and the Aegean.   Delaville Le Roulx
seems to imply that the whole fleet started from Venice which is not in conformity with the actual organization of the campaign.

[5] Gibbons, *Foundations of Ottoman Empire*, 100–3.

Amedeo's crusade, the Byzantine Empire was feeble, factious and incapable of repelling the Muslim invader, while Turkey was ruled by an active and able Sultan, Murad I (1359–89), who was taking full advantage of the condition of the Balkan states to expand his realm with bewildering rapidity. Yet it would be a serious mistake to overestimate the military achievements of the Ottomans at a stage when they still owed most of their triumphs to the weakness of their neighbours. The time was ripe for a crusade strong enough to wreck the nascent empire of the Turks in Europe, and no better strategic point could have been chosen by the army of the Cross for this purpose than Gallipoli. How far the Count of Savoy realized these facts, is impossible to know with precision. The chief reason for landing in Gallipoli may have been the obvious one of its situation as the first Ottoman colony in Europe on the way to Constantinople. Whatever their tactical motive may have been, the fact remains that the crusaders left Negropontis on 15 August, and within two days they landed at Gallipoli and at once set siege to it. The town happened to be inadequately defended by a small garrison stationed in its fortresses, and thus presented no serious resistance to the Christians. A breach made in its walls provided the besiegers with an entrance for hand-to-hand fighting with the Turks inside the fortifications. An English knight named Richard Musard, who acted as the Count's banner bearer, gave the sign for the onslaught and the crusaders poured into the town which was finally seized on 23 August. Among the Christians who succumbed in the fighting, were Rolland de Vaissy, the seigneur de Saint-Amour, Jean de Verdon and Giraud the Marshal.[1] Their remains were later carried to Pera and interred with great honour in one of its Catholic churches. The next step was the massacre of the Muslims who survived the battle and failed to escape. The Count then appointed Aymon Michel as captain of the citadel and Jacques de Lucerne as governor of the town. A

---

[1] Demetrius Cydonius, *Oratio de non Reddenda Callipoli*, in MPG, CLIV, 1009 et seq. (cf. Golubovich, V, 129–30); *Chron. de Sav.*, 305–9; Datta, 98–101.

garrison of about two hundred men was left to guard the conquest. These included the German company, and in their number were constables, arbalesters, archers and valets.[1]

After this achievement, Amedeo decided to withdraw the rest of his army to the fleet and sail to Constantinople, instead of marching to that city by land and purging the surrounding country of the Ottomans. They arrived there early in September to find that its unhappy Emperor had been seized by Šišman III who ruled central Bulgaria.[2] It was at this juncture that Pierre I de Lusignan, on hearing of Amedeo's arrival at Constantinople, dispatched a French knight named sire Pierre de Levat to ask him to come to Cyprus and join him in attacking the Egyptian Sultan's possessions; but the Count explained to him that the Venetians had informed him of the establishment of peace in that field, thus rendering his services unnecessary to the King. It was then too late for the Count to comply with the King's request while his own cousin the Emperor was held in captivity. Savoy's first duty was to achieve John's freedom.[3] In his great distress as a result of continued Ottoman aggression, John V Palaeologos had decided to go to the court of Lewis of Hungary to negotiate another union of the Churches and thus obtain aid from him. Fearing a surprise by the Turkish pirates if he went by the Black Sea, he had preferred to take the road through Bulgaria to the confines of Hungary. Šišman had been informed of the Emperor's presence in his territory, and as he had an old grievance against the Hungarians and the Greeks who had inflicted defeat and humiliation upon his

---

[1] Datta, 103.

[2] After the death of Czar Alexander of Bulgaria in 1365, the country was divided among his three sons. Western Bulgaria was inherited by Stracimir with Widdin as his capital. Central Bulgaria, extending from the Danube to the Rhodope Mountains was ruled by John Šišman from Tirnovo. Western Bulgaria was under prince Constantine, except the Dobrudja and the upper coast of the Black Sea which became subject to Dobrotič. Šišman's influence, however, became preponderant in the whole country after the capture of Stracimir by Lewis of Hungary. The other two princes owed him allegiance as their senior. Gibbons, *Foundations*, 140–1.

[3] Makhairas (ed. Dawkins), I, § 186, pp. 164–7.

father, he arrested John and his retinue, and carried them to Widdin, his capital.[1]   The Empress therefore received the Count as the deliverer of her husband and supplied him with 12,000 gold parperos [2] towards the cost of the expedition against Bulgaria.   The fleet was further reinforced by five galleys—two equipped by the Empress, two by the Genoese in Pera, and one constructed at the Count's own expense.   These and other preparations were completed in the course of September.[3]

Before the actual campaign, there was a prelude.   Two French nobles, the seigneurs d'Urtières and de Fromentes [4] were given a Genoese galley with orders to sail across the Black Sea and up the Danube to Widdin, the central Bulgarian capital, in an attempt to save the Emperor. There are no details extant of their instructions; but it may be conjectured that their mission was a purely diplomatic one, since a solitary galley was insufficient to intimidate King Šišman's forces.   The ambassadors, however, never reached their destination.   Their galley was battered by a fierce tempest in the Bosphorus, and they had to take refuge in the Girol [5] harbour until the winds abated for them to return home without accomplishing anything. The failure of this armed embassy decided Amedeo's course of action.   The only alternative left for him was to conduct a campaign into Bulgaria to secure the liberty of his cousin.   As a precautionary measure, he entrusted part of his army under the leadership of Gaspart de Montmayeur with the defence of Constantinople if the Ottomans threatened it during his absence.[6]

---

[1] On the story of the captivity of the Emperor, see Demetrius Cydonius, *Oratio pro subsidio Latinorum*, in MPG, CLIV, 975–6 (cf. Golubovich, V, 130–1).   See also Datta, 1 et seq.; Delaville Le Roulx, I, 152; Iorga, *Mézières*, 334–5.

[2] Bollati di Saint-Pierre, 3–4.

[3] Datta, 117 et seq.; Delaville Le Roulx, l.c.

[4] Delaville Le Roulx, l.c.

[5] ib., I, 153, note 1; cf. Berger de Xivry, *Mém. sur . . . Manuel Paléologue*, in *Mém. de l'Acad. des Inscript.*, XIX (1853), II, 91.   Girol, Girout or Bocca di Giro, sometimes identified as Hieron or Hierum on the Eastern coast of the Bosphorus north of Scutari.

[6] Delaville Le Roulx, I, 153.

When all preparations had been made and all precautions taken, the fleet sailed through the Bosphorus and is reported to have been at 'Lorfenal' [1] on 6 October 1366. Travelling along the Western coast of the Black Sea which was mostly in Bulgarian hands, the crusaders finally landed at the port of Sisopolis [2] on the 17th of the same month. The town, which was ill-defended owing to its remoteness at a time when every soldier was needed by the central government to deal with the marauding Turks inland, fell to the Latins without difficulty. Other towns in the same region, including Manchopolis and Scafida,[3] suffered the same fate. At the latter, several Turkish ships were found and were all sunk when they attempted resistance. The next important stage in the campaign was the siege of Mesembria,[4] the best fortified port of the district. The fleet under Francesco Gattilusio, Latin lord of the island of Mytilene, blockaded the town from the sea. On land, the army was divided into two large corps. The first was led by Basset and Lesparre, assisted by Guillaume de Granson and Jean de Grolée. The second, including the contingents of Savoy, Burgundy and the Dauphiné, was under the personal command of Amedeo with a number of close military advisers such as the seigneurs de Génève, Châlons, Urtières and Clermont. In the face of a strong and organized army, the defence could not hold out long. The castle commanding the harbour was seized and the town itself surrendered soon afterwards. The Count stationed a body of his troops in it and placed Berlion de Forax and Guillaume de Chalamont in command on 22 October.

---

[1] id., l.c., note 2, suggests the reading of 'l'Arsenal' instead, to signify the port where the Byzantine Empire kept its own arsenal. Situated at the entrance of the Bosphorus from the Black Sea, however, was the Phanar to which reference is made.

[2] Suzopoli in the *Chron. de Sav.*, 310—the Greek Sozopolis and the modern Sozopol or Sizoboli at the southern entrance to the gulf of Burgas.

[3] Also Manchopoly and Schafida. *Chron. de Sav.*, l.c. Delaville Le Roulx, l.c., note 4, suggests that the first was probably Macropolis north of Mesembria. The second was situated on the inner coast of the gulf of Burgas south of Mesembria.

[4] For the siege of Mesembria, see *Chron. de Sav.*, 311–12; Delaville Le Roulx, I, 153–4.

The army then marched a little south of Mesembria and
seized Axillo [1] and then, in the reverse direction north of
that town, Lemona [2] opening its gates to them.   Two small
garrisons were placed there under Pierre Vibodi and Antoine de Champagne.   Hitherto, the campaign had been so
easy that some of the younger knights who were not present
at the attack on Lemona hungered for an opportunity to
prove their valour.   Therefore, single-handed, they planned
to surprise an exceptionally well-fortified castle known as
Colocastro.   In this, they failed with a loss of five knights
and ten squires.   The older generation in the army then
organized a more formidable attack and the fort succumbed,
its inhabitants were massacred and its government was
transferred to the Greeks. [3]   The next point in the campaign was at Varna, the greatest and strongest of the Bulgarian towns on the Black Sea.   Owing to its situation at
a considerable distance from the field of Latin operations,
it was decided that the crusaders should proceed to it by
sea.   The fleet arrived in the waters of the town on 25
October.   The army landed safely in the surrounding
country and, finding that the fortifications were impregnable, set siege to the town and opened up negotiations
with its inhabitants.   Jean de Vienne and Guillaume de
Granson represented the crusaders in the discussions held
with twelve delegates of Varna, and it was agreed that in
return for a respite from violence and siege the town should
supply the army with provisions and send ambassadors to
Šišman to treat on behalf of the Count for the deliverance
of the captured Emperor of Constantinople. [4]

The ambassadors started on 29 October for the court of

[1] Delaville Le Roulx, op. cit., I, 154, note 3; Datta, 127–8; Spruner-
Menke's Atlas, Map 88.   Axillo, also known as Anxialus, Anchialus,
Achelous, Lassillo and Lessilta.

[2] Delaville Le Roulx and Datta, l.c.   See also *Chron. de Sav.*, 311–13;
Spruner-Menke's Atlas, l.c.   Lemona, Limeno, Lymeno, Emmona or Cavo
di Lemano.   The *Chroniques de Savoye* wrongly place the capture of Lemona
and Colocastro during the period of inactivity while the crusaders were
besieging Varna.   This seems impossible owing to the distance between
them, unless part of the army was left behind for that purpose.

[3] *Chron. de Sav.*, 312–13.

[4] ib.. 312.

Šišman at Adrianople.[1]   Although including a strong
Bulgarian element from Varna, the embassy was headed
by the Latin Patriarch of Constantinople,[2] and accompanied by the seigneur de Fromentes, Adalbert of Bohemia, Guiot Ferlay and Gabriel Riblia.[3]   The King of
Bulgaria was anxious to settle his differences with the Latins
who were invading his country in order to save Varna and
peacefully arrest their progress.   He dispatched his own
representatives to meet Amedeo's envoys half-way at
'Trevo'[4] where the parties held their meetings.   The
issues at stake were three in number—the freedom of the
Byzantine Emperor, the surrender of the Latin prisoners
seized by the Bulgarians in recent battles, and the restoration of occupied territory to its rightful suzerain in return
for the first two concessions.   The first and most vital issue
was settled without difficulty, and the Emperor was actually
set free on 21 December.   As regards the second, although
the King of Bulgaria promised to grant all his captives [5]
their freedom, he refused to do so later without the payment of ransom.   The third problem was solved by a
compromise.   Varna was to be spared by the crusaders,
who were not really anxious to prolong a siege of whose
results they were doubtful.   Meanwhile the Count was
allowed to retain Mesembria and his conquests on the
south-western coast.   The last of the terms was fulfilled
without delay.   Amedeo raised the siege of Varna on the
day of the Emperor's recovery of his freedom, that is, on

[1] ib., 313.   Adrianople became the first Ottoman capital in Europe in
1366.   In the absence of exact chronology, if we believe the statement of the
Chroniques de Savoye that the embassy went to Adrianople instead of Widdin or
Tirnovo, it must be assumed that the fall of Adrianople to the Turks took
place very late in 1366.

[2] Paul, who became Archbishop of Smyrna in 1355, Archbishop of Thebes
in 1364 and Patriarch of Constantinople on 17 April 1366 in succession to
Pierre de Thomas.   Mas Latrie, *Patriarches Latins de Constantinople*, in
ROL, 3e année (1895), 440.

[3] *Chron. de Sav.*, 314; Datta, 130 et seq.; Delaville Le Roulx, I, 155 and
note 3.

[4] Probably Tirnovo.

[5] These included Antonino Visconti, Guy de Pontarlier, Marshal of
Burgundy, and Bandiguere and Poypi.   Delaville Le Roulx, I, 156,
note 1.

21 December, and the homeward journey was immediately begun.[1]   On the 26th of the same month, the crusaders reached Mesembria, which Amedeo handed over with the other smaller towns and forts to John V after long negotiations conducted mainly at Sisopolis, where the two cousins stayed from 9 January to 20 March 1367.   It was stipulated that the Emperor should pay Amedeo the sum of 15,000 florins in exchange for these new additions to his realm.   Finally, the fleet sailed to the Bosphorus, came within sight of the harbour of 'Lorfinal'[2] on 6 April, and shortly afterwards the crusaders made a triumphant entry into Constantinople and were warmly received by its inhabitants.[3]

The campaign ended with two more minor victories over the Ottomans.   The Count, who had engaged his army for the period of one year, still had two months' service due to him from the crusaders.   So he conducted a spirited attack by sea and land on the forts of Eueacassia and Coloveyro.[4]   Little is known about these two places except that they were situated on the European shores of the Marmora.[5]   In both cases, the seamen and the infantry showed great prowess in their encounter with the stubborn Turkish garrisons.   Notwithstanding a resolute defence, both fortresses were captured and burnt on 14 May 1367.

The rest of the month of May was spent partly in the payment of the troops and partly in negotiations with John V to bring the schism of the Churches to a happy end. The first seems to have weighed very heavily on the finances of the Count.   The money acquired from the bankers of Lyons together with Amedeo's own savings, the large sum advanced by the Empress towards the campaign in Bulgaria for the deliverance of her husband, the sum which the Emperor paid in exchange for the surrender of Mesembria

---

[1] *Chron. de Sav.*, l.c.; Datta, 133–5.   [2] *vide supra*, 391, n. 1.

[3] *Chron. de Sav.*, l.c.; Datta, 137 et seq.; Delaville Le Roulx, I, 155–6.

[4] Datta, 141–3.

[5] Delaville Le Roulx, I, 157, note 1, suggests that Coloveyro is probably the Greek καλόγερος, meaning a monastery for men; but this does not help in solving the problem of identifying the place.

to him,[1] and the exactions from the natives of the conquered territories [2]—all proved inadequate to meet the
payment of the troops. Amedeo, therefore, had to raise
several loans from the Latin merchants of Pera to make up
the deficit,[3] and was thus left alone to bear the financial
burden of an expensive campaign.

In the matter of the union of the Churches, Savoy exerted
a final effort to prove his fidelity and devotion to the Church
of Rome. The moment seemed a propitious one to bring
the East and the West together. The Emperor was under
a personal obligation to his Latin cousin for saving him
from imprisonment. The citizens of Constantinople had
also acclaimed him as a great benefactor and as a saviour
of their sovereign. As the time was approaching for
Amedeo's return to his own country, he urged John V to
show his gratitude by following him to Rome to offer his
allegiance to the Pope. Reluctantly, the Emperor promised
to do so, but in the meantime explained the impossibility
of fulfilling his promise in the near future, as the state
of his Empire necessitated his presence in Constantinople.[4]
The news of this vague promise, however, seems to have
leaked out of the imperial palace, and the feeling of
undying hatred for Roman Catholicism was again stirred
up in the hearts of the Greeks. As the Count of Savoy
was boarding his galley for the homeward journey, the
Patriarch of Constantinople and a Greek knight came
to inform him that their Emperor was compelled to re-

---

[1] It was stipulated on the cession of the town to the Emperor on 9 March
that the Count should receive 15,000 gold florins. It appears, however, that
the sum actually paid amounted to only 11,028 parperos. Bollati di Saint-
Pierre, 3–4; Datta, 145–6.

For further details of the expedition accounts kept by the Count's treasurers,
Pietro Gervasio and Antonio Barberio, see Bollati di Saint-Pierre, Section I.
The editor of these documents does not give any reasoned analysis of them.
This remains to be done. The usefulness of the text of these receipts is not
confined to their demonstration of the heavy cost of the campaign; they also
serve to check the chronology of the crusade.

[2] The sum of 17,568 and a half gold parperos was raised from the town of
Mesembria. Bollati di Saint-Perre, 5.

[3] Summary of receipts and payments as presented by Gervasio and
Barberio, in Bollati di Saint-Pierre, 26–7 and 277–8.

[4] *Chron. de Sav.*, 315–16.

nounce his vow to come to Rome, as his subjects threatened
to depose him and elect another in his place if he left the
capital.[1]   Amedeo then seized the Patriarch and four
Greek barons whom he surrendered to the Pope later as
hostages until the submission of the Greeks to Rome became a reality.[2]   This way, however, proved as ineffective
as the rest; for even if the Emperor wished in all good faith
to unite the Greek and the Roman Churches, his subjects
as a whole were determined at any cost not to submit to
the papacy.[3]

On 4 June 1367, Amedeo of Savoy and his companions
sailed from Pera to Negropontis, Coron, Modon and along
the Dalmatian coast of the Adriatic to Venice.   They
arrived in the Republic of St. Mark on 31 July, and the
Count himself remained there until 8 September, when he
decided to travel direct to Rome before returning to his
own lands.[4]   Urban V, who had preached the crusade from
the Avignonese curia, was able to realize his cherished
ambition of returning to the Vatican in April 1367.   Thus
Amedeo, who had taken the Cross from Urban's hands
at Avignon, now went to report to him in Rome on the
accomplishment and result of the crusade.   The Pontiff
and his Cardinals were very gratified with the news
of the defeat of the Turks and the Bulgarians and of the
prospect of the union of the churches.   Amedeo handed
his Greek hostages to the convened church dignitaries, and
then took the road to his native parts.[5]

The expedition of Amedeo VI of Savoy, originally conceived as part of the crusade of Pierre I de Lusignan in
1365, was deflected from its original course by the misleading news fabricated by the Venetians for their own ends
and by the unfortunate coincidence of John V's imprison-

[1] *Chron. de Sav.*, 316–17.   [2] ib., 318–19.   [3] *vide supra*, Cap. XI.
[4] *Chron. de Sav.*, 318–19; Datta, 141 et seq.
[5] Amedeo's crusade is commemorated by an impressive bronze monument
in the Piazza Palazzo di Città, Turin.   The Count is represented in a
warlike attitude with a drawn sword in the right hand and a small shield in the
left.   Two Saracens lie at his feet—one dead with a broken weapon in hand
and the other fallen and desperately trying to shield himself from an impending blow of the crusader's sword.   The monument was a gift of
King Carlo Alberto, unveiled on 7 May 1853.

ment in Bulgaria.   Therefore, it became a single-handed
attempt with two definite purposes in view—first, a modest
attack against the Turks in Europe; and second, the
deliverance of the Emperor from captivity.   In these two
fields, it met with all the success that could be expected in
the circumstances.   On the other hand, in the wider issues
of the future, it had many and mixed results of a different
nature.   The Ottomans were indeed beaten in Gallipoli;
but they remained strong elsewhere and the recovery of
their losses was a· foregone conclusion.   The invasion of
part of the Bulgarian coast and the capture of the important
town of Mesembria for the Emperor of Constantinople
only paved the way for its fall to the Turks.   The Bulgarians had lost it and the Empire was too weak to keep it.
A war with Bulgaria, moreover, only fanned the flames of
hatred and fostered the spirit of division in the Balkans.
Instead of meeting their common enemy with a united
front, the princes of the East continued to drift apart, thus
enabling the Ottoman Sultans to pursue their career of
triumph in Europe without any serious opposition.   The
Kingdom of Bulgaria was perhaps further weakened and
its collapse accelerated by this crusade.   Before the end
of Murad's reign, the whole of that country was virtually
in the clutches of the Ottomans, and Šišman himself became a tributary to the Sultan in 1388.   Notwithstanding
the satisfaction expressed in Rome as to the union of the
Churches, this imaginary achievement of Amedeo's crusade
was quickly exposed by the hatred of the Greeks.   The
triumph of the Latin host was a transitory factor in the
history of south-eastern Europe.   The holy warriors passed
out of the Empire within a year, but the Turks remained
and watched for its final ruin.   The crusade undoubtedly
brought fame to Amedeo at the Roman curia and at the
European courts as well as in Italy [1] itself, but it also
brought him bankruptcy at home.   This was probably the
most enduring and most painful of its immediate effects.

---

[1] He became arbiter of many quarrels in Italy, and in 1382 prepared an
army for Louis d'Anjou in his attempt to reconquer the Kingdom of Naples.
He was universally lamented on his sudden death in 1383.   *Art de vérifier
les dates*, 836.

CHAPTER XVII

CRUSADE OF LOUIS II DE BOURBON

Idea and precursors of action against North Africa. France, Genoa and the crusade. Object and cause of the expedition: Tunis and piracy. Itinerary. Al-Mahdiya and its siege. End of expedition. Effect

THE idea of the crusade against North Africa was not foreign to Europe in later medieval times. In the thirteenth century Ramon Lull,[1] as a result of his personal contacts with the Moors in Spain and Barbary, had been its greatest exponent, and Philippe de Mézières[2] did not overlook it in his propagandist treatises for holy war during the following century. Action in this sphere also had a notable precedent in the last of St. Louis' crusades undertaken against the Kingdom of Tunis in 1270; but perhaps the direct precursor of the expedition of 1390 was that of 1388, when a combined fleet of three large Sicilian, five Pisan and twelve Genoese galleys surprised and occupied the island of Jerba in the Gulf of Gabès. At that time the island was a possession of Abul-'Abbās Abu-Bakr, King of Tunis, and the leader of the Christian army was Manfredo de Chiaramonte. Although Jerba was conquered mainly by Genoese galleys, Manfredo annexed it to the realm of Marie, Queen of Sicily, after paying the Genoese helpers a sum of 36,000 gold florins for their services. In the following year, Pope Urban VI, from whose hands Queen Marie had herself received the Kingdom of Sicily in fief, invested Manfredo with the lordship of Jerba and all the other smaller islands situated in the same Gulf near the shores of Tunis.[3]

[1] *vide supra*, Cap. IV.   [2] *vide supra*, Cap. VII.
[3] Stella, *Annal. Genuen.*, in Muratori, RIS, XVII, 1128; Reynaldus, XXVI, *ad ann.* 1389, no. 6; Mas Latrie, *Traités de paix et de commerce et documents divers sur les relations des chrétiens avec les arabes de l'Afrique Septentrionale au moyen âge*, 239–40.

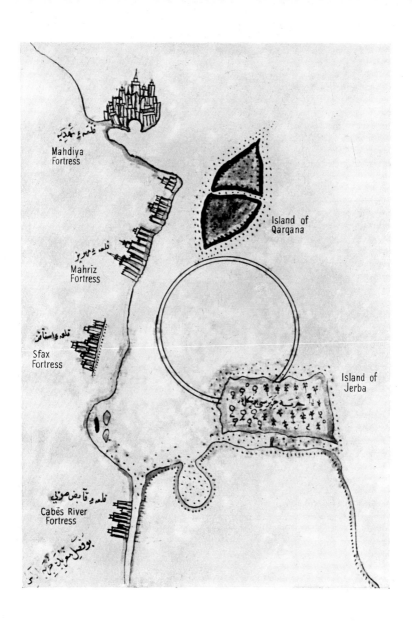

Meanwhile the situation, not only in Genoa, but also in France, seemed ripe for another expedition on a large scale against the African mainland itself.   Since the termination of the first part of the Hundred Years' War by the Treaty of Brétigny in 1360,[1] France had enjoyed a period of comparative peace; and under the wise and able government of Charles V (1364–80), the country had made a surprising recovery from the series of blows which it had sustained during the previous reigns.   At the accession of Charles VI (1380–1422), the age of prosperity, inaugurated by his predecessor, seemed to continue, at least during the first few years of the reign.   While England was in the throes of its internal struggles of the reign of Richard II (1377–99) and the Holy Roman Empire but a shadow of past power, France was spreading its influence in more than one direction.   Within the confines of the kingdom, there was a strong government, capable of putting an end to the urban revolts in Paris, Rouen and other north French towns. Outside the country, 'foreign' activity was shown chiefly in two centres.   In the first place, Philippe le Hardi, duc de Bourgogne, was extending his power in the Low Countries, and the King and his nobles assisted in the defeat of the Flemish armies at the battle of Rosebecke on 27 November 1382, carried out another campaign in Flanders in 1383, forced the peace of Tournai upon that country in 1385 in spite of English aid to it, and even invaded the Duchy of Gueldres in 1388.   In the second place, Louis II d'Anjou, cousin of King Charles, carried French arms into Italy and seized the Kingdom of Naples for himself.   This conquest was begun in 1382 under the auspices of France and with the blessing of the Holy See against the rival claims of Charles of Durazzo, a descendant of the first Angevin house of Naples who was assassinated in Hungary in February 1386 while under pain of excommunication.   In fact, the foundations of French activities in Italy, destined to become a more general and more direct affair in the reign of Charles VIII, must be traced to the last two decades of the fourteenth century.   At this time, too, Florence was

---

[1] Cosneau, *Grands traités de la Guerre de Cent Ans*, 33–68.

seeking an alliance with France in order to check the
ambitious schemes of the Dukes of Milan in Tuscany.[1]

In these circumstances, it was not surprising that Genoa
should turn to France for support in her troubles. Both
her internal and external conditions called for a policy
which ended in the surrender, at least nominally, of the
authority of the Republic to France and the appointment of Marshal Boucicaut as its governor on behalf of
Charles VI in 1396.[2] At home Genoa was the prey of
factions among her own nobles. The Doge Antoniotto
Adorno had acted as accomplice in the torture and murder
of six cardinals dragged in chains to Genoa by Urban VI
as a penalty for siding with the 'anti-pope' Clement VII.
This act of cruelty, coupled with excessive measures of
tyranny towards his own compatriots, created a profound
feeling of horror in Genoa, and Adorno's position became a
very precarious one. Moreover, the Milanese menace on
the northern boundaries of the Republic was becoming more
and more serious every day. To save himself from impending civil war at home and to save Genoa from the danger
of invasion by Milan from abroad, the astute doge decided
to sign a treaty with France acknowledging Charles VI as
'Defender of the Commune and the People' in 1396.[3]
Although this voluntary surrender to France came six years
after the accomplishment of the crusade of Louis II de
Bourbon, it gives some indication of the disposition of the
Republic towards her great Western neighbour before the
conclusion of the afore-mentioned treaty.[4] By sea, how-

---

[1] N. Valois, *France et Grand Schisme*, II, 19 et seq.; Coville, *Premiers
Valois et la Guerre de Cent Ans*, in Lavisse, *Hist. de France*, IV, 1ère partie,
288 et seq.; E. Mirot, *Siège de Mahdia*, 1–5; T. A. Trollope, *Commonwealth
of Florence*, II, 271.

[2] Delaville Le Roulx, *France*, I, 403.

[3] The Doge was generally styled as 'Januensium dux et populi defensor'. The treaties and documents connected with the surrender of Genoa
to France have been published by E. Jarry, *Origines de la domination française
à Gênes*, 369 et seq.

[4] Jarry, op. cit., 33, also points out that the response of France to the
Genoese request of 1390 in connexion with the Barbary expedition made the
name of Charles VI very popular in the Republic and paved the way for the
closer *rapprochement* of 1396.

ever, Genoa remained a great power and a formidable rival to Venice. Between them, the two republics shared most of the Eastern trade. The influence of the Genoese was particularly strong in the Black Sea where they owned the colony of Caffa and in the western part of the Mediterranean where they monopolized a good deal of the trade with the Barbary kingdoms, especially Tunis. Although superior by sea, Genoa was in need of reinforcement by land, and so found yet another reason for looking westward to France for support in her project for an expedition against Tunis.[1]

The state of the Moorish kingdoms in North Africa was a great source of anxiety for the Genoese. The empire of the Almohades, which had sustained many defeats in Spain, was further weakened by internal revolutions, and finally collapsed before the end of the thirteenth century. On its ruins, there arose four smaller and much less illustrious dynasties—the Naṣrides of Granada, the Merinides of Fez, the 'Abd al-Wadides of Tlemsen, and the Ḥafṣides of Tunis.[2] The last of these was the object of a series of Christian attacks of which the crusade of 1390 was only one. Tunis formed an admirable centre for the African trade, and its proximity to the Italian maritime republics attracted many Western merchants to the great souks of its capital and of the ports of Soussa, al-Mahdiya, Sfax and Gabès as well as to the island of Jerba seized by Sicily in 1388. Cereals, dates, rugs, leather coats of mail, and Muslim slaves formed part of Tunisian exports.[3] Christian funduqs are known to have been in existence at al-Mahdiya, Sfax, Gabès and Jerba.[4] If Tunis attracted ships from the West, it also became the home of the Barbary corsairs. These had small fleets of light craft which they manœuvred with skill in attacking and plundering the heavy trade galleys. Unable to suppress piracy on their own shores, the weak kings of Tunis appear to have gone to the other extreme by encouraging it. The audacity of these pirates

[1] Petitot, *Livre des faicts du mareschal Boucicaut*, in *Coll. des mémoires*, VII, 4 et seq.; Mirot, op. cit., 5–8; J. T. Bent, Genoa, 36–7, 178–80.
[2] Ch. A. Julien, *Hist. de l'Afrique du Nord*, 409, 418.
[3] ib., 429–30.   [4] ib., 431.

grew with the passing of time.   On many occasions they
reached and raided the coasts of Sicily and Italy.   Nothing
could be more menacing for the states whose welfare was
based solely on commerce and the security of the seas.   A
crusade against Tunis as visualized by the Genoese, was
not merely an act of piety, but a matter of necessity for their
livelihood.   It was above all meant to chastise the pirates
and deal a blow to Abu-Bakr, King of Tunis, for his acqui-
escence in, if not patronage of, this reign of lawlessness on
the seas.   This was therefore the immediate and also the
ultimate cause of the Barbary expedition from the Genoese
point of view.   The choice of the town of al-Mahdiya as
the object of the coming siege was not haphazard.   In
Mahdiya, the piratical navies appear to have found a stronghold to which they resorted with their plunder.   Hence
the Genoese directed the expedition to the chief source of
their troubles.[1]

Towards the end of the year 1389, Charles VI was travelling in Languedoc to receive homage from his southern
vassals, to reassure himself of the good faith of some of the
unruly and powerful barons especially Gaston Phoebus,
comte de Foix, to invest his cousin Louis II of Anjou with
the crown of the Kingdom of Naples while he was at Avignon,
and to end the scandal of the schism in the Church.   After
a long and circuitous journey, he arrived at Toulouse on
29 November 1390.[2]   It was there that the King received
a Genoese embassy which sought his support for their project of Crusade.   According to some Italian writers, the
ambassadors delivered a great oration in his presence, extol-
ling him as the defender of the faith whose renown
had spread over the world and whose name was feared
by all infidels.   The word 'Frank' in the East had long been
regarded as the synonym of 'Christian', and the piety and

---

[1] Mirot, op. cit., 7–9; Delaville Le Roulx, op. cit., I, 166–7; Julien, op. cit.,
431.
[2] Froissart (Kervyn), XIV, 30 et seq.; E. Petit, *Séjours de Charles VI*
(1380–1400), in *Bulletin du Comité des Travaux historiques et scientifiques*,
section d'histoire et de philologie (Paris, 1887), 43–5; cf. Mirot, op. cit., 2
and note 2.   The King left Paris on 2 September 1389, and with him many of
his nobles and councillors.   Charles was only twenty at the time.

courage of the French people were now needed for the holy
cause in aid of the Genoese against the Saracens; and
although the outcome of the planned campaign would be
limited, the harvest of glory from it would be great and
everlasting.[1]   On the other hand, the French chroniclers
make only a plain statement of the relevant facts put forward
by the ambassadors.   Their spokesman, a clerk, asked for
the King's help to suppress the terrorization of the seas by
the Saracen pirates, and, on behalf of his republic, offered
to supply the expedition with the necessary fleet to convey
the crusaders to al-Mahdiya.[2]   Moreover, Genoa would
furnish all the provisions and an army including twelve
thousand archers in addition to eight thousand well-equipped
valets (*gros valets*) for the duration of the campaign.[3]
After listening to the Genoese plan and offer, the King
promised to give the ambassadors his reply in two days,[4]
during which he retired to consider the whole matter with
his council.   In the secret deliberations which followed,
there were evidently two opposed parties.   The Marmousets including such men as Bureau de la Rivière and Jean
le Mercier, promoted from the ranks of the *bourgeoisie* by
Charles V and employed by Charles VI as his personal
advisers until the disastrous period of his madness, approached the subject with great caution.   France was in
need of her men, they asserted, especially as the negotiations
for a stable and abiding peace with England were still in
progress and the relations between the two countries were
not yet founded on a permanent basis.   It would therefore be folly to encourage a project by which the flower of
French chivalry should be engaged in foreign fields while
the situation at home remained precarious.   On the
other hand, the nobles, especially the young and impulsive

---

[1] Foglietta, *Dell'Istorie di Genova*, 348 et seq.; cf. Mirot, 10.

[2] Known in the French chronicles as 'ville d'Auffrique en Barbarie'.   See
for example, Cabaret d'Orville, 218 *passim*; Froissart (ed. Kervyn), XIV,
152 et seq., 269 et seq.   *Vide infra*, 411 n. 4.

[3] Cabaret d'Orville, 218-20; Froissart, XIV, 152-3; *Religieux de Saint-
Denis* (ed. Bellaguet), I, 648-51; Jean Juvenal des Ursins (ed. Michaud et
Poujoulat, in *Nouv. Coll. des Mémoires*, II), 383.

[4] Cabaret d'Orville, 220.   According to the *Religieux*, I, 650, the King
regretted that he was unable himself to lead the crusade.

among them, adopted a totally different attitude. The cessation of the war with England had deprived them of opportunities to display their valour and they wished to occupy their time in a holy cause. Their advice was accepted, but with some reservation, probably owing to the influence of the Marmousets. The King informed the Genoese ambassadors that he was willing to grant their republic aid and comfort.[1] The 'ordonnance' of the crusade, however, imposed certain limits to this aid. Every knight or esquire who wished to participate in the forthcoming campaign, must equip himself, not from the state revenues, but entirely at his own expense. The great barons of the land were not free to employ men from outside their own domains for this expedition. Knights and squires alone had the right to join, but valets were excluded from this privilege, at least as long as they were not gentlemen. Finally, the total number of the French contingent was not to exceed fifteen thousand.[2]

The choice of the leader of the crusade was then made without great difficulty. The Genoese requested that this dignity should be conferred upon a prince of the blood. First among the candidates was the King's brother Louis, comte de Valois and duc de Touraine. His youth, for he was only eighteen years of age at the time,[3] and his inexperience in matters of warfare decided the King and his council against his appointment.[4] Next in importance and social standing, were the King's uncles. Jean, duc de Berry,[5] had not distinguished himself in war, diplomacy or administration, and his deplorable career in Languedoc was in all minds. On the other hand, Philippe le Hardi, duc

---

[1] Cabaret d'Orville, 220–4; *Religieux*, I, 650–3; Juvenal des Ursins, l.c.

[2] Mirot, 12.

[3] Born 13 March 1372, Louis became comte de Valois in 1376, duc de Touraine in 1386 and duc d'Orléans in 1392. He married Valentina Visconti, daughter of Giovanni Galeazzo and Isabelle de France in 1389. His assassination on 23 November 1407 was a crucial event in the dissensions in France which ultimately gave rise to the Armagnac party as against the Burgundian in the period 1407–22.

[4] Froissart, XIV, 154.

[5] Jean was duc de Berry and d'Auvergne as well as comte de Montpensier et de Poitou.

de Bourgogne[1] and comte de Flandre, was the greatest
figure in French diplomacy and one of the wealthiest nobles
in France.   All eyes must have turned to him as the
most eligible leader, but he was much too engrossed in
his own schemes in the north-east of France and in asserting his influence at the court of Paris, to embark on
a foreign campaign.   The last candidate was Louis II de
Clermont, duc de Bourbon and the King's maternal uncle,
a man of mature age and considerable experience in
affairs of state and in matters of war.[2]   An able and prudent
captain, he was also surnamed the 'Good Duke' on account
of his generous, pious and chivalrous character.   Gentle in
manner, benign in speech, energetic in action and attractive
in person and manner, he drew all to him.[3]   Moreover, his
past had been glorious.   He had fought by the side of
Jean II le Bon and shared captivity with him in England
for eight years (1360–8).   After recovering his liberty, he
participated in the famous campaigns of Bertrand du Guesclin in Brittany and Guyenne.   On the death of Charles V,
he was nominated one of the young King's guardians along
with the ducs d'Anjou, de Berry, and de Bourgogne.
He fought with Charles VI at the battle of Rosebecke
in 1382 and was one of the promoters of the Spanish
expedition of 1386.   He was considering an expedition
to Italy to assist Louis of Anjou when the project for
crusade emerged to attract his attention.[4]   His ideal of
chivalry found a notable expression in the establishment of
a new order of Knighthood which he called the Order of

[1] Christine de Pisan, *Livre des fais* (Michaud et Poujoulat), II, 20,
describes him as 'Prince . . . de souverain sens et bon conseil, doulx . . . et
aimable à grans, moyens et à petis; . . . large comme un Alixandre, en court
et estat magnificent'.

[2] Born on 4 August 1337, Duke Louis was fifty-three years old at the
time of the crusade.   Cabaret d'Orville, xxvii, 4.

[3] One of the best accounts of Bourbon's character in his youth is written by
Christine de Pisan, op. cit., 22:
'En sa jeunesse, fu prince bel, joyeux, festoyant et de honnorable amour
amoureux et sanz péchié, selon que relacion tesmoigne; joyeux, gentil en ses
manières, bénigne en parolles, large en dons, avenant en ses faiz, d'acceuil si
gracieux, que tiroit à luy amer princes, princesses, chevaliers, nobles et toutes
gens qui le fréquentoyent et véoyent'.

[4] Cabaret d'Orville, *passim*; Valois, *Grand Schisme*, II, 14; Mirot, 11.

the Golden Shield (Escu d'or).[1]   Its motto was 'ALLEN',
to signify action in the service of God and country wherever
the conquest of honour by feats of chivalry could be pursued.[2]   When there was some hesitation in the King's
council as to the nature of the response to be given to the
Genoese, the Duke was foremost in expressing noble sentiments in favour of the crusade.   It was a project after his
own heart.   He pleaded with the King to grant him the
leadership of the host and permission to fight in the King's
name and in God's service;[3] for no glory could equal that
of marching in the steps of Louis IX and fighting in the
regions where the Saint himself had spent the last days of
his life in defence of a holy cause.[4]   The King's objections,
according to Cabaret d'Orville,[5] were twofold—the great
work which was awaiting accomplishment at home, and the
difficulty of finding soldiers who were prepared to undertake
so distant a journey.   The Duke assured Charles that in his
own domains, he had the knights and squires who would
not fail him, but follow him in his great enterprise.   Finally,
the King complied with the Duke's wish and informed the
Genoese ambassadors of his decision.   These hastened
back to their republic with the good tidings, while the news
of the crusade spread rapidly throughout the Kingdom of
France and reached England and Spain.[6]   Pope Clement
VII granted the Duke and all those who might follow him
plenary absolution from sins.[7]

After having received the pontifical blessing at Avignon
for his undertaking, Louis de Bourbon proceeded to Paris

---

[1] Cabaret d'Orville, 12–15.

[2] ib., 13.   The Duke's speech to the knights of his Order included the
following significant phrase as an explanation of the motto chosen by him:
'Allen est à dire: allons tous ensemble au service de Dieu, et soyons tous ung
en la deffense de nos pays, et là ou nous porrons trover et conquester honneur
par fait de chevalerie'.

[3] ib., 221; 'que je me puisse employer pour vous, et au nom de vous, au
service de Dieu: car c'est la chose au monde que j'ai plus désirée, et après les
fais mondains, il est belle chose de servir Dieu'.

[4] *Religieux*, I, 652–3.   [5] *Chron. du bon duc*, 221.

[6] *vide infra*, recruits from these countries.

[7] Cabaret d'Orville, 223; 'absolucion de poine et de coulpe, à lui et à ses
gens'.

in order to raise the necessary funds for the preparations.[1]
Louis de Touraine, the King's brother, furnished him with
a loan of twenty thousand florins [2] and the King with a
donation of twelve thousand gold francs.[3]   Nor were the
other French barons forgotten in these generous transactions.   Charles placed at their disposal twenty thousand
six hundred and thirty gold francs, Philippe le Hardi gave
two thousand to Philippe de Bar, and Louis de Touraine
distributed thirteen thousand five hundred and thirty francs
to various members of his own court.[4]   While these
measures were being taken, Louis de Bourbon went to his
duchy to arrange the government of his domains in his
absence and to institute a small council of five members
of his Chambre des Comptes de Moulins to supervise the
recruitment of his own contingent.   It was also on this
occasion that he wrote his last will and testament in readiness
for the unknown.[5]

The news of the crusade circulated far and wide.   Nobles,
knights, men-at-arms and squires begged for permission
to take the Cross under the ducal banner before the total
number of fifteen thousand should be completed in accord-

---

[1] He stopped on his way to Paris only for a short interview with Philippe le
Hardi at Chançeaux near Sémur on 17 February 1390.   E. Petit, *Itinéraires
de Philippe le Hardi et de Jean sans Peur*, in *Coll. des documents inédits de
l'hist. de France* (Paris, 1888); cf. Mirot, 12 and note 4.

[2] Huillard-Bréholles et Lecoy de la Marche, *Titres de la maison ducale de
Bourbon II*, 38 no. 3790, dated wrongly Paris 18 March 1380 instead
of 1390, whereby the duc de Bourbon mortgaged all his property, especially the revenue accruing from his county of Clermont for the payment
of that sum 'pour accomplir le voyage que, à l'aide de Dieu, il entend à faire
en Barbarie'.   Ib., no. 3791, dated Paris 26 March 1390, whereby Louis de
Touraine ordained that his 'valet de chambre, Simon de Dammartin, changeur
et bourgeois de Paris' should receive from the officers of the Bourbonnais in
the county of Clermont all the payments made towards the afore-mentioned
loan.

[3] B.N., P. or. 455, dos. Bourbon no. 20; cf. Mirot, 13 n. 2.

[4] Arch de la Côte-d'Or, B 1479, f. 680 vo.; Mirot, 13, 41 et seq.   Burgundy's donation was made on 11, the King's on 22 March 1390.   Touraine
entrusted his treasurer Jean Poulain with the distribution of the sums contributed by him.

[5] Cabaret d'Orville, 224; Delaville Le Roulx, op. cit., I, 170; Mirot, 13.
The government of the Bourbonnais was entrusted to Pierre de Norris, a
Nivernais.

ance with the royal ordinance.[1] Gentlemen from many parts of France,[2] from England and its Continental empire,[3] from Aragon,[4] and from Hainault and Flanders[5] came in detachments of no mean size to join the movement. The rendezvous of the French contingents was Marseilles, that of the foreign troops was Genoa. As regards the accumulation of provisions for these armies, an unforeseen difficulty had to be solved by the Duke. The Genoese had promised to furnish all the needs of the crusade; but the Doge wrote to inform Louis that unless he mediated with the comte de Provence who had no sympathy for the Genoese and with the Angevin authorities in the Kingdom of Naples for permission to buy some of the necessary articles in which the Ligurian territories were poor, there might be a serious shortage. The Duke at once wrote to Provence and delegated Charles de Hangast[6] to the court of Naples to procure the authorization for Genoese purchases. At Marseilles, however, these were found inadequate, and Bourbon had to supply the deficiency.[7] He probably came to this port

---

[1] *vide supra*, 404.

[2] Such as Philippe de Bar, Philippe d'Artois comte d'Eu, Enguerrand VII de Coucy, Guy and Guillaume de la Trémouille, Jean de Vienne admiral of France and others of whom many served later in the Crusade of Nicopolis. *Vide infra*, Cap. XVIII and Appendix IV.

[3] These included Jean Harpedenne, seneschal of Bourdeaux, John Beaufort, natural son of the Duke of Lancaster, Philippon Pelourde, Lewis Clifford, Lord Neville, John Clinton, John Cornwall and William Fotheringay. Cabaret d'Orville, 223; Mirot, 16; Delaville Le Roulx, I, 176; see also Appendix IV. Juvenal des Ursins, 383, says that 'le comte de Derby, un vaillant chevalier d'Angleterre, délibéra d'aller avec lesdits seigneurs de France, et vint vers eux avec une compagnie de ceux de son pays non mie grande'.

[4] Such as the vicomte de Rosas and Pierre de Planella; Mirot, l.c., see also Appendix IV. It is interesting to note that the Aragonese members of the expedition were not sent out of sympathy for the Genoese whom they hated, but merely to make certain that the army did not land on any territory belonging to their kingdom, especially as Genoa disputed with them the possession of the island of Sardinia. Mirot, 19–20.

[5] Such as le comte d'Ostrevant, Jean de Lannoy and Jean de Ligne; Mirot, l.c., see also Appendix IV.

[6] Cabaret d'Orville, 225. Mirot, 17, puts him as Jean de Hangast.

[7] ib., 227. This included 'deux cens tonneaulx de vin, et deux cens lars, avecques foison potages, et telles provisions ... Et fit mettre deux mil chiefs de poulailles ... pour les malades.'

on 20 June and spent the rest of the month in supervising and completing the preparations.[1]   The troops behaved well and paid their way, so that wherever they went, they had a cordial reception.[2]   In the harbour were twenty-two Genoese galleys [3] awaiting them, and all was ready at the beginning of July, when the fleet set sail to Genoa.   While the bulk of the French army thus came by sea, the foreign contingents including the English under the command of John Beaufort, the Flemings and also the Burgundians arrived at the republic by the land route.[4]   Philippe de Bar and Guy de la Trémouille had been sent ahead of the Duke not later than 13 May to supervise the Genoese preparations.[5]   On reaching the Ligurian waters, the Duke ordained that the army must not land and that the galleys should remain three miles off the coast [6] in order to avoid unnecessary confusion and waste of time; but he himself and a small number of nobles paid a hurried visit to Antoniotto Adorno and were received with great joy and honour by the citizens.[7]   The Genoese army as estimated by the *Religieux de Saint-Denis* consisted of one thousand arbalesters, two thousand men-at-arms, and about four thousand mariners.[8]   According to the same writer's estimate, their

[1] *En route* to Marseilles, Louis visited his nephew Amé VII in Turin. With him were Enguerrand de Coucy, the comtes d'Eu and d'Harcourt, the admiral Jean de Vienne, and a physician named Jean de Grandeville.   Saraceno, *Registri dei principi di Casa d'Acaia* (*Miscellanea di storia italiana*, XX), 186; Cabaret d'Orville, 223–4; cf. Mirot, 17.

[2] Juvenal des Ursins, 383. 'Et partout ou ils passoient on leur faisoit bonne chere, car ils payoient complètement ce qu'ils prenoient.'   In that age, this seems a remarkable and unusual feature of the campaign.

[3] Cabaret d'Orville, 226.

[4] Foglietta, l.c.; *Religieux*, I, 652–3.

[5] Arch. de la Côte-d'Or, B 1479, f. 83; letters dated 13 May 1390 to the said nobles in Genoa; cf. Mirot, 18 n. 3.   Froissart, XIV, 155–6, mentions these two among others who had gone to Genoa for the same purpose.

[6] Cabaret d'Orville, 228.

[7] Froissart, XIV, 156; Cabaret d'Orville, 228–9.   The Duke's companions on his visit to the Doge were the comte d'Eu, the sire de Coucy and Souldich de l'Estrau (or Soudic de la Trau).   When leaving, they were given 'foison d'épices, sirops, prunes de Damas, et autres liqueurs' to comfort the sick.

[8] *Religieux*, l.c.   Juvenal des Ursins, l.c., gives an estimate of a thousand arbalesters and four thousand other well-armed combatants.

fleet was composed of eighty galleys and other vessels;[1] and
if we add to these the twenty-two galleys conveying the
French,[2] the total would exceed a hundred in all.[3] Giovanni
Centurione, surnamed d'Oltramarino, a relative of the Doge
and an experienced sailor, was appointed admiral in command of the fleet.[4] There only remained the ceremony of
blessing the expedition before sailing in accordance with the
general usage on occasions of crusades. This presented
the leaders with some difficulty owing to the schism in the
Church and the presence of contingents from countries
which supported Boniface IX in Rome and others which
obeyed Clement VIII at Avignon. To satisfy all, representatives of both popes were brought to the army and a
double benediction was given.[5]

Finally, the fleet set sail to its destination, one day early
in July [6] when the sea was calm and the wind favourable.
The details known of the itinerary show that the galleys
must have followed the short route between Genoa and the
Kingdom of Tunis by crossing the Tuscan, Tyrrhenian and
Mediterranean Seas to the Gulf of Gabès. Passing by the
small islands of Gorgona and Elba, and sailing along the
coast of Sardinia, they halted nearly midway at Cagliari and
the little island of Ogliastro for re-victualling. As they
crossed the part of the sea called by Froissart 'le gouffre de
Lion', much feared by the medieval sailors, they underwent
great peril of dispersion and foundering owing to a tempest
which swept that region. In the end, however, the fleet
reached the island of Conigliera, only sixteen leagues off the

---

[1] *Religieux*, l.c.

[2] Cabaret d'Orville, *vide supra*, 409 and n. 3.

[3] Froissart, XIV, 157, speaks of one hundred and twenty galleys, two
hundred other vessels for men-at-arms and arbalesters, and more than a
hundred transports for provisions.

[4] *Religieux*, I, 654; Paolo Interiano, *Ristretto delle historie Genovesi*, f. 132
ro. Interiano estimates the fleet at sixty galleys and twenty other ships.

[5] *Religieux*, l.c.; Juvenal des Ursins, 383–4.

[6] Mirot, 21, suggests that the exact date was 3 July 1390. Delaville Le
Roulx, I, 178, says that on the third day after leaving Marseilles, the Duke
himself landed at Genoa. Froissart, XIV, 158, records the arrival of the
fleet at Porto Fino, a maritime suburb of Genoa, on the third day after sailing
and at Porto Venere, an eastern frontier town of the republic, on the fourth
day. The fleet remained for one night at each of the two ports.

African coast, probably in the neighbourhood of Monastir, a little north of al-Mahdiya.[1]   This last island had been fixed beforehand as their meeting-place in case of dispersion by weather.   There, they stopped for nine days [2] for the soldiers to recuperate from the weariness and sickness of a hard journey, and for the leaders to hold a council of war and decide on the steps to be taken for immediate action on the mainland.

Al-Mahdiya,[3] invariably known in the French sources as the city of Africa [4] (cité d'Auffricque), was chosen as the object of their offensive operations.   This choice, it has already been remarked,[5] was made on account of the fact that the town had become the chief stronghold of piratical bands who made a habit of plundering Christian ships and raiding the towns and villages on the coasts of Sardinia, Sicily and Italy.   Ibn Khaldūn states in this connexion that the Barbary corsairs seized many of the Christian inhabitants of those regions and either sold them in the slave-markets of Algeria and Tunisia or received a heavy ransom for their liberation.[6]   Another reason was perhaps that al-Mahdiya had twice been the object of Christian attacks before that time, and on both occasions it had succumbed to the arms of the invaders.   In 1087, it was occupied by a combined force of the Genoese, Pisans and Normans of Sicily; and in 1148 it was again seized by the Normans and remained as a Sicilian colony for twelve years before it was recovered by the Almohad 'Abd al-Mu'min.[7]   If the town had thus

---

[1] Cabaret d'Orville, 229 (*seize lieues*); Froissart, XIV, 158, (*trente milles*); Juvenal des Ursins, 384.   Gorgona is a little island in the Tuscan Sea, Ogliastro another situated near the coast of Sardinia and Conigliera probably the modern Kuriat, a fishing island, near the southern coast of the Gulf of Hammāmet east of Monastīr and north of Moknine in the kingdom of Tunis.

[2] Cabaret d'Orville, 229; Froissart, XIV, 159, 212.

[3] Another town bearing the same name, but formerly known as al-Mamura, exists in Morocco on the Atlantic coast at the mouth of Wādī Sabu.

[4] Probably from the name of Cape Africa upon which the town of al-Mahdiya is situated between the Gulfs of Hammāmet to the north and Gabès to the south.   *Vide supra*, 403 n. 2.

[5] *vide supra*, 401–2.   [6] *Kitāb al-'Ibar*, VI, 399.

[7] Yāqūt, *Mu'jam al-Buldān* (ed. Wüstenfeld), IV, 696; Qazwīnī, *'Āthar al-Bilād* (ed. Wüstenfeld), II, 184; ibn al-Athīr, *al-Kāmil* (ed. Tornberg), XI, 83–5.

been twice taken by Christian arms, it must have seemed possible for the host of God in 1390 to repeat the same experience with the same or even greater measure of success. Moreover, al-Mahdiya was one of the best-fortified towns on the coat of Tunisia. Its capture would break the power of the Barbary kings and furnish the Christians with a valuable base for further operations against the enemies of the true faith.[1] This view was to lead to complete disillusionment, partly owing to the duplicity of the Genoese who merely aimed at ensuring the safety of their fleets and at obtaining trade privileges for themselves, and partly as a result of the invulnerable nature of the fortifications of the town itself. The western sources, indeed, speak of the strength of the beleaguered city, but they offer no systematic description of it beyond what the reader may glean from their account of the siege. This gap is filled by the Oriental geographers and chroniclers, of whom many must have visited the town in their wide travels. Al-Mahdiya, we are told, was (and still is [2]) a double town. The main town was built on a small peninsula projecting into the sea like the 'palm of the hand', connected with the mainland by means of an isthmus which resembled the 'wrist'.[3] Its founder,[4] al-Mahdī 'Ubaid Allāh, from whom it derived its name, intending to adopt it as the capital of his Fatimid realm, spared no effort and no money to render it worthy of his dignity as a Caliph and a monarch. Apart from the peninsular founda-

---

[1] In the deliberations of the crusaders on the island of Conigliera as quoted by Froissart (XIV, 215), al-Mahdiya is regarded as the key to the kingdoms of North Africa, and its fall, moreover, would make all the Saracens as far as Nubia and Syria tremble.

[2] Professor H. A. R. Gibb (Oxford), who has visited the Mahdiya district, says that although now in ruins, the town still bears signs of its double structure and past strength.

[3] Yāqūt, op. cit., IV, 694–5; Qazwīnī, op. cit., II, 183; Abul-Fedā, Taqwīm al-Buldān (ed. Reinaud and de Slane), 144–5; al-Dimashqī, Nukhbat al-Dahr (ed. Fraehn and Mehren), 234–5. The peninsula is about one mile in length and 500 yards in breadth; article al-Mahdiya by G. Marçais, in EI, III, 121.

[4] The date of its foundation was A.H. 300/A.D. 912. It took about four years to build, since its completion is reported by Yāqūt (IV, 695) in the month of Dhulqi'da 303/916 and that of its walls even later in 305/917. Al-Mahdī, however, did not settle there until 308/920.

tion, the Caliph established another town close to the first on the mainland. The first was adopted as the residential quarter and the second was mainly a business centre. Both towns, however, were strongly fortified with walls and lofty towers. Heavy iron gates served as outlets to the sea and to the land.[1] A special system for the storage of water in addition to a regular fresh supply by canal was devised to ensure the ability of the town to resist long sieges.[2] The entrance to the harbour was guarded by two towers and a chain across the bay, which accommodated a large number of ships.[3] In attacking a town of this description, the crusaders would evidently be confronted with a task of considerable magnitude. Nevertheless, the decision of Conigliera was unanimously accepted by the host, and the fleet set sail to al-Mahdiya.

On the Muslim side, the news of the expedition seems to have reached the King of Tunis some time before the arrival of the Christians. Ibn Khaldūn, the only Arab historian who gives a fairly detailed account of the siege, says that the King prepared for the coming encounter by

---

[1] Yāqūt, l.c.; Qazwīnī, l.c.; al-Dimashqī, l.c.; *Description de l'Afrique Septentrionale* par El-Bekrī, trans. de Slane, 65–6. Yāqūt describes one of the gates as weighing 1,000 Qintars including nails, each weighing 6 Ratls. (1 Qintār = 100 Ratls, i.e. approximately 100 lb). Its length was 30 Shibrs, i.e. about 15 feet. Piri Re'īs, the sixteenth-century Turkish navigator who visited al-Mahdiya and drew the earliest-known plan of it, says that there were seven gates on the land side, one of bronze and the rest of iron—each surmounted by a tower. He also states that he had never seen a site like that of al-Mahdiya, as it was almost an island, and he admires its walls and fortifications. P. Kahle, *Piri Re'īs Bahrija*; Cap. 89. In the course of their account of the siege the Western sources refer to three land gates. The difference in the sources as to the number of gates may be explained by the fact that al-Mahdiya was a double town. One gate or passage connected the two foundations, but more than one connected the mainland town with the interior of the country.

[2] Yāqūt and Qazwīnī, l.c., state that 360 huge cisterns were made to hold water sufficient for one year's requirements at the rate of approximately one cistern every day.

[3] Yāqūt, IV, 695–6, says that it accommodated thirty, and Qazwīnī, II, 183–4, says two hundred, but a footnote rectifies this to thirty. El-Bekrī, op. cit., 67–8, states that the harbour was large enough for thirty vessels and that the Sultan had two hundred ships including two large galleys in the neighbourhood of the palace.

sending his son, Abu Fāris, to raise an army of volunteers and watch for the hostile fleet in that district.[1] The Christian galleys, however, sailed to the shores of al-Mahdiya, and the army landed without meeting any resistance. Froissart reports a discussion which arose in the Moorish council of war as to whether they should resist the disembarkation of the Christian troops.[2] Although the details furnished by the chronicler may belong to the world of fiction, the story in its broad outline has the appearance of truth, judging by subsequent events. Two Saracen 'knights', he says, named Mandifer and Bellius, advanced two different views before the council. The first asserted that it was their duty to defend al-Mahdiya from the outset by preventing the enemy from landing. The second, an old and experienced man, opposed this suggestion. The Christians, he argued, would force their way to a landing under cover of the redoubtable Genoese arrows against which the defence had no protection. Moreover, a defeat of the Muslim vanguard might lead to the total loss of the city before the advent of further reinforcements, more especially as the French and their companions were known to be expert and subtle warriors.[3] On the other hand, they had no horses with which they might overrun the countryside, while the city was impregnable and the climatic conditions were unfavourable.[4] The weather was hot, and it would become still hotter. They would necessarily be encamped under the scorching African sun while the Sara-

[1] *Kitab al-'Ibar* (Bulāq ed.), VI, 400.

[2] Froissart, XIV, 217–21.

[3] ib., XIV, 219; 'car les François et ceulx qui sont venus en leur compaignie pour faire armes, sont trop expers en armes et trop subtils'.

[4] This point is probably not without foundation in truth. At an early stage in the negotiations with the Genoese ambassadors, they informed the Duke of Bourbon that the Republic could mass sufficient vessels for 6,000 men-at-arms if these were available, for horses would be unnecessary ('car il n'y fault nulz chevaulx'); Cabaret d'Orville, 223.

In a miniature of a combat near al-Mahdiya (MS. of Froissart's chron., B.N., fonds français, 2646, f. 79, reproduced by Mirot, 42–3), several pictures of horses can be seen, but in all the miniatures of the Harley MS. of Froissart (B.M. Harleian 4379, ff. 60 vo, 89 vo, 104 vo) reproduced in this study and also in Coulton's Studio vol. called *Chronicler of Chivalry*, 26, 29, 46, no horses are represented at all.

cens passed their days in the shade of trees.[1] Their provisions were limited, while the resources of the country
remained at the disposal of the native troops. Finally, sickness and death would prevail among them and ensure their
retreat. The revenge of the Arabs would be accomplished
without striking a single blow.[2] Whatever the origin of
this story may have been, the elaborate military preparations
of the Christians for disembarkation proved unnecessary,
since the Berber army avoided action at this stage, except
for a few volleys of missiles fired from the outlying towers
on the fleet as it entered the harbour.[3] The order of landing
had been planned at the island of Conigliera. The vanguard, consisting of six hundred men-at-arms and a thousand
Genoese arbalesters occupying the lighter craft under the
command of Enguerrand de Coucy and the comte d'Eu,
approached the shore first. Next came the main battle,
including the majority of the French contingents under the
personal command of the Duke accompanied by the members of his own household. Then the foreign contingents
with the English and the rest of the Genoese followed in
the rear.[4] In this order a perfect and undisturbed landing
was accomplished, probably in the latter part of the month
of July.[5] Then, in accordance with the modes and con-

---

[1] Froissart, XIV, 220. 'L'air est chault, et encoires sera-il plus chault.
Ils seront logiés au soleil, et nous en fueillies.'

[2] id., l.c. 'Ainsi en serons-nous bien vengiés et sans cop férir.'

[3] Juvenal des Ursins, 384, and the *Religieux de Saint-Denis*, I, 656–9,
make special mention of a heated battle in which the English bowmen played
a prominent part on landing; but this is confuted by the sequence of events
and by the authoritative account of Cabaret d'Orville and ibn Khaldūn on the
French and Arabic sides.

[4] Cabaret d'Orville, 229–30.

[5] The exact date of the landing is uncertain. The *Religieux*, I, 654,
contends that the fleet was, for a whole month after leaving the shores of
Europe, exposed to the greatest of peril in a wild tempest—a statement which
implies that the landing took place early in August. Froissart, XIV, 223,
says that the Christians 'se logièrent sur la terre de leurs ennemis à la veue des
Sarrazins à ung Mercredy la nuit de la Magdalene', that is, 22 July. In
Barcelona, news circulated that the army had landed at Bona in the neighbourhood of the frontier between Tunisia and Algeria on 27 July and captured
a Berber king (Arch. Barcelona, Reg. Cancell. 1959, f. 82); and a document
of 7 August refers to the news of landing as already known in Genoa (Prato,
Arch. Dalini, fundaco Genova; Florence, cart. 34); cf. Mirot, 26 note 2.

ventions of the time, new knights were made on the field of
battle; among these were Jean de la Ligne and his cousin
Henri d'Antoing from the duchy of Hainault.[1] To the
crusaders' amazement, however, the enemy did not emerge
from their strongholds for the expected encounter, and there
was no sign to indicate that they intended taking any
immediate action. The host therefore spent the rest of the
day in pitching camp in the plain separating the city and
its garrison from the Muslim armies stationed on the hills
beyond. In the centre of the camp stood the Duke's
pavilion, surmounted by the banner of France in the middle
of which there was a white space decorated with the image
of a seated Madonna with the shield of Bourbon at her
feet.[2] On the right were the tents of Guy and Guillaume
de la Trémouille and those of many gentlemen from France,
Hainault and Holland; and on the left those of the sire
d'Offiment, John Beaufort and others. The Genoese arbalesters occupied the furthest extremities of the encampment
and covered a wide space. The provisions were left on
board the transports and conveyed daily by means of
small rowing boats according to the requirements of the
host.[3]

The first day passed without any engagement whatever
between the hostile forces, although, within the town itself,
drums had given the alarm from the high ramparts of the
towers as soon as the Christians were sighted.[4] On the
following morning, Duke Louis ordered the beginning of
the siege by land and by sea. The Genoese, of whom many
must have returned to their galleys, blockaded the city by
sea, while the French and foreign contingents guarded the
'three' land gates and cut all communications between
al-Mahdiya and Berber reinforcements coming from the
interior of the country.[5] For three days, the siege was
rigorously pursued without a sally from within the town
or battle by the Moorish army from without. At the
close of the third day, however, when the Christians

---

[1] Froissart, XIV, 222.   [2] Froissart, XIV, 223.
[3] ib., XIV, 223–6.   [4] ib., XIV, 216.
[5] Cabaret d'Orville, 230–1. On the land gates of al-Mahdiya, *vide supra*,
413 n. 1.

were taking their supper, the camp became silent and without movement and the occasion seemed to the inhabitants
an auspicious one for surprising their enemies. The garrison has been estimated at six thousand by one chronicler
and twelve thousand strong by another.[1] A considerable
number of these suddenly poured out of the land gates;
but, to their dismay, they found the other party fully prepared for these contingencies. The crusaders had installed
a guard of two hundred men-at-arms and one thousand
Genoese arbalesters [2] to guard against attacks of this kind.
Hugues de Chastellus, seigneur de Châteaumorand,[3] his
two sons Jean and Guichard, le sire de Négrepelisse, le sire
de l'Espinasse, Henri Antoing and others in command of
these detachments, not only defended their position with
courage, but also pursued the assailants to the very gates
of the town. The Saracens left three hundred dead on the
field in this encounter.[4] Afterwards they did not dare to
undertake another sally and were contented with the defence
of their fortified position behind the walls, leaving the whole
burden of hand-to-hand fighting in the open plains for the
combined armies and forthcoming reinforcements from
Tunis and elsewhere.

[1] Cabaret d'Orville, 230, gives the larger estimate which is adopted by
Mirot, 28. The *Religieux*, I, 656–7, on the other hand, gives the more
reasonable number of 6,000. A third estimate is also extant. Juvenal des
Ursins, 384, says that the King of Tunis placed 2,000 combatants inside al-
Mahdiya which he calls 'Carthage'; but this appears to be much too small a
garrison for a town so renowned for its strength.

[2] Froissart, XIV, 228. The same chronicler places this attack on the
second day after the organization of the encampment.

[3] The seigneur de Châteaumorand may be regarded as the real author of the
Chronique du bon duc. It was he, nearly forty years after the campaign, who
furnished Cabaret d'Orville with all details for the said chronicle. Châteaumorand was a member of the Bourbon household and he appears to have
been a close companion of the Duke in his expeditions and adventures. The
information furnished by him is therefore authoritative, although it suffers
from two defects—first, his intent on the glorification of his master in whose
praise he dictated his history to Cabaret d'Orville, and second, the usual
errors in dates and minute details as a result of dictating from memory after the
lapse of many years. On Cabaret d'Orville and Châteaumorand, see
Chazaud's introduction, x–xix; and the *Chronicle* itself, *passim*; Delaville Le
Roulx, I, 184–5.

[4] Cabaret d'Orville, 231; Froissart, XIV, 228–9.

It is not easy to fix the number of these combined forces
with precision, as we have to depend in this solely on the
Western sources which usually exaggerate the numerical
superiority of the enemy in order to magnify the achievement of the crusaders.   Mention has already been made of
the volunteer corps of unknown size, commanded by Abu
Faris, son of the King of Tunis, who had reached the
outskirts of al-Mahdiya before the landing of the Christians.
The main body of the regular troops was still to follow
some days later after the advent of the volunteers.   While
the siege operations were in progress, we are told by
Cabaret d'Orville,[1] two Genoese galleys which had been
reconnoitring the coast of Tunisia came to report the
approach of the kings of Tunis, Bugia and Tlemsen with a
force of cavalry sixty thousand strong.   The *Religieux de
Saint-Denis*,[2] on the other hand, says that the King of Tunis
commanded an army of forty thousand men outside the
town, and his estimate is echoed by Juvenal des Ursins [3]
and Froissart.[4]   In the absence of any definite information
about the volunteer corps, we may therefore regard
the Muslim forces as roughly between forty and sixty
thousand.   With a number so large as this, a pitched battle
could have been fought with no mean chance of success.
Yet the Berber kings wisely averted unnecessary bloodshed
and adopted the equally effective tactics of fast skirmishing
on horseback until the enemy was exhausted.   The army
arrived with the sounds of trumpets, drums, cymbals, fifes
and clarions.[5]   When they came within reach of a bowshot of the Christians, a minor engagement took place, and
their losses are estimated to have been sixty horse and
a hundred foot.[6]   They did not approach any further, and
at nightfall pitched their camp in a fortified position on a
small hill facing the enemy.   The Christians, for their

---

[1] *Chron. du bon duc*, 232.   [2] *Chron.*, I, 656–7.

[3] *Hist. de Charles VI*, 384.

[4] Froissart, XIV, 228, specifies the elements of the army as 30,000 archers
and 10,000 horsemen.

[5] Cabaret d'Orville, 235; 'à tous leurs naquères tambours cimballes
frestaulx et glais'.

[6] ib., 236.

part, aimed at two things—first, to render the spasmodic attacks of the Moors ineffective or even impossible, and second, to try and bring them out of their fortified camp into an open general battle.   As soon as the news of the approach of the large Muslim army reached the crusaders, the Duke summoned a council of war consisting of the sire de Coucy, the comte d'Eu, the comte Dauphin, the sire de Graville, the soudic de la Trau, the vicomte d'Uzès and others as well as the captains of the Genoese [1] to confer on the best military procedure to achieve these aims.   The Genoese who knew the tactics of the Moors better than the others advised the leader to encircle the camp from the coast south of al-Mahdiya to that on the north with a line of stakes and cord four feet high to prevent the horses from jumping into the Christian camp and harassing it.   This having been done, the Genoese fixed crossed galley oars and lances along this boundary line to enable their archers, thus protected, to aim at their targets with deadly effect.[2]   Small bodies each composed of one hundred men-at-arms and fifty arbalesters under the command of a captain were posted on guard at intervals of one hundred and twenty feet.[3]   The Duke himself commanded a thousand knights and five hundred arbalesters [4] in the rear to prevent the city garrison from sallying by the land gates and so pressing the crusaders between two hostile forces.

While the Christians thus defended their position with these elaborate preparations, the enemy systematically avoided entanglement in an open battle, and the remaining operations were limited to a series of minor skirmishes. These took place almost every day and sometimes in the dead of night throughout the period of forty-two days,[5] and prodigies of valour were displayed by all classes in the

[1] ib., 232–3.   [2] ib., 233.

[3] ib., 233–4.   Cabaret d'Orville's actual estimate is that every detachment of 150 should defend 'vingt cinq brasses'; but as each 'brasse' equals only six feet, it seems hardly feasible that less than one foot was allotted to each man, and it must therefore be inferred that Cabaret d'Orville meant the posting of these bodies at intervals of twenty-five 'brasses'.

[4] ib., 234.   The Duke's banner was carried on this occasion by Robert de Damas and his pennon by Jean de Châteaumorand.

[5] ib., 238.

host.   French, English,[1] Aragonese and Genoese—all distinguished themselves by acts of heroism.   God, too, and
the holy saints were on their side, for the miraculous happened on various occasions.   One night, the barking of a
watchdog brought by the Genoese gave the alarm of an
unexpected attack at a late hour and saved the Christians
from a difficult situation.[2]   Another nocturnal attack was
arrested by a miracle.   As the Saracens were quietly advancing towards the Christian camp under cover of darkness, a
'congregation' of ladies all dressed in white and carrying a
large white ensign (*gonfanon*) decorated with a red Cross
intercepted them and struck fear into their hearts.   At sight
of this apparition, their ranks fell into confusion and they
took to their heels.[3]   Whether this story was invented in
the course of the expedition to encourage the host or woven
by the chronicler to heighten the effect of his account of the
crusade, is difficult to judge, more especially as it can be
traced nowhere outside Froissart's chronicle.   Perhaps the
most serious of these skirmishes was the last one.   Froissart, whose flair for the dramatic was great, tells us of the
curious way in which this battle was inaugurated.   A young
Saracen named Agadinquor, the son of one 'duc d'Oliferne',
had fallen in love with Alsala, the only daughter and sole
heiress of the King of Tunis.[4]   In order to justify his plea
for her hand, he wished to distinguish himself by extraordinary feats of arms in the present campaign.   One day,
he sent an interpreter to propose on his behalf a duel
between himself and a picked member of the Christian army.
Boucicaut at once took the lead and suggested a combat of
one, ten, twenty or forty from the two sides of a closed field.
While these negotiations were in progress, many other
knights gathered round Boucicaut.   The news reached
the Duke; and he set out with two thousand men to put
an end to this foolhardy project.   It was, however, too

---

[1] Juvenal des Ursins, 384, pays a special tribute to the English archers in
the following words: 'Et firent bien hardiment les archers d'Angleterre, et
tellement que les Sarrasins reculèrent.'

[2] Froissart, XIV, 235.

[3] ib., XIV, 234–5.

[4] For the whole episode and the attack on the Saracen camp, see Froissart,
XIV, 229, 244–5; Cabaret d'Orville, 242–6; Juvenal des Ursins, l.c.

late to refrain from action, for he noticed that the Saracens had vacated their camp and were coming forward in
battle array.   Instead of moving towards the Muslim army,
Louis de Bourbon estimated it more profitable to hasten to
their empty camp and ruin it.   So a signal was given to
this effect, and the French and foreign contingents as well
as detachments of Genoese arbalesters attacked the camp
where they remained for an hour pillaging, destroying and
burning Muslim tents.   The comte d'Eu then warned the
Duke that the Saracens contemplated a reprisal on the
Christian camp which was deserted at the time, for only the
sire de Coucy and a handful of men together with the sick
troops were left behind.   The comte's reminder was
accepted by the Duke, and, at the sound of trumpets, all
emerged from the ruined camp in readiness for the retreat.
Strict orders were issued that the men should not be induced
to follow the Saracens, but should fight their way back in a
solid block.   Moreover, five hundred Genoese arbalesters
and two hundred men-at-arms were placed on the wing
exposed to attack.   The Moors attacked the Christian
column four or five times but were repulsed in each case
with heavy casualties.   Of the crusaders but few perished,
and these not by Saracen arms on the homeward march, but
in the camp as a result of exhaustion under the weight of
their coats of mail and the difficulty of free movement in
the soft sands of the desert.[1]

Throughout the succession of skirmishes, the Christians

---

[1] Cabaret d'Orville, 245, states that the Christian dead were only six
including the sire de Vailly, brother of the comte de Sancerre, Geoffrey de la
Celle-Guenon and four squires, and that their death was caused 'par deffaulte
d'allaine, ou sablon, dont ne se povoient ravoir, par ce qu'estoient trop fort
armés'.   The *Religieux de Saint-Denis*, I, 668–9, on the other hand, gives a
higher death-roll.   In addition to the names given by Cabaret d'Orville, he
mentions also messire de Blot, Jean de Pierre-Buffière, messire de Bellefaye,
Guichard de Malère, Yon de Cholet, Guichard de Palerne, Guy le Villain,
Jean Périer, Robert de Hangot, messire de Bours, Geoffrey de Dinan,
Guillaume Andureau, Jean des Îles, messire Jean de Trye, messire de Machecoul, Eustache de Mailly, messire Bertrand de Chesnac, messire Guy de
Vaise, Étienne du Port, an English gentleman named Fotheringay 'cum
multis aliis Anglicis', Alain de Champigny, and eight members of the household of the sire de Rieux 'quorum nomina non teneo, eciam ultimum diem
signaverunt'.

managed to keep al-Mahdiya itself in complete isolation and
without access to the mainland. But this was only half the
battle. The town remained intact, and the siege might have
dragged over a very long period until the crusaders' provisions were finished. The one way of surmounting this
difficulty was to try to seize the beleaguered city by assault.
Such an attempt probably took place just before the burning
of the Saracen camp. The Duke had summoned a council
of war in which the Genoese captains were consulted on the
matter. They had brought with them, they said, scaffold-
ing and timber material sufficient for the construction of a
high tower [1] and two 'hawks-bills' (*becs de faulcon* [2]) for
scaling the fortifications. The completion of this task
would take barely eight days. [3] According to information
previously gathered by the agents of the republic, these
structures should be applied at a certain tower by the
sea, where the walls and the defence were less invulnerable.
It was also considered that the holders of that front would
dominate the rest of the town and break all resistance. The
suggestion was regarded as excellent and another decision
was also taken by the council to the effect that part of the
army should storm the land gates and draw the garrison
from the sea wall to ensure the full use of the new structures,

[1] Cabaret d'Orville, 239; 'un eschaffault de trois estages de hault, et de
trois brasses et demie en carreure'. Cf. *Religieux*, I, 664; 'castellum ligneum
tricameratum, longitudinis quadraginta pedum totidemque latitudinis'.

[2] Cabaret d'Orville, l.c. 'Et d'autre partie devers la mer, dirent Gennois,
avons intencion de faire sur quatre gallées deux becs de faulcon, et en chascun
bec de faulcon une eschiffe à mettre quinze hommes d'armes, et dix arbalestiers.' The *Religieux*, l.c., provides further information regarding these 'hawk's
bills'—'Ut per mare, quod a latere muro continguum erat, hostes possent
eciam expugnari, prefati artifices super navem, quam defixis anchoris red-
diderant stabilem, ligneam turrim erexerant pontem in summitate habentem
qui superponeretur muro, ut manutentim pugnaretur.' It may be inferred
in this case that the 'bec de faucon', usually consisting of a wooden rod with
an iron head projecting in the shape of a hawk's beak for hooking on to
other objects, must have been of considerable size so as to support the
number of men given by Cabaret d'Orville. It may also be assumed that it
was mounted by special ladders hung on one side of the anchor at the top,
while the other side was intended to hook on to the wall.

[3] The account of the construction of the wooden tower and the battle on
the walls is given by Cabaret d'Orville, 238–42, and the *Religieux*, I, 664–7,
as well as the Arab historian ibn Khaldūn, VI, 400.

while another body guarded the rear against the attacks of
the Maghribine kings.   The Genoese at once set to work
and the host rejoiced, and every one thought that the
fall of al-Mahdiya was a foregone conclusion.[1]   The bitterness of their disillusionment was, however, as great as the
hopefulness of their expectation.   Neither the elaborate
tower, nor the ingenious adaptation of the 'becs de faucon' to
the circumstances of the siege, nor even the fierce storming
of the gates was of any avail.   All came to nothing in the
end.   The watchfulness of the beleaguered citizens was unflagging.   As soon as they became aware of the Genoese
activity, they reinforced the garrison on all sides.   It would
even appear that they must have guessed the object of the
wooden tower, for they brought their heavy artillery to the
spot against which the action was conducted.   Moreover,
the Religieux or rather his informant accuses the Genoese of
tardy movement.[2]   The tower was fixed on wheels and drawn
by men in the direction of the sea wall.   Its slow progress
gave the Saracens ample opportunity to bombard it for a
whole day and a night until they reduced it to a heap of
burning cinder before it reached its objective.   Cabaret
d'Orville says that the stones used in the bombardment were
covered with inflammable material,[3] and ibn Khaldūn mentions the use of naphtha. [4]   The 'becs de faucon' also proved
of little practical value.   When they were attached to the sea
wall, two Norman knights, who wished to show their prowess by being the first to climb to the ramparts, lost their lives
in the attempt.   One of them was cut to pieces and his
mutilated body thrown back to intimidate the crusaders,
while the other was dropped into the sea and drowned.[5]
Genoese sailors who succeeded in reaching the ramparts after
a prodigious effort, were foiled by a Saracen invention to
counteract the use of the 'becs de faucon'.   A closed
wooden structure was hurriedly built on the tower likely to
be attacked by the Genoese.   Crevices were left open in its
roof for the use of arms, and the interior was filled with

---

[1] Cabaret d'Orville, 240; 'les Chrestiens de l'ost furent si lies et joieulx
qu'il sembloit que tout fust nostre'.

[2] *Religieux*, I, 664–5.   [3] *Chron. du bon duc*, 240.

[4] *Kitāb al-'Ibar*, VI, 400.   [5] *Religieux*, l.c.

soldiers. The barefooted mariners who attempted to cross this area had their feet seriously wounded by Moorish swords and arrows from the most unexpected direction and were glad to retire to their ships.[1] The vigorous attack on the land side resulted, indeed, in the destruction of one of the gates; but the defence was so strong that the Duke's men could go no further.[2] Their only achievement in this fighting was the repulse of the Berber kings who came with their combined armies, now reduced to forty-six thousand men, to break into the crusaders' camp while the main battle was raging at the gates.[3]

The complete failure of the crusaders either to seize the town by storm or to annihilate the Maghribine army had a very discouraging effect on the mind of the host. The siege had been in operation for more than nine weeks,[4] the object of the campaign remained unaccomplished, and there was no sign to indicate that its fulfilment was nearer than at the first landing on infidel soil. Fighting was becoming more and more burdensome every day; and the heavy Western armour, suited for warfare in cooler climates and devised mainly for combat on horseback, became a serious handicap in the stifling heat of the African desert, and the invaders had but a scanty supply of horse. The

---

[1] Cabaret d'Orville, 241.   [2] id., l.c.

[3] ib., 241–2. The number given by Cabaret d'Orville on this occasion implies that the total loss of the Moors must have amounted to fifteen thousand, as he had previously (*vide supra*) stated that the combined Maghribine forces were sixty thousand when they first came to the relief of al-Mahdiya.

[4] Froissart, XIV, 231, refers to the period of nine weeks of skirmishing. Cabaret d'Orville, 238, 240, 245, 250, gives the duration of parts of the operations on various occasions—forty-two days of skirmishing before the decision to storm the town, eight days in the construction of the tower and the 'becs de faucon', fifteen days' skirmishing after the attack on the Saracen camp, and three days' negotiations before boarding the fleet; that is sixty-eight days in all, besides the additional days on which the serious fighting and the assault on the town took place, for they are not included in these calculations. Towards the end of the account of Cabaret d'Orville (248), a specific reference to the duration of the campaign is made as being two months and a half. The *Religieux*, I, 666–7, also refers to more than ten weeks 'in hac inaquosa et regione arenti'. But Froissart, XIV, 274, whose chronology of the campaign is somewhat confused, states that the crusaders boarded the fleet for the return journey on the sixty-first day after their arrival on African soil.

Christian armour compared badly with the Saracen leather suits [1] which, though offering less protection than the steel coats of mail worn by the knights and men-at-arms, gave them the advantage of a freer movement, and their light Arab steeds ensured swift action. The Genoese stock of provisions was running low, and the lack of fresh water was a matter of grave anxiety. After each battle, those who survived were suffocated by the heat and bathed in sweat; and, with gaping mouth and open nostrils, they panted for breath and searched for anything to quench their thirst.[2] The wine imported by the Genoese from Apulia and Calabria for the expedition was much too dry and strong for the French,[3] and no doubt it had an adverse effect on their spirit for battle owing to the general state of fatigue and lassitude which this unaccustomed drink must have produced in the ranks. The sick among them were many, and the number was increasing with the passing of time.[4] Moreover, the change of season was imminent, when the crossing of the sea would become perilous on account of the frequency of violent gales at that time of the year.[5] Knights and men-at-arms began to grumble and the Genoese complained that their ships were lying idle and their engines burnt.[6] The general feeling was in favour of raising the siege, the utility of which was doubted by all except perhaps the Duke himself and a handful of nobles. On the Saracen side, too, the tendency was against the prolongation of hostilities. They had all to lose and nothing to gain by a war waged on their own soil. Their numbers, if we believe Cabaret d'Orville,[7] were depleted by at least fifteen thousand, and they were unable to inflict any crushing defeat upon their enemy. Their armour and their traditional methods of warfare prevented them from coming into open battle with the Christians, whose balistas wrought havoc

[1] Froissart, XIV, 230; 'se arment le plus de cuir, et portent targes à leurs cols moult légières, couvertes de cuir bouly de Capadoche, où nul fer ne se puelt prendre, ne attachier, se le cuir n'est trop eschaufé'.

[2] *Religieux*, I, 668–70. '. . . ore patulo et naribus aera captantes, contra sitim petebant humoris remedium'.

[3] Froissart, XIV, 236.

[4] Juvenal des Ursins, 384; Froissart, XIV, 270.

[5] *Religieux*, I, 666–7.   [6] Cabaret d'Orville, 246.   [7] *vide supra*, 417.

among them. Al-Mahdiya, too, was hard pressed by the stringency of a siege which left no gap either on land or by sea. It was only natural in these circumstances that an overture for peace should be heartily welcomed on both sides. The mediators for the ending of the crusade were its initiators —the Genoese—by virtue of their long-standing relations with the people of Tunisia and their knowledge of the country. The Genoese were, moreover, not interested in the crusade as a holy war, but, like all Italian republics, they regarded it as a war for the furtherance of their trade privileges beyond the sea. If such privileges were ensured without territorial acquisitions for Christendom as a whole, the Genoese would be the first in the host to accept them without scruple and without consideration for the main object of the campaign as seen by the enthusiastic and pious Duc de Bourbon.[1]

Without regard to their leader's personal opinion and sentiments, the Genoese started the negotiations with the envoys of the King of Tunis for a treaty and for the subsequent raising of the siege. After four days' discussion, the two parties reached agreement on the provisional terms of peace, which may be summed up under four headings. In the first place, there should be a truce for ten years, during which the King of Tunis would do no harm to Christians in his territories.[2] In the second place, the King's annual revenue (*rente*) from the town of al-Mahdiya, should be paid to the Genoese for fifteen years. In the third place, the government of Tunis was bound in the course of the first year following to pay the sum of twenty-five thousand ducats to both the Duke and the Commune as a war indemnity for the cost of the expedition. In the fourth place, the wealthy Catalan, Neapolitan and Sardinian merchants resident in al-Mahdiya [3] should be guarantors of these terms. When the project for a treaty was submitted to the leader of the crusade, he summoned a council

---

[1] Cabaret d'Orville, 247. The Duke's remark on overtures for peace is significant. The crusaders, he asserted, did not come 'pour faire paatis, mais pour . . . conquester'. In a note, the editors define the word 'paatis' as 'Traité de paix à prix d'argent, comme en faisaient les grandes compagnies.'

[2] ib., 246–7.　　　　　　　　　　　　　　[3] ib., 247.

THE RAISING OF THE SIEGE OF AL-MAHDIYA, THE
STRONG TOWN OF AFRIQUE (M. cixx, p. 404) MS. HARL.
4379, Fol. 104

of the French and English captains to decide the issue.
The first speaker was le soudic de la Trau, on account
of his age, valour and experience.   In his opinion, a war
waged against three kings for two months and a half had
achieved some measure of success.   The terms offered,
he stated, were as honourable to the crusaders as the capture
of the town.   Al-Mahdiya was reduced to tribute and to
servitude, and the treaty must not be rejected.[1]   Then the
English spokesmen [2] were called upon to express their
views, and afterwards several Frenchmen including the
comte Dauphin, Enguerrand de Coucy and the comte d'Eu.[3]
All were one in supporting the soudic's words.   Bourbon
had no choice but to accede to their wishes; and, on the
third day of their deliberations, he ordered the army divisions
to board the fleet, saying to the seigneur de Coucy—
'Good cousin, you were the first at the descent on land,
when we came before Africa, and I wish to be the last to
mount a galley at the departure'.[4]   Before embarkation,
however, a precautionary measure was taken in order to
safeguard the retreat of the troops.   A body of two hundred
men-at-arms and one hundred arbalesters were secretly
installed in a mosque behind an old wall, two hours before
daybreak.   They were instructed on pain of death to remain
quiet in their hiding-place, ready for prompt action in case
of treachery on the part of the Saracens while the troops
were retiring to the vessels.   This proved to be a wise and
far-sighted act; for, while the retreat was taking place, the
Berber kings unscrupulously sent a cavalry battalion of
six hundred to harass it.   No sooner was this done, than
the Duke revealed his ambushed troops who routed the
truce-breakers.   These left a number of dead estimated as
between a hundred and a hundred and twenty.   Then, un-

---

[1] ib., 248.   Le soudic de la Trau ended his speech with the personal
remark—'et quant a moi, qui ne suis que ung povre chevalier, je tiens ceste
chose aussi honnourable que si j'avoie esté en trois batailles'.

[2] ib., 248–9.   These were 'Jehannicot d'Ortenie, anglois, l'ung des
vaillants chevaliers' and 'le sire de Cliffort chief des Anglois'.

[3] ib., 249–50.

[4] ib., 250.   'Beau cousin, vous fustes le premier à la descente en terre,
quand nous venismes devant Auffricques, et je vueil estre le dernier à monter
en gallée, au despartir.'

disturbed, all went aboard, and the fleet sailed on the same day to the island of Conigliera where the crusaders dropped anchor until the following morning,[1] probably to decide the homeward itinerary before resumption of the journey.

Some were dissatisfied with the outcome of the campaign and requested that they might be taken to Naples, Sicily, Cyprus, Rhodes or even Syria for further feats of arms on the road to Jerusalem.[2] The state of mind of those who thirsted for more fighting was not utterly disregarded. Bourbon consulted Giovanni Centurione as to the possibility of sailing to a convenient place where the army could still be used against the infidels.[3] The Genoese admiral at once conceived the idea of using the crusaders in other fields of interest to his Republic. The port of Cagliari in Sardinia, he said, was a nest of Catalan pirates as well as a regular station for re-victualling the Barbary corsairs' fleets, and it was the duty of the holy warriors to end this by invading the town and entrusting it to the devout care of his countrymen.[4] Behind this pious reason in Oltramarino's mind, however, was the dispute between a Genoese noble, Brancaleone Doria, and the King of Aragon over the former's right to Sardinia by virtue of his marriage to Eleanore des Beaux of the province of Arborea in that island.[5] The Duke accepted the admiral's suggestion at its face value and his army had no difficulty in substituting a Genoese garrison for the existing one. Their next objective was the island of Ogliastro near the east coast of Sardinia. This, too, succumbed to the same fate as Cagliari; and afterwards the crusaders sailed in the direction of Naples. It has been said that the motive of the projected journey to Naples was to chastise its inhabitants for supplying the African pirates with victuals.[6] Nevertheless, it is easy to conjecture that Bourbon's purpose was to assist Louis II of Anjou in subjugating the kingdom recently

[1] Cabaret d'Orville, 251.   [2] Froissart, XIV, 274.
[3] Cabaret d'Orville, 251.   [4] ib., 251–2.
[5] Loray, *Jean de Vienne*, 250; Delaville Le Roulx, I, 195–6; Mirot, 34
[6] Delaville Le Roulx, I, 196. Cabaret d'Orville, 253, on the other hand says that 'le duc de Bourbon et les Gennois . . . vouloient fort tirer devers Naples, pour ce que avitailloient Auffricque, pour eulx monstrer le traictié que avoit esté fait.'

acquired by his father, Louis I, the founder of the second
Angevin house. The fleet was, however, deflected from its
course by a sudden strong tempest during the night. Most
of the galleys were driven to Messina, where Manfredo de
Chiaramonte, the powerful lord of half the island of Sicily,
received the stranded crusaders with great honour. One
galley, carrying the soudic de la Trau and Jean de Châteaumorand, was wrecked on the western coast of the island
near Trapani, but all on board were saved with the loss
of their goods. Later, on hearing the news, the Duke
dispatched a special galley which carried them to Messina
to enjoy the great festivities celebrated by Manfredo for his
noble guests. Before their departure from Sicily, Manfredo
asked that he might be knighted by Louis de Bourbon.
The ceremony was performed, and the Duke presented the
new knight with a golden girdle on which was inscribed
Bourbon's motto—'Espérance'. Manfredo then supplied
the galleys with wine, biscuits, salted meat and other provisions.[1] The Genoese admiral thus led the fleet to
Terracina on the Tyrrhenian coast of Italy which had a
reputation for providing Arab pirates with refuge and provisions. The lower parts of the town surrendered at once
and the castle was captured after two days' siege, and, like
the other conquests, entrusted to the Genoese. Then
sailing along the Italian coast, they reached Piombino, a
naval base belonging to Pisa. Here Centurione tried to
persuade Bourbon to settle an old dispute between Pietro
Gambacorta, lord of Pisa, and the Ligurian Republic by
force of arms. This unfair request for the undisguised
use of the holy warriors against their fellow-Christians
in the interest of the Genoese was rejected, although the
Duke offered to mediate between the two parties, and his
mediation produced the same result as the use of arms, for
Gambacorta was so intimidated by the presence of Bourbon's
host that he gave way to the Genoese demands.[2] After this
inequitable settlement, in which the Duke was the moral and
Pisa the material victim of Genoese cunning, the fleet sailed
in the direction of Elba and finally dropped anchor at
Porto Fino, a maritime suburb of Genoa. After landing at

---

[1] Cabaret d'Orville, 253–5.   [2] ib., 255–6.

this point, a number of soldiers died as a result of fatigue and long sickness.[1]

According to a story given by Cabaret d'Orville, the Duke, supported by the principal leaders of the French army such as Coucy, Eu and others, insisted on remaining in the ships until they reached Marseilles, much to the disappointment of the Republic which had prepared a triumphal reception for him. Bourbon, continues Cabaret d'Orville, had made a solemn vow to return to the port of his original embarkation and was determined not to break it in spite of Genoese supplications.[2] The party was therefore taken by sea to Marseilles, and there they stayed ten days [3] for repose after their long and exhausting wanderings and in order to visit the holy shrines of the district.[4] Thence each went to his home and the Duke entered his own county of Forez whose inhabitants gave him a great reception. In the Bourbonnais, he met his agent sire Jean de Norris and procured horses, clothing, gold and silver from him for the rest of the journey, and at the town of Montbrison, he joined his wife and two sons, Jean and Louis, for a period of eight days.[5] This detailed story is, however, without foundation, for Jean de Châteaumorand who furnished Cabaret d'Orville with it after many years from memory, confused the events of 1390 with those of the following year.[6] The truth was that the Duke actually left his galley at Genoa some time before 15 October, and thence went to see Giovanni Galeazzo Visconti at Vercelli.[7] Afterwards he met his nephew, Amé VII of Savoy, at Santhia on 3 November; and three days later, took the road to Milan. At

---

[1] Cabaret d'Orville, 257. These included the sire de Saint-Sévère, Guichard de Chastellus, son of Jean de Châteaumorand, the sire de Castillon, the sire de Caillart and twelve Englishmen.

[2] ib., 257.   [3] id., l.c.   Not eight days as quoted by Mirot, 35.

[4] id., l.c.   The shrines were those of Saint-Antoine de Viennois and Notre-Dame de Pui.

[5] ib., 258.

[6] The story is accepted by Delaville Le Roulx, I, 198, but refuted by Mirot, 35-6.

[7] G. Gabotto, *Gli ultimi giorni del conte Rosso e i processi per la sua morte*, in *Bibl. della Soc. Stor. Subalpina*, (Pavia, 1912) LXVI, 15-16; cf. Mirot, 36 note 1.

Ciria, the count of Savoy met him again on 18 November. Accompanied by Lucchino de Saluces and his own physician, he left Ciria and reached Susa by way of Avigliana. At this juncture, many crusaders joined him, and the party crossed the Alpine paths of Mont-Cenis and descended on French soil [1] where they were eagerly awaited by their friends and relatives who had prayed for a fair wind to bring them back home in safety.[2] The crusaders went on to Paris, and their presence at the royal court aroused great enthusiasm for holy war. In the excitement of the moment, Charles VI himself and the duc de Touraine his brother took the Cross.[3] This was the immediate effect of Bourbon's expedition to Barbary. The idea of a royal crusade to crush the power of the Saracens and carry the banner of France far and wide was resuscitated for the moment. Although there is no reason for doubting the sincerity of this vow, it never came to fulfilment. The pressure of events in France made it impossible for the King to leave the country. On the other hand, the French chivalry continued to hunger for war with the infidels, a fact which helps to explain the great popularity of the cause when, five years after, preparations were begun for the greatest fourteenth-century expedition and the last real crusade to be undertaken against the Turks.[4]

The other results of Bourbon's expedition are remarkable for their insignificance. Although begun and executed as a crusade by the French and foreign contingents it had no effect on the course of events in the Levant, and the situation in the Holy Land remained unaltered. By some curious misconception, the Western mind in medieval times failed to

---

[1] Mirot, 36.

[2] According to Froissart, XIV, 279, the wives of several nobles were much perturbed by the long absence of their husbands. Eustache Deschamps, (*Soc. des anciens textes*, IV, 266), expressed the general feeling of the noble ladies in a special ballad on the Barbary Expedition. In 'L'Envoy' of that ballad, he says:

> 'Princes, baron, chevalier, escuierie,
> De bien faire ne vous fault que penser:
> Dame n'avons par déçà qui ne die
> Que le bon vent vous puist tost ramener!'

[3] Froissart, XIV, 280–1.

[4] *vide infra*, Cap. XVIII on the Crusade of Nicopolis.

estimate the isolation of the Maghribine and the Near
Eastern Muhammadan countries. Except for sundry
trade contacts and the ties of a faith common to both,
the two lived in almost water-tight compartments, and the
weakening of the one could never react favourably or unfavourably on the other. In this respect, therefore, the
crusade did not help the real cause of the Latins in the
Levant. The long-lost Kingdom of Jerusalem remained
as forlorn in 1390 as it had already been after the disastrous
and abortive crusade of St. Louis in 1270. The Barbary
expedition of Louis de Bourbon, nevertheless, seems to have
impressed the contemporary mind as a result of another
misconception. The Duke, it was firmly believed, had
wrested from the Berber kings an honourable treaty which
was a justification for the campaign. His return to Europe
was a triumphant one; and except for the solitary voice of
Froissart,[1] who held the view that Coucy was more suited
for the leadership of the host than Bourbon, the writers of
the time almost unanimously acclaimed him as a champion
of the faith and a victor over the unfaithful. In reality,
the crusade neither made territorial acquisitions in Africa
nor humiliated the Barbary kings in any practical sense.
Al-Mahdiya was left undamaged and the Berber army far
from annihilated. The Arab chronicler of the Mgharib,
ibn Khaldūn, simply mentions the end of the expedition as a
defeat for the Christians and a triumph for the arm of Islam.[2]
The terms of the treaty as concluded before the embarkation
of the host, although favourable to Genoese interests, fell
short of the main object of the campaign. It would even
seem doubtful whether the Arab monarch was not merely
playing for time. The attack of his horsemen on the
Christians as they boarded the galleys after his approval of
the terms of peace indicates that he was not too ardent in his
intention to keep them. It was, indeed, not until 17
October of the following year after much procrastination
that a stable treaty [3] was concluded with Genoa. By this,

---

[1] See, for example, XIV, 251.   [2] *Kitāb al-'Ibar*, VI, 400.

[3] Arch. di Stato, Genova, Materie politiche, Mazzo 10; cf. Mas Latrie,
Traités de paix, 243–4. The Genoese envoys to the court of Abul-'Abbas
Abu-Bakr at Tunis were Gentile de Grimaldi and Lucchino de Bonavey.

the interests of both parties were respected.   From the
Genoese standpoint, it would be misleading to call the
expedition a crusade.   Faithless and materialistic as the rest
of the Italian republics, Genoa could hardly be regarded as a
crusading state.   The attacks by the Genoese on Chios and
other parts of the Christian Empire of the East and later
on the Latin Kingdom of Cyprus which formed the last bulwark of Catholicism in the Levant, their shameful behaviour
in the crusade of the Dauphin de Viennois, their piracy in
the Eastern Mediterranean, and their long-standing reputation as the best furnishers of slaves to reinforce the
Mamlūk army irrespective of papal bans—all these are
matters treated at some length elsewhere in this study, and
all prove that the Genoese cared little for holy war as an act
of devotion and gave their support to it only when it served
their ends.   It was natural that they should encourage the
prevalent contemporary belief that the African campaign
was a crusade; but actually it was only one of a series of
expeditions to safeguard their trade interests in North Africa
and the undisturbed passage of their fleets in the Mediterranean.   Like the expedition of 1388, that of 1390 had
those two aims in view.   When the offer of a treaty ensuring their privileges was made and provisionally executed,
the captains of the fleet appear to have lost their ardour
for the siege.   This was undoubtedly not the sole factor
at work in the ending of the crusade, but it was nevertheless a potent influence.   The French army, it would seem,
was merely a 'cat's paw' for the Genoese.   Their tentative
suggestion of the choice of the duc de Touraine as the
leader of the expedition when their embassy approached
the King of France at the beginning of 1390 was probably
made with the idea of putting into their own hands a help-

They demanded in general the renewal of a previous treaty concluded by
Frederico Lecavelo and asked for the deliverance of the Christian prisoners
numbering 260 (according to the letter of a Venetian consul dated 1392).
It appears, however, that only a number equal to that of the Muslim prisoners
was exchanged without payment and the republic had to ransom the rest.   It
is significant that other treaties, similar to that of the Genoese in respect of
trade interests, were later made with Pisa, Venice, and Sicily, in spite of the fact
that they did not collaborate in the crusade of 1390 (cf. Mas Latrie, op. cit.,
244 et seq.).

less youth whom they might employ in accordance with their will. The Duke of Bourbon, despite his mature age, did not escape from being used by the Genoese in this manner. Under cover of extirpating Saracenic influence, the astute Giovanni Centurione d'Oltramarino succeeded in persuading Louis de Bourbon to subdue Cagliari, Ogliastro and Terracina for the Genoese, and even used the weight of the Duke's influence to end the dispute with Pisa in favour of his own republic. There was, however, a totally different aspect to this growing inter-relation between the Genoese and the French. As a result of the crusade, France became very popular in Genoa. A further stage had been reached in the series of events and *rapprochements* which led to the voluntary cession of the Republic to France in 1396.[1] The conclusion of the matter is, therefore, that the crusade failed to achieve its original purpose as a holy war, and only helped the Genoese to realize some of their ambitions as against a number of impotent Christian states. The disappointment of the foreign contingents must have been great. The adventurers from many lands who enlisted for pay and plunder returned empty-handed from the attack on the impregnable town of al-Mahdiya. They were to swell the ranks of the next crusade.

[1] *vide supra,* 399–401.

CHAPTER XVIII

THE CRUSADE OF NICOPOLIS

Europe and the Crusade; propaganda; preparations. March of the crusaders: Buda, Widdin, Rahova and Nicopolis. Siege of Nicopolis and march of the Ottomans. The hostile forces; preliminary skirmishes; battle of Nicopolis; defeat and massacre of the crusaders. Ransom and return of the captives. Results of the Crusade

THE memory of the Barbary expedition stimulated the spirit of the French and English chivalry to undertake another crusade, and the conclusion of the peace between Charles VI and Richard II left the combatants of the Hundred Years' War free to pursue their activities in fields other than France. Indeed the situation throughout Europe during the last decade of the fourteenth century appeared to be favourable to holy war. The pressure of the Ottomans on the south-eastern frontiers of Catholic countries was calling for prompt action; and the fall of Widdin (1390) on which Sigismund had a long-standing claim, rendered Hungary the bulwark of Catholic Christendom against these new and redoubtable enemies. On the one hand, their incursions north of the Danube alarmed the Hungarians and Wallachians, and on the other, the expulsion of a Turkish garrison stationed at Nicopolis Minor (1393) encouraged the Christians of many countries to participate in the forthcoming campaign of 1396.[1] As early as 1394, the Roman Pope, Boniface IX, issued two bulls [2] proclaiming the crusade in Eastern Europe; and in

---

[1] *Nicopolis*, 1 et seq. The present chapter is not intended to incorporate all the details included in my full study of the subject. To avoid unnecessary repetition, I have here embodied the result of my previous researches without dwelling on the controversies connected with many aspects of the crusade or reproducing all the references to the sources and secondary authorities which the reader will find in my *Crusade of Nicopolis*, London (Methuen), 1934.

[2] The first, *Cogimur ex debita charitate* (3 June), enjoined Archbishop John of Neopatras to proclaim the holy war in Bosnia, Croatia, Dalmatia and

the following year, the Avignonese Pope, Benedict XIII, issued a number of other bulls releasing Jean de Nevers from certain vows and granting him and his companions in arms plenary absolution and the power to communicate with the infidels in case of emergency.[1]   In 1395 Philippe de Mézières, the greatest propagandist of the time, wrote his *Epistle to Richard of England* by order of Charles VI, in order to bring their respective countries into harmony and closer association during the impending crusade.[2]

The preachers of the crusade were the heralds of official embassies exchanged between Sigismund and the princes of the West.   In 1393, the comte d'Eu and a hundred French knights appeared at Buda to offer the King of Hungary their services against the miscreants.   The King had just won the battle of Nicopolis Minor and so invited the French detachment to assist in combating the Bohemian heretics instead of renewing uncertain hostilities beyond his southern border.   It is possible that in the distress of these years he also intimated to them the need for a real crusade against the Turks and asked them to mediate on his behalf for the promotion of the movement at the court of France.   In 1394 Guillaume de la Trémouille, marshal of Burgundy, was instructed to proceed to Buda to inform Sigismund of the willingness of the Dukes of Burgundy, Orleans and Lancaster to consider an appeal for a crusade.   In 1395 the official negotiations were actually begun in the Republic of St. Mark whose geographical situation was favourable for all parties and whose consent and collaboration were essential for the success of

---

Slavonia; and the second *Ad Apostolatus nostri* (13 October) extended this proclamation over Treviso, Venice, the Patriarchate of Grado, the See of Salzburg with its suffragan dioceses and the Duchy of Austria.   Reynaldus, *ad ann.* 1394, no. 23; cf. *Nicopolis*, 33–4.

[1] cf. *Nicopolis*, 34.   Benedict on this occasion sent Pierre Berthiot, a secretary of Philippe le Hardi, to the comte de Nevers with presents including horses and mules.

[2] *Nicopolis*, 29–31.   The *Epistle* is analysed elsewhere in the present study; *vide supra*, Cap. VII.   A much shorter letter sent by the French to the English King on 25 May 1395, by the hand of Robert l'Hermite, a Norman knight, aims at the same object and bears signs of Mézières' pen; ib., 171 note 63; cf. Kervyn, Froissart, XV, 388–91, and Iorga, *Mézières*, 479–82.

THE KING OF FRANCE RECEIVES NEWS OF THE
TURKISH VICTORY AT NICOPOLIS (M. ccxv, p. 448)
MS. HARL. 4380, Fol. 98.

any crusade. The first to appear on the scene were the Byzantine delegates whose arrival at Venice is recorded in December 1394. Early in the following year, de la Trémouille, Renier Pot and twelve squires were present in the Signory (4 February), and after awaiting the Hungarian ambassadors for twelve days, they appealed to the Senate for a decision which was denied to them owing to the absence of the principals in the matter. After the departure of the French, three Hungarian representatives under the leadership of Nicholas of Kanizsay, Archbishop of Gran and Sigismund's treasurer, landed at Venice on 10 March; and after some procrastination, the Senate agreed to supply a number of galleys equal to one quarter of the coalition fleet, on condition that the Venetian contribution should not exceed twenty-five sail.[1]

The ambassadors then travelled to Lyons where the Duke of Burgundy welcomed them and presented them with precious vases and a table-cover decorated with pearls, sapphires and diamonds. Then he ordered his chamberlain, Renier Pot, to accompany them to Paris; but owing to the absence of the King's uncles at Avignon, Kanizsay went on to Dijon (17–19 May) to see the Duchess of Burgundy and to Bordeaux to meet the Duke of Lancaster; and the latter assured him of his resolve to support the holy enterprise. On the return of the ambassador to Paris, he found the princes of the regency in the capital, and in their presence Kanizsay placed Sigismund's letter in Charles's hands, delivered a speech depicting the great Turkish menace to the eastern frontier of Christendom, and implored the King of France not to fail his relative of Hungary. The appeal was favourably received by the King and enthusiastically supported by the nobles; and Kanizsay and his companions returned to their country with valuable gifts and many promises of aid and comfort against the Ottomans. It is possible that they travelled by the land route through Central Europe in order to extend their appeal to the German free towns and princes who were to contribute no mean share to the crusade.[2]

In France and particularly in Burgundy, the Hungarian

---

[1] *Nicopolis*, 34–8 and 174–5 notes.   [2] ib., 38–9 and 175–6 notes.

expedition had been the subject of important financial legislation even before the advent of the embassy from Buda. The Duke of Burgundy, who was the principal promoter of this crusade in the West, issued a minute in 1394 specifying the ordinary and extraordinary taxes in his territories, the aids and loans from the royal and ducal demesnes, and the loans from the clergy and from Milan, which were required for the 'voiage d'Onguerie' and for the knighting of his eldest son. The aggregate anticipated by the Duke was 700,000 francs, a sum of considerable magnitude in those days.[1] Guy VI de la Trémouille raised more than 24,000 francs for his own preparations, and his accounts may serve as a specimen of what must have been done by other nobles of France.[2] These exorbitant levies were lavishly spent on the sumptuous and elaborate equipment. Tents, pavilions, banners, standards, horse-covers—all were made of rich green velvet, and all were heavily embroidered with the arms of Nevers in Cypriot gold-thread. There were twenty-four cartloads of pavilions alone. Saddles and harness were decorated with gold, silver, ivory and precious stones. More than three hundred pennons were ornamented with silver, and the four great banners of the expedition were embroidered with the image of Our Lady and the arms of France and Nevers in gold-thread. According to Froissart, nothing was overlooked in equipment, furniture, rich clothing, and gold and silver plate.[3] Magnificence rather than efficiency was the keynote to these vast and elaborate preparations.

Philippe le Hardi's eldest son, Jean comte de Nevers, a youth of twenty-four years of age, whom his father wanted to see knighted in the eastern field amid deeds of valour against the infidels, was chosen as leader of the Franco-Burgundian army. The movement was very popular throughout the realm of France. One thousand

---

[1] Delaville Le Roulx, *France*, II, 18, 21–2; Bavyn MS., f. 343; Plancher, III, 148; *Nicopolis*, 39, 139 (Appendix IV–A), 201 notes.

[2] *Les la Trémouille pendant cinq siècles*, 13–15; *Nicopolis*, 39, 140 (Appendix IV–B).

[3] Froissart, XV, 224; Bavyn MS., ff. 348 ro–349 ro; *Nicopolis*, 40–1, 141–2 (Appendix V–A), 176 notes.

knights and an equal number of squires enlisted for the
campaign; and every prince of the blood brought with him
a large band of retainers in his own pay.   Jean le Meingre
(Boucicaut) had in his train as many as seventy, of whom
fifteen were fully-fledged knights.   In addition to the
knights and squires some eight thousand men of all classes
joined the host.[1]   By the 'Ordonnance'[2] of 28 March
1396, the council of war was appointed and the disciplinary
measures for the campaign were enacted.   A body of five
councillors was selected to advise the young comte de
Nevers in matters of war.   This included Philippe de Bar,
the admiral Jean de Vienne, Guy and Guillaume de la
Trémouille, and Odard de Chasseron.   Two other groups
of subsidiary advisers were provided for further consultation whenever the Count should deem this necessary.
To secure order in the ranks, certain rules of medieval
justice were laid down by this document.   A gentleman
causing tumult would lose his horse and harness, a varlet
using a knife, his fist, and any one committing robbery an
ear.   Finally, the 'Ordonnance' fixed 20 April 1396 for
the various detachments to meet at Dijon where four
months' wages would be paid to them at the rate of forty
francs the knight, twenty the squire and twelve the archer.

[1] The total number of the Franco-Burgundian contingent cannot be traced
in the French sources; but fortunately the German chroniclers who probably
witnessed its passage through their country made a record of it.   König-
shofen, 814 (cf. Brauner, 17), gives the total of 10,000, and Schiltberger, 3,
estimates it at 6,000.   The Bavyn Memoir, f. 347 vo, confirms the first.
If we accept the proportions provided by the 'Ordonnance' of 28 March 1396
(vide infra), the constituent elements of the contingent may be approximately
calculated as follows:

Knights	1,000
Squires	1,000
Archers	500
Arbalesters	1,000
Other men-at-arms and infantry. . . .	6,500
Total . . .	10,000

The Bavyn Mem., l.c., states that, excluding the members of the count's
household, one month's salary of the knights, squires and others in his pay
amounted to 36,190 livres.   *Nicopolis*, 41–2, 176 notes.

[2] ib., 144–8 (Appendix VI, where the whole of this important document is
newly edited from the original Dijon MS.).

Although no statement was made as to the wages of the unmounted man, this could be roughly calculated from various accounts at ten francs per month.[1]

While these preparations were on foot in France and Burgundy, other auxiliary contingents were being actively massed in Germany and England. The Count Palatine Ruprecht Pipan, eldest son of Duke Robert III of Bavaria, the Count of Katznellenbogen, Count Herman II of Cilly and Burgrave John III of Nuremberg were foremost among the German princes who took the Cross.[2] The German contingent as a whole may be estimated at 6,000 strong.[3] On the other side of the channel there were raised a thousand men-at-arms, probably under the command of either John Holand, Earl of Huntingdon and a younger brother of Richard II, or John Beaufort, a son of the Duke of Lancaster.[4] Others from Spain, the Italian republics, Poland, Bohemia and Wallachia[5] were also forthcoming; but the greatest numbers were supplied by Hungary. Sigismund had brought together an army of sixty thousand[6] men ready for the struggle and awaited the arrival of the Western contingents.[7]

[1] Judging by the total wages as stated in the Bavyn MS. and the wages of the knights, squires and archers given in the 'Ordonnance'; *Nicopolis*, 42–3.

[2] Strömer, 48; Petrus de Rewa, *De Monarchia*, 652; *Klindenberger Chron.* and *Annal. Mellic.*, cf. Brauner, 9; Aschbach, *Gesch. Kaiser Sigmund's Zeit*, I, 99; *Nicopolis*, 43–4 and 177 notes.

[3] Kiss, 266; *Nicopolis*, 67.

[4] Antonio Fiorentino, in AM, XXVII, pt. ii, 208; *Nicopolis*, 44–8, 177–8 notes.

[5] *Nicopolis*, 48–9, 178 notes. For details of estimate, *vide infra*, note.

[6] Froissart (Kervyn), XV, 245; *Nicopolis*, 67, 184 notes.

[7] The units of the crusading army may be estimated as follows:

French	10,000
English	1,000
German	6,000
Hungarian	60,000
Wallachian	10,000
Bohemian, Polish, Spanish and Italian volunteers and mercenaries.	13,000
Total	100,000

Nicopolis, 66–7, 184 notes. A somewhat different estimate by Kiss (266) is reproduced in *Nicopolis*, 184, note 25. Kiss's estimate takes no account of the English contingent.

Buda was the general rendezvous of the various crusading bodies. The Franco-Burgundian forces were present
at Dijon on 20 April 1396 in accordance with the terms
of the 'Ordonnance', and proceeded thence to Montbéliard. Jean de Nevers, who was in Paris on 6 April
and arrived at Dijon on 13 April, left the Burgundian
capital ten days later than his army and took command at
Montbéliard.[1] Proceeding through the Franche-Comté
and Upper Alsace, the army crossed the Rhine south of
Strasbourg and gained the upper valley of the Danube in
Bavaria. At Ratisbon, the German auxiliaries, led by John
of Nuremberg and Count Palatine Ruprecht, joined the
army of Nevers; and the combined forces travelled to
Straubing, Passau and Vienna. At Straubing, a great
reception was given in honour of Jean de Nevers by his
brother-in-law Albert of Bavaria, while Artois and Boucicaut continued with the vanguard of the army to Austria.
They arrived in Vienna at Whitsuntide (21 May) and
Nevers reached the same destination on St. John's Day
(24 June). Leopold IV, Duke of Austria and a second
brother-in-law of the comte de Nevers, received them with
great honour, furnished them with several shiploads of
provisions and wine, and gave their leader a loan of 100,000
ducats, while a Flemish knight named Walter de Ruppes
was sent ahead of the army to announce its approach to
King Sigismund. The crusaders reached Buda probably
late in July 1396. The English contingent, too, is known
to have been present by this time; and a general council
of war was held to consider plans.[2] Sigismund wished
to adopt defensive tactics and wait for the enemy in his
Hungarian strongholds; but his prudent suggestions were
unanimously rejected by the commanders of the foreign
contingents who, according to Froissart, came 'to conquer
the whole of Turkey and to march into the Empire of

---

[1] Froissart (Kervyn), XV, 230; *Religieux*, II, 428–9; Plancher, III, 149;
cf. *Nicopolis*, 50, 178 notes.

[2] *Nicopolis*, 50–6, 178–80 notes. Except for a small body under Henri de
Bar and Enguerrand de Coucy who went by way of Lombardy, Venice and
the eastern Alpine paths to Buda, the bulk of the army therefore followed the
land route as delineated through Germany and Austria.

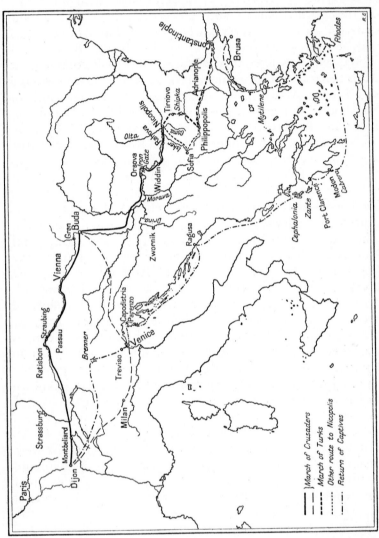

Paris
Strassburg
Montbeliard
Dijon
Ratisbon
Straubing
Passau
Vienna
Gran
Buda
Brenner
Milan
Treviso
Venice
Capodistria
Parenzo
Zwornik
Ragusa
Drina
Morava
Widdin
Orsova
Iron Gate
Olta
Nicopolis
Rahova
Timova
Shipka
Istar
Osma
Sofia
Philippopolis
Adrianople
Constantinople
Brusa
Mytilene
Rhodes
Cephalonia
Zante
Port Clarence
Modon
Cabrera

March of Crusaders
March of Turks
Other route to Nicopolis
Return of Captives

THE ROUTES

R.C.

442

Persia, . . . the Kingdom of Syria and the Holy Land'.[1]
Their spokesman, Enguerrand de Coucy, finally succeeded
in imposing the will of his colleagues upon the King; and
the combined armies marched along the left bank of the
Danube as far as Orsova, and then crossed the Iron Gate
in the neighbourhood of that town.[2]

The campaign was actually begun south of the Danube.
It was here that the crusaders were guilty of terrible atrocities against the poor Orthodox peoples whose chief crime
was that they had succumbed to the Ottomans. They
left behind them a trail of pitiless plunder and destruction in spite of the remonstrances of the clergy.[3] On
their way to Nicopolis, they seized Widdin and Rahova.
The first, which was held by a Bulgarian prince (probably
Stracimir) under Ottoman suzerainty, surrendered without
serious resistance and the handful of Turks stationed in its
forts were massacred, while new knights were made on the
field of battle in conformity with the traditions of medieval
chivalry. At Rahova, on the other hand, the invaders
encountered some difficulty The town was surrounded by
double walls and a moat and guarded by a strong Turkish
garrison. Moreover, the fate of their fellows at Widdin
decided them to make a firm stand within their fortifications
and defend the town to the death. In spite of all these circumstances, the comte d'Eu and Boucicaut together with a
band of foolhardy Frenchmen who hungered for victory and
wished to have for themselves all the honour of occupying
this new town, decided to storm the walls. Their assault,
however, would have resulted in a defeat or a protracted
siege, had Sigismund's reinforcement not come to their aid.
This was indeed the decisive factor—the town fell, its inhabitants were put to the sword except for a thousand

---

[1] Froissart (Kervyn) XV, 242; *Nicopolis*, 55–6, 180 notes.

[2] The army marched in three sections: first, a Hungarian detachment
under Nicholas of Gara forming the vanguard and leading the way by roads
with which they were fully acquainted; second, the foreign contingents under
the comtes d'Artois, d'Eu and de la Marche and the sire de Coucy; and third,
the rest of the Hungarians with Sigismund and Jean de Nevers. Froissart
states that the crossing of the Iron Gates lasted eight days. *Nicopolis*,
56–7, 180 notes.

[3] ib., 57, 180 notes.

wealthy townsmen who were carried into captivity in the
hope of heavy ransom, and, after pillage, Rahova was set on
fire and a garrison of two hundred crusaders installed in its
ruins.[1]

The next important city held by the Turks in that part
of the Danube valley was Nicopolis.[2] Situated near the
estuary of the Osma and facing the valley of the Aluta, it
commanded two of the main Danubian arteries which
penetrated both Bulgaria and Wallachia; and built on a
small plateau which sloped precipitously to the southern
plain and towered over the river on the northern side, its
site presented the assailant with immense difficulties.
With double walls and lofty towers, furnished with a strong
and watchful Turkish garrison under the able command
of Dogan Bey, Nicopolis proved to be invulnerable to attacks
from without, and the ample provisions stored within made
the prospect of a successful siege both slight and remote.
The crusaders approached the city by land, while the
Venetian and Genoese fleet, probably with the Knights of
Rhodes under the Grand Master Philibert de Naillac, came

---

[1] Nicopolis, 58–9, 180–1 notes. It is interesting to note that Froissart gives
a totally different account of the march of the crusaders to Nicopolis. They
attacked, he says, the three towns of Comette, Le Quaire and Brehappe,
which Kervyn identifies in a rather far-fetched explanation as Timok, Kaara
and Ro-du-Timok on the route to Belgradtschi which is situated ten leagues
south-west of Widdin. Although Brehappe had fallen to the invaders, its
adjacent castle was valiantly defended by Cordabas, a Turk, and his three
brothers—Maladius, Balachius and Ruffin, of whom the last was sent under
cover of night to warn the Sultan of the progress of the Christians. The
story of Froissart or rather his informant is evidently a fable, although it has a
moral, for the Turkish residents of Widdin and Rahova who managed to flee
to the south must have forewarned Bayezid of the campaign. Froissart, XV,
246–57; XXIV, 80, 387; XXV, 233.

[2] The modern 'Nikopol' and Turkish 'Nigheboli', known in the French
sources with slight variation as 'Nicopoli', in the German as 'Siltach, Schiltach,
Schiltaw, Schiltarn, &c.', in the Hungarian as 'Nicopolis Major' to distinguish it from 'Nicopolis Minor' on the Wallachian side of the river.
Founded by Heraclius in 629, it is usually confused in medieval literature
with the earlier Nicopolis ad Istrum or Haemum on the bank of the Rossitza
near the village of Nikup in the interior of Bulgaria. On the Nicopolis
district, see account of my visit, in Crusade of Nicopolis, Appendix VIII,
152–4, 'Nicopolis To-Day (1932): City and Battlefield'; also 60, 181 note
66.

by way of the Black Sea and upstream as far as this point.[1] Their arrival may be dated as 10 September 1396.[2] The crusaders, indeed began the siege operations at once. The fleet blockaded the outlet of the 'port' of Nicopolis on the riverside, while the land forces surrounded the city on the south side. Ladders were made by the French for mounting the walls, and the Hungarians are said to have dug out two large mines leading to the fortifications. It soon became evident, however, that these primitive methods were insufficient for an effective assault on the impregnable Nicopolis, and the crusaders possessed no artillery such as 'balistae, catapults and siege engines'.[3] Imagining their task to be a light one and considering that they were going to fight only a disorderly and undisciplined horde of heathens such as many of them had found in Lithuania, the crusaders had neglected to provide themselves with the implements of fourteenth-century siege warfare before proceeding against the Ottomans. They soon discovered the hopelessness of their undertaking and had to face a siege prolonged until Nicopolis should be starved into surrender and the Sultan's army defeated. It was during this period of inactivity that the character of the troops deteriorated. Gluttony, gambling, drinking and debauchery were some of the vices which the clergy tried in vain to repress among all ranks. Festivities and orgies, unworthy of a host of God, continued without interruption for fifteen days, and the army lived in 'heedless security'.[4] Men refused to believe that Bayezid could dare to face the flower of Western chivalry in open battle, and those who spread any such rumour in the companies lost their ears as a penalty by order of Marshal Boucicaut.[5]

Bayezid was engaged in the siege of Constantinople when the news of the campaign reached him. He summoned at once all his Asiatic and European troops including a body of eleven thousand Sipahis who were at the Byzantine capital. The siege of the city was suspended for the time being, and the Sultan marched to Adrianople

[1] ib., 54–5, 60–1.   [2] ib., 61, 182 note 70.
[3] *Religieux*, II, 407–8.   [4] Delaville Le Roulx, *France*, I, 257.
[5] *Religieux*, II, 500–1; *Nicopolis*, 61–2, 182 notes.

and up the valley of the Maritza to Philippopolis where the Asiatic and the majority of the European troops were assembled. The armies then took the direct road across the Balkan mountains by way of the Shipka Pass, and after a short halt at Tirnovo, where they were joined by the Serbian contingent led by Stephen Lazarović, a Christian vassal of Bayezid, they advanced to the region of Nicopolis and pitched camp on 24 September [1] on fortified heights about four miles south of the Danube. Between them and the river lay first the plain over which Nicopolis looked on the landward side and then the fortress city itself. This plain was already in part occupied by the Christian host.

It will be helpful at this juncture to pause for a while to consider the strength, both numerical and moral, of the hostile parties and their leaders as well as some aspects of the tactics which were to bring defeat upon the Christians and to ensure victory for the Ottomans. The allegation that the unhappy end of the army of the Cross was the result of Muslim superiority in numbers seems to be entirely without foundation. The Christians, as has already been noted, were approximately 100,000; [2] and the Ottomans, according to the most trustworthy authorities, could not have exceeded 104,000. [3] If we accept this fair estimate, a fraction of four thousand can hardly be considered as a decisive factor in a battle where such numbers were engaged. Medieval estimates are usually magnified and have to be considered with reservation, if not suspicion; but the main point in the present case is that the two contestant parties met on an equal footing as regards numbers. The battle of Nicopolis was won by the side which possessed unity of word and action, superior discipline, prudent tactics and wise leadership.

[1] *Nicopolis*, 62–5, 182–3 notes.   [2] *vide supra*, 440.
[3] The Turkish divisions, according to the *Religieux de Saint-Denis* (II, 503–4) on the authority of an unbiased eye-witness, are estimated in this wise:

A vanguard of infantry	34,000
'Main battle' of cavalry	30,000
Rearguard and Sultan's bodyguard (cavalry) . .	40,000
Total . . .	104,000

Nicopolis, 68–9; 185 notes.

Jealousy and disunity among the Christians had already been demonstrated in the general council of war at Buda as well as in the campaign itself until the siege of Nicopolis. The defensive policy of Sigismund who knew the real strength of the enemy and his tactics was rejected by the foreigners from the outset, owing partly to the aggressive temperament of the French nobility and partly to the fact that others had come from remote countries in search of booty in hostile territories. The capture of Rahova had already furnished a striking example of the impulsive egoism of the young nobles of France who aimed at seizing the town single-handed and even resented the assistance afforded by the Hungarians at a moment when the failure of their attempt seemed certain.[1] When the Ottoman army came on the scene, Sigismund first sent his marshal [2] and afterwards went himself to implore the French to remain in the rear for decisive action while the Hungarians, who knew Turkish methods of war, conducted the preliminary fighting; but the younger generation protested on the ground that the King was scheming to have the flower of the victory and of honour [3] for himself, and so his plans were defeated and the older men such as Coucy and Vienne who supported him were accused of treachery by their young and inexperienced countrymen.[4] If the French and foreign leaders displayed a lamentable hostility to the King's plans, the doubtful loyalty of the Wallachians to a cause which was mainly Hungarian did not leave Sigismund unperturbed.[5] The heterogeneous nature of the Christian army with its conflicting hopes and aspirations fostered faction and ended in disaster. On the other hand, the Ottomans' unity of purpose and rigorous discipline presented a completely different picture. Although the Janissaries, famous in later history, were hardly of serious value in the fourteenth century,[6] the Turkish 'Timar System' [7] and the despotic power of the Sultan ensured

---

[1] *vide supra*, 443.
[2] According to Froissart, XV, 313, named 'messire Henri d'Esteuillem-chale' (*sic*). [3] ib., XV, 314.
[4] ib., XV, 313–14; *Religieux*, II, 502–3; cf. *Nicopolis*, 70.
[5] *Nicopolis*, 70–1. [6] ib., 74–5, 186 notes.
[7] ib., 185–6 note 47, on the etymology of the word 'timar'.

united action in his army. By the 'Timar System', all fiefs (timars) were held in return for military service at the Sultan's good pleasure and not for a limited number of days as in the West. All Timarlis (feoffees) and Ziams (za'ims or chiefs) owed allegiance to the Sultan alone and had to furnish his army with an equipped horseman for every three hundred aspers of their income. By this means, the Sultan was able in the fourteenth century to raise about 75,000 men. These were divided into 'Toprakli' bodies (cavalry) and 'Piadé' or 'Yaya' (infantry). Realizing, however, the precariousness of an exclusive dependence on the land-holding classes for their military strength, the far-sighted Ottoman rulers founded two new bodies whose sole vocation was military service. The one was a bodyguard of 'Sipahis' or mounted soldiers who constituted the most important section of the Sultan's forces and may rightly be considered the first standing army in medieval Europe. The other body included the Janissaries (Yeni-tcheri, or new soldiers)—a nascent regular infantry whose importance, as we have stated, should not be exaggerated at this stage. The rest of the army units consisted of the irregular 'Akinjis' (horse) and 'Azebs' (foot) who played a prominent part in Ottoman tactics as they were usually sent ahead of the main troops, partly for plunder and partly to exhaust the enemy and, by feigning flight, draw him into battle with the regulars.[1] An army so well organized, would seem not only capable of withstanding attacks by a medley of soldiers and adventurers from the West, but also of routing them. Moreover, the moral qualities of the individual Turk added to the strength of the Ottoman army as a whole. 'Wine, women and gambling' were banned in the Ottoman camp, and men often spent their spare moments in prayer; but of all their virtues, obedience was the greatest.[2] Their

---

[1] *Nicopolis*, 71–5.

[2] Foglietta, *De Causis magnitudinis Turcarum imperii*, in *Opuscula nonnulla*, 48–65, of which there is an old English version edited by R. Carr, *The Mahumetane or Turkish Historie . . . Adioyned a Finall Discourse concerning the Causes of the Greatness of the Turkish Empire*, ff. 110–23; cf. *Nicopolis* 75–6.

firm conviction that they were fighting for the just and holy cause of Islam encouraged them not to shrink from a death which would bring forth the crown of martyrdom and the glory of a paradise everlasting; and the plunder of infidel property was sufficient recompense for those who survived the fray.[1] The outstanding characteristics of Bayezid, sole leader of the Ottoman army, presented a remarkable contrast to Sigismund's weakness and the stubborn vanity of his French companions. The contemporary Arabic chronicler, ibn Ḥajar,[2] describes him as 'one of the best kings in the world'. 'He was feared' adds the annalist of the time, 'and he loved learning and learned men, and revered those who knew the Qur'ān . . . Anyone who had a grievance could submit it to him, and he would immediately remove it. Security spread in his country to such an extent that a man with a load of goods could travel without being intercepted by anyone. He made two conditions for all those in his service—that they should be neither liars nor traitors.' The same author does not overlook the Turkish vices in his account, for he says that the Sultan allowed his men to indulge in licentious practices, both natural and unnatural. Such indulgence, however, Bayezid had forbidden in the camp. The Western methods of war, too, proved to be inferior to those of the 'Turks'. The shock tactics of the iron-clad knight lost their deadly effect in the face of the elusive mobility of the light Turkish steed which harassed the flanks of the Christian line and the extraordinary Turkish skill in the use of the arrow.[3] Such was the general state of the forces which were about to come into conflict of arms and of faith in the plains south of Nicopolis.

Some skirmishing had occurred in the hills and mountain paths before the Ottomans pitched their camp in the position already noted. Coucy and other knights, tired of the inactivity of the blockade, had decided to march into

---

[1] *Nicopolis*, 76.

[2] *Inbā' al-Ghumr*, BM. MS. Rich. 7321, f. 139 vo. Ibn Ḥajar makes this statement on the authority of an Egyptian envoy who visited the Ottoman court at Brusa. Cf. *Nicopolis*, 78.

[3] *Nicopolis*, 79–80, 188–9 notes.

the interior of the country in search of the enemy. They took with them a detachment of a thousand, of whom five hundred were crossbowmen, together with a few Hungarian guides to lead the way. Froissart,[1] to whom we owe our knowledge of this preliminary phase of the campaign, says that the Christians discovered a Turkish body of 20,000 guarding the only pass (probably the Shipka) connecting the northern and southern plains of the peninsula in that region. To draw them from their fortified position, Coucy instructed a hundred horsemen to approach the enemy and then feign flight, while the rest of the Christians lay in ambush in the woods. The plan succeeded and the Turks were attacked in the rear while pursuing the fleeing enemy. Many were slain and a few saved themselves by taking refuge in the mountains. The triumph of this minor raid, however, incurred the wrath of the comte d'Eu and Boucicaut, who accused their senior in years of having robbed his leader Jean de Nevers of the honour of victory.[2] At last the news of the approach of Bayezid with the principal Turkish army reached the crusaders on Monday 25 September 1396.[3] Sigismund then visited the leaders of the French before sunrise on Tuesday in a last and desperate attempt to convert them to his view on the matter

[1] Kervyn ed., XV, 265–8; cf. *Nicopolis*, 82–4.

[2] Although this episode is reproduced here, the balance of opinion appears to be against its literal acceptance. *Nicopolis*, 84.

[3] Broadly speaking the German medievalists accept the authority of Strömer (ed. Hegel, *Chron. d. deutsch. Städt.*, Nürnberg, I; 50) in putting the date of the battle as Thursday, 28 September, while French scholars accept the evidence of the *Religieux* (II, 500)), Froissart (XV, 312), the *Istoire et chron. de Flandres* (ed. Kervyn, *Chron. belges inéd.*, II, 419) and the *Res Gestae* (ed. Kervyn, in Froissart, XV, 410) by adopting Monday, 25 September, as the correct date. The independent Arabic authority of the Damascene writer, ibn al-Jazarī (BM. MS. Or. 2433, f. 278 ro) supports the argument for the French chronology. Ibn al-Jazarī refers to the 'third day' after the battle of 'Yankaboli' as 25 Dhulḥijja A.H. 798 which, according to the Wüstenfeld-Mahler'sche 'Tabellen' corresponds to Friday, 29 September. As, however, the Wüstenfeld-Mahler calculations are often one day behind time, it may follow that the battle ended on 26 September—the day of the massacre—and the actual encounter on 25 of that month. *Nicopolis*, 149–51 (Appendix VII); see also F. Giese, *Turkische und abendländische Berichte zur Gesch. Sultan Bajazids I*, in Harrassowitz's *Ephémérides orientales*, no. 34—April 1928, 2–11.

of tactics. He met with another rebuff and returned to his camp without modifying their suicidal plan. Neither the argument of his mistrust in his vassals Mircea and Laczković whom he wished to post in the van in order to guard against their defection, nor the support given him by the minority of older members of the French contingent such as Coucy and Vienne, was of any avail in bringing the young soldiers to listen to reason. This lack of unity among the leaders of the campaign was to lead to their ultimate discomfiture. The disheartened Sigismund retired to his quarters to arrange his line of battle independently and the Frenchmen decided to take the offensive alone in the hope of reaping all the harvest of glory for themselves. Meanwhile, news of the imminent battle spreading in the ranks of the alien contingents caused much excitement among them. Before marching into the field, they massacred the prisoners of Rahova. This ominous beginning of the day had its repercussions on Bayezid's mind and hardened his heart against the culprits when they appealed for mercy after their rout.[1]

The order of battle on both sides seems clear. On the part of the Christians, the French and other alien troops including the English formed the van. Sigismund, who had with him the Grand Master and the Knights of Rhodes, divided the Eastern European forces into three sections— the centre under royal command, the right wing consisting of Transylvanians led by their voyevode Stephen Laczković, and the left wing of Wallachians under Mircea.[2] On the Turkish side, Bayezid also divided his army into three battles, but arranged them in a different way. The vanguard included the 'Akinjis' or irregular cavalry, who concealed behind them a dense field of pointed stakes inclined towards the enemy and sufficiently long to pierce a horse's chest. Next was the 'main battle' consisting of the Turkish foot-archery, probably with the Azebs and Janissaries. These two 'battles' were placed in a fortified position on the slope of the hills at the southern extremity of the plain occupied by the Christians. Beyond the skyline, the Sultan arranged the flower of his army including the

---

[1] *Nicopolis*, 84–6. [2] ib., 87, 93.

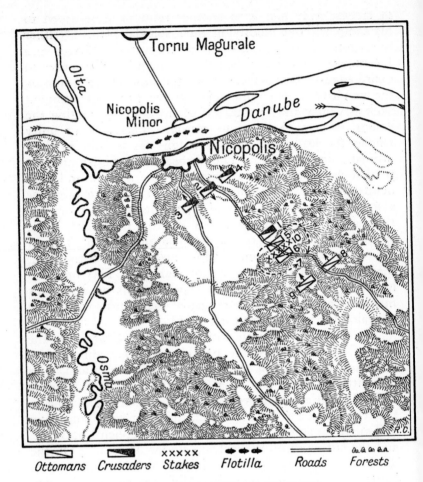

PLAN OF THE BATTLE OF NICOPOLIS

1. John of Burgundy and French and Foreign army
2. Sigismund and Hungarians, Poles, Bohemians, etc.
3. Laczković and Transylvanians
4. Mircea and Wallachians
5. Ottoman irregular cavalry—first position
6. Ottoman irregular infantry and Janissaries
7. Ottoman irregular cavalry—second position
8. Bayezid and Sipahis
9. Lazarović and Serbs
10. Field of Stakes

Sipahi cavalry in the rear, and Stephen Lazarović and his mounted Serbian auxiliaries took their post by their suzerain.[1]

The battle itself was started by the French who, after making new knights in the field, proceeded with the foreign contingents at full gallop, crying wildly 'Vive St. Denis!' and 'Vive St. Georges!' The 'Akinjis' could not sustain the heavy shock of the Christian horse, and they fled to the right and left with considerable loss. Nevertheless, they regained their formation behind the Turkish foot. This reversed the order of their lines of battle and revealed the forest of stakes which paralysed the advance of the Christian horse while the Ottoman archers showered volleys of arrows on the enemy. At this stage, the majority of the Christians in the van dismounted and began to uproot the stakes which prevented them from coming into a hand-to-hand fight with the Turkish infantry.[2] A desperate battle then ensued; and the Ottomans who fought without armour, according to the eye-witness quoted by the *Religieux de St.-Denis*,[3] lost ten thousand dead and the survivors took to their heels. So the first stage in the battle ended in victory for the Christians. Then the leaders of the host ceased operations for a short period of repose and in order to consider the next step. Having decided to pursue the same course against the Ottoman cavalry, now within a bowshot, and in the belief that Bayezid himself was in command of that body, they conducted a spirited attack on the Turkish lines and struck vigorously to right and left until they had created a gap in the centre. This enabled the crusaders to rush to the rear and use their daggers with deadly effect from this unexpected angle. Five thousand[4] of the Muslim army were slaughtered in this encounter and the rest galloped to safety beyond the summit of the hill. The usual procedure in Western warfare at this juncture would have been

---

[1] *Nicopolis*, 86-7.

[2] For a digest of opinion on the disputed question of the crusaders' dismounting, the evidence derived from the sources, and an estimate of the circumstances of the battle, see *Nicopolis*, 37-9, 190 notes.

[3] *Chron.*, II, 506-9.　　　　　　[4] *Religieux*, II, 508.

to re-mount and chase the enemy. This was impossible
in the circumstances, since the horses had been discarded
earlier in the day and were now out of reach. Instead of
contenting themselves with the happy results hitherto
achieved, the foolhardy Christians pursued the fleeing men
on foot uphill. This marked the turn of the tide. On
reaching the summit and seeing Bayezid's forty thousand
Sipahis, they were seized with dismay and the 'lion in them
turned into a timid hare'.[1] In a state of utter exhaustion
and within easy reach of a formidable foe, their confusion
was great and many fell down the steep ascent and lost
their lives while others remained in the field and fought
to the end. Jean de Vienne, admiral of France, vigorously
defended the banner of Notre-Dame of which he was the
bearer. Six times the banner fell and six times he raised
it again before his death. When the Admiral's body was
found later in the day, his hand still clutched the great
ensign whose defence had cost him his life.[2] As the
Turkish swordsmen approached Jean de Nevers, a number
of faithful retainers surrounded him and implored the
attackers to spare his life. Their request was granted, but
Jean was carried into captivity.[3]

In order to estimate the part played by the Hungarians
in the battle of Nicopolis, we must return to its earlier
stages. Sigismund had arranged his line of battle in
the rear independently and without any communication
or co-ordination with the foreigners who occupied the van.
Although he knew that they had marched alone against the
enemy, the King remained in the dark as to their further
movements. After the rout of the Turkish irregulars
and the dismounting of the Western Christians, the horses
were left behind without control. A stampede followed with disastrous results. At the sight of riderless
horses, the Hungarians became convinced that the alien
troops had been defeated, and this unmasked the real sentiments of the disloyal contingents and caused great confusion
in the loyal ranks. Laczković and Mircea who commanded the right and left wings retired from the field

---

[1] *Religieux*, II, 510.   [2] ib., II, 514–15; Froissart, XV, 318.
[3] *Nicopolis*, 91–2.

without lifting a finger to aid their suzerain. Nevertheless, Sigismund ordered the loyal units in the 'main battle' to advance to the rescue of the French and alien armies, then believed to be in distress. It is said that he and his men encountered a Turkish body of twelve thousand foot who 'were all trampled upon and destroyed'.[1] These were probably the Azebs and Janissaries, survivors of the French attack, who had failed to take refuge behind the Turkish horse. Thereupon, the Hungarians came into direct contact with Bayezid's cavalry, which, having ridden through the exhausted foreigners at the hill-top, had now reached the plain. A desperate battle took place with considerable loss on both sides and the issue swayed between the two contestants until Stephen Lazarović, the Christian Despot of Serbia, came up with five thousand men to the aid of his Ottoman suzerain. The Serbs overthrew the royal banner, and their action proved to be a decisive factor in favour of the Turks. Seeing that the end was approaching and that the fate of the King was in the balance, John Burgrave of Nuremberg, Philibert de Naillac Grand Master of Rhodes, Nicholas Kanizsay Archbishop of Gran, John Gara and other leaders of the host persuaded Sigismund with difficulty to leave the field and conducted him to a barge on the Danube. The party then drifted downstream, followed by Turkish arrows, until they were picked up by a Venetian galley. Only John Gara was landed on the left bank to proceed to Hungary and manage the affairs of the Kingdom, as Sigismund who feared treachery on the part of the Wallachians decided to pursue the long sea route to Buda by way of Constantinople, Rhodes and Ragusa.[2]

The remaining history of the battle is a sad tale of desperate attempt at flight by few and of a merciless massacre of many. Some tried to reach the open western plains and were cut down by Turkish sabres. Others boarded the craft in the Nicopolis harbour and many ships were overladen and sank. Others tried to swim the river and were drowned under the weight of their heavy armour. The rest were captured and a grim fate awaited them on the

---

[1] Schiltberger, 3. [2] *Nicopolis*, 94, 98–9.

following day. Approximately three thousand in number,[1] they were stripped of their clothes and driven in groups tied together with ropes before the Sultan on the morning of 27 September. Bayezid's fury was aggravated when he realized the magnitude of his losses, estimated at 30,000 men,[2] and he resolved to take his revenge on the defenceless prisoners. Recognizing Jacques de Helly who had served him in his eastern campaigns and who knew the Turkish language, he asked him to indicate the leaders of the expedition for whose lives he might raise heavy ransoms. In this manner, Jean de Nevers, Philippe d'Artois comte d'Eu, Jacques de Bourbon comte de la Marche, Enguerrand de Coucy, Henri de Bar, Guy de la Trémouille and other nobles were separated from the mass. All those under twenty years of age with the possibility of many years of servitude before them were set aside. The rest were massacred in cold blood from 'morning till vespers', for not until evening did the executioners' hideous task come to an end. Three hundred remained yet to face their doom. These were, however, spared decapitation only to be carried into slavery to Brusa. Many of them were sent to the Muslim potentates of the East with Bayezid's messengers announcing his victory over the Christians. Schiltberger provides an example of these presentations. The Ottoman Sultan 'sent a lord

---

[1] *Religieux*, II, 518–19. This estimate is adopted here on account of the fact that the informant of the Monk of St. Denis, an eye-witness of the battle, seems to have been a temperate and unbiased person. Other estimates, however, are extant. Justinger (184) says that the slaughtered Christians were 100,000, Delayto (Annal. Est., in Muratori, RIS, XVIII, 936) 40,000 on both sides, the *Chronik aus Kaiser Sigmund's Zeit* (*Chron. d. deutsch. Städt.*, Nürnberg, I, 359) 24,000, Sozomenus (*Spec. Hist.*, in Murat., RIS, XVI, 1162) 20,000, Posilge (cf. Köhler, *Schlacht*, 32) 12,000, Antonio Fiorentino (in AM, XXVI, pt. ii, 209) more than 10,000, Schiltberger (5) 10,000, the Res Gestae (in Kervyn's Froissart, XV, 410) 8,000, Strömer (*Chron. d. deutsch. Städt.*, Nürnberg, I, 49) 400, and Froissart (XV, 327), Juvenal des Ursins (in Michaud et Poujoulat, II, 409) and Rabbi Joseph (ed. Bialloblotsky, I, 252) 300.

[2] *Religieux*, II, 518–19. Froissart (XV, 323) puts the proportion of the killed at thirty Muhammadans to every Christian, the *Hist. de Boucic.* (VI, 463) at twenty to one, Juvenal des Ursins (l.c.) at ten to one, and Antonio Fiorentino (l.c.) and Sozomenus (l.c.) at six to one.

named Hoden of Hungary with sixty boys, as a mark of
honour to the King-Sultan (of Egypt); and he would have
sent me (Schiltberger) to the King-Sultan, but I was
severely wounded'.[1]

The few who escaped from the stricken field suffered
tortures on their homeward journey. Count Ruprecht
Pipan arrived in Bavaria a dying man in beggar's clothes.
He passed away a few days later at Amberg.[2] The hard
lot of those who reached Hungary and Lombardy was
vividly described by Eustaches Deschamp [3] in a special
ballad. Robbed of their clothing and all their slight
possessions and left to the mercy of the snowy winter of
Central Europe and the wild beasts of the Hungarian
mountains, many perished and only few came to their homes
to spread the news of the great calamity. At first these
rumours were generally discounted as incredible and those
who circulated them were imprisoned in the Châtelet by
order of Charles VI until the truth was revealed. The King
had not long to wait for confirmation. Jacques de Helly
was set free to go to the West to announce the defeat of his
countrymen and Bayezid's willingness to accept a ransom
for the captives. He reached Paris on Christmas Eve; and
the Christmas festivities were turned into universal mourning.[4] The nobles of the court of France had already sent
a number of envoys to Venice and Constantinople before
Helly's arrival to inquire about the fate of their relatives.[5]
Afterwards a solemn embassy was appointed in the early
days of January 1397. This consisted of Jean de Châteu-

---

[1] Schiltberger, 3, 113; *Nicopolis*, 96–7, 118.

[2] Onsorgius, in *Rer. Boic. Script.*, I, 375; Trimethius, *Chron. Duc. Bav.*, I,
117; Brauner, 48; *Nicopolis*, 95–6.

[3] *Contre la Hongrie et la Lombardie*, in Œuvres, ed. Saint-Hilaire, VII,
Balade MCCCIX, 66–7; ed. Tarbé, I, 119; cf. *Nicopolis*, 128–9.

[4] Eustache Deschamps, in a ballad 'Faicte pour ceuls de France quant ilz
furent en Hongrie', notes the state of the country in the following words:
          'Je ne voy que tristesce et plour
          Et obseques soir et matin.'
Saint-Hilaire, VIII, 85–6; Tarbé, I, 163; Champollion-Figéac, *Louis et
Charles, ducs d'Orléans*, 209; Delaville Le Roulx, *France*, I, 339; *Nicopolis*,
101, 131–2.

[5] See details of these preliminary embassies in *Nicopolis*, 100–2, 194–5
notes.

morand a Barbary crusader and member of the King's Council, Jean de Vergy governor of the Franche-Comté and Gilbert de Leuwerghem governor of Flanders, all men of experience and diplomatic skill.[1] They were accompanied by Jean Blondel and Robert d'Anguel, first squire and secretary of the Duke of Burgundy, Jean Wilay representing the Duke of Orleans, and twenty-four valets and ten falconers.[2] They carried with them loads of precious gifts for the Sultan. Horses, dogs, falcons, hunting equipment, jewellery, and cloth and tapestry of the best workmanship from Rheims and Arras with designs symbolic of the life of Alexander the Great, of whom Bayezid considered himself the rightful heir, were among the gifts.[3] First, Jacques de Helly was sent in haste to obtain safe-conduct for the ambassadors who proceeded later on 20 January[4] in two groups. Jean de Vergy in charge of the valets and the presents took the direct land route to Buda by way of Germany and Austria, while the rest went to Milan to request its duke to assist in the negotiations and joined the others at the capital of Hungary.[5] In the Levant, the prisoners had much aid and comfort from the Latin Christians of the Archipelago and Cyprus. Boucicaut and Guy de la Trémouille were freed on parole in order to enable them to raise funds towards the ransom. They sailed to Rhodes to ask the knights to persuade the merchant princes of the Aegean islands to support the prisoners at the court of Bayezid and to provide the money urgently needed for their deliverance. Boucicaut then left Rhodes on a solitary journey, for his companion died in that island at Easter 1397.[6] In Mytilene, Francesco Gattilusio received him

---

[1] Froissart, XV, 338–9; Delaville Le Roulx, II, 26; *Nicopolis*, 102–3.

[2] *Chron. de la traison et mort de Richart &c.*, 165–6 note 1; Champollion-Figéac, III, 40; Delaville Le Roulx, I, 202–3; *Nicopolis*, 102–3.

[3] Bavyn Mem., ff. 353 ro–54 ro, transcription in Appendix V–B, *Nicopolis*, 142–3; Froissart, XV, 427; Delaville Le Roulx, I, 303 and II, 26–32.   [4] Froissart, XV, 345.

[5] Delaville Le Roulx, I, 304; *Nicopolis*, 104. Froissart, XV, 348–52, 358, gives an imaginary account of the ambassadors' passage through Buda, where Sigismund is alleged to have detained them and to have restored their liberty only after strong intercession by the Grand Master Philibert de Naillac.

[6] Kervyn, XVI, 52, 264.

with honour, lent him 36,000 francs, and assured him of
every possible effort on behalf of the French at the court of
Brusa.[1]   Nicholas of Aenos, too, lent him 2,000 ducats and
presented him with fish, bread and sugar, while his wife
added some linen cloth to the provisions.[2]   King Jacques I
of Cyprus sent Bayezid a model ship of fine gold valued at
20,000 ducats and lent Nevers and his fellow-captives
15,000 gold florins (24 June 1397).[3]

On the arrival of the solemn embassy at Brusa, the ransom
was fixed at 200,000 gold florins. Of this huge sum,
28,000 florins were immediately paid, but only on loan, by
Jean de Lusignan lord of Beyrouth and two wealthy merchants of Pera named Brancaleon Grillo and Nicholas
Matharas. The settlement of the balance was promised
within a month; and Francesco Gattilusio held himself
responsible for 110,000 florins, Nicholas of Aenos for
40,000, and Gaspard de Pagani of Pera and Nicholas
Paterio of Foglio Nuova jointly for 11,000.[4] Meanwhile
the prisoners, now set free, pledged themselves to pay back
these loans to the Latin merchants without delay; and Jean

[1] Miller, *Latin Orient*, 320; Delaville Le Roulx, I, 308.

[2] *Hist. de Boucic.*, VI, 472; Miller, 320; *Nicopolis*, 105.

[3] Froissart, XVI, 31–5, 352–5; *Chron. Fland.*, I, 350; Delaville Le Roulx,
I, 311; *Nicopolis*, 105, 196 notes.

[4] The following sums are known to have actually been raised:

Jean de Lusignan.	28,000	ducats
The Knights of Rhodes	30,000	,,
The King of Cyprus .	15,000	,,
The Genoese merchants of Pera .	30,000	,,
Venetian loan .	15,000	,,
Loan from a Dominican of Capodistria .	15,000	,,
Dino Rapondi, Lombard merchant of Paris, in the name of the King of Hungary .	100,000	,,
Loan from Italian bankers .	53,000	,,
Total .	286,000	,,

If this estimate may be accepted, the surplus (86,000 ducats) must have been
used towards the cost of the homeward journey. The first four sums
represent payments to Bayezid before the release of the captives, but it is
doubtful whether the remaining sums, at least the loans from Rapondi and
the Italian bankers, were sent to Gattilusio on whom the dead-weight of
the immediate settlement of the balance of the ransom must have fallen.
Nicopolis, 106–11.

de Nevers, Henri de Bar and Jacques de Bourbon promised
to remain at Venice until the fulfilment of their pledge.   In
spite of the solemnity with which their word was given
at the time of distress, the western nobles failed to carry out
in full their obligations to the eastern merchants; and as late
as 1400, Gattilusio sent Ansaldo Spinola to remind Philippe
le Hardi of an unpaid debt of 108,000 ducats overdue to
him.[1]   Although there was undoubtedly a good deal of
misappropriation of loans and levies [2] by the Duke of Burgundy, it must be remembered that his magnanimous offer
to take all the responsibility for the ransom proved to be an
immense burden for his resources.   Even if we overlook
the fabulous cost of the preparations made before the
departure of the crusaders from Dijon and the debts con-
tracted by the comte de Nevers on the way to Buda, the rest
of the Duke's debts could hardly be confined to 200,000
ducats.   The presents to the Sultan, the cost of sending
dispatches and embassies to the East, the extravagant
journey of the prisoners to the West, the gifts in money and
otherwise to Nevers' companions on their arrival in France
and Burgundy [3]—all these and many unforeseen and
incidental expenses approximately doubled the net cost of
the ransom.   Moreover, the unscrupulous behaviour of the
Venetians added much to the Duke's financial entanglements.   They had owed Sigismund an annuity of 7,000
ducats which he sold to Dino Rapondi in return for the
payment of the Hungarian contribution of 100,000 ducats
towards the ransom.   The Venetians refused to discharge
this obligation to Rapondi and even shamelessly demanded
the settlement of Nevers' small debt of 15,000 ducats to
them.[4]   The negotiations over this matter continued

---

[1] *Nicopolis*, 111.

[2] Levies in the royal and ducal domains together with some additional loans
amounted to 1,102,000 francs. *Nicopolis*, Appendix IX, 155–6.

[3] Presents in cash amounted to nearly 57,000 livres. *Nicopolis*, Appendix
V–C, 143.

[4] ib, 111–12. It must be noted, however, that the Venetians ultimately reduced this loan to 5,000 ducats and offered to allow it to be
reckoned as part of the annuity of 7,000 ducats. In so doing, they admitted
the transfer of their debt to Rapondi in principle, but insisted on refusing
payment nevertheless.

throughout the reigns of Philippe le Hardi, Jean Sans Peur and Philippe le Bon; and the Venetians came to terms in July 1424, only when they realized the danger which threatened their commerce in Flanders.[1] The unworthy dealings of the Republic on the one hand, and the loss of men and money on the other, played their part in fostering a spirit of indifference to the crusade among the rulers and nations of the West.

The financial difficulties which immediately followed the crusade, did not affect the elaborate preparations for the reception of the surviving crusaders. On 24 June 1397, they were discourteously dismissed by the Sultan with a challenge and some ignoble gifts.[2] Before the departure of Nevers and his companions in captivity from Brusa, the ambassadors hastened by sea to announce the news to the Duke and the princes of France. Leuwerghem died at Mytilene, but the rest continued the journey to Venice and overland to Paris. The prisoners themselves left the coast of Asia Minor about the end of July and landed at Mytilene, where, after remaining for more than a month as the honoured guests of Francesco Gattilusio, they visited the Grand Master of Rhodes for another period. Afterwards they sailed to Venice by way of Modon, Cabrera, Zanta, Clarenza (Clarence), Cephalonia, Ragusa, Parenzo and Capodistria. They stayed in the Republic of St. Mark for a short time in fulfilment of their pledge to the Eastern merchants, but soon took refuge in Treviso owing to the appearance of the plague in the city and ultimately obtained permission to return to their homes. Their numbers were then depleted by the death of Coucy at Brusa, Philippe d'Artois at Mikalidsch, Guy de la Trémouille at Rhodes and Henri de Bar at Venice. The remaining knights traversed the Tyrol and Switzerland, and finally descended on Burgundy. Proceeding by slow and easy stages to

---

[1] Delaville Le Roulx, I, 327–34; *Nicopolis*, 112.

[2] Froissart, XV, 47, puts a speech in Bayezid's mouth on this occasion and asserts that the Sultan strongly expressed his readiness to meet any western prince in the field. Barante, II, 210, describes the presents as a mace of iron, Turkish coats of mail made of linen and human intestines, and a Turkish drum. Cf. *Nicopolis*, 107.

Dijon (22 January 1398), Fougères (6 March), Ghent, Paris (10 March), Arras (16 March), Lille, then Ghent a second time (23 March), Antwerp (29 March), Ypres and Termonde, Tournay (25 April) and Grammont, Nevers had a great welcome. Everywhere men rejoiced, minstrels sang, musicians played, processions were held and presents offered in honour of the Count and his companions. The general atmosphere was one of triumph rather than defeat, and the disastrous end of the fallen thousands at Nicopolis was forgotten.[1] One solitary spirit, however, neither forgot the humiliation of the Christians by the Turks nor discarded the idea of another crusade. From the depth of his seclusion in the Abbey of the Celestines in Paris, Philippe de Mézières wrote his last epistle analysing the causes of the defeat and prescribing the remedies which would ensure the success of another expedition.[2] Among other recommendations, he advanced his plan for the new military Order of the Passion and concluded with an exhortation to the Duke of Burgundy and to the King of France to avenge the recent calamity by reviving holy war against the miscreants. 'But Philippe de Mézières was a forlorn voice in a world of change. Universal action had become impossible, and the downfall of Western chivalry at Nicopolis had tolled the knell of the age of new Orders and the age of the great Crusades.'[3]

[1] *Nicopolis*, 107–9.
[2] *Épistre lamentable et consolatoire*; *vide supra*, Cap. VII.
[3] *Nicopolis*, 125.

OF THE RAN-
SOMED CAP-
TIVES OF THE
CRUSADE OF
NICOPOLIS IN
FRANCE

(M. ccxxi, p. 453)
MS. HARL. 4380,
Fol. 131b.

THE PAYMENT
OF RANSOM FOR
THE COMTE
DE NEVERS
(M. ccxx, p. 453)
MS. HARL. 4380,
Fol. 118.

CHAPTER XIX

THE AFTERMATH OF THE CRUSADES

The Ottomans and their 'Counter-Crusades': the Balkans, Byzantium, Hungary and Venice. Egypt and its 'Counter-Crusades': 'Counter-propaganda', Armenia, Cyprus and Rhodes. The Levant a Turkish colony: Mamlūk downfall, decay of Eastern trade, and beginning of age of discoveries. Belated projects for Crusade

THE disaster to Western chivalry at Nicopolis marked the end of the crusades as an organized movement of Christendom against Islam for the deliverance of the Holy Land. The Turks defended their foothold on the Continent with such astounding success that the monarchs and peoples of the West became discouraged and Eastern Europe was left to its fate. One of the earliest and most critical chapters in the history of the Eastern Question was then closed in favour of the Ottomans who were accepted as a new European state in spite of their alien origin and religion. Hungary became the bulwark of Catholic Christendom and to stem the Turkish advance towards the heart of Europe was its only chance of survival as an independent country. In 1396, after the battle of Nicopolis, the Hungarian armies were almost annihilated and the meagre numbers that survived the massacre of the Christian forces were dispersed without any immediate hope of bringing them together again. Sigismund was therefore unable for a time to organize any further resistance and the road to Buda was open to the invaders if they chose to pursue their progress in that direction. Nevertheless Bayezid I, probably owing to the exhaustion of his troops and to his own illness,[1] preferred to stay south

---

[1] According to Chalkokondylas (MPG, CLIX, 83), Bayezid had a sudden attack of gout which hindered him from taking action against Hungary; cf. *Nicopolis,* 97 and 194 note 98.

of the Danube. Although the Ottomans had for nearly half a century been penetrating the Balkans, and although the rulers of Bulgaria and Serbia were among the Sultan's vassals and even the Byzantine Emperor paid him an annual tribute, the peninsula as a whole was still far from being an Ottoman dominion. Many wide areas in it remained yet to be conquered; and for that matter, Asia Minor itself was divided among numerous independent Turkish dynasties of which the Ottomans were but one, and not the strongest, unit. It was to this primary work of consolidation that the far-sighted Sultans had to devote all their attention for several generations to come, and Bayezid was no exception. North of the Danube, he limited his operations to the recovery of his interrupted suzerainty over the principality of Wallachia and to some raids in the Hungarian provinces of Styria and Syrmia. South of the Danube, he displayed more vigour in the exploitation of his great victory of 1396. The annexation of Bulgaria and Serbia was completed; and the Ottomans crossed the Morava and the Drina to the West, and penetrated Bosnia as far as Zwornik. In the south, too, a good opportunity presented itself to the Sultan, when the Greek Bishop of Phocis invited him to come on a hunting expedition into Thessaly and Epirus. The Sultan, whose passion for the chase was great, welcomed this invitation. The hopes of both host and guest, however, were not confined to a mere pleasure trip. The Bishop intended to use the Sultan's formidable army for the re-establishment of his shaken authority in his diocese against Latin and Greek rivals; but the astute Bayezid and his armies hastened to lay their hands, not only on Phocis, but also on Doris, Locris and several other districts in Livonia and the Morea. Turkish settlements were planted in many depopulated regions of Greece to replace the natives who had been carried off into slavery.

While the Sultan's generals, Everenos and Ya'qūb, were entrusted with the execution of the rest of his plans in the Morea, Bayezid himself resumed the siege of Constantinople. This siege, begun before September 1396 and interrupted by the war with the Western knights, was again

undertaken without further delay.[1] The capture of that
'great city' had been the chief object of the Ottoman Sultans
for some time, and its fall seemed imminent in the period
that followed the collapse of the crusade of Nicopolis. The
rulers of the West, even if they were not impotent to
contribute any material help to its defence, were reluctant to
put more men into the Eastern field which had so recently
brought disaster upon them. Emperor Manuel's western
journey of 1399–1402 to beg for aid against the Turks
aroused little more than sympathy and empty promises
among the Catholic rulers of Europe.[2] All the assistance
that was to reach him from these quarters had been rendered
before his departure, when Boucicaut and a band of adventurers numbering one thousand and two hundred men
landed at Constantinople in 1399.[3] This could hardly be
described as a crusade, in spite of the fact that Boniface IX
had twice preached the holy war in April 1398 and March
1399.[4] Monarchs and princes who were capable of leading
the host were much too engrossed in their own affairs to lend
ear to the words of the Pope, and no one was in the mood
to take his preaching seriously except probably the Venetians and the Genoese whose trade interests in Constantinople were directly affected by the Turkish menace. The
majority of Boucicaut's men were not pious volunteers for
the defence of the Cross. They were chiefly fighting for
pay from their employer and for booty from their victim.
When they found from their few encounters with the enemy
that the Ottomans offered no substantial material for pillage
and, moreover, that the Byzantine emperor was too poor to
reward them, they sailed back to the West after fighting a
few minor engagements in the neighbourhood of the city.
The Marshal of France and governor of Genoa left behind
him Jean de Châteaumorand and a very small number of

[1] Von Hammer, *Gesch. d. osman. Reich.*, I, 204 et seq.; Gregorovius,
Athen, I, 241 et seq. and II, 219 et seq.; Gibbons, *Foundations*, 229–31;
Delaville Le Roulx, *France*, I, 249–54; *Nicopolis*, 117–18.

[2] Delaville Le Roulx, op. cit., I, 256–8; *Nicopolis*, 119–20.

[3] *Livre des faicts du bon messire Jean le Maingre* in *Coll. complètes des
mémoires* (Petitot, 1ere série), VI, 482 et seq.; Delaville Le Roulx, I, 259 et
seq.; Gibbons, 236–9.

[4] Reynaldus, *ad ann.* 1398, no. 40, and 1399, nos. 1–4.

men to supervise the defence until his return.[1]   It is said
that he proposed that the Emperor should do homage to the
King of France for his empire in return for French assistance,
and that Venice, Genoa and the Order of St. John of Jerusalem sanctioned his suggestion.   But Boucicaut did not
return to the forlorn city, nor did Charles VI accede to the
plan of imposing his suzerainty over an empire which was
tottering to its fall.[2]

It would, however, be an error to magnify the ease with
which the Ottomans might have seized Constantinople
at this stage in their career.   Numerous factors were
against them.   They had neither heavy artillery to storm
the walls nor a fleet [3] strong enough to blockade the city on
all sides.   If we remember that it was these two elements
that proved decisive in the final siege of 1453 by Sultan
Muhammad II, we may realize how difficult Bayezid's task
must have been in 1399–1400.   Moreover, the garrison
itself was temporarily strengthened by the advent of
Boucicaut and his Latin army.   The Ottomans could only
intercept access from the city to the Balkans by land and
thus reduce its supplies.   Although a siege under these
circumstances promised to be long, Bayezid appeared to be
determined to carry it to a successful issue at any cost, and
his operations against Byzantium broke down only under
the weight of Timur's invasion of Asia Minor.   The battle
of Angora (1402) and the capture of the Sultan postponed
the downfall of the city for half a century, during which the
Ottomans recovered from the Tatar blow and fought the
Christians in several battles with varying fortunes.   Murad
II (1421–51) started another siege of Constantinople after
his accession to the throne, but was compelled to raise it in
1422 [4] for the lack of effective artillery and navy—the
two factors which had handicapped Bayezid I in 1399.
On the other hand, his wars with the Hungarians under the

---

[1] *Livre des faicts*, VI, 494–8.   [2] Gibbons, 238–9.

[3] On the subject of Turkish artillery, *vide infra*, note on sources for Siege
of Constantinople.   On Turkish navy, see Piri Re'īs (ed. P. Kahle), op. cit.,
and Hajji Khalīfa, *Tuhfat al-Kibār*, trans. J. Mitchell.

[4] Vasiliev, *Emp. byz.*, II, 334; Gibbon, VII, 143 et seq.; De la Jonquière,
I, 90.

leadership of John Hunyadi, a Transylvanian hero whose
name passed into legend, culminated in a crushing defeat of
the Christians at Varna (1444).[1]   This campaign, like many
others, was styled as a crusade and the Pope was represented
in it by Cardinal Julian Cesarini; but actually it was little
more than one episode in the Turco-Hungarian wars
of the fifteenth century.   Muhammad II (1451–81) was
more fortunate than his predecessors in regard to Constantinople.   He concentrated his forces round the city on
6 April 1453.   The garrison consisted of the disheartened
and demoralized Greeks together with some four hundred
Genoese men-at-arms under the command of Giovanni
Giustiniani.   The Emperor Constantine Dragases and his
helpers fought valiantly but with little effect against the
heavy Ottoman artillery constructed at Adrianople for the
purpose of the siege.   On 29 May 1453, the 'Conqueror'
marched into the city of Constantine and so a painful
chapter was closed in the history of the great controversy
between Christendom and Islam.[2]   The capture of that
city, though foreseen for a long time before this date, produced much alarm and consternation in Europe.   Talks of
another crusade were revived and the hopes of men were
fixed on Philippe le Bon, Duke of Burgundy, and the
enthusiastic Aeneas Sylvius, later Pius II, of whose efforts
and their tragic end much has already been said elsewhere.[3]
It is not within the scope of the present study to dwell upon
the details of the Hungarian struggle by land or the Venetian
battles by sea in an attempt to arrest Ottoman encroach-

---

[1] Vasiliev, op. cit., II, 330.

[2] It is unnecessary to enlarge upon the details of the siege and fall of Constantinople.   The subject has been fully treated by many scholars, and most
of the Byzantine and Turkish histories include many useful references to it.
For the original sources, see Bury's account in his edition of Gibbon's *Decline
and Fall*, VII, 332–5, and P. Pogodine, 'Studies on the Sources of the
History of the Siege and Capture of Byzantium by the Turks in 1453', in the
Journal of the Ministry of Public Instruction, vol. 264 (1889), pp. 205–58
(in Russian).   Monographs on the history of the fall of Constantinople
include—G. Schlumberger, *Siège, prise et sac de Constantinople par les Turcs
en 1453*; and E. Pears, *Destruction of the Greek Empire and Capture of Constantinople*.

[3] *vide supra*, Cap. IX; see also Barante, *Ducs de Bourgogne*, V, 3 et
seq.

ments in Europe. It will suffice here to state that the battle of Mohacz [1] (1526) precipitated the fall of Hungary, and that the famous battle of Lepanto [2] (1571), though won by Venice, was of little practical value since the Venetians came to terms with the Supreme Porte.

If the advance of the Ottomans into Europe can be regarded as one aspect of the reaction of Islam towards Christianity, Egypt was, during the last century of her existence as an independent state, far from idle in that Muslim holy warfare (Jihād) which may be appropriately described as the 'counter-crusade'. The history of this interesting and important movement, rich in Arabic documentary evidence, is worthy of a special study covering the period from the great Saladin to Muhammad the Conqueror. Much has been written on the crusade, yet little is to be found on the 'counter-crusade' save isolated and disconnected references. Although the need for that study is pressing, its irrelevance to the present work can allow little more than a rapid survey of some aspects of the literature and events leading to the triumph of Egypt over Christendom in many fields in the Levant. The Muslim point of view in regard to the sanctity of the Holy Land was singularly similar to that of the Christians. Hence arose a new counter-propagandist literature preaching that Syria was the land of promise and the natural heritage of those who professed the true faith of Islam. Its ancient shrines and temples, of which many had already been converted into mosques, were second in holiness only to those of Mekka and Medina. Muslim tradition, according to the numerous versions extant during the Later Middle Ages, imposed the duty of pilgrimage to those places on all those who could afford to perform it. The abundance of such literature is a notable feature of the fourteenth century.[3]

[1] De la Jonquière, I, 152–5.

[2] See monograph on Lepanto by Julien de la Gravière, *Guerre de Chypre et bataille de Lépante*, II (Paris, 1888). See also Daru, *Venise*, IV, 174–88.

[3] A selection of this literature, still mainly in manuscript, is included in the Bibliography, Section I, Pt. 2, under the title 'Miscellaneous'. Note, for example, the first two anonymous works as well as those by al-Herawi, ibn Kathīr, al-Khazrajī, al-Maqdisī, al-Tadmurī, and ibn al-Zayyat. Little of

The analysis of one of these treatises may help to illustrate the nature of Muslim counter-propaganda. A Cambridge manuscript known as the *Book of the Virtues of Jerusalem* (Kitāb Faḍā'il Bayt al-Maqdis) in which is incorporated another called the *Book of the Virtues of Syria* (Kitāb Faḍā'il al-Shām) and dated in the second half of the fourteenth century,[1] includes much material of great interest. It is said, states the author of the book, that the Prophet recommended a pilgrimage to Jerusalem to all his followers; and those unable to perform this duty should send oil for the lanterns of its sanctuaries, as the angels would pray for the giver as long as the oil burnt therein.[2] A prayer said in the great mosque of Jerusalem was equal to forty thousand prayers elsewhere, and one said in the mosque of Damascus to thirty thousand.[3] If a man knelt eight times in prayer at Jerusalem, he would become the companion of the prophet Abraham in paradise; and when he had completed the ten, he would even rise to the place of David.[4] Another version of the 'Ḥadīth' (tradition) went further. A pilgrim to Jerusalem would earn the reward of a thousand martyrs and his flesh would be saved from the flames of the abyss in the future world.[5] The reasons for urging Muslims to visit Syria and to settle in it, however, were not purely sentimental and pious. The writer of the second tract (Faḍā'il al-Shām) tries to prove that Syria possessed nine-tenths of the wealth [6] of the world. His far-fetched statements and hypotheses, despite their evident weakness, have a moral. It behoved men to come to that country, not only for pious practices, but also to avail themselves of its agricultural and trade amenities, and thus they might enjoy prosperity in this world and ensure a place in paradise in the world to come. All these great expectations

---

this material has been published, and it has received small attention from competent scholars. This neglected chapter in Arabic literature is nevertheless worthy of some consideration.

[1] MS. Qq. 912, f. 139 vo, 1 Rajab 765/ 4 April 1364.
[2] ib., f. 32 vo.
[3] ib., f. 33 ro.
[4] ib., 34 vo.   [5] ib., ff. 35 ro–36 vo.
[6] ib., f. 88 ro & vo.

coupled with the principle of holy war (al-Jihād [1]) and the tradition of efficient military training [2] in Mamlūk Egypt, explain the moral and physical vigour with which the 'counter-crusade' fulfilled the triumph of Islam in Syria and elsewhere in the Levant.

The re-conquest of Syria, begun in earnest and with effect by Saladin or even before his time, was completed at the beginning of our period with the capture of 'Akka and Ṭarābulus in 1291. This marked the end of the first stage in the counter-crusade. The second consisted of the invasion of the Christian Kingdom of Armenia which became an Egyptian province in 1375.[3] Both of these stages have been treated in the foregoing pages. With the fall of Armenia, the Mamlūk dominions were bounded by the Muslim principalities of the Turks in Asia Minor, over which they had neither a religious claim nor, probably, military superiority. The conquering arm of Egypt had to extend in another direction. To attain more victories against the Christians, it was necessary for them to equip a strong fleet for the conveyance of their troops beyond the sea. Their want of ships arrested their progress for half a century, although we must remember that during that

[1] Much diversity of opinion exists on the problem of 'al-Jihād' ranging from Arnold's view in *The Preaching of Islam* to Massignon's thesis in his lecture ed. H. A. R. Gibb in *Whither Islam?* I do not propose to take sides in this rather delicate controversy, and have, instead, made a record of most of the Qur'ān texts where the subject is mentioned. See al Qur'ān, Sūra II, texts 185–9, 212, 215; III, 136, 160–5, 194; IV, 76–9, 86, 97; V, 39; VIII, 40, 66, 75–6; IX, 13–14, 29, 41, 87–9, 112, 124; XVI, 111; XXII, 76–7; XXV, 54; XXIX, 5, 69; XLVII, 4–6, 33; XLIX, 15; LVII, 10; LX, 1; LXI, 4, 11–13; LXXIII, 20. Except for Sūras XVI, XXII, XXV, XXIX, LVII, LXI and LXIII, in which 'al-Jihād' is not particularly elaborated, the bulk of 'al-Jihād' texts are Medinese, that is, they belong to the period after the prophet's flight (*hijra*) to Medina and the failure of preaching and persuasion among his own tribesmen in Mekka. For pronouncements on the same subject by the Prophet, see Wensinck's Indexes to the Traditions under 'jāhada' and 'jihād'.

[2] *vide supra*, Cap. I, *et infra*, Bibliography, Section I, Pt. 2 under 'Art of War'. See also another list of tracts on war preserved in the Istanbul libraries, in an article by H. Ritter, Kleine Mitteilungen und Anzeigen: 'La Parure des Cavaliers' und die Literatur über die ritterlichen Kunste, in *Der Islam*, XVIII (1929), 116–54.

[3] *vide supra*, Cap. II et XI.

period the Ottomans continued the movement against the Byzantine Empire and the Balkan states with bewildering rapidity.

The third stage in the Egyptian counter-crusades was inaugurated in 1424 against the Latin Kingdom of Cyprus. The Mamlūks had an old grievance against the house of Lusignan since the crusade of Pierre I which ruined Alexandria in 1365.[1] The Sultans never forgot this disaster and their minds were continually bent on chastising the island-kingdom that had inflicted so much damage on one of their most prosperous towns. Another factor which decided Egypt to take action against Cyprus was the recurrence of 'Frankish' piratical raids on Muslim property both at sea and on the mainland. A number of these raids have already been mentioned in connexion with the crusade of Alexandria. In the fifteenth century they seemed to become a permanent menace to Egypt, and the Cypriots were regarded at the court of the Sultan as guilty of harbouring and encouraging this unprovoked piracy.[2] In July or August 1422, two 'Frankish' grabs descended on the coast of Alexandria, destroyed Muslim craft carrying one hundred thousand 'dinārs' worth of goods, and went off unharmed.[3] In August 1423, news of another impending attack reached the amīrs of Alexandria, Damietta and Rosetta;[4] and in March or April 1425, similar rumours compelled the Mamlūks to concentrate a strict watch on the coast.[5] In the same year, the Cypriot chronicler reports a raid on Syria in which Philippe de Picquigny, bailiff of Limassol, and Jean Gasel, commander of Aliki, were confederates.[6] This was probably the encounter reported by Maqrīzī on 2 May 1425, in which a Muslim trading ship carrying fifty men from Laodicia was seized and burnt and its crew killed without exception.[7] The Egyptians could

---

[1] *vide supra*, Cap. XV.

[2] Makhairas (ed. Dawkins), § 651.

[3] Maqrīzī, *Kitāb al-Sulūk*, IV (Gotha MS., Pertsch, 1620), f. 49 ro et vo.

[4] ib., f. 54 vo.   [5] ib., f. 63 vo.

[6] Makhairas, § 651.

[7] Maqrīzī, op. cit., f. 64 vo. Another in the same year (ff. 63 vo–64 ro) is reported on Ṣūr and the country between Ṭarābulus and Ḥalab.

no longer bear this state of affairs. In the previous
year (1424), the Sultan [1] had dispatched a small flotilla of
six ships and a detachment of men to protest to King
Janus of Cyprus. The men fulfilled their mission and
further pillaged some Venetian goods stored at Limassol.
After setting this port on fire, they returned to Cairo.[2] This
was the first of three expeditions which ended in the complete defeat of the Cypriot arms.[3] The second took place
in the following year, when a fleet of more than forty units
sailed from Bulāq to Famagusta by way of Damietta and
Tarābulus, carrying an army of about a thousand who
defeated the Cypriot forces with heavy loss, pillaged
the western part of the island, and returned with their ships
laden with booty and prisoners.[4] The third and final
expedition was manned in 1426. On this occasion very
elaborate preparations were made by the Sultan to ensure
the crushing of the power of Cyprus. A fleet of a magnitude unknown in Mamlūk history was brought together
in the Bulāq arsenal. According to Khalīl al-Dhāhirī,[5]
it consisted of one hundred and eighty sail; and Makhairas [6]
estimates it at one hundred and fifty and the Saracen army
at five hundred Mamlūks, two thousand Turkmens and six
hundred Arabs. The leadership of the army was entrusted
to two able commanders, Taghrī Bardī al-Maḥmūdī and
'Ināl al-Jakamī.[7] The situation in Cyprus had long
been ripe for the coming downfall. The period of cruel
intrigue which was inaugurated with the murder of Pierre I
(1369), the strongest monarch in the history of the Lusignan
dynasty, rent the kingdom into endless factions and turned it

---

[1] The reigning Sultan was Bursbay (al-Ashraf Saif-al-Dīn); see Genealogical
Tables, Appendix V.

[2] Makhairas, §§ 651–2; Khalīl Dhāhirī, cf. Mas Latrie, II, 506–8; Abul-
Mahāsin b. Taghrī Bardī (al-Nujūm, ed. Popper), VI, 582.

[3] A valuable article on 'The Mamlūk Conquest of Cyprus in the Fifteenth
Century' by M. M. Ziada may be found in the *Bulletin of the Faculty of Arts,
Egyptian University*, Vol. I, Pt. I, 90–113 and Vol. II, Pt. I, 37–57.

[4] Makhairas, §§ 654–9; Khalīl Dhahirī, cf. Mas Latrie, II, 508–10;
Maqrīzī, op. cit., 64 vo–66 ro; ibn Taghrī Bardī, VI, 590–4.

[5] op. cit., II, 511.   [6] op. cit., § 672.

[7] Ibn Taghrī Bardī, VI, 601; Maqrīzī, o.c., ff. 71 vo–72 ro; Khalīl
Dhahirī, l.c.; Makhairas, l.c.

into a field of battle for the conflict between Venice and Genoa. Each of these two astute republics strove to dominate the island irrespective of religious fellowship and regardless of established treaties.[1] Their selfish motives led to ruinous war on the soil of Cyprus; and, to add to the troubles of the ill-fated island, its nobles became disunited and the central administration was unable to control them. Plague, too, exacted its toll of death and damage among the population.[2] It was a sad inheritance which fell to the lot of King Janus. The arm of the Mamlūk Sultan proved too formidable for his resources and, at the battle of Kherokitia near the Vassilipotamo River on 7 July 1426, his power sank and he himself was captured and carried to Egypt.[3] The account of the annihilation of the Cypriot army and the merciless ravages that followed the victory of the Egyptians as told by Makhairas, and the pitiful events of the captivity of Janus in Cairo as told in the contemporary chronicles of Egypt, belong to a history other than that of the crusades. Janus paid a heavy penalty for the great crime which his ancestor, Pierre I, had committed against Alexandria in 1365. His humiliation was but the beginning of his serious troubles, for his release from imprisonment was only granted on condition that he should pay an immediate ransom and a future tribute to be rendered every year in return for holding his crown in vassalage to the Sultan.[4]

The downfall of Cyprus constituted the third stage of the Egyptian counter-crusade. As a natural corollary, this led to the fourth and final stage in which the Mamlūks waged wars with the Knights of St. John in Rhodes. The success of their expeditions against an enfeebled Cyprus whetted their appetite for another triumph in Rhodes, especially as they were now in possession of a proved navy

---

[1] Makhairas, §§ 328 et seq.; gives many of the details of the Veneto-Genoese struggle in Cyprus.

[2] Makhairas, §§ 623, 636, 637, 643, records the occurrence of plagues in the years 1393, 1409, 1410, 1419 and 1420.

[3] ib., §§ 678 et seq.

[4] Maqrīzī, op. cit., f. 72 vo; ibn Taghrī Bardī, VI, 617-20; Khalīl Dhāhirī, cf. Mas Latrie, II, 514.

to convey their troops beyond the sea and Rhodes was situated within easy reach of their vassal island of Cyprus. Nevertheless, they found the knights to be of a different metal from that of the Cypriots; and their campaigns against Rhodes met with a severe rebuff. This was due to the strong fortification of that island, to the rigorous observance of discipline in the ranks of the Order, its unity in counsel and in action, and to an elaborate system of espionage which forewarned the Grand Master of the movements of the enemy and thus kept the Order in full readiness to repulse all attacks. Three times did the Egyptians attempt to reduce Rhodes to subjection, and three times were their efforts frustrated by the valiance and preparedness of the knights. The first of these campaigns occurred in 1440 when a fleet of fifteen grabs was manned at Bulāq for the attack on Rhodes. Sailing by way of Cyprus and Alaya for revictualling, the fleet was reinforced by two more ships provided by the Turkish amīr of the latter place, and the combined fleet reached Rhodes. To their dismay, they found the enemy waiting for them. Their incursion was repulsed with a loss of twelve Mamlūks and many seriously wounded. Seeing the hopelessness of their situation, they withdrew to Egypt.[1] The defeat of the Sultan's [2] arms gave him a new grievance against Rhodes and decided him to undertake another expedition to punish the masters of that island and destroy their power. He started his preparations with this object in 1442, and approximately one year later a fleet carrying one thousand five hundred regular troops in addition to a large number of volunteers under the command of 'Īnāl al-'Alā'ī was brought to Damietta on the way to Ṭarābulus where it was planned that they should be reinforced by more men from Syria. The Egyptian fleet was, however, battered and dispersed on a tempestuous journey, and its arrival delayed. Some ships reached Beirūt and others Ṭarābulus, only to find

---

[1] Maqrīzī, *Kitāb al-Sulūk*, IV (B.M. MS. Or. 2902), ff. 216–17; ibn Taghrī Bardī, op. cit., VIII, 114; Vertot, *Chevaliers de Malte*, II, 363 et seq.; Weil, *Abbasidenchalifat*, II, 234.

[2] The reigning Sultan was Jaqmaq (al-Ẓāhir Saif-al-Dīn), and the Grand Master of Rhodes Jean de Lastic; see Genealogical Tables, Appendix V.

that the Syrian contingent had gone ahead of them to Cyprus—then a safe base for Muslim operations against Rhodes. The various forces at last united in the neighbourhood of the ports of Larnaca and Limassol, and after plundering the defenceless inhabitants, set out to Paphos (al-Bāf) for revictualling, presumably at the expense of the King and people of Cyprus. Thence they proceeded by way of the friendly towns of Alaya and Adalia on the south coast of Asia Minor to the little island-fortress of Castellorizzo (Qashṭīl al-Rūj) which belonged to the Knights of St. John. Its towers were pulled down and destroyed and its garrison massacred after some resistance (October 1443). At this juncture, it was found that winter was approaching and, realizing the impregnability of Rhodes and the danger of being cut off from Egypt for the season, the commanders of the army decided to retire direct to Damietta and Cairo.[1] Like the first expedition, the second, therefore, achieved nothing of its original purpose. The third campaign in 1444 was as luckless as the rest. In the spring of that year a body of a thousand Mamlūks, together with many volunteers, equipped with siege engines, left Alexandria and Damietta for Ṭarābulus where they were reinforced by a Syrian contingent and the joint army sailed to Rhodes. Some besieged the capital, while others raided the neighbouring towns and villages. Their efforts, however, proved to be without avail against the invulnerable fort of St. Nicholas, and their numbers were continually depleted in the strenuous fighting that followed. Three hundred Mamlūks were killed in the field and five hundred wounded, while a number of Latin converts to Islam deserted the Egyptians and went over to the Knights. In the meantime, the summer season was drawing to a close and the prospect seemed very unpromising. Defeated and disheartened, the survivors raised the siege and returned to Egypt.[2]

[1] The chief source for the Second Expedition against Rhodes is *Inbā' al-Ghumr* (BM. MS. Add. 7321, ff. 361–4) by ibn Ḥajar on the authority of one Burhān-al-Dīn al-Buqaʿī. See also ibn Taghrī Bardī, op. cit., VII, 122; al-Sakhāwī, *al-Tibr al-Masbūk* (continuation of al-Maqrīzī's *Sulūk*), 62–5; Weil, II, 235.

[2] Sakhāwī, 87–9; ibn Taghrī Bardī, VII, 132–6; Weil, II, 236–7. Peace was finally concluded, thanks to the good offices and great influence of the

It is doubtful whether the Mamlūk attacks on Rhodes had any permanent effect on the Order of St. John. The damage done to their stronghold was temporary and their power appears to have remained almost unshaken. Nevertheless, Egypt established a dangerous precedent for its Ottoman successors who twice besieged the Knights and finally brought disaster upon the island. Muhammad II made the first attempt to subdue the island in 1448, but it was not until 1522 that Sulaiman I succeeded in the expulsion of the Order in the days of the Grand Master Philippe Villiers de l'Isle-Adam after one of the most heroic defences in the history of Rhodes.[1] During the interval between the end of Egyptian and the beginning of Ottoman counter-crusades against Rhodes, many developments had taken place in the history of the Levant. The star of the Ottomans was in the ascendant. Constantinople became the capital of their new empire in 1453, and their power in Asia Minor was consolidated at the expense of the Turkish amīrs whose principalities, large and small, were swallowed by the Sultans. In 1516 the battle of Marj Dabiq was fought in the vicinity of Aleppo between Salim I and Qanṣūh al-Ghaurī. The death of the latter on that field precipitated the invasion of Syria by the Turks. In 1517 the battle of al-Raydaniya (the modern Abbasieh quarter, north-east of Cairo) sealed the fate of Egypt; and after several minor encounters, al-Ghaurī's successor, Ṭūmān-Bāy was captured and hanged at the Zuwailah Gate of the city. The triumph of the Ottomans in both battles was not due to their numerical and tactical superiority or even their courage in hand-to-hand fighting, but to their use of artillery and gunpowder which were almost unknown to the army of Egypt.[2] As we have seen, the downfall of

French merchant prince, Jacques Coeur, at the court of Egypt. His mediation between the two belligerents was carried out with the approval of Charles VII of France. Vertot, II, 373–4; L. S. Costello, *Jacques Coeur* (London, 1847), 203–4; A. B. Kerr, *Jacques Coeur* (London, 1927), 141.

[1] Vertot, III, 212 et seq.; Atiya, article *Rhodes* in EI.

[2] The sources for the Turkish conquest are the histories of ibn Iyas (new ed. in Bibl. Islamica of the DMG by P. Kahle and M. Mustafa), ibn Ṭūlūn (tract ed. Hartmann) and ibn Zunbul. A new edition collated from the

Constantinople long before the occupation of Cairo may also be ascribed largely to the efficiency of the Turkish artillery. Whatever the causes of success may have been, the effects which mattered most were that the Levant became a large Turkish colony with disastrous results to the flourishing trade of Egypt and the Italian republics. All the eastern trade routes were now in Turkish hands, and Cairo, Alexandria and Damascus began to lose their medieval importance. Constantinople had become the great capital of the Sultans and of Islam; and Latin embassies in search of markets and privileges now made their way, not to Cairo, but to the metropolis of the new empire of the Ottomans.[1] Meanwhile, the great movement of Oceanic exploration which led to the rounding of the Cape and the finding of the New World, though inaugurated before that time, was accelerated; and the Near Eastern commerce became a memory.

In the tumult of new movements and a modern age, the crusade for the salvation of the Holy Land sank into oblivion. Now and again we hear of a project to revive holy war against the Turks; but it was quickly evident that this was little more than idle talk and a vain echo from the past. In 1515, Leo X, Francis I and Maximilian I discussed a crusade, and Francis expressed his wish to lead a campaign for the re-conquest of Jerusalem.[2] When we remember that Francis did not shrink from concluding an alliance with the Turks against the Holy Roman Empire at one stage in his career, we can estimate the degree of

manuscripts in Cairo, Gotha, Munich, Vienna, London, Manchester and Glasgow is in preparation by the author and will, it is hoped, appear in print in the near future.

[1] It is also to be noted that after the capture of Constantinople by the Turks and of Granada by the Christians, the Moors of Spain addressed their grievances to the Ottoman Sultans. An instance is quoted in the Bibliography—*vide infra* Section 6 (Oriental), Pt. I (Official), of a letter to Bayezid II.

[2] Charrière, *Négotiations de la France dans le Levant*, in *Coll. des documents inédits* (Paris, 1849), I, cxxviii-cxxxi; Zinkeisen, *Gesch. d. osman. Reich. in Europa* (Gotha, 1840–63), III, 807; ib., *Drei Denkschriften über die orientalische Frage, vom Papst Leo X, Franz I und Maximilian I* (Gotha, 1854); cf. Iorga, *Un projet relatif à la conquête de Jérusalem*, in ROL, II (1894), 183–4.

his sincerity in regard to a Christian holy war. During
the rest of the sixteenth century, however, men were so
completely absorbed in the Reformation, and Europe itself
was so deep in the throes of international wars and civil
strife, that even mere talk of a crusade became more remote
than ever. In the seventeenth century, on the other hand,
old ideas began to reappear and new plans were drawn up
for the recovery of the Eastern Empire. The duc de
Nevers, Richelieu and Father Joseph—all dreamt of reviving
the old cause.[1] Ferdinand I of Tuscany actually landed
in Cyprus and established relations with the Asiatic chief-
tains who were in open revolt against the authority of
the Ottoman Sultan in 1607–8, but nothing of worth
came from their alliance and Ferdinand himself died on
7 February 1609.[2] A curious propagandist document of
the same year illustrates the seriousness with which these
belated schemes were taken in some quarters. Father
Giovanni Dominelli, an Italian resident in Cairo, writing
in his mother tongue, formulated an elaborate plan for a
campaign against the Ottomans to save 'the most Holy
Sepulchre and the holy places of Jerusalem'.[3] Circumstances within the Turkish Empire seemed to him favourable. The Sultan was at war with Hungary in Europe
and with Persia in Asia, while rebels were up in arms
against him in Asia Minor. He could hardly be victorious
in all these fields, especially if the Catholics chose to take
advantage of his entanglements by attacking his vast realm
on all sides—in the Archipelago, at Constantinople, Qaramania, Rhodes and Alexandria. When Byzantium was
pressed, the Greeks would rise against their oppressors.
Alexandria was almost unguarded and would succumb to
the arms of the Cross without difficulty. The garrison of
the city consisted of two hundred men, and, in fact, the
whole army stationed in Egypt was only four thousand.

---

[1] B.N. MS. fr. 3259; Zinkeisen, *Gesch. d. osman. Reich.*, III, 859 et seq.
and IV, 267–9; cf. Iorga, op. cit., 184.

[2] Zinkeisen, IV, 268; Galluzzi, *Istoria di granducato di Toscana sotto il
governo della casa Medici* (Florence, 1781), III, 156–8, 236–42, 251–3; cf.
Iorga, l.c.

[3] Iorga, op. cit., 185–6; 'e dalle mani d'Infideli saria stato levato il thesoro
del santissimo sepolchro et j lochi santi d'Hierusalem'.

In Syria, the situation of the Ottomans was not a very happy one. The amīr of Ṣaida (Sidon) hated them, and, assisted by the Maronite Christians of Lebanon, he would become a serious menace. The Muslim Fakhr-al-Dīn and the Christian natives would furnish the Syrian contingent with arms, artillery and provisions, and would aid and comfort the invaders.[1] The time appeared to Father Giovanni ripe for universal action by all good Catholics against the infidel usurper of the Holy Land; but the Reverend Father who lived in the East forgot that the day for universal action had gone and that the nations of Europe, now torn asunder between Catholic and Protestant camps, had long lost their enthusiasm for holy war. The crusade was a thing of the past.

[1] Iorga, op. cit., 185–9.

CHAPTER XX

CONCLUSION

General view of the Crusade in the Later Middle Ages.   Main causes and consequences of its failure

The fall of 'Akka and the remaining Latin outposts on the Asiatic mainland caused alarm and consternation in Western Christendom.   The idea had been cherished of using 'Akka as a base for renewed operations against the Saracens, and now 'Akka with other strongholds had passed to the enemy.   The spirit of despair which prevailed in the mind of the age was reflected in the propagandist literature reviewed and analysed in the first book of the present study.   Immediate action became imperative if the Holy Land were to be saved.   Men of letters and men of action, diplomats and ecclesiastical dignitaries, councils of state and councils of the church, pilgrims and travellers—in fact all classes of medieval society, high and low, religious and secular, participated in the propagandist movement and keenly felt the need for crusade. Finally, their efforts came to some fruition when Latin princes and nobles of Europe and the Levant conducted a series of expeditions against Muhammadan rule in various quarters.   The movement may be considered to have reached its high-water mark with the invasion and sack of Alexandria in 1365.   The Crusade of Nicopolis may justly be regarded as the last serious attempt organized by Europe as a whole, not only to crush the Ottomans in the Balkan Peninsula, but also to reach Jerusalem in the heart of the Mamlūk Empire by armed force.   Afterwards, indeed, expeditions bearing the name of crusades did not cease; but they were single-handed efforts mainly undertaken in self-defence, and Holy War lost its original significance as being a universal movement for the recovery of the Holy Land.   If the fourteenth century was the golden age of the later medieval crusade, the fifteenth was that of Muslim supremacy. Egypt became mistress of the Levant, while the Ottomans rapidly completed their conquest of the Balkans. The abortive attempt of Pius II to raise arms against the Turks in the sixties of the fifteenth century is but one instance of the hopelessness of reviving a cause which belonged to the past.

The failure of the movement in the end to achieve any of its original aims may be ascribed to many causes. Disunion played a prominent part in bringing disaster upon the leaders of the Cross and their contingents. This is undoubtedly symptomatic of the wider issues of a period in which the old conception of world-government by Empire and Papacy had been undermined by the rise of new states grouped round royal persons with a growing sense of nationality. Men's minds, too, were distracted from the crusade by multiple troubles at home and in the Church. England and France were involved in the ruinous Hundred Years' War, imperial prestige was weakened in Germany and Central Europe, the Italian Republics were engaged in wars amongst themselves and in the process of trade expansion beyond their own confines, and Christian Spain had to deal with the Moors in the Iberian Peninsula. The Spanish 'crusades' were battles for national freedom—a subject apart—and are therefore overlooked in the present study. In the Church, the Babylonish Captivity ended in the Great Schism and the Conciliar Movement, which monopolized the attention of the West and stood between the public mind and the crusading idea. Then, the insincerity and arrogance which marked the behaviour of many crusaders did nothing to promote the justice of their cause and crown their efforts with a permanent triumph. The sacrilege committed by the Latins at Alexandria and their unworthy flight on the approach of the enemy bore disquieting witness to the spirit of the crusader. The sincere members of the expedition such as King Pierre I and his Chancellor Philippe de Mézières and the Apostolic Legate Pierre de Thomas did not misinterpret these portents. Further, the Italian Republics were engaged in constant intrigue against the crusading movement during the period under review. A war waged with the Muslims, who controlled all routes to the East, might impair their commercial prosperity and deplete their resources, and they were not disposed to sacrifice their material interests for the cause of God. The Genoese were sufficiently unscrupulous to practise the slave trade and carry young Mamlūks to reinforce the Egyptian armies in defiance of all papal bans and bulls. The haughty character of the French chivalry, too, increased the difficulties of all serious enterprises against a redoubtable enemy. This led them to ruin at Nicopolis, when they rejected Sigismund's wise plans in the vain hope of gaining for themselves all the glory of victory. In addition to these causes, we have to remember that the crusaders fought on alien soil, and that neither their armour nor their method of warfare were suitable for the new circumstances. Their weighty coats of mail hampered free movement and exhausted their strength in warmer climes, while their heavy horse and their shock-tactics proved to be of little avail in face of the swift harassing attacks of the light cavalry of the enemy. The Christians were also under the illusion that they were to face a horde of disorderly miscreants. This false conception was a source of many and great mistakes and misfortunes. Both in Egypt and in Turkey existed standing armies of the highest order—among the first of their kind in medieval history. Men whose sole vocation was war, trained in the best military tradition of the Mamlūks and the Ottomans, with blind obedience and strict discipline as the keynotes to their action, constituted the Muslim battalions which routed the heterogeneous medley of Western knights with their antiquated tactics. Like the crusaders, the Muslim combatants firmly believed that they were fighting against an aggressive infidel; and their loyalty to their cause on the whole surpassed that of their enemy. Medieval chroniclers tried on many occasions to find excuses for the discomfiture of their countrymen in the numerical superiority of the Muslims. This view, it is hoped, has been disproved in the foregoing pages. Victory was won not by greater numbers, but by better tactics and the stricter observance of discipline.

The final collapse of the crusading impulse in the West had far-reaching effects on the course of events in the East. Egypt was left in full command of the situation in the Levant, and Turkey became a European as well as an Asiatic power. Egypt then embarked on a series of counter-crusades which precipitated the downfall of the Christian kingdoms near its boundaries. Armenia soon disappeared as an independent state and became a Mamlūk province, while the enfeebled Latin Kings of Cyprus from the disastrous reign of Janus de Lusignan were constrained to pay annual tribute to the Sultans in Cairo. In the meantime, the conquering arm of the Ottomans extended far and wide into south-eastern Europe. After Adrianople, Byzantium became their capital and the throne of Constantine devolved upon Muhammad II and his successors in 1453. The process of incorporating the derelict Latin outposts in the Morea was continued with unflagging vigour; and once their new empire had been consolidated, the Sultans began that northern march into east-central Europe which led them to the gates of Vienna. The crusaders of Nicopolis failed to arrest this great movement at its earliest stage and the Eastern Question remained one of the chief factors in European politics throughout modern history. At last when Egypt and the Holy Land fell before the Ottoman power in the sixteenth century, their fate was, henceforward, bound up with that of Muslim Turkey. The recovery of Jerusalem by forces from Western Europe and all the continents, old and new, was achieved only towards the close of the Great War. Muhammadans fought on both sides, and this war was not for the recovery of the Holy Places, but for the defeat of the Ottoman and his allies. The older cause had sunk into oblivion five centuries before the Allied Armies entered Jerusalem on 10 December 1917.

APPENDICES

APPENDIX I

PRO RECUPERATIONE TERRAE SANCTAE, PETITIO RAYMUNDI PRO CONVERSIONE INFIDELIUM

(Munich MS., Lat. 10565)

ADVERTAT sanctitas vestra sanctissime pater domine Bonifaci papa ac vos Reverendi patres domini cardinales quod cum Deus creaverit homines ut eum cognoscant diligant et honorent et recolant in veritate, et cum infideles sint multo plures quam christiani qui a mundi principio usque nunc persistentes in errore non cessant descendere ad poenas perpetuales infernales quantum deceret quod vos sanctissime pater qui per Dei gratiam primatum tenetis in populo christiano et vos Reverendi domini cardinales aperiretis ecclesiae sanctae thesaurum ad procurandum quod omnes qui verum Dei cultum ignorant ad veritatis lumen perveniant ut finem valeant assequi ad quos (*sic*) Deus eos ex sua benignitate creavit.

Thesaurus iste quem per divini cultus multiplicationem ipsis infidelibus dicimus reserandum duplex est spiritualis videlicet et corporalis.

Thesaurus spiritualis potest ipsis infidelibus communicari sive modo scilicet quod in diversis locis ad hoc aptis per terram christianorum ac in quibusdam locis etiam Tartarorum fiant studia idiomatum diversorum in quibus viri sacra scriptura competenter imbuti tam religiosi quam saeculares qui cultum divinum per orbem terrarum desiderant ampliari valeant ipsorum infidelium idiomata diversa addiscere et ad eorum partes pro praedicando evangelio [pro] Dei utiliter se transferre et quod uni Dominorum cardinalium hoc pium Dei negotium committatur de cuius ordinatione et licentia illi tales ponantur in studiis et ad praedicandum mittantur qui eis prout decens fuerit provideat in expensis.

Thesauro corporali uti poteris isto modo scilicet quod similiter uni domino Cardinali ordinatio committatur ad procurandum et certandum passagium pro terra sancta laudabiliter acquirenda et acquisita etiam conservanda potenter ordinato ad hoc certo numero bellatorum et quemcunque (*sic*) contingit mori aliquos eorundem totidem vel plures vel pauciores secundum quod expedire videbitur sine dilatatione mittantur per ordinationem dicti Domini Cardinalis eisdem in expensis necessariis provisuri.

Cum autem praedicta sine magnis sumptibus non valeant adimpleri decimam ecclesiae pro acquisitione et aliam competentem collectam pro conservatione sub constitutione perpetua ad hoc expedit assignari ut ubique terrarum perpetuo reddatur honor debitus summo Deo.

Multum etiam expedit quod Graeci et alii scismatici reuniantur ecclesiae sacrosanctae quod fieri poterit disputando per authoritates et rationes necessarias quibus per Dei gratiam ecclesia latina sufficienter abundat. Ipsis enim ecclesiae reunitis facilius poterimus eorum subsidio mediante qui viciniores existunt impugnare et de terra jure nostra expellere Sarracenos, ac etiam, quod non est modicum, participare cum Tartaris ad quorum conversionem debemus per praedicationem et disputationem viriliter laborare. Ipsi enim cum adhuc gentiliter sint viventes ad legem nostram quam possumus inter eos libere praedicare faciliter (f. 84 vo) possunt trahi, cum etiam non sit curae principibus Tartarorum cuiusque secta sint eorum subditi professores quod vero nullatenus est a fidelibus negligendum. Nam Judaei et Sarraceni qui sunt dominationi Tartaricae subiugati habere illos ad sectam propriam quilibet elaborant.

Sed si traherentur ad aliquam illarum quod absit vel tertiam per seipsos sicut Mahometus fecit instituerent possent ecclesiae Dei maximum damnum inferre.

Si vos sancte pater quibusdam Sarracenorum regibus scribetis quod vobis mitterent aliquos Sarracenos eorum qui discretiores et subtiliores inter alios reputantur, tales prout credo vobis mittere non differrent quibus inter nos per aliquot annos commorantibus possemus disputando benigne et amicabiliter conferendo veritatem ostendere quam de fide nostra tenemus. Ipsi enim estimantes nos irrationabiliter et fatue de Deo et eius operibus secundum articulorum nostrae fidei invincibilem veritatem credere ac sentire ac nos esse promptos ad ostendendum rationes quas infideles apponunt contra fidem nostram non esse necessarii (*sic*) nec aliquid contra nos secundum veritatem concludere, rationes vero nostras pro fide sic esse invincibiles quod nullum ex ipsis omnino inconveniens sequitur. Imo sublimitas inestimabilis divinae essentiae et eius oppositionum gloriosior humano intellectui declaratur ex quo valde inconvenientes et necessariae comprobantur quae quidem rationes in sacra pagina seminatae sunt et plantatae et per philosophiam significatae prout apparet intuentibus diligenter in quibus scientes quidam modum novum inquirendi et inveniendi ad hoc ex divina bonificentia noviter in . . .[1] licet immerito

---

[1] Blank space with cross in margin. Probably in(venerunt).

et valde indigno concessum (*sic*) possunt copiosius abundare vel reciperent
fidem nostram aut multum haesitantes de secta sua recederent et suis
compatriotis quid et quomodo sentimus et credimus de Deo et eius
operibus recitarent.

Consideretis ergo sancte pater et vos reverendi domini Cardinales
quomodo prae caeteris hominibus tenemini honorem Dei et ecclesiae
utilitatem totis viribus procurare cum Deus vos prae caeteris honor-
averit vos suos vicarios et gregis sui pastores constituens, et quomodo
per Tractatum praedictorum potest universali ecclesiae magna utilitas
evenire, et licet sit longum negotium est tamen executione dignum
cum sit amabile et Deo gratum ac valde omnibus gratiosum.

Nec est praetermittendum propter eius proplexitatem a viris
magnanimis tantum bonum considerantibus quo mundani homines
aggrediuntur laboriosa et valde ardua propter bona transitoria
acquirenda et quomodo reges terrae guerras maximas et valde peri-
culosas assumunt, quomodo etiam anicellini hakasini seipsos morti
scienter exponunt et ad hoc faciendum ab infantia nutriuntur ut genus
suum tradere valeant libertati.

Consideretis etiam si placet quomodo Christiani terras amittunt et
audatiam quam contra Sarracenos habere solebant et quomodo perit
respectus et sunt fere ab omni Christiano neglectae et quomodo clamant
laici contra clerum.

Quare ex praedictorum ordinatione haberent in vobis et vestris bonis
operibus exemplum laici ad bona publica procuranda ex quo auferretur
grande onus a vobis cum damnum et detrimentum christianitatis pro
maiori parte nostrae negligentiae imputetur.

Si autem dicat quis quod fiet infidelium conversio non modo sed
alias quando Deo placuit meditetur diligenter et cogitet ille talis utrum
Deus velit quod semper et ubique sibi in veritate a suo populo serviatur
et utrum velit omnes homines salvos fieri (f. 85 ro) et ad finem ad quos
(*sic*) creavit eos venire acsi de hoc dedit Dominus Jesus Christus
exemplum et sui discipuli per mundum universum laborosissime discur-
rentes ad cultum Dei omnibus hominibus statuendum.

Plures ad hoc possunt adduci rationes authoritates et sanctorum
exempla et plura alia particularia sunt in christianitate necessarie
ordinanda quae devotioni aliorum dimitto cum merito timeam in
tantorum dominorum praesentia plura loqui.

Et si in hiis quae proposui nimis praesumptuosissime in aliquo sim
locutus flectens cordis genua veniam postulo et requiro humiliter
quantum possum me paratum exhibens praedictis omnibus ordinatis
quae prout per se patet possibilia sunt laudabilia sunt et decentia et ipsis
ordinatoribus inestimabiliter meritoria primum mitti vel inter primos
ad terras Sarracenorum quorum linguam didici ad cultum divinum
ampliandum domini nostri Jesu Christi subsidio mediante (f. 85 vo).

APPENDIX II

PILGRIMS AND TRAVELLERS

THE following list is intended to illustrate the extent of propagandist literature of the fourteenth and fifteenth centuries with special reference to pilgrimages. It has been compiled on the basis of Röhricht's *Bibliotheca Geographica Palaestina* and Golubovich's *Biblioteca Bio-Bibliografica della Terra Santa*, together with additions and modifications from our own studies. To avoid duplication of work already executed by these two scholars, we have limited the material quoted here to the author's name, the time at which he wrote, the title of his work, and, unless very incomplete and insufficient, the most recent edition thereof. In some cases where the works have not been edited, references to MSS. extant are provided. We have arranged them chronologically without separating the anonymous tracts under one heading and grouped those of uncertain date at the end of their century. Pilgrims whose names are known to us from the various state archives as well as the Papal and Venetian Archives, but who left no written account of their travels are excluded from this list. For further specialized study of any particular work here cited, the researcher is strongly advised to consult Röhricht and Golubovich in addition to the cross references made to the various chapters of Part I of the present study.

1. FIDENZIO OF PADUA (1274–91).—*Vide* Cap. II.
2. LA DEVISE DES CHEMINS DE BABILOINE (1289–91).—Michelant-Raynaud, *Itin. franç.*, I, 236–51; cf. Ch. Schéfer, *Étude sur la devise, &c.*, in AOL, II A, 89–101.
3. LES CASAUS DE SUR (*c.* 1290).—*Itin. franç.*, I, 253–6.
4. THADDEO OF NAPLES (1291).—*Vide supra*, Cap. II.
5. RICOLDO DI MONTE CROCE (1294).—*Vide* Cap. VIII.
6. HAYTON (*c.* 1300).—*Vide* Cap. III.
7. MARINO SANUDO TORSELLO, THE ELDER (*c.* 1310).—*Vide* Cap. V.
8. ODORIC OF PORDENONE (1320).—*Vide* Cap. X.
9. BERNARDUS THESAURARIUS (1320).—*De acquisitione Terrae Sanctae.* In Muratori, RIS, VII, 687–9 and 711–15.

10. FRANCISCUS PIPINUS DE BONONIA (1320).—*Tractatus de locis Terrae Sanctae.* Tobler, Dritte Wanderung (Gotha, 1859), 400–12.

11. FRANCESCO GIORGI DA VENEZIA, *alias* Paolini (1324).—*Libro della Terra Santa scritto nel* 1324. Bonifacius Stephanus, *Liber de perenni cultu Terrae Sanctae,* ed. Cyprianus de Tarvisio (Venice, 1875), 298.

12. ANTONIO DE REBOLDIS OF CREMONA (1327).—*Itinerarium ad sepulchrum Domini,* ed. Röhricht, in *Zeitschr. des Deutschen Palaestinae-Vereins,* (1890), 153 et seq.

13. PAULINUS PUTEOLANUS (*c.* 1330).—*De passagiis in Terram Sanctam.* Excerpta ex 'chronologia magna' codicis latini CCCXCIV bibliothecae ad d. Marci Venetiarum auspice Societate illustrandis Orientis latini monumentis, ed. G. M. Thomas, Venice and Paris, 1879.

14. JOHANNES FEDANTIOLA (*c.* 1330).—*Descriptio Terrae Sanctae cum indice omnium ejusdem locorum.* Sbaralea, *Supplem. ad SS. Minorum,* II, 418 as mentioned in *Bibliotheca Gratarod Bergom. Medicin. Doctoris* probably identical with the Vat. Codex: Minoritae liber descriptionis Terrae Sanctae, cited by Montfaucon, *Bibl. bibliothecarum,* I, 18. See also Wadding, *SS. ordin. Minorum,* I, 141 and Vermiglioli, *Biografia degli scrittori Perugiani* 1829, I, 15–16.

15. SIMEON SIMEONIS and HUGO ILLUMINATOR (1332).—*Itinerarium fratrum Symeonis et Hugonis Illuminatoris ordin. fratrum minorum professorum* ed. J. Nasmith, Cambridge, 1778.

16. WILHELM VON BOLDENSELE (1332).—*Vide* Cap. VIII.

17. BURCARD (1332).—*Vide* Cap. VI.

18. LUDOLF VON SUCHEM (1335–41).—*Vide* Cap. VIII.

19. JEAN DE BOURGOGNE 'MANDEVILLE' (*c.* 1335).—*Vide* Cap. VIII.

20. GIACOMO DI VERONA (1335).—*Vide* Cap. VIII.

21. ANONYMUS COLONIENSIS (*c.* 1338–48).—*Dar na dat geschreven is van deme heilgen lande in die koufmanschaf en wissen ouch alle lude nijet &c.* Röhricht and Meisner in *Zeitschr. für deutsche Philologie,* XIX, 1–86.

22. NICOLAS ROSSELL (*c.* 1340).—*Liber locorum sanctorum Terre Jerusalem;* also *Nomina Episcoporum et patriarcharum Jerosolimitanorum,* Bover, *Bibl. de escrit. Baleares,* Palma, 1868, II, 298, No. 1084, §§ 26, 27.

23. FRAY BLAS DE BUYSA (*c.* 1342).—*Relacion verdadera y copiosa de los Sagrados Lugares de Jerusalem y Tierra Santa . . .* ordenado por el P. Fray Blas y Buysa, Madrid, 1622 and Salamanca, 1624.

24. ITINERARIUM CUJUSDAM ANGLICI (1344)—*Terram Sanctam et*

alia loco sancta visitantis anno 1344. Golubovich, IV, 395–6, 427–60.

25. NICCOLÒ DA POGGIBONSI (1345).—*Libro d'Oltramare*, ed. Alberto Bacchi della Lega, 2 vol., Bologna, 1881–2, in *Scelta di curiosità letter. inedite o rare dal secolo XIII al XVII.* See also Golubovich, V, 1–24.

26. RUDOLF VON FRAMEYNSBERG (1346).—*Itinerarium in Palaestinam, ad montem Sinai et in Aegyptum.* Canisius, *Antiquae lectiones*, ed. Basnage, IV, 358–60.

27. PHILIPPE DE MÉZIÈRES (c. 1347).—*Vide* Cap. VII.

28. NICOLAUS DE HUDA (1348).—*Notabilia de Terra Sancta.* Neumann, in AOL, II B, 305 ff.

29. ANONYMO TRECENTISTA (c. 1348).—In Carlo Gargiolli, *Viaggi in Terra Santa*, Florence, 1862, 443–50.

30. FR. VALENTINO and MESSER DOLCIBENE OF FLORENCE (1349).—*Viaggio del santo Sepolcro.* Golubovich, V, 50–1.

31. GIOVANNI DE' MARIGNOLLI (1350).—*Vide* Cap. X.

32. BARTHOLOMAEUS ANGLICUS, DE GLANVILLA (c. 1350).—*De genuinis rerum coelestium, terrestrium et infernorum proprietatibus*, Frankfurt, 1609.

33. DESCRIPTIO QUORUNDAM TERRAE SANCTAE MEMORABILIUM (c. 1350).—Werlauff, *Symbol. ad geograph. medii aevi*, Hauniae, 1821, 55–9.

34. COLA DI RIENZO (1351).—*Correspondence relating to the East.* Golubovich, V, 56–8.

35. JOHANN VON OSTERREICH (1356–7).—*Tractatus de Terra Sancta* of which a MS. is mentioned by Wadding and Sbaralea in Acta SS. 19 Jan., Cap. 14, Note.

36. PIERRE DE THOMAS [1] (1360).—*Vide* Cap. VII.

37. HUGH BERNARD OF IRELAND (1360).—*Itinerarium Terrae Sanctae.* Golubovich, V, 80.

38. ACCOUNT OF TRAVEL TO THE HOLY PLACES (c. 1360).—*Vide* J. Martinov, in *Monuments of Early Literature*, St. Petersburg, 1882, XIV, 17–28 in Russian. French trans. in AOL, II B, 389–93.

39. JEAN GODJEALIS (c. 1361).—*Itinerarium Terrae Sanctae*; Rignon, 1861, 83; and Bonifacius Stephanus, 298.

40. JOHANNES POSITI (c. 1363).—*Peregrinaggio e descrittione de Gerusalemme*; Rignon, 1861, 83.

41. FRANCESCO PETRARCA (c. 1364).—*Itinerarium Syriacum.* Ed.

[1] Although Pierre de Thomas wrote nothing of a propagandist nature, his activities as crusader, propagandist and pilgrim justify the inclusion of his name in this list.

Lumbroso, in *Atti della reale acad. d. Lincei*, 1888, IV. Serie, IV, 390–403.

42. WALTER WIBURN (*c.* 1367).—*De proprietatibus Terrae Sanctae.* Wadding, *SS. Minor*, 149.

43. MEMORIA PEREGRINATIONUM TOTIUS TERRAE SANCTAE (1373).—Vienna, MS., 140 s. XV, ff. 104–10.

44. EPITOME BELLORUM SACRORUM, IN QUA ETIAM DESCRIPTIO PALAESTINAE (1374 and 1422).—Canisius-Basnage, *Antiquae lectiones*, IV, 426–46.

45. IOHANN VON BODMAN (1376).—*Fahrt zu dem heiligen würdigen Grab zu Jerusalem.* Röhricht, *Deutsche Pilgerreisen*, Gotha, 1889.

46. HERTEL VON LICHTENSTEIN (1377).—*Philippi Liber de terra sancta oder Hertels v. Lichtenstein Pilgerbüchlein deutsch von Leupolt Augustiner-Lesemeister*, Vienna, 1872.

47. VIA PRIMA QUAE EST DIVERSORUM LOCORUM MUNDI DISTANTIA DEMONSTRATIVA (*c.* 1380).—Lelewel, *Géographie du moyen âge*, III, 281–308.

48. LIONARDO FRESCOBALDI (1384).—*Vide* Cap. IX.

49. GIORGIO GUCCI (1384).—*Viaggio al luoghi santi.* In Gargiolli, *Viaggi in Terra Santa* (Florence, 1862), 271–438.

50. SIMONE SIGOLI (1384).—*Viaggio in Terra Santa* (Turin, 1873), in *Bibl. della Gioventa Italiana*, LVIII. (Also Florence, 1883.)

51. LORENZ EGEN (1385).—*Wie Lorenz Egen von Augsburg . . . zoch gen Sant Kathareinen.* Ed. Keinz in: *Ausland*, 1865, 917–19.

52. PETER VON SPARNAU and ULRICH VON TENNSTÄDT (1385).—*Reise nach Jerusalem.* Röhricht, 109–10.

53. IOHANNES DE HESE (1389).—*Peregrinatio Ioannis Hesei ab urbe Hierusalem instituta et per Indiam, Aethiopiam aliasque quasdam remotas mundi nationes ducta; Vide* Oppert, *der Priester Iohannes*, Berlin, 1864, 180–93.

54. IGNATIUS VON SMOLENSK (1389–1405).—*Vide* Cap. VIII.

55. HENRY BOLINGBROKE, EARL OF DERBY (1392–3).—*Vide* Cap. VIII.

56. THOMAS BRYGG and THOMAS DE SWYNBURNE (1392–3).—*Vide* Cap. VIII.

57. NICCOLÒ DI MARTHONO (1394).—*Vide* Cap. VIII.

58. OGIER VIII SEIGNEUR D'ANGLURE (1395).—*Vide* Cap. VIII.

59. RELATION D'UN VOYAGE DE METZ A IERUSALEM ENTREPRIS EN 1395 PAR QUATRE CHEVALIERS MESSINS (1395).—In: *L'Austrasie, Revue du Nord-Est de la France*, Metz, 1838, III, 149–68, 221–36. The four travellers were (236):

Iehan de Raigecourt, Remion de Mitry, Poince Le Gournaix
and the author of this bulletin Nicolle Louve.

60. IEAN VOET D'UTRECHT (1398).—'In den jaer ons heeren MCCC
ende XCVIII ick heer Johann Voet van Utrecht heb
geweest tot Jherusalem.' O'Kelly, Le Héraut d'Armes
(Bruxelles, 1873) III, 278, *Mém. sur l'ordre de St. Sépulcre*
180 and in *Comptes rendus de la commiss. d'histoire*, 1862, III,
146–7.

UNDATED FOURTEENTH-CENTURY TRACTS

61. *Bethel sive Declaratio Jerusalem Versibus Leoninis Composita.*
Breslau, Stadtbibl. Abth. Rhediger., 89, s. XIV.

62. *De Habitantibus Terre Sancte. De Assassinis.* Turin, Athen.
E. V. 8, s. XVI, ff. 10–11.

63. *De Septem Nationibus Terrae Sanctae.* Crivellucci, *I codici
della libreria . . . nel convento di S. Maria delle grazie presso
Monteprandone*, 1889, 85–91.

64. *De Sepulchro Domini.* Zwettl, Stiftsbibl., 167, s. XIV–XV.

65. *De Situ Civitatis Antiochene.* Florence, Bibl. naz. (Magliab.),
XXIII, 122, s. XIV (II, ii, 327), f. 163 vo.

66. *De Situ Jerusalem.* Cambridge, Corp. Christ. Coll., 301,
s. XIV, f. 177.

67. *Descriptio Locorum Venerabilium Sanctae Civitatis Jerusalem,
Quorundam Oppidorum et Notabilium Locorum Terre Promissionis* and *Descriptio Regni Syriae et Egypti.* Florence, Bibl.
Naz. (Magliab.), XXIII, 122, s. XIV (II, ii, 327), ff. 163,
166 vo–71 vo.

68. *Descriptio Palaestinae.* Vienna 2162, s. XIV, f. 102.

69. *Descriptio Palestine.* B.M., Sloane 2319, s. XIV.

70. *Descriptio Parochiae Jherusalem.* Paris, B.N. fonds lat. 6186,
s. XIV, f. 133 vo.

71. *Descriptio Terrae Sanctae.* B.M. Harleian MS. 2333, s. XIV.

72. *Descriptio Terrae Sanctae.* B.M., Caligula A III in the
Chronicle of Nicol. of Gloucester, ff. 24 v.–6.

73. *Enarratio Locorum Terrae Sanctae.* 'Odo autem mi reverende
domine et eam Antoniam vocavit.' Lucca, Bibl. capituli 545,
s. XIV–XV, ff. 98 vo–107.

74. *Fragmentum Descriptionis Terrae Sanctae.* 'Alexandria distat a
Hierusalem contra Orientem per Jericho.' Vienna, 509,
s. XIV, ff. 23 vo–26 ro.

75. *Viaggio del S. Sepolchro, Il Quale Fecie Uno Fiorentino.*
Golubovich, V, 345–7.

76. *Peregrinationes Terrae Sanctae.* Golubovich, V, 347–50.

77. *Peregrinationes Tocius Terre Sancte.* Golubovich, V, 450–5.

78. *Processionale Jerosolymitanum.* Golubovich, V, 356–65.
79. *Processionale Terrae Sanctae.* Golubovich, V, 365–7.
80. *Fragmentum Descriptionis Terrae Sanctae.* Rome, Reg. Christ. 863, s. XIV, ff. 64–71.
81. *Hee Sunt Peregrinaciones et Loca Terre Sancte.* Oesterr. kath. Vierteljahrschrift 1872, 9–11.
82. *John of Ashburne. Peregrinationes Terrae Sanctae.* Oxford, Bodleian MS. 99, s. XIV, ff. 274–99.
83. *Incipit Liber Terre Sancte Jherusalem.* Evreux, 36, s. XIV, ff. 58–65.
84. *Iter de Venetiis ad Ioppen.* B.M., Sloane 683, s. XIV, f. 42.
85. *Itinerarium ad Sanctam Civitatem.* Avignon, 400, s. XIV.
86. *Itinerarium Hierosolymitanum.* s. XIV, Amiens, Escalopier, Catal. II, No. 5174.
87. *Itinerarium in Terram Sanctam.* 'Et visitavi in terra sacra leucas est locus, ubi beatus Georgius dicitur esse natus.' (Mülhausen i. Elsass, pergam., s. XIV, 103 ff.; only short report on the Holy Places and Sects of Palestine.)
88. (*Itinerarium Terrae Sanctae.*) '. . . tam cito et in tali momento oculi qui est benedictus in secula seculorum. Amen.' Conrady, *Vier rheinische Palaestina-Pilgerschriften*, Wiesbaden 1882, 20–46; cf. 1–19.
89. *Loca Peregrinationis Terre Sancte.* Oxford, Bodl. Rawlins. C. 958, s. XIV.
90. '*Nu wil ich sagen, wie iz Gestalt in Deme Tempele zu Jerusalem, da daz Heilige Grab inne ist.*' Saechs. Weltchronik, Thüring. Fortsetz. 1350 in *Mon. Germ. histor. auctores ling. vernacul.*, II, 1877, 298–9.
91. *Ordo Peregrinationum in Jherusalem.* (Monteprandone, N. 30, s. XIV–XV; cf. Crivellucci, *I codici della libreria . . . nel convento di S. Maria delle grazie presso Monteprandone*, Livorno, 1889, 62–4.
92. *Pèlerinages et Stations de la Terre Sainte.* Paris, B.N. fonds franç. 25550, s. XIV, ff. 19 vo–45 vo.
93. *Peregrinationes que sunt in Sancta Civitate.* (Padua, Univers. 1728.)
94. *Peregrinationes Sanctae.* Vienna 3763, s. XIV, ff. 249 vo–53 ro.
95. *Peregrinationes Sanctae Terrae Repromissionis.* B.M. Arundel 507, ff. 216–29, s. XIV.
96. *Peregrinationes Terrae Sanctae (Quae a Modernis Peregrinis Visitantur. 'Et est Sciendum').—Peregrinationes civitatis sancte Jherusalem et totius Terre Sancte cum peregrinationibus totius urbis Romae. Impressum alma in urbis Andegavensis*

universitate per me Iohannem de Latour, 1493.   Cf. L'Escalopier, II, No. 5175.

97. *Pilgrimage to Jerusalem.*   Oxford, Cod. Regin. 375, s. XIV,
ff. 42–83.

98. *Spese de li Pelegrini Desmonta di a zafo Prima per Dreto del
Soldan Pagane al Zafa.*   Vat. 5255, s. XIV, ff. 140 ro–
41 vo.

99–107. *Nine Anonymous Pilgrimages.*   Briefly analysed by Golubovich, V, 356, 367–9.

108. BJÄRN (*c.* 1400).—*Itinerarium per Italiam et Palaestinam, per
Hispaniam et Groenlandiam, known to Arn. Jona, Specimen
histor. de Islandia*, 154 (cf. F. Johannaeus, *Ecclesiae Islandiae
historia*, II, 395–7) and now lost.

109. GRETHENIOS (*c.* 1400).—*Vide* Cap. VIII.

110. GHILLIBERT DE LANNOY (1403–4, 1421–2, 1446–7).—*Voyages
et ambassades.*   *Vide* Cap. IX.

111. IOHANN SCHILTBERGER (*c.* 1410).—The bondage and travels of
Iohann Schiltberger, a native of Bavaria, translated by Commander J. Buchan Telfer, with notes by F. Bruun, London,
1879.   (Hakluyt Society.)

112. JOHANNES OF AZAMBUJA (1410), Cardinal-Bishop of Lisbon.
Barbosa, Bibl. Lusitanica 1747, II, 652–4.

113. NICCOLÒ DA ESTE (MARCHESE) (1413).—*Vide* Cap. IX.

114. *Viaggium Terrae Sanctae* (1415).—Upsala, Clm. 43, s. XV,
ff. 18 vo.–20 vo.

115. DIETRICH VON NIEM (*c.* 1415).—In his account of the Holy
Land, he follows the work of Fulcherius Carnotensis
(Alphons Fritz, *Zur Quellenkritik der Schriften Dietrichs von
Niem*, Paderborn, 1886, 59–60, 65).

116. EPIPHANIUS (1415–7).—*Itinéraire à Jérusalem du moine
Epiphane* (*c.* 1416).   Fr. trans. Mme B. Khitrovo, Geneva,
1888, 193–6 (Soc. de l'Orient latin, Série géogr. V, Itineraires
Russes).

117. IACOPO DA SANSEVERINO (1416).—*Viaggio fatto da Iacopo da
Sanseverino con altri gentiluomini e da esso descritto*, Lucca,
1868.

118. HANS PORNER (1418).—*Itinerarius.*   L. Hänselmann, in
Zeitschr. d. hist. Vereins für Niedersachsen, 1875, 113–56.

119. NOMPAR DE CAUMONT (1418).—*Voyage d'oultremer en Iherusalem* par le Seigneur de Caumont, ed. le marquis de La
Grange, Paris, 1858.

120. ZOSIMUS (1419–22).—*Vie et pèlerinage.* Fr. trans. Mme B. Khitrowo, Geneva, 1888, 197–221 (Société de l'Orient latin, Série géogr. V, Itinér. Russes).

121. *Diario di Felice Brancacci Ambasciatore con Carlo Federighi al Cairo* (1422).—Ed. Dante Catellacci, in *Archivio storico ital.,* 1881, VIII, 158–88.

122. JOHANNES POLONER (1422).—*Peregrinatio ad Terram Sanctam.* T. Tobler, *Descriptiones Terrae Sanctae,* 1874, 225–78.

123. COPPART DE VELAINE (1423).—*Voiages.* Bibl. Ashburnham, Barrois, 472, s. XV, ff. 17–27; now in Paris.

124. JOHANNES BASSENHAMMER (1426).—See Herschel im *Anz. für d. Kunde d. Deutsch.,* Vorzeit, 1863, 319–22.

125. *A Poem in Old English Verse (c.* 1426).—Containing directions for a pilgrimage to Jerusalem. B.M., Cotton. Vitellius 113, s. XV.

126. MAGISTER JOHANNES DE FRANKFORDIA (1427).—*Itinerarium ab Heydelberg Jerusalem. Vide* Röhricht, Bibl., 107.

127. GASPARE DI BARTOLOMEO DI SIENA (1431).—*Itinerario al S. Sepolcro.* Florence, Bibl. naz. (Magliab.) XIII, 30. Cf. Mariti, *Viaggi,* IV, 80.

128. MARIANO DA SIENA (1431).—*Del viaggio in Terra Santa.* Florence, 1822. Parma, 1865.

129. BERTRANDON DE LA BROCQUIÈRE (1432–3).—*Vide* Cap. IX.

130. GRAF PHILIPP VON KATZENELLENBOGEN (1433).—Röhricht u. Meisner, *Die Pilgerfahrt des letzten Grafen Ph. v. K.* in: *Zeitschrift für deutsches Alterthum,* 1882, New Series XIV, 348–71.

131. THOMAS, *Ordin. Minorum* (1434).—*Instructorium peregrinorum.* (Paris, B.N. fonds lat. 8751 E, s. XV, ff 30–1 v.; cf. ibid. 2049, s. XV, ff. 226 r.–32 r.)

132. *Description of a Pilgrimage from Venice to Beirut* (1434).—E. Henrici in: *Zeitschr. für deutsch. Alterth.,* 1881, 59–70.

133. JOHANN AND ALBRECHT, MARKGRAFEN VON BRANDENBURG (1435).—F. Geisheim, *Die Hohenzollern am heiligen Grabe zu Jerusalem, insbesondere die Pilgerfahrt d. Markgrafen Iohann u. Albrecht v. Brandenburg,* Berlin, 1858, 205–53.

134. PERO TAFUR (1435–9).—*Vide* Cap. IX.

135. GEORG PFINZING (1436 and 1440).—Kamann. *Die Pilger-fahrten Nürnberger Bürger nach Jerusalem (Mitth. d. Vereins für Gesch. d. Stadt Nürnberg,* Heft II, 1880).

136. HERZOG FRIEDRICH VON OESTERREICH (1436).—*Meerfahrt.* Ed. Röhricht, in *d. Zeitschr. für german. Philologie,* 1890, 26–41.

137. GIACOMO DALFINI (1437).—Correspondence from the Holy Land, in the Archives of Florence.

138. HANS VON DER GRUB (1440).—Röhricht, *Deutsche Pilgerreisen* (Gotha, 1889), 144.

139. HANS ROT (1440).—*Hist. Gesellsch. zu Basel*, 1881, Neue Folge, 326–91.

140. GIRNAND VON SCHWALBACH (1440).—*Walfart.* Röhricht and Meisner, *Deutsche Pilgerreisen*, 97–9.

141. *Vya Pergendi de Venetiis versus Jherusalem et Distancia Locorum* (c. 1440).—The Hague, L. 27, s. XV, ff. 80 vo–82 ro.

142. *Hie ist zu Wissen der Ablass vnd Gnad vnd die Walfart des Helgen Landes vber Mere* (1441).—Röhricht and Meisner, op. cit., 100–2.

143. ANDREA VETTORI (1443).—Florence, Bibl. naz. (Magl.) XIII, 79.

144. GANDOLFO (1444).—*Relatio de statu rerum Orientalium*, in Wadding, *Annal. Minor.*, *ann.* 1444.

145. *Reise Eines Anonymus von Venedig Nach Jerusalem* (1444).— Birlinger, in *Herrigs Archiv für neuere Sprachen*, XL, 1867, 301–22.

146. *Arenga super Passagio Generali* (c. 1445).—Brussels 226, s. XV.

147. JÖRG MÜLICH VON AUGSBURG (1449).—*Walfart.* Röhricht, *Deutsche Pilgerreisen*, 135.

148. STEFFAN VON GUMPENBERG (1449–50).—Goldmayer, in *Zeitschr. für Bayern u. d. angränzenden Länder*, Munich, 1817, II, Heft I, 237 et seq.

149. WILHELM WALTER DE ZIERIXSEE (1449–50).—*Descriptio de tota terra promissionis cum Jherusalem.* Wolfenbüttel, Cod. Aug. 18, 2 qu., ff. I ro–43 ro.

150. HENRICUS DE LUBECK ET TROSSELMANN (1450).—*Iter a Lubeck Jerusalem.* Copenhagen, Alter fond 2077, s. XV, ff. 10 et seq.

151. *Eene Pelgrimsreis naar het Heilig Land* (1450).—Ed. J. Habets, in *Publications de la Société hist. de Limbourg*, IX, 1872, 204–16 (cf. XII, 1875, 85–95).

152. JACOBUS GUTTERBUCK (c. 1450).—*Tractatus de duabus civitatibus Iherusalem et Babilonia et civibus earundem.* Wolfenbüttel, Cod. Helmstad. 309, ff. 99–110.

153. *Breviary of a Pilgrim* (c. 1450).—W. Fröhner, in *d. Zeitschr. für deutsches Alterthum*, 1859, XI, 34.

154. *Van den Gestant ende Gelegentheit des heiligen landes*, (c. 1450).— Röhricht, op. cit., 136.

155. CLAUDE DE MIRABEL (1452).—*Voiages de Jerusalem et de Saincte Katérine.* St. Génois, *Voyageurs Belges*, I, 34–6.

156. GUILLAUME DE CHÂLONS (1453), *comte de Tonnerre, sire d'Arguel, de Bouclas et de Montfaucon, plus tard prince d'Orange.* E. Travers, in *Revue nobiliaire* (1869), V, 257–9.

157. PETER ROT (1453).—Röhricht, op. cit., 139–41.
158. *Von der Schickung u. Gestalt* (1454) *des heil. grabes zu Jerusalem und des heilighen landes.* Munich, Cgm. 1276, s. XV, 25 ff.
159. GEORG VON EHINGEN (*c.* 1455).—F. Pfeiffer, in *Bibl. d. Stuttg. litt. Verein,* I, 1842.
160. NICOLAS SCHOUTET (1455–91).—St. Genois, *Voyageurs Belges,* I, 193–7.
161. LUDOVICUS DE ANGULO (1456).—*Palaestinae descriptio tripartita.* Tobler, Dritte Wanderung, 937.
162. JEHAN FRANCELOT (*c.* 1456).—*Voyaige d'Oultremer. Bibl. protypograph. ou librairie des fils du roi Jean,* Paris, 1830, 307–8, No. 2179.
163. GABRIELE CAPODILISTA (1458).—*Itinerario della Terre Santa et del Monte Sinai.* Perugia (*c.* 1472).
164. ANTON PELCHINGER (1458).—*Von der schickung vnd gestalt des heiligen grabs vnsers herren Jhesu Christ zu Jerusalem.* Vienna, 3012.
165. ROBERTO DE SAN SEVERINO (1458).—G. Maruffi, *Viaggio in Terra Santa di Roberto da Sanseverino,* Bologna, 1888 (Scelta di curiosità lett. ined. o rari dai sec. XIII–XVII).
166. WILLIAM WEY (1458 and 1462).—*Vide* Cap. IX.
167. *Incipit Terre Sancte Descripcio et Locorum* (1459).—Vienna 4739, s. XV, ff. 104–23.
168. BERNHARD VON EPTINGEN (1460).—*Beiträge für vaterland. Geschichte,* Basel, 1885, New Series II, Heft 1, 1–75.
169. HANS COPLÄR (1461).—*Reise in das heil. Land.* Vienna, Cgm. 3080 (563), s. XV.
170. GRAF HEINRICH D. AELTERE VON STOLBERG (1461).—*Meerfahrt nach Jerusalem u. in d. gelobte Land.* Ed. E. Jacobs, in *Zeitschr. d. Harz-Vereins,* I, 1868, 173–92; cf. also XII, 1881, 484–8.
171. LANDGRAF WILHELM DER TAPFERE VON THÜRINGEN (1461).— J. G. Kohl, *Die Pilgerfahrt d. Landgrafen Wilhelm d. Tapferen v. Thüringen zum heil. Lande,* Bremen, 1868, 67–157.
172. FRATER NICOLAUS (1461).—*Peregrinatio Terrae Sanctae.* Milan, Ambros. F. 45, s. XV; and St. Petersburg, Oeffentl. Bibl. No. 2, s. XV.
173. GABRIELE MEZZAVACCA DI BOLOGNA (*c.* 1461).—*Descrizione di Terra Santa.* Bonifacius Stephanus, 286.
174. BENEDETTO DEI (1462–77).—Pagnini, *Della decima,* II, 135–280.
175. SEBALD RIETER SENIOR (1464).—Röhricht and Meisner, *Reisebuch d. Familie Rieter,* Tübingen, 1884 (Stuttgarter Literar. Verein CLXVIII), 14–36.
176. GABRIEL MUFFEL? (1465).—'Hie vahet sich an die gotliche fart

des heiligen grabs vnsers herrn Jesu Christi hin vnd herwider zu faren.' B.M., Egerton Add. 1900 s. XV.

177. BASILIUS (1465–6).—*Pèlerinage du marchand Basile.* Fr. trans. Mme B. Khitrovo, Geneva, 1888, 241–56. (Société de l'Orient latin, Série géogr. V, Itinéraires russes.)

178. ZWIENEK LEW VON ROZMITAL (1465–7).—J. A. Schmeller, *Des böhm. Herrn Leos v. Rozmital Ritter- Hof- und Pilger-Reise durch die Abendlande,* 1465–7, Stuttgart Liter. *Verein,* VII, 1844.

179. *Dies ist der Wege zu schiffen vber mere von Venedige kenn Jherusalem* (before 1466).—Breslau, *Universitätsbibl.,* IV, ff. 105 (*de anno* 1466), 145.

180. HANS VON REDWITZ (1467).—*Wallfahrt.* In *Archiv für d. Gesch. u. Alterthumskunde von Oberfranken,* I, 2, 6–17.

181. NICOLAUS AND WILHELM VON DIESBACH (1467–8).—*Pilgerfahrt.* Röhricht, op. cit., 130.

182. PIER ANTONIO BUONDELMONTE (1468 and 1474).—*Viaggio al santissimo sepolcro.* Florence, Bibl. naz. (Magliab.) XIII, 76 s. XV–XVI, ff. 1–16 vo.

183. MYNSINGER (1468).—*Peregrinatio Eberhardi Barbati in Terram Sanctam.* Röhricht, op. cit., 150–3.

184. IOHANNES KETTNER VON GEISENFELD (1469).—W. A. Neumann, *Beiträge zur Bibliogr. der Palastinliteratur im Anschluss an eine Besprechung,* in *Zeitschr. des Deutschen Palaestina-Vereins,* IV (Leipzig, 1881), 235.

185. ANSELME D'ADHORNE (1470).—Anselme Adorne, Sire du Corthuy, pèlerin de Terre Sainte. Récit historique by M. E. de la Coste, Brussels, Ghent and Leipzig, 1855.

186. FILIPPO BONACCORSI DI S. GEMINIANO (1470).—Zeno, *Dissertazioni* (Venice, 1752–3), II, 198.

187. ULRICH BRUNNER (1470).—*Annales des voyages,* 1854, I, 29–32.

188. GRYPHON FLAMENGUS (*c.* 1470).—*Itinerarium seu topographia Terrae Sanctae.* Wadding, *Annal. Minor.,* ann. 1475, No. 18.

189. WERNER ROTH (Zurich) (*c.* 1470).—*Meerbuch.* Röhricht, op. cit., 155.

190. WILHELM TZWERS (T'SWEERTS) (*c.* 1470).—*Descriptio Terrae Sanctae.* Wolfenbüttel, Cod. Weiss. 52, s. XV, fol. 1–93.

191. FRANCESCO PUICHARD (1472).—*Viaggio al S. Sepolcro ed al S. Giacopo di Galizia.* B.N., fonds ital. 900 s. XV.

192. ULRICH LEMAN (1472–80). *Walfart nach Jerusalem.* Johanniterblatt, 1880, No. 1; also Röhricht, op. cit., 316.

193. SEBASTIEN MAMEROT (1472–88).—*Comte de Marsy, Les pèlerins Picards à Jérusalem,* Amiens, 1881, 12–13.

194. HANS VON WALLENRADE (WALLENROD) (before 1473).—Röhricht, op. cit., 155.

195. ALESSANDRO DI FILIPPO RINUCCINI DA FIRENZE (1474).—*Viaggio al Santo Sepolcro.* Florence, Bibl. naz. XIII, 11, 76, s. XV–XVI, ff. 69–108; and Milan, Bibl. Trivulz. 82, s. XV.

196. HIPPOLYTA (1474).—*Peregrinatio Terrae Sanctae per Jacobum servitorem Hippolyte ducissae Calabriae.* R. Röhricht, *Die Wallfahrt der Herzogin Maria Hippolyta v. Calabrien nach dem heiligen Lande,* in Zeitschr. des Deutschen Palaestina-Vereins, XIV (Leipzig, 1891), 12–16.

197. PETRUS DE DENGRA (?), ALIAS DE LEYSTERGATE (1475).—*Peregrinatio Terrae Sanctae.* Amiens, L'Escalopier 5182, s. XV, ff. 172–9.

198. JOHANN FRIDACH VON DUSSELDORF (before 1475 or 1494). Röhricht, *Deutsche Pilgerreisen,* 198.

199. JOHANNES AB INDAGINE (1475–6).—Röhricht, op. cit., 155–6.

200. ALESSANDRO ARIOSTO (1475–8).—*Viaggio nella Siria, nella Palestina e nell' Egitto,* ed. G. Ferraro, Ferrara, 1878.

201. MARTIN KÖTZEL (1476).—Rhenanus, *Reise nach d. gelobten Land im Jahre* 1476, in *Altes u. Neues für Geschichte u. Dichtkunst von Bothe u. Vogler,* 1832, I, 28–103.

202. RUDOLPHUS DE LANGHEN (1476).—*Urbis Hyerosolimae templique in ea origo variaeque fortunae prophanationes et excidia libri II.* Daventriae, J. de Breda (1477), Coloniae 1517.

203. HERZOG ALBRECHT VON SACHSEN (1476).—*Peregrinatio seu Passagium ad Terram Sanctam.* Röhricht, op. cit., 156–71.

204. GIAN GIACOMO TRIVULZIO in *Terra Santa* (1476).—E. Motta, in *Archivio storico Lombardo,* 1886, III, 866–78.

205. *Buch umb ten weg zu ten Heiligen Grab* (1477).—Paris, B.N., Réserve 1271.

206. *Prologus Arminensis (c.* 1478).—Cf. P. J. Bruns, *Die älteste gedruckte bisher unbekannte Beschreibung von Palästina,* in *Götting. Biblioth. d. neuesten theol. Literatur,* Göttingen, 1797, III, 2tes Stück, 159–204.

207. *Ein Hübscher Tractat* (1479)—*wie durch Hertzog Gotfried von Pullen und ander mer christenlicher Fürsten und herren das gelobte landt und das heylig grab gewunnen ist worden als man zahlt* 1099 *iar auch von dem weg darauff dahin geet, Nota als man schreibt nach Christi unseres herren geburt* 1479 *jare also schreiben die heiden nach Mahomets tod* 834 *jar, getruckt zu Augspurg durch Erhart Oeglin.*

208. JACOB KREYCK AND DERYCK VOGEL (1479).—*Reize van Zutphen toe Jerusalem na den heiligen grave Christi anno* 1479 (Middlehill; cf. Haenel, Catalogue 873); now in Brussels.

209. SEBALD RIETER JUN. (1479).—Röhricht and Meisner, *Reisebuch der Familie Rieter*, Tübingen, 1884 (Stuttgarter Liter. Verein CLXVIII), 36–149.

210. JOHANNES TUCHER (1479).—H. Kuntzel, *Drei Bücher deutscher Prosa* (Frankfort, 1838), 104–96.

211. WENGK VON NÜRNBERG (1479).—Cf. von Hormayr, *Taschenbuch* (1840), 284.

212. SANTO BRASCA (1480).—*Viaggio del sepulchro con le sue antichita et oratione de loco in loco*, Milan, 1519.

213. *Voyage de la Saincte Cyté de Hierusalem* (1480).—Ch. Schéfer, in *Recueil de voyages et de documents pour servir à l'histoire de la géographie depuis le XIII jusqu'à la fin du XVI siècle*, II (Paris, 1882).

214. FELIX FABER (1480 and 1483).—*Vide* Cap. IX.

215. PAULUS WALTER (1481–3).—*Itinerarium*. M. Sollwerk, in *Stuttgarter Literar. Verein*.

216. NIKLAS BAKALAR (1482).—Description of the Holy Places (in Czech.). Cf. Dobrowsky, *Gesch. d. böhmisch. Sprache*, 277.

217. BERNHARD VON BREIDENBACH (1483).—*Peregrinationes*. Several editions and translations into French, Spanish, German, Flemish and English. *Vide* Allgemeine Deutsche Bibliographie and other bibliographies.

218. GEORG VON GUMPPENBERG (1483).—*Reise zum heil. Grabe*. Röhricht, op. cit., 180–1.

219. PAOLO TREVISANO (1483).—Morelli, *Dissertaz. intorno ad alcuni viaggiatori Veneziani* 1803, 8.

220. JAN AERTS (1484).—E. Neefs: *Un voyage au XVe siècle en Terre Sainte Egypte &c.*, in *Revue catholique* (Louvain, 1873), IX, 268–91, 321–36, 425–51, 553–81.

221. GRAF LUDWIG VON HANAU-LICHTENBERG (1484).—Märcker, in *Anz. für d. Kunde d. Vorzeit*, 1862, 79–82.

222. GRAF PHILIPP JUN. VON HANAU-MÜNZENBERG (1484).—Röhricht, op. cit., 181.

223. CLAES VAN DUESEN (1484–96).—Conrady, *Vier rheinische Pal.-Pilgerschriften*, 189–222.

224. FRANCESCO DA SURIANO (1485).—*Itinerario de Hierusalem*, Venice, 1524.

225. IOOS VAN GHISTELE (1485).—In *Revue générale*, Brussels, 1883, XXXVII, 723–64; XXXVIII, 46–71, 193–210.

226. GEORGES LENGHERRAND (1485–6). *Voyage de Georges Lengherrand, mayeur de Mons en Haynaut, à Venise, Rome, Jérusalem, Mont Sinai et le Kayre* ed. par le marquis de Godefroy Ménilglaise (Mons, 1861), Société d. bibliophiles Belges séant à Mons, No. XIX.

227. ALEXIS, PRIOR OF BURY (1486).—*Dialogue du Crucifix et du Pèlerin*; Gouget, Bibl. Francisc. X, 119.

228. GIROLAMO DE CASTELLIONE (1486).—*Trattato de le parte ultra mare zioe Terra santa*, Milan, 1491.

229. CONRAD GRÜNEMBERG (1486).—Röhricht, op. cit., 182–4.

230. *Voyage à la Terre Sainte, au mont Sinai et au couvent de Sainte Cathérine*, (1486).—E. Morin, *Notice sur un manuscrit de la bibl. de Rennes*, in *Revue des sociétés savantes des départements*, 1860, II Série, V, 235–46.

231. JEAN DE CUCHERMOIS (1487).—*Voyage de . . . en Hierusalem* 1490.

232. JEHAN DE TOURNAY (1487).—J. J. Voisin, *Principaux passages d'un voyage en Terre Sainte fait par Jehan de Tournay en* 1487 (Tournay, 1863).

233. NICOLAS DE PONTEAU (1487).—Kobler, *Katholisches Leben im Mittelalter*, 1887, I, 668–75.

234. THOMAS BASIN (1488).—*Breviloquium peregrinationum ad Terram Promissionis.* Paris, B.N., fonds lat. 5970 A, s. XV, ff. 59–63.

235. THOMAS RAYMUNDUS (*c.* 1488).—*Peregrinatio ad loca Sancta.* Fabricius, *Bibl. medii aevi* 1746, VI, 729.

236. *Viaggio de Firenze a Jerusalem* (1489–90).—G. Mariti, *Illustrazioni di un anonimo viaggiatore del secolo XV* (Livorno, 1785).

237. SEBASTIAN BRANDT (1490).—*De origine et conuersatione bonorum Regum et laude Ciuitatis Hierosolymae cum exhortatione ejusdem recuperande.* (Hain, No. 3735.) German trans.—Von dem Anfang und Wesen der heiligen statt Jerusalem aus dem Lat. ins Deutsche übersetzt von Conrad Frey, 17 Brachmonat (i.e. June) 1518 in Strassburg, J. Knoblock.

238. SIEUR DE LABASTIE (1490).—*Pèlerinage.* Lyons, Bibl. du collège 717 (590), s. XV.

239. PHILIPPE DE VOISINS (1490).—*Voyage à Jérusalem. Archives historique de la Gascogne*, 1883, 13–45.

240. NICOLAUS DE FARNAD (*c.* 1490).—*Compendium locarum Terre Sancte.* Vienna s. anno.

241. AMBROSIUS VON GLAUBURG (*c.* 1490).—Röhricht, op. cit., 185.

242. MARTIN KABATNIK (1491).—Hanusch, *Quellenkunde u. Bibliographie der böhmisch-slovenischen Literaturgesch.* (Prague, 1868), 58.

243. STEPHAN KAPFMANN (1491).—*Reise in's Gelobte Land.* Röhricht, op. cit., 186.

244. DIETRICH VON SCHACHTEN (1491).—Röhricht and Meisner, op. cit., 165–245.

245. *Escript de un Voiage Faict en Jerusalem l'an* 1491 *retournant l'an*
(1491).—Valenciennes, B.B. 3, 1, ff. 5–8.

246. BERNARDINO DI NOLI (1492).—*Ierosolimitana peregrinatione.*
Lucca, Bibl. publ. 1301, s. XV.

247. PETER FASSBENDER VON MOLSBERG (1492).—*Bedvartt nahe dem
heiligen Grabe zu Jerusalem.* Röhricht and Meisner, op. cit.,
246–77.

248. HERZOG CHRISTOPH VON BAYERN (1493).—Röhricht and Meisner, op. cit., 297–307.

249. JOHANN V. LOBKOWITZ U. HASSENSTEIN (1493).—*Nouv. Annales
des voyages,* 1854, I, 33.

250. CHURFÜRST FRIEDRICH DER WEISE VON SACHSEN (1493).—*Pilgerfahrt nach d. heil. Lande.* Röhricht, op. cit., 187–93.

251. GRAF BOTHO VON STOLBERG (1493).—Ed. Jacobs: *Ueber die
Meerfahrt Graf Bothos des Glückseligen zu Stolberg,* in *Zeit-
shrift des Harzvereins,* 1868, I, 192–220.

252. HEINRICH VON ZEDLITZ (1493).—*Pilgerfahrt nach d. heil Lande.*
Röhricht, op. cit., 196–8.

253. IAN VAN BERCHEM (1449).—St. Genois, *Iean van Berchem
voyageur |brabançon du XV. siècle,* in *Messager des sciences
historiques de Belgique,* 1855, 460–8.

254. PIETRO CASOLA (1494).—*Viaggio di Pietro Casola a Gerusalemme*
(Milan, 1855).

255. PFALZGRAF ALEXANDER BEI RHEIN (1495).—*Beschreibung der
Meerfahrt zum heiligen Grab im Reyssbuch,* 1584, 30–47 and
1609, I, 55–86.

256. WOLFF VON ZÜLNHART (1495).—Röhricht and Meisner, op. cit.,
308–14, 512.

257. PETER RINDFLEISCH (1496).—*Walffartt zum heiligen Grab.*
Röhricht and Meisner, op. cit., 319–44.

258. ARNOLD VON HARFF (1496–9).—*Pilgerfahrt.* Ed. E. von
Grote (Cologne, 1860).

259. HIERONIMO CASIO DI MEDICI (1497).—Harrisse, *Excerpta Colombiniana,* 196, No. 278.

260. BONSIGNORE DI FRANCESCO (1497).—*Viaggio di Gerusalemme per
via di Constantinopoli.* Florence, Bibl. naz.(Magliab.)XIII,93.

261. HERZOG BOGISLAUS X. VON POMMERN (1497).—*Des Herzogs B.
v. Pommern Pilgerreise nach d. gelobten Lande,* Berlin, 1859.

262. HANS SCHÜRPFF (1497).—*Pilgerfahrt nach Jerusalem.* Ed.
J. V. Osterstag, in *Geschichtsfreund* (Einsiedeln, 1852), 182–
249.

263. *Fragment of a Pilgrimage* (1497).—To be found at the end of
an Arras MS. 266 (cf. Catalogue général d. manuscrits des
bibliothèques des départements, IV, 100).

264. STEPHAN BAUMGARTNER (1498).—Röhricht, op. cit., 208–12.
265. JEHAN DE ZILLEBEKE (1499).—*Voyage à Notre Dame de Lorette et à Jérusalem.* St. Genois, *Voyageurs Belges*, I, 38–40.
266. ZANOBI DELLA VACCHIA (1499).—*Viaggio ai Luoghi Santi.* Florence, Bibl. Riccard. 1923, s. XV.

UNDATED FIFTEENTH-CENTURY TRACTS

267. *Ablass in Jerusalem* (Saec. XV.).—Wolfenbüttel, Cod. Helmst. 1130, s. XV, ff. 41–5.
268. *Travel Guide to Jerusalem* (in Middle High German). W. A. Neumann, *Beiträge zur Bibliographie der Palästinaliteratur im Anschluss an eine Besprechung*, in *Zeitschr. des Deutschen Palaestina-Vereins*, IV (1881), 234–5.
269. *Benedictiones Peregrinorum.* Munich, Clm. 6007, s. XV, f. 185.
270. *Description of the Holy Land* (in Middle High German). Wolfenbüttel, Cod. Helmst. 1293, s. XV, ff. 72–89.
271. *Another Description.* S. Florian, XI, 575.
272. AMADEUS BOUERIUS. *Libellus peregrinationis Terrae Sanctae.* Paris, B.N., fonds lat. 4826, s. XV.
273. *Brevis Descriptio Terrae Sanctae.* Wolfenbüttel, Cod. Helmst. 354, s. XV, ff. 292 vo–4 ro.
274. *Fragment of a XV Cent. Pilgrimage.* (Korth, in *Anzeig. des germ. Mus.*, 1883, 316–8.)
275. BENEDETTO DANDOLO '*patrizio Veneto che nella prima metà del secolo XV percorse la Siria ed altri paesi raccogliendo con zelo indefesso antiche medaglie*' (Amat, I, 220).
276. '*Daz ist dye Andächtige Processio dye die romischen pilgrein tuen in Jerusalem.*' Munich, Clm. a. 1805, s. XV, f. 42; 14574, s. XV, ff. 161–5; 14909, s. XV, f. 67 (lat.).
277. *De Civitate Hierusalem Descriptionis Libellus.* Bodl. Canon, 168, s. XV.
278. *De Civitatibus Jerusalem et Babylon.* Wolfenbüttel, Cod. Helmst. 237, s. XV, ff. 262–72.
279. *De Duabus Civitatibus Scil. Babilon et Jerusalem.* Mayence, Stadtbibl. Cod. Carthus. 454, § 2, Sammelband s. XV.
280. *De Introitu Peregrinorum.* Munich, Clm. 569, s. XV, ff. 182–4.
281. *De Passagio Terrae Sanctae.* Trier, Stadtbibliothek 1217 (1324), § 12, s. XV.
282. *De Patriarchatu et Metropolitanis et Eorum Suffraganeis Terre Sancte Ierusalem.* Munich, Clm. 721, s. XV, ff. 71–3.
283. *De Peregrinatione Quomodo Debet Fieri Cum Exemplo.* Munich Clm. 17628, s. XV, f. 320.

284. *De Peregrino.* Cologne, Bibl. der drei Gymnasien 223, s. XV.
285. *De Regnis Ultramarinis.* Wolfenbüttel, Cod. Aug. 18, 2 qu. s. XV, f. 72.
286. *De Situ Terrae Sanctae.* Wolfenbüttel, Cod. Aug. 18, 2 qu. s. XV, f. 72.
287. *De Terra Sancta.* Munich, Clm. 18768, s. XV, ff. 245–6.
288. *De Terra Sancta.* Wolfenbüttel, Cod. Helmst. 442, s. XV, f. 89.
289. *Déclaration de tous les lieux ou il y a pardons en la Terre Saincte.* Paris, B.N., fonds franç. 6110, s. XV.
290. *Descriptio Jerosolimitana.* Wolfenbüttel, Cod. Helmst. 552, s. XV, ff. 261–2.
291. *Descriptio Locorum Terrae Sanctae et Iter et Via ad S. Catharinam.* Mayence, Stadtbibl., No. 239.
292. *Descriptio Palestinae Incerti Auctoris.* Pertz, *Archiv*, XI, 803.
293. *Descriptio Quorundam Locorum Sacrorum.* Munich, Clm. 14909, s. XV, ff. 73–80.
294. *Descriptio Terre Promissionis.* Munich, Clm. 215, s. XV, f. 45.
295. *Descriptio Terrae Sanctae.* Mayence, Stadtbibl. Cod. Carthus. 272, s. XV.
296. *Descriptio Terrae Sanctae.* Munich, Clm. 721, s. XV, ff. 71 vo–8 vo.
297. *Descriptio Terrae Sanctae.* Frankfurt a. M., Stadtbibl. Praedicat. 1277 Miscell., s. XV, ff. 1–51 ro.
298. *Die Heiligen Orte in u. um Jerusalem.* Munich, Cgm. 3890, s. XV, ff. 211–16.
299. *Die Heil. Plätze.* Jacobs and Ukert, *Beitr. zur älteren Litteratur*, Leipzig, I, 1835, 445.
300. *Die Heil. Stätten in Jerusalem u. ihre Umgebungen.* Munich, Cgm. 736, s. XV, ff. 87–91.
301. *Die Heiligen Stätten u. die Ablässe zu Jerusalem.* Munich, Cgm. 1113, s. XV, ff. 93–5.
302. *Die Reigerung (sic) vff dem wege gen Jherusalem zu.* Munich, Clm. 441, f. 188, s. XV.
303. *Distributio Locorum circa urbem Hierosolyma.* Leiden, Cod. Voss. graec. 13, s. XV, ff. 69–101.
304. *Dit syn die Heilige Stede.* Leiden, Bibl. Acquoy.
305. *'Dit synt die Heilige Stede des Heiligen Lants.'* Conrady, *Vier rheinische Palästina-Pilgerschriften*, 72–181.
306. LOUIS DE LA FONTAINE, SEIGNEUR DE SALMONSART. Lengherand ed. Menilglaise, XIII.
307. *Fragmentum Descriptionis Hierusalem.* Vienna, 509, s. XV, f. 23.

308. *Geistliche Pilgerfahrt.* Von. Liebenau, in *Kathol. Schweizer Blätter*, 1888, IV, 686.

309. *Goldwag der Ewigen Stadt Jerusalem.* Munich, Cgm. a. 501, ff. 360–2, s. XV; 831, ff. 42–7, s. XV.

310. HENRICUS DE HISPANIA. *De locis terre sancte et vestigiis ejus.* Cheltenham, 6650, s. XV.

311. *Hie Sind Vermerkt die Heiligen Stett.* Munich, Clm. 14919, s. XV, f. 148.

312. *Historia de Duobus Peregrinis Quorum unus Alterum Occidit.* Munich, Clm. 18361, s. XV, ff. 54–6.

313. '*Hy Hebt sich an daz Heilig Land.*' Wernigerode, Zb, 10.

314. '*In Ecclesia S. Sepulcri de Jerusalem ista sunt loca Peregrinationis.*' Padua, Univ. 2029, s. XV.

315. *Instructio ad Peregrinationem in Terram Sanctam.* Vienna, 2982, s. XV, ff. 25 ro–46 vo.

316. '*Item das sind die Hailigen Stet.*' Berlin, Cgm. 989, s. XV, ff. 57–75.

317. *Itinerario del Terra Sancta.* Florence, Bibl. naz. (Magl.), XXXVIII, 47 s. XV.

318. *Itinerarium Jerosolimitanum cum Missa in Veneracione S. Sepulcri.* Cambridge, J. J. Smith, Catalogue 162, s. XV, ff. 111–41.

319. *Itinerarium Terrae Sanctae.* Pertz, *Archiv*, VIII, 608.

320. *Itinerary from Venice to Joppa.* Thomas Wright and O. Halliwell, *Reliquiae antiquae*, 1841, I, 237.

321. *Itinerary with Distances from Nuremberg to London and Edinburgh, thence through France, Spain and Italy and by Venice to Ierusalem and Mount Sinai and thence through Constantinople to Denmark, Sweden and Norway.* B.M., Egerton Add. 1901, s. XV, f. 31.

322. *Itinerary with Distances from Prague through Germany and Flanders to London and Edinburgh, thence through France, Spain and Italy and by Venice to Ierusalem and Mount Sinai and thence through Constantinople to Denmark, Sweden and Norway.* B.M., Egerton Add. 1901, s. XV, f. 151–4.

323. *Luoghi di Terra Santa.* Paris, B.N., nouv. acquis. lat. 1154, s. XV, ff. 180–3.

324. *Mauritius Parisiensis. Declaratio mappae Terrae Sanctae.* Munich, Clm. 18736, s. XV, ff. 201–12.

325. MELLIADUSE ESTENSE. *Viaggio in Terra Santa.* Modena, Archives s. XV, cart. 66.

326. *Memoriale pro Peregrinis.* Melk, Stiftsbibl. H. 42, s. XV, ff. 266–70.

327. *Of Mountains in Greece and Places in the Holy Land.* Bodl. Digby, 88, s. XV, ff. 28–9.

328. *Narrative of Pilgrimage to Jerusalem.* Bodl. Colleg. Reg. 357, s. XV.

329. *Nota ditz Regimen auf Dieser Walfart.* B.M., Egerton Add. 1900, s. XV, f. 154.

330. *Peregrinatio ad Terram Sanctam.* Brussels 2357, s. XV.

331. *Peregrinatio in Terram Sanctam.* Trier, Stadtbibl. 790 (797), s. XV.

332. *Prayers for Indulgences at the Holy Places at Jerusalem arranged according to the days of the week written by 'een weerdich priester ghenaemt heer Bethleem.'* B.M., Addit. 24937 s. XV.

333. *Qualiter Peregrini Debent se Habere in Itineratione.* Wolfenbüttel, Cod. Helmst. 653, s. XV, ff. 7–8.

334. *Relation d'un Gentilhomme arrivé de Jérusalem.* Turin, s. XV.

335. HORATIO MARCO TIGRINO. *Breve descrittione e dichiaratione delli disegni del Tempio, della città di Jerusalem e della Terra Santa.* B.M., Addit. 10226 s. XV; Berlin, Cod. ital. 16, s. XVI, ff. 230–41; Paris, B.N., copy of B.M. MS.

336. *Tractatus de Peregrinatione ad Loca Sancta.* B.M., Harleian. 635, s. XV, f. 277.

337. *Tractatus de Peregrinationibus.* Admont, Stiftsbibl. 155, s. XV.

338. *Tractatus de Regionibus.* Bodl. Canon. miscell. 355, s. XV, 24 vo–8 ro.

339. *Tractatus sive Descriptio Terrae Sanctae.* Wolfenbüttel, Cod. Helmst. 18, 2 qu. s. XV, f. 67–9.

340. *Vejleder for Pilgrimme.* Copenhagen, Arna Magn. 792, s. XV.

341. *Veteris Cujusdam Scriptoris Itinerarium in Terram Sanctam,* s. XV scriptum. Hamburg, Stadtbibl. Cod. geogr. 72, s. XV.

342. *Via ad Terram Sanctam* (S. XV). St. Genois, *Voyageurs Belges,* II, 205.

343. *Via ad Terram Sanctam.* Atiya, *Nicopolis,* 23–4; also *vide supra,* Cap. VIII.

344. *Viaggi e Cosmographie di duo peregrini.* Harrisse, *Excerpta Colombiniana* (Paris, 1887), 219, No. 355.

345. *Viaggio in Terra Santa.* Florence, Bibl. Riccard. 2760, s. XV.

346. *Viaggio in Terra Santa.* Florence, Naz. 38, 8, 47.

347. *Von den Heiligen Stätten in Palästina.* Munich, Cgm. 2886, s. XV.

348. *Von der Kinncklichen Heilgen stat zu Jerusalem.* B.M., Add. 22622, s. XV, ff. 79–80.

349. *Le Voyage de Turquie et de la Saincte Terre. Bibl. protypo-*

graphique ou librairie des fils du roi Jean (Paris, 1830), 165, No. 1078.

350. *Wallung Oder Kirchfart zu den heiligen stätten.* Munich, Cgm. 735, s. XV, ff. 16–30.

351. *Descriptio Terrae Sanctae.* Utrecht, Univers. 285, s. XV.

APPENDIX III

ARAGON AND EGYPT

THE relations between Aragon and Egypt during the first three decades of the fourteenth century are little known, in spite of their importance for the wider history of the relations between the East and the West, including both matters of commerce and of crusades. On the Western side a number of Aragonese letters have been published by Finke [1] and Golubovich [2]; but, on the Oriental side, no trace can be found of the Arabic correspondence of the Mamlūk Sultans in answer to the aforementioned letters in either the secondary authorities or the published primary sources. These we have been fortunate enough to discover in the Archivio de la Corona de Aragon in Barcelona and bring to light for the first time. Original documents of this kind, preserved almost intact, are extremely scarce either inside or outside Egypt. It will therefore be helpful to tabulate their contents, beginning with some reference to the Aragonese letters as a preliminary measure for drawing our conclusions and for the reconstruction of the embassies exchanged between the two countries.

ARAGONESE LETTERS [3]

1. From Jaime II (1291–1327) to Sultan al-Malik al-Nāṣir (second reign 1298–1308), dated Villafranca de Panades (in the neighbourhood of Barcelona), 1 June 1303.[4] This includes the requests for the following:

    (a) Reopening of the Christian Churches closed in Cairo and 'Babilonia' in return for the safe-conduct and freedom of worship accorded to the Moorish subjects of Aragon.

---

[1] *Acta Aragonensia*, II, nos. 461 and 472, pp. 744–5 and 758–9 respectively.

[2] *Biblioteca Bio-Bibliografica*, III, 73–85, 185–7, 309–18. See also H. Lammens, Correspondance diplomatique, in ROC (1904), 166–7; A. Rubiò, in *Anuari de l'Institut d'estudis catalans*, II (1908), 590; Campany, *Memorias historicas sobre la marina, comercio y artes de la antigua ciudad de Barcelona* (Madrid, 1779–82), II, 73, and IV, 80; L. Nicolau Olwer, *Expansio de Catalunya en la Mediterrània Oriental*, 24–31.

[3] Archivio de la Corona de Aragon, Reg. 334.

[4] Golubovich, III, 75–6.

(*b*) Liberation of the Aragonese subjects Lupo de Liranes, G. de Vilalba, Bartholomeo de Villafranca, and G. Dostarrich, taken prisoner by the Sultan from Ṭarābulus (Tripoli).

(*c*) Restoration of 12,000 besants unjustly taken from the merchants of the city of Barcelona by the customs authorities in Alexandria.

2. From Jaime II to al-Nāṣir, dated Barcelona, 1 September 1305 [1] refers to the Sultan's embassy under 'Mir Facardi' [2] and requests:

(*a*) That all Christians carrying an Aragonese royal brief for a pilgrimage to the Holy Sepulchre may be allowed to travel, stay, and return safe and sound from the Sultan's dominions without payment of customs, duty, or tribute (anar, estar et tornar salu et segur per tota vostra terra et senyoria, ne pagan ne donan negun dret ne tribut).

(*b*) That the Sultan may, like all good princes, accord to the Christians resident within his realm and under his protection, freedom of action as in the reign of his noble predecessor.

(*c*) That Giovanni Perez Calvets, Vasco Periz Fajardo and Alfonso Peris, subjects of Jaime's nephew, Ferdinand IV of Castille, as well as Bertrando de la Popia, who are the Sultan's prisoners, may be set free.

3. From Jaime II to al-Nāṣir (third reign 1309–40), dated 8 September [3] 1314, sent with two ambassadors—Guglielmo de Casandal and Arnaldo Sa-Bastida (or de Bastida)—who bore instructions to treat at the Sultan's court for the following:

(*a*) Ending the vexatious persecution of Christians.

(*b*) Freedom and safety for pilgrims to the Holy Land.

(*c*) Liberation of Christian prisoners.

4. From Jaime II to al-Nāṣir, dated Barcelona, 27 August 1318 [4] —the ambassadors this time being F. de Villafranca, a knight and archer of the king (alguazirus regis),[5] and Arnaldo de Bastida (see third embassy):

---

[1] ib., III, 77–9. Undoubtedly this is the embassy recorded by the anonymous author of *Tashrīf al-Aiyam*, B.N. MS. fonds arabe 1705, ff. 61 ro–62 ro.

[2] Probably al-Amīr Fakhr-al-Dīn 'Othman al-Nāṣiri, the Sultan's ambassador in 1304; *vide infra*, Roll 2. Also appears as Fracaldi; Golubovich, III, 186.

[3] Golubovich, III, 185–7.   [4] ib., III, 187.

[5] This is apparently the Arabic 'al-qaus' (the bow), often pronounced 'al-gaus' in colloquial Arabic. Golubovich suggests that 'al-uatar' (the arrow) is the origin of the Latin 'alguazirus' and the Spanish 'alguacil', both

     (*a*) To thank the Sultan for his response to the King's request
by setting three Christians free.

     (*b*) To renew the friendly relations between the two monarchs.

     (*c*) To ask for the freedom of all other Christian prisoners.

5. From Jaime II to al-Nāṣir, dated September 1322,[1] requesting:

     (*a*) That the Sultan may grant the custody and administration of
the Holy Sepulchre to the Order of the Preaching Friars.

     (*b*) That these new custodians may be installed in the dwelling
of the 'Patriarch', owing to its proximity to the Holy
Sepulchre.

     (*c*) That the Sultan, as a signal proof of his amity, may sur-
render to the royal ambassadors some holy relics said to
be in his treasures and including the real Cross and
Christ's own Chalice as well as the body of St. Barbara.

6. From Jaime II to Nāṣir, dated Barcelona, 20 August 1327:[2]

     (*a*) Asking for the freedom of Bananat, a Catalan of Barcelona,
Johan Roderigue of Navarre, Jaquet, an English interpreter (angles Torçimayn [3]), and others whom the bearer
of the letter, P. de Mijavilla, will name by word of mouth.

     (*b*) Pressing the Sultan to allot a section of the Basilica of the
Holy Sepulchre to the Minorite friars and to provide
them with a dwelling-place in the vicinity thereof.

EGYPTIAN LETTERS

These consist of the following manuscripts:

1. 'Carta árabe en papel.'   No. worn out.   Dated 15 Rajab A.H.
699/6 April A.D. 1300.

2. 'Carta árabe en papel.'   No. worn out.   Dated 13 Shawwal A.H.
703/19 May A.D. 1304.

3. 'Carta árabe en papel.'   No. worn out.   Dated 1 Sha'ban A.H.
705/16 February A.D. 1306.

4. 'Documentos árabes del Archivio de la Corona de Aragon; 4ª
Seccion, Cartas Orientales, Caja 4, doc. 19.'   One of four rolls
without number.   Dated in the 'first ten' days of Sha'ban A.H.
705/16–26 February A.D. 1306.

5. 'Carta árabe en papel.'   No. worn out.   Dated 'Bairam Day'
(i.e. 10 D̲h̲ulhijja) A.H. 714/17 March A.D. 1315.

---

of which mean 'archer', and further asserts that the colloquial for 'al-uatar'
is 'al-guatar', which is evidently a mistake.

   [1] Golubovich, III, 233–4 ; Finke, II, 756.

   [2] Golubovich, III, 312–14; Finke, II, 758–9.

   [3] This is the Arabic 'turjuman' which has passed into European languages
as 'dragoman'.

6. Same section as no. 3, 'Caja 5, Carta árabe en papel no. 492'.
Dated 15 Ṣafar A.H. 723/23 February A.D. 1323.

7. Same as no. 3, 'Caja 4', without special number of document.
Dated 15 Jumāda I A.H. 728/29 March A.D. 1328.

8. Same as nos. 3, 5 and 6, 'Caja 5, Carta árabe en papel no. 159'.
Dated 1 Jumāda I A.H. 730/20 February A.D. 1330.

All these rare original documents present themselves in the form of rolls of varying lengths, some reaching approximately eighty feet, and about one foot in width. They are carefully written in large attractive Mamlūk 'thuluth' court hand. Their style is flowery, but contains useful examples for students of Egyptian diplomatics in the fourteenth century. They were issued during the second and third reigns of Sultan al-Nāṣir, son of Qalawūn. The first six are addressed to Jaime II (1291–1327) and the last two to Alfonso IV (1327–36).

The following is a separate analysis of the contents of each of these documents:

First Roll:

(a) Lengthy introduction referring to the Tartar raids in Syria and stressing the vigour with which the Sultan's army had repulsed their hordes.

(b) Acknowledgement of receipt of King's letter as well as the verbal messages of his envoys.

(c) Guarantee in regard to the Aragonese merchants who frequent Egypt, that their safe-conduct and the protection of their goods and chattels will be ensured by decree.

(d) Promise of facilities and protection to Christian pilgrims to Jerusalem.

(e) Statement that the Aragonese envoys are returning, accompanied by Egyptian ambassadors with presents to the King.

Second Roll:

(a) Declaration of the liberation of Christian prisoners.

(b) Reference to the Sultan's envoy to Aragon, al-Amīr Fakhr-al-Dīn 'Othman al-Naṣiri,[1] who had ascertained the King's amity.

---

[1] This is apparently the embassy recorded in the B.N. MS. of the *Tashrīf*; *vide supra*, note. The embassy consisted of Fakhr-al-Dīn (who was 'Istādār' or 'Major-domo' of al-Amīr 'Izz-al-Dīn Aybak al-Aqzam), and one of the Sultan's judges (qāḍis). *Tashrīf*, f. 61 vo. It is interesting to note that the same work refers to the King of Aragon by name as 'al-Funsh' (Alfonso) apparently at a time when Jaime II was still alive. This may prove that the *Tashrīf* was written after the death of the latter and the accession of Alfonso in 1427, and hence the confusion.

(c) Notice of the persecution of the Copts and closing of churches. Here the Sultan points out that the verdict on this matter lies with the holy Muslim law which enforces the closing of churches constructed after the publication of the Covenant of 'Umar. Nevertheless, the Sultan has acceded to the re-opening of two churches in Cairo.

Third and Fourth Rolls:—Evidently these two are connected with one and the same embassy. The third, probably issued a few days before the fourth, deals with the following:

(a) Pilgrimages to the Holy Land, which may be undertaken in peace and security.

(b) An order issued to the governor of Alexandria to ensure the safety of all Aragonese subjects and merchants.

(c) Release of Christian captives, with a note that no Aragonese were to be found in the Sultan's prisons owing to the friend-ship of the two monarchs.

The Fourth Roll contains a list of presents sent by the Sultan to the King of Aragon with al-Amīr 'Othman al-Afarmi.

Fifth Roll:—Refers to the King's ambassadors mentioned by name in Aragonese Letter (*vide supra*, no. 3), emphasizes his friendliness in lengthy terms, and accedes to the liberation of 'Ifrīr Kiliam, Ifrīr Almat' (Friars Guillaume and Almata?), and six others in honour of the King's request despite the fact that they were cap-tured while fighting with the enemy against the forces of Islam.

Sixth Roll:—The Sultan

(a) Returns Christian prisoners in safety.

(b) Accedes to the King's request in regard to the monks sent by him.

(c) Assures the King that he treats his Christian subjects with respect and gives them protection, in return for which he requests that the King should also allow the Muslim subjects of Aragon to retain their own customs, say their prayers, and enjoy royal protection.

Seventh Roll:—Acknowledges receipt of the King's letter [1] and assures him that 'if he proceeds with the despatch of good ships with abundant goods', the body of St. Barbara will be handed to him.

---

[1] In *Nihāyat al-Arab*, Leiden MS. V, Cod. 19, under the year A.H. 727, Nuwairi refers to the coming of envoys of 'al-Bāb' (the Pope) and 'Faransīs' to mediate for the Sultan's clemency towards 'ahl al-dhimma' (People of the Covenant, i.e. the native Christians of Egypt and Syria). Whether

Eighth Roll:—Acknowledgement of receipt of presents sent with 'Afrancīs Morkos' (Francesco Marco?) and other envoys of the King.

REMARKS AND CONCLUSIONS

1. When we try to co-ordinate these diplomatic exchanges, it becomes clear that:
   - (*a*) Roll 2 from Egypt answers Letter 1 from Aragon.
   - (*b*) Rolls 3 and 4 from Egypt answer Letter 2 from Aragon.
   - (*c*) Roll 5 answers Letter 3.
   - (*d*) Roll 6 answers Letters 4 and 5.
   - (*e*) Roll 7 answers Letter 6.

Then, Rolls 1 and 8 remain without counterpart on the Western side. On the other hand, it is evident that the Sultan did not take the initiative in writing them. Roll 1 refers to receipt of a letter of the King of Aragon, and Roll 8 to arrival of embassy with presents.

2. The letters indicate the existence of a spirit of goodwill between Egypt and Aragon in the first three decades of the fourteenth century, a period in which trade with Muslim territories was prohibited by papal bulls and attempts were made to blockade the coasts of Egypt and Syria by European maritime leagues. It is significant, however, that all these diplomatic exchanges took place during the second and third reigns of Nāṣir on the one hand, and the reign of Jaime II on the other. Although Roll 7 is explicitly addressed to Alfonso IV, the letter which it answers was sent by Jaime II. Outside these two reigns in Egypt and Aragon, it is difficult to trace any similar attempts at a serious *rapprochement*.

3. The main objects of the Aragonese letters were:
   - (*a*) Friendship with Egypt.
   - (*b*) Mitigation of the sufferings of the persecuted Copts.
   - (*c*) Facilities for Western pilgrims.
   - (*d*) Advancement of Aragonese trade with Egypt.

4. Two aspects of the Egyptian letters, which cannot be examined here owing to their irrelevance, are worthy of special consideration and independent study:
   - (*a*) Egyptian diplomatics in the Later Middle Ages as revealed by these original documents including the Sultan's full title, the

---

this is Jaime's last embassy to the Sultan, or another from Charles IV, King of France (1322–8), who is known to have intervened for the Eastern Christians (Lot, 'Essai sur l'intervention de Charles . . . en faveur des Chrêtiens d'Orient', in BEC (1875), XXXVI), remains uncertain, although Nuwairi's own reference (ib., f. 126 vo) to the fact that no embassy had been received from France since the days of the Aiyubid al-Ṣāliḥ Najm-al-Dīn (1240–9) appears to decide in favour of the argument for the latter.

titles given to foreign princes in the West, and the redaction and arrangement of official correspondence.[1]

(b) The list of Egyptian presents to the King of Aragon, accompanying the Fourth Roll, may throw much light on the articles of luxury used in fourteenth-century Egypt.

---

[1] H. Lammens, op. cit., l.c., has translated the title of the King of Aragon from al-Qalqashandi, *Ṣabḥ al-A'sha*; cf. Golubovich, III, 73. Still far more important as a source for this matter of titles than al-Qalqashandi are —first, the official correspondence aforementioned, and, second, the inscriptions published by G. Wiet in *Catalogue général du musée arabe du Caire, Objets en cuivre* (Cairo, 1932). The second is, of course, confined to the title of the Mamlūk Sultans.

APPENDIX IV

LISTS OF THE CRUSADERS

THE following three lists comprising the names of those known to have participated in the crusades of Alexandria, Barbary and Nicopolis are here reproduced for reference. They are necessarily incomplete as a result of gaps in the sources. We have based them on the work done by Delaville Le Roulx (*France en Orient*, II, 12–17, 78–80) and L. Mirot (*Siège de Mahdia*, 41–50), as well as the charter of the crusade of Nicopolis (ed. Atiya, in *Crusade of Nicopolis*, 144–8). Our present additions to these lists are small except in the first list where we have been able to trace many additional names in *Makhairas' Chronicle* (ed. Dawkins, §§ 163 and 167). Those whose names are marked with a † are known to have died in the course of the campaign).

I. CRUSADERS OF ALEXANDRIA (1365)

Amé III, Comte de Genvévois

Antioch (Prince of). See Lusignan (J. de)

Antioche (sire Jean d') [2]

Antioche (sire Thomas d') [2]

Airasca (Ferlino d'), grand admiral of the Order of Rhodes

Archiac (sire Foulques d')

Argentem (sire Jean d') [1]

Babin (messire Raymond) [2]

Bailliada (sire Robert)

Basqueville (sire Guillaume VI, Martel de)

Beaufort (Guillaume-Roger de), viscount of Turenne

Beauvillier (sq. Jean de)

Beauvillier (sire Jédouin de)

Beduin (sire Hugues) [2]

Bellangues (seigneur de)

Benauges. See Grailly

Blaru (sire Saquet de)

Bon (sq. Baudri de)

Bon (sq. Bonau de) †

Bonne (sq. Robesson)

Boutellin (sq. Hostes)

Brabant (sq. Endruet de)

Brie (sire Badin de) [2]

Brie (sire Jean de) [2]

---

[1] *Anonimalle Chronicle*, 51, which also includes the name of Sir Miles de Stapilton of Bedale (Co. York). This, however, must be regarded as incorrect owing to Miles' death in the December prior to the expedition, leaving a minor son. See Editor's note, 170.

[2] Makhairas, § 163.

Brunswick [1]
Cassi (sire Pierre de) [2]
Cayeu (Jean de), seigneur de Vimes in Vimeu
Chastelet (sq.)
Chenevières (sire Raus de)
Clairvaux (seigneur de)
Cologne (sire Perceval de), chamberlain of the King of Cyprus
Contes (sq. Jean de)
Corbon (sq., bastard of)
Coutances (Aimé de)
Estouteville (sire Nicolas d'), seigneur de Torcy
Fay (sire Oisellet du)
Ferté (sire Jean de la) [2]
Flavigny (seigneur de)
Friquans (Jean de)
Galilee (prince of). See Lusignan (H. de)
Gauvain
Génévois (count of). See Amé III
Giblet (sire Eudes de)
Giblet (messire Henri) [3]
Giblet (sire Jean de) [2]
Grailly (sire Bertrand de), bastard of Benauges
Grésille (sire Pierre de la)
Grimani (messire Pierre de) [3]
Grimort (Perrin de)
Guerrot, sq.
Guibelin. See Ibelin (J. de)
Handressi (sq. Raoulin d')
Henri le Cypriote [2]
Herefort (comte de)
Ibelin (sire Jacques d')
Ibelin (Jean d')
Ibelin (sire Nicolas d')
Jaucourt (Philippe de)

La Bove (sire Gobert de)
La Conté (sq. Lambequin de)
Lamenevain (sq. Hervé de)
Laskaris (messire Jean) [3]
Le Baveux (sire Gui)
Le Baveux (sire Renaud)
Le Baveux (sire Robert)
Le Coche (sire Hervé)
Le Cordelier. See Puignon
Le Petit (sire Renier)
Le Roux (sire Robert)
Lesparre (Florimont, sire de)
Lor (sire Gautier de)
Lornis (sire Jean de)
Lusignan (Hugues de), prince of Galilee
Lusignan (Jacques), prince of Antioch
Lusignan (Pierre I de), King of Cyprus
Mailly (sire Jacques de)
Malocella (messire Pierre) [3]
Mar (sire Jean de) [3]
Martel. See Basqueville
Mézières (Philippe de), chancellor of Cyprus
Mimars (sire Gui de) [3]
Monstry (Jean de), admiral of Cyprus
Montgesart (sire Hamerin de) [3]
Montgesart (sire Jacques de) [3]
Montgesart (sire Lepass de) [3]
Montolif (sire Hugues de) [3]
Montolif (sire Roger de) [3]
Montolif (sire Thomas de) [3]
Morpho (Jean de), comte d'Edesse, admiral of Cyprus
Montbouchier (seigneur de)
N... (sire, Scottish) †
Nantouillet (sire Renard de)
Navarre (sire Balian de) [3]

---

[1] Makhairas, § 167. [2] ib., § 163.
[3] ib., § 167.

Norès (Jacques de), turkopolier of Cyprus
Norès (sire Louis de) [1]
Omont (sire Philippe d') †
Pastez (sire Jean)
Petit (Jacques)
Plessie (sire Balian de) [2]
Poissy (sire Gilles de)
Pont (sire Thibaut du)
Preaux. See Rivière (J. de la)
Puchay (seigneur du)
Puignon (sire Le Cordelier de)
Rabette
Reims (sq. Jean de)
Resigny (sq. Mansart de)
Rhodes (admiral of). See Airasca (F. de)
Rivière (sire Jean de la), seigneur de Préaux
Rochefort (sire Jean de)
Rohais (comte de). See Morpho (J. de)
Saint-Martin (seigneur de)
Sassenage (seigneur de)
Saus (sire Guillaume de)

Saus (sire Jean de)
Sovains (sire Jean de)
Sur (sire Jean de), admiral [1]
Taillanville (sire Jean de), seigneur d'Yvetot
Thinoly (Simon), chamberlain of the King of Cyprus
Thomas (Pierre de), Apostolic Legate
Torcy. See Estouteville
Tribouville (Tribouillart de)
Turenne (Vicomte de). See Beaufort (Guillaume-Roger de)
Vasa (seigneur de) [2]
Vendieres (sire Jean de)
Verneuil (Hue de)
Verni (sire Thomas de) [1]
Vimes en Vimeu (seigneur de). See Cayeu (Jean de)
Visconti (sire Guillelmo)
Voulte (Bremond de la), chamberlain of the King of Cyprus
Yvetot. See Taillanville (J. de)

2. CRUSADERS OF BARBARY (1390)

Albret (sire Charles d')
Amboise (sire Ingelger d')
Antoing (sire Henri d')
Arcy (Giraud d') Master of the pantry to the Duke of Touraine
Arenton (sq. Blondelet d') †
Auberchicourt (sire François de)
Audenay (sq. Guillaume d') †
Audureau (Guillaume) †
Aunay (le vicomte d')
Aunoy (sire Robert, called le Gallois)

Bailledart (messire Robert), maître d'hôtel to duke of Touraine
Balleure (messire Gaudri de)
Bar (sire Philippe de)
Beau (Nicolas de)
Beaufort (John)
Bellefaye (sire de) †
Bellefrère (sire de) †
Béraud (Philippe)
Berneval (Robert de) †
Bertrand called d'Espalt, sire †
Bethencourt (sire Jean de), chamberlain to the duke of Touraine

[1] Makhairas, § 163.　　　　[2] ib., § 167.

Bieussy (Jean de)
Blot (le sire de) †
Bochut
Boschet (Raoul de)
Boucicaut (sire Geoffroi Le Meingre, le jeune)
Bourbon (Louis II, duke of)
Bours (sire de)
Boutervilliers (Sanglier de)
Boutillier (sire Jean le)
Boves (Perrinet de)
Bressolles (Renaut de)
Budes (Alain), duke of Touraine's Master of the Stables
Bus (Ivonet du)
Cabroles (sire Robert de)
Caillart (le sire du) †
Calain (sire Boniface de)
Calviste (sire Gui de la) †
Carma (Jean de)
Castillon entre Deux Mers (sire de) †
Catenas (sire Jean de) †
Celle-Guenand (Geoffroi de la) †
Centurione, surnamed Oltramarino (Giovanni)
Chambly (Charles de)
Champagne (sire Alain de) †
Champagne (sire Jean de) †
Chantemelle (Taupin de)
Chapelle (sire Rofroi de la) †
Charny (Geoffroi de, sire)
Chastel-Montagne (le sire de)
Chastellus (sire Guichard de) †
Chastellus (sire Hugues de)
Chastellus (sire Jean de), surnamed Châteaumorand
Châtillon (sire Gaucher de)
Chauvigny (Philippe de) †
Chesnac (Bertrand de) †
Chin (le sire de)
Cholet (Yon de) †
Ciboulle (Jean) Genoese sq.
Claroy (Guillotin de)

Clervaux (sire Eustache de) †
Clifford (Lewis)
Clinton (John)
Clues (Le Borgne de) †
Coich (Burgaud Le)
Cornwallis (John)
Coucy (Enguerrand VII, sire de)
Courcy (le sire de)
Courtiambles (Jacques de)
Cousay (sire Amé de) †
Craon (sire Amaury de) †
Cressonnière (Robin de la)
Croilly (le sire de) †
Cuise (Jean de), Master of the Waters and Forests of Normandy and Picardy; seigneur de Puis
Damas (sire Robert de)
Dancelles (Charles) †
Dauphin (sire Hugues)
Dignaut (sire Jean de) †
Disnau (Geoffroi de) †
Egreville (Guiot d')
Escaufours (sire Fouques d') †
Escaufours (sq. Gautier d') †
Esneval (sire Robert d')
Espinasse (le sire de l')
Essarts (Pierre des)
Estouteville le jeune (Jean d')
Eu (le comte d')
Eu (Guillaume, sénéchal d')
Foix (Ivain, bâtard de)
Fotheringay (sq. William) †
Franc (Jean)
Franqueboth, sq. †
Frésier (sire Geoffroi) †
Fresnes (Richard de), sq. of the Duke of Touraine
Gacelli (sire Guillaume de) †
Garde (sire Guichard de la) †
Garencières (le sire de)
Garet (sire Guillaume de) †
Giresme (Cordelier de)

Glené (Tochar de), bailiff of the Bourbonnais

Grandville (Jean de), physician of the Duke of Bourbon

Graville (Guillaume, sire de)

Hainaut, comte d' Ostrevant (Guillaume de)

Hangest (Charles d')

Hangest (Robert d'), chamberlain of the Duke of Touraine †

Harcourt (Jean VII, comte d')

Harcourt (Robert d') †

Hargiers (sire Jean d')

Harpedenne (sire Jean)

Harville (Guillaume d')

Havenières (Raoul d')

Havré (sire Gérard II d')

Hervilliers (Philippe d')

Heuze (Le Baudrain de la)

Houdan (Philippe de) †

Huniquet (sq. Huguenin)

Huses (vicomte de) †

Isles (sq. Jean des)

Isques (Desir d')

Jaucourt (Geoffroi de)

Jaucourt (Philippot de), sq. and cup-bearer of the Duke of Burgundy

Jaucourt (Guillaume de), surnamed Sauvage, King's first master of the pantry

Lambert (Jacques), King's usher

Lanay (sq. Jean de) †

Lande (sq. Jean de la) †

Lebrun (Guichard)

Lemoine (sq. Jean) †

Levillain (sq. Gui) †

Liège (sq. Foucaut de) †

Ligne (le sire de)

Ligne (sire Jean de)

Linières (le sire de)

Lisques (sire Grison de)

Longueval (le sire de)

Longwy (le sire de)

Louin (sire Guerard de)

Loup (Blain), surnamed Le Louvart, marshal of the Bourbonnais

Loup, surnamed Blomberis, brother of Blain Loup †

Luyères (sq. Geoffroi de) †

Machecoul (le sire de) †

Mailly (Eustache de) †

Malere (Guichard de) †

Mamines (sq. Pierre de) †

Marc (Antoine) genoese

Martel (Guillaume), chamberlain of the King

Matefelon (le sire de)

Mauni (Alain de)

Mauvoisin (Jean), sq. and cup-bearer of the Duke of Touraine

Michaille (Gauvain)

Mignotel †

Molletin (Simon), valet

Mont (Robert du) †

Montaigut (Louis Aycelin de), seigneur de Chateldon, Breuil, Montgilbert, Roche-Milay, and governor of Nivernais and Donziois

Montdoucet (Robert, surnamed Le Borgne de)

Montecoe (sire Jean de) †

Montigny (Jean de), surnamed Friant

Morillon (sq. Jean) †

Morles (sire Guillaume)

Mothe (Aleaume de la) †

Mothe (sq. Aubert de la) †

Motte (sq. Jean de la) †

Mouleraye (sire Guichard de la) †

Mouleraye (sire Tristan de la) †

Moulin (sire Guillaume du)

Naillac (Elion de)

Nancelles (Bertier de)

Nantouillet (Renaud de)
Négrepelisse (le sire de)
Neufville
Offemont (le sire d')
Ortingas (sq. Jeannicot d')
Palerne (Guichard de) †
Paquières (sq. le Borgne de), master of the pantry of the Duke of Burgundy
Parc (sq. Guillaume de) †
Paviot (Pierre), first chamberlain of the Duke of Touraine
Perier (sq. Jean) †
Pierre Buffière (Jean de) †
Planella (Pierre de), Councillor of the King of Aragon
Poitiers (Louis de)
Poitiers (Philippe de)
Port (Etienne du) †
Porte (Perrinet de la)
Puille (Robert de) †
Quesnes (Karados des)
Rieux (le sire de)
Rocheguion (le sire de la)
Rocque (Floridas de la) †
Ronnay (Gui de)
Rosas (le vicomte de)
Rous (le sire de), Breton
Roussay (Guiot de)
Roye (sire Jean de)
Russel (John)
Saigne (le sire de la)
Sainte-Sévère (le sire de) †
Saint-Germain (le sire de)
Saint-Polques (le sire de)
Saint-Priest (le sire de)
Salle (Gadifer de la), chamberlain of the King, of the Duke of Berry, and of the Duke of Touraine, seneschal of Bigorre
Sancerre (Étienne de), sire de Vailli †
Sancerre (Jean III, comte de)

Sarrebière (sire Étienne de) †
Scalet (sire Lyon) †
Siffrevast (sq. Jean de)
Soisy (Jean de)
Souastre (Perducat de) †
Stapella (sire Guillaume de) †
Surgères (sire Jacques II, sire de)
Tignonville (sire Guillaume de)
Tirant (sq. Robert le)
Tors (le sire de)
Tourney (sire Amé de) †
Trau (sire Jean de Préchac, soudic de la)
Tremagon (Jean de), sq. of the Duke of Touraine
Trémouille (sire Guy de la), seigneur de Sully
Trémouille (sire Guillaume de la), seigneur d'Usson
Trémouille (sire Jean de la), seigneur de Jonvelle
Trie (sire Jean de), chamberlain of the King and marshal of the Duke of Touraine †
Trie (sire Jean, bâtard de) †
Trie (Renaud de)
Uzès (sire Elzéar, vicomte de)
Vaise (sire Gui de) †
Val-Auger (Denis de) †
Vernay (Barthomier du)
Viausse (sire, le Borgne de)
Vienne (Guillaume de), seigneur de Saint-Georges
Vienne (Jean de), admiral
Vieulxpont (Yves de)
Villain (sq. Jean) †
Villenove (le sire de)
Vilnove (sire Floridas de)
Vincy (J. de)
Voudenay (Eustache sire de), chamberlain of the Duke of Burgundy
Vrolant (Robin de)

3. CRUSADERS OF NICOPOLIS (1396)

Agram. See Gran
Agreville. See Egreville
Anthoing (Henri d') †
Antoing (Hue d')
Ardentun (Robert)
Artois (Philippe d'), comte d'Eu †
Aumont (Jacques d')
Aunoy (Guillaume d')
Auxonne (Jean d')
Aynne (Louis d') †
Bahagnon (Claux de) †
Bailleur (sire Gauvanet le)
Bar (Henri de), seigneur d'Oisy †
Bar (sire Philippe de) †
Barrois (le)
Bateteau
Baudrain de Cauny (le)
Bauffremont (Gautier de), seigneur de Vauvillars et Ruppes
Beaucouray (Jean de), sq. of honour to the Duke of Orléans
Beaucouroy (le petit)
Beaumenil, cousin of the comte d'Harcourt
Beauvais (le Châtellain de). See Bordes (Jean des)
Bebek (Demetrius)
Beigne (Guillaume de la) †
Besançon (le Porcelot de)
Beverhout (sq. Alard de)
Blaisy (sire Jean de)
Bloet (Ogien) archer
Bloume (sq. Guy)
Bochout (sq. Jean de)
Bodem (Hans von). See Sracimir (John)
Boislève (sire Jean)
Boloine. See Boulogne
Bonneu

Bordes (Guillaume des), standard-bearer of France
Bordes (Jean des); Beauvais (le Châtellain de)
Boucicaut (Jean II, surnamed le Meingre), Marshal of France
Boulogne (sire Antoine de)
Bourbon (sire Jacques de), comte de la Marche
Bouterville or Boutarvillier (Philippe de), surnamed Sanglier, pantry sq. of the Duke of Orleans
Boves (sire Jean de)
Braqueton (le petit)
Breteau (Guillaume), pantryman
Breteau (Simon), maître d'hôtel
Briffault
Brocart, archer
Bruwere (sq. Bertrand le)
Bruwere (sire Roland le)
Bugnot (Jean)
Buignet (Jean), pantry-keeper of the Duke of Burgundy †
Bus (sq. Guillaume de)
Busère (Gauhier de, sq.)
Buxeuil (Damas de) †
Buxeuil (Jacques de)
Cadzaud (Jean de) Grand Admiral of Flanders †
Caedsaud. See Cadzuad (J. de)
Cajaut. See Cadzaud (J. de)
Campighem (sire Roger de)
Carnes (Jean), archer
Caronuel (Thomas de)
Centumarante
Cépeaux (Jean de)
Châlon (sire Henri de)
Châlon (Hugues de), seigneur d'Arlay †
Champdio (Hugues de) †

Chandio (Pierre de)

Charny (sire Geoffroy de)

Chartres (sire Bertrand de) †

Chasseron (Marc) †

Chasseron (sire Odart de) †

Chastel Belin (le seigneur de)

Chastillon (son of the seigneur de)

Châtelot.   See Neuchatel (Thibaut de) †

Chavigny (sire Regnaud de)

Chevenon (Hugues de), standardbearer of Marshal Boucicaut

Chiffreval

Cilly (Hermann II, Count of)

Cognignehault (Laurent), archer

Coligny (Jacques de), eldest son of Jean de Coligny, seigneur de Crescia

Coligny (Jean de), seigneur de Crescia †

Collet (Hannotin)

Condebourch (Nicle de)

Cops (Donatien du), archer

Cortiambles (Jacques de)

Cortiambles (son of Jacques de)

Coucy (Enguerrand VII, sire de) †

Courtroisin (sq. Jean de)

Craon (Guillaume de)

Crescia.   See Coligny (Jean de)

Cressonnière (Robert de la)

Cressonnière (Robin de la)

Crux (sire Jean de)

Damas (Huguenin de), sire de la Bazole

Damas (Joceran de) †

Delayto (Jacques de)

Delft (sire Pierre de la)

Demetrius (the three sons of), Ban of Sclavonia †

Descosieu (sq. Laurent)

Deve (mess.)

Distergo.   See Demetrius

Doue (Louis)

Douve (sq. Jorge de la)

Druickham.   See Sans Terre (Jean)

Dugay (Louis), 1st. sq.

Egreville (sire Jean d')

Enguerammet

Ensteinchalle.   See Esteulemchale

Espinasse (le sire de l')

Essarts (sire Tort des)

Estavayé (Gérard d'), Marshal of Hungary.   See Esteulemchale

Esteulemchale (Henry d'), Marshal of the King of Hungary

Estouteville (sire Charles d')

Eu (comte d').   See Artois (Philippe d') †

Eu (Guillaume d'), seneschal of the Comte d'Eu †

Eyne.   See Aynne

Fay (sq. Jacques du)

Flandres (le Haze de).   See Haze (called Louis le)

Flandre (sire Raoul de)

Flandre (Renault, bâtard de)

Flandre (Victor, bâtard de)

Forgach (Jean de) †

Fougières (sq. le Galois de)

Francho (lo), treasurer of Sigismund

Francho (two brothers of)

Fravenberger von Haag (Christian)

Fravenberger (Georges or Guillaume)

Fravenhofen (Georges von)

Friant.   See Montigny (J. de)

Frison (Louis le) †

Fünfkirchen (nephew of Valentine, Bishop of) †

Gadifer, archer

Gara (Nicolas), Grand Palatine of Hungary

Gara (son of Nicolas), standard-bearer †

Garancières (son of the Seigneur de)

Gaucourt (sire Raoul de)

Gaudin (Robert)

Gauvignon

Gemage (Jean de)

Germigny (sq. Etienne de)

Germigny (Jean de), bailiff of Autun †

Giac (Louis de), seigneur de Chateaugay †

Goscalc

Gran (John, arch. de), son of John of Kanyzsay

Granson (sire Jean de)

Graville (le sire de)

Gray (Jean de), attendant at the Hôtel d'Artois in Paris, prob. †

Greiff (Herr Hans) †

Gruthuse (sq. Jean de la), standard-bearer

Guindot (Geoffroy), châtelain d' Avallon

Guitton (Gilles de) of Rhodes

Haluwin (sq. Jean de)

Haluwin (sire Olivier de)

Hamme (sq. le Leu de la)

Hangest (Jean de), seigneur de Heugeville

Harcourt (Robert d') †

Hauweel (sire Roland) †

Haye (Pierre de la)

Haze (Louis le), bâtard de Flandre †

Heliot (Berthélot), valet de chambre of the Duke of Burgundy

Helly (sire Jacques de)

Heugeville (le seigneur d'). See Hangest (J. de)

Heuse (Jean de la) †

Hodierne (Michelet), maître de la chambre aux deniers †

Holand (John, Count of Huntingdon) [1]

Houlfort (Enguerrammet de), châtelain de Montbard †

Huron (Jean)

Illsua (Eustache de), Palatine of Hungary.

Jabeuf (Matherot) †

John, bishop of Grosswardein †

Kanyzsay (Stephen), Chief Janissary, count of Samoyye-Var

Kapolia (John) †

Katzenellenbogen (Eberard v., count of)

Kocrimel (sire Thomas de) †

Kolandus (sire, son of Sansinus) †

Kuchler (Ulrich) †

Kulski (sire Thomas)

Lalemant (Mathé)

Langon (Lancelot de)

Lannoit (sire Philippe de)

Laszković (Stephen) of Transylvania

Lejeune. See Monnoyer

Lembèque (sire Jean de) †

Lentzenawer (Wernher) †

Linières (sire Godemart de)

Linières (sire Jean de)

Lohes (sire Jacques de)

Longvy (seigneur de)

Lucgères (Geoffroy de) pantry sq. of the Duke of Orleans

Lugny (Guillaume de) †

Lugny (Huguenin de)

Malicorne (son of madame de)

Marchant (sire Robert le)

[1] See *Nicopolis,* 47–8.

Marche (Comte de la). See
    Bourbon (Jacques de)
Mareschal (sire Louis le)
Marothy (John) †
Mathery
Maubuisson
Maumes (messire de)
Mehun (Seigneur de).† See
    Tournon (Jacques de)
Mello (sire Guillaume de)
Mes (sq. Jean du)
Messem (sire Tristan de)
Metten-Eye (sire Jean)
Metten-Eye (Louis), citizen of
    Bruges
Milli (sire Robert de)
Mircea, Voyevode of Wallachia
Molnheym (Johann Ulrich von)
Molnheym (Bertold Hans von)
Mongascon, grandson of Robert
    VII, comte d'Auvergne †
Monnetoy (sire Hugues de)
Monnoyer (le jeune)
Monseaugeon (Étienne de)
Montaubert (sire Jean de)
Montbéliard (sire Henri de)
Montbéliard (brother of mess.
    Henri's wife)
Montcavrel (sq. le Borgne de) †
Montcavrel (le sire de)
Montcavrel (son of le sire de) †
Montigny (Jean, sire de), sur-
    named Friant
Montquel (sq. le Borgne de)
Muart
Mussy (sire Philippe de) standard-
    bearer †
Naillac (sire Hélion de) †
Naillac (Philibert de), Grand
    Master of Rhodes †
Nanton (Guillaume de)
Nanton (Phelipot de)
Neufchatel (Thibaut de), seig-
    neur de Châtelot †

Nevers (Jean, comte de)
Normandea(u) (le), maître d'hôtel
Nuremburg (John III, burgrave
    of)
Nybs (comte de)
Octeville
Pacy (sire Regnault de)
Paillard (Copin), kitchen squire
Pasquot (Adam), archer
Pasztoh (Jean de)
Paymiel (sire Fouque)
Petit (André le), archer
Pierre (friar, Cordelier)
Pipan (Ruprecht), count palatine
Plancy (le sire de)
Pommart (sire Anceau de)
Pontallier (Jacques de)
Pontallier (sire Jean de)
Pot (Renier), chamberlain to the
    Duke of Burgundy.
Poulain (Guillaume), pantry-
    squire of the Duke of
    Orleans
Proost (sire Hughe de)
Prunelle (sire Jean)
Quiéret (Guillaume)
Qui s'arme (Jean), valet des
    chevaux du Comte de
    Nevers †
Ragny (Girard de)
Ranty (Rasse de)
Rascie (Etienne, comte de)
Rasse (le Bégue de)
Ray (le sire de)
Reichartinger (Leonhard),
    Bavarian †
Reingaerdsvliet (sire Jean de)
Renel (Berthelot de), archer
Reneval (sire Raoul de)
Renty (Bâtard de)
Renty (le Galois de)
Rez (Peter von)
Rigny (Georges de)
Rigny (sire Jean de)

Robichon (Jean), archer

Rochechouart

Rochefort (Jean de)

Roussay (sire Guiot de)

Roye (Dreux, surnamed Lancelot de) †

Roye (Jean de), seigneur de Plessis, de Roye, de Muret et de Buzancy †

Roye (Mathieu de), son of Jean

Roye (sire Regnault de), chamberlain and councillor of the King

Rozgon (comte Simon)

Ruaut (sire Guillaume)

Ruppes (Gauthier de). See Bauffremont

Rye (sire Henri de)

Saint Aubin (sire Jean de), seigneur de Deuzy

Saint Chatier (Bertrand de)

Saint Croix (sire Jean de) †

Saint Germain (Jean de)

Saint Pol (le sire de)

Saint Py

Saint Seigne (Thierry de)

Salins (sire Henri de)

Sanglier. See Bouterville

Sansinus, châtelain de Wisegrad †

Sans-Terre (Jean), surnamed seigneur de Druickham †

Sarcus (Jean de)

Sarrazin (sire Jean le)

Saucourt (Huet de)

Sauvegrain (Jean), surnamed Normendel †

Sauvement (Henri de), bailiff of Aumont †

Savoisy (sire Jean de)

Savoy (bâtard du comte de)

Scenya. See Swantoslaus

Schiltberger (John)

Schmichar (sire Etienne)

Scyborius, sire

Semsey (Ladislas) †

Semur (Gauvignon de), captain of Doudain in Charolais †

Siffrenast (sq. Jean de)

Sigismund, King of Hungary

Simontornya (Stephen), nephew of Stephen Laszkovich

Sonday (Tribouillard de) †

Sracimir (John), King of Bulgaria

Steiner (der kleine)

Stiborricze (Stiborius de)

Strömer (Erhart) †

Sunx (Jacquot de)

Swantoslaus, surnamed Scenya

Synüher (Stephen). See Simontornya

Tauques (sire Jean de)

Tauques (Rasse de)

Temesvar (brother-in-law of the count of) †

Temesvar (brother of the former) †

Temseke (Jean de), citizen of Bruges

Ternaut (Jean de), cup-bearer

Thouars. See Vivonne (Savari de)

Toulongeon

Tournon (Jacques de), seigneur de Mehun †

Tramerie (Pierre de la)

Tremangon (sire Jean de), chamberlain of the Duke of Orleans †

Trémouille (sire Guillaume de la), seigneur d'Usson, marshal of Burgundy †

Trémouille (Guy de la), seigneur de Sully †

Trémouille (sire Philippe de la), son of Guillaume †

Trye (sire Jean de)

Utenhove (sire Jean)

Utenhove (Nicolas)
Utenzwane (sire Galois)
Varadiensis episcopus. See Jean
Varsenaere (sq. Jean de)
Vautravers (Guillaume de)
Vé (le seigneur de), chamberlain
of the Duke of Burgundy †
Vergy (sire Guillaume de)
Vergy (sire Jacques de)
Vernot (Louis de)
Vienne (sire Guillaume de)
Vienne (sire Jacques de), seigneur
de Longvy †
Vienne (Jean de), admiral of
France †
Vienne (son of Jean de) †

Vienne (Jean de), seigneur de
Longvy
Villers (Boelin)
Villiers (Anceau de)
Villiers (sire Philibert de)
Vivonne (Savari de), seigneur de
Thouars †
Vries (Louis de) †
Wolkenstein (Oswald de)
Zeno (Niccolò) †
Zolerne (Frederic, count of),
Grand Prior of the Teu-
tonic Order in Germany †
Zwaesberghe (sire Gille de)
Zwenenghem (sire Louis de)
Zweveghem. See Zwenenghem.

APPENDIX V
CHRONOLOGICAL TABLES[1]

I. EMPERORS

1. HOLY ROMAN EMPERORS

1298	Albert I (Hapsburg)
1308	Henry VII (Luxemburg)
1314	Lewis IV (Bavaria). Frederick of Austria (rival emperor)
1347	Charles IV (Luxemburg). Günther of Schwartzburg (rival emperor)
1378	Wenzel (Luxemburg)
1400	Rupert (Palatinate)
1410	Sigismund (Luxemburg). Jobst of Moravia (rival emperor)
1438	Albert II (Hapsburg)
1440	Frederick III
1493–1519	Maximilian I

2. EASTERN EMPERORS

1261	Michael VIII Palaeologos
1282	Andronikos II. (Michael IX co-emperor, 1295–1320)
1328	Andronikos III ⎱ John VI Kantakuzenos, rival em-
1341	John V ⎰ peror, 1341–54 (ob. 1383)
1391	Manuel II. John VII, co-emperor, 1399–1403
1425	John VIII
1448–53	Constantine XI Dragases

[1] In a special study like the present, these general tables may seem superfluous. Nevertheless, in the course of our work, we have found it necessary to refer continually to a large variety of books for the confirmation of our dates. To avoid this inconvenience and to save the reader's time, we publish them in this Appendix with some reluctance. The Western reader is further asked to note that the familiar lists of Popes, Emperors and Kings are not so familiar to Eastern readers. It is hoped that their usefulness may justify the space allotted to them. In compiling these lists, we have used the works of Zambaur, Lane-Poole, Stockvis, Bouillet (*Atlas d'hist. et de géogr.*), Mas Latrie, Weil, Gibbons, Delaville La Roulx, Neale, Butcher, Kidd and others.

3. TITULAR LATIN EMPERORS OF CONSTANTINOPLE [1]

1272	Philippe de Courtenay
1274	Catherine de Courtenay
1308	Catherine de Valois
1346	Robert de Tarente
1364	Philippe de Tarente
1368	Jacques de Beaux (ob. s.p. 1383)

II. POPES, ANTI-POPES AND PATRIARCHS

1. POPES AND ANTI-POPES

1294	Boniface VIII		
1303–4	Benedict XI		
1305–14	Clement V. (Beginning of Babylonish Captivity)		
1316	John XXII. (Nicholas V, Anti-Pope, 1328–30)		
1334	Benedict XII		
1342	Clement VI		
1352	Innocent VI		
1362	Urban V		
1370	Gregory XI	Anti-Popes and Beginning of Schism	
1378	Urban VI.	1378–1394	Clement VII
1389	Boniface IX.	1394–1415	Benedict XIII
1404	Innocent VII.	1410–15	Gregory XII (as
1406	Gregory XII		rival Pope)
1409	Alexander V		
1410–15	John XXIII		
1417	Martin V. (End of Schism)		
1431	Eugenius IV.	1439–49	Felix V
1447	Nicholas V		
1455	Calixtus III		
1458	Pius II		
1464	Paul II		
1471	Sixtus IV		
1484	Innocent VIII		
1492–1503	Alexander VI		

2. PATRIARCHS OF CONSTANTINOPLE FROM THE GREEK RESTORATION TO THE OTTOMAN CONQUEST

	Greek	1275	John XI
1261	Arsenius	1282	Joseph I (2)
1267	Germanus	1283	Gregory II
1268	Joseph I (1)	1289–93	Athanasius I (1)

[1] Cf. Bouillet, op. cit., 385.

1294	John XII	1450	Athanasius II
1303	Athanasius I (2)	1453–9	Gennadius II
1311–15	Nephon I		
1316	John XIII		*Latin*
1320–1	Gerasimus I	1253	Pantaleon
1323	Jesaias	1286	Pietro I Corrario
1334	John XIV	1302	Leonardo Faliero
1347–49	Isidore I	1305	Hugolin
1350	Callistus I (1)	1308	Nicholas
1354	Philotheus (1)	1324	Peter II
1355–63	Callistus I (2)	1330(?)	Cardinalis
1364	Philotheus (2)	1335	Gozio Battaglini
1376–9	Macarius (1)	1338	Robert
1380–88	Nilus	1341	Enrico d'Asti
1389	Antonius IV (1)	1345	Guillelmo I de
1390	Macarius (2)		Castello
1391	Antonius IV (2)	1346	Stephen
1397	Matthias	1346	Guillelmo II
1410	Euthymius II		Pustrella
1416–39	Joseph II	1364	Pierre de Thomas
1440	Metrophanes II	1366	Paul
1443	Gregory III	1368	Philippe de Cabassole

3. PATRIARCHS OF ALEXANDRIA

	Coptic [1]		*Latin* [2]
1271	John VII	1245	Unknown
1294	Theodosius II	1310	Gilles de Ferrara
1311	John VIII	1323	Odo de Sala
1321	John IX	1328	John I of Aragon (son of
1327	Benjamin II		King James II)
1340	Peter V	1342	Guillaume de Chanac
1348	Marcus IV	1351	Humbert de Viennois
1363	John X	1361	Arnaud Bernard du Pouget
1371	Gabriel IV	1371	Jean II de Cardaillac
1375	Matthew I	1386	Pierre Amily de Brunac
1409	Gabriel V	1391	Simon de Cramaud
1427	John XI	1401	Leonardo Delfino
1453	Matthew II	1402	Hugo Roberti de Tripoli
1467	Gabriel VI	1429	Vitalis de Mauléon
1475	Michael VI	1435?	Giovanni Vitelleschi
1481–1521	John XII	1451	Jean d'Harcourt
		1505	Bernardino Caraffa

[1] Cf. Mrs. Butcher's list.
[2] Cf. Mas Latrie, *Patriarches Latins d'Alexandrie*, in ROL. *Vide* Bibliography.

Melkite [1]

1276–1308	Athanasius III
c. 1320	Gregory II
?	Gregory III
c. 1367	Nephon
?	Marcus III
?	Nicholas III
?	Gregory IV
1437–50	Philotheus I
?	Athanasius IV
c. 1523	Philotheus II

III. WESTERN RULERS

France

1270	Philippe III
1285	Philippe IV
1314	Louis X
1316	Jean I
1316	Philippe V
1322	Charles IV
1328	Philippe VI
1350	Jean II
1364	Charles V
1380	Charles VI
1422	Charles VII
1461–83	Louis XI

England

1272	Edward I
1307	Edward II
1327	Edward III
1377	Richard II
1399	Henry IV
1413	Henry V
1422	Henry VI
1461	Edward IV
1483	Edward V
1483	Richard III
1485–1509	Henry VII

Doges of Venice

1289	Pietro Gradenigo
1311	Giorgio Marino
1312	Giovanni Soranzo
1329	Francesco Dandolo
1339	Bartolomeo Gradenigo
1343	Andrea Dandolo
1354	Marino Faliero
1355	Giovanni Gradenigo
1356	Giovanni Delfino
1361	Lorenzo Celsi
1365	Marco Cornaro
1368	Andrea Contarini
1382	Michele Morosini
1382	Antonio Venier
1400	Michel Steno
1414	Thomaso Mocenigo
1423	Francesco Foscari
1457	Pasquale Malpiero
1462	Cristoforo Moro
1472	Niccolò Tron
1473	Niccolò Marcello
1474	Pietro Mocenigo
1476	Andrea Vendramin
1478	Giovanni Mocenigo
1485	Marco Barbarigo
1486–1501	Agostino Barbarigo

[1] Little is known with any certainty on the Melkite succession. This list is drawn from *L'Art de vérifier les dates* and Kidd's *Churches of Eastern Christendom*.

Doges of Genoa

1339	Simone Boccanera
1344	Giovanni di Murta
1350	Giovanni da Valente
(1353–6	Milanese Domination)
1363	Gabriele Adorno
1370	Domenico da Campofregoso
1378	Niccolò Guarco
1383	Leonardo Montaldo
1384	Antoniotto Adorno
1390	Giacomo Campofregoso
1392	Antonio Montaldo
1393	Francesco Guistiniano
1394	Niccolò Zoaglio
1396	Antoniotto Adorno
(1396–1409	French Domination)
(1409–13	Domination of Montferrat)
1413–15	Giorgio Adorno
1415	Bernabò de Goanno
1413–21	Tommaso da Campofregoso
(1421–36	Milanese Domination)
1436	Isandro da Guarco
1436–42	Tommaso da Campofregoso
1443	Raffaele Adorno
1447	Bernabò Adorno
1447	Giano da Campofregoso
1448	Luigi da Campofregoso
1450	Pietro da Campofregoso
(1458–60 and 1515–22	French Domination)

Dukes of Burgundy

1363	Philippe le Hardi
1404	Jean Sans Peur
1419	Philippe le Bon
1467–77	Charles le Téméraire

IV. THE LATIN EAST

Cyprus (Lusignans)

1285	Henri II
(1306–9	Amaury of Tyre)
1309	Henri II
1324	Hugues IV
1359	Pierre I
1369	Pierre II
1382	Jacques I
1398	Janus
1432	Jean II
1458	Charlotte de Lusignan and Louis de Savoie
1460	Jacques II
1473	Jacques III de Lusignan and Catherine Cornaro, his mother
1474–89	Catherine Cornaro, alone
(1489–1570	Venetian Domination)

Armenia

1196–1219	Leo I
(1219–52	Isabel)
1222–5	Philip
1226–70	Hethoum I

1270–89	Leo II	1305	Foulques de Villaret
1289–97	Hethoum II	1319	Hélion de Villeneuve
1293–5	Thoros	1346–53	Dieudonné de Gozon
1296–8	Sempad	1354	Pierre de Cornillon
1298–9	Constantin I	1355	Roger de Pins
1301–7	Leo III	1365	Raymond Berenger
1308–20	Ochin	1374	Robert de Juillac
1320–42	Leo IV	1377	Jean Fernandes
1342–4	Guy or Con-		d'Hérédia
	stantin II	1396	Philibert de Naillac
1344–63	Constantin III	1421	Antoine Fluvian
(1363–5	Leo the Usurper)	1437	Jean de Lastic
1365–73	Constantin IV	1454	Jacques de Milli
(1373–4	Mariam)	1461	Pierre-Raymond
1374–5	Leo V (ob. s.p.,		Zacosta
	Paris 1393)	1467	Jean-Baptiste des
			Ursins

Rhodes (Grand Masters of
the Hospital)

		1476	Pierre d'Aubusson
		1503	Emeri d'Amboise
1285–93	Jean de Villiers	1512	Gui de Blanchefort
1294	Eudes des Pins	1513	Fabrice Caretto
1296–1304	Guillaume de Vill-	1521–34	Philippe Villiers de
	aret		l'Isle-Adam

V. MUSLIM MONARCHIES
Egypt (Mamlūks)

1290	al-Ashraf Ṣalaḥ-al-Dīn Khalīl (9th of the Baḥrī Mamlūk line)
1293	al-Nāṣir Nāṣir-al-Dīn Muḥammad (1)
1294	al-ʿĀdil Zayn-al-Dīn Qitbugha
1296	al-Manṣūr Ḥusām-al-Dīn Lājīn al-Manṣūri
1298	al-Nāṣir Nāṣir-al-Dīn Muḥammad (2)
1308	al-Muẓaffar Rukn-al-Dīn Baibars II al-Jashankīr
1309	al-Nāṣir Nāṣir-al-Dīn Muḥammad (3)
1340	al-Manṣūr Sayf-al-Dīn Abu-Bakr
1341	al-Ashraf ʿAlāʾ-al-Dīn Qujuq
1342	al-Nāṣir Shibāb-al-Dīn Aḥmad
1342	al-Ṣāliḥ ʿImād-al-Dīn Ismāʿīl
1345	al-Kāmil Sayf-al-Dīn Shaʿbān
1346	al-Muẓaffar Sayf-al-Dīn Hajjī
1347	al-Nāṣir Nāṣir-al-Dīnal-Ḥassan (1)
1351	al-Ṣāliḥ Ṣalāḥ-al-Dīn Ṣāliḥ
1354	al-Nāṣir Nāṣir-al-Dīn Ḥassan (2)
1361	al-Manṣūr Ṣalāḥ-al-Dīn Muḥammad

1363	al-Ashraf Nāṣir-al-Dīn Shaʻbān
1376	al-Manṣūr ʻAlā'-al-Dīn ʻAlī
1381	al-Ṣāliḥ Ṣalāḥ-al-Dīn Hajjī (1)
1382	al-Ẓāhir Sayf-al-Dīn Barqūq (beginning of the Burji Mamlūk line, *vide infra*)
1389	al-Ṣāliḥ Ṣalāḥ-al-Dīn Hajjī (2)—with title al-Muẓaffar (temporary return of the Baḥrī line)
1390	al-Ẓāhir Sayf-al-Dīn Barqūq
1398	al-Nāṣir Nāṣir-al-Dīn Faraj (1)
1405	al-Manṣūr ʻImād-al-Dīn ʻAbd-al-Azīz
1406	al-Nāṣir Nāṣir-al-Dīn Faraj (2)
1412	al-ʻĀdil al-Muʻtaṣim (Abbasid Caliph)
1412	al-Mu'ayyad Sayf-al-Dīn Shaikh
1421	al-Muẓaffar Aḥmad
1421	al-Ẓāhir Sayf-al-Dīn Ṭaṭar
1421	al-Ṣāliḥ Nāṣir-al-Dīn Muḥammad
1422	al-Ashraf Sayf-al-Dīn Bursbay
1438	al-ʻAzīz Jamāl-al-Dīn Yūsuf
1438	al-Ẓāhir Sayf-al-Dīn Jaqmaq
1453	al-Manṣūr Fakhr-al-Dīn ʻOthmān
1453	al-Ashraf Sayf-al-Dīn 'Ināl
1460	al-Mu'ayyad Shibāb-al-Dīn Aḥmad
1461	al-Ẓāhir Sayf-al-Dīn Khushqadam
1467	al-Ẓāhir Sayf-al-Dīn Bilbay
1468	al-Ẓāhir Timūrbugha
1468	al-Ashraf Sayf-al-Dīn Qāitbay
1496	al-Nāṣir Muḥammad
1498	al-Ẓāhir Qanṣūh
1499	al-Ashraf Jānbalāṭ
1500	al-ʻĀdil Sayf-al-Dīn Ṭumānbāy
1501	al-Ashraf Qanṣūh al-Ghaūrī
1516–17	al-Ashraf Ṭumānbāy

Turkey (Ottomans)

1299	Othman I
1326	Orkhan
1360	Murad I
1389	Bayezid I
1402	Muhammad I
1421	Murad II
1451	Muhammad II (the Conqueror)
1481	Bayezid II
1512	Selim I
1520–66	Sulaiman I (the Magnificent)

BIBLIOGRAPHY

THE wide scope of this study necessarily makes the present bibliography both lengthy and intricate; for the history of the Crusade in the Later Middle Ages extends beyond Europe and the Levant to the Far East. An original list of nearly 2,000 entries has been considerably reduced for reasons of space. Works of a purely general nature and minor articles and tracts on secondary points which have been consulted in the course of my researches have, broadly speaking, been omitted, and for particulars of these, the reader may be referred to the footnotes. Moreover, books in my bibliography of the *Crusade of Nicopolis* (London, 1934) have been left out except in cases where certain studies covered a wider field than that crusade. The strict rule of economy, however, has not been rigidly observed in regard to the primary sources, eastern and western, manuscript and printed. The need for some critical remarks on the intrinsic value of each source is felt; but, on the other hand, it is to be noted that this aspect is treated with fullness in the text and footnotes of the chapters. To reduce the complexity of the bibliography, we have classified it in the following manner:

I. *Manuscripts.*

    (*a*) Western.
    (*b*) Oriental—arranged alphabetically and not according to their provenance, under the sub-headings:
        I.   Official.
        II. Encyclopedic works.
        III. Chronicles.
        IV. Art of War.
        V. Miscellaneous: Geography and Travel, Pilgrimage and Counter-propaganda, &c.
        These were mainly drawn from the libraries and archives of London, Oxford, Cambridge, Manchester, Paris, Leiden, Berlin, Gotha, Vienna, Rome, Madrid, the Escorial, Barcelona, Cairo and Algiers.

II. Official Sources in Print [1]

    (*a*) Western.
    (*b*) Oriental.

III. Literary Sources of the West in Print

    (*a*) Propaganda, Missionary, Pilgrimage and Travel. (Especially relating to Pt. I of the book.)
    (*b*) France.
    (*c*) England.
    (*d*) Italy.
    (*e*) Central and Eastern Europe.
    (*f*) Byzantine and Balkan States.
    (*g*) Miscellaneous: Spain, Cyprus, Rhodes, Armenia and Western Jews.

IV. Literary Sources of the East in Print

V. Secondary Authorities

    (*a*) Monographs and special Works on or relating to the Later Crusades.
    (*b*) Miscellaneous Works of Reference.

The following abbreviations have been used for works frequently quoted in the footnotes:

AOL	. .	Archives de l'Orient Latin
AM.	. .	Archivio Muratoriano
AS	. . .	Acta Sanctorum
ASI.	. .	Archivio Storica Italiano
BGAL .	.	Brockelmann, Gesch. d. Arabischen Literatur
BM.	. .	British Museum
BN .	. .	Bibliothèque Nationale
CSBH .	.	Corpus Script. Byz. Hist.
DNB	. .	Dictionary of National Biography
EI .	. .	Encyclopedia of Islam
JA .	. .	Journal Asiatique
JRAS	. .	Journal of the Royal Asiatic Society
MPG .	.	Migne, Patrologia Graeca
MPL	.	Migne, Patrologia Latina
Nicopolis	.	Atiya, Crusade of Nicopolis
PRO	. .	Public Record Office

[1] The titles of sub-sections are at times inevitably somewhat arbitrary; and we are aware, for instance, that the placing of some of the works listed under 'Official' is open to criticism.

Rieu. . . Supplementary Catalogue of the Arabic MSS. in the
British Museum
RIS . . . Rerum Italicarum Scriptores (Muratori)
ROC . . Revue de l'Orient Chrétien
ROL . . Revue de l'Orient Latin
RS . . . Rolls Series
WGA . . Wüstenfeld, Geschichtschreiber d. Araber
ZDPV . . Zeitschrift der deutschen Palaestina-Vereins

I. MANUSCRIPTS

(a) WESTERN

London: British Museum
Une poure et simple epistre dun vieil solitaire des Célestins de
Paris (Philippe de Mézières) adressant à . . . Richart par la
grace de Dieu Roy d'Angleterre, &c. No. 20, B. VI.

London: Public Record Office
Account by Henry of Godard of a journey to Paris and the
Emperor of Constantinople. No. E. 101–320–17.

Oxford: Bodleian Library
Nova religio passionis (*vide Nicopolis*, 136–8), Nos. 813 and 865.
Via ad Terram Sanctam. No. Ashmol. 342

Brussels: Bibl. Royale
Traités de paix. No. Roy. 7381

Paris: Bibl. Nat.
Mémoires du voiage fait en Hongrie par Iean dit Sans Peur, Conte
de Neuers &c. . . . Par Prosper Bauyn. (*vide Nicopolis*,
141–3.) Coll. de Bourg., 20, Rois et ducs, ff. 339–66.
Le Songe du Vieil Pélerin (Philippe de Mézières). Fonds
fr. 22542.
Histoire des comtes de la Marche et d'Angoulesme, roys de Chypre,
de Hierusalem et d'Armenie, du nom de Lezignan et
d'Antioche. . . . Par Pierre Gaucher, dit Scevole de Sainte-
Marthe, escuyer &c. Fonds fr. 24211.

Paris: Bibl. de l'Arsenal
Diplomatic letters of Philippe de Mézières. No. 499 D.

Paris: Bibl. Mazarine
Noua religio miliciae passionis ihesu christi pro acquisicione sancta
ciuitatis iherusalem et terre sancte. (*Vide* Molinier, Deux
MSS., in AOL, I, 351 et seq.) No. 1943.
Oratio Tragedica. No. 1651.

Dijon: Archives Communales. Chambre de ville
Série B. 140. Délibérations, 1397 à 1398.
Série B. 140. Registres, 1397 à 1398.
Administration générale. Pièces politiques. Trésor des chartes.
A. 12. Liasse l^{re}. Côte 23.

Dijon: Archives de la Côte d'Or
Ordonnance de Philippe le Hardi. Côte B. 11876. (*Vide*
Nicopolis, 144–48.)

Venice: Archivio di Stato
Liber este continet omnes Partes Secretas captas in Consilio
Rogatorum &c.
Deliberationes mixtae secretas. Indices et Regesti. (Misti.).
I Libri Commemoriali della Repubblica di Venezia. Regesti 9
Tomes. (Cf. Thomas, G. M., and G. L. P. Tafel:
Urkunden zurältern Handels etc.; also Thomas and R.
Pridelli, Diplomatarium Veneto-Levantinum etc., Pts. 1
and 11 to 1454. In—Monumenti Storici pubblicati della
R. Deputazione Veneta di Storia Patria, Serie Prima, Docu-
menti, vols. VIII and IX. Venice, 1880–90.)
Liber Albus. (Treaties, privileges, &c., with the Levant powers
to 1348.)

Genoa: Archivio di Stato
Diversorum Filze.
Diversorum Registri.
Materie Politiche.
Magistrorum rationalium introitus et exitus.

Turin: Archivio di Stato
Viaggio di Levante. Mazzo 1, nos. 1–12; Mazzo II, nos. 1–2.

Turin: Archivio Camerale
Accounts of the Treasurers of Savoy: Pietro Gervasio and
Antonio Barberio, 1360–70.

Munich: Staatsbibliothek
Tracts and Petitions by Ramon Lull. Lat. 10565.

(*b*) ORIENTAL

I. Official

Copy of Letter from the Muslims of Spain to Bayezid II (A.H. 886–
918) describing their sad lot after the Christian conquest of
the Kingdom of Granada. Algiers MS. no. 1620. Fagnan,
p. 450. 'Inān (Miṣr al-Islāmiya), pp. 134 et seq., refers to
petitions of this nature submitted to the Sultan of Egypt.

Documentos Arabes del Archivio de la Corona de Aragòn in Barcelona:

A.—1. Seccion.—Documentos pertenecientes al reyno de Granada. Caja 1, nos. 1–76
2. Seccion.—Cartas marroquies. Caja 2, nos. 77–114
3. Seccion.—Documentos de la Ifriquia o sea de Bugia, Tunez y Tripoli. Caja 3, nos. 115–44.
4. Seccion.—Cartas Orientales. Caja 4, 5, y 4 rollos; nos. 145–55.
5. Seccion.—Cartas Valencianes. Caja 3, nos. 156–60.

B.— Series of documents transcribed by Don Manuel de Bofarull and preserved in the same Archives.

C.— Carta árabe en Papel. Nos. (?) worn out. Consist of four large rolls of parchment, bearing four letters from the Sultans of Egypt to the Kings of Aragon, dated in the years A.H. 699, 703, 705 and 714.

II. Encyclopedias

al-Nuwairī, Abul-'Abbās A. b. 'Abd-al-Wahhāb b. A. Shihāb-al-Dīn . . . al-Bakrī al-Taīmī al-Kindī al-Shāfi'ī; (ob. A.H. 732/A.D. 1332): Nihāyat al-Arab fī funūn al-Adab. Vatican MS. no. 741. (BGAL, II, 139–40; WGA, no. 399.)

al-'Umari, Shihāb-al-Dīn Abu'l-'Abbās A. b. Yaḥya b. Faḍlallah . . . al-Qurashī al-Shāfi'i; (ob. A.H. 748/A.D. 1348, year of the Black Death):—Masālik al-Abṣār fī Mamālik al-Amṣār. (Part trans Fr. by Gaudefroy-Demombynes, *L'Afrique moins l'Égypte*, Paris, 1927.) Cairo MS., Encyc. 556, 557 and 8M, including photographs of the Aya-Sofia MS. in 43 vols. (BGAL, II, 141, WGA, no. 411.)

III. Chronicles

al-'Ainī, Abu Maḥmūd b. A. b. Mūsa b. A. b. Ḥussain b. Yūsuf Badr-al-Dīn . . . al-Ḥanafī; (ob. A.H. 855/A.D. 1451): 'Iqd al-Jumān fī Tārikh Ahl al-Zamān. Paris, B.N. MS. fonds ar. 1544. (BGAL, II, 52–3; WGA, no. 489.)

Ibid.—Tārikh al-Badr fī Awṣāf Ahl al-'Aṣr. Large History in 10 volumes of which the following are known to exist: 1.—Vol. covering years A.H. 149–99; Upsala, 254. 2.—Vol. covering years 717–98; B.M., 935. (BGAL and WGA, l.c.)

Anonymous.—Kitāb Tawārikh al-Miṣr (*sic*) wal-Ḥalab (*sic*) wal-Quds wa-Baghdād wal-Yaman wa-Sā'ir Bilād al-'Ibād. Camb. MS., Dd. 5, 11. (Browne, Hand-List, 52.)

Anonymous.—History of the Mamlūk Sultan al-Malik al-Nāṣir, son of Qalāwūn. Paris MS., B.N., fonds ar. 1705. (De Slane, 317.)

Baibars, al-Amīr Rukn-al-Dīn . . . al-Dawadār al-Nāṣirī al-Manṣūrī al-Miṣrī; (ob. A.H. 725/A.D. 1325): al-Tuḥfa al-Mulūkiya fī al-Dawla al-Turkiya. Vienna MS., Mixt. 665. (BGAL, II, 44; WGA, 390.)

al-Basṭāmī, 'Abd-al-Raḥmān b. M. b. 'Ali b. A. . . .: Tawḍiḥ Manāhij al-Anwār wa-Taftīḥ Mabāhij al-Azhār. B.M. MS., Or. 4306. (Rieu, no. 481, pp. 289–90.)

al-Ba'ūnī, Abu 'Abdallah M. b. Shihāb-al-Dīn Abul-'Abbās A. . . . al-Shāfi'ī al-Dimashqī; (ob. A.H. 871/A.D. 1465): Urjūzat al-Khulafā' wal-Salāṭīn 'Umarā' al-Mu'minīn. B.M. MS., Or. 1550. (Rieu, no. 487 II; BGAL, II, 41.)

Boḥtor, Ṣāliḥ b. Yaḥya (ob. A.H. 845/A.D. 1442): Tārīkh Beirūt. B.N. MS. 1760. (De Slane, 312; BGAL, II, 38–9; WGA, 482)

al-Dhahabī, Shams-al-Dīn M. b. A. b. 'Uthmān b. Qaīmāz b. 'Abdallah . . . al-Turkumānī al-Fāriqī al-Shāfi'ī; (ob. A.H. 748/A.D. 1348): (a) Tārīkh al-Islām. B.M. MS., Or. 1540 and 1558. (BGAL, II, 46 et seq.; WGA, 410.) Oxford MS., Laud. 279.

(b) Kitāb al-'Ibar fi al-Tawārīkh. B.M. MS., Or. 6428. Oxford MS., Digby Or. 15. (BGAL and WGA, l.c.)

ibn Duqmāq, Ibrāhīm b. M. . . . Ṣārim-al-Dīn al-Miṣrī al-Ḥanafī; (ob. A.H. 809/A.D. 1406): (a) al-Jawhar al-Thamīn fī Tārīkh al-Khulafā' wal-Salāṭīn. Oxford MSS., Digby Or. 28, and Pocock, 352. (BGAL, II, 50; WGA, 457.)

(b) Nuzhat al-Anām fī Tārīkh al-Islām. Paris MS. 1597; and Gotha MSS., 1570–2. (BGAL and WGA, l.c.)

'Imād-al-Dīn, al-Mālik al-Mu'ayyad. . . . Isma'īl b. 'Alī b. M. b. 'Umar b. Shāhinshāh b. Ayyūb al-Ayyūbī of Ḥamāh (ob. A.H. 732/A.D.1321): al-Tibr al-Masbūk fī Tawārīkh Akābir al-Mulūk. Cairo MS., Hist. 68 M II. (Cairo Cat., V, 121.)

al-Fāsī, Taqī-al-Dīn M. b. M. 'Alī al-Hussainī . . . al-Makkī al-Mālikī: al-Muqni' fī Akhbar al-Mulūk wal-Khulafā' wa-Wulūt Makka al-Shurafā'. John Ryland MS., Ar. 80.

Ibn al-Furāt, Nāṣir-al-Dīn b. 'Abd-al-Raḥmān b. 'Alī A. b. M. b. 'Abd-al-'Azīz M. al-Miṣrī, known as . . .; (ob. A.H. 807/A.D. 1405): Tārīkh al-Duwal wal-Malūk. Vienna MSS., A.F. 117–25. (BGAL, II, 50; WGA, 454.)

Ibn Ḥabīb, Shihāb-al-Dīn . . . al-Ḥalabī al-Shāfi'ī; (ob. A.H. 779/A.D. 1377): (a) Third vol. of Durrat al-Aslāk fī Dawlat al-

Atrāk. Oxford MS., Marsh. 319. (BGAL, II, 36–7; WGA, 440.)

(b) Juhainat al-Akhbār fī Dhikr Mulūk al-Amṣār, known as al-Musajjaʿ. Vatican MS., Ar. 277. (BGAL and WGA, l.c.)

Ibn Ḥajar, Shihāb-al-Dīn A. b. ʿAli . . . al-ʿAsqalānī; (ob. A.H. 852/A.D. 1449): Inbā' al-Ghumr bi-Abnā' al-ʿUmr. B.M. MS., Bibl. Rich. 7321. (BGAL, II, 67–70; WGA, 487.)

al-Jaʿfarī, Nāṣir-al-Dīn b. M. b. M. b. M. b. al-Ḥasan . . . al-Shāfiʿī; (ob. after A.D. 1494): al-Sālik wal-Maslūk ila Tārīkh al-Khulafā' wal-Salāṭīn wal-Mulūk. Paris MS., fonds ar. 1607. (De Slane, p. 302; BGAL, II, 53–4.)

al-Jazarī, M. b. . . .; (ob. c. A.D. 1429): Dhāt al-Shifā' fī Sīrat al-Nabī wal-Khulafā'. B.M. MS., Or. 2433. Vide Rieu, no. 516, pp. 317–18.

al-Karamānī, A. b. Yūsuf b. A. . . .: Kitāb al-Duwal wa-Akhbār 'Āthār al-'Uwal. Madrid MS. 5153.

Ibn Kathīr, Abulfidā Ismāʿīl . . . al-Baṣrawī al-Shāfiʿī; (ob. A.H. 774/A.D. 1373): Tārīkh al-Bidāya wal-Nihāya. Oxford MS., Marsh. 676. (BGAL, II, 49; WGA, 434.)

al-Maqrīzī, Taqī-al-Dīn &c.; (ob. 1442): (a) Kitāb al-Sulūk li-Ma'rifat Duwal al-Mulūk. Vol. I Camb. MS., Qq. 276. Vol. II B.M. MS., Or. 9542. Vol. III Oxford MS., Marsh. 260. Vol. IV B.M. MS., Or. 2902 and Gotha MS. A 1620. (BGAL, II, 38–41; WGA, 482.)

(b) al-Durar al-Mudī'a fi Tārīkh al-Duwal al-Islāmiya. Camb. MS., Qq. 2. (Browne, Hand-List, 71.)

Al-Nuwairi, M. b. Qāsim b. M. . . . al-Iskandarānī (ob. after A.H. 775/A.D. 1373). Al-Ilmām bil-I'lām fī mā jarat bihi al-Aḥkām wal-'Umūr al-Maqdīya fī Waq't al-Iskandariya. Vol. I (in 2 pts.), Berlin MSS. We. 359–60, and vol. II, Cairo MS., Hist. 1449. (Held anon. by Ahlwardt, 9815 and BGAL, II, 35–6. Vide supra, Cap. XV notes.)

Ibn Qāḍī Shuhba, Abu Bakr b. A. b. M. b. ʿUmar Taqī-al-Dīn . . . al-Asadī al-Dimashqī al-Shāfiʿī; (ob. A.H. 851/A.D. 1448): al-I'lām bi-Tārīkh al-Islām; and Mukhtaṣar al-'Ibar, (Abridgement and continuation of al-Dhahabī, vide supra). Paris MSS. 1598–1600; Oxford MS. Marsh. 143. (BGAL, II, 51; WGA, 486.)

al-Ṣafadī, AbuʿAlī al-Ḥasan b. Abī M. 'Abdallah al-'Abbāsī al-Hāshimī known as . . . ; (ob. after A.H. 711/A.D. 1311): Nuzhat al-Mālik wal-Mamlūk fi Mukhtaṣar Sīrat man waliya Miṣr min al-Mulūk. Paris, B.N. MS., fonds ar. 1706. (De Slane, 317; BGAL, II, 35.)

al-Salāmī, Shihāb-al-Dīn A.: Mukhtaṣar al-Tawārīkh (to A.H. 806/A.D. 1403–4). Cairo MS. Hist. 1435.

Ibn Shākir, M. . . . b. A. b. ʿAbd-al-Raḥmān Ṣalāḥ-al-Dīn al-Ḥalabī al-Dārātī al-Dimashqī al-Kutubī; (ob. A.H. 764/A.D. 1363): ʿUyūn al-Tawārīkh (Gotha, 1567; Paris, 1586–8; B.M. Supplt., 472; Lee, 72; Vatican, Bibl. It., XLVI, 32). (BGAL, II, 48; WGA, 422.)

IV. Art of War

al-Aḥdab. Description of the technique of 72 lance manoeuvres according to the military system of Najm-al-Dīn Ḥassan al-Rammāḥ al-Aḥdab. (Without title page.) Paris MS., B.N., fonds ar. 2827, ff. 1 vo–13 vo. (Vide De Slane, p. 509.)

Anonymous. Kitāb al-Furūsiya wal-Jihād. Oxford MS., Hunt. 76. (Vide Uri, I, 101.)

Anonymous. Kitāb al-Furūsiya. Paris MS., B.N., fonds ar. 2829. (De Slane, pp. 509–10.)

Anonymous. Treaties on military pyrotechnics including prescriptions for the manufacture of inflammable materials for use as missiles. (Without title page.) Paris MS., B.N., fonds ar. 2827, ff 26 ro–51 vo. (De Slane, p. 509.)

Baktūt, Badr-al-Dīn . . . al-Ram nāḥ al-Malikī al-Ẓāhirī (ob. A.H. 711/A.D. 1311): (a) Nihāyat al-Suʾl wal-Umniya fī Taʿlīm al-Furūsiya. B.M. MS., Or. 3631 I. (Vide Rieu, no. 820, pp. 555–6.)

    (b) Manual of the equestrian art, the manipulation of weapons on horseback, and the veterinary treatment of horses. B.M. MS., Or. 3631 II. (Rieu, l. c. BGAL, II, 135.)

al-Khwārizmi, Rukn-al-Dīn Jamshār . . .: Treatise on archery. (Without title page.) B.M. MS., Or. 3631 III. (Rieu, no. 820, pp. 555–6.)

Ibn Minkalī, al-Qizz M. . . . (c. A.H. 778/A.D. 1376): (a) Uns al-Malā bi-Waḥsh al-Falā. Paris MS., B.N., fonds ar. 2832. (De Slane, p. 773; BGAL, II, 136.)

    (b) al-Tadbīrāt al-Sulṭāniya fī Siāsat al-Ṣināʿa al-Ḥarbīya. B.M. MS., Or. 3734. (Rieu, no. 822, pp. 557–8.)

al-Ṭarābulsī, M. b. Lājīn al-Ḥusāmī, known as . . .; (circa A.H. 780/A.D. 1379): (a) Tuḥfat al-Mujāhidīn fī al-ʿAmal bil-Mayādīn. Oxford MS., Hunt. 76/11. (Uri, I, 101; BGAL, II, 136.)

    (b) Ghāyat al-Maqṣūd fī al-ʿAmal wal-ʿIlm bil-Bunūd. Paris MS., B.N., fonds ar. 2827, ff 14–26 ro. Leiden 1418. (De Slane, 509; De Jong and de Goeje, III, 297; BGAL, II, 135.)

al-Yūnānī, Taibugha al-Ashrafī al-Baqlamīshī . . . (c. A.H. 770/A.D. 1368): Ghunyat al-Ṭullāb fī Maʿrifat al-Ramy (wal-Nishāb). Camb. MSS. Qq. 176 and Qq. 240. (Rieu, no. 821; Browne, 127–8; BGAL, II, 135–6.)

V. Miscellaneous: Geography and Travel, Pilgrimage and Counter-Propaganda, &c.

Anonymous. Awrāq Jumiʿat fīha faḍāʾil Miṣr. Camb. MS., Qq. 91.[1] (Browne, Hand-list, p. 135.)

Anonymous. Kitāb Faḍāʾil Bait al-Maqdis wafīh Kitāb Faḍāʾil al-Shām. Camb. MS., Qq. 91[2]. (Signed 1 Rajab, A.H. 765; *vide* f. 139 vo.)

al-Badrī, Abul-Tuqā (or Baqā) Abu-Bakr b. ʿAbdallah b. M. . . . al-Dimashqī al-Shāfiʿi; (*circa* A.H. 887/A.D. 1482)—Nuzhat al-Anām fī Maḥāsin al-Shām. John Ryland MS., Ar. 107. (cf. B.M. MS., Or. 1559; BGAL, II, 132.)

al-Fazarī, Ibn al-Firkāh (?) (ob. A.H. 729/A.D. 1329): Faḍāʾil al-Shām. Camb. MS., 3236. (Browne, 134; BGAL, II, 130; WGA, 394.)

al-Herawī, Abul-Ḥasan ʿAli b. Abu-Bakr . . . (ob. A.H. 611/A.D. 1214): Kitāb al-Ishārat fī Maʿrifat al-Ziārat. John Ryland MS., Ar. 69.

Ibn Abi-Ḥajla, Shihāb-Dīn A. b. Yaḥyā b. Abi-Bakr ʿAbd-al-Wāḥid al-Talmasānī, known as . . . (ob. A.H. 776/A.D. 1375): Sukar-dān al-Sulṭān. John Ryland MSS., Ar. 93/95. (BGAL, II, 12–13; WGA, 437.)

Ibn Kathīr (*vide supra*): al-Ijtihād fī Ṭalab al-Jihād. Cairo MS., Hist. 408.

al-Khazarjī, Muwaffaq-al-Dīn Abū M. ʿAbd-al-Raḥmān . . . al-Anṣārī (c. A.H. 780/A.D. 1378): (*a*) Murshid al-Zuwwār ila Qubūr al-Abrār fī Ziārat al-Muqaṭṭam. B.M. M.S., Or. 4635. (Rieu, 663; BGAL, II, 34.)

(*b*) al-Durr al-Munaẓẓam fī Ziārat al-Muqaṭṭam. B.M. MS., Or. 3049. (Rieu, no. 668, pp. 448–9.)

al-Maqdisī, Shihāb-al-Dīn Abū Maḥmūd b. M. b. Ibrāhīm b. Hilāl b. Tamīm b. Surūr al-Shāfiʿī (ob. A.H. 765/A.D. 1364): Muthīr al-Gharām fī Ziārat al-Quds wal-Shām. Paris MS., B.N., fonds ar. 1667, ff. 3 ro.–119 vo. (BGAL, II, 130–1; WGA, 425.)

al-Tadmurī, Abulfidā Isḥāq b. Ibrāhīm b. A. b. M. b. Kāmil . . . al-Shāfiʿī (ob. A.H. 833/A.D. 1429): Muthīr al-Gharām li-Ziyārat al-Khalī &c. Paris MS., B.N., fonds ar. 1667, ff. 120 ro.–188 vo. (De Slane, 311, BGAL, II, 131.)

Ibn. al-Zayyāt, Naṣr-al-Dīn M. b. Jalāl-al-Dīn ʿAbdallah b. Abi-

Ḥafṣ Sirāj-al-Dīn ʿUmar al-Anṣārī al-ʿAbbāsī al-Suʾūdī . . .;
(circa A.H. 804/A.D. 1401): al-Kawākib al-Sayyāra fī Tartīb al-
Ziāra fī al-Qarāfatain al-Kubrā wal-Ṣughrā. Cairo MS., V,
119. (BGAL, II, 131.)

II. OFFICIAL SOURCES IN PRINT

(a) WESTERN

Aeneas Sylvius Piccolomini (Pope Pius II). *Opera omnia.* Bâle,
  various editions and dates.
Amari, M. *Trattato stipulato Giacomo II d'Aragona col Sultano
  d'Egitto il 29 gen.* 1293. In *Atti academici dei Lincei*, 3rd
  series, Vol. XI. Memorie; 1882–3.
Bliss, W. H., and J. A. Twemlow (ed.). *Calendar of Entries in the
  Papal Registers relating to Great Britain and Ireland.* Papal
  Letters. Vol. IV (1362–96). London, 1902.
Boutaric, E. *Notices et extraits des documents inédits relatifs à
  l'histoire de France sous Philippe le Bel.* In *Notices et extraits des
  MSS. de la Bibliothèque Impériale et autres bibliothèques*; T. XX,
  pp. 83–237. Paris, 1862.
Brown, R. (ed.). *Calendar of State Papers; Venetian* (1202–1607).
  London, 1864.
Chevalier, L'abbé C. Ulysse. *Documents historiques sur le Dauphiné.*
  Montbéliard and Lyons, 1874.
Cosneau, E. (ed.). *Les grandes traités de la Guerre de Cent Ans.*
  Paris, 1889.
Delaville Le Roulx, J. *La France en Orient au XIVe siècle.* Ex-
  péditions du maréchal Boucicaut. Vol. II, Pièces justificatives.
  In *Bibl. des Éc. fr. d'Athènes et de Rome*; fasc. 45. Paris, 1886.
Dominicans. *Monumenta Ordinis Fratrum praedicatorum historica.*
  10 vols. Rome, 1897–1901.
Douet d'Arcq, L. *Choix de pièces inédites relatives au règne de
  Charles VI, publiées pour la Société de l'histoire de France.*
  2 vols. Paris, 1863–4.
Ducange, G. *Familles d'outre mer.* Ed. E. G. Rey in *Collection de
  documents inédits sur l'histoire de France.* Paris, 1869.
Durrieu, P. *Procès-verbal du martyre de quatre frères mineurs* (1391).
  AOL, I. Paris, 1881.
Ehrle, F. (ed.). *Zur Vorgeschichte des Conzils von Vienne.* In
  Archiv. für Lit. und Kirchengesch. des Mittelalters.
Eubel, C. *Hierarchia Catholica Medii Aevi.* 3 vols. Münster,
  1898–1910.
Finke, H. *Acta Aragonensia.* 3 vols. Berlin and Leipzig, 1908–22.

Gams, P. B. *Series episcoporum ecclesiae catholicae.* Ratisbon, 1873. Supplement, 1886.

Gauthier, L. *Les Lombards dans les Deux Bourgognes. Bibl. de l'École des hautes études;* fasc. 156. Paris, 1907.

Golubovich, G. *Biblioteca bio-bibliografica della Terra Santa e dell' Oriente francescano.* 5 vols. Florence, 1906–27.

Guérard, L'abbé Louis (ed.). *Documents pontificaux sur la Gascogne d'après les Archives du Vatican. Pontificat de Jean XXII* (1316–34). Textes publiés et annotés pour la Société historique de Gascogne. 2 vols. Paris, 1896–1903.

Hardy, Sir T. D. *Syllabus (in English) of the Documents, &c., in the Collection known as 'Rymer's Foedera'.* 2 vols. London, 1873.

Hingeston, F. C. (ed.). *Royal and Historical Letters during the Reign of Henry the Fourth.* Vol. 1 (1399–1404). In RS. London, 1860.

Huillard-Bréholles, M., and M. Lecoy de la Marche. *Titres de la Maison ducale de Bourbon.* 2 vols. In *Inventaires et documents publiés par la Direction générale des Archives Nationales.* Paris, 1867–74.

Iorga, N. *Notices et extraits pour servir à l'histoire des croisades au XVe siècle.* 6 séries. Paris and Bucharest, 1899–1916.

Jarry, E. *Les origines de la domination française à Gênes* (1392–1402). Documents diplomatiques. Paris, 1896.

Kohler, C. (ed.). *(a) Lettres pontificales concernant l'histoire de la Petite Arménie au XIVe siècle.* In *Florilegium ou Recueil de travaux d'érudition dédié à M. le marquis Melchior de Vogüé &c.* Paris, 1909.

   (b) Lettres des Papes à Guillaume d'Adam, archevêque de Sultanyeh. In ROL, X, 16 et seq.

Laborde, Le comte de. *Les ducs de Bourgogne. Études sur les lettres, les arts et l'industrie pendant le XVe siècle, et plus particulièrement dans le Pays-Bas et le duché de Bourgogne.* 3 tomes. Paris, 1849–52.

Lizérand. *Le dossier de l'affaire des Templiers.* In *Classiques de l'histoire de Fr.,* 1924.

Ljubić, S. (ed.). *Monumenta spectanta historiam Slavorum meridionalium.* Vol. IV (1358–1403). Agram, 1874.

Mas Latrie, M. de (ed.) *(a) Commerce et expéditions militaires de la France et de Venise au moyen âge. Collection de documents inédits sur l'histoire de France.* Mélanges historiques. Vol. III. Paris, 1835, &c.

   (b) Documents gênois concernant l'île de Chypre, in AOL II. Paris, 1884

   (c) Traités de paix et de :ommerce et documents divers con-

cernant les relations des chrétiens avec les arabes de l'Afrique septentrionale au moyen âge. Paris, 1866.

Miklosich, F. (ed.). *Monumenta Serbica spectanta historiam Serbiae, Bosnae, Ragusii.* Venice, 1858.

Mont, J. du (ed.). (*a*) *Corps universel diplomatique du droit des gens &c.* T. I–II. Amsterdam and The Hague, 1726.
(*b*) *Supplément au corps universel diplomatique du droit des gens.* Amsterdam, 1739.

Muller, G. *Documenti sulle relazioni delle città tuscane coll'Oriente cristiano e coi Turchi fine all'anno 1531.* Florence, 1879.

Petit, E. (*a*) *Itinéraires de Philippe le Hardi et de Jean sans Peur.* In *Coll. des documents inédits de l'hist. de Fr.* Paris, 1888.
(*b*) *Séjours de Charles VI* (1380–1400). In *Bull. du Comité des Travaux historiques et scientifiques, section d'histoire et de philologie.* Paris, 1887.

Plancher, Dom Urban. *Histoire générale (de Bourgogne) avec notes, des dissertations et les preuves justificatives composées sur les auteurs originaux, les registres, les cartulaires &c. &c.* 4 tomes. Dijon, 1739–81.

Reynaldus, Od. *Annales ecclesiastici.* Continuation of Baronius; several editions; last ed. 37 vols. Bar-le-Duc and Paris, 1864–83.

Röhricht, R. (ed.). (*a*) *Lettres de Ricoldo de Monte-Croce.* In AOL, T. II, pp. 258–96. Paris, 1884.
(*b*) *Annales de Terre Sainte.* In AOL, II, 427–61. Paris, 1884.
(*c*) *Regesta regni Hierosolymitani* (*MXCVII–MCCXCI*). Oeniponti, 1893.

Rymer's Foedera &c. Several editions; see Gross, *Sources and Literature of English History* (London, 1915), no. 2097.

Sathas, G. H. *Documents inédits relatifs à l'histoire de la Grèce au moyen âge* (1400–1500). 2 vols. Paris, 1880–1.

Secousse, — (ed.). *Ordonnances des rois de France de la troisième race.* 23 vols. Paris, 1745, &c.

Smith, Lucy T. (ed.). *Expeditions to Prussia and the Holy Land made by Henry, Earl of Derby (afterwards King Henry IV), in the years 1390–91 and 1392–93.* Camden Society Publications. London, 1894.

Tardif, J. *Inventaire et documents, publiés par l'ordre de l'empereur sous la direction de M. le marquis de Laborde.* Monuments historiques. Paris, 1866.

Theiner, A. (ed.). *Monumenta vetera historium Hungariae sacram illustrantia &c.* 2 vols. Rome, 1859–60.

Thomas, G. M., (a) and G. L. P. Tafel, *Urkunden zur ältern Handels, und Staatsgeschichte der Republik Venedig.* Vienna, 1856.

(b) and R. Predelli, *Diplomatarium Veneto-Levantinum sive acta et diplomata res Venetas, Graecas atque Levantinas.* Pts. I–II, to 1454. *Monumenti storici pubblicati dalla R. Deputazione Veneta di Storia Patria.* Seria prima. Documenti. Vols. VIII–IX. Venice, 1880–99.

Viard, J. *Documents parisiens du règne de Philippe VI de Valois* (1328–50). *Extraits des registres de la chancellerie de France.* T. I (1328–38), and T. II (1339–50). Paris, 1899–1900.

(b) ORIENTAL

Amari, M. (ed.). (a) *I Diplomi Arabi del R. Archivio Fiorentino.* Testo originale con traduzione e illustrazione. Florence, 1868.

(b) *Biblioteca Arabo-Sicula.* Leipzig, 1855.

Bonaparte, Prince Roland (ed.). *Documents de l'époque mongole des XIIIe et XIVe siècles.* Paris, 1896.

Faridün Bey. *Majmuaʿ-i-Munshāʾatu-s-Salatin.* (Correspondence of the Ottoman Sultans in Turkish.) 2 vols. Istanbul, A.H. 1264–5 (1867–9).

Hammer-Purgstall, J. von. *Les ordonnances égyptiennes sur les costumes des Chrétiens et des juifs, tirées de l'histoire de Nuweiri.* In *JA*, Série V, 1855, T. 5, pp. 393 et seq.

Kotwicz, Wladyslaw. *En marge des lettres des il-Khans de Perse retrouvées par Abel-Remusat.* Collectanea Orientalia, no. 4. Lwow, 1933.

Mas Latrie, L. *Traités de paix et de commerce &c.* (*Vide supra*, Section IIa).

Noradounghian, Gabriel Effendi (ed.). *Recueil d'actes internationaux de l'empire Ottoman.* 3 vols. (Vol. I, 1300–1789.) Paris, 1897–1903.

Sylvestre de Sacy. *Mémoire sur une correspondance inédite entre Tamerlan et le roi de France Charles VI.* Extrait du Moniteur, no. 226 (1812).

Testa, Le baron G. de; contd. by A. and L. de Testa (ed.). *Recueil des traités de la Porte Ottomane avec les puissances étrangères.* 11 vols. Paris, 1864–1911.

III. LITERARY SOURCES OF THE WEST IN PRINT

(a) PROPAGANDA, MISSIONARY, PILGRIMAGE AND TRAVEL

(Especially relating to Pt. I of the book [1])

Adam, Guillaume d'; dominicain, archevêque de Sultanyeh. *De modo Sarracenos extirpandi* (*circa* 1310). Ed. Kohler. *Documents arméniens des croisades*, II. See also, *Documents relatifs à Guill. d'Adam*, in ROL, T. X (1903–4), 16 et seq.

Aeneas Silvius (Pope Pius II). *Opera*. (For editions and list of works, see C. M. Ady, *Pius II*, London, 1913.)

Carmesson, J. *Vita S. Petri Thomae, patriarchae Constantinopolitani, legati apostolici, ex ordine B. Mariae Virginis*. Ed. Daniel de Sainte-Marie, in *Speculum Carmelitarum*, Antwerp, 1666.

Dubois, Pierre. (*a*) *De recuperatione Terre Sancte*. Ed. V. Langlois. In *Coll. de textes pour servir à l'étude et l'enseignement de l'histoire*. Paris, 1891. Cf. Anon. in Bongars, *Gesta Dei*, II.

  (*b*) *Oppinio cujusdam suadentis regi Francie ut regum Jerosolimitanum et Cipri pro altero filiorum suorum, ac de invasione regni Egipti*. Ibid., pp. 132 et seq.

Fidenzio di Padua. *Liber Recuperationis Terrae Sanctae*. In Golubovich, T. II, 9 et seq.

Germain, Jean. *Le Discours du voyage d'Oultremer au très victorieux roi Charles VII prononcé en* 1452. Ed. Ch. Schefer, in ROL (1895).

Golubovich, G. *Bibl. bio-bibliografica della Terra Santa*. (See Section II*a*.)

Koehler, H. (Ed.) *L'Église chrétienne du Maroc et la Mission Franciscaine*, 1221–1790. Paris, 1934.

Kohler, Ch. (Ed.) *Deux projets de croisade en Terre-Sainte composés à la fin du XIIIe siècle et au début du XIVe*; in ROL, T. X (1903–4), 406–57.

Levanto, Galvano de (Physician of Philippe le Bel, *circa* 1295). *De recuperatione Terrae Sanctae*. Ed. Kohler, in ROL, VI, 343 et seq.

Lull, Ramon. *Opera Omnia*. 8 vols. Ed. Ivo Salzinger; Mayence, 1721–37.

  Three dissertations on R. L. and a contemporary *Vita ab Anonymo* in AS, June, T. VII, 581–639; cf. E. Alison Peers,

---

[1] For Pilgrims and Travellers, see special Appendix and footnotes of respective chapters in Part I.

A Life of R. L. written by an unknown hand about 1311. London, 1927.

Mézières, Philippe de. (*a*) *Epistre lamentable et consolatoire*. Ed. Kervyn, in Froissart, XVI. Brussels, 1872.

(*b*) *Vita S. Petri Thomasii*, in AS, III, 605–11. Paris, 1863.

(*c*) *Une lettre apocryphe sur la bataille de Smyrne* (1346), in ROL, II (1895), 27–31.

(*d*) *Militia Passionis Jhesu Christi*; *Description de deux MSS.*, by A. Molinier, in AOL, I. Paris, 1881. (See also Western MSS. Full list of Mézières works may be found in Iorga's monograph.)

Molay, Jacques de, grand maître du Temple (Crusade memoir, *circa* 1307). *Baluze*, ed. Mollat, III, 145 et seq.; Delaville Le Roulx, *France en Orient*, II, 3–6.

Nogaret, Guillaume de. *Mémoire de . . . sur la possibilité d'une croisade*; in *Notes et extraits de documents inédits relatifs à l'histoire de France sous Philippe le Bel*; in *Notes et extraits des manuscrits de la Bibl. Impériale*, &c., T. XX (Paris, 1862), Pt. II, 199 et seq.

Pietro de Penna. *Libellus de Locis Ultramarinis*. Ed. Ch. Kohler, in ROL, T. IX (1902), nos. 3–4, pp. 313–83.

Piloti, Emanuele. *De modo, progressu ac diligenti providentia habendis in passagio Christianorum pro conquesta Terrae Sanctae tractatus.* Ed. Reiffenberg, in *Coll. des chroniques belges inédites, IV.* Brussels, 1846.

Sanudo, Marino . . . dictus Torsellus (Patricius Venetus). *Liber secretorum fidelium crucis super Terrae Sanctae recuperatione et conservatione.* In Bongars, *Gesta Dei per Francos*, T. II. Hanover, 1611. Eng. trans. of Pt. XIV, Bk. III, by A. Stewart, in Palestine Pilgrims' Text Society. London, 1896.

(*b*) *Epistolae*. In *Gesta Dei per Francos*, T. II. Hanover, 1611. Cf. Dorez and Roncière, in BEC, 1895, LXI, 34–44.

Thaddeo of Naples. *Hystoria de Desolacione et Conculcacione Civitatis Acconensis et Tocius Terre Sancte*, in A.D. MCCXCI. Ed. Comte Riant. Geneva, 1873.

Villaret, Foulques de, grand maître de l'Hôpital, *Mémoire*, ed. Petit, in BEC, 1889.

(*b*) FRANCE

Bacha, E. (ed.). *La chronique liègoise de* 1402. (Latin.) Commission royale d'histoire. Brussels, 1900.

Bel, Jean le. *Chronique* (1326–61). Ed. J. Viard and E. Déprèz. 2 vols. Paris, 1904–5. (Soc. Hist. Fr.)

Bellaguet, M. L. (ed.). *Chronique du Religieux de Saint-Denys, contenant le règne de Charles VI, de* 1380 *à* 1422. (Latin text and Fr. trans.) Coll. des doc. inéd. sur l'hist. de France. 4 vols. Paris, 1839–52.

Bonet, Honoré. (*a*) *L'arbre des batailles.* Lyons, 1477 and 1481. Anthoine Verard, Paris, 1483. Michel le Noir, Paris, 1505. Oliuier Arnoullet, Lyons, *sine anno.* An English version by Prof. G. W. Coopland of Liverpool University is in course of preparation.

(*b*) *L'apparicion de Jehan de Meun*; and *Somnium super materia scismatis.* Ed. Ivor Arnold, in Publications de la Faculté des lettres de l'Université de Strasbourg, fasc. 28. Paris, 1926.

Brandon, J. *Chronondrum.* Ed. Kervyn de Lettenhove, in *Chroniques relatives à l'hist. de Bourgogne*, T. I. Brussels, 1870.

Cabaret d'Orville, Jehan. *La chronique du bon duc Loys de Bourbon.* Ed. A. M. Chazaud. Paris, 1876.

Cuvelier. *Chronique de Bertrand du Guesclin.* Ed. E. Charrière, in *Coll. de doc. inéd. sur l'hist. de Fr.* 2 vols. Paris, 1839.

Deschamps, Eustache. *Oeuvres inédites d'.* Ed. P. Tarbé in 2 vols. Reims, 1849. Better ed. *Oeuvres complètes*, 11 vols., by le marquis de Queux de Saint-Hilaire; in publications of the Société des anciens textes français; Paris, 1878–1903.

Enguerrand de Monstrelet. *Chronique.* Ed. Douet d'Arcq. Vol. I. Paris, 1857. Eng. trans. Th. Johnes. London, 1867.

Froissart, Jean. *Chroniques.* Ed. (*a*) Kervyn de Lettenhove. 25 vols. Brussels, 1870–77.

(*b*) Luce, S., G. Raynaud, and L. Mirot. 12 vols. Paris, 1869, &c.

English translations:

(*a*) Bourchier, John, Lord Berners. 4 vols. London, 1523–5. New ed. G. G. Macaulay. London, 1899.

(*b*) Johnes, T. Numerous editions. Hafod ed. in 5 vols. 1805; and 12 vols. 1805–10. Bohn ed. in 2 vols. London, 1849.

Godefroy, T. (ed.). *Histoire de messire Jean de Boucicaut, maréchal de France, gouverneur de Gênes. Collections complètes des mémoires relatifs à l'histoire de France.* Other editions: Petitot; Michaud et Poujoulat; and Buchon. Paris, 1620, &c., and 1853, &c.

Gui de Blois, Un serviteur de. *Relation de la croisade de Nicopoli.* Ed. Kervyn de Lettenhove, in *Oeuvres de Froissart*, vols. XV and XVI. Brussels, 1871.

Joinville, Sire Jean de. *Histoire de Saint Louis*, ed. N. de Wailly, Paris, 1874. Eng. trans. Th. Johnes, Hafod Press, 1807.

Kervyn de Lettenhove (ed.). (*a*) *Le livre des trahisons de France envers la maison de Bourgogne. Chroniques relatives à l'hist. de la Belgique sous la domination des ducs de Bourgogne*, T. II. Paris, 1870, &c.

  (*b*) *La geste des ducs Philippe et Jehan de Bourgogne* (1393–1411). Same series, T. II.

  (*c*) *Res gestae ab MCCCLXXXIII ad annum MCCCCV.* Same series, T. III.

  (*d*) *Istore et chronique de Flandre. Collection de chroniques belges inédits*, T. II. Brussels, 1880.

Luce, S. (ed.). *Chronique des quatre premiers Valois* (1327–93). Paris, 1862. (Soc. Hist. Fr.)

Moranvillé, H. (ed.). *Chronographia regum Francorum* (1270–1380). 2 vols. Paris, 1891–3. (Soc. Hist. Fr.)

Nangis, Guillaume de. *Chronique latine de . . . de* 1113 *à* 1300. Ed. H. Géraud. Paris, 1843.

Nangis, Guillaume de. *Les continuateurs de . . . de* 1300 *à* 1368. 2 vols. Ed. H. Géraud, in *Soc. de l'hist. de Fr.* Paris, 1843.

Pisan, Christine de. *Le livre des fais et bonnes meurs du sage roy Charles.* In *Collection des mémoires pour servir à l'histoire de France, depuis le XIIIe siècle jusqu'a la fin du XVIIIe.* Ed. Michaud et Poujoulat. Vols. I and II. Paris, 1836, &c.

Smet, J. J. de (ed.). (*a*) *Chronicon Comitum Flandrenensium. Corpus chronicorum Flandriae*, T. I. Brussels, 1837, &c.

  (*b*) *Chronicon Flandriae inde a Liderico I° usque ad mortem Joannis ducis Burgundiae et comitis Flandriae, Anno MCCCXIX.* Same series, T. I.

  (*c*) *Chroniques des Pays Bas, de France, d'Angleterre, et de Tournai.* Same series, T. III.

Ursins, Jean Juvenal des; archevêque de Reims. *Histoire de Charles VI, roy de France, et des choses mémorables advenues durant quarante-deux années de son règne, depuis* 1380 *jusques à* 1422. In *Nouvelle collection des mémoires pour servir à l'histoire de France, depuis le XIIIe siècle jusqu'à la fin du XVIIIe.* Ed. Michaud et Poujoulat. Vol. II. Paris, 1836.

(*c*) ENGLAND

Anonimalle Chronicle. Ed. V. H. Galbraith. Manchester, 1927.

Chaucer, Geoffrey. *Works.* 7 vols. Ed. W. W. Skeat. Oxford, 1894–7.

Evesham, Monk of. *Historia Vitae et Regni Ricardi II Angliae Regis.* Ed. T. Hearne. Oxford, 1729.

Gower, John. Complete works. 4 vols. Ed. G. G. Macaulay. Oxford, 1899–1902.

Higden, Ranulph. *Polychronicon.* Ed. C. Babington and J. R. Lumley. 9 vols. In RS. London, 1856.

Knighton, Henrici. *Chronicon.* 2 vols. Ed. J. R. Lumley. In RS. London, 1889–95.

Langland, William. *The Vision of William concerning Piers the Plowman.* In three parallel texts. 2 vols. Ed. W. W. Skeat. Oxford, 1886.

Malmesbury, Monk of. *Eulogium historiarum sive temporis.* (From the creation to 1366, with a continuation to 1490). 3 vols. Ed. P. S. Haydon. In RS. London, 1858–63.

Murimuthensis, Adami, *Chronica sive temporis* (1303–46), *cum eorundum continuatione (ad* 1380) *a quodam anonymo.* Ed. T. Hogg. London, 1846.

Sherley, Sir Anthony, and his Persian Adventure. Ed. Sir E. Denison Ross, in Broadway Travellers. London, 1933.

Thompson, E. M. (ed.). *Chronicon Angliae* (1328–88). In RS. London, 1874.

Trokelow, Johannis de, *Chronica et Annales.* In RS. London, 1866.

Walsingham, Thomas. *Historia Anglicana.* Ed. H. T. Riley. In RS. London, 1864.

Wavrin, Jean de. *Les chroniques d'Engleterre.* Ed. Mlle du Pont. 2 vols. Paris, 1856–63.

Wendover, R., and Mat. Paris. *Relations touching the Tartars, taken out of the Historie of . . ., with Certaine Epistles on the Subject,* A.D. 1240–43. In *Purchas His Pilgrims,* Vol. XI, Cap. III. Glasgow, 1905. Original in RS.

Wyclif, John. (*a*) *Select English Works.* 3 vols. Ed. T. Arnold. Oxford, 1869.

    (*b*) *Tracts and Treatises.* Ed. R. Vaughan, in The Wycliffe Society Publications. London, 1845.

(*d*) ITALY

Annales Mediolanenses, Anonymi Scriptoria. Ed. Muratori; RIS, T. XVI. Milan, 1730.

Antonio Fiorentino. *Cronica Volgare* (1385–1409), *già attributa a Piero di Giovanni Minerbetti.* Ed. Elina Bellondi. AM; T. XXVII, Pt. II. Bologna, 1915–17.

Bisticci, V. da. *The Vespasiano Memoirs, Lives of Illustrious Men of the XVth Century.* London, 1926. Original It. ed. in 3 vols. Bologna, 1892.

Camugliano, G. N. di. *Chronicles of a Florentine Family* (1200–1470). London, 1933.

Cribellus, L. *De expeditione Pii papae II in Turcas libri duo.* In

Muratori, RIS, XXII, 21–80. (Cf. new ed. Carducci, in AM.)

Dandolo, Andrea. *Cronica* (to 1339—cont. Raphael Caresino to 1388). In Muratori, RIS, XII, 1–524. (Cf. new ed. Carducci, AM.)

Delayto, Jacoli de. *Annales Estenses.* Ed. Muratori. RIS, T. XVIII. Milan, 1731.

Foglietta, Vberti. (*a*) *De cavsis magnitudinis Turcarum imperii.* Rome, 1574. Eng. version in R. Carr, *The Mahumetane or Turkish Historie. . . . Adioyned a finall discourse concerning the causes of the greatnesse of the Turkish Empire.* London, 1600. (*b*) *Historia Genuensium libri XII.* Genoa, 1585.

Galeazzo, Bartolomeo e Andrea Gatari. *Cronaca Carrarese* (1318–1407). Ed. A. Medin and G. Tolomei, in AM, T. XVII, Pt. I, fasc. 5–6. Bologna, 1900, &c.

Giustiniani, A. *Annali della repubblica di Genova.* 2 vols. Genoa, 1855. (Early ed. Genoa, 1537.)

Gubbio, Ser Guerriero da. *Cronaca* (1350–1472). Ed. G. Mazzatinti, in AM, T. XXI, Pt. IV, fasc. 1–2. Bologna, 1900, &c.

Pegolotti. *Pratica della mercatura.* In G. F. Pagnini, *Della decima e di altre gravezze imposte dal comune di Firenze, della moneta e della mercatura, &c.* 4 vols. Lisbon and Lucca, 1765–6.

Paulo Interiano. *Ristretto delle Historie Genovesi.* Lucca, 1551.

Petrarca, Francesco. *Epistolae de Rebus Familiaribus et Variae.* Ed. J. Fracassetti, 3 vols. Florence, 1859–63. It. trans. by same, 2 vols., Florence, 1869–70.

Platina, B. *The Lives of the Popes.* 2 vols. Eng. trans. W. Benham, in the Ancient and Modern Library of Theological Literature. London s.d.

Sanudo, Marino (The Younger). (*a*) *Vite de' Duchi di Venezia* (1421–93). In Muratori, RIS, XXII, 399–1252. Cf. new ed. Carducci, in AM.

  (*b*) *Diarii.* Ed. G. Berchet. 56 vols. Venice, 1877–1900.

Savoy, Chronicle of. In *Monumenta historiae patriae de Savoia, Scriptores,* I. Turin, 1840.

Sozomeni Pistoriensis Presbyteri. *Chronicon Universale.* Ed. G. Zaccagnini, in AM, T. XVI, Pt. I, fasc. 59. Bologna, 1900, &c. Also Muratori, RIS, vol. XVI.

Stella, G. *Annales Genuenses* (1298–1409). In Muratori, RIS, XVII, 917 et seq. Cf. new ed. Carducci, AM.

Villani, G. (ob. 1348). *Historia universalis.* In Muratori, RIS, XII, 1–1002. Cf. new ed. Carducci et al. AM. Eng. trans. of parts T. E. Selfe, ed. P. H. Wicksteed. London, 1896.

Villani, M., and his son Filippo. *Historia ab* 1348 *ad* 1365. *Continuation of G. Villani's Historia.* In Muratori, RIS, XIV, 1–770. Cf. new ed. Carducci et al. AM.

(*e*) CENTRAL AND EASTERN EUROPE

Detmar. *Chronik von* 1105–1386. In *Chron. der deutschen Städte,* Lübeck, I.

Dlugosz, J. *Historia Polonica.* Libri XII. 2 vols. Leipzig, 1711–12.

Emler (ed.). *Vita Karoli IV,* and *Chronicon Aulae regiae.* Both in *Fontes rerum Bohemicarum,* T. II and IV. Prague, 1878–82.

Hegel, K. (ed.). *Chronik aus Kaiser Sigmund's Zeit bis* 1434. *Die Chroniken der deutschen Städte.* Nürnberg. Vol. I. Leipzig, 1862.

Justinger, Conrad. *Die Berner-Chronik.* Ed. G. Stüder. Bern, 1871.

Liliencron, R. von. *Die historischen Volkslieder der Deutschen vom* 13. *bis* 16. Jahrhundert. 4 vols. Leipzig, 1865–9.

Pertz, G. H., &c. (ed.). *Annales Mellicenses. Mon. Ger. Hist. Script.,* T. IX. Hanover, 1826, &c.

Pray, George de. *Annales Regum Hungariae* (997–1564). Ed. Schwandtner, *Script. Rer. Hung.,* &c., vol. II. Vienna, 1764, &c.

Rewa, Petrus de. (*a*) *De Sacra Corona Regni Hungariae.* Ed. Schwandtner. *Script. Rer. Hung.,* &c., vol. II. Vienna, 1746, &c.

  (*b*) *De Monarchia et S. Corona Regni Hungariae.* Same ed., vol. II.

Schiltberger, I. Ed., K. F. Neumann: *Reisen des Johannes Schiltberger.* Munich, 1859. Also Hammer: *Reise in den Orient.* Munich, 1813. Eng. trans., J. B. Telfer, with notes by Prof. P. Bruun of Odessa, published in the Hakluyt series: *The Bondage and Travels of Johann Schiltberger.* London, 1879. Cf. P. Bruun: *Geogr. Bemerkungen zu Schiltbergers Reisen* in *Sitzungsberichte der kgl. Bayer Akad. d. Wiss.* Munich, 1869 (vol. II).

Strömer, Ulman. *Puchel von mein geslechet und von abenteur,* 1349 *bis* 1407. *Chron. d. deutsch. Städte;* Nürnberg. Vol. I. Leipzig, 1862.

(*f*) BYZANTINE EMPIRE AND BALKAN STATES

Avril, A. de. *La bataille de Kossovo. Rhapsodie serbe, tirée des chants populaires et traduite en français.* Paris, 1868.

Chalkokondylas, L. *Historiarum de origine ac rebus gestis Turcarum.*

Gr. text and Lt. trans. in MPG, vol. clix.   Fr. trans., *Blaise de Vigénaire*.   2 vols.   Paris, 1662.

Chronicon Breve (Anonymi).   MPG, vol. clvii.   Paris, 1866.

Ducas, Johannes (1341–1462).   Hist. Byz.   Bonn, 1834.   MPG, vol. clvii.

Hopf, K.   (*a*) *Les Giustiniani, dynasties de Chio*.   Fr. trans., E. A. Vlasto.   Paris, 1888.

   (*b*) *Veneto-byzantinische Analekten*.   In *Sitzungberichte der Wiener Akad.*, XXXII.   Vienna, 1859.

   (*c*) *Chroniques gréco-romanes*.   Berlin, 1873.

Kantakuzenos, Johannes VI (1320–57).   3 vols.   Bonn, 1828–32.   MPG; vols. cii–civ.

Manuel I Palaeologos (1388–1407).   MPG, clvi.

Muller, J.   (*a*) *Byzantinische Analekten*.   In *Sitzungsberichte d. k. Akad. d. Wiss. hist. phil. kl.*, IX, 336 et seq.   Vienna, 1852.

   (*b*) *Uber einige byzantinische Urkunden von 1324 bis 1405*.   Ibid., VII.   Vienna, 1852.

Nicephorus Gregoras (1204–1351).   Byz. Hist. 2 vols.   Bonn, 1855.   Paris, 1702.

Pachymeres (1258–1308).   2 vols.   Bonn, 1835.   Rome, 1660.

Panaretos, Michael (1204–1386).   *Annale of Trebizond*, ed. J. F. Tafel in *Opuscula*.   Frankfort, 1832.   Another edition by Fallmerayer in *Abhandlung der k. Bayerischen Akad. der Wissenschaften*.   Munich, 1844.

Phrantzes, George (1259–1477).   Bonn, 1838.   MPG, vol. clvi.

(*g*) MISCELLANEOUS: SPAIN, CYPRUS, ARMENIA, AND WESTERN JEWS

Amadi et Strambaldi.   *Chroniques*.   In It., ed. Mas Latrie. 2 pts.   Paris, 1891/3.

Bustron, Florio.   *Cronica* (1191–1489).   Chron. of Cyprus in It., ed. L. de Mas Latrie; in *Mélanges historiques*, V, 1–532.   Paris, 1886.   Cf. C. N. Sathas; *Bibliotheca Graeca medii aevi*; vol. II.   Venice, 1873.

Dordel, Jean, Évêque de Tortiboli.   *La chronique d'Arménie*.   Ed. U. Robert, in AOL, T. II, Sect. A, Critique des sources.   Paris, 1884.

Hayton.   *Histoire Orientale ou des Tartares. Recueil de divers voyages curieux faits en Tartarie, en Perse et ailleurs*.   Leiden, 1729.   For various editions, *vide Nicopolis*, pp. 20, 166 notes.

Héthoun II, roi d'Arménie.   *Poème de . . . (circa 1292)*.   In *Recueil des historiens des croisades, historiene arméniens*, vol. I, pp. 550 et seq.   Paris, 1869.   (Contains Armenian text and French translation.)

Joseph, Rabbi. *The Chronicles of Joseph Ben Joshua Ben Meir, the Sphardi.* 2 vols. Trans. from Hebrew by C. H. F. Bialloblotsky. London, 1836.

Lusignan, P. Estienne de. (*a*) *Description de Chypre.* Paris, 1580. (*b*) *Généalogie des rois de Chypre.* Paris, 1579.

Machaut, Guillaume. *La prise d'Alexandrie ou chronique du roi Pierre Iᵉʳ de Lusignan.* Ed. Mas Latrie. Soc. de l'Or. Lat. Geneva, 1877.

Makhairas, Leontios. *Recital concerning the Sweet Land of Cyprus entitled 'Chronicle'.* 2 vols. Greek text with Eng. trans. and notes by R. M. Dawkins. Oxford, 1932. Other ed. of Greek text and Fr. trans. by E. Miller and C. Sathas. 2 vols. Paris, 1881–2. Also Greek text by Sathas, in *Bibl. graeca medii aevi,* II. Venice, 1873.

Morel-Fatio, A. (ed.). *Libro de los Fechos et Conquistas del Principado de la Morea, compilado per comandamiento de Don Fray Johan Fernandez de Heredia, Mastro del Hospital de S. Johan de Jerusalem.* (Chronique de Morée aux XIIIe et XIVe siècles.) Publiée et traduite pour la première fois pour la Société de l'Orient Latin; Série Historique, IV. Geneva, 1885.

Muntaner, Ramon. *Chronica o descripeio dela fets e hazanayes del inclyt rey Don Jaime, &c.* Fr. trans. by Buchon. 2 vols. Paris, 1827. Ger. trans., K. F. W. Lanz. 2 vols. Leipzig, 1842.

Raynaud, G. *Gestes des Chiprois.* In *Soc. de l'Or. Lat.* Paris, 1887.

Sempad, Le connétable. *Chronique du royaume de la Petite Arménie* (*c.* 1335). In *Recueil des historiens des croisades, Historiens arméniens,* vol. I, pp. 610 et seq. (Continuation to the downfall of the kingdom *circa* 1405, pp. 701 et seq.) Paris, 1869.

IV. LITERARY SOURCES OF THE EAST IN PRINT

Abd-al-Latif, Arab Physician of Bagdad: Kitāb-al-Ifāda wal-Ítibār fī al-'Umūr al-Mushāhada wal-Ḥawādith al-Mu'āyana bi-'Arḍ Miṣr. *Relation de l'Égypte, suivie de divers extraits d'écrivains orientaux et d'un état des provinces et des villages de l'Égypte dans le XIVᵉ siècle,* trad. Silvestre de Sacy. Paris, 1810.

Abulfida (ob. A.H. 732/A.D. 1331). Taqwīm al-Buldān. Ed. Reinaud and MacGuckin de Slane. Paris, 1840. Fr. trans. Reinaud and S. Guyard, 2 pts. Paris, 1848–83. Lithograph of texts of BM. and Dresden MSS. by Ch. Schier. Berlin and London, 1846.

Anonymous Turkish Chronicle, trans. into French, by Buchon in

Froissart, vol. XIII. Paris, 1825, &c. (Cf. Uruj. *Vide infra*.)

Ibn 'Arabshāh, Abul-'Abbās A. b. M. b. 'Abdallah b. . . . Shihāb-al-Dīn al-Dimashqī al-Ḥanafī (ob. A.H. 854/A.D. 1450): 'Aja'ib al-Maqdūr fi Akhbār Timūr. Leiden, 1636.

Ibn al-Athīr, 'Izz-al-Dīn Abu-l-Ḥasan 'Alī Abū-l-Karam M.b. M. b. 'Abd-al-Karīm b. 'Abd-al-Wāḥid (ob. 1233): al-Kāmil fi al-Tārīkh. (Famous Universal History of Islam.) 12 vols. Leiden, 1851.

al-Bakrī (lived *c.* 1068). *Description de l'Afrique Septentrionale.* Trans. MacGuckin de Slane, Algiers and Paris, 1913.

Ibn Baṭṭūṭa's Travels. Ed. and Fr. trans. C. D. Defréméry and B. R. Sanguinetti. 4 vols. Paris, 1853, &c. Eng. Selection, H. A. R. Gibb, in Broadway Travellers, London, 1929.

al-Dimashqī, Shams-al-Dīn b. 'Abdallah M. Abū-Ṭalib al-Anṣarī (ob. A.H. 727/1327). Nukhbat al-Dahr fi 'Aja'ib al-Barr wal-Baḥr. Arabic Text ed. Fraehn and A. F. Mehren. Leipzig, 1923. Fr. trans. A. F. Mehren. Copenhagen, 1874.

Ibn Ḥajar al-Asqalānī, Aḥmad b. 'Ali b. M. b. M. b. 'Alī b. Aḥmad (ob. A.H. 852/A.D. 1449): al-Durar al-Kāmina fi A'yān al-Mi'a al-Thāmina; ed. S. Krenkow, 4 vols., Hyderabad, A.H. 1348–50.

El-Herewy, Aboul Ḥassan. Documents divers. Extraits d'. Ch. Schéfer. In AOL, T. I, pp. 587–609. Paris, 1881.

Idrisi's Geography. A. Jaubert, *Géographie*, 2 vols. Paris, 1838–40. Latin version, G. Sonita and J. Hesronita. Rome, 1619.

Ibn Khaldūn, Abd al-Raḥman b. M. (ob. 1406)—al-'Ibar wa-Dīwān al-Mubtada wa-l-Khabar. 7 vols. Cairo, A.H. 1284 (1867–8). For trans., *vide*:

    (*a*) McG. de Slane, *Prolegomènes.* Paris, 1863–8.

    (*b*) Ibid., *Hist. des Berbères.* Algiers, 1852.

Khalil Ed-Dahiry—Zoubdat Kachf El-Mamâlik. *Tableau politique et administratif de l'Égypte, de la Syrie et du Hidjâz sous la domination des sultans mamlouks du XIII⁰ au XV⁰ siècle.* Ed. P. Ravaisse, in Publications de l'École des langues orientales vivantes. Paris, 1894.

Leunclavius, J. *Annales Sultanorum Othmanidarum a Turcis sua Lingua Scripti*; and *Pandectes Historiae Turcicae*; in MPG, T. 159, pp. 573–650 and 717–923.

Lonicerus, F. *Chronicorum Turcicorum.* (Based on Turkish histories.) Frankfort, 1878.

al Maqrīzī (*vide supra* MSS.). (*a*) Al-Mawā'iẓ wal-I'tibar bi-Dhikr al-Khiṭaṭ wal-Athār. Bulāq (A.H. 1270). Ed. M. Quṭṭah al-

'Adawī, 2 vols. New ed. and Fr. trans. Gaston Wiet and Paul Casanova, in progress. Cairo, 1911, &c.

(b) Histoire des Sultans Mameloukes d'Égypte. Trad. E. Quatremère. Paris, 1837, &c. New ed. of text begun by M. M. Ziada. Cairo, 1934. (See Kitāb al-Sulūk, in MSS.)

al-Omari, Ibn Fadl-Allah. L'Afrique moins l'Égypte, Fr. trans. Gaudefroy-Demombynes. Paris, 1927. (Vide supra MSS.)

Piri Re'īs Bahrija. Die turkische Segelhandbuch für das mitteländische Meer von Jahre 1521. Ed. and Ger. trans. P. Kahle, 2 vols. Berlin and Leipzig, 1926.

al-Qalqashandī, Abu-l-'Abbās Aḥmad (ob. 1418). Ṣubḥ al-a'sha. (Encyclopaedia.) 14 vols. Cairo, 1913, &c.

al-Qazwīnī, Zakariya b. M. b. Maḥmud (ob. A.H. 682/A.D. 1283). 'Aja'ib al-Makhlūqāt; and Āthār al-Bilād. 2 vols. Ed. F. Wüstenfeld. Göttingen, 1848–9.

Sa'd-al-Dīn, M. b. Ḥasan (Khoja Effendi). Tāj-al-Tawārīkh. 2 vols. Istanbul, 1862. (For list of translations see Gibbons' Foundations, 360 and Nicopolis, 218.)

al-Sakhāwī, Shams-al-Dīn M. b. 'Abd-al-raḥmān (ob. 1496). al-Tibr al-Masbūk fī Dhail al-Sulūk. (Continuation of Maqrīzī's Kitāb al-Sulūk. Vide supra, Or. MSS.) Ed. Aḥmad Zakī. Cairo, 1896.

Ibn Taghrī Bardī, Abul-Maḥāsin Jamāl-al-Dīn Yūsuf (ob. A.H. 874/A.D. 1469). Al-Nujūm al-Zāhira fi Mulūk Miṣr wal-Qāhira. Ed. Popper, University of California Publications in Semetic Philology, in progress. Berkeley (California), 1909, &c. Ed. Dār al-Kutub. Cairo.

Uruj b. 'Adīl al-Qazzaz, Tawārīkh 'Āl 'Othman. (Fifteenth century chronicle in Turkish). Ed. F. Babinger, Quellenwerke des islamischen Schriftums, 2 vols. Hanover, 1925.

Yāqūt al-Ḥamawī, Shihāb-al-Dīn Abū-'Abdallah al-Rūmī (ob. A.H. 626/A.D.1229). Mu'jam al-Buldān. Leipzig (1866), ed. F. Wüstenfeld, 6 vols. Cairo (1906), ed. M. Amin al-Khānjī and Aḥmad b. al-Amīn al-Shanqīṭī, 10 vols.

Zetterstéen, K. V. Beiträge zur Geschichte der Mamlukensultane in den Jahren 690–741 der Hiǵra nach arab. HSS. Leiden, 1919.

V. SECONDARY AUTHORITIES

(1) MONOGRAPHS AND SPECIAL WORKS ON OR RELATING TO THE LATER CRUSADES

Ady, C. M. Pius II (Aeneas Silvius Piccolomini), the Humanist Pope. London, 1913.

André, M. Le bienheureux Raymond Lulle. Paris, 1900.

Atiya, A. S. (a) *The Crusade of Nicopolis*. London, 1934.

(b) Articles 'Nikopolis', 'Rhodes' and 'Rosetta' in EI; 'The Crusade of Nicopolis and a Classified Bibliography of the Crusade in the Fourteenth Century', in *Bulletin of the Institute of Historical Research*, XI (1934), 185.

(c) *A Fourteenth Century Fatwa on the Status of Christians in Mamlūk Egypt*. In *Studien zur Geschichte des Nahen und Fernen Ostens*. Festschrift Paul Kahle. Leiden, 1935.

Barber, W. T. A. *Raymond Lull: The Illuminated Doctor*. A Study in Mediaeval Missions. London, 1903.

Berger de Xivry. *La vie et les ouvrages de l'empereur Manuel Paléologue*. In *Mémoires de l'Académie des Inscriptions*, XIX, pt. 2, pp. 1–301. Paris, 1853.

Bosio, I. *Dell'istoria della . . . religione . . . e militia di S. Giovanni Gierosolimitano*. 3 vols. Rome, 1594–1602. Other ed., Rome, 1621; Rome and Naples, 1629–34. Vol. III, Rome, 1676 and Naples, 1695.

Boislisle, De. *Projet de croisade du premier duc de Bourbon*. In *Bulletin de la Soc. d'hist. de Fr.*, 1872.

Bréhier, L. *L'église et l'Orient au moyen âge: les croisades*. 5th ed. Paris, 1928.

Cahour, J. *Les dernières croisades et l'Europe musulmane au moyen âge*. Laval, 1926. (Autolithographie.)

Capitanovici, G. J. *Die Eroberung von Alexandria*. Berlin, 1894.

Chapman, C. *Michel Paléologue, restaurateur de l'empire byzantin* (1261–82). Brussels, 1926.

Chevalier, U. *La croisade du dauphin Humbert II* (1345–7). Paris, 1920.

Datta, P. *Spedizione in Oriente di Amedeo VI conte di Savoia*. Turin, 1826.

Delaville Le Roulx, J. (a) *La France en Orient au XIVᵉ siècle. Expéditions du maréchal Boucicaut*. In *Bibl. des Écoles françaises d'Athènes et de Rome*, fasc. 44–5. Paris, 1886.

(b) *Les Hospitaliers en Terre Sainte et à Chypre* (1100–1310). Paris, 1904.

(c) *Les Hospitaliers à Rhodes jusqu'à la mort de Philibert de Nailhac* (1310–1420). Paris, 1913.

(d) *Mélanges sur l'Ordre de S. Jean de Jérusalem*. Paris, 1910.

Dézert, Desdevises du. *Les croisades*. Clermont, 1895.

Faure, C. *Le Dauphin Humbert II à Venise et en Orient* (1345–47). In *Mélanges d'archéologie et d'histoire*, published by L'École française de Rome, XXVII (1907), 509–62.

Gabotto, F. *L'età del conte verde in Piemonte, secondo nuovi documenti* (1350–83). Rome, 1895.

Gay, J. *Clément VI et les affaires d'Orient.* Paris, 1904.

Gottron, A. *Ramon Lulls Kreuzzugsideen.* In *Abhandlungen zur Mittleren und Neueren Geschichte*, ed. G. v. Below, H. Finke u. F. Meinecke, Heft 39. Berlin and Leipzig, 1912.

Grousset, R. *Histoire des croisades et du Royaume Franc de Jérusalem.* 3 vols. Paris, 1934–6.

Hauréau. *Raimond Lulle.* In *Hist. Litt. de la Fr.*, XXIX.

Häussler, M. *Felix Fabri aus Ulm und seine Stellung zum Geistigen Leben seiner Zeit.* Leipzig and Berlin, 1914.

Heidelberger, F. *Kreuzzugsversuche um die Wende des 13. Jahrhunderts.* Berlin and Leipzig, 1912.

Helferich. *Raymund Lull und die Anfänge der katalonischen Literatur.* Berlin, 1858.

Herzsohn, I. J. P. *Der Ueberfall Alexandrien's.* Diss. Bonn, 1886.

Hirsch-Gereuth, A. v. *Studien zur Geschichte der Kreuzzügsidee nach den Kreuzzügen.* Munich, 1896.

Hintzen, J. D. *De Kruistochts-plannen van Philips den Goede.* Rotterdam, 1918.

Iorga, N. (a) *Philippe de Mézières* (1327–1405) *et la croisade au XIVe siècle.* Bibl. de l'Éc. des hautes études; fasc. 110. Paris, 1896.

    (b) *Un Projet relatif à la conquête de Jérusalem* (1609), in ROL, II (1894), 183–9.

    (c) *Une collection des lettres de Philippe de Mézières*, in *Rev. Hist.*, XLIX (1892), 39–57 and 306–22.

    (d) *Relations entre l'Orient et l'Occident au moyen âge.* Paris, 1923.

Jarry. *Le retour de la croisade de Barbarie.* In BEC, 1893.

Jenkins, R. C. *The Last Crusader: or the Life and Time of Cardinal Julian of the House of Cesarini.* London, 1861.

Kahle, P. *Die Katastrophe des mittelalterlichen Alexandria.* In *Mémoires de l'Institut Français*, T. LXVIII, Mélanges Maspéro, vol. III, 137–54. Cairo, 1935.

Kohler, Ch. *Étude sur Guillaume d'Adam, archevêque de Sultanyeh.* In *Doc. armén. des crois.*, II, 1906, pp. clxviii et seq.

Kunstmann, F. *Studien über Marino Sanudo den älteren.* In *Abhandlungen der k. Bayrischen Akad. der Wissenschaft.* hist., VII, pt. 1. Munich, 1855.

Lacaille, H. *Étude sur la vie d'Enguerrand VII, sire de Coucy, comte de Soissons* (1340?–1397). In *Positions des thèses &c. de la promotion &c.* Mâcon, 1890.

Loray, Terrier de. *Jean de Vienne, amiral de France*, 1341–96. Paris, 1877. (Soc. bibliogr.)

Lorentz, P. R. *Les missions dominicaines en Orient au XIVe siècle.* In *Archivium Fratrum Praedicatorum*, II. Paris and Rome, 1932.

Lot, H. (*a*) *Projets de croisade sous Charles le Bel et sous Philippe de Valois.* In BEC, 4e série, 1859, V, 503–9.

(*b*) *Essai d'intervention de Charles le Bel en faveur des chrétiens d'Orient.* Ibid., Paris, 1875, XXXVI, 588–600.

Mas Latrie, L. de. (*a*) *Histoire de l'île de Chypre sous le règne des princes de la maison de Lusignan* 3 vols., Paris, 1855–61.

(*b*) *Patriarches latins d'Antioche*, in ROL, I (1894), 192–205

(*c*) *Patriarches latins de Constantinople*, in ROL, III (1895), 433–56.

(*d*) *Patriarches latins d'Alexandrie*, in ROL, IV (1896), 1–11.

(*e*) *Archevêques latins de l'île de Chypre*, in AOL, II (Paris, 1884), 207–328.

Magnocavallo, A. *Marin Sanudo il Vecchio e il suo progetto di Crociata.* Bergramo, 1901.

Manfroni, C. *La battaglia di Gallipoli e la politica veneto-turca.* Venice, 1902.

Meyer, E. H. *Die Staats und völkerrechtlichen Ideen von Peter Dubois.* Leipzig, 1908.

Michaud, J. F. *Histoire des croisades.* New ed. in 7 vols. Paris, 1824–9. Eng. trans. W. Robson: *History of the Crusades*; 3 vols.; London, 1852.

Mirot, L. *Une expédition française en Tunisie au XIVe siècle. Le siège de Mahdia* (1390). Paris, 1932.

Norden, W. *Das Papsttum und Byzanz: die Trennung der beiden Mächte und das Problem ihrer Wiedervereinigung bis 1453.* Berlin, 1903.

Paris, P., and l'Abbé Lebeuf. *La vie et les voyages de Philippe de Mézières.* In *Mém. de l'acad. des Inscript.*, nouv. série, vol. XV, pt. 1, pp. 359–98.

Parisot, V. *Cantacuzène, homme d'état et historien, ou examen critique comparatif des 'Mémoires' de J. C. et des sources contemporaines.* Paris, 1845.

Parraud, Abbé A. *Vie de Saint Pierre Thomas.* Avignon, 1895.

Pears, E. *Destruction of the Greek Empire and Capture of Constantinople by the Turks.* London, 1903.

Peers, E. Allison. *Ramon Lull, A Biography.* London, 1929.

Pelliot, P. *Les Mongols et la Papauté.* Three extracts from ROC, 1923, &c.

Perroquet, A. *Apologie de la vie et des oeuvres du bien-heureux Raymond Lulle.* Vendôme, 1667.

Powicke, F. M. *Pierre Du Bois.* In *Historical Essays,* ed. Tout and Tait, pp. 169–91. London, 1902.

Prutz, H. (*a*) *Rechnungen über Heinrich von Derbys Preussenfahrten.* In *Verein für die Gesch. der Provinzen Ost-und Westpreussen.* Leipzig, 1893.

(*b*) *Kulturgeschichte der Kreuzzüge.* Berlin, 1883.

Rabanis, J. *Notice sur Florimont sire de Lesparre, suivie d'un précis historique sur cette seigneurie.* Bordeaux, 1843.

Rémusat, A. *Biographie de Jean de Montecorvin.* In *Biographie universelle Didot.*

Riber, Ll. *Vida i actes del reverend mestre i benaventurat màrtir Ramon Lull.* Mallorca, 1916.

Röhricht, R. (*a*) *Geschichte der Kreuzzüge im Umriss.* Innsbruck, 1898.

(*b*) *Geschichte der Königreichs Jerusalem* (1100–1291). Innsbruck, 1898.

(*c*) *Beiträge zur Geschichte der Kreuzzüge,* 2 vols., Berlin, 1874–8.

(*d*) *Kleine Studien zur Geschichte der Kreuzzüge.* Berlin, 1890.

(*e*) *Bibliotheca Geographica Palaestinae.* Berlin, 1890.

(*f*) *Deutsche Pilgerreisen nach dem Heiligen Lande.* Innsbruck, 1900.

(*g*) *Deutsche Pilgerreisen &c.* (With H. Meisner). Berlin, 1880.

Saint-Esprit, M. de. *Vie admirable de saint Pierre Thomas.* Paris, 1652.

Schlumberger, G. (*a*) *Récits de Byzance et des croisades,* 2 vols., Paris, 1916–22.

(*b*) *Fin de la domination franque en Syrie après les dernières croisades: prise de Saint-Jean d'Acre en l'an 1291 par l'armée du Soudan d'Égypte.* Paris, 1914.

(*c*) *Expédition des 'Almugavares' ou routiers catalans en Orient.* Paris, 1924.

(*d*) *Le siège, la prise et la sac de Constantinople par les Turcs en 1453.* Paris, 1926.

Stevenson, W. B. *The Crusaders in the East.* Cambridge, 1907.

Vertot, L'Abbé. *Histoire des chevaliers de Malte,* 7 vols. Paris, 1819.

Wadding, L. *Annales Minorum seu historia trium ordinum a S. Francisco institutorum.* 8 vols. Various editions.

Wallon, H. *Saint Louis et son temps.* 2 vols. Paris, 1875.

Weitbrecht, H. W. *Raymond Lull and Six Centuries of Islam.* London, 1915.

Wilken, F. *Geschichte der Kreuzzüge.* 7 vols. in 8. Leipzig, 1807–32.

Wright, J. K. *The Geographical Lore of the Time of the Crusades.* New York, 1925.

Zeck, E. *Der Publizist Pierre Dubois: seine litterarische Denk-und Arbeitsweise im Traktat, 'De recuperatione terre sancte'.* Berlin, 1911.

Zurlauben, Baron de. *Abrégé de la vie d'Enguerrand VII du nom, sire de Couci, avec un détail de son expédition en Alsace et en Savoie.* In *Mém. de l'Acad. des Inscriptions,* 1ere série, T. XXV.

Zwemer, S. M. *Raymund Lull: First Missionary to the Moslems.* New York and London, 1902.

(2) MISCELLANEOUS WORKS OF REFERENCE

Adeney, W. F. *Greek and Eastern Churches.* Edinburgh, 1908.

Allen, W. E. D. *History of the Georgian People.* London, 1932.

Arnold, T. W. *Preaching of Islam.* 3rd ed. photographed from 2nd. London, 1935.

L'Art de vérifier les dates. One vol. ed. Paris, 1770.

Baddeley, W. St. Clair. *Queen Joanna I of Naples, Sicily, and Jerusalem.* London, 1893.

Barante, M. de. *Histoire des ducs de Bourgogne de la maison de Valois,* 1364–1482. 8 vols. Paris, 1860.

Baschet, A. *Archives de Venise. Histoire de la Chancellerie secrète.* Paris, 1870.

Barthold, W. *Turkestan down to the Mongol Invasion.* 2nd ed. Trans. H. A. R. Gibb. London, 1928.

Bent, J. T. *Genoa, How the Republic Rose and Fell.* London, 1881.

Blanc, P.-S. *Histoire ecclésiastique,* vols. 1–2. Paris, 1860.

Bouvat, L. *Empire Mongol.* Paris, 1927.

Bratianu, G. I. *Recherches sur le commerce génois dans la mer noire au XIIIe siècle.* Paris, 1929.

Breccia, A. *Porto d'Alexandria d'Egitto, studio di geografia commerciale. Mém. de la Soc. Roy. de Géogr. d'Egypte,* XIV. Cairo, 1927.

Brockelmann, C. *Geschichte der arabischen Litteratur.* 2 vols. Berlin, 1898–1902. Supplement, Leiden, 1936, in progress.

Brown, Horatio F. (a) *Venice. An Historical Sketch of the Republic.* London, 1893.
    (b) *Studies in the History of Venice.* 2 vols. London, 1907.

Browne, E. G. *A Literary History of Persia.* 4 vols. 2nd ed. Cambridge, 1929–30.

Browne, L. E. *Eclipse of Christianity in Asia.* Cambridge, 1933.

Budge, Sir E. A. Wallis. *A History of Ethiopia, Nubia and Abyssinia.* 2 vols. London, 1928.

Buri, V. *L'unione della Chiesa Copta con Roma sotto Clemente VIII. Orientalia Christiana* (Rome), vol. XXIII 2, no. 72.

Butcher, E. L. *Story of the Church of Egypt.* 2 vols. London, 1897.

Cahun, L. *Introduction à l'histoire de l'Asie, Turcs et mongol des origines à* 1405. Paris, 1896.

Daru, P. *Histoire de la république de Venise.* 9 vols. 4th ed. Paris, 1853.

Finlay, G. *History of Greece from its Conquest by the Romans to the Present Time.* Ed. H. T. Tozer. 7 vols. Oxford, 1877.

Fleury, C. *Histoire ecclésiastique.* 20 vols. Paris, 1836–7.

Flick, A. C. *Decline of the Medieval Church.* 2 vols. London, 1930.

Fortescue, A. (*a*) *The Uniate Eastern Churches.* Ed. G. D. Smith. London, 1923.

  (*b*) *Orthodox Eastern Church.* London, 1911.

  (*c*) *Lesser Eastern Churches.* London, 1913.

Gaudefroy-Demombynes. *La Syrie à l'époque des Mamelouks d'après les auteurs arabes; description géographique, économique et administrative.* Paris, 1923.

Gibbon, E. *The History of the Decline and Fall of the Roman Empire.* Ed. by J. B. Bury. 7 vols. London, 1902.

Gibbons, H. A. *The Foundations of the Ottoman Empire* (1300–1403). Oxford, 1916.

Gieseler, J. C. I. *Ecclesiastical History.* Trans. F. Cunningham. 3 vols. Philadelphia, 1836.

Gregorovius, F. (*a*) *Geschichte der Stadt Rom im Mittelalter.* 8 vols. 5th ed. Stuttgart, 1903, &c. Trans. Annie Hamilton: *History of the City of Rome in the Middle Ages*; 8 vols. in 13. London, 1894–1902.

  (*b*) *Gesch. d. Stadt Athen im Mittelalter.* 2 vols. Stuttgart, 1889.

Hackett, J. *History of the Orthodox Church of Cyprus.* London, 1901.

Hammer-Purgstall, J. von. *Geschichte des osmanischen Reiches.* 10 vols. Pest, 1827–34. Fr. trans. with Atlas, Hellert and author. 18 vols. Paris, 1843.

Hasluck, F. W. *Christianity and Islam under the Sultans.* 2 vols., Ed. Margaret M. Hasluck. Oxford, 1929.

Hazlitt, C. *The Venetian Republic. Its Rise, its Growth and its Fall* (421–1797). 2 vols. London, 1900.

Hélyot, P. *Histoire des ordres monastiques, religieux et militaires, et des congrégations séculières.* 8 vols. Paris, 1711–21. Ed. Migne (alphabetically arranged). 4 vols. Paris, 1847–59

Hemilly. *Histoire de Majorque et de Minorque.* Maëstricht, 1777.

Heyd, W. *Geschichte des Levantehandels im Mittelalter,* 2 vols. Stuttgart, 1879. Standard Fr. trans. Furcy-Raynaud and author, 2 vols. Paris, 1885–6 (Lithographed, Leipzig, 1936).

Histoire littéraire de la France. Vols. I–XXXVI. Paris, 1733–1927. Begun by the Religieux Bénédictins de la Congrégation de Saint-Maur and continued by the Membres de l'Institut. (1st 26 vols. analysed by Franklin, pp. 585–97.)

Hodgson, F. C. *Venice in the Thirteenth and Fourteenth Centuries.* London, 1910.

Hogarth, D. G. *The Nearer East.* London, 1905.

Howorth, H. H. *History of the Mongols from the 9th to the 19th Centuries.* 2 vols. in 3. London, 1876–80. Pt. IV with indexes, 1928.

Hudson, G. F. *Europe and China, Survey of their Relations from the Earliest Times.* London, 1931.

Jonquière, Vte de la. *Histoire de l'empire ottoman.* New. ed. 2 vols. Paris, 1914.

Julien, Ch.-A. *Histoire de l'Afrique du Nord.* Paris, 1931.

Kidd, B. J. *Churches of Eastern Christendom.* London, 1927.

Kindermann, H. *'Schiff' im Arabischen. Untersuchung über Vorkommen und Bedeutung der Termini.* Zivickau i. Sa., 1934.

Köhler, G. *Die Entwickelung des Kriegwesens und der Kriegführung in der Ritterzeit von Mitte des, II.* Jahrhunderts bis zur den Hussitenkriegen. 2 vols. Breslau, 1886.

Landon, E. H. *Manual of Councils.* 2 vols. Revised ed. London, 1893.

Lane-Poole, S. (a) *Egypt in the Middle Ages.* London, 1925.
 (b) *Mohammadan Dynasties.* Photographed ed. Paris, 1925.

Loserth, J. *Geschichte des spätern Mittelalters von 1197 bis 1492.* Munich, 1903.

Lussan, Mlle de. *Histoire et règne de Charles VI.* 9 vols. Paris, 1743.

Lybyer, A. H. *The Government of the Ottoman Empire in the Time of Suleiman the Magnificent.* Harvard University Press, 1913.

Maclear, G. F. *A History of Christian Missions during the Middle Ages.* Cambridge and London, 1863.

Macpherson, D. *Annals of Commerce.* 4 vols. London, 1805.

Manfroni, C. *Il dominio del Mediterraneo durante il medio evo.* Rome, 1900. (Reprint from the *Rivista marittima*, 1900.)

Marengo, E. *Genova e Tunisie* (1388–1515), *relazione storica.* In *Atti della Società ligure di storia patria*, vol. XXXII (1901).

Miller, W. *Essays on the Latin Orient.* Cambridge, 1921.

Milman, H. H. *History of Latin Christianity.* 9 vols. London, 1883.

Morgan, J. de. *Histoire du peuple arménien.* Paris and Nancy, 1919.

Mosheim, J. L. von. *Institutes of Ecclesiastical History, Ancient and Modern.* Trans. J. Murdock and ed. H. Soames. 4 vols. London, 1845.

Moule, A. C. *Christians in China before the Year* 1550. London, 1930.

Muir, Sir W. *The Mameluke or Slave Dynasty of Egypt* (A.D. 1260– 1517). London, 1896.

Neale, J. M. *History of the Holy Eastern Church.* (*a*) General Introduction. 2 vols. London, 1850.

　　　　(*b*) Patriarchate of Alexandria. 2 vols. London, 1847.

　　　　(*c*) Patriarchate of Antioch. London, 1873.

Neander, J. A. W. *Allgemeine Geschichte der christlichen Religion und Kirche* (to 1430). 6 vols. Hamburg, 1826–52. Trans. J. Torrey: *General History of the Christian Religion and Church.* 9 vols. London, 1847–55.

Newton, A. P. (ed.). *Travel and Travellers of the Middle Ages.* London, 1926.

Olwer, L. Nicolau d'. *L'expansio de Catalunya en la Mediterrànea Oriental.* Vol. I in *Enciclopèdia 'Catalunya'.* Barcelona, 1926.

Oman, Sir Charles. *History of the Art of War in the Middle Ages.* 2 vols., London, 1924.

Pagano, C. *Delle impresse e del dominio dei Genovesi nella Grecia.* Genoa, 1846

Pastor, L. *Geschichte der Päpste seit dem Ausgang des Mittelalters.* Eng. trans. F. I. Antrobus and R. F. Kerr in 18 vols. London, 1891.

Pigeonneau, H. *Histoire du commerce de la France.* Vol. I. Paris, 1885.

Quatremère. *Notice de l'ouvrage qui a pour titre Mesalik* &c. In *Not. et Extr. des MSS. de la Bibl. nat.*, XIII. Paris, 1836.

Ramsay, Sir W. M. *Historical Geography of Asia Minor.* London, 1890.

Roncière, C. de la. *Histoire de la marine française.* 5 vols. Paris, 1889–1920.

Robertson, J. C. *History of the Christian Church.* 8 vols. London, 1876.

Stephens, W. *From the Crusades to the French Revolution,* A History of the La Trémoille Family. London, 1914.

Strange, G. le. *Palestine under the Moslems.* Description of Syria and the Holy Land from A.D. 650 to 1500. Trans. from Med. Arab Geogr. London, 1890.

Tozer, H. F. *The Church and the Eastern Empire.* London, 1888.

Tritton, A. S. *The Caliphs and their Non-Muslim Subjects.* A Critical Study of the Covenant of Umar. Oxford, 1930. Supplemented by article, Islam and the Protected Religions, in JRAS, April, 1931.

Trollope, T. A. *History of the Commonwealth of Florence.* 4 vols. London, 1865.

Valbonnais. (a) *Mémoires pour servir à l'histoire du Dauphiné.* Paris, 1711.
(b) *Histoire des dauphins de la troisième race.* 2 vols. Geneva, 1721.

Valois, N. *La France et le Grand Schisme d'Occident.* 4 vols. Paris, 1896–1902.

Vasiliev, A. A. *Histoire de l'empire byzantin.* 2 vols. Trans. P. Rodin and A. Bourguina. Paris, 1932.

Wachter, A. *Ueberfall des Griechentums in Kleinasien im XIV. Jahrhundert.* Leipzig, 1905.

Weil, G. *Geschichte des Abbasidenchalifats in Egypten.* 2 vols. Stuttgart, 1860–2.

Wiet, G. *Précis de l'histoire de l'Égypte,* T. II, Pt. 2. Cairo, 1932.

Wüstenfeld, F. *Die Geschichtschreiber der Araber und ihre Werke.* Göttingen, 1882.

Zambaur, A. de. *Manuel de généalogie et de chronologie pour l'histoire de l'Islam.* Texte, tableaux et cartes. Hanover, 1927.

INDEX

Economy has been observed in sub-headings and subject-matter where these can easily be found in the detailed Table of Contents. Bold-type is used in some entries to indicate the chief references to the subject of each entry. References to persons are arranged alphabetically according to Christian names and not to surnames, except in very few cases where the surname is too well-known to be overlooked. Authors are included only when they appear in chapter texts and not in footnotes.
Abbreviations used are: Abp. = Archbishop; b = ibn; Bp. = Bishop; Cple. = Constantinople; Emp. = Emperor or Empire; K. = King; Lat. = Latin; n. = note; nn. = notes; Patr. = Patriarch; sgr. = seigneur; T.S. = Terra Sancta.

ADDENDUM TO APPENDIX I

(pp. 487–9)

Compare I. Longpré—*Deux opuscules inédits du B. Raymond Lulle*, in France franciscaine, 18 (1935), 145–54. This includes the *Petitio pro Conversione Infidelium*. M. Longpré's text is derived from the B.N. MS. Lat. 15450, and mine from the Munich MS. Lat. 10565. Evidently both texts were in preparation at the same time, and the decision to leave my text as it stands is due to the fact that Longpré's work has been made known to me only at the final stage in the publication of my book. The Munich text, moreover, may prove useful for purposes of comparison and further collation with the Paris MS., and this may be sufficient justification for the space here given to it.